READINGS IN INFORMATION SYSTEMS:

A Managerial Perspective

READINGS IN INFORMATION SYSTEMS:

A Managerial Perspective

Edited by

JAMES C. WETHERBE
School of Management
University of Minnesota

V. THOMAS DOCK
School of Business Administration
University of Southern California

STEVEN L. MANDELL
School of Business Administration
Bowling Green State University

Cover Art: Karl Benjamin

WEST PUBLISHING COMPANY
50 W. Kellogg Boulevard
P.O. Box 64526
St. Paul, MN 55164-1003

Printed in the United States of America

Library of Congress Cataloging-in-Publication Data

Readings and information systems.

Includes index.
1. Management information systems. I. Wetherbe, James C. II. Dock, V. Thomas. III. Mandell, Steven L.
T58.6.R417 1988 658.4'038 88-2517
ISBN 0-314-65767-3

To Shannan Benschoter for her conscientious efforts and dedication. Without her skills this project could not have been completed.

TABLE OF CONTENTS

EDITORS' PREFACE

There is no more dynamic field than information systems (IS)! If any one characteristic pervades this field, it is *change*. Advances in computer systems have received a great deal of attention. Significant gains have been made in both hardware technology and software techniques. Along with these advances in computer systems have come advances in the approaches and concepts of information processing for organizations. The area of IS, with respect to supporting managerial functions, is continuously developing. One result of this development is that an IS body of knowledge has been constructed.

The objective of this book is to bring together articles that provide insight into the primary concepts of information systems. The selections provide students with essential background material on information systems that is needed by managers and end-users of these systems. The readings reflect this perspective and recognize the contribution of IS as a means, rather than an end. The book includes articles that are already considered classics, along with many other timely pieces. The text is intended for use in a wide variety of courses in which the topic of information systems is discussed.

J.C.W.
V.T.D.
S.L.M.

contributors

RUSSELL L. ACKOFF
BRANDT ALLEN
IZAK BENBASAT
ROBERT I. BENJAMIN
GORDON BOCK
BRENT BOWMAN
W. M. A. BROOKER
JAMES F. COX
GORDON DAVIS
JO ELLEN DAVIS
KIMBERLEY DAVIS
JOHN DEARDEN
GERARDINE DESANCTIS
CHARLES DICKINSON, JR.
V. THOMAS DOCK
OMAR A. EL SAWY
JAMES C. EMERY
GORDON C. EVEREST
WARD A. FREDERICKS
DAVID H. FREEDMAN
BRENT GALLUPE
RICHARD D. HACKATHORN
JOHN C. HENDERSON
MADELINE M. HENDERSON
BLAKE IVES
HUGH F. JUERGENS
FREMONT E. KAST
PETER G. W. KEEN
EUGENE R. KLEINBERG
ROBERT L. LEITHEISER
HENRY C. LUCAS, JR.
VINCENT P. LUCHSINGER
MARJORIE A. LYLES
IAN C. MACMILLAN
M. LYNNE MARKUS
ROBERT J. MOCKLER
ROBERT I. MANN
RICHARD O. MASON
HARVEY P. NEWQUIST III
MARY LIPPITT NICHOLS
MARGRETHE H. OLSON
GERALD F. PRICE
NICK RACKOFF
ALFRED RAPPAPORT
DANIEL ROBEY
JOHN F. ROCKART
JAMES E. ROSENZWEIG
JAMES A. SENN
CHRISTOPHER R. SPRAGUE
RALPH H. SPRAGUE, JR.
KEN STONECIPHER
RONALD N. TAYLOR
EDWARD M. TOLLIVER
MICHAEL E. TREACY
EFRAIM TURBAN
WALTER A. ULLRICH
PAUL R. WATKINS
HUGH J. WATSON
JAMES C. WETHERBE
EDGAR G. WILLIAMS
CHARLES WISEMAN
STANLEY YOUNG
ROBERT W. ZMUD

sources

Academy of Management Journal
Business Horizons
Business Week
California Management Review
Computerworld
DATA BASE
Data Management Magazine
Datamation
Harvard Business Review
High Technology
Information Management Review
Journal of Business Strategy
Journal of Information Systems Management
Journal of Systems Management
Management Accounting
Management Science
McGraw Hill Book Company
MIS Quarterly
MSU Business Topics
North-Holland Publishing Company
Sloan Management Review
Systems and Procedures Journal
The Colgate Darden Graduate School of Business Administration, University of Virginia
The Systems Approach: A Primer

UNIT ONE

Systems: A Management Perspective

The "systems approach," a growing area of study and practice, has been highly touted for its great potential for solving problems and improving the performance of organizations. Unfortunately, there has been no clear agreement about what the "systems approach" actually is. The purpose of Unit 1 is to explore the fundamentals of systems theory and their application to the business organization.

Section 1, General Systems Theory, attempts to clarify some of the structural and sematic aspects of systems in order to show what they are and what they do. Special emphasis is placed on the theme of integration in purposive and function systems. This section explores what the systems approach can and cannot do for organizations, and how it can help improve their performance.

Section 2, The Organization as a System, examines the application of the systems approach to the practice of management. This application is intriguing and challenging; the day-to-day problems of practical management provide a worthy test of the effectiveness of the systems approach as a management tool.

Section 3, The "Total Systems" Approach, is devoted to management systems that encompass entire organizations. This has been a controversial area. Although "total systems" seem to be a worthy goal to strive for, they appear easier to discuss in theory than to achieve in practice. This section evaluates attempts to use a holistic approach in system design and the prospects for the ultimate success of these efforts.

SECTION ONE

General Systems Theory

READING 1

An Anatomy of Systems

article by
VINCENT P. LUCHSINGER
and V. THOMAS DOCK

A system is a collection of interrelated parts which is unified by design to obtain one or more objectives. Scientists are concerned with a system of knowledge, particularly in the case of astronomy where solar systems and bodies within that system are the objects of study. Of concern in the space age is the relationship that exists between elements in solar systems, and attributes of bodies in those systems. An inherent conclusion from the above definition indicates that systems are designed to perform some kind of task.

The word "systems" is used quite often in our literature today. Almost daily, we read or hear about various kinds of systems, such as defense systems and school systems. Looking at the role of management in a systematic context, we can view its execution by the managers of an organization in its environment as a systematic endeavor.

Source: Vincent P. Luchsinger and V. Thomas Dock, *The Systems Approach: A Primer* (1976). Reprinted by permission of the authors.

The term "system" has five fundamental implications. These are:

1. A system must be designed to accomplish an objective.
2. The elements of a system must have an established arrangement.
3. Interrelationships must exist among the individual elements of a system, and these interrelationships must be synergistic in nature.
4. The basic ingredients of a process (the flows of information, energy, and materials)[1] are more vital than the basic elements of a system.
5. Organization objectives are more important than the objectives of its elements, and thus, there is a de-emphasis of the parochial objectives of the elements of a system.

The objective of a systems study is the recognition of the managerial functions and the interrelations between the subsystems of the organization. We are not attempting to learn mathematical formulas, production processes, or the intricacies of the computer. Rather, our objective is the awareness of the variables involved in executing managerial functions so that decisions will be made in light of the overall effect upon the organization and its objectives. These decisions must consider not only the organization, but also the suprasystems (industry, environment, etc.) in which the organization operates.

An understanding of the systems approach requires familiarity with the basic concepts of general systems theory. To provide this basic foundation, the following topics are discussed in this reading.

- Characteristics of systems
- Elements of systems
- Types of systems
- Methods of system study
- The organizational system

The systems approach to management is simply keeping the organization's objectives in mind throughout the performance of all activities. It requires a communication network and coordination among all the parts (subsystems) of the organization (system). As emphasized by Johnson et al., "essentially, management is the process whereby those unrelated resources are integrated into a total system for objective accomplishment."[2]

A basic understanding of the systems concept and the essential elements of systems will promote sound management decisions. There is no guarantee that all systems could, or should, be computerized. On the contrary, the major basic management decisions are made by human systems rather than by computer systems. Why then should we study systems? If we can innovate ways to integrate human and computer systems, we can combine the superior qualities of both types of system and free the human system from repetitive tasks more suited to computers.

We will be looking at organizations and their operations in a systematic manner, taking note of the fact that they are composed of parts and that they are reapplied and integrated by design so that they may best meet their objectives, singly and in unison. In keeping with what we will come to know as systems thought, we will find methods and concepts which will be of great value to the manager as he views his role within his organization, as well as the role of parts of his organization, not to mention the environment of which his organization is a part.

General systems theory has been emerging for several decades, and has reached a position where it is making important contributions in an interdisciplinary sense. As such, systems theory is not merely a theoretical framework; rather, it is providing contributions in fields of applied science, technology, and behavioral sciences. Since Albert von Bertalanffy first proposed a general systems theory in 1950, the thread of systems thinking has been developed by scientists in increasing number. Kenneth Boulding, a prominent contemporary economist, wrote on general systems theory as the skeleton of the science in 1956. That article and other works, such as C. P. Snow's "The Two Cultures of the Scientific Revolution" in 1959, propelled the study and application of systems thought. Boulding proposed various levels of systems which were contained within each other, ranging from smaller units to larger and more comprehensive structures which contain interacting elements. At the present time, the Society for General Systems Research is an organization that is strongly promoting the organismic viewpoint as a means of providing structure and meaning for man's attempt to solve problems he finds in his world. It is particularly significant to note that an attempt to derive order is present in studies which are reflecting an increasingly interdisciplinary nature.

Characteristics of Systems

The world contains a multitude of systems, but one can identify a few characteristics that are present in all systems. These are:

1. Organization
2. Interaction
3. Interdependence
4. Integration
5. Central objective

Organization implies structure and function. It indicates that components of a system are arranged to permit the type of function which would help the organism or organization achieve its objectives.

The literature indicates that hierarchal relationships are found among systems, the concept of organization indicates that there is a meaningfulness in the manner in which those parts are assembled as an organization.

Interaction refers to the function of systems and parts of systems with one another. It does indicate that there is a transactional relationship of some type between parts of a system. It means that parts of systems and systems which contain those parts do not operate in a vacuum, but continually relate with other units with whom they try to exchange or maintain some types of relationship. In a business sense, this indicates that each part of a business organization can easily be expected to interact and relate with other parts of that organization, and that there would also be relationships between parts of a system that can be found at various levels. For example, a purchasing department must interact with the production division, and the advertising department must certainly interact successfully with the sales department for the entire organization as a system to attain any effectiveness.

The third characteristic is that of *interdependence*, which means that parts of the organization depend upon one another. It is not merely that they relate and interact with each other, but that they have an interdependence. It means that parts of an organization provide mutual satisfaction for needs and a means of attainment for other parts of the organization. In a sense, each part of the organization that is designed and operated in a systematic manner needs each other part of the organization. While the nature and amount of this need may vary between differing parts of organizations and systems, the need exists nevertheless. This characteristic can be compared to the cobweb which displays a set of interlocking relationships, so that a disturbance anywhere upon that cobweb means that the disturbance may be transmitted to other parts of that cobweb. Decisions made in one part of the organization will affect other parts of the organization.

A fourth characteristic of systems is *integration*. This means the holism of systems is emphasized. While much concern is often placed on analysis, the accompanying synthesis is very important for integrating those parts so that the purposes of the organization can be achieved. Perhaps more than any other characteristic, integration is a concept which makes the systems approach pay its way. Here one is concerned with ways in which the organization is tied together. Notice that by definition, the parts of a system are tied together by design to achieve one or more objectives. This unification is more than sharing a physical location or a common company name, but means that parts of that system share objectives of the entire organization, having recognized their condition of interdependency and interaction with other parts of the organization. Proper integration can introduce a synergistic effect where units acting in concert can produce more impact than the mere unintegrated collection of individuals operating separately.

The *central objective* of a system is its measure of performance. Hopefully, this will be the output of the system. Objectives may be classified as *real* or *stated.* The *real* objective of the system will not be sacrificed to achieve other goals. For example, if one's real objective is to maximize income, one will sacrifice entertainment and other activities that decrease available work time. But, this also means that one must not sacrifice components of one's health subsystem that are necessary to one's ability to perform work. The *stated* objective may be the *real* objective, but it is not uncommon for an organization to print one objective and to operate by a different objective. An analysis of the company's system will reveal the *real* objective. An organization may state that its objective is a quality product, but in reality it sacrifices quality to increase profits. Obviously, this is not a comprehensive example because the objective may have several constraints. Therefore, it is important to accurately identify the objectives when developing or analyzing a system for the organization.

Elements of Systems

To reconstruct or construct organizations in the systems framework, the elements of systems must be considered. The elements that are most appropriate for consideration are:

1. Outputs
2. Inputs
3. Processor
4. Subsystems
5. Suprasystem or environment
6. Boundaries—interface

7. Control
8. Feedback

Illustration 1 shows the schematic for a system. This system helps to portray those elements which are integrated by design to achieve the objectives of that system.

Outputs are a major consideration as a system element. The objective of any system is to render an output that has value to its environment. Only by coping with the environment in an adaptive manner can the system exchange goods, products, and service for other considerations of value. The reason for the system's existence is the rendering of outputs which have value for its environment. This output can be an automobile, it can be an insurance policy that is underwritten, it can be an educated student, it can be a consulting service, or it can be medical care. Whatever the output, it must find usefulness through a transaction in which the environment finds utility or satisfaction in that output.

The *input* consists of those factors which are applied to the system. In classical economics, these factors might be the production factors of land, labor, capital and entrepreneurship. In a more modern sense, the inputs may be information, energy, and resources. From another perspective, the inputs into an organization might be human, technological, and social. The inputs also refer to the configuration, the rate, or the energizing of the application of resources that are applied to the system that in a final form will be rendered as outputs. In a very real sense, an input-output function is the contribution that is rendered by any kind of organizational system.

Illustration 1 A schematic of a system

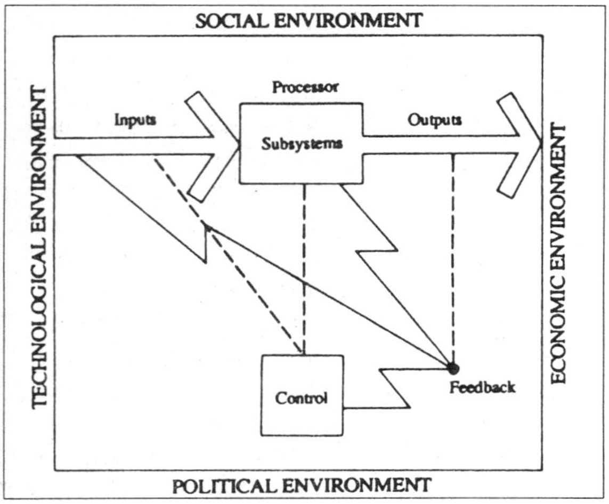

The *processor* is that element of the system which involves a transformation or conversion process which modifies the input into the output format. By this process, the nature of input may be modified or at least treated in some manner so as to add value to the output which has been rendered by the processor. Part of any organization is a processor function which may be difficult to disassemble or analyze, but which does represent the operational efforts of the organization.

Subsystems are elements which lie within the processor or the system under consideration, and which may have unique and identifiable functions. For instance, the personnel department could be considered a subsystem of an organization which performs a function on behalf of the organization. It does have an identity, but needs to recognize the role it has with the entire organization. As such, each subsystem performs a necessary role in the processing which is accomplished by the system, and contributes something to the transformation of input resources into the output which is finally rendered.

The *suprasystem* or environment is the larger setting in which the system exists. It constitutes the ecology of the system and is composed of all those elements which impinge on the system and which may find some meaningful relationship with the system. This suprasystem, which has the system as one of its subsystems, may provide constraints upon the system we are analyzing.

The basic characteristics of a system's environment are:

1. The system can do very little about the environment's behavior or characteristics.
2. It determines in part how the system performs.
3. It is the requirement schedule—"demand" is in the environment.

From the system's point of view, if the system cannot do anything about *it* and *it* matters, relative to the objectives of the system, the *it* is part of the environment.

In the hierarchal sense mentioned as a characteristic of systems, every system has a suprasystem within which it exists. For example, a business organization is within a larger system of its industry, or the economy. As in Illustration 1, the suprasystem has technological, social, economic, and political dimensions. The suprasystems encompasses the system under scrutiny. One might further note that there would be transactions involving interchange or information, energy, and resources between the system and the suprasystem. Particular concern can be stressed for the relationship between the outputs of the system and the suprasystem which should absorb those outputs and find them of transactional value.

The *boundaries* provide an interface between the system under concern and parts of adjoining systems. As such, the boundaries may be defined arbitrarily, but they must be observable. The boundaries are limitations or parameters that provide interface with elements of the same organization or other organizations. While boundaries may be considered a form of limit, they do provide a surface of interface through which inputs and outputs pass into and out of the heart of the system (the processor).

The *control* element provides managerial guidance for the system. Since it is the information network that connects the managerial function with the processor, the output function, the input function, and the suprasystem, the control element is heavily involved in decision considerations. This means that desired outputs can be established and pursued by means of the operational function of the system through the guidance of the control element.

The *feedback* system is an element which measures output with regard to a standard, usually in a cybernetic system which involves communication and control. The evaluations of variances can be feedback to the control element or into the input or processor element to reduce the negative variation between output and desired outcome.

Each element of the system has a specific function. Working in harmony, they provide the integrated operation that is the desired activity for the organization under our examination.

Types of Systems

Within general categories, systems can be classified in several different ways. Some of the more common ways for classifying systems that would be of concern to students of management are:

1. Physical or abstract
2. Natural or man-made
3. Manned
4. Open or closed

The frame of reference within which one views systems is of great consequence to the use of the systems approach as a framework for studying management. For example, systems can be viewed as physical systems. *Physical* systems are tangible entities which have physical presence. Physical systems can be determined to be static or dynamic. A building is an example of a static system, whereas an organization is an example of a dynamic system. Much of the concern of managers is with physical systems which represent the transformation of distribution of goods and products which have physical attributes, and which can be seen, counted, weighed, or measured. *Abstract* systems are those which may be conceptual, but in almost every case are nonphysical. An abstract system may constitute a set of variables which are of concern to a manager as they relate to a problem. An equation can be considered an abstract system, as might the double entry bookkeeping system. Major concerns in abstract systems are variables or constants that constitute that abstract system as well as the relationship between variables. Of particular concern is the use of models to represent abstract systems. In a very practical sense, the executive uses models, abstract conceptualizations of physical situations, or operational problems as he attempts to make decisions or solve problems in his role as an executive. While physical and abstract systems may appear to be at opposite ends of a continuum, there is a concern for relating the two in the sense that much of the task of managers is to relate from physical systems to abstract systems for decision making and problem solving, and then to successfully transform the outcome of those abstract deliberations back into a physical world with physical systems to achieve results.

Natural systems are to be found in the environment of the organization or system of concern. Much concern is expressed today over the conservation of natural systems, such as the landscape, shores, and beaches, and the atmosphere. More immediate acquaintanceship to most students of management are *man-made* systems. Man-made systems display many properties of natural systems except that those systems are designed by man to be more adaptive in the sense that they help man cope with his environment. Forest products from the natural system are converted into housing as a shelter to help man deal with the elements. An organization or a company is a man-made system. The man-made system may exist in an environment which may be somewhat natural, but a man-made organization is designed to help man adapt to his environment, more and more of which is becoming man-made. Concern about pollution and environmental restoration revolve about the attempts of man to restore balance in the natural environment. The major concern of this work will be with man-made systems. Man-made systems include social systems, production systems, and legal political systems. The sociotechnical system is one of the more complex and challenging forms of a man-made system.

Manned systems are a behavioristic description of systems which involve the participation of man. As such, manned systems can be described in the following ways:

1. Man-man systems or behavioral systems
2. Man-machine systems
3. Machine-machine systems

Man-man systems or *behavioral* systems involve interaction between men as major parties. In this case, man interacts and transacts with man. The role of man as a receiving an initiating party in these negotiations not only adds a humanistic flavor to manned systems, but also provides for variety and possible misunderstanding. These constructs will place particular stress on the social, psychological, and cultural sensitivity of man in the way in which he deals with other persons in his environment. Man as a social being has become an increasingly important concept in the study and practice of management in recent years.

Man-machine systems provide an interesting case in which man interacts with machines to achieve desired outcomes. In the production function, and in the interest of improving the operation of the activity of the organization, machines ordinarily are introduced into an operation to replace functions which previously were performed by man. In this sense, man operates with typewriters, automobiles, conveyors, and elevators in order to do his business in a more efficient and effective manner. A general decision influence in man-machine systems is that an objective of the use of machines is to free man for that type of activity in which he can be most effective.

Machine-machine systems refer to automated systems in which man has a role only in initiating the system or in terminating the system. While man may also be involved in monitoring the system, machines interact with machines in such a manner as to test goods or to perform certain activities and free man for other kinds of endeavor. Automation is becoming an increasingly important concept in the organization today whereby men may be freed upon routine or heavily physical tasks to perform more creative and innovative kinds of work. This has introduced much controvery into the picture of industrial relations and labor relations, but does purport to improve the effectiveness of the system.

A *closed* system is considered to be isolated from its environment. It does not exchange energy with the environment when it is in a state of equilibrium. L. von Bertalanffy concluded that "a system is closed if no material enters or leaves it. To perform work, however, the system must be, not in equilibrium but tending to attain it."3

The boundaries of the system are strictly observed, and the interface surfaces are impermeable. The thermostat is the classic example of the closed system in which environmental influences are ignored as the sensor of the thermostat determines when and how long heat may be applied to maintain a steady state. For purposes of analysis, some organizations can be considered as closed systems. While this may be somewhat unrealistic, it may permit a form of analysis that is easier if the assumptions of the closed system are accurately handled.

Most organic systems are *open* systems. Open systems permit and facilitate exchange of energies, informaion, and resources with the suprasystem. Most organizations are open systems. In that sense, the organizations do interact with their environments as they render outputs that purportedly have value to that environment, and they receive inputs of some type as information, energy, or other resources that are applied to the processor. The concept of the open system is of great value and importance to the study of the organization as will be seen in later readings.

In our discussion of the types of systems, one must emphasize the distinction between types of systems and *feedback loops*. When one discusses information and control systems, one will identify a *"closed loop sequence"* and an *"open loop sequence."*

The *closed loop sequence* represents feedback measurement of the output and resultant adjustments in the input to bring about the desired results. The control device is an element of the system it serves and the system can be an open system or a closed system. The heating system employing the thermostat is a closed system with a closed loop sequence. The business organization interacting with its environment is an open system with a closed loop sequence in that it receives feedback in its output and adjusts input accordingly.

The *open loop sequence* involves control by a device or person that is not an integral part of the system. An example is a street light controlled by a timer. The timer does not measure the objectives of the lights. It simply controls the switch to turn the lights on and off at certain hours. If the weather is overcast and lights are needed, the *timer* does not recognize the variable. The control is not exerted in terms of operation.

Methods of System Study

Two methods are most useful in studying a system. These methods are the black box system and the analytic system.

In the *black box* approach, the system is considered as an entity which is impenetrable, but which can be studied in terms of input-output relationships. Considering the output as a dependent variable which is a function of the application of inputs as independent variables, relationships can be observed. Intervening processes native to the processor, the black box, are derived which may permit us to make certain observations about the processor. In the origin of black box studies, in electronics, it was assumed that the so-called black box was not capable of analysis. In one sense, the human mind might be used this way, but one can infer what happens in the mind by relating the outputs of mental activity to the inputs that were applied. The economic tool of analysis, called input-output analysis, is an example of this type of reasoning. Certain types of experimentation operate on the same principle.

An *analytic* form of study is also available. In this method, several steps are taken. The normal procedure is to:

1. Determine the identity of the system. What is a system? What are its boundaries, and exactly what does the system purport to do?
2. What are the objectives of the system? What outputs does the system purport to generate? What is its function or what are the goals that it seeks as it attempts to cope with its environment?
3. What are the parts of the system and what is the objective of each of those subsystems? In what ways do the subsystems relate with each other?
4. How are the subsystems integrated so that they operate in a truly holistic form?

The most crucial question is the question of integration. A system should operate in a manner befitting the identity it claims in order to achieve the objectives it entertains. Questions in the analytic format are of major concern to any organization, but may be used in a general scheme which involves the analysis or breakdown of the organization followed by the synthesis or the integration of those parts into a meaningful, applicable, integrated whole.

The Organizational System

An organization is very appropriately viewed as a system. The Seiler model in Illustration 2 shows an organizational nature. The actual behavior or processor or the organizational system consists of activities, interactions, and sentiments. The outputs rendered by that organizational system can be defined as productivity, satisfaction, and development. It can be noted that each of those are engaged in interaction with other units. In the context of the organizational system as a largely behavioral system, it is interesting to note that the particular flavor of this side of the model has evolved from work done by Homans in sociological literature. Such a view of the organization as a system supports the contention of many authors and scholars that organizations can be viewed as a sociotechnical system or as a psychosocial system.

This type of delineation reflects the major flavor of the organization or the way in which it is viewed as an abstract system. Another very useful way of viewing the organization as a system is to evaluate some basic considerations proposed by Churchman about the meaning of systems. He submits some steps of system description, such as:

1. The total system objectives and more specifically the performance of the whole system.
2. The system's environment; the fixed constraints.
3. The resources of the system.
4. The components of the system, the activities, goals, and measures of performance.
5. The management of the system.[4]

Each of those considerations relates directly to the elements of the system outlined earlier, but pertains to a managerial consideration of organizations as systems. In this manner, (1) the *organization* can be described as a system in very operational terms to include profit or growth as a measure of performance, (2) The *environment* can be considered as a constraint on capital, prices, demand, and technology, (3) *resources* can be considered dollars, personnel, or materials, (4) *components* can be equated with product lines, and (5) *management* can be represented by decision making about resources.

Discussion Questions

1. What are some common ways in which we use the word "system"? How do they differ in meaning? What aspects of meaning do they share?
2. Think of a system with which you are familiar. Identify the following elements of the system: stated central objective, real central objective, subsystems, suprasystems, inputs, outputs, processor, boundaries, control, feedback. How does the system interact with other systems and its environment? In what ways are the system's component parts interdependent? How are the parts integrated into a total system?
3. Provide examples of systems from your own experience, and answer each of the following descriptions: physical, abstract, natural, manufactured, behavioral, human-machine, machine-machine, closed, open. Which of

Illustration 2 An elementary framework for diagnosing human behavior in organizations

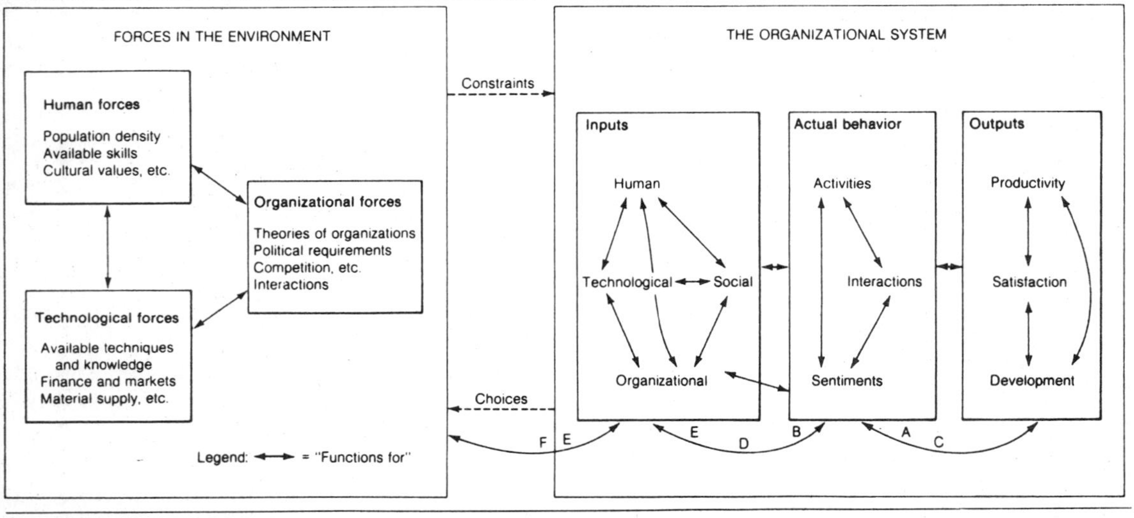

Reproduced with permission from Systems Analysis in Organization Behavior by J. Seiler (Homewood, IL: Richard D. Irwin, Inc., 1967), p. 33.

these descriptions apply to the system you used in answering Question 2?

4. What is the difference between the "black box" approach and the analytic approach? In what circumstances would each be useful? Is it reasonable to apply both approaches to the same system? Why or why not?

Footnotes

1. Eric W. Leaver, "How Automatic Can We Get?" in *Keeping Pace with Automation*, American Management Association, Special Report 7, 1956, pp. 1-2.
2. Richard A. Johnson, Fremont E. Kast, and James E. Rosenzweig, *The Theory and Management of Systems* (New York: McGraw-Hill Book Company, 1973), p. 129.
3. Ludwig von Bertalanffy, "The Theory of Open Systems in Physics and Biology," *Science*, Vol. III (1950), p. 23.
4. C. West Churchman, *The Systems Approach* (New York: Dell Publishing Company, 1968), pp. 29-30.

READING 2

General Systems Theory: Applications for Organization and Management

article by
FREMONT E. KAST and
JAMES E. ROSENZWEIG

Biological and social scientists generally have embraced systems concepts. Many organization and management theorists seem anxious to identify with this movement and to contribute to the development of an approach which purports to offer the ultimate—the unification of all science into one grand conceptual model. Who possibly could resist? General systems theory seems to provide a relief from the limitations of more mechanistic approaches and a rationale for rejecting "principles" based on relatively "closed-system" thinking. This theory provides the paradigm for organization and management theorists to crank into their systems model all of the diverse knowledge from relevant underlying disciplines. It has become almost mandatory to have the word "system" in the title of recent articles and books (many of us have compromised and placed it only in the subtitle).[1]

Source: *Academy of Management Journal*, December 1972, pp. 447-465.

But where did it all start? This question projects us back into history and brings to mind the long-standing philosophical arguments between mechanistic and organismic models of the 19th and early 20th centuries. As Deutsch says:

> Both mechanistic and organismic models were based substantially on experiences and operations known before 1850. Since then, the experience of almost a century of scientific and technological progress has so far not been utilized for any significant new model for the study of organization, and in particular of human thought [1, p. 389].

General systems theory even revives the specter of the "vitalists" and their views on "life force" and most certainly brings forth renewed questions of teleological or purposeful behavior of both living and nonliving systems. Phillips and others have suggested that the philosophical roots of general systems theory go back even further, at least to the German philosopher Hegel (1770-1831) [2, p. 56].

Thus we should recognize that in the adoption of the systems approach for the study of organizations we are not dealing with newly discovered ideas—they have a rich genealogy.

Even in the field of organization and management theory, systems views are not new. Chester Barnard used a basic systems framework.

> A cooperative system is a complex of physical, biological, personal, and social components which are in a specific systematic relationship by reason of the cooperation of two or more persons for at least one definite end. Such a system is evidently a subordinate unit of larger systems from one point of view; and itself embraces subsidiary systems—physical, biological, etc.—from another point of view. One of the systems within a cooperative system, the one which is implicit in the phrase "cooperation of two or more persons," is called an "organization" [3, p. 65].

And Barnard was influenced by the "systems views" of Vilfredo Pareto and Talcott Parsons. Certainly this quote (dressed up a bit to give the term "system" more emphasis) could be the introduction to a 1972 book on organizations.

Miller points out that Alexander Bogdanov, the Russian philosopher, developed a theory of tektology or universal organization science in 1912 which foreshadowed general systems theory and used many of the same concepts as modern systems theorists [4, pp. 249-50].

However, in spite of a long history of organismic and holistic thinking, the utilization of the systems approach did not become the accepted model for organization and management writers until relatively recently. It is difficult to specify the turning point exactly. The momentum of systems thinking was identified by Scott in 1961 when he described the relationship between general systems theory and organization theory.

> The distinctive qualities of modern organization theory are its conceptual-analytical base, its reliance on empirical research data, and above all, its integrating nature. These qualities are framed in a philosophy which accepts the premise that the only meaningful way to study organization is to study it as a system. Modern organization theory and general system theory are similar in that they look at organization as an integrated whole [5, pp. 15-21].

Scott said explicitly what many in our field had been thinking and/or implying—he helped us put into perspective the important writings of Herbert Simon, James March, Talcott Parsons, George Homans, E. Wight Bakke, Kenneth Boulding, and many others.

But how far have we really advanced over the past decade in applying general systems theory to organizations and their management? Is it still a "skeleton," or have we been able to "put some meat on the bones"? The systems approach has been touted because of its potential usefulness in understanding the complexities of "live" organizations. Has this approach really helped us in this endeavor or has it compounded confusion with chaos? Herbert Simon describes the challenge for the systems approach:

> In both science and engineering, the study of "systems" is an increasingly popular activity. Its popularity is more a response to a pressing need for synthesizing and analyzing complexity than it is to any large development of a body of knowledge and technique for dealing with complexity. If this popularity is to be more than a fad, necessity will have to mother invention and provide a substance to go with the name [6, p. 114].

In this article we will explore the issue of whether we are providing substance for the term *systems approach* as it relates to the study of organizations and their management. There are many interesting historical and philosophical questions concerning the relationship between the mechanistic and organistic approaches and their applicability to the various fields of science, as well as other interesting digressions into the evolution of systems approaches. However, we will resist those temptations and plunge directly into a discussion of the key concepts of general systems theory, the way in which these ideas have been used by organization theorists, the limitations in their application, and some suggestions for the future.

Key Concepts of General Systems Theory

The key concepts of general systems theory have been set forth by many writers [7] and have been used by many organization and management theorists [8]. It is not our purpose here to elaborate on them in great detail because we anticipate that most readers will have been exposed to them in some depth. Figure I provides a very brief review of those characteristics of systems which seem to have wide acceptance. The review is far from complete. It is difficult to identify a complete list of characteristics derived from general systems theory; moreover, it is merely a first-order classification. There are many derived second- and third-order characteristics which could be considered. For example, James G. Miller sets forth 165 hypotheses, stemming from open systems theory, which might be applicable to two or more levels of systems [9]. He suggests that they are *general* systems theoretical hypotheses and qualifies them by suggesting that they are propositions applicable to general systems *behavior* theory and would thus exclude nonliving systems. He does not limit these propositions to individual organisms, but considers them appropriate for social systems as well. His hypotheses are related to such issues as structure, process, subsystems, information, growth, and integration. It is obviously impossible to discuss all of these hypotheses; we only want to indicate the extent to which many interesting propositions are being posed which might have relevance to many different types of systems. It will be a very long time (if ever) before most of these hypotheses are validated; however, we are surprised at how many of them can be agreed with intuitively, and we can see their possible verification in studies of social organizations.

We turn now to a closer look at how successful or unsuccessful we have been in utilizing these concepts in the development of "modern organization theory."

A Beginning: Enthusiastic But Incomplete

We have embraced general systems theory but, really, how completely? We could review a vast literature in modern organization theory which has explicitly or implicitly adopted systems theory as a frame of reference, and we have investigated in detail a few examples of the literature in assessing the "state of the art" [10]. It was found that most of these books professed to utilize general systems theory. Indeed, in the first few chapters, many of them did an excellent job of presenting basic systems concepts and showing their relationship to organizations; however, when they moved further into the discussion of more specific subject matter, they departed substantially from systems theory. The studies appear to use a "partial systems approach" and leave for the reader the problem of integrating the various ideas into a systematic whole. It also appears that many of the authors are unable, because of limitations of knowledge about subsystem relationships, to carry out the task of using general systems theory as a conceptual basis for organization theory.

Furthermore, it is evident that each author had many "good ideas" stemming from the existing body of knowledge or current research on organizations which did not fit neatly into a "systems model." For example, they might discuss leadership from a relatively closed-system point of view and not consider it in relationship to organizational technology, structure, or other variables. Our review of the literature suggests that much remains to be done in applying general systems theory to organization theory and management practice.

Some Dilemmas in Applying GST to Organizations

Why have writers embracing general systems theory as a basis for studying organizations had so much difficulty in following through? Part of this difficulty may stem from the newness of the paradigm and our inability to operationalize "all we think we know" about this approach. Or it may be because we know too little about the systems under investigation. Both of these possibilities will be covered later, but first we need to look at some of the more specific conceptual problems.

Figure I Key concepts of general systems theory

Subsystems or components—A system by definition is composed of interrelated parts or elements. This is true for all systems—mechanical, biological, and social. Every system has at least two elements, and these elements are interconnected.

Holism, synergism, organicism, and gestalt—The whole is not just the sum of the parts; the system itself can be explained only as a totality. Holism is the opposite of elementarism, which views the total as the sum of its individual parts.

Open systems view—Systems can be considered in two ways: (1) closed or (2) open. Open systems exchange information, energy, or material with their environments. Biological and social systems are inherently open systems; mechanical systems may be open or closed. The concepts of open and closed systems are difficult to defend in the absolute. We prefer to think of open-closed as a dimension; i.e., systems are relatively open or relatively closed.

Input-transformation-output model—The open system can be viewed as a transformation model. In a dynamic relationship with its environment, it receives various inputs, transforms these inputs in some way, and exports outputs.

System boundaries—It follows that systems have boundaries which separate them from their environments. The concept of boundaries helps us understand the distinction between open and closed systems. The relatively closed system has rigid, impenetrable boundaries; whereas the open system has permeable boundaries between itself and a broader suprasystem. Boundaries are relatively easily defined in physical and biological systems but are very difficult to delineate in social systems such as organizations.

Negative entropy—Closed, physical systems are subject to the force of entropy which increases until eventually the entire system fails. The tendency toward maximum entropy is a movement to disorder, complete lack of resource transformation, and death. In a closed system, the change in entropy must always be positive; however, in open biological or social systems, entropy can be arrested and may even be transformed into negative entropy—a process of more complete organization and ability to transform resources—because the system imports resources from its environment.

Steady state, dynamic equilibrium, and homeostasis—The concept of steady state is closely related to that of negative entropy. A closed system eventually must attain an equilibrium state with maximum entropy—death or disorganization. However, an open system may attain a state where the system remains in dynamic equilibrium through the continuous inflow of materials, energy, and information.

Feedback—The concept of feedback is important in understanding how a system maintains a steady state. Information concerning the outputs or the process of the system is fed back as an input into the system, perhaps leading to changes in the transformation process and/or future outputs. Feedback can be both positive and negative, although the field of cybernetics is based upon negative feedback. Negative feedback is informational input which indicates that the system is deviating from a prescribed course and should readjust to a new steady state.

Hierarchy—A basic concept in systems thinking is that of hierarchical relationships between systems. A system is composed of subsystems of a lower order and is also part of a suprasystem. Thus, there is a hierarchy of the components of the system.

Internal elaboration—Closed systems move toward entropy and disorganization. In contrast, open systems appear to move in the direction of greater differentiation, elaboration, and a higher level of organization.

Multiple goal seeking—Biological and social systems appear to have multiple goals or purposes. Social organizations seek multiple goals, if for no other reason than that they are composed of individuals and subunits with different values and objectives.

Equifinality of open systems—In mechanistic systems there is a direct cause-and-effect relationship between the initial conditions and the final state. Biological and social systems operate differently. Equifinality suggests that certain results may be achieved with different initial conditions and in different ways. This view suggests that social organizations can accomplish their objectives with diverse inputs and with varying internal activities (conversion processes).

Organizations as Organisms

One of the basic contributions of general systems theory was the rejection of the traditional closed-system, or mechanistic view of social organizations. But did general systems theory free us from this constraint only to impose another, less obvious one? General systems theory grew out of the organismic views of von Bertalanffy and other biologists; thus, many of the characteristics are relevant to the living organism. It is conceptually easy to draw the analogy between living organisms and social organizations. "There is, after all, an intuitive similarity between the organization of the human body and the kinds of organizations men create. And so, undaunted by the failures of the human-social analogy through time, new theorists try afresh in each epoch." [11, p. 660]. General systems theory would have us accept this analogy between organism and social organization. Yet, we have a hard time swallowing it whole. Katz and Kahn warn us of the danger:

> There has been no more pervasive, persistent, and futile fallacy handicapping the social sciences than the use of the physical model for the understanding of social structures. The biological metaphor, with its crude comparison of the physical parts of the body to the parts of the social system, has been replaced by more subtle but equally misleading analogies between biological and social functioning. This figurative type of thinking ignores the essential difference between the socially contrived nature of social systems and the physical structure of the machine or the human organism. So long as writers are committed to a theoretical framework based upon the physical model, they will miss the essential social-psychological facts of the highly variable, loosely articulated character of social systems [12, p. 31].

In spite of this warning, Katz and Kahn do embrace many of the general systems theory concepts which are based on the biological metaphor. We must be very cautious about trying to make this analogy too literal. We agree with Silverman, who says, "It may, therefore, be necessary to drop the analogy between an organization and organism: organizations may be systems but not necessarily *natural* systems" [13, p. 31].

Distinction Between Organization and An Organization

General systems theory emphasizes that systems are organized—they are composed of interdependent components in some relationship. The social organization would then follow logically as just another system. But we are perhaps being caught in circular thinking. It is true that all systems (physical, biological, and social) are by definition organized, but are all systems organizations? Rapoport and Horvath distinguish "organization theory" and "the theory of organizations" as follows:

> We see organization theory as dealing with general and abstract organizational principles; it applies to any system exhibiting organized complexity. As such, organization theory is seen as an extension of mathematical physics or, even more generally, of mathematics designed to deal with organized systems. The theory of organizations, on the other hand, purports to be a social science. It puts real human organizations at the center of interest. It may study the social structure of organizations and so can be viewed as a branch of sociology; it can study the behavior of individuals or groups as members of organizations and can be viewed as a part of social psychology; it can study power relations and principles of control in organizations and so fits into political science [14, pp. 74-75].

Why make an issue of this distinction? It seems to us that there is a vital matter involved. All systems may be considered to be organized, and more advanced systems may display differentiation in the activities of component parts—such as the specialization of human organs. However, all systems *do not* have purposeful entities. Can the heart or lungs be considered as purposeful entities in themselves or are they only components of the larger purposeful system, the human body? By contrast, the social organization is composed of two or more purposeful elements. "An organization consists of elements that have and can exercise their own wills" [15, p. 669]. Organisms, the foundation stone of general systems theory, do not contain purposeful elements which exercise their own will. This distinction between the organism and the social organization is of importance. In much of general systems theory, the concern is primarily with the way in which the *organism* responds to environmentally generated inputs. Feedback concepts and the maintenance of a steady state are based on internal adaptations to environmental forces. (This is particularly true of cybernetic models.) But what about those changes and adaptations which occur from *within* social organizations? Purposeful elements within the social organization may initiate activities and adaptations which are difficult to subsume under feedback and steady state concepts.

Open and Closed Systems

Another dilemma stemming from general systems theory is the tendency to dichotomize all systems as open or closed. We have been led to think of physical systems as closed, subject to the laws of entropy, and to think of biological systems as open to their environment and, possibly, becoming negentropic. But applying this strict polarization to social organizations creates many difficulties. In fact, most social organizations and their subsystems are "partially open" and "partially closed." Open and closed are a matter of degree. Unfortunately, there seems to be a widely held view (often more implicit than explicit) that *open-system thinking is good and closed-system thinking is bad*. We have not become sufficiently sophisticated to recognize that both are appropriate under certain conditions. For example, one of the most useful conceptualizations set forth by Thompson is that the social organization *must seek* to use closed-system concepts (particularly at the technical core) to reduce uncertainty and to create more effective performance at this level.

Still Subsystems Thinking

Even though we preach a general systems approach, we often practice subsystems thinking. Each of the academic disciplines and each of us personally has limited perspective of the system we are studying. While proclaiming a broad systems viewpoint, we often dismiss variables outside our interest or competence as being irrelevant, and open our system only to those inputs which we can handle with our disciplinary bag of tools. We are hampered because each of the academic disciplines has taken a narrow, "partial systems view" and find comfort in the relative certainty which this creates. Of course, this is not a problem unique to modern organization theory. Under the more traditional process approach to the study of management we were able to do an admirable job of delineating and discussing planning, organizing, and controlling as separate activities. We were much less successful in discussing them as integrated and interrelated activities.

How Does Our Knowledge Fit?

One of the major problems in utilizing general systems theory is that we know (or think we know) more about certain relationships than we can fit into a general systems model. For example, we are beginning to understand the two-variable relationship between technology and structure. But when we introduce another variable, say, psychosocial relationships, our models become too complex. Consequently, in order to discuss all the things we know about organizations, we depart from a systems approach. Perhaps it is because we know a great deal more about the elements or subsystems of an organization than we do about the interrelationships and interactions between these subsystems. And general systems theory forces us to consider those relationships about which we know the least—a true dilemma. So we continue to elaborate on those aspects of the organization which we know best—a partial systems view.

Failure to Delineate a Specific System

When the social sciences embraced general systems theory, the total system became the focus of attention and terminology tended toward vagueness. In the utilization of systems theory, we should be more precise in delineating the specific system under consideration. Failure to do this leads to much confusion. As Murray suggests:

> I am wary of the word "system" because social scientists use it very frequently without specifying which of several possible different denotations they have in mind; but more particularly because, today, "system" is a highly cathected term, loaded with prestige; hence, we are all strongly tempted to employ it even when we have nothing definite in mind and its only service is to indicate that we subscribe to the general premise respecting the interdependence of things—basic to organismic theory, holism, field theory, interactionism, transactionism, etc. . . . When definitions of the units of a system are lacking, the term stands for no more than an article of faith, and is misleading to boot, insofar as it suggests a condition of affairs that may not actually exist [16, pp. 50-51].

We need to be much more precise in delineating both the boundaries of the system under consideration and the level of our analysis. There is a tendency for current writers in organization theory to accept general systems theory and then to move indiscriminately across systems boundaries and between levels of systems without being very precise (and letting their readers in on what is occurring). James Miller suggests the need for clear delineation of levels in applying systems theory: "It is important to follow one procedural rule in systems theory in order to avoid confusion. Every discussion should begin with an identification of the level of reference, and the discourse should not change to another level without a specific statement that this is occurring" [9, p. 216]. Our field is replete with these confusions about systems levels. For example, when we use the term "organizational behavior" are we talking about the way the organization behaves as a system or are we talking about the behavior of the individual participants? By goals, do we mean the goals of the organization or the goals of the individuals within the organization? In using systems theory we must become more precise in our delineation of systems boundaries and systems levels if we are to prevent confusing conceptual ambiguity.

Recognition that Organizations are "Contrived Systems"

We have a vague uneasiness that general systems theory truly does not recognize the "contrived" nature of social organizations. With its predominate emphasis on natural organisms, it may understate some characteristics which are vital for the social organization. Social organizations do not occur naturally in nature; they are contrived by man. They have structure; but it is the structure of events rather than of physical components, and it cannot be separated from the processes of the system. The fact that social organizations are contrived by human beings suggests that they can be established for an infinite variety of purposes and do not follow the same life-cycle patterns of birth, growth, maturity, and death as biological systems. As Katz and Kahn say:

> Social structures are essentially contrived systems. They are made of men and are imperfect systems. They can come apart at the seams overnight, but they can also outlast by centuries the biological organisms which originally created them. The cement which holds them together is essentially psychological rather than biological. Social systems are anchored in the attitudes, perceptions, beliefs, motivations, habits, and expectations of human beings [12, p. 33].

Recognizing that the social organization is contrived, again cautions us against making an exact analogy between it and physical or biological systems.

Questions of Systems Effectiveness

General systems theory with its biological orientation would appear to have an evolutionary view of systems effectiveness. That living system which best adapts to its environment prospers and survives. The primary measure of effectiveness is perpetuation of the organism's species. Teleological behavior is therefore directed toward survival. But is survival the only criterion of effectiveness of the social system? It is probably an essential but not all-inclusive measure of effectiveness.

General systems theory emphasizes the organism's survival goal and does not fully relate to the question of the effectiveness of the system in its suprasystem—the environment. Parsonian functional-structural views provide a contrast. "The *raison d'etre* of complex organizations according to this analysis is mainly to benefit the society in which they belong, and that society is, therefore, the appropriate frame of reference for the evaluation of organizational effectiveness" [17, p. 896].

But this view seems to go to the opposite extreme from the survival view of general systems theory—the organization exists to serve the society. It seems to us that the truth lies somewhere between these two viewpoints. And it is likely that a systems viewpoint (modified from the species survival view of general systems theory) will be most appropriate. Yuchtman and Seashore suggest:

> The organization's success over a period of time in this competition for resources—i.e., its bargaining position in a given environment—is regarded as an expression of its overall effectiveness. Since the resources are of various kinds, and the competitive relationships are multiple, and since there is interchangeability among classes of resources, the assessment of organizational effectiveness must be in terms not of any single criterion but of an open-ended multidimensional set of criteria [17, p. 891].

This viewpoint suggests that questions of organizational effectiveness must be concerned with at least three levels of analysis. The level of the environment, the level of the social organization as a system, and the level of the subsystems (human participants) within the organization. Perhaps much of our confusion and ambiguity concerning organizational effectiveness stems from our failure to clearly delineate the level of our analysis and even more important, our failure really to understand the relationships among these levels.

Our discussion of some of the problems associated with the application of general systems theory to the study of social organizations might suggest that we completely reject the appropriateness of this model. On the contrary, we see the systems approach as the new paradigm for the study of organizations; but, like all new concepts in the sciences, one which has to be applied, modified, and elaborated in order to make it as useful as possible.

Systems Theory Provides the New Paradigm

We hope the discussion of GST and organizations provides a realistic appraisal. We do not want to promote the value of the systems approach as a matter of faith; however, we do see systems theory as vital to the study of social organizations and as providing the major new paradigm for our field of study.

Thomas Kuhn provides an interesting interpretation of the nature of scientific revolution [18]. He suggests that major changes in all fields of science occur with the development of new conceptual schemes or "paradigms." These new paradigms do not represent just a step-by-step advancement in "normal" science (the science generally accepted and practiced) but rather a revolutionary change in the way the scientific field is perceived by the practitioners. Kuhn says:

> The historian of science may be tempted to exclaim that when paradigms change, the world itself changes with them. Led by a new paradigm, scientists adopt new instruments and look in new places. Even more important, during revolutions scientists see new and different things when looking with familiar instruments in places they have looked before. It is rather as if the professional community has been suddenly transported to another planet where familiar objects are seen in a different light and are joined by unfamiliar ones as well. . . . Paradigm changes do cause scientists to see the world of their research-engagement differently. Insofar as their only recourse to that world is through what they see and do, we may want to say that after a revolution scientists are responding to a different world [18, p. 110].

New paradigms frequently are rejected by the scientific community. (At first they may seem crude and limited—offering very little more than older paradigms.) They frequently lack the apparent sophistication of the older paradigms which they ultimately replace. They do not display the clarity and certainty of older paradigms which have been refined through years of research and writing. But a new paradigm does provide for a "new start" and opens up new directions which were not possible under the old.

> We must recognize how very limited in both scope and precision a paradigm can be at the time of its first appearance. Paradigms gain their status because they are more successful than their competitors in solving a few problems that the group of practitioners has come to recognize as acute. To be more successful is not, however, to be either completely successful with a single problem or notably successful with any large number [18, p. 23].

Systems theory does provide a new paradigm for the study of social organizations and their management. At this stage it is obviously crude and lacking in precision. In some ways it may not be much better than older paradigms which have been accepted and used for a long time (such as the management process approach). As in other fields of scientific endeavor, the new paradigm must be applied, clarified, elaborated, and made more precise. But it does provide a fundamentally different view of the reality of social organizations and can serve as the basis for major advancements in our field.

We see many exciting examples of the utilization of the new systems paradigm in the field of organization and management. Several of these have been referred to earlier [19], and there have been many others. Burns and Stalker made substantial use of systems views in setting forth their concepts of mechanistic and organic managerial systems [20]. Their studies of the characteristics of these two organization types lack precise definition of the variables and relationships, but their colleagues have used the systems approach to look at the relationship of organizations to their environment and also among the technical, structural, and behavioral characteristics within the organization [21]. Chamberlain used a system view in studying enterprises and their environment which is substantially different from traditional microeconomics [22]. The emerging field of "environmental sciences" and "environmental administration" has found the systems paradigm vital.

Thus, the systems theory paradigm is being used extensively in the investigation of relationships between subsystems within organizations and in studying the environmental interfaces. But it still has not advanced sufficiently to meet the needs. One of the major problems is that the practical need to deal with comprehensive systems of relationships is overrunning our ability to fully understand and predict these relationships. *We vitally need the systems paradigm but we are not sufficiently sophisticated to use it appropriately.* This is the dilemma. Do our current failures to fully utilize the systems paradigm suggest that we reject it and return to the older, more traditional and time-tested paradigms? Or do we work with systems theory to make it more precise, to understand the relationships among subsystems, and to gather the informational inputs which are necessary to make the systems approach really work? We think the latter course offers the best opportunity.

Thus, we prefer to accept current limitations of systems theory, while working to reduce them and to develop more complete and sophisticated approaches for its application. We agree with Rapoport who says:

> The system approach to the study of man can be appreciated as an effort to restore meaning (in terms of intuitively grasped understanding of wholes) while adhering to the principles of *disciplined* generalizations and rigorous deduction. It is, in short, an attempt to make the study of man both scientific and meaningful [23, p. xxii].

We are sympathetic with the second part of Rapoport's comment, the need to apply the systems approach but to make disciplined generalizations and rigorous deductions. This is a vital necessity and yet a major current limitation. We do have some indication that progress (although very slow) is being made.

What Do We Need Now?

Everything is related to everything else—but how? General systems theory provides us with the macro paradigm for the study of social organizations. As Scott and others have pointed out, most sciences go through a macro-micro-macro cycle or sequence of emphasis [5]. Traditional bureaucratic theory provided the first major macro view of organizations. Administrative management theorists concentrated on the development of macro "principles of management" which were applicable to all organizations. When these macro views seemed incomplete (unable to explain important phenomena), attention turned to the micro level—more detailed analysis of components or parts of the organization, thus the interest in human relations, technology, or structural dimensions.

The systems approach returns us to the macro level with a new paradigm. General systems theory emphasizes a very high level of abstraction. Phillips classifies it as a third-order study [2] that attempts to develop macro concepts appropriate for all types of biological, physical, and social systems.

In our view, we are now ready to move down a level of abstraction to consider second-order systems studies or mid-range concepts. These will be based on general systems theory but will be more concrete and will emphasize more specific characteristics and relationships in social organizations. They will operate within the broad paradigm of systems theory but at a less abstract level.

What should we call this new midrange level of analysis? Various authors have referred to it as a "contingency view," a study of "patterns of relationships," or a search for "configurations among subsystems." Lawrence and Lorsch reflect this view:

> During the past few years there has been evident a new trend in the study of organizational phenomena. Underlying this new approach is the idea that the internal functioning of organizations must be consistent with the demands of the organization task, technology, or external environment, and the needs of its members if the organization is to be effective. Rather than searching for the panacea of the one best way to organize under all conditions, investigators have more and more tended to examine the functioning of organizations in relation to the needs of their particular members and the external pressures facing them. Basically, this approach seems to be leading to the development of a "contingency" theory of organization with the appropriate internal states and processes of the organization contingent upon external requirements and member needs [24, p. 1].

Numerous others have stressed a similar viewpoint. Thompson suggests that the essence of administration lies in understanding basic configurations which exist between the various subsystems and with the environment. "The basic function of administration appears to be coalignment, not merely of people (in coalitions) but of institutionalized action—of technology and task environment into a viable domain, and of organizational design and structure appropriate to it" [25, p. 157].

Bringing these ideas together we can provide a more precise definition of the contingency view:

> The contingency view of organizations and their management suggests that an organization is a system composed of subsystems and delineated by identifiable boundaries from its environmental suprasystem. The contingency view seeks to understand the interrelationships within and among subsystems as well as between the organization and its environment and to define patterns of relationships or configurations of variables. It emphasizes the multivariate nature of organizations and attempts to understand how organizations operate under varying conditions and in specific circumstances. Contingency views are ultimately directed toward suggesting organizational designs and managerial systems most appropriate for specific situations.

But it is not enough to suggest that a "contingency view" based on systems concepts of organizations and their management is more appropriate than the simplistic "principles approach." If organization theory is to advance and make contributions to managerial practice, it must define more explicitly certain patterns of relationships between organizational variables. This is the major challenge facing our field.

Just how do we go about using systems theory to develop these midrange or contingency views? We see no alternative but to engage in intensive comparative investigation of many organizations following the advice of Blau:

> A theory of organization, whatever its specific nature, and regardless of how subtle the organizational processes it takes into account, has as its central aim to establish the constellations of characteristics that develop in organizations of various kinds. Comparative studies of many organizations are necessary, not alone to test the hypotheses implied by such a theory, but also to provide a basis for initial exploration and refinement of the theory by indicating the conditions on which relationships, originally assumed to hold universally are contingent. . . . Systematic research on many organizations that provides the data needed to determine the interrelationships between several organizational features is, however, extremely rare [26, p. 332].

Various conceptual designs for the comparative study of organizations and their subsystems are emerging to help in the development of a contingency view. We do not want to impose our model as to what should be considered in looking for these patterns of relationships. However, the tentative matrix shown in Figure II suggests this approach. We have used as a starting point the two polar organization types which have been emphasized in the literature—closed/stable/mechanistic and open/adaptive/organic.

We would consider the environmental suprasystem and organizational subsystems (goals and values, technical, structural, psychosocial, and managerial) plus various dimensions or characteristics of each of these systems. By way of illustration we have indicated several specific subcategories under the Environmental Suprasystem as well as the Goals and Values Subsystem. This process would have to be completed and extended to all of the subsystems. The next step would be the development of appropriate descriptive language (based on research and conceptualization) for each relevant characteristic across the continuum of organization types. For example, on the "stability" dimension for Goals and Values we would have High, Medium, and Low at appropriate places on the continuum. If the entire matrix were filled in, it is likely that we would begin to see discernible patterns of relationships among subsystems.

We do not expect this matrix to provide *the* midrange model for everyone. It is highly doubtful that we will be able to follow through with the field work investigations necessary to fill in all the squares. Nevertheless, it does illustrate a possible approach for the translation of more abstract general systems theory into an appropriate midrange model which is relevant for organization theory and management practice. Frankly, we see this as a major long-term effort on the part of many researchers, investigating a wide variety of

Figure II Matrix of patterns of relationships between organization types and systems variables

Organizational supra- and subsystems	Continuum of organization types	
	Closed/Stable/Mechanistic	Open/Adaptive/Organic
Environmental relationships		
General nature	Placid	Turbulent
Predictability	Certain, determinate	Uncertain, indeterminate
Boundary relationships	Relatively closed; limited to few participants (sales, purchasing, etc.); fixed and well defined	Relatively open; many participants have external relationships; varied and not clearly defined
Goals and values		
Organizational goals in general	Efficient performance, stability, maintenance	Effective problem solving, innovation, growth
Goal set	Single, clear-cut	Multiple, determined by necessity to satisfy a set of constraints
Stability	Stable	Unstable
Technical		
Structural		
Psychosocial		
Managerial		

organizations. In spite of the difficulties involved in such research, the endeavor has practical significance. Sophistication in the study of organizations will come when we have a more complete understanding of organizations as total systems (configurations of subsystems) so that we can prescribe more appropriate organizational designs and managerial systems. Ultimately, organization theory should serve as the foundation for more effective management practice.

Application of Systems Concepts to Management Practice

The study of organizations is an applied science because the resulting knowledge is relevant to problem-solving in on-going institutions. Contributions to organization theory come from many sources. Deductive and inductive research in a variety of disciplines provides a theoretical base of propositions which are useful for understanding organizations and for managing them. Experience gained in management practice is also an important input to organization theory. In short, management is based on the body of knowledge generated by practical experience *and* eclectic scientific research concerning organizations. The body of knowledge developed through theory and research should be translatable into more effective organizational design and managerial practices.

Do systems concepts and contingency views provide a panacea for solving problems in organizations? The answer is an emphatic *no*; this approach does not provide "ten easy steps" to success in management. Such cookbook approaches, while seemingly applicable and easy to grasp, are usually shortsighted, narrow in perspective, and superficial—in short, unrealistic. Fundamental ideas, such as systems concepts and contingency views, are more difficult to comprehend. However, they facilitate more thorough understanding of complex situations and increase the likelihood of appropriate action.

It is important to recognize that many managers have used and will continue to use a systems approach and contingency views intuitively and implicitly. Without much knowledge of the underlying body of organization theory, they have an intuitive "sense of the situation," are flexible diagnosticians, and adjust their actions and decisions accordingly. Thus, systems concepts and contingency views are not new. However, if this approach to organization theory and management practice can be made more explicit, we can facilitate better management and more effective organizations.

Practicing managers in business firms, hospitals, and government agencies continue to function on a day-to-day basis. Therefore, they must use whatever theory is available; they cannot wait for the *ultimate* body of knowledge (there is none!). Practitioners should be included in the search for new knowledge because they control access to an essential ingredient—organizational data—and they are the ones who ultimately put the theory to the test. Mutual understanding among managers, teachers, and researchers will facilitate the development of a relevant body of knowledge.

Simultaneous with the refinement of the body of knowledge, a concerted effort should be directed toward applying what we do know. We need ways of making systems and contingency views more useable. Without oversimplication, we need some relevant guidelines for practicing managers.

The general tenor of the contingency view is somewhere between simplistic, specific principles and complex, vague notions. It is a midrange concept which recognizes the complexity involved in managing modern organizations but uses patterns of relationships and/or configurations of subsystems in order to facilitate improved practice. The art of management depends on a reasonable success rate for actions in a probabilistic environment. Our hope is that systems concepts and contingency views, while continually being refined by scientists/researchers/theorists, will also be made more applicable.

Discussion Questions

1. How accurate is the analogy between organizations and organisms? In what ways is the analogy misleading? Is it totally without validity? How can it be limited or modified so that it remains a useful guide for understanding organizations?
2. What do the authors mean when they say that social organizations are "contrived systems"? Why are such systems able to continue beyond the lifetimes of the people who create them? What forces can cause them to break down or change?
3. Think of a specific example of a social organization with which you are familiar. How can its effectiveness as a system be measured from the standpoint of its environment? Of the organization itself? Of its human participants? Are these criteria of effectiveness in conflict? Are the conflicts unavoidable, or can they be reconciled?
4. What is the difference between the "contingency view" proposed by the authors and the traditional "principles of management" approach? What deficiencies in the older approach have led Kast and Rosenzweig to propose a new viewpoint? Can you foresee any difficulties in adopting the "contingency view"?

References

1. Karl W. Deutsch, "Toward a Cybernetic Model of Man and Society," in *Modern Systems Research for the Behavioral Scientist*, edited by Walter Buckley (Chicago: Aldine Publishing, 1968).
2. D. C. Phillips, "Systems Theory—A Discredited Philosophy," in *Management Systems*, edited by Peter P. Schoderbek (New York: Wiley, 1971).
3. Chester I. Barnard, *The Functions of the Executive* (Cambridge: Harvard Univ. Press, 1938).
4. Robert F. Miller, "The New Science of Administration in the USSR," *Admin. Sci. Quart.*, Sept. 1971.
5. William G. Scott, "Organization Theory: An Overview and an Appraisal," *Acad. Management J.*, April 1961.
6. Herbert A. Simon, "The Architecture of Complexity," in *Organizations: Systems Control and Adaptation*, Vol. 2, edited by Joseph A. Litterer (New York: Wiley, 1969).
7. Kenneth E. Boulding, "General Systems Theory: The Skeleton of Science," *Management Science*, April 1956; Walter Buckley, editor, *Modern Systems Research for the Behavioral Scientist* (Chicago: Aldine, 1968); David Easton, *A Systems Analysis of Political Life* (New York: Wiley, 1965); A. D. Hall and R. E. Eagen, "Definition of System," *General Systems, Yearbook for the Society for the Advancement of General Systems Theory*, Vol. 1, 1956; James G. Miller, "Living Systems: Basic Concepts," *Behav. Sci.*, July 1965; Talcott Parsons, *The Social System* (New York: Free Press of Glencoe, 1951); Ludwig

von Bertalanffy, *General Systems Theory* (New York: Braziller, 1968).
8. C. West Churchman, *The Systems Approach* (New York: Dell Publishing, 1968); F. E. Emery and E. L. Trist, "Socio-technical Systems," in *Management Sciences: Models and Techniques*, edited by C. W. Churchman and Michele Verhulst (New York: Pergamon, 1960); Fremont E. Kast and James E. Rosenzweig, *Organization and Management Theory: A Systems Approach* (New York: McGraw-Hill, 1970); Daniel Katz and Robert L. Kahn, *The Social Psychology of Organizations* (New York: Wiley, 1966); Joseph A. Litterer, *Organizations: Structure and Behavior*, Vol. 1 (New York: Wiley, 1969); Joseph A. Litterer, *Organizations: Systems, Control and Adaptation*, Vol. 2 (New York: Wiley, 1969); E. J. Miller and A. K. Rice, *Systems of Organizations* (London: Tavistock, 1967); Edgar Schein, *Organizational Psychology*, rev. ed. (Englewood Cliffs: Prentice-Hall, 1970).
9. James G. Miller, op. cit., note 7.
10. Fremont E. Kast and James E. Rosenzweig, op. cit., note 8; Daniel Katz and Robert L. Kahn, op. cit., note 8; Joseph A. Litterer, op. cit., note 8; A. K. Rice, *The Modern University* (London: Tavistock, 1970); James D. Thompson, *Organizations in Action* (New York: McGraw-Hill, 1967).
11. Kurt W. Back, "Biological Models of Social Change," *Amer. Sociological Review*, August 1971.
12. Daniel Katz and Robert L. Kahn, op. cit., note 8.
13. David Silverman, *The Theory of Organizations* (New York: Basic Books, 1971).
14. Anatol Rapoport and William J. Horvath, "Thoughts on Organization Theory," in *Modern Systems Research for the Behavioral Scientist*, edited by Walter Buckley (Chicago: Aldine, 1968).
15. Russell L. Ackoff, "Towards a System of Systems Concepts," *Management Science*, July 1971.
16. Henry A. Murray, "Preparation for the Scaffold of a Comprehensive System," in *Psychology: A Study of a Science*, edited by Sigmund Koch (New York: McGraw-Hill, 1959).
17. Ephraim Yuchtman and Stanley E. Seashore, "A System Resource Approach to Organizational Effectiveness," *Amer. Sociological Review*, Dec. 1967.
18. Thomas S. Kuhn, *The Structure of Scientific Revolutions* (Chicago: Univ. of Chicago Press, 1962).
19. Walter Buckley, editor, op. cit., note 7; David Easton, op. cit., note 7; Daniel Katz and Robert L. Kahn, op. cit., note 8; Joseph A. Litterer, op. cit., note 8; E. J. Miller and A. K. Rice, op. cit., note 8; A. K. Rice, op. cit., note 10; James D. Thompson, op. cit., note 10.
20. Tom Burns and G. M. Stalker, *The Management of Innovation* (London: Tavistock, 1961).
21. E. J. Miller and A. K. Rice, op. cit., note 8.
22. Neil W. Chamberlain, *Enterprise and Environment: The Firm in Time and Place* (New York: McGraw-Hill, 1968).
23. Walter Buckley, editor, op. cit., note 7.
24. Jay W. Lorsch and Paul R. Lawrence, *Studies in Organizational Design* (Homewood, Ill.: Irwin-Dorsey, 1970).
25. James D. Thompson, op. cit., note 10.
26. Peter M. Blau, "The Comparative Study of Organizations," *Industrial and Labor Relations Review*, April 1965.

Footnotes

1. An entire article could be devoted to a discussion of ingenious ways in which the term "systems approach" has been used in the literature pertinent to organization theory and management practice.

SECTION TWO

The Organization as A System

READING 3

The Systems Approach to Business Organization and Decision Making

article by
ROBERT J. MOCKLER

System theory has had a revolutionary effect on business operations. Many an executive has found the revolution chaotic, for it has come in the form of the intrusion of the computer and computer personnel into his operations. He has felt his authority and control slowly stripped away by a movement he little understands and because of this has resisted it.

The computer is not, however, the villain. What normally happens is that the introduction of the computer sets in motion a systematic reevaluation of what the business is and how it can operate most efficiently. This reevaluation exposes the real problem—the gradual fragmentation of decision-making systems within a company over the years. The exposure of the problem in turn leads to an effort to reestablish smoothly working, fully coordinated decision-making systems for the business.

Systems theory provides a conceptual basis, as well as principles and guidelines, for establishing a more efficient system for planning, control, and operational decision making.

The Theory of Systems

A system may be defined as an orderly grouping of separate but interdependent components for the purpose of attaining some predetermined objective.[1] Three important aspects of systems are implied by this definition:

- The arrangement of components must be orderly and hierarchical, no matter how complex it is.
- Since the components of the system are interdependent, there must be communication among them.

Source: © 1968 by The Regents of the University of California. Reprinted from the *California Management Review*, vol. XI. no. 2, pp. 53-58, by permission of The Regents.

• Since a system is oriented toward an objective, any interaction among the components must be designed to achieve that objective.

A number of authorities working in diverse fields of specialization have contributed to the development of systems theory. Four of the better known are Ludwig von Bertalanffy, Kenneth Boulding, Norbert Wiener, and Herbert Simon.

A biologist, von Bertalanffy, is considered the originator of the general systems theory.[2] Disturbed by the increasing fragmentation and specialization of knowledge in this century, he attempted to find a unifying framework for the separate scientific disciplines. His work led to the development of a general theory of systems, which he felt provided such an integrating approach to the study and development of a wide range of scientific disciplines: "The notion of a 'system' being defined as 'any arrangement or combination , as of parts or elements, in a whole' applies to a cell, a human being, a society, as well as to an atom, a planet or a galaxy."[3]

Kenneth Boulding carried the general systems theory a step further by defining nine levels of systems, starting with the most simple and static (the anatomy and geography of the universe) and ending with the most dynamic (transcendental systems).[4] He thus conceived of a hierarchical arrangement of separate systems, which are in turn components of larger systems.

Both Boulding and von Bertalanffy recognized the dangers that resulted from the increasing fragmentation of science into more and more subgroups and the growing difficulty of communicating among the scientific disciplines. One of the main objectives of the general systems theory was to develop "a framework of general theory to enable one specialist to catch relevant communications from others."[5]

Since systems theory focuses on the dynamic interrelationship and interaction of entities, information and communication theory are important to the development of systems theory. In his study of information theory and communication, Norbert Wiener drew many parallels between the communication processes in living beings and in the newer communication machines, such as computers. Both have special apparatuses for collecting information from the outside world, storing it, and using it as a basis for action. Through this mechanism both human beings and information-processing machines have the capacity to compare actual performance to expected performance and to correct any deviations by "the sending of messages which effectively change the behavior of the recipient."[6] Thus, Wiener saw communication and information theory as a basis for understanding and explaining the planning, control, and decision-making processes.[7]

Herbert Simon, in his study of business management, considered "decision-making" and "managing" as synonymous.[8] He saw the business organization within which the manager works as a decision-making information system. Simon thus extended the scope of Wiener's information and communication theory and von Bertalanffy's general systems theory by applying them to business operations, where they can be viewed as vehicles for effectively achieving corporate objectives.

Systems theory and the various applications of it explored by these four men are important to business managers primarily for these reasons:[9]

• Since the systems concept is objective-oriented, systems organization automatically centers attention upon the objectives for which the firm has been established and helps to generate concerted and coordinated activity toward attainment of these objectives.
• Systems theory stresses the interdependence of elements, so that a manager is continually forced to view the business firm as a component of the overall operating economy.

From a systems theory viewpoint, therefore, a business organization can be viewed on one level as a complete, integrated decision-making system designed to achieve some specific objective, such as producing automobiles or paper products. On another level this internal business system can be viewed as a component or subsystem of a larger system—the economic, social, and competitive environment within which the business operates.

The Environmental System

Looking upon the social, economic, and competitive environment as an integrated system, of which a particular business is a subsystem, aids management planning and decision making.

1. In planning and operating a particular company its managers are led to give greater consideration to the political and social values of the environment and potential impact that these values, and the legislation they produce, have on the business.
2. Managers become more aware of the economic forces influencing the business. The company's long- and short-range planning is thus influenced to a greater degree by such economic factors as supply and demand; population growth and labor force trends; gross national product and income estimates; technological development; trends in governmental receipts and expenditures; fluctuations in industrial production, price levels, business, and the economy in general; and seasonal factors.[10]
3. A company's managers are made more aware of the specific influences of the competitive system on their operations. As a result, a company's sales forecasting is improved, for greater consideration is given to such market and industry factors as anticipated market standing and share, competitive strategy and action, and new product and market development. Projected profit levels, rates of return on investment, and specific production, marketing, and financial plans are also developed with more precise estimates of competitive conditions in mind.

The effects of these external factors can then be weighed with other information on internal company resources—the strengths and weaknesses of the particular business under study—to develop final corporate plans and to make operating decisions.

A business manager acquires such an approach to planning and decision making by following the principles of scientific business planning.[11] However, the systems approach supplements and reinforces the disciplines laid down in scientific planning, by impressing upon the manager the relationship between his internal business operation and its economic and social environment.

The Relation of Systems Theory to Business Organization for Decision Making

Systems theory has had an even greater impact on the internal organization of, and the decision-making processes within, individual business enterprises.

The systems approach forces the manager to look upon his business organization as an information network, with the flow of information providing the decision makers at varying management levels with the information needed to make decisions of all types. As a result, business information systems, which were once considered mainly accounting record-keeping systems, are now being called upon to support all the planning, control, and operational decision-making processes within a company. As such, these systems are required to store and process not only information concerning internal operations, but also information concerning competitor plans, strategies, programs, and performance, as well as significant information on the economic and social environment—in short, all the information needed for executive decision making.

These information-communication systems necessarily link together the components needed to operate a business successfully, i.e., the people, plants, and machines assembled for the purpose of achieving both the general corporate objective of making money and the individual corporate objective of making money by engaging in a specific type of profit-making business enterprise.

In organizing the components of a business to achieve its objectives, traditional business organization theory has emphasized the relationships between people by focusing on the tasks to be performed, the job positions related to performing these tasks, and the appropriate authority and responsibility for each job position.

In *Management Systems*, McDonough and Garrett[12] give some of the principles of organization that show the traditional, people-oriented approach to organization:

1. Be sure that adequate provision is made for all activities.
2. Group (departmentalize) activities on some logical basis.
3. Limit the number of subordinates reporting to each executive.
4. Define the responsibilities of each department, division, and subdivision.
5. Delegate authority to subordinates wherever practicable.
6. Make authority and responsibility equal.
7. Provide for controls over those to whom authority is delegated.
8. Avoid dual subordination.
9. Distinguish clearly between line authority, functional authority, and staff relationships.
10. Develop methods of coordination.

These principles clearly focus on the person-to-person relationships within an organization, and on the physical and functional departmentalization of the business unit. The commonplace block-diagram organization chart reflects this concept. Such relationships are, of course, important in thinking about organizations, but overemphasis of these relationships can obscure the information and communication links so vital to effective decision making within the corporation.

When changes are introduced within the traditional organization structure, new departments or units are normally added or new responsibilities given to existing departments. Sometimes these additions or changes are made to meet new business needs, sometimes to take maximum advantage of an individual executive's particular combination of talents, and sometimes merely to adjust to the personalities of individual executives. Such a fragmented development process almost invariably leads to some decrease in the effectiveness of the decision-making processes within an organization.

The systems concept of organization attempts to avoid this problem by focusing on the dynamic interaction and intercommunication among components of the system. Systems theory subordinates the separate units or departments of a business to decision-making information and communication networks. Understanding this difference is fundamental to understanding how systems theory has affected business organization and decision making.

The initial chart picturing a business organization restructured around the information flows, instead of around the authority and responsibility units, does not look substantially different, for during the first phases of the changeover only a few departments have been added and some job responsibilities shifted. The change in basic organization philosophy has a profound effect, however, for it creates major changes in the way an organization functions—changes that affect the lives of all the individuals operating within the business system and changes that after a period of time produce major adjustments in the structure of the business organization. Both in theory and in practice, therefore, the theory of systems is revolutionary for an established business.

The revolution has in fact occurred in most larger companies, for the introduction of electronic data processing, with its enormous capacity for storing and processing information and its enormous expense, is forcing business to use a systems approach to organization development. The computer has in a sense been the catalyst for reevaluation and change. For some companies the transition has been smooth; for others it has been chaotic.

When introducing a computer, many companies tend to approach the changeover in the traditional way—piecemeal, department by department. Such an approach only reinforces the fragmentation and disruption of information and decision-making systems.

The Catalyst for Change

Instead, as most companies sooner or later discover, before major decisions concerning computerization are made, management must step back and reevaluate the entire flow of business, not merely the individual operations being computerized, in order to isolate the major decision-making areas, their inter-relations, and the information needed to make these decisions most effectively. In other words, the systems approach has proved in practice to be the best one.

For example, in a large mail-order business which has recently been changing to computerized order processing and information handling, the first inclination was to write programs in steps, first for marketing, then for order processing, billing, inventory control, and so on, for each of the components or departments currently operating in the company.

It soon became apparent that this was not the best approach. At this time management directed the systems group to study the nature of the business in which the company was then engaged, the business in which the company hoped to be engaged within the next five years, and the environment in which the company would operate in the future.

The group next constructed a chart of the flow of the business operation, starting with the coupon-advertisement offering the product and asking for the order, and following the customer's order through processing and billing until the product is shipped, the merchandise restocked, and the bill paid. For each phase in the flow chart a supplemental list was made of the significant planning, control, and operational decisions necessary to perform that phase well. The information needed to make these decisions and the form in which this information was needed was then determined.

Only after the above studies were completed was a decision made as to which aspects of the business process could most economically be computerized, which would best be done clerically, and which were of sufficiently minor importance to the overall functioning of the business that they would be done in a less than ideal way or not be done at all.

As a final step, the actual organization of the operation was restructured around the picture of the business which had been developed in the systems studies.

The diagram of the restructured organization may have looked to the casual observer like the traditional organization chart of the former organization, for there were departments for marketing, order processing, billing and credit, product procurement and inventory control, and liaison among all these operations. But the changes made to bring the organization into line with the known decision-making needs of the business were enormous.

On closer examination it was clear that the new organization set up to handle the business had little relation to the old organization. Pockets of personal strength had been wiped out, and antiquated reporting relationships had been changed drastically. Major adjustments had been made in the daily interworkings between departments and in the groupings of functions within each department. For example, advertising was now a marketing department, order processing included customer service, and product procurement and warehousing were combined. In other words, what is commonly called an "authority" organization structure had given way to a "systems" organization structure.

The reevaluation showed that the organization had not grown dynamically with the business but was a conglomeration of old operating procedures, compromises made to accommodate personality differences, and the like. Although the changeover was painful, it revitalized the operation.

The advantages of following the systems approach may seem obvious to the reader. Yet it is still an approach rarely followed in practice. In an existing business concern the tendency is to look at the business as a series of departments, with department heads who perform various functions, the totality of which is the "business." What this business is, how it flows, and how its parts interrelate is likely to be known only by those who grew up with the business and now head it. And even they may not have a clear understanding of some of the newer aspects of the business.

The mail-order company cited in the example above was fortunate. In spite of the problems caused by the introduction of systems thinking into the organization, the company finally adjusted to and profited from the systems approach. Many companies faced with computerization have taken the easy way out. Instead of starting with a thorough reevaluation of their businesses from a systems viewpoint, they have computerized their operations piecemeal. Letting presently established organizational structures control the systems study and development creates problems, among them: it leaves the antiquated organization structure intact and hinders the development of an effective mechanism for improved decision making; and it leads to inefficient use of the new, automated, computerized processing equipment.

The systems approach is revolutionizing business decision making, for it can provide more comprehensive information, faster, at the point and in the form it is needed to make better business decisions. Adapting the organization to the information systems needed for effective planning, control, and operational decision making enables a company to take advantage of new facilities for storing and processing information, which can in turn lead to competitive advantages and greater profits.

Conclusion

Drastic organizational changes do not necessarily have to occur at the time a study of the business system is made, for a company may have grown and developed in tune with its growing business. But this is the exception. Some changes will always occur, and over the long run they are usually major.

The executive familiar with the fundamental changes in business philosophy forced upon business by the introduction of electronic data processing and the development of systems theory will be better prepared to meet the challenges they present. He will not be confused by the continuing change brought about by the systems approach to organization and decision making, nor will he consider electronic data processing a threat to his position. Instead, he will be able to control and guide that change in the most profitable directions and at the same time expand his capacity for more effective management performance.

Discussion Questions

1. Recall the definition of an organization's environment, which was given in a preceding article: the environment comprises all of the factors that affect the organization's performance, but are beyond the control of the organization's managers. Why is it important to include environmental considerations in the firm's decision making? What techniques exist for coping with uncertainty about the environment?
2. What are the advantages of structuring a business along lines of information and decision flow rather than lines of authority and responsibility? Can you think of any potential dangers? How does the use of computers favor one form of organization over the other?
3. How might organizational restructuring increase the effectiveness of computers to a business firm? What does this suggest about the usefulness and limitations of computers?
4. In applying the systems approach to a business organization, should the organization be structured to suit the system, or should the system be designed to fit the organization? Is a compromise possible between these extremes?

Footnotes

1. Many variations of this definition exist, e.g., Warren Brown, "Systems, Boundaries, and Information Flow," *Academy of Management Journal*, IX:4 (December 1966), p. 318, defines a system as "a group or complex of parts (such as people, machines, etc.) interrelated in their actions towards some goal," and Richard A. Johnson, Fremont E. Kast, and James E. Rosenzweig, *The Theory and Management of Systems* (New York: McGraw-Hill Book Company, Inc., 1973), p. vii, state that "a system may be defined as an array of components designed to achieve an objective according to plan."

2. Johnson, Kast, and Rosenzweig, p. 6, No. 1, assert that von Bertalanffy was the first to use this term. For further information on von Bertalanffy's systems theory, see his *Problems of Life: An Evaluation of Modern Biological and Scientific Thought* (London: C. A. Watts and Co., Ltd., 1952) and a series of papers by von Bertalanffy, Carl G. Hempel, Robert E. Bass, and Hans Jonas, published as "General Systems Theory: A New Approach to Unity of Science," in *Human Biology*, XXIII:4 (December 1951), pp. 302-361.

3. von Bertalanffy, "General Systems Theory," p. 303.

4. Kenneth E. Boulding, "General Systems Theory—The Skeleton of Science," *Management Science*, II:3 (April 1956), pp. 197-208.

5. *Ibid.*, p. 199.

6. Norbert Wiener, *The Human Use of Human*

Beings: Cybernetics and Society (Boston: Houghton Mifflin Company, 1950), p. 8.
7. *Ibid.*, p. 15.
8. Herbert A. Simon, *The New Science of Management Decision* (New York: Harper & Row, Publishers, 1960), p. 1.
9. A number of recent authors have studied the application of systems theory to business operations: Robert N. Anthony, John Dearden, and Richard F. Vancil, *Management Control Systems: Cases and Readings* (Homewood, Ill.: Richard D. Irwin, Inc., 1965); John Dearden and F. Warren McFarlan, *Management Information Systems: Text and Cases* (Homewood, Ill.: Richard D. Irwin, Inc., 1966); Daniel O. Dommasch and Charles W. Laudeman, *Principles Underlying Systems Engineering* (New York: Pitman Publishing Corp., 1962); Donald G. Malcolm and Alan J. Rowe, *Management Control Systems* (New York: John Wiley & Sons, Inc., 1960); Adrian M. McDonough and Leonard J. Garrett, *Management Systems: Working Concepts and Practices* (Homewood, Ill.: Richard D. Irwin, Inc., 1965); Henry M. Paynter, *Analysis and Design of Engineering Systems* (Cambridge, Mass.: M.I.T. Press, 1961); and Thomas R. Prince, *Information Systems for Management Planning and Control* (Homewood, Ill.: Richard D. Irwin, Inc., 1966).
10. A review of the kinds of environmental information needed for business planning, control, and operational decision making can be found in the following: V. Lewis Bassie, *Economic Forecasting* (New York: McGraw-Hill Book Company, Inc., 1958); Elmer Clark Bratt, *Business Cycles and Forecasting*, 5th ed. (Homewood, Ill.: Richard D. Irwin, Inc., 1961); John F. Due and Robert W. Clower, *Intermediate Economic Analysis: Resource Allocation, Factor Pricing, and Welfare*, 5th ed. (Homewood, Ill.: Richard D. Irwin, Inc., 1966); and Milton H. Spencer, Colin G. Clark, and Peter W. Hoguet, *Business and Economic Forecasting* (Homewood, Ill.: Richard D. Irwin, Inc., 1961).
11. The following is a simplified statement of the planning process: (1) Define specifically what the company's planning effort is expected to achieve and to what use the plans will be put; develop an approach (including organization and management planning policies) to carry out the planning function within the corporation. (2) Determine the key factors (planning premises) which will have a major influence on planning, through a study of both the environment (the economy, society, public policy, industry, and market) and the company's strengths and weaknesses. (3) In the light of the planning premises, develop and evaluate alternative directions the company might follow over the long range and select the corporation objective (i.e., kind of company) which will enable the company to most profitably exploit the market opportunities identified during the premising stage of planning. (4) After developing and evaluating alternative policies and programs which will achieve the objective, determine the policies, programs, and procedures that best fulfill the corporate objective and still meet market, industry, and company criteria (premises), and establish a suitable organization structure and adequate budgetary and operational controls. (5) Review and refine the program periodically.

For further information on the approach to scientific planning, see: Melville C. Branch, *The Corporate Planning Process* (New York: American Management Association, 1962); Preston P. LeBreton and Dale A. Henning, *Planning Theory* (Englewood Cliffs, N.J.: Prentice-Hall, Inc., 1961); Bruce Payne, *Planning for Company Growth* (New York: McGraw-Hill Book Company, 1963); and Brian W. Scott, *Long-Range Planning in American Industry* (New York: American Management Association, 1965).
12. McDonough and Garrett, p. 9. (See footnote 9).

READING 4

Organizational Systems

article by
VINCENT P. LUCHSINGER
and V. THOMAS DOCK

Organizations are one of our most typical systems. Man spends much of his life working in the organizational context. Scott has pointed out that:

> The distinctive qualities of modern organizational theory are its conceptual-analytical base, its reliance on empirical research data and, above all, its integrating nature. These qualities are framed in a philosophy which accepts the premise that the only meaningful way to study organization is to study it as a system.[1]

March and Simon point out that organizations are vastly important to every aspect of modern life. The work force spends one third of its waking hours in them. Our every lifetime need from food to entertainment to health care is served by organizations.

Source: Vincent P. Luchsinger and V. Thomas Dock, *The Systems Approach: A Primer* (1976). Reprinted by permission of the authors.

The emerging field of contingency theory is closely tied to the systems view of organization. While the contingency approach holds to no one best way of organizing, the use of systematic thinking leads to an appreciation of situational factors in organization design and structure. In general, a contingency approach advocates the open systems, adaptive mode of operation. Special sensitivity for environmental conditions (both external and internal to the organization) is a basic tenet of the contingency approach.

Still, the contingency approach and the systems approach are not identical. The contingency approach is characterized by situation-orientation, responsiveness, and sensitivity to changes in conditions. The systems approach is characterized chiefly by integration, wholeness, interdependence, and super- and subsystem awareness. While the two approaches are complementary and overlap to some extent, there are essential differences which enhance their mutual contributions in use.

Blau defines organization as:

> a number of men that have become organized into a social unit that has been established for the explicit purpose of achieving certain goals.[2]

Presthus defines organizational systems as:

> a system of structural interpersonal relations. . . . Individuals are differentiated in terms of authority, status, and role with the result that person interaction is prescribed. . . . Anticipated reactions tend to occur, while ambiguity and spontaneity are decreased.[3]

Scott further defines the organization as:

> a vehicle for accomplishing goals and objectives. . . . A mechanism having the ultimate purpose of offsetting those forces which undermine human collaboration.[4]

Organization theory is a new and eclectic field, i.e., it borrows from several disciplines. Organization theory concentrates on human social organizations, generally large and complex. It is closely related to and is a special element of general systems theory. Johnson et al. say:

> The organization function is the means, or bonding agent, by which separate human and material resources are fused together to form an integrated, operating system.[5]

Considering an organization as a system, Johnson et al. say a system is:

> an organized or complex whole; an assemblage or combination of things or parts forming a complex or unitary whole. . . . The word system connotes plan, method, order, and arrangement. . . . The focus of systems management is on providing a better picture of the network of subsystems and interrelated parts which go together to form a complex whole.[6]

Organized systems are purposive. They are directed toward objective accomplishment according to a plan. "The organization is an assemblage of people, materials, machines, and other resources geared to task accomplishment through a series of interactions and integrated into a social system."[7] The systems approach is a conceptual guide, a way of thinking, a model. The systems concept focuses on the relationships of these parts or subsystems and how their performance affects the whole system. Under a systems approach, one changes his view of organizations from looking at structure to looking at flows and processes. Systems theory is concerned with dynamics, flows, and interrelations rather than static hierarchies with traditional linkages. Newer technologies require a newer view of organization design and conceptualization. The system is designed around the technological core and its relation to the environment. The input is economic resources, and the output is economic welfare. Chin defined open systems as "systems in contact with their environment and with input and output across system boundaries."[8] The simplified model of a business system in Illustration 1 portrays the cycle of energy events and their significant interface relations and transactions with environmental elements.

Characteristics of Open Organizational Systems

Systems have constant exchange with their environment through a continuous inflow and outflow of energy through permeable boundaries. Systems can be viewed by tracing these energy patterns and viewing how the output reactivates the cycle.

Importation of Energy

Open systems import various forms of energy from the external environment. Stogdill defines input as "the variables that generate the total system when they are operated upon in various combinations." He says:

> Performances, interactions, and expectations can be treated as input variables that generate group structure, operations, and interpersonal relationships.[9]

Inputs are material, financial, informational, and human resources. Human inputs are often measured in work hour units. Social organizations draw their energy supply or input from various environmental elements including other organizations.

Illustration 1 The business firm: an environment-sensitive open system

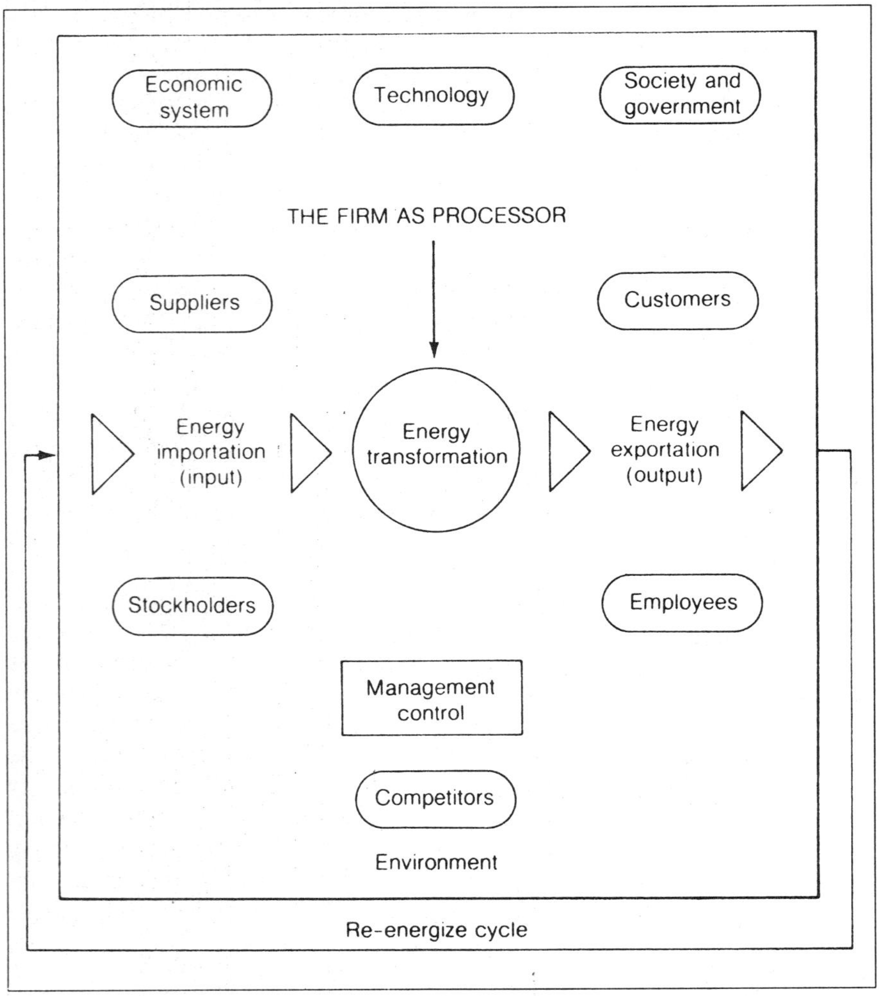

Throughput and Transformation Process

The system manipulates, transforms, or alters the input energy. This is the major purpose for processing materials into a product or providing a service. This is reorganizing or adjusting the output. In systems, one views the dynamic nature of flows of men, materials, money, and information through the system and within the system. Productivity is a function of the transformation process. Stogdill discusses productivity as:

> the changes in organizational expectancy values that result from the operations of the organization. . . . The productive outcome is some resultant decision or action that satisfies in some positive or negative degree the goal expectations of the organization.[10]

The Output

Open systems export a product or service into the environment. Outputs are the reason for being. Society allows an organization to exist and rewards it for its output. Outputs are measured in productivity, the efficient combination of input resources resulting from system operations.

Systems as Cycles of Events

The pattern of energy flow is in a cycle. Input, throughput, output, and then recycle. The output provides new energy. If it is a product, it is sold and the money is used to purchase new inputs. Katz and Kahn say:

> The structure is to be found in an interrelated set of events which return upon themselves to complete and renew a cycle of activities. It is events rather than things which are structured, so that social structure is a dynamic rather than a static concept. Activities are structured so that they comprise a unity in their completion or closure.[11]

Negative Entropy

Open systems store energy. This is a move to stop the entropic process and acquire negative entropy. Biological organisms run down and eventually perish. Organizational systems import more energy than they export, increase the ratio of imported to expended energy, and store energy. During a period of crises or negative returns, they can live off the stored energy.

Information Input, Negative Feedback, and the Coding Process

Information inputs from the environment are signals or cues to guide system operation. Negative feedback allows the system to find out how output deviates from objectives or plans and correct. Chin discusses feedback and how it is gathered:

> While affecting the environment, a process we call output, systems gather information about how they are doing. Such information is then fed back into the system as input to guide and steer its operations.[12]

Feedback is a control mechanism which measures output, compares output to a standard, and adjusts new inputs and operations based on this information. Johnson et al. define control as:

> that function of the system which provides direction in conformance to the plan, or in other words, the maintenance of variations from system objectives within allowable limits. . . . The objective of the system is to perform a specified function, while the objective of control is to maintain the output which will satisfy the system requirements.[13]

As the environment is scanned for information cues, only significant cues are absorbed. This reduction and selectivity is the coding process which simplifies data and makes it manageable.

The Steady State and Dynamic Homeostasis

A system moves toward a basic stability or steady state through a uniform input and output energy flow. In a dynamic organization this is not a true equilibrium but a ratio of energy exchange that is relatively stable. External forces or environmental pressures that disrupt the system (disequilibrium) are countered by forces which stabilize and restore the system. A social organization builds up energy reserves to call on when needed. Systems almost appear to grow naturally by ingesting or acquiring environmental elements that are essential for survival. If a business firm is dependent on a single source of raw material supply, it may acquire or merge with that organization. The purpose is to insure the character and survival of the system. Johnson et al. say:

> An organism is an open system which maintains a constant state while the matter and energy which enter it keep changing (so-called "dynamic equilibrium"). The organism is influenced by, and influences, its environment and reaches a state of dynamic equilibrium in this environment.[14]

Organizations also seek an equilibrium in dealing with system employees. Barnard and Simon see this based on motivation. A system will induce members' contributions through rewards and therefore survive as long as those contributions of energy are forthcoming at a near equal level of flow.

Differentiation

Open systems move to role elaboration and functional specialization. This is a division of labor by departments (subsystems) and workers. With increased organizational complexity, interdependent subsystems handle certain tasks. The output of one subsystem becomes the input of another.

Litterer says:

> When work is divided, boundaries are drawn between various work elements, grouping them into jobs, positions, or organizational units.[15]

Any organization has a goal set, a group of desired outcomes or outputs. These are arranged in a hierarchy of goals, based on importance. With differentiation, the creation of subsystems to do units of work, one develops goals for the subsystems. This can create suboptimization where the parts of subsystems pursue their own subgoals. Since the parts affect the whole, it is desirable for subsystem goals to be consistent with overall system goals, but differentiation naturally creates potential goal conflict. In discussing differentiation into subsystems and the impact of the systems concept, Simon says:

> Organizations will still be hierarchal in form. The organization will be divided into major subparts, each of these into parts, and so on, in familiar lines of departmentalization. The exact basis for drawing departmental lines may change somewhat. Product divisions may become even more important than they are today; while the sharp lines of demarcation among purchasing, manufacturing, engineering, and sales are likely to fade.[16]

Equifinality

Equifinality implies that a system can reach the same final state from differing initial conditions and by a variety of paths. Once organizations have established realistic objectives, plans, strategies, alternatives, and courses of action must be set as a roadmap of the path toward the target objective. In most systems there is more of a consensus on goals than on paths to reach the goals.

Characteristics of Social Organizations

Organizations are contrived, purposive sociotechnical systems. They include men and machines working together toward goals. Organizations are contrived in that they are designed where people can benefit from cooperative effort. Scott says:

> Organization enhances the predictability of human action, because it limits the number of behavioral alternatives available to the individual.[17]

An organizational system is contrived or invented by men and therefore exists in the greater culture and is shaped by attitudes, beliefs, habits, motivations, perceptions, and expectations. Organizations are based on the benefits of social cooperation. They are characterized by symbiosis—the mutual living together of diverse organisms. The patterns of cooperation and linkage of system parts working together toward mutual goals leads to synergy—the total output the system can command is greater than the parts could produce if they were not linked.

Organization

System members take roles (institutionalized behavior patterns or jobs), obey system rules, and remain because the system rewards them in pay or psychic satisfaction. Ideally, system members internalize through their value systems the same goals of the system. Common values, system norms, and formal rules all reduce the human variability. Katz and Kahn say:

> The network of standardized role behaviors constitutes the formal structure of the organization. A formalized role system then, is one in which rules defining the expected interdependent behavior of incumbents of system positions are explicitly formulated and sanctions are employed to enforce the rules.[18]

Norms and values are an integrating force. They are shared beliefs. Norms prescribe sanctioned behavior. Values are an individual's system of ideology. There is generally conformity to norms and values in an organizational system. To discuss cohesive value systems would imply more congruence and common values than generally exist. Value conflicts are negotiated or resolved. As Buckley says:

> A social system is always characterized by multiple and contradictory value systems and their many shades of interpretation in concrete action and interaction. . . . A social system is always characterized by an institutionalized value system. The social system's first functional imperative is to maintain the integrity of that value system.[19]

Types of Organizational Subsystems

Parts of organizations can be viewed as subsystems performing certain subordinate functions. The following discussion describes those subsystems after the schema of Katz and Kahn, 1967.

Productive or Technical Subsystems

The productive subsystem is concerned with the throughput, the work that gets done in transforming inputs into outputs. Organizations are classified according to their main productive process, i.e., manufacturing, educational, etc.

Supportive Systems

Supportive systems are those that carry on exchanges with the environment across permeable boundaries. This can be selecting inputs or disposing of outputs. Boundary-spanning functions such as purchasing, sales, and public relations are all supportive.

Maintenance Subsystems

Maintenance subsystems keep the system parts functioning. They do not do the work described as throughput. The personnel function of selection, socialization, training, and rewarding is a maintenance function. Patterning role behavior ties people into the system in relation to the task to be performed. Maintenance is concerned with preservation of the system through selection and rewarding of personnel. Reward, sanction, and motivation systems are geared to get people to join and stay in the system and perform as desired.

Adaptive Subsystem

The supportive subsystems face outward toward the environment for procurement and disposal. The production and maintenance subsystems face inward and are concerned with the internal workings and interaction of the system. The system is environment-sensitive and needs to take action in a changing complex environment to insure survival. This is the role of the adaptive subsystem which faces outward, acts as a sensor in detecting environmental cues, and is future-oriented. Any external changes—in society, in competitors, in demand for output, in politics—can dictate the need for rapid systems change. The degree of change receptivity can spell doom or survival for the organization. Adaptive subsystems anticipate changes and include research and development, long-range planning, and market research. Adaptation is reacting to feedback. Survival of an organization depends on a continual relationship with its environment and coping with environmental change. Preparing for change based on a reading of the environment is adapting through planning which is "intelligent cooperation with the inevitable . . . a predetermined course of action . . . the vehicle for accomplishment of system change."[20]

Managerial Subsystems

Johnson et al. say, "The organization is an assemblage of people, materials, machine and other resources geared to task accomplishment through a series of interactions and integrated into a social system."[21] The assembling of resources, the selection of goals, the design of tasks, and the programming of subsystem interactions is the job of management.

The organization exists to solve problems of the environment. Transferring problems into solutions is the role of management. Young defines the management subsystem as:

> that subsystem of the organization whose components consist of a subset of individuals (man to man) whose duties are to receive organizational problems (inputs) and thereupon to execute a set of activities (process) which will produce organizational solutions (output) for either increasing the value of return of the total organizational activity (satisfying) or for optimizing some function of the total organizational inputs and outputs.[22]

Management combines input resources of men, money, and machines and integrates these into a total system to accomplish objectives. The heart of management is decision making based on information. In the control function, this information is feedback. Johnson et al. say:

> Large social organizations, such as business and government, have developed complex information systems which attempt to facilitate decision making and focus it on goal accomplishment.[23]

Management acts both as an executive system (authority structure) and a regulatory mechanism (feedback/control). "The essence of authority structure is the acceptance of directives as legitimate. . . . Every organization has an executive system for carrying out policy or the implementation of administrative decisions."[24] For more information on subsystems, see Table 1, which presents the Katz and Kahn perspective on organizational subsystems.

The Organization and Its Environment

An organization can be viewed in relation to its supporting environment, the continuing exchanges and significant interfaces. Stogdill says, "An organization may be regarded as an agent of exchange with its environment."[25]

Systems, Subsystems, and Suprasystems

Any system is made up of a set of subsystems. The system is itself a supplement of the greater society. Systems interact with and are dependent on other systems. (See Table 1.) To study any system one looks at the next higher level of system, and views its dependence on this suprasystem. The reason for the existence of a business, hospital, or university is that society, a suprasystem, desires its output. The output of one system will be the input of another.

An organization that is viewed in relation to other organizations is a "focal organization" when viewed in relation to the major system with which it has frequent exchanges. In Illustration 1, one sees a "focal organization" and its "organizational set." Evan says:

> The relations between the focal organization and its organization-set are conceived as mediated by (a) the role-sets of its boundary personnel, (b) the flow of information, (c) the flow of products or services, and (d) the flow of personnel.[26]

Within the organization, the systems approach means the subsystems transact and communicate vertically as well as horizontally. Under the systems approach, the scalar nature of the hierarchy does not disappear but becomes a set of layers of interacting subsystems. The subsystem boundaries (departments) become more permeable, more open to flows of information, people, and material because there is more clearly perceived goal unity.

System Openness, System Boundaries, and System Coding

System openness refers to the degree to which the system is receptive to all types of inputs. These permeable boundaries are subject to flows of people, technology, information, resources, and influence. The degree of openness is important to survival in this period of rapid social and technological change. A rigid, closed system which resists fresh inputs would rapidly become obsolete. The rational, machine theory, or mechanistic approach to management viewed an organization as a rational and efficient machine of functional parts perfectly integrated to achieve goals. This traditional approach viewed the system as more or less closed and not as dependent on its environment. The conflicting theory is open systems which Johnson et al. say:

Table 1 Formal subsystems of organizations: their functions, dynamics, and mechanisms

Subsystem	Function	Dynamic	Mechanisms
I. **Production: primary processes**	Task accomplishment; energy transformation within organization	Proficiency	Division of labor; setting up of job specification and standards
II. **Maintenance of working structure**	Mediating between task demands and human needs to keep structure in operation	Maintenance of steady state	Formalization of activities into standard legitimized procedures; setting up of system rewards; socialization of new members
III. **Boundary systems**			
A. Production supportive: procurement of materials and manpower and product disposal	Transactional exchanges at system boundaries	Specifically focused manipulation of organizational environment	Acquiring control of sources of supply; creation of image
B. Institutional system	Obtaining social support and legitimation	Societal manipulation and integration	Contributing to community; influencing other social structure
IV. **Adaptive**	Intelligence, research and development, planning	Pressure for change	Making recommendations for change to management
V. **Managerial**	1. Resolving conflicts between hierarchical levels	1. Control	1. Use of sanctions of authority
	2. Coordinating and directing functional substructures	2. Compromise vs. integration	2. Alternative concessions; setting up machinery for adjudication
	3. Coordinating external requirements and organizational resources and needs	3. Long-term survival; optimization, better use of resources, development of increased capabilities	3. Increasing volume of business; adding functions; controlling environment through absorbing it or changing it; restructuring organization

Source: D. Katz and R. L. Kahn, *The Social Psychology of Organizations* (New York: John Wiley and Sons, 1966), p. 86.

focuses on an organization's properties, processes, and adaptive mechanisms, as a dynamic, operational unit. It is basically an open model within which the organization is operating with varying degrees of uncertainty and must develop means of adapting to its changing environment.[27]

Chin says a system boundary is:

the line forming a circle around selected variables, where there is less interchange of energy (or communication, etc.) across the line of the circle than within the delimiting circle.[28]

Another view of boundary is that it encompasses all system members. According to Litterer, a member is "someone who participates in the operation of an organization, the selection of its objectives, or both."[29]

The boundary is the barrier condition between the system and the environment, between people on the inside and people on the outside. Energy and information intake over the boundary is done through a selection process known as system coding. This is selecting and transforming of inputs to correspond to the nature of the system.

The Internal Environment

All organizations have an internal climate or unique culture. Katz and Kahn say, "many organizations have formal induction and socialization procedures for instilling the behavior, attitudes, and values which differentiate the system from the outside environment."[30] This culture has taboos, folkways, mores, norms, and values. The understanding of systems theory is incomplete without a recognition of the behavioral dimensions of organizational systems.

Levels of Management

The organizational system can be also described in terms of levels after the framework of Parsons. Parsons suggested three levels of management in the complex organization: "the institutional or community level, the managerial (organizational) level, and the technical or production level."[31] Each level contributes a unique function under the guidance of management so as to respond beneficially to the environmental forces impinging or bearing on it.

The institutional or community level of management interacts with society in relating the work and outputs of the organization to the community. The organizational level of management supervises functions within the organization so as to successfully integrate and process the inputs. As such, the organizational level of management directs the technical or production level which is processing information, energy, and materials.

The technical-production level of management conducts the basic tasks of the firm. Here are conducted activities of production and transformation, marketing-distribution, and finance. The tasks involved may be labor-intensive with the heavy use of labor, or may be intensive in technical processes, research, equipment, or analysis depending upon the work of the operating unit. This is the operational level of the firm. The description of the levels is portrayed in Illustration 2 as they relate to each other as stacked systems.

Contingency-Situational Approaches to Organization

The contingency-situational approach to organization is a movement that is appropriate for mention at this point. The systems approach is indicative of the responsive and adaptive strategy followed by the organization in coping with environmental demands and opportunities. Rigidity, inflexibility, and simplistic approaches to organization are inadequate to meet today's challenges to complex and dynamic organizations. In terms of organizational design, the contingency-situational approach attempts to configure the organization in the best manner to get the job done *in a given situation*. As a contingency represents a possible event, the contingency-situational approach to organization promotes the flexibility and responsiveness to adapt to changes in the environment, changes in processes of the organization, and changes in the relationships within and without the organization.

Organic (adaptive and responsive) formats for the organization are suggested as replacements for mechanistic orientations. This change to an organic posture is related to the recognition of complexities and changes in the environmental and technological forces which must be contended with. The contingency approach toward organization is uniquely appropriate to the systems approach in that the system itself is output-sensitive in interacting with the environment. Relationships between important variables become extremely important, depending on the situation at hand, or the projected possibilities.

Lawrence and Lorsch are given considerable credit for advancing the contingency approach in

Illustration 2 Managerial levels or layers of the firm

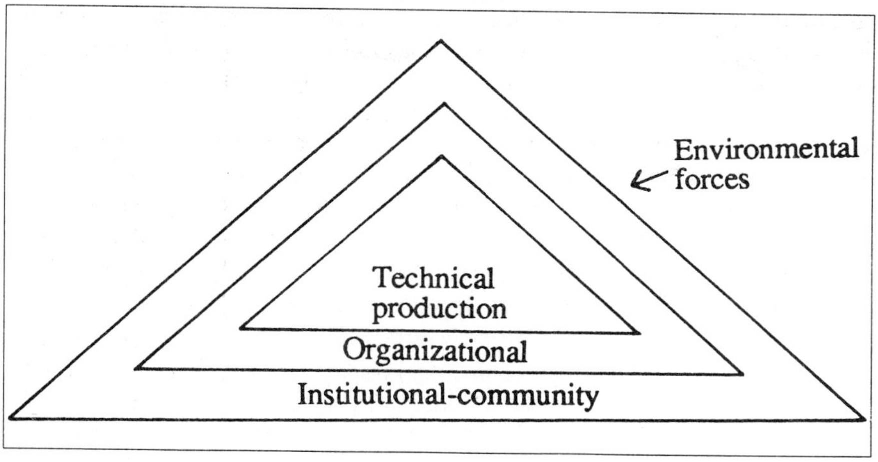

Illustration 3 Schema of Lawrence and Lorsch's model

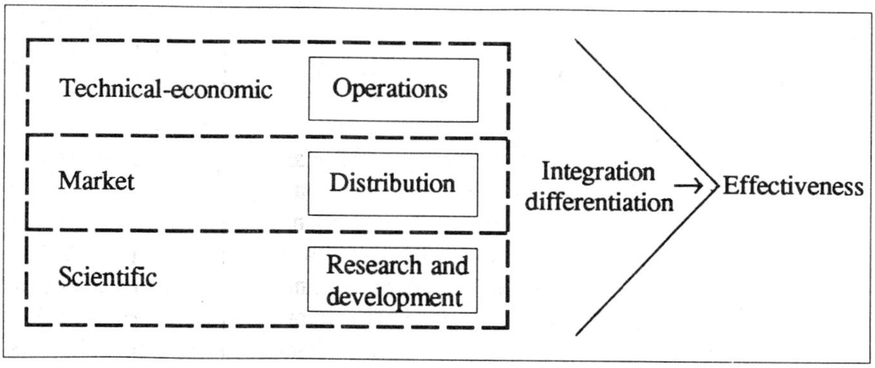

organization with their research and interpretations based on experiences of firms. Out of that research, three key concepts are proposed for consideration in organization design.

- *Differentiation*—the state of segmentation of the organizational system into subsystems, each of which tends to develop particular attributes in relation to the requirements posed by its relevant external environment.
- *Integration*—the process of achieving unity of effort among the various subsystems in the accomplishing of the organization's tasks.[32]
- *Environment*—as conceptualized by outward looks from the system.

The environment was further broken into the subenvironments of market (sales and distribution), technical-economic (production or operations), and scientific (research and development) activities. The integration needed by the firm was directly related to the differentiation required in conducting the affairs of the firm. The effectiveness of the firm then depended upon the differentiation that was indicated for the firm to do its business in coping with the environmental constraints and opportunities. The more the firm's operations diversified to meet conditions, the more important integration became. In turn, the effectiveness of the firm depended on being diversified and responsive enough (in the sense of differentiation) to meet challenges and opportunities.

The contingency approach says there is no one best way to organize. Depending upon the situation and the contingencies, the organization should differentiate to meet multiple conditions, to adjust to changes, and to obtain the information needed about the environment to cope with the environment. Truly then "it depends upon the situation," or upon the contingencies which may arise that we want to be ready for when we think about preparing our organization to operate most effectively.

In Retrospect

The organization area is one of the most useful and graphic areas for application of the systems approach. An organization is a system, and thus the systems approach adds to the integrating essence of the traditional organization consideration. The emphasis on micro and macro elements, the links, and goals in systemic organization focus on aspects that are involved in the dynamic nature of organizations. The organization is a classic example of the open system which interacts and imports energy from the environment, while generating outputs which are hopefully found functional by that same environment. Organizations have unique social and behavioral dimensions as the humans, as actors, in the organization behave so as to energize the organizational framework, and thus convert the organizational structure into the purposive goal-seeking system that most organizations are intended to be.

Discussion Questions

1. Are systems and organizations the same thing? Is every system an organization? Is every organization a system? What do your answers imply about the applicability of general systems theory to the study of organizations?
2. What is entropy and how does it apply to the study of systems? Why is negative entropy necessary to maintain a steady-state equilibrium? Why can open systems achieve negative entropy, whereas closed systems cannot? What is the role of feedback in maintaining a steady state?
3. In what forms do business organizations receive energy from their environment? What processes are involved in transforming this energy into outputs? In storing it internally for later use? In utilizing such stored energy to maintain the organization's steady state?
4. How can an organization cope with the conflicting goals of its specialized subsystems and the multiple and contradictory value systems of its human members? Can such conflicting goals and values be made compatible with those of the parent organization? Can they be used to the organization's advantage?
5. How is the idea of an open system related to the "contingency-situational" approach to organizations? Are the contingency approach and the systems approach in conflict? If one is adopted, must the other be abandoned? In what areas is each most likely to be useful?

Footnotes

1. W. G. Scott, "Organization Theory: An Overview and an Appraisal," *Journal of the Academy of Management* 4:1 (April 1961), p. 42.
2. P. M. Blau and W. G. Scott, *Formal Organizations* (San Francisco: Chandler, 1962), p. 1.
3. R. V. Presthus, "Toward a Theory of Organizational Behavior," *Administrative Science Quarterly* (June 1958), p. 50.
4. Scott, op. cit. pp. 664-665.
5. R. A. Johnson, et al., *The Theory and Management of Systems* (2nd ed.; New York: McGraw-Hill, 1967), p. 65.
6. Richard A. Johnson, et al., *The Theory and Management of Systems* (3rd ed.; New York: McGraw-Hill, 1973), pp. 4-6.
7. *Ibid.*, p. 5.
8. R. Chin, "The Utility of System Models and Developmental Models for Practitioners," in W. G. Bennis, K. D. Benne and R. Chin, eds., *The Planning of Change* (2nd ed.: Holt, Rinehart, and Winston, Inc., 1969), p. 303.
9. R. M. Stogdill, "Dimensions of Organization

Theory," in J. D. Thompson, ed., *Approaches to Organizational Design* (University of Pittsburgh, 1963), p. 29.
10. *Ibid.*, p. 34.
11. D. Katz and R. L. Kahn, *The Social Psychology of Organizations* (New York: Wiley, 1966), p. 21.
12. Chin, op. cit., p. 303.
13. Richard A. Johnson, et al., *The Theory and Management of Systems* (3rd ed.; New York: McGraw-Hill, 1973), p. 72.
14. *Ibid.*, p. 11.
15. J. A. Litterer, *The Analysis of Organizations* (New York: Wiley, 1965), p. 202.
16. H. A. Simon, *The New Science of Management Decision* (New York: Harper and Row, 1960), pp. 49-50.
17. Scott, op. cit., p. 7.
18. Katz and Kahn, op. cit., p. 49.
19. W. Buckley, *Sociology and Modern Systems Theory* (Englewood Cliffs, N.J.: Prentice-Hall, 1967), p. 26.
20. Johnson, et al., op. cit., pp. 51 and 53.
21. *Ibid.*, p. 47.
22. S. Young, *Management: A Systems Analysis* (Glenview, Ill.: Scott, Foresman, 1966), p. 15.
23. Johnson, et al., op. cit., p. 67.
24. Katz and Kahn, op. cit., pp. 44-45.
25. Stogdill, op. cit., p. 44.
26. W. M. Evan, "The Organization-Set," in Thompson, ed., op. cit., p. 178.
27. Johnson, et al., op. cit., p. 26.
28. Chin, op. cit., p. 300.
29. Litterer, op. cit., p. 6.
30. Katz and Kahn, op. cit., p. 61.
31. T. Parsons, *Structure and Process in Modern Societies* (New York: Free Press of Glencoe, 1960), p. 60.
32. P. Lawrence and J. Lorsch, "Differentiation and Integration in Complex Organizations," *Administrative Science Quarterly*, Vol. 12 (June 1967), pp. 3-4.

SECTION THREE

The "Total Systems" Approach

READING 5

Organization as a Total System

article by
STANLEY YOUNG

Increasingly, organizations are being considered from a systems point of view in both descriptive and normative context.[1] Ashby's work would exemplify some of the descriptive work. Systems Development Corporation, Strategic Air Command, and Lockheed are effectively using the systems concept to redesign major phases of organizations in an operational and normative sense.[2] Many companies have expanded similar efforts to certain subsystems, such as steel-rolling mills, oil refineries, and so on.[3]

Our conception of the organization is changing from one of structure to one of process. Rather than visualizing the organization in its traditional structural, bureaucratic, and hierarchical motif, with a fixed set of authority relationships, much like the scaffolding of a building, we are beginning to view organization as a set of flows, information, men, material, and behavior. Time and change are the critical aspects. When we consider the organization from a normative point of view, we find another reason for this trend which is of more immediate concern. This is the working hypothesis of my article. Only when the organization is designed (organization planning) from a systems engineering orientation will it be able to take full advantage of the new and emerging managerial technologies, such as quantitative methods, the computer, information sciences, and the behavioral sciences. The engineering sciences have illustrated unusual success in the rapid creation and application of new technology and will, therefore, represent the guiding model of this analysis.

However, before taking up my thesis, let us note the current problems concerning the effective utilization of managerial technology. One problem relates to the absence of a construct as to how this new technology is to be used in an integrated and systematic manner; or consider it as the absence of a meaningful gestalt, or whole, into which such a technology would logically fit. What does exist might be categorized as a tool chest or "bits and pieces" state.

For example, let us suppose that a personnel manager has a problem of excessive absenteeism. Given the external and internal environment of the firm, the organizational constraints he has as a manager, and a set of behavioral information and managerial tools that he has acquired, how does he reduce the absenteeism rate? He knows something about psychology—perception, cognition, learning, and motivation theory. From social psychology, he should be aware of theories of attitudes formation and resistance to change. From sociology, he recalls the implication of group theory. He can calculate the median, mean, and mode, run a correlation, and find a derivative. He is a qualified MBA student. Yet, what specifically should he do to reduce the absenteeism rate? Students and practitioners are given a tool chest filled with some mathematics, some psychology, and so on, and the manager is then admonished to build a better house.

Although one can appreciate the value of these various approaches, one is still confronted with the problem of their integrated application in order to be relatively assured of achieving a desired result. What is missing is the bridge or discipline between tools and organizational results. The engineering sciences represent such a discipline.[4]

Although one can raise many serious questions as to the reality, validity, predictability, and effectiveness of the classical principles approach, nevertheless it can be said that it roughly holds together as a whole or single unit, and its parts are related in logical fashion. Starting with the concept of private property and the delegation of authority, the organizational chart is drawn; authority is allocated; a division of labor is specified; and the functions of management, planning, organizing, and staffing are outlined. A certain internal logic is present, not unlike the economist's model of perfect competition. The parts are related to each other in a particular manner. Viewed as a single construct, the traditional model is understandable and operational to students and practitioners alike.

A Systems Approach

The same cannot be said for the newer managerial technology. The general management or organization theorist's domain is the whole. One is concerned with the problem of organization space or the distance between subfunctions, subprocesses, tools, and techniques—the interface problems. To those who are concerned with the whole, the partial approach of the new technology is disconcerting. Where and how do all these parts fit together, and what is the relationship between one and another? Sprinkling behavioral and quantitative courses about a business curriculum is of questionable effectiveness. Therefore, as far as the newer technologies are concerned, a gestalt, or general, model has been missing which will integrate all the parts meaningfully. What is being suggested is that the systems approach will provide this model.

Another problem which has emerged, which requires that the organization be designed as a total system, is that all too frequently the organizational context into which the newer technologies are inserted tends to be inappropriate. We are attaching sophisticated techniques to a primitive vehicle—the bureaucratic structure. Organizations should be designed around the technology; technology should not be forced to fit an existing structure. Thus, some corporations, to be fashionable, have created operations research departments which in fact have been given little or nothing to do. One case was reported in which the primary duty of the O.R. official was to solve the school mathematics problems of the corporate president's daughter!

In the history of innovation, one frequently finds that when a new device is invented it is attached to the existing model. For example, when the gasoline motor was first invented, it was connected to a buggy. However, as additional innovations occurred, the vehicle itself eventually had to be modified. If advantage was to be taken of additional improvements, obviously one could not unite a 300-horsepower motor to a light wooden shay. If innovation follows its usual course, we can expect the new managerial techniques to force a modification in the traditional organizational arrangements. This, indeed, has been taking place. The exploitation of the computer has led to a weakening or abolishment of the traditional divisional or departmental lines of authority. Improvements in the control and measurement of operations have the same consequences.

The differences between administrative and engineering analyses that will be taken up are:

- The engineering sciences view of the operation to be analyzed as a system or subsystem.
- The design and implementation of such systems as a sequential analysis of a team effort composed of appropriate specialized personnel.

Research, development, hardware specifications, and pilot and field studies are conducted with at least one purpose: to create and apply an improved technology to the functional operations being considered. Further, historically, the engineering sciences have incorporated the basic sciences of physics, chemistry, and quantitative methods into their analyses.

To demonstrate how the organization may be treated from an engineering point of view, it will first be analyzed as a system, and then the design process will be briefly outlined. In the presentation of the organization as a system, the approach will be analytical—a successive breakdown of the whole into increasingly smaller parts.

Organization as a Total System

In Figure 1, the business organization is presented in its most simplified form. The basic input is economic resources, the organization is the process, and the output is economic welfare. Other organizations can be represented by changing the inputs and outputs. For example, the hospital has a human input (sick patient) and a healthy patient as the output.

In Figure 2, the control or feedback mechanism is added to the organization, which is represented by management. Or, in terms of control theory, the management segment constitutes the basic control element of the organization. Thus, given a certain welfare objective or expected welfare output (a profit increment), actual welfare is measured against expected welfare. If a difference exists, then a problem is indicated. This information is sent to the management segment which formulates a solution that is then input into the organization process. This feedback device will operate until the actual and expected welfares are approximately equal.

In Figure 3, the control unit is further broken down into a series of parts, in order to provide an adaptive capability for the organization.[5] Given a change in certain environmental inputs, one initially has an input analyzer, which indicates the nature of such changes. This is an information-gathering or sensory device; somewhat analogously, market research might be so categorized in terms of sensitizing the organization to some of the external variables, as accounting functions for the internal changes. One has also a display device, the identifier, which indicates the state of the organization or any of its subprocesses at any given time.

Hence, if the subprocess were a production plant, the identifier at a given time could indicate the productive capacity, current running capacity, order backlog, inventory conditions, orders in process, production lines in operation, and machine breakdown. Such information is fed to a decision-making unit along with the information from the environment. We assume that a set of rules has been programmed, one of which will be selected for a particular environmental input and a given process point to achieve a certain output.

For example, if the initial input is a large order with a required completion data, the rule may be to go to overtime. This information is called a control signal and is sent to the control unit. The control

Figure 1 Organization as a system

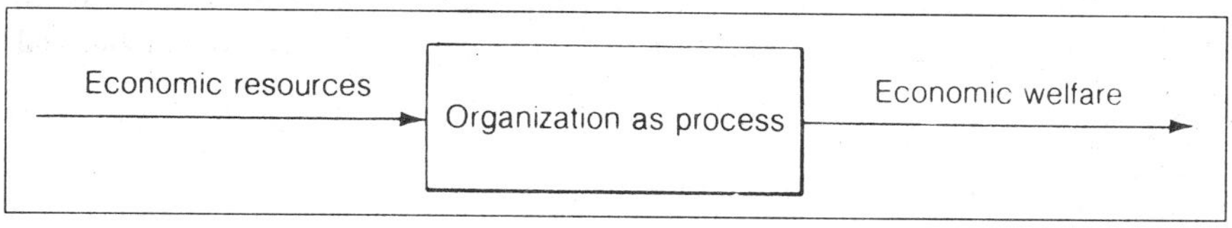

Figure 2 Organization with control unit

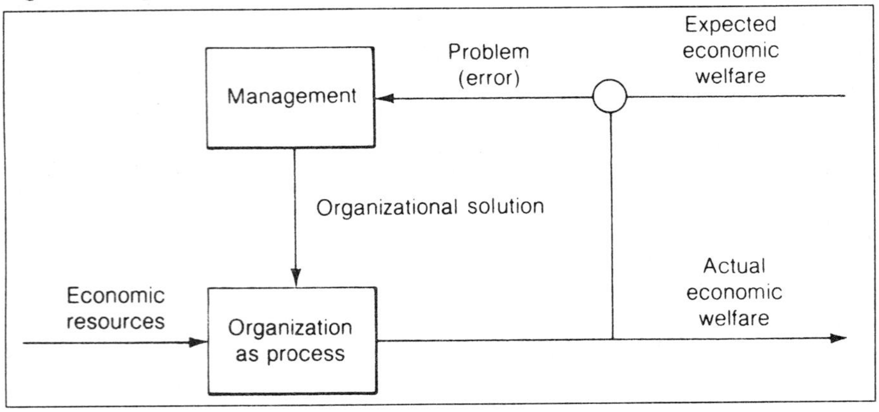

Figure 3 Organization as an adaptive system

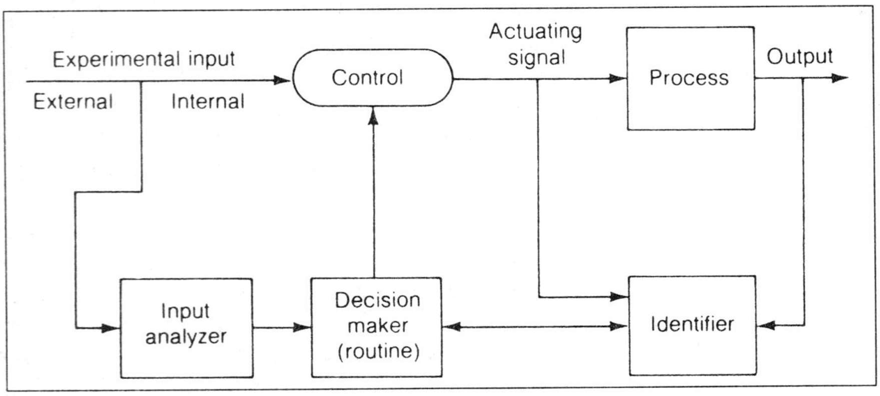

unit is that element which actually changes the input before it enters the system, or the process itself. The order could have been put into a queue. Such information is simultaneously sent to the identifier. Therefore, at any given time, the identifier tells us what inputs have entered the process, the state of the process, and its outputs.

Because the control signal and the control unit are frequently confused, the difference between the two should be explained. The example that is usually given is the driving of an automobile. If one wants to stop an automobile by depressing the brake pedal, information is relayed to the brakes of the car. It is not the brake pedal that stops the car, but the brakes, which constitute the control unit. Similarly, in a man-to-man system, the control signal and the control unit would appear as shown in Figure 4.

Let us suppose that the total employee population is the basic system, and we want a higher work output. Further, assume that we know exactly what the relationship is between need satisfaction input and expected work output. Given the figure for expected work output, the decision maker will increase or decrease the amount of need satisfaction (for example, money) via a control signal to the financial department, where need satisfaction is stored in the form of money. This department would release funds until the expected work output was achieved. It is not the decision to increase work output or its relay to the employee that constitutes the control element or even the

Figure 4 The control signal and the control unit

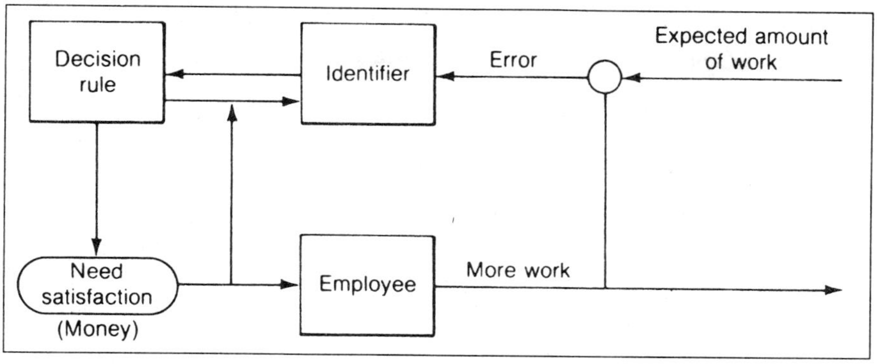

decision to augment wages and salaries, but the reservoir and release of funds that is the control element. In other words, a salary may be to the employee what brakes are to an automobile. For our particular purposes, those subparts of the organizational control mechanism—input analyzer, and so on—give the process an adaptive capability or the ability to adapt to changing inputs so as to maintain a desired or expected output.

In Figure 5, the organization is further broken down into a series of major subprocesses: marketing, production, and so on, each with its own adaptor. The adaptor consists of an input analyzer, decision rules, identifier, and control for each subprocess. Moreover, it is assumed that each of these subprocesses can be identified and separated from other subprocesses. A super-adaptor applies a series of decision rules for subdecision makers, to assure appropriate adjustment between processes. It is further assumed that each subsystem's adaptor has this same capability concerning subprocesses. Consequently, the production system may have subsystems of purchasing, inventory control maintenance, and so forth. The inputs and outputs of these subsystems would have to be controlled appropriately with the proper decision rules.

In Figure 6, a learning capability in the form of a designer is added to the adaptive system. A learning capability can be thought of as the ability of the system to redesign itself or learn from past mistakes so as to improve system performance. Given the environmental state of the system and the application of what is thought to be the correct rule, the expected output may still not be produced. This indicates design problems.

The designer would receive information as to system performance. Then, to increase welfare output, he would attempt to improve the adaptive mechanism: by formulating more effective decision rules for the decision-making routine, by improving the identifier in terms of more and better information, by achieving a more rapid response in information from the input analyzer, by improving the sensory devices, and by improving the control mechanisms.

In Figure 7, we now see the total system in some detail. We have our environmental inputs on the left, both external and internal (psychological, sociological, etc.). Two basic subsystems are shown: marketing and production, in which the marketing output becomes a production input. Each of these subsystems has its own adaptor, and although not shown, a coordinating adaptor to integrate the two. Further, each subsystem has its own design capability.

The only new feature of the schematic is the box at the top: Design of System Design. This particular function would integrate the work of subdesigners. For example, if the organization is viewed as an aircraft, the design of which is generally broken down into such areas as weight and structures, air frame, power, information system, and so on, design coordination is required. Moreover, this function would also advise as to design technique and strategy, and, ideally, one should be able to reach a stage in which the design itself of subsystems could be programmed.

Thus, in looking at Figure 7, we see in some detail the organization as a total system which is self-regulating and self-learning, at least partially

Figure 5 Major subprocesses, each with its own adaptor

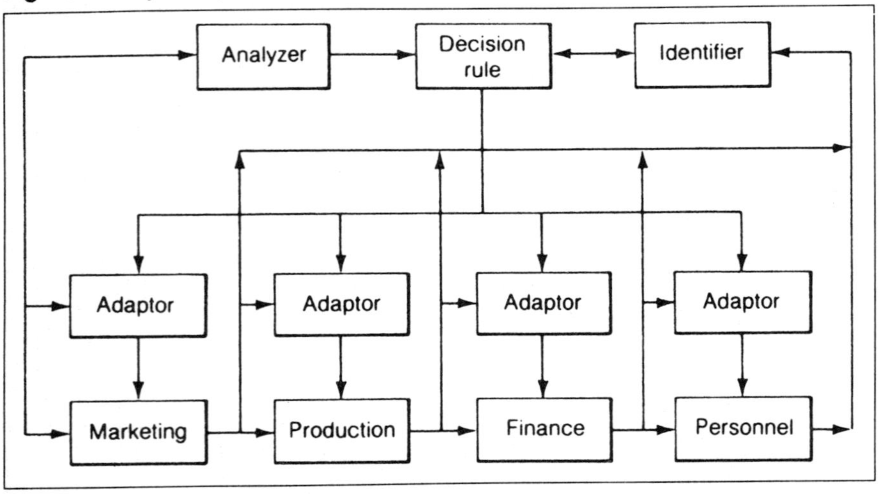

Figure 6 Adaptive system with learning capability

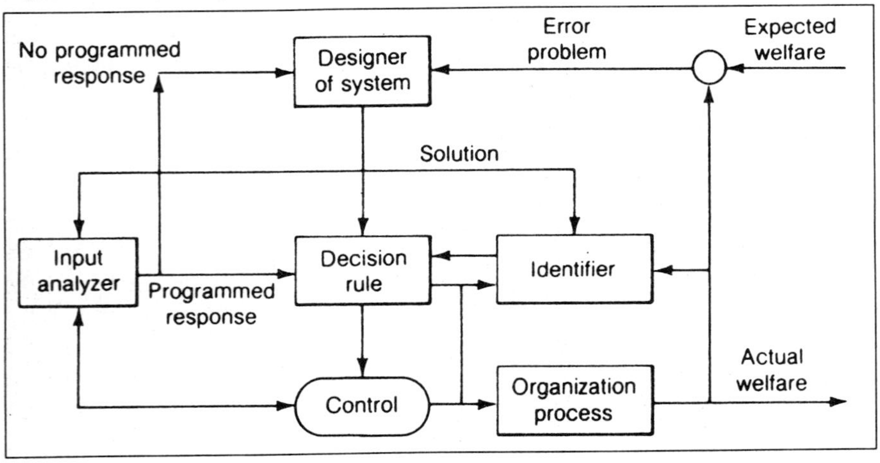

closed, in which the environment can be detailed and in which subsystems are integrated. Further, the adaptor provides for appropriate internal adjustments between subsystems. In other words, the organization without too much difficulty can be considered as a total system. All of its essential elements can be incorporated into a design. Also, with an appropriate index, one can detail the subsystems. Each subsystem can be broken down into its subsystems, and so forth. The indexing of the system's subparts is a complex but not an insurmountable problem. For example, it is estimated that the blueprints for a new aircraft may finally weigh two or three tons—more than the aircraft itself!

System Design

In Figure 8, we can briefly go through the design process, which further analyzes the function of the designer. Given a statement of the problem or the type of system with which one is concerned, the next, and key, step is the construction of a model of

Figure 7 Organization as a total adaptive system

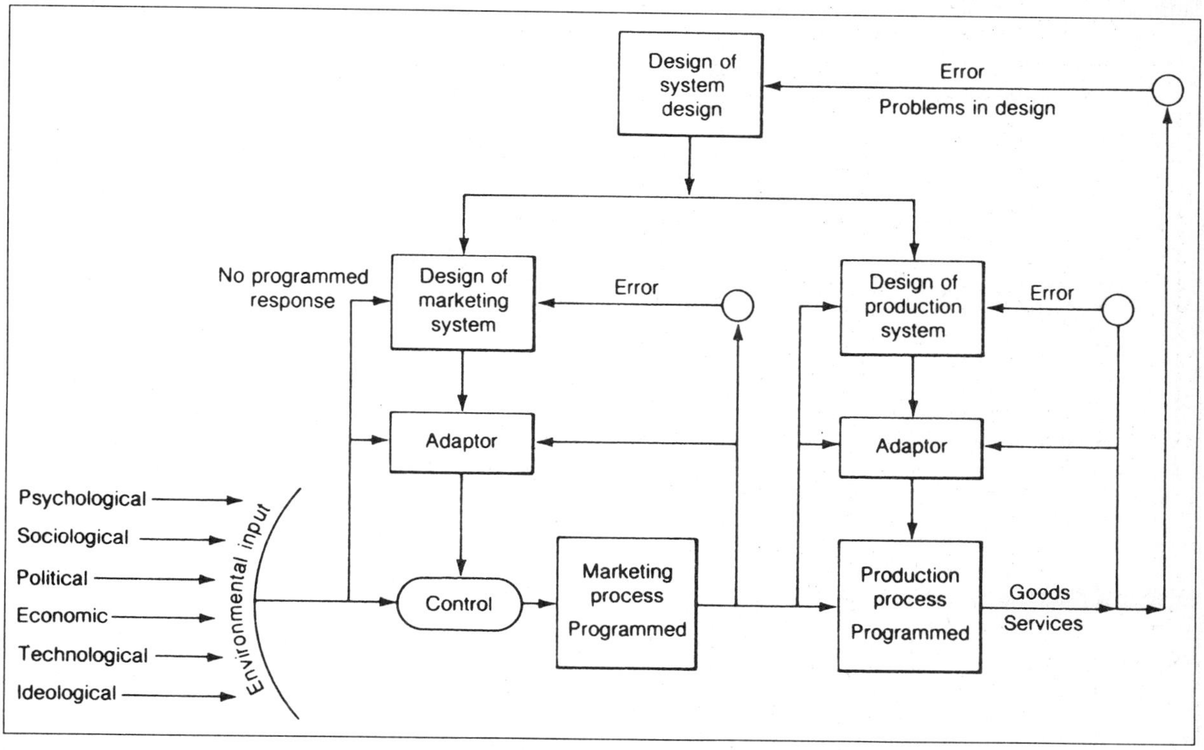

the system. Such a model would be essentially stochastic in nature and would stipulate the output or mission of the system and the inputs, of which there are three:

- The input upon which the process is to operate or that input which enters the system.
- Environmental inputs which affect the process.
- Instrumental or control inputs which modify the operation of the process or the process itself—and here we are concerned with the technology of processing the load inputs. For example, in a marketing subsystem, if the initial input is a potential customer, he has to be processed through the subsystem so that a sale will result.

The system's logic relates to the set of decision rules or, given certain inputs, the state of the system and a certain control capability, such as more or less advertising—what particular decision rule should be utilized to achieve some expected output? Information requirements related to the classification, amount, and timing of information, so that the system will operate as expected. Hence, concerning the environmental variables, what information about which variables should be gathered? How often? How much? And how soon would this information have to reach the decision role?

At the outset, it would be a highly worthwhile investment to construct a complete stochastic model of the system with which one is concerned, in which output is the dependent variable, and inputs, environmental and instrumental, are the independent variables. For example, one might be concerned with a personnel selection subsystem in which the output is a certain number of qualified employees. The environmental inputs might be the labor demand for certain occupations, amount of unemployment, the number of graduates, and so on; the instrumental variables might be the recruiting budget, the number of recruiters, the training program, etc.

It is more efficient to construct one model to

Figure 8 System design

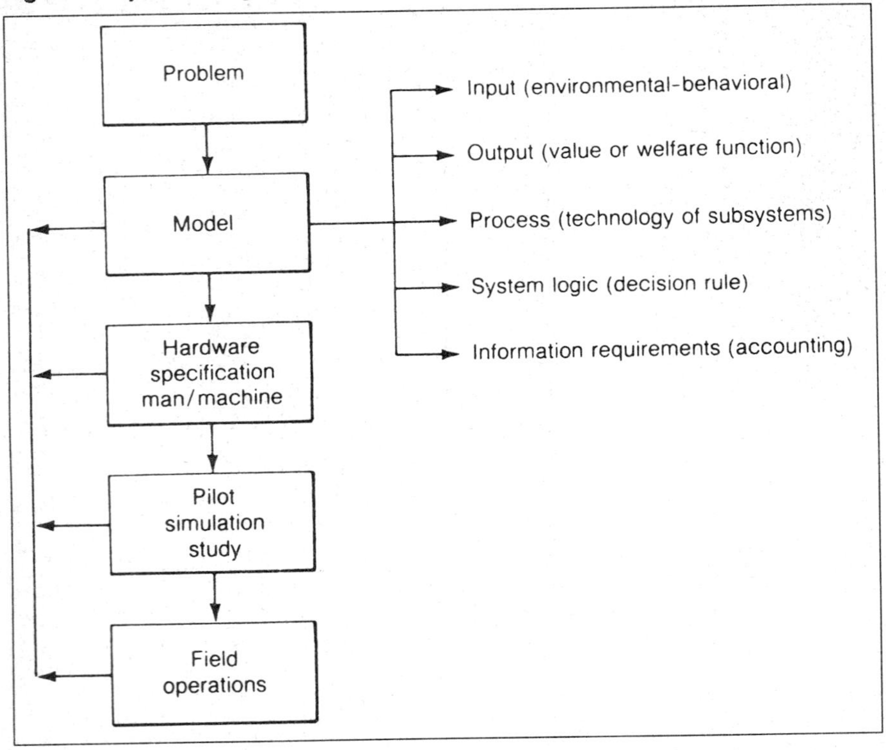

which various decision rules can be applied than to construct a new model every time a new decision rule is formulated. With the latter approach, one would always be reconstructing the model, given a change in tools. Once the model is constructed, the research and development begins. One can experiment—try different decision rules and different hardware specifications—in terms of devising appropriate controls and measuring devices.

Experimentation requires a certain ingenuity. A grocery chain may have to set aside one of its representative stores for research purposes. It would not only be important to establish the consequences of various pricing strategies, but if possible, the causes for such consequences or, at least, the ability to predict their outcome. Given a new rule on a pilot basis, one can apply it to actual hardware. Naturally, one has to be sure that the data from pilot studies are meaningful in terms of the total system with which one is concerned. Research and development represent the essence of the engineering effort. Experimentation is costly and uncertain, but there is little doubt that the payoff is greater than using an intuitive approach.

If it is successful, the new rule can be applied, and data can be fed regularly to the designer, so that he can continually improve and refine his initial model. Although one may begin with a relatively unrefined model, with successive experimentation and field experience, hard data will constantly flow back to the designer. This will enable him to improve his model in terms of the nature of the variables, the preciseness of the parameters, and the model's predictability.

Over time, an improvement in the state of the art should occur, if research development is effectively executed. Our grocery chain should have an ever-improving pricing strategy. As for hardware specifications, apart from the consideration of costs, one is concerned with providing components that will execute the operations as specified.

In terms of Figure 8, of particular concern is the problem of how to convert what is essentially a paper model into something that approaches operating reality. We can construct reasonably good stochastic or econometric models which can be used to simulate different decision rules, but the conversion of these into operating reality with appropriate hardware is a different matter. In an operating context, the stochastic model or identifier becomes an information panel for a decision or rulemaker. In terms of hardware, information collection or sensory devices are needed which survey the environment and send such data to a central location, so that the values of the variables of the model can be displayed. An example is the control room in a public utility, in which the operator watches continually the changing values of significant variables. Only with such a display can appropriate action be taken. However, wiring such a system is a particularly difficult task.

For example, as a member of a team that has been given the responsibility of designing a metropolitan poverty program as a total system, the primary inputs are poverty families, and the outputs are supposed to be self-sufficient economic units. Although there exists some technical assurance that a stochastic model can be constructed, we have not yet been able to reach this design step, because we are at the initial stage of inventing a sensory machine that will give us some running idea of the nature of our changing inputs which, in this instance, is the changing mix of the characteristics of our poverty families. This program appears in Figure 9.

Another area that requires additional work is the control element, which actually modifies the operation of the system. In a man-to-man system, we do not have sufficient information about which variables to vary and by how much, in order to achieve the desired human behavior. The crude reward and punishment system that we have all too often gives us dysfunctional results. Presumably, in the design process, when serious deficiencies arise, research and development should be directed to those areas.

Managerial Technology as Utilized in System Design

Although this view of the organization as a total adaptive system and the design process has been brief, it has been sufficient to indicate how one can take advantage of the newer managerial techniques in the use of systems analysis.[6] In terms of the system presented, where and how do these techniques fit? As for the behavioral sciences, our environmental inputs or variables are behavioral in nature. To build a model and eventually a display panel, such knowledge is essential. In the decision box, we would utilize our various decision rules, such as Linear Programming, Game Theory, Dynamic Programming, PERT, and so forth. Because system design requires one to deal eventually with a total subsystem such as marketing, in all likelihood we will become increasingly concerned with the problem of combining various decision rules. For example, Gerald Thompson has indicated that we must combine appropriate decision rules to achieve the most satisfactory system output. Under what conditions is it advisable to move from Linear Programming to rule of thumb, and then back to Linear Programming? As Professor Thompson has noted,

> We need to develop heuristics about using heuristics. That is, an executive program that would accept a problem and then decide which of a list of heuristics (decision rules) should be employed to give its solution.[7]

The information sciences relate to the input analyzer and the collection, manipulation, and relay of information. Here we have all our data collection and processing problems. The control element relates to the area of control theory, specifically, the direction of human effort. Finally, in designing a specific subsystem, such as personnel or marketing, one should have some knowledge with regard to the technology of these systems; for example, one should be able to use employment tests correctly in the selection process.

In designing the organization as a total system, it would appear rather apparent that one would not only have to be familiar with but also be able to use a wide array of sophisticated managerial techniques and knowledge. The understanding and use of managerial techniques is an integral part of the design process. This is distinctly counter to the bureaucratic structure, which merely attaches such techniques to it with little purpose or place.

Figure 9 Poverty program as a system

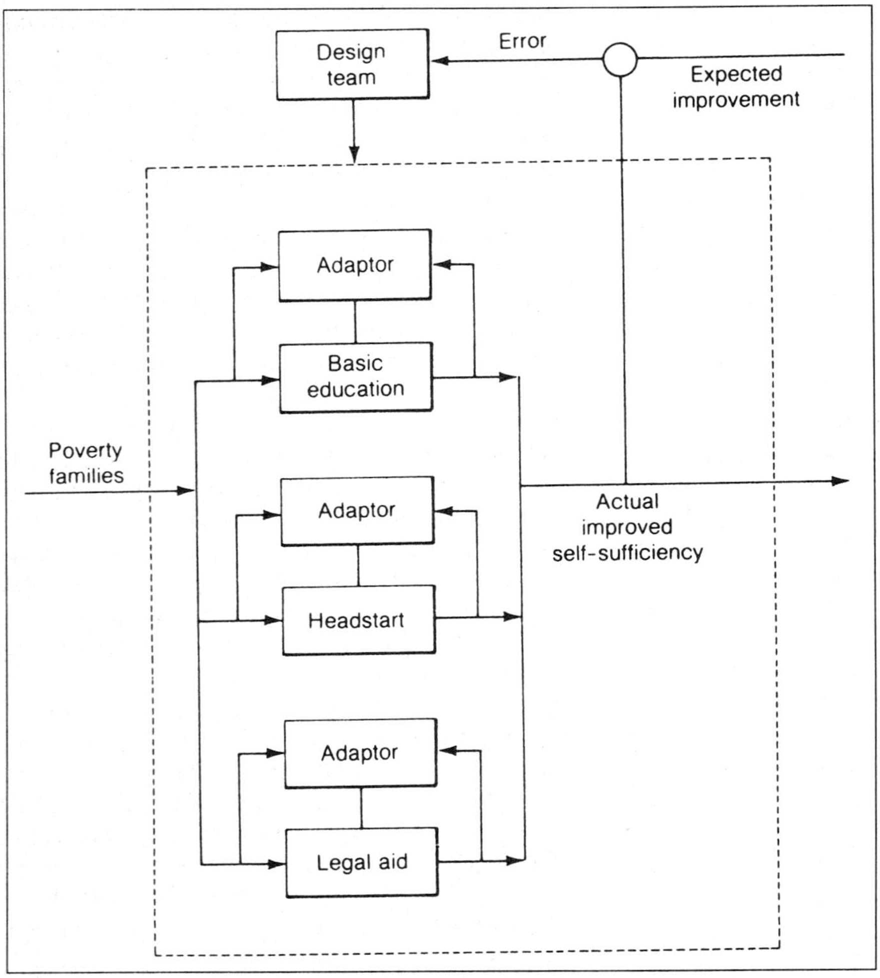

Design Criteria

Design criteria are rules which are utilized to evaluate designs as to their acceptability. Given a number of designs, which one is the best? Although there are numerous rules, the most widely used are: *measurability, feasibility, optimality, reliability,* and *stability.* We will consider only the first three.

Measurability is the system's ability to evaluate its performance. If its performance cannot be measured, a system's desirability or undesirability cannot be established. Its particular excellences or deficiencies cannot be known. When models are measurable, the superior system can be inferred from the specific measuring devices used in each. In the model that has been suggested, the identifier as a display panel is the primary measuring mechanism, in that we would know the actual inputs, process, outputs, and decision rules. If the model is not working as expected, the errors would be fed to the designer on a more or less continual basis, so that the system could be redesigned for more effective results.

One of the most serious weaknesses of the bureaucratic design as a management system is that it lacks measurability. When the bureaucratic system is redesigned, for example, from a product to a functional arrangement or when the line of command is lengthened by the introduction of additional levels of managers, no measuring devices exist either in the previous or subsequent design that will indicate what improvements, if any, have occurred.

Feasibility relates to the question of whether or not the model will operate as planned. As the model must be realistic, it must be capable of being installed, of achieving expected payoff, and of performing its task requirements winthin the environment of the system. If a particular quantitative decision-making tool is suggested, can we be reasonably certain that it can be employed in an operational context? The use of pilot studies or experimental models relates to the question of feasibility.

Given any managerial device, we of course want to know if it will increase organizational payoff when it is utilized; will stockholders, employees, and consumers be better off than before? Organizations are normative systems. All too often, the student and practitioner are exposed to quantitative manipulations and behavioral research that are interesting, but either no directions are provided as to how these findings are to be incorporated into the operations of the firm or no measuring devices are suggested that will establish the quantity of welfare that the research results will actually produce.

The end purpose of the manager, as it is viewed in this analysis, is to design subsystems which will actually increase human well-being. The manager is not, per se, a mathematician, statistician, sociologist, or psychologist. However, he must rely on these disciplines in much the same way that the engineer has to rely on physics. This does not mean that continuous research is not required in these disciplines, if designs are to improve. However, such research will not automatically lead to improvements. It is only when the designer is able to incorporate findings into an operating reality that he can achieve the full value of the research.

A corollary to the feasibility criterion relates to the question of balance between the parts of the system. All parts of the system must not only be integrated, but they must also be mutually consistent. One would not put into practice a primitive input analyzer and follow this with a complex regression analysis in the identifier. The final system output will be no more productive than the least productive part of the system. Each part acts as a constraint on all other parts. Consequently, the identifier can never be any better than the input analyzer, and so on. The absence of integration and/or balance is self-defeating.

For example, we frequently find information systems personnel providing voluminous data; that is, the input analyzer is well developed. However, the rest of the system may be missing; there is no identifier or set of decision rules. In other instances, we may have analyses of the use of a single decision rule, linear programming, but nothing else.

As long as we find this type of analysis, managers will always revert, out of necessity, to the most primitive part of the total system, because this part represents the primary constraint. In such a context, increasing sophistication will not meet the criterion of feasibility. Even if it is used, no increment in organizational payoff will result.

For example, in the design of the poverty program system that was mentioned earlier, the staff's initial impulse was to design an econometric model of the program including exogenous variables. We immediately ran into the constraints of the rest of the system and realized that, until we had a relatively effective input analyzer, a set of decision rules, and a control element, we could not move to the sophisticated model we wanted. In other words, when one designs a total system, he is generally forced to start with a fairly elementary model. Then, when all the parts are developed, he can progress to a more complex system.

The management sciences may be overly concerned with the *optimality* criterion and ignore such other criteria as measurability and feasibility, on the assumption that if one has an optimal solution there is little else that has to be done. But unless all criteria are considered, we will not get the hoped-for results. To have a solution that is optimal but nonfeasible is meaningless. Obviously, a solution has to be measurable, feasible, and reliable, before we can consider its optimality.

For the most part, operating managers stress the feasibility criterion. At the outset, they want something that will work and actually function and are not overly concerned with optimality. In dealing with a complex system, I am sure what constitutes an optimal solution. Russell Ackoff has said:

> One of the things Operations Research has learned about putting results to work is having considerable effect on its methods. This means the team must either translate elegant solutions into approximations that are easy to use or sidestep the elegance and move directly to a quick and dirty decision rule. Operations Research is learning that an approximation that is used may be a great deal better than an exact solution that is not.[8]

Because design methodology imposes a specific discipline on the designer, we can be assured that new techniques will be effectively utilized.

Some Implications

Although this has been a rather broad treatment of the organization as a total system, certain implications can be inferred.

1. On a normative basis, organizations should be viewed as a *total system* if we are to increase organizational output. Different organizations, corporations, universities, poverty programs, and so on can be categorized. Further, although this is by and large an article of faith, nevertheless some empirical evidence does exist (certainly in the area of complex weapons systems) that, if organizations are viewed as a total system, better results will be obtained. We are in the initial stages of this development, and, at this time, we can only block out the basic characteristics of total systems.
2. There has been an attempt to demonstrate that the systems approach is a highly conducive vehicle for the *incorporation of current managerial technologies*, unlike the bureaucratic structure. Irrespective of the developing managerial concepts, the bureaucratic structure itself represents such a serious constraint that only minimal advantages would accrue.
3. When viewed in this context, the *essential role of the manager is that of designer of organizational or behavioral systems*, just as the engineer is the designer of machine systems. The design of a large complex system, however, will necessitate a team effort: mathematicians, psychologists, and information specialists. But, as in large machine systems, system specialists will be required to integrate the team effort. There is little reason why efforts cannot be organized to design a marketing system in the same fashion as the F-111 aircraft was designed.

In conclusion, the engineering and management sciences face the same fundamental problem—the creation of improved systems. Both suggest that quantitative modeling be performed, based on their respective underlying sciences, physical and social. However, in the engineering sciences the design and implementation of machine-to-machine systems tends to be organizationally highly systematic, whereas such a development is yet to occur with respect to the management sciences in their designs of man-to-man systems.

Discussion Questions

1. How much validity is there in Young's analogy between the engineering and management sciences? At what points does the analogy fail? What are the implications for practical management?
2. Do you think the author offers a realistic model of the way businesses are, or should be, organized? What meanings does he give to the terms "input analyzer," "identifier," "adaptor," and "decision rule"? How might these components of the system be realized in practice?
3. What does Young mean by the statement that "a salary may be to the employee what brakes are to an automobile"? Is this comparison plausible? Do you believe research and development can discover "which variables to vary and by how much, in order to achieve the desired human behavior"? Should business firms involve themselves in such issues? Why or why not?
4. What are stochastic models? Why are they useful? How can such models be designed so that they have the flexibility to experiment

with alternative decision techniques and incorporate new ones as they become available? What might be learned from such experiments? What are some limitations of this approach?

5. List some possible criteria of system design other than measurability, feasibility, and optimality. Are such criteria always compatible? If different system designs satisfy different criteria, how should a choice be made?

Footnotes

Portions of this article were presented at the Midwest Academy of Management, Spring Meeting, 1966, Lexington, Kentucky.

1. For example, see Joseph Litterer, *Analysis of Organizations* (New York: John Wiley & Sons, Inc., 1965); Claude MacMillan and Richard Gonzales, *Systems Analysis* (Homewood: Richard D. Irwin, Inc., 1965), Chaps. 11-14; Ross Ashby, *An Introduction to Cybernetics* (New York: John Wiley & Sons, Inc., 1958), Chaps. 10-14.
2. For example, see Donald G. Malcolm, *et al.*, *Management Control Systems* (New York: John Wiley & Sons, Inc., 1960).
3. See Cornelius Leondes, *Computer Control Systems Technology* (New York: McGraw-Hill Book Company, Inc., 1961), Chaps. 15-20.
4. See Arthur D. Hall, *A Methodology for Systems Engineering* (Princeton: D. Van Nostrand Company, Inc., 1962); and Harry E. Goode and Robert E. Machol, *Systems Engineering* (New York: McGraw-Hill Book Company, Inc., 1957).
5. For a review of adaptive systems, see El. Mishkin and Ludwig Braun, Jr., *Adaptive Control Systems* (New York: McGraw-Hill Book Company, Inc., 1961); and J. H. Westcott, *An Exposition of Adaptive Control* (New York: The Macmillan Company, 1962).
6. For a more complete review, see Goode and Machol, *System Engineering*.
7. Gerald L. Thompson, "Some Approaches to the Solution of Large Scale Combinatorial Problems," Carnegie-Mellon University, Pittsburgh, working paper, p. 25.
8. Russell L. Ackoff, "The Development of Operations Research," *Scientific Decision Making in Business*, Abe Schuchman, ed. (New York: Holt, Rinehart and Winston, Inc., 1963), pp. 59-60.

READING 6

The Total Systems Myth

article by
W. M. A. BROOKER

The purpose of this article is to examine critically the value of the total systems concept and to make predictions on the effects of its application. As is implied in the title, the author does not regard the concept itself as having the practical value claimed by its followers. On the other hand, the belief in this concept is a powerful motivating force among those who have accepted it as a frame of reference.

Why and what is untrue about the total systems concept? The basic error in the total systems concept is the assumption that the total systems approach is the most fruitful; that systems analysis in any situation is the most powerful kind of planning that can precede planned and profitable change for a company.

This article will discuss the foundations of the systems concept, the value of this concept and the limitations of its application. These limitations amount to an inadequacy as to the totality of pervasiveness of the approach, notwithstanding its value in an auxiliary role. We shall then discuss the requirements of an overall approach and outline an alternative in which systems theory occupies a significant but auxiliary role.

Source: *Systems & Procedures Journal*, July-August 1965, pp. 28-32.

Foundations of the Systems Concept

The foundation of the systems concept seems to rest on the work of von Bertalanffy, who apparently coined the term "general systems theory." Hall, who is referred to by von Bertalanffy, defines the system as

> a set of objects with relationships among the objects and among their attributes. Objectives are simply the parts or components of a system.[1]

More specifically, systems are defined in terms of flows. According to Forrester, the business system is

> a system in which the flows of information, materials, manpower, capital equipment and money set up forces that determine the basic tendencies towards growth, fluctuation and decline.[2]

The flows of a business system, according to Optner, are in the form of a closed system which

> can be defined as one which is free of variation or disturbance . . . the concept of the black box[3]

of which the basic model is thus:

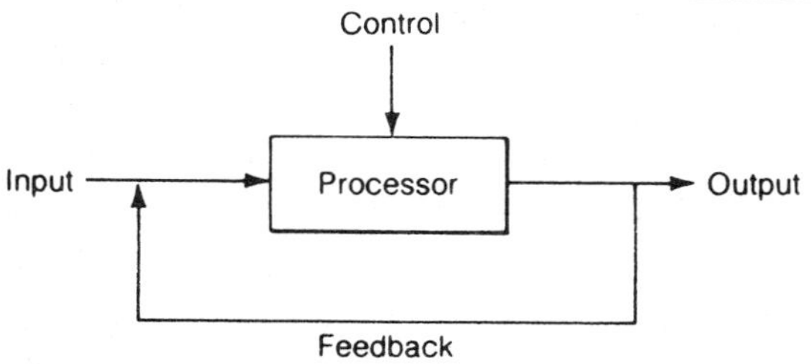

In its business form, this model becomes:

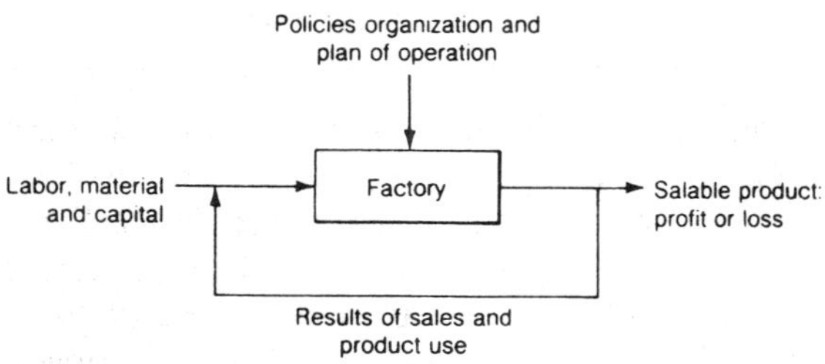

An advantage of the systems approach is that it focuses attention on broader issues than may be contained in a single department. This is because of the emphasis on inputs and outputs. What goes on *inside* the black box is of secondary importance. Naturally this has a healthy effect on any departmental narrowness of viewpoint.

The second advantage of the systems approach is that it aids in the formulation of purposes or objectives for a particular department or operating area. The reason for the existence of any operating area can very neatly be expressed in the formula:

$$P = O - I$$

where P is purpose, O is output and I stand for input.

A third advantage of the systems approach is that it can sometimes be related to decision making. Forrester, for example, in his model for industrial dynamics (p. 62), shows information flows controlling valves in material and money flows.[4]

Forrester, incidentally, develops this theme very well in demonstrating the effect of varying sales volume on inventory levels.

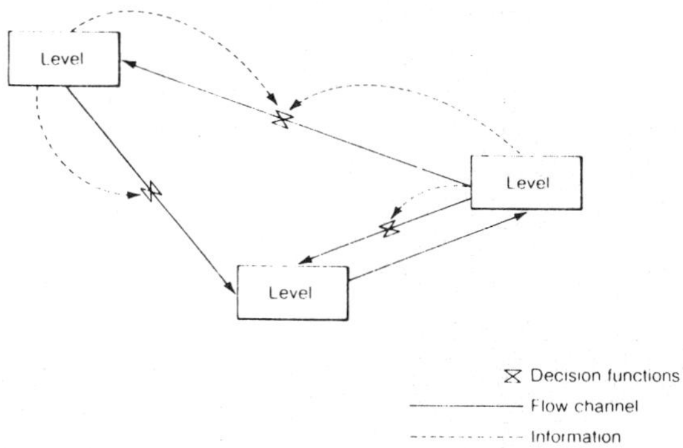

Disadvantage of the Total Systems Approach

The author's main quarrel with the approach is that many of the followers of systems theory seem to have translated *general* systems into total systems; they give the impression that if systems are omnipresent they must somehow, like God, be omnipotent. General systems theory is a valid field of interdisciplinary study. Those who profess general systems theory realize its limitations, which are not recognized by those who take the *total* systems approach. As an example of an understanding of the limitations of the approach, let's refer again to Hall. Following his definition of a system quoted previously in this article he continues:

> Systems may consist of atoms, stars, switches, springs, wires, bones, gases, mathematical variables, equations, laws and processes.[5]

Nowhere in this list does he refer to businesses or people; nowhere in his book does he suggest the use of systems engineering models in business.

Bertalanffy remains conservative: "General systems theory in its present form is one—and still very imperfect—model among others." Even then, this organismic picture would not claim to be a "nothing but" philosophy: it would remain conscious that it only presents "certain aspects of reality . . . but never exhaustive, exclusive or final."[6]

In contrast is the Forrester definition quoted above. Later, in his book, he says:

> Industrial dynamics models in their purpose and origin will be . . . similar to models of engineering systems . . . concentration must be on those factors that determine the characteristics of information feedback systems—structure, amplification and delays.

Even more ambitious is Wiener:

> It is the thesis of this book that society can only be understood through a study of the messages and the communication facilities which belong to it. . . .[7]

The Error in the "Total" Approach

In a nutshell the objection to the "totality" of systems approach is that there is an assumption that this approach is the most important one.[8] This assumption is translated into practice by writers who define the role of change agents such as systems analysts in terms of the total systems concept.

In terms of this concept, the role of the change agents is to design the business system in terms of *flow* of information, materials, money and people, and to persuade members of the enterprise to adopt the system or subsystem so designed. The author has never come across a situation where this has actually been achieved nor has he read an account of where this has been done. This may be coincidental or it may be because of the following:

1. The total systems approach in business makes no attempt to explain, predict or understand why the human members of the business system act the way they do. It is concerned with components of a business system in the same way as communication theory is concerned with electronic components in a communications system, but it offers little or no understanding of those components either as individuals or as members of business organizations.
2. If it cannot explain the way things are, the total systems approach cannot be expected to explain the way things are going to be. Insofar as the total systems approach is weak analytically with regard to the most significant aspects of the business system (viz., the people), it must also be weak in predicting future developments with regard to people.

Illustrations of the Myth

In order to demonstrate the points we have been making we are going to discuss two articles, both heavily influenced by the total systems concept.

The first is "Analyzing an Overall System" by Charles J. Berg. Early in his article he defines a business system as a

> . . . set of policies, rules, and procedures which defines the actions, responsibilities, and authorities of all elements of a business organization in the day-by-day conduct of its normal activities.[9]

This is all-encompassing, and justifies us in classifying it as being a holistic or total approach. How does Mr. Berg use it? The core of his article is concerned with the stepwise

> analytical technique for defining our present position and for use as a systems reference point. Step One is the use of the conventional flow chart of the existing system, with each step analyzed and measured showing the amount of time, money and physical distance required in each processing component. It is not unusual to find at this stage that unnecessary transportation, time and money are incorporated into the system. Step Two relies on the information previously produced, but it is a modified form of the same information. This is the input-output analysis

chart. This technique clearly depicts the multitudinous uses of various data. Generally it can be stated that where many inputs are used to devise many outputs, potential systems improvements are of a high order. Step Three is to relate the present system as described in Steps One and Two above into financial terminology. What lines on the statement are affected and what are the potential improvements available? Step Four is the allocation of people responsibility for the planned systems improvement, along with specific financial objectives to be attained. Step Five is to accomplish the improvements resulting from the analysis of the above information.

Diagramatically Berg expresses his approach as shown in Figure 1.

But the author does not fulfill his promise. In terms of his own definition of a business system his analytical technique is mainly concerned with "procedures and actions." He refers to policies, rules, responsibilities and authorities *of all elements of a business organization* in his definition of a business system quoted above, and says precious little about them in his analytical technique. Under which of his stepwise analytical techniques could one consider the following problems which have to be considered in any business organization?

What business should we be in? For example, should be diversify our operations, or consolidate? Should our business be divisionalized along product lines, customer grouping, or geographic areas? Should our engineering function be centralized or decentralized or along some combination of both?

In fact these problems cannot be subsumed under the techniques proposed because they are too narrow. The promise of total systems—evident in the definition—remains unfulfilled in the proposals for its creation.

Similar objections come to mind with a second article by Dr. R. L. Martino.[10] But in this case the gap between promise and proposal is even more blatant. The promise lies in the title: "The Development and Installation of a Total Management System."

Most business people are inclined to accept the simple notion that management is concerned with governing and controlling of the activities of a company, somewhat analogous to the executive branch of the government of a state. To enlarge "management" to "total management system" emphasizes the pervasiveness of the phenomenon and also its completeness and orderliness. This promise is not borne out by the following:

Figure 1 The stepwise analytical techniques shown here are too narrow to fulfill the promise evident in the definition of total systems.

ONE: If you have a manufacturing order and this is combined with an engineering specification, bills of material and manufacturing information, manpower and the facilities required can be determined.

TWO: With material requirements being compared to raw material inventories, purchases and material receipts schedules can be derived.

THREE: Returning now to the manpower and facilities requirements, combining and comparing this with planning information, we can evolve specific production plans.

FOUR: Material receipts schedules and pay cards, along with production standards and the production plans, can be integrated to produce payrolls, production data and finished goods inventory.

FIVE: Coordinating the information of a sales order with that of the finished goods inventory, we can produce shipments, invoices, bills of lading and sales receipts.

SIX: Finally, we can build management decisions into the systems which are necessary to operate most effectively.

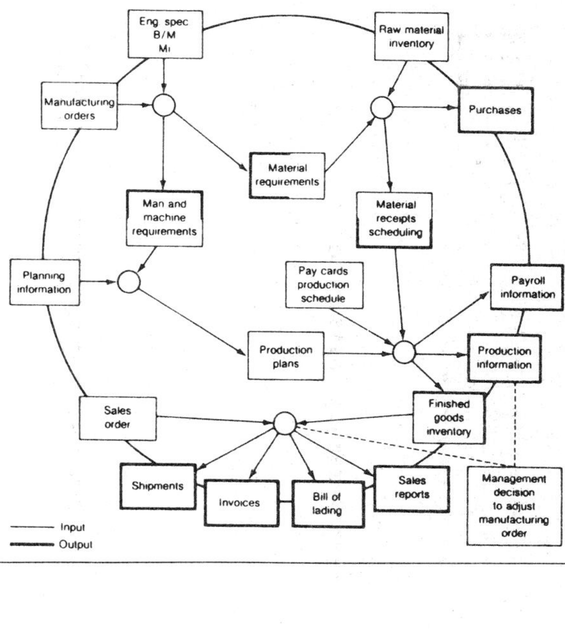

> The primary objective in developing a total management system should be the production of detailed up-to-the-minute summaries of the past and the use of these summaries to project future activity. In essence the functions of a total management system are: (1) To predict; (2) To compare the prediction with actual results; and (3) To produce the deviations between the predicted and the actual.

In other words, the total system conceptualizers, when they really get down to it, talk of designing flows of information to enable management to do its job better. Martino represents this diagramatically in Figure 2.

The figure shows what management does with various kinds of information. In Martino's model, management *itself* is not part of the total management system, for nowhere is there any phase where management looks at itself or the organization of which it is a part. It is as though management were something like the driver of a car, detached; as though, like a car driver, management made the decisions, the "systems" carried them out.

Factories, warehouses and saleshouses and other industries, services, utilities—whatever the business exists for—consist of much more than information handling systems glorified into some state of "totality." Just as a map of a country may cover the whole of it, it is not a "total" depiction of it, because in a country there are other dimensions and features that cannot be shown on a map. Similarly, in a business there are other dimensions and features which cannot be subsumed under the kinds of total systems we have been discussing.

Requirements of a General Business Theory

What then, are the theoretical requirements of change agents in business? The following thoughts are offered as criteria for a basic theory:

Figure 2 This diagram shows what management does with various kinds of information. Management itself, however, is not part of the total management system, for nowhere is there any phase where management looks at itself or the organization of which it is a part.

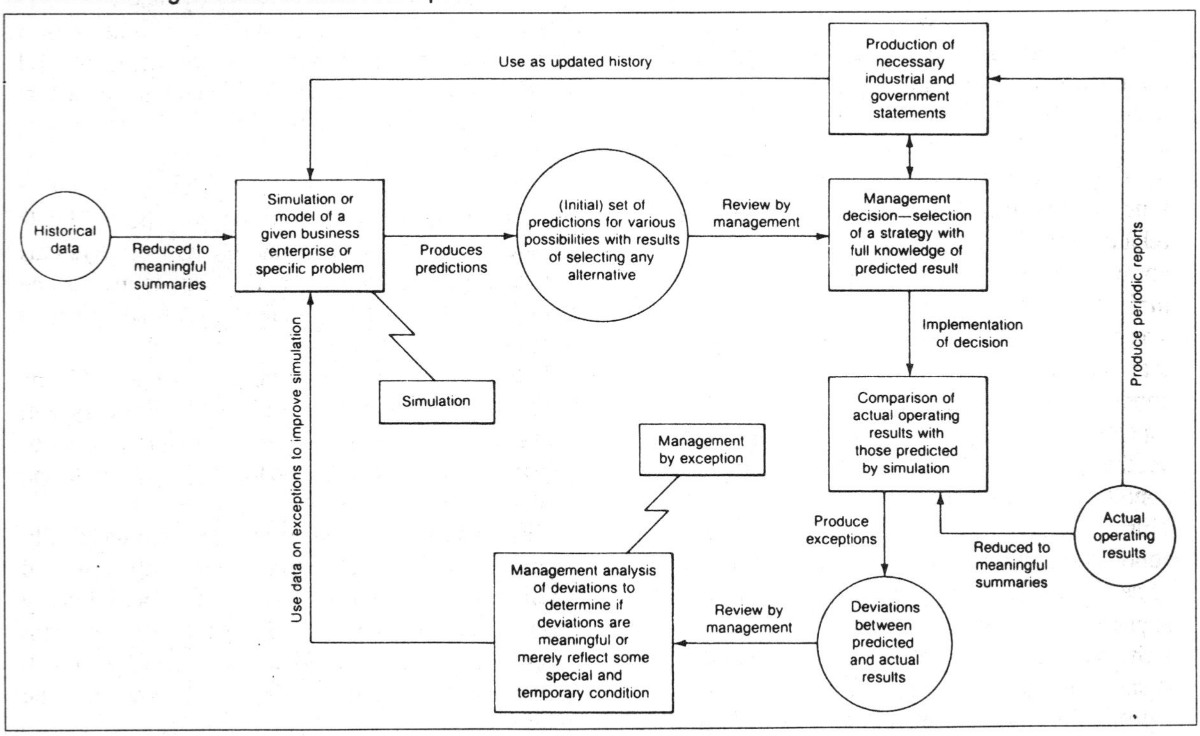

A. **Understanding for action**

1. It must be capable of understanding current problems of business. Therefore,
2. It should be capable of realistic predictions on consequences of proposed actions.
3. It should provide a basis for establishing direction for proposed change.

B. **Basis for theoretical development**

An acceptable basic theory should be broad enough to include other more specific theories. If, for example, we reject total systems theory as a basic tool, the basic tool we do adopt should be capable of covering the valuable aspects of such a theory.

Outline of a Basic Theory

What follows is a skeletal account of a theory which meets these requirements:

1. A business is primarily a social human group. The machines, however vast, are originated by and operated by human beings. Therefore, the theoretical basis should be human-oriented.
2. There are three aspects of human groups which are important to the understanding of a business. They are objectives, or purpose; activities, or the actual work performed; and relationships which include cooperative and functional as well as the ever-present man/boss relationship. In addition, there are three corresponding concepts pertaining to the individual: values, status, and activities.
3. The basis of the approach suggested is, first, that there are certain desirable or healthy conditions for these group and individual aspects, particularly in their relationship to one another. Second, it can be assumed that these conditions do not necessarily apply at all times. Third, it is suggested that the lack of desirable conditions applying will lead to the occurrence of certain effects or symptoms. Fourth, the approach envisages the use of various techniques to reveal these symptoms. Fifth, it is suggested that the symptoms can be used to identify the *causes* of malfunction, and sixth, that planning and executing projects which rectify causes are the proper work of systems analysts, or other change agents, in business.
4. The activities of business are only one of many aspects. Only when this aspect is viewed against its proper background of group purpose (or objectives) and structure, and individuals' values and status, should it be elaborated into a "totality" of system.
5. It is entirely possible to make use of the valuable aspects of systems theory (discussed in the early part of this article) within these other concepts, but then the systems aspect is no longer "total" but ancillary.

A Proposed Role for Systems Analysis

How can the role of the systems analyst be met in view of these criticisms? The senior systems man in a company may be analogous to a cabinet minister in charge of communications (embracing, for instance, tele-, postal, road, rail, and air communications). A minister of communications is concerned with the development of channels for the transmission of information in whatever form. Similarly, the VP of communications with a firm should be concerned with the development and maintenance of communication networks which best achieve company, and divisional if necessary, purpose(s).

This is far-reaching in that it would be extending throughout the whole but it is not holistic or "total" in the Wiener or Forrester sense. Systems departments, therefore, are not analogous to the management of a *real* whole (e.g., a company, a plant or a division).

Let us again take a geographic analogy. All the cities in North America are connected by a system of roads, but urban development—as in the case of corporate development—means working with the wholes in the situation.

City management and development undoubtedly requires auxiliary and parallel development and modification in the road system, and occasionally cities have to adjust to a road development program under the control of a wider authority which constitutes a natural whole,[11] such as a state government.

Roads in this way are analogous to the communications networks of business. Corporations as natural wholes are composed of other, smaller wholes (divisions, operating departments, staff functions, etc.), and the role of management is the continuous mutual adjustment of these parts to one another in order to achieve company goals. This process of continuous adjustment requires the continuous development of new communications transmittal, reception and storage, and it is the role of the systems analyst to carry out this development.

Sometimes, as in the case of a city having to adjust to the road development by a wider authority, the natural wholes (e.g., divisions, departments) within a company have to adjust to the communications system imposed upon them by the company as a whole.

The total systems concept implies—indeed some of its exponents, as we have seen, are quite explicit—that the communications system is the basis for understanding and changing society, or the micro-society that the corporation forms. This is not true; the systems concept is not that "total."

Discussion Questions

1. Are the human members of a business firm part of the total system? Why does the total systems approach tend to neglect the human element? What difficulties does this present for management?
2. Do you agree that the total systems approach cannot answer general questions about the organization's overall objectives? Why or why not? If not, can the approach be modified to deal with such questions?
3. Why is it important for management to monitor its own performance? Is this possible using the total systems approach?
4. Is Brooker's proposed theory of business a workable alternative to the total systems approach? What kind of knowledge does it presuppose? Does it offer help in areas where the total systems approach breaks down?

Footnotes

1. Arthur D. Hall, *A Methodology for Systems Engineering*, Van Nostrand, Toronto, 1962, p. 60.
2. J. W. Forrester, "Industrial Dynamics: A Major Breakthrough for Decision-Makers," *Harvard Business Review*, July-August 1958, p. 52.
3. Stanford L. Optner, *Systems Analysis for Business Management*, Prentice-Hall, Englewood Cliffs, NJ., 1960, pp. 3-15.
4. From J. W. Forrester, *Industrial Dynamics*, John Wiley & Sons, New York, 1961, p. 67.
5. Hall, *loc. cit.*
6. Ludwig von Bertalanffy, *General Systems Theory—A Critical Review*, Yearbook of the Society for General Systems Research, Vol. VII, 1962, p. 10.
7. Norbert Wiener, *The Human Use of Human Beings—Cybernetics and Society*, Doubleday-Anchor, New York, 1954, p. 16.
8. The reason for the error lies in what the author calls the Magical Fallacy.
9. Charles J. Berg, "Analyzing an Overall System," *Systems & Procedures Journal*, November-December 1963.
10. R. L. Martino, "The Development and Installation of a Total Management System," *Data Processing for Management*, April 1963, p. 31.
11. J. C. Smuts, *Holism and Evolution*, Compass Books, New York, 1961.

UNIT TWO

Management Information Systems: Conceptual Foundations

Management information is useful knowledge that is produced as output of data processing operations and acquired for specific purposes. It is basic to the conduct of business; it is needed by managers to support the decisions they must make to achieve organizational goals.

From its inception, the computer has been recognized as a powerful tool with vast potential for improving the quality of decision-making information supplied to management. There has been far less general agreement however, on the ways in which the new technology can best be harnessed to serve the needs of management, and on the forms that management information systems should take. The articles in Unit II provide an overview of the subject and a sample of the views of the proponents and detractors of MIS.

Section 4 (The MIS Idea) offers a variety of viewpoints from the academic and business worlds. Among the important topics addressed are the nature of management information systems, their potential benefits, the kinds of information they can provide, strategies for their implementation, and management issues raised by their introduction into the business organization.

In spite of the optimistic early predictions, many MIS projects have not lived up to user's expectations. The attempt to diagnose the reasons for failures has given rise to a flourishing critical literature that reexamines the assumptions underlying the MIS idea. In Section 5 (Dissenting Views), the critics get their turn at bat. A number of explanations are advanced for the disappointing results of MIS some efforts; most focus on human and organizational problems external to the information system itself. Two of the critical articles are presented with rebuttals from MIS advocates; readers are urged to evaluate the arguments and form their own opinions.

SECTION FOUR

The MIS Idea

READING 7

A Manager's Perspective of Management Information Systems

article by
WARD A. FREDERICKS

A plethora of seminars, speeches, articles, and scholarly books extolling the virtues of MIS (management information systems) has descended upon the business community. *Online*, *real-time*, *data base*, and *teleprocessing* have become part of the "compleat" manager's vocabulary, albeit with less understanding of meaning than usual. In fact, management has accepted the reality of the concept of MIS with open arms, trusting that the types of key decisions which have to be made daily will somehow become easier when the promised data appear in precisely organized formats.

Major companies have mounted massive efforts aimed at designing MIS with results ranging from disaster to partial success. It is still appropriate to say that well-designed and operating MIS are much easier to find in the pages of technical and management journals than in real life.

Source: *MSU Business Topics*, Spring 1971, pp. 7-13. Reprinted by permission of the publisher, Division of Research, Graduate School of Business Administration, Michigan State University.

In order to look at the concept and the application of MIS, an appropriate starting point is to look at management and its most fundamental actions and processes to see what role systems can play in aiding managers in the attainment of their objectives.

The term *top management* as used in this article will cover those members of management whose perspective must include the operation of the entire company—typically the president and executive vice-president in centralized companies, and division general managers in decentralized companies.

Textbooks list planning, controlling, organizing, and so on, as the major functions of management. In an ongoing business enterprise, however, top management makes key decisions relating to certain aspects of the business which determine the size, character, and long-term viability of the organization. These decisions are made in every company, regardless of size, and represent the most difficult part of the management process. They set the tone for the entire enterprise. To simplify the perspective in these key decisions and actions, a five-way categorization would be: (1) decisions and actions which affect pricing, (2) decisions and actions which affect volume, (3) decisions and actions which affect overhead or structural cost, (4) decisions and actions which affect product (or service) cost, and (5) decisions and actions which affect asset turnover.

In every business enterprise it is the interaction of the decisions made in each of the above categories which determines the viability and profitability of the organization. Any MIS effort, then, should address, both in cause and effect terms, the impact of having systems which can influence the outcome of these various decisions and actions.

Profitability: A Complex Result

In order to put proper emphasis upon the complex interaction of the five main areas for management action just listed, let us investigate the "anatomy of a profit." Profit is certainly one of the major objectives of business enterprise, although not the only objective in today's complex society. Continued existence of the enterprise is dependent upon the generation of acceptable profit, however, and therefore management thrust must be directed toward this result.

Management action aimed at producing profit in an ongoing business enterprise may be looked at in terms of the four parts to the profit equation below:

$$(1)\quad (P \times V) - PC - SC = PROFIT$$

$$(2)\quad \frac{Profit}{Assets} = \text{Return on Investment}$$

Simply stated, price times volume equals gross revenue for the enterprise, from which is subtracted product cost and structural cost (or overhead). Profit-oriented management action must be aimed at impacting one or more of the variables in the equation to have a favorable effect on the result. Return on investment of the enterprise is a function of profit, certainly, but turnover of assets involved in the business plays a major role in determining the resultant rate of return.

It is prudent to begin an analysis with simple truths in order to follow the flow of logic to the desired end. In terms of the actions of management and the impact of various kinds of decisions on profitability and return on assets employed, the "truths" exposed above are certainly simple and both mathematically and judgmentally provable to the most practical manager.

Where does the impact of various elements of the MIS come into the picture? Basically, operating systems in any company form the basis for the information system, and these operating systems impact the profit equation by their very existence.

Systems Impact on the Process of the Business

Perhaps the easiest way to visualize the interrelationships between the business, operating data processing systems, and the overall MIS is to visualize the total enterprise as being made up of intertwined key processes. Then it can be seen that the planning, control, and administration of these key processes constitutes the overall management of the company.

The major interacting processes which together make up the entity called the company include:

- The financial analysis and control process
- The market-research—product definition—product introduction
- The sales planning—forecasting—monitoring process
- The purchasing—provisioning—manufacturing—finished-product-distribution process

Each one of the four processes needs to be managed at strategic, tactical, and operational levels. In order to properly manage each process, an information system must exist which provides data to the manager which is a symbolic representation of the process itself. The information system needs to provide the *planning*, *control*, and *administrative* data necessary to constantly evaluate and take appropriate action upon the process to bring it under control. Therefore, in each area or department of the business, management must go through a disciplined thought process in order to: (1) define the process (or processes) for which the function is responsible; (2) define the information necessary to plan, control, and administer the process; (3) design the operating and/or information systems which will provide operational assistance and reports necessary to plan, control, and administer the process; (4) determine the level of cost which the present and proposed techniques will require to carry out the process; and (5) determine what changes in the method or technique of handling the process are required to minimize costs or allow for greater volume at minimum expenditure.

Let us take the process of acquiring raw materials, transforming them into finished product, and distributing the product, as an example. Let us examine it at operational, tactical, and strategic levels, and then look at the implications. Table 1 summarizes the aspects of the process.

It is evident that in the development and implementation of information systems in a company, when we view the problem as one supporting the planning, control, and administrative functions of a major process, we must define the operational, tactical, and strategic requirements and considerations which permit management of that process on a continuous basis under constantly changing circumstances.

Conversely, when we are looking at the strategic, tactical, and operational management needs of the corporation, we have to take into consideration and formalize the planning, control, and administrative systems necessary to manage the major processes.

It is obvious that with this approach we are no longer talking about *the* MIS, as if it were some mythical beast like the unicorn; we are talking about an interlocking, coordinated set of management systems designed to optimize the planning, control, and administration of specific processes operationally, tactically, and strategically. Modularity is essential in our approaches to management concepts and to system design.

A Sense of Strategy: MIS

Management information systems don't just happen, they have to be uniquely constructed to fit the enterprise they are to serve.

We have already seen that the management perspective of MIS implies that there are operational elements as well as tactical and strategic planning elements in the hierarchy of systems which together make up an MIS.

From a strategic standpoint, development of an MIS must start with development of operational systems which have immediate benefits to the enterprise in terms of reducing overhead costs or some other major variable in the profit equation.

Information to be used in MIS originates at the operating levels within the company, and in the marketplace. In order to develop an MIS one does not set out to design one, but one should set out to design specific operational and control systems required for the ongoing management of individual processes and functions in the company. Further, each operational and control system in a given functional area consisting of a series of specific applications needs to be evaluated and brought into being only after identifying the business goals of the system and performing initial cost/benefit analysis prior to expenditures on design and installation.

In terms of a basic strategy of systems development, one of the key management goals in a manufacturing company is the control of cost goods sold. In a situation where material is the dominant element of the total cost of finished goods, a key system to be developed would be a manufacturing and logistical control system primarily oriented toward optimizing work in process and raw material inventories, and toward optimization of assets used in the production process, machine tools, toolage, and so forth. Justification of such a system would lie in increased utilization of assets, reduction of inventories in relation to throughput, and, in general, increased throughput through the factories for a given level of investment.

Similarly, in the marketing area as far as control of the flow of finished goods from factory door to retail is concerned, information on order status through the distribution system leads to better information on product mix and volume. Relating production mix to demand mix makes lower inventories in the distribution pipeline possible for any given level of sales activity. This again leads to conservation of assets employed in realizing a given level of revenue.

We find that if we define and implement an information system designed to control the process which has to be carried out (such as purchasing,

Table 1 Aspects of the Business Logistics Process

Functions	Operational Level	Tactical Level	Strategic Level
Planning	(a) Plan the receiving and progress chasing schedule of material deliveries.	(a) Forecast of sales in detail of each specific product within lead time of material acquisition.	(a) Determine future product line requirements and strategies.
	(b) Plan releases on suppliers to be processed next day.	(b) Translation into future build program.	(b) Estimate long range demand for existing and planned products by demand region.
	(c) Plan machine shop schedule for next day.	(c) Determination of sourcing pattern.	(c) Determine production and warehousing facilities requirements.
	(d) Plan next day's assembly schedule.	(d) Planning of inventory levels of raw material, work in process, and finished goods.	(d) Plan management, administrative, labor, and other resources required for planned growth.
	(e) Plan inspection, packing, and shipping schedule for next day.	(e) Planning of purchasing quantities and orders on suppliers.	(e) Determine capital requirements and financial conditions for successful growth.
	(f) Plan minimum/maximum in-process inventories (short lead items).	(f) Planning and scheduling of utilization of existing facilities and available labor.	
		(g) Planning of requirements for cash to finance any seasonal needs.	
Control	Control all activities (processes) against documented plan prepared yesterday; report and take appropriate action on variances.	Monitoring of accuracy of all forecasts up to cut-off point determined by lead time of materials and components. Continuous feedback in response to market changes and production achievement, modifying tactical plan on a continuous basis.	Control against predicted performance to adjust strategic plans on a continuous basis in response to: economic trend changes, inflationary changes, political situations, industry and competition, technological developments, and current performance accomplishment.
Administration	Prepare and communicate all operational control documentation and capture for future analysis and extrapolation of historical performance. (Receiving documentation, machining orders and instructions, scrap reports, assembly tallies, packing instructions, shipping documentation, production volume data, and so forth.)	Maintenance and communication of all tactical planning and feedback information. Acquisition, maintenance, and extrapolation of historical data.	Maintain continuously updated planning data base containing feedback from the tactical control system and monitoring of external environment.

production control, machining, assembly line scheduling, wholegoods warehousing, wholegoods distribution, and so forth), the data which have to be maintained to do so almost automatically include information needed to control costs—to account for the operation and to develop historical data for statistical and forecasting purposes. It is really right at the basic level of operational control data that a computer-aided MIS is anchored, because it is at that level that facts for planning, extrapolation, and monitoring of progress have to be captured.

These examples are given in an attempt to illustrate the point that the foundation of an MIS is in the information and operating systems designed to control and support operations in the manufacturing, distribution, marketing, financial, and logistics areas.

Back to the Basics

We began this analysis with a discussion of the basic tools open to the manager and of the arena in which he could take actions to increase profits. Where, then, does the construction of an MIS aid him in the manipulation of the variables which determine the result of his efforts? Let's look again at the variables and indicate where the elements of an MIS impact each and what abilities the manager has with operating management systems which he would otherwise forego:

1. Structural Costs (Overheads)

Perhaps the most difficult group of decisions made by top management revolve around the ongoing costs of administering the company. Early EDP (electronic data processing) applications typically address segments of this expense in terms of mechanizing payroll, accounting, and billing. The key decision factors in mechanizing these areas are those which relate to the relative simplicity of accomplishing the EDP application and the high level of predictability that savings in overhead will, in fact, occur as a result of the mechanization effort. Order processing, warranty claim processing, purchase order preparation, and work in process inventory status are all applications which form the most basic parts of an overall MIS, and which, if properly conceived and executed, should provide for a reduction in overhead cost at expected levels of volume.

Many technical writers bemoan the fact that companies tackle the administrative and accounting applications first rather than some abstruse decision-making types of functions. Business logic and the realities of commercial life strongly suggest that these applications are, in fact, the most appropriate bases upon which to build an MIS effort.

2. Price and Volume

It is the marketing and sales area of price and volume that creativity in systems design can pay off for the knowledgeable businessman. The customer of any company is looking for a supplier and a product which minimizes his total cost of doing business. Development of systems which make it easier to do business with your company than with competitors can provide opportunity to maximize price without attendant loss of volume. Providing the customer with an inventory control system and maintaining his inventory records allows for reductions in his costs while giving sales management useful information on product movement.

Price and product cost analyses with the kind of detail possible by use of EDP systems may suggest different pricing approaches where basic models of the product are sold at low margin while typical add-ons carry higher profit. In addition, the relatively fixed nature of the cost of mechanically handling administration activities may make it possible to go after incremental volume at less than fully absorbed price when circumstances are appropriate.

3. Product Cost

While product cost may be reduced by better scheduling of manpower and assets utilized in the company, many other opportunities also exist to employ EDP-generated intelligence to minimize costs. Product-by-product cost/price analysis will invariably show up specific products where inflation or other factors have seriously deteriorated margins. Decisions can then be made on pricing action or product phase out. Purchasing systems which analyze bought-out materials by commodity type, vendor, frequency of usage, commonality of usage, or multiple vendors in various geographic locations are relatively straightforward systems applications which typically yield profitable results. These applications will often provide summarized data which establish different make/buy situations than had been previously recognized.

4. Asset Turnover

The critical elements which lead to improved asset turnover are summarized in the ability to tightly and precisely schedule usage of assets, and in the ability to react to changes in need for assets quickly enough to avoid acquisition of unnecessary dollars of inventory. Sales analysis and forecasting systems can provide intelligence on shifts in needs for inventory and production. Combined with appropriate production control and material provisioning systems, lead times to react to market changes may be reduced by months. The ability to react to change should, in fact, be the overriding objective in design of material and production control systems, since an overly precise result which cannot be changed quickly in the face of market shifts will straitjacket management instead of providing the flexibility necessary to maximize resulsts.

The Management Questions

We have seen that an MIS is not one system but a series of interrelated operating elements which support different ongoing processes of the business. How then does operating top management select and determine priorities of effort in the systems area, and how does the management know when the efforts it is sponsoring are paying off?

Basically, there is a set of questions to which management needs to know the answers in order to effectively run the business. The questions are simple, their answers straightforward, and their interrelationships obvious. They are:

- What are we selling?—Product and dollars
- Where are we selling it?—Geography and product mix
- What will we be selling and where?—Forecast—units and dollars
- What do we own?—company inventories—product and dollars and age
- Where it it?—Locations of inventory
- What are we producing for sale?—Production schedules
- When will it be ready for sale?—Future product availability
- What will it cost us?—Product cost
- What should we be producing and selling tomorrow?

Any MIS which is truly responsive to the needs of top management should provide the answers to these questions—accurately and quickly. The system will be composed of a number of sub-systems which address certain aspects of one or more questions—and which are used by operating personnel as an inherent part of their activities. The answers to the questions will provide management with data indicating whether action needs to be taken in the arena of price, volume, structural cost, product cost, or asset turnover—and should indicate the basic area for action. And it should be paying for itself, in reduction of structural costs or product costs; the MIS benefit should be a product of the "gestalt" equation where 2 + 2 = 5.

If the EDP systems in a company can answer the questions posed above then they represent truly an MIS.

It is management's responsibility to ask "why not?" if the systems efforts in their company do not appear to produce the desired end results. If systems in a company do not provide answers to the key questions, then management hasn't been providing enough input to the systems development process and the technicians have been practicing their own brand of footwork. One can consider the projects currently underway in any systems group and determine if they meet all the tests of relevance contained below:

- Will existence of the system being designed help to answer one or more of the nine key top management questions about the business?
- Has the system been cost justified by the operating area which is to use it?

• Are the systems people working with (and for) the staff of the operating area of the busines which is the sponsor of the effort?
• Are there explicit time targets for the systems people to meet in order to finish the project?
• Does overall systems management know and recognize where this systems effort will fit into the total information system needs of the company?

If systems efforts in a company can meet the tests of relevance, chances are good that an overall MIS is coming into being. If not, management is not being served, and whatever is to be produced by the systems effort will not aid in making the kinds of decisions necessary to produce profits.

It remains up to management to produce an MIS which will produce profits instead of costs for the company. The final product of management is, after all, profits.

Discussion Questions

1. In what specific ways can the acquisition of an MIS affect the variables in a firm's profit equation? Are such effects always predictable? Are they always beneficial (i.e., in the direction of greater profit)?
2. How is Fredericks' position on the "transitional versus apocalyptic" issue influenced by his management background? Would a programmer or a systems analyst agree with him? Why or why not? Is compromise possible between the two extreme positions on this question?
3. Why are administrative and accounting applications typically among the first to be automated? How do the potential benefits compare with those offered by more sophisticated information processing applications? What about the predictability of the benefits?
4. Are all of Fredericks' "tests of relevance" equally important in judging the feasibility of an MIS proposal? Which do you think are the most important? Why?

SECTION FIVE

DISSENTING VIEWS

READING 8

Myths of Automated Management Systems

article by
EDWARD M. TOLLIVER

Today, many top executives are worried because competitors are reportedly using computers to make major breakthroughs in executive level management techniques and effectiveness. These executives tend to have an uneasy feeling that somehow they have failed to exploit the potentials of modern management science—and that the penalty will soon become painfully visible in the profit and loss statement.[1]

Relax, Mr. Worried Executive. Computers have not resulted in major breakthroughs in executive level management and none are in prospect. Computers have done little more than perform clerical tasks such as the day to day processing of sales, production and accounting actions. Computers have performed such routine tasks in an efficient manner. But these tasks involve the processing of decisions that have already been made and the principal by-product of value to executives is historical data.

In contrast, the success of a business is largely dependent on decisions concerning future events. Such decisions do benefit from a good and timely analysis of historical happenings which an automated management system can provide. But the basic ingredients of such decisions (and thus of business success) are judgment, initiative and common sense. An automated management system cannot be endowed with these ingredients. An automated system will no more insure the success of a business than a scalpel will insure the success of a surgical operation. A good automated system is to an executive what a good scalpel is to a surgeon: both increase the chance of success but are certainly no substitute for ability and know-how.

Nevertheless, the purveyors of automated management system miracles continue to promote myths such as the following (Oversimplication is employed for the sake of brevity):

Source: *Journal of Systems Management*, vol. 22, no. 3 (March 1971).

Myth: the successful executive will soon have a computer terminal on his desk

About as useful as a typewriter on his desk. A computer can provide perhaps 10% of the ingredients of a good executive decision. The executive and his human associates must continue to provide the remaining 90%. (But humor the senior executive who has taken a computer course and wants a computer terminal to play with—he is entitled to some diversion and will likely tire of the gadget before he seriously disrupts the system.)

Myth: think big—I: don't just automate the old way of doing things: restructure the company's operations to fully exploit the potential of modern computers

Not if the company's success is dependent on making a profit. It is hard to make really major breakthroughs in management processes while concurrently teaching the computer to do complex new things. Don't venture into uncharted waters too far too fast. Find out how far others have successfully gone, take advantage of their accomplishments and mistakes, and go a bit further. If you have a long-range system vision, describe it the best you can and try to channel interim system development in a compatible manner.

Myth: think big—II: a fully integrated corporatewide system will revolutionize the company

It sure will. Responsibility is likely to be so diffused that almost everyone will have an excuse. An error or failure at one point may jam the gears in several departments. We still can't fully integrate functions without disproportionate risk of operational and economic penalty. Concentrate on automating information near its point of origin and making it available to every concerned department for use by that department as it sees fit. Promote the multiple use of common items of information.

Don't be too concerned about some duplication in the automated processing of information once it is in computer useable form; computer power is relatively cheap and getting cheaper. Letting each department run its own part of the business will promote initiative and innovation with more effective results in the long run. It is, however, desirable to have a few persuasive but diplomatic system experts around to discover and promote opportunities for integrating across departmental boundaries.

Myth: think big—III: take advantage of the growing capability to transmit a tremendous volume of data in microseconds over long distances

Business and government are already being buried in an avalanche of data of marginal value. The need is to decrease the flow of data—not increase it. There are valid requirements to transmit electronically over long distances relatively small quantities of data, such as stock transactions and reservations. In contrast, there are very few valid requirements to rapidly transmit large volumes of data hundreds or thousands of miles for business purposes. The next most important goal is to cull out and transmit only what serves a substantially useful purpose.

The next most important goal is to transmit it in the most economical manner—getting business data there in a day or two is usually as satisfactory as getting it there in a microsecond. But, keep in mind that the cost of long distance electronic data transmission is going to decrease very substantially—possibly by 50% or more in the next five years—so don't base a cost-effective evaluation on today's prices.

Myth: stop the foot dragging—create an automated system czar at the senior vice-president level

Another excellent way to diffuse responsibility. Just try holding the sales manager responsible for sales when he is convinced (rightly or wrongly) that the Czar isn't giving him the information he needs, is requiring the sales staff to create useless computer input, and is permitting the computer to mistreat customers.

A better way is to create an automated management service (not Czar) good enough so that the sales manager will go to it for help in implementing his ideas. There is merit in having a senior executive to insure that the service is good, to insure that the service is being fully exploited but not abused, and to impose minimum standardization and other guidelines to the extent clearly justified to achieve corporate-wide objectives.

Myth: centralize system design to more effectively utilize systems experts

Your objective is to operate the company more effectively—not to utilize systems experts more effectively. System design is nothing more nor less than figuring out a better way to get a job done—using rubber stamps, quill pens, computers or anything else that best achieves results. The person who can figure out the best way is usually the department head responsible for the day to day accomplishment of objectives. Make available systems experts to help him.

In contrast, systems experts, left to their own devices, will usually end up solving the wrong problem or the right problem the wrong way. Much of what they create may not be used—or may become just an additional (not a replacement) process. After the responsible department head has determined rather specifically how things should be done, it's OK to have the details worked out by a centralized staff of systems experts.

Myth: our department heads aren't smart enough—get outsiders to create a major new automated system

If department heads aren't smart and flexible enough to be cruise directors in developing an automated management system they aren't capable of doing their present job and should have been replaced long ago. Probably department heads need only some leadership from you, enough relief from day to day pressures to do some constructive thinking, and the assistance of experts who have know-how in the automated techniques involved.

An essential ingredient in successful development of an automated system is knowledge of the job to be done and understanding of the environment in which it must be accomplished. Another essential ingredient is in-house enthusiasm for a new system. Department heads tend to have a monopoly on both of these essential ingredients. They can very quickly learn enough about computer capabilities to be cruise directors. In contrast, it would take a great many months for a systems expert to acquire a real understanding of your business even if you could find such an expert who has the aptitude and motivation. But don't overlook the potential value of an outside management firm that has actually solved the specific kind of problem you have.

Myth: executives must determine their information needs

Wait for executives to determine their information needs in the detail meaningful to a computer and you are not likely to develop a good automated management system. Executives get to be executives because they are good at solving broad intangible problems. Computers get to be computers because they are built to handle specific tangible problems. An executive typically doesn't think on a wavelength meaningful to a computer. You can and must get executives to meaningfully express their information needs from an overall operational or functional perspective. These needs must then be translated by functional staff people into specific information requirements meaningful to ADP experts.

Myth: automated management systems are flexible—just put data in and the computer can use it to answer almost any management question you can think of

A computer can only answer questions you have anticipated well in advance and taught it to answer. Teaching a computer to answer a question is far more costly and time consuming than teaching an individual to answer a question. So depend primarily on individuals—not automated systems—to answer nonrepetitive questions. This is also another reason why most executives will never have a computer terminal on their desk.

Myth: but a "data management system" can automatically reorganize data almost any way you want

It sure can reorganize it, like restacking in a variety of ways. But that doesn't help much in making management decisions such as how, why or where you should build a brick house. And you have to be somewhat of a computer technician to persuade the Data Management System to restack the bricks.

Myth: our automated management system costs too much—I

So do groceries, but you don't stop eating. You consider what each item of food contributes to your well being, either nutritionally or emotionally, and you perhaps eliminate filet mignon. You don't cut out vegetables because the penalties and alternatives are not in your best interest. Apply the same common sense to your automated management system. Its segments, like items of food, must be individually evaluated in terms of what they do for you. Such an evaluation should be a continuing process. It makes no more sense to condemn the cost of an automated management system as a whole than to condemn the cost of food as a whole.

Myth: our automated management sytem costs too much—II

Not the system—but your decisions to do things of marginal value. It's mighty sporty and impressive to know the status of every customer order every hour—but what does it do for you or the customer? Is your decision to have such information costing you $10 for every $1 of benefit? Such illogical decisions/requirements are the principal cause of excessive system costs. (A strictly secondary cause might be the efficiency of the automated system itself.)

Myth: our automated management sytem costs too much—III

Probably not enough. The really big potential today is in promoting the automation of functions that could be accomplished far more efficiently by automation—even if you have to bribe a major department or facility with a computer of its own.

Myth: don't discourage automation by prorating costs among departments

If you don't prorate costs you'll have the biggest computer system in town and most of what it does won't be cost-effective. First discontinue charging each department with the travel and entertainment costs it incurs: you'll learn the same lesson for less.

Myth: to have a successful automated management system depend on an outside firm (computer utility) for computer service as you do for electric service

Follow this logic and you can reduce the size of your organization to a president and a few staff assistants. You could contract out your sales, production, accounting and most other functions to various firms of specialists. But you don't because such functions are essential to your success and you can't precisely define the requirements or measure the results. It's not like arranging for so many kilowatts and volts of electricity. The same is true of stenographic or computer services. Thus most successful firms (except the smallest) will continue to have in-house computer capability to meet basic requirements and will depend on outside facilities to meet specialized or peak needs.

Myth: automated systems revolutionize management process

To date computers have generally discouraged really major changes in management processes by making it economically feasible to continue doing things the old way. And once the old way is automated, change becomes more difficult and expensive. In some instances, however, the definitive analysis of management processes essential to automation has even revealed significant opportunities for improvement—even if the automated system didn't work as promised.

Myth: automated management sytems are a myth—There aren't any such things

Almost true. Mostly, there are automated clerical systems. A very few firms have successfully automated some of the more routine management functions, but to date benefits have usually not justified the expense. A tremendous gap exists between what is theoretically possible and what is operationally and economically feasible.

But don't stick your head in the sand—the potential is there. During the next decade or so the more routine management functions will be gradually automated with substantial payoff. Just avoid the major expense and operational penalties of being a pioneer unless your organization has a great deal to gain.

Discussion Questions

1. What dangers does Tolliver see in thinking too big? What are the dangers of thinking too small? Which is more dangerous? Why?
2. Do executives always know their own information needs? Is there a difference between knowing them and being able to formulate them precisely? How can the executive's specific knowledge of his/her job be combined with the ADP expert's knowledge of computers to produce the results needed?
3. What factors should be considered when deciding whether and how far to automate the management process? Is there such a thing as too much automation? Might some firms be better off without any? Why or why not?
4. Summarize Tolliver's attitude toward computers. How does it compare with the views expressed in Section 4? With which of Tolliver's points do you agree and disagree most strongly, and why?

Footnotes

1. The system management concepts in this article are written from the perspective of private business where the success of a system can ultimately be judged by its impact on the profit and loss statement. Such system management concepts are not always applicable in government where the criterion of success is not profit.

READING 9

Management Misinformation Systems

article by
RUSSELL L. ACKOFF

The growing preoccupation of operations researchers and management scientists with Management Information Systems (MIS's) is apparent. In fact, for some the design of such systems has almost become synonymous with operations research or management science. Enthusiasm for such systems is understandable: it involves the researcher in a romantic relationship with the most glamorous instrument of our time, the computer. Such enthusiasm is understandable but, nevertheless, some of the excesses to which it has led are not excusable.

Contrary to the impression produced by the growing literature, few computerized management information systems have been put into operation. Of those I have seen that have been implemented, most have not matched expectations and some have been outright failures. I believe that these near- and far-misses could have been avoided if certain false (and usually implicit) assumptions on which many such systems have been erected had not been made.

There seem to be five common and erroneous assumptions underlying the design of most MIS's, each of which I will consider. After doing so I will outline an MIS design procedure which avoids these asssumptions.

Give Them More

Most MIS's are designed on the assumption that the critical deficiency under which most managers operate is the *lack of relevant information*. I do not deny that most managers lack a good deal of information that they should have, but I do deny that this is the most important informational deficiency from which they suffer. It seems to me that they suffer most from an *overabundance of irrelevant information.*

Source: Reprinted by permission of Russell L. Ackoff, "Management Misinformation Systems," *Management Science*, Volume 14, Number 4, December, 1967, pp. B147-B156.

This is not a play on words. The consequences of changing the emphasis of an MIS from supplying relevant information to eliminating irrelevant information are considerable. If one is preoccupied with supplying relevant information, attention is almost exclusively given to the generation, storage, and retrieval of information: hence emphasis is placed on constructing data banks, coding, indexing, updating files, access languages, and so on. The ideal which has emerged from this orientation is an infinite pool of data into which a manager can reach to pull out any information he wants. If, on the other hand, one sees the manager's information problem primarily, but not exclusively, as one that arises out of an overabundance of irrelevant information, most of which was not asked for, then the two most important functions of an information system become *filtration* (or evaluation) and *condensation*. The literature on MIS's seldom refers to these functions let alone considers how to carry them out.

My experience indicates that most managers receive much more data (if not information) than they can possibly absorb even if they spend all of their time trying to do so. Hence they already suffer from an information overload. They must spend a great deal of time separating the relevant from the irrelevant and searching for the kernels in the relevant documents. For example, I have found that I receive an average of forty-three hours of unsolicited reading material each week. The solicited material is usually half again this amount.

I have seen a daily stock status report that consists of approximately six hundred pages of computer printout. The report is circulated daily across managers' desks. I've also seen requests for major capital expenditures that come in book size, several of which are distributed to managers each week. It is not uncommon for many managers to receive an average of one journal a day or more. One could go on and on.

Unless the information overload to which managers are subjected is reduced, any additional information made available by an MIS cannot be expected to be used effectively.

Even relevant documents have too much redundancy. Most documents can be considerably condensed without loss of content. My point here is best made, perhaps, by describing an experiment that a few of my colleagues and I conducted on the OR [operations research] literature several years ago. By using a panel of well-known experts we identified four OR articles that all members of the panel considered to be "above average," and four articles that were considered to be "below average." The authors of the eight articles were asked to prepare "objective" examinations (duration 30 minutes) plus answers for graduate students who were assigned the articles for reading. (The authors were not informed about the experiment.) Then several experienced writers were asked to reduce each article to 2/3 and 1/3 of its original length only by eliminating words. They also prepared a brief abstract of each article. Those who did the condensing did not see the examinations to be given to the students.

A group of graduate students who had not previously read the articles were then selected. Each one was given four articles randomly selected, each of which was in one of its four versions: 100%, 67%, 33%, or abstract. Each version of each article was read by two students. All were given the same examinations. The average scores on the examinations were then compared.

For the above-average articles there was no significant difference between average test scores for the 100%, 67%, and 33% versions, but there was a significant decrease in average test scores for those who had read only the abstract. For the below-average articles there was no difference in average test scores among those who had read the 100%, 67%, and 33% versions, but there was a significant *increase* in average test scores of those who had read only the abstract.

The sample used was obviously too small for general conclusions but the results strongly indicate the extent to which even good writing can be condensed without loss of information. I refrain from drawing the obvious conclusion about bad writing.

It seems clear that condensation as well as filtration, performed mechanically or otherwise, should be an essential part of an MIS, and that such a system should be capable of handling much, if not all, of the unsolicited as well as solicited information that a manager receives.

The Manager Needs the Information That He Wants

Most MIS designers "determine" what information is needed by asking managers what information they would like to have. This is based on the assumption that managers know what information they need and want it.

For a manager to know what information he needs he must be aware of each type of decision he should make (as well as does) and he must have an adequate model of each. These conditions are seldom satisfied. Most managers have some conception of at least some of the types of decisions they must make. Their conceptions, however, are likely to be deficient in a very critical way, a way that follows from an important principle of scientific economy: the less we understand a phenomenon, the more variables we require to explain it. Hence, the manager who does not understand the phenomenon he controls plays it "safe" and, with respect to information, wants "everything." The MIS designer, who has even less understanding of the relevant phenomenon than the manager, tries to provide even more than everything. He thereby increases what is already an overload of irrelevant information.

For example, market researchers in a major oil company once asked their marketing managers what variables they thought were relevant in estimating the sales volume of future service stations. Almost seventy variables were identified. The market researchers then added about half again this many variables and performed a large multiple linear regression analysis of sales of existing stations against these variables and found about thirty-five to be statistically significant. A forecasting equation was based on this analysis. An OR team subsequently constructed a model based on only one of these variables, traffic flow, which predicted sales better than the thirty-five variable regression equation. The team went on to *explain* sales at service stations in terms of the customers' perception of the amount of time lost by stopping for service. The relevance of all but a few of the variables used by the market researchers could be explained by their effect on such perception.

The moral is simple: one cannot specify what information is required for decision making until an explanatory model of the decision process and the system involved has been constructed and tested. Information systems are subsystems of control systems. They cannot be designed adequately without taking control into account. Furthermore, whatever else regression analyses can yield, they cannot yield understanding and explanation of phenomena. They describe and, at best, predict.

Give a Manager the Information He needs and His Decision Making Will Improve

It is frequently assumed that if a manager is provided with the information he needs, he will then have no problem in using it effectively. The history of OR stands to the contrary. For example, give most managers an initial tableau of a typical "real" mathematical programming, sequencing, or network problem and see how close they come to an optimal solution. If their experience and judgment have any value thay may not do badly, but they will seldom do very well. In most management problems there are too many possibilities to expect experience, judgment, or intuition to provide good guesses, even with perfect information.

Furthermore, when several probabilities are involved in a problem the unguided mind of even a manager has difficulty in aggregating them in a valid way. We all know many simple problems in probability in which untutored intuition usually does very badly (e.g., What are the correct odds that two of twenty-five people selected at random will have their birthdays on the same day of the year?). For example, very few of the results obtained by queuing theory, when arrivals and service are probabilistic, are obvious to managers; nor are the results of risk analysis where the managers' own subjective estimates or probabilities are used.

The moral: it is necessary to determine how well managers can use needed information. When because of the complexity of the decision process, they can't use it well, they should be provided with either decision rules or performance feedback so that they can identify and learn from their mistakes. More on this point later.

More Communication Means Better Performance

One characteristic of most MIS's which I have seen is that they provide managers with better current information about what other managers and their departments and divisions are doing. Underlying this provision is the belief that better interdepartmental communication enables managers to coordinate their decisions more effectively and hence improves the organization's overall performance. Not only is this not necessarily so, but seldom is so. One would hardly expect two competing companies to become more cooperative because the information each acquires about the other is improved. This analogy is not as far fetched as one might first suppose. For example, consider the following very much simplification of the case does not affect any of its essential characteristics.

A department store has two "line" operations: buying and selling. Each function is performed by a separate department. The Purchasing Department primarily controls one variable: how much of each item is bought. The Merchandising Department controls the price at which it is sold. Typically, the measure of performance applied to the Purchasing Department was the turnover rate of inventory. The measure applied to the Merchandising Department was gross sales; this department sought to maximize the number of items sold times their price.

Now by examining a single item let us consider what happens in this sytem. The merchandising manager, using his knowledge of competition and consumption, set a price which he judged would maximize gross sales. In doing so he utilized price-demand curves for each type of item. For each price the curves show the expected sales and values on an upper and lower confidence band as well. (See Figure 1.) When instructing the Purchasing Department how many items to make available, the merchandising manager quite naturally used the value on the upper confidence curve. This minimized the chances of his running short which, if it occurred, would hurt his performance. It also maximized the chances of being overstocked but this was not his concern, only the purchasing manager's. Say, therefore, that the merchandising manager initially selected price P_1 and requested that amount

Figure 1 Price-Demand Curve

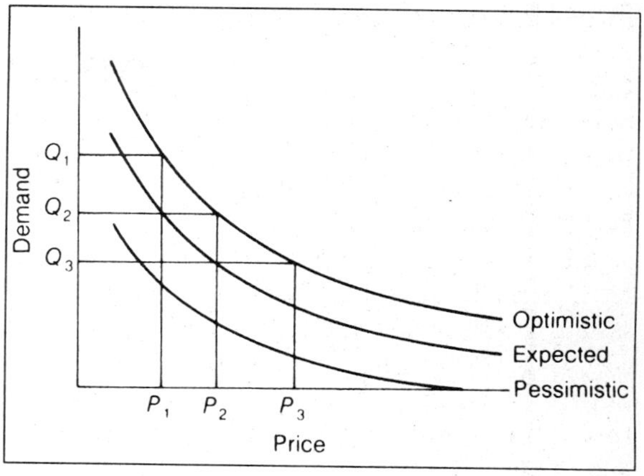

Q_1 be made available by the Purchasing Department.

In this company the purchasing manager also had access to the price-demand curves. He knew the merchandising manager always ordered optimistically. Therefore, using the same curve he read over from Q_1 to the upper limit and down to the expected value from which he obtained Q_2, the quantity he actually intended to make available. He did not intend to pay for the merchandising manager's optimism. If merchandising ran out of stock, it was not his worry. Now the merchandising manager was informed about what the purchasing manager had done so he adjusted his price to P_2. The purchasing manager in turn was told that the merchandising manager had made this readjustment so he planned to make only Q_3 available. If this process—made possible only by perfect communication between departments—had been allowed to continue, nothing would have been bought and nothing would have been sold. This outcome was avoided by prohibiting communication between departments and forcing each to guess what the other was doing.

I have obviously caricatured the situation in order to make the point clear: when organizational units have inappropriate measures of performance which put them in conflict with each other, as is often the case, communication between them may hurt organizational performance, not help it. Organizational structure and performance measurement must be taken into account before opening the floodgates and permitting the free flow of information between parts of the organization. (A more rigorous discussion of organizational structure and the relationship of communication to it can be found in "Systems Theory from an Operations Research Point of View.")[1]

A Manager Does Not Have to Understand How an Information System Works, Only How to Use It

Most MIS designers seek to make their systems as innocuous and unobtrusive as possible to managers lest they become frightened. The designers try to provide managers with very easy access to the system and assure them that they need to know nothing more about it. The designers usually succeed in keeping managers ignorant in this regard. This leaves managers unable to evalute the MIS as a whole. It often makes them afraid to even try to do so lest they display their ignorance publicly. In failing to evaluate their MIS, managers delegate much of the control of the organization to the system's designers and operators who may have many virtues, but managerial competence is seldom among them.

Let me cite a case in point. A Chairman of the Board of a medium-sized company asked for help on the following problem. One of his larger (decentralized) divisions had installed a computerized production-inventory control and manufacturing-manager information system about a year earlier. It had acquired about $2,000,000 worth of equipment to do so. The Board Chairman had just received a request from the Division for permission to replace the original equipment with newly announced equipment which would cost several times the original amount. An extensive "justification" for doing so was provided with the request. The Chairman wanted to know whether the request was really justified. He admitted to complete incompetence in this connection.

A meeting was arranged at the Division at which I was subjected to an extended and detailed briefing. The system was large but relatively simple. At the heart of it was a reorder point for each item and a maximum allowable stock level. Reorder quantities took lead-time as well as the allowable maximum into account. The computer kept track of stock, orderd items when required and generated numerous reports on both the state of the system it controlled and its own "actions."

When the briefing was over I was asked if I had any questions. I did. First I asked if, when the system had been installed, there had been many parts whose stock level exceeded the maximum amount possible under the new system. I was told there were many. I asked for a list of about thirty and for some graph paper. Both were provided. With the help of the system designer and volumes of old daily reports I began to plot the stock level of the first listed item over time. When this item reached the maximum "allowable" stock level it had been reordered. The system designer was surprised and said that by sheer "luck" I had found one of the few errors made by the system. Continued plotting showed that because of repeated premature reordering the item had never gone much below the maximum stock level. Clearly the program was confusing the maximum allowable stock level and the reorder point. This turned out to be the case in more than half of the items on the list.

Next I asked if they had many paired parts, ones that were only used with each other; for example, matched nuts and bolts. They had many. A list was produced and we began checking the previous day's withdrawals. For more than half of the pairs the differences in the numbers reordered as withdrawn were very large. No explanation was provided.

Before the day was out it was possible to show by some quick and dirty calculations that the new computerized system was costing the company almost $150,000 per month more than the hand system which it had replaced, most of this in excess inventories.

The recommendation was that the system be redesigned as quickly as possible and that the new equipment not be authorized for the time being.

The questions asked of the system had been obvious and simple ones. Managers should have been able to ask them but—and this is the point—they felt themselves incompetent to do so. They would not have allowed a hand-operated system to get so far out of their control.

No MIS should ever be installed unless the managers for whom it is intended are trained to evaluate and hence control it rather than be controlled by it.

A Suggested Procedure for Designing an MIS

The erroneous assumptions I have tried to reveal in the preceding discussion can, I believe, be avoided by an appropriate design procedure. One is briefly outlined here.

1. Analysis of the Decision System. Each (or at least each important) type of managerial decision required by the organization under study should be identified and the relationships between them should be determined and flow-charted. Note that this is *not* necessarily the same thing as determining what decisions *are* made. For example, in one company I found that make-or-buy decisions concerning parts were made only at the time when a part was introduced into stock and were never subsequently reviewed. For some items this decision had gone unreviewed for as many as twenty years. Obviously, such decisions should be made more often; in some cases, every time an order is placed in order to take account of current shop loading, underused shifts, delivery times from suppliers, and so on.

Decision-flow analyses are usually self-adjusting. They often reveal important decisions that are being made by default (e.g., the make-buy decision referred to above); and they disclose interdependent decisions that are being made independently. Decision-flow charts frequently suggest changes in managerial responsibility, organizational structure, and measure of performance which can correct the types of deficiencies cited.

Decision analyses can be conducted with varying degrees of detail, that is, they may be anywhere from coarse to fine grained. How much detail one should become involved with depends on the amount of time and resources that are available for the analysis. Although practical considerations frequently restrict initial analyses to a particular organizational function, it is preferable to perform a coarse analysis of all of an organization's managerial functions rather than a fine analysis of one or a subset of functions. It is easier to introduce finer information into an integrated information system than it is to combine fine subsystems into one integrated system.

2. An analysis of information requirements. Managerial decisions can be classified into three types:

a. Decisions for which adequate models are available or can be constructed and from which optimal (or near optimal) solutions can be derived. In such cases the decision process itself should be incorporated into the information system thereby converting it (at least partially) to a control system. A decision model identifies what information is required and hence what information is relevant.

b. Decisions for which adequate models can be constructed but from which optimal solutions cannot be extracted. Here some kind of heuristic or search procedure should be provided even if it consists of no more than computerized trial and error. A simulation of the model will, as a minimum, permit comparison of proposed alternative solutions. Here too the model specifies what information is required.

c. Decisions for which adequate models cannot be constructed. Research is required here to determine what information is relevant. If decision making cannot be delayed for the completion of such research or the decision's effect is not large enough to justify the cost of research, then judgment must be used to "guess" what information is relevant. It may be possible to make explicit the implicit model used by the decision maker and treat it as a model of type (*b*).

In each of these three types of situation it is necessary to provide feedback by comparing actual decision outcomes with those predicted by the model or decision maker. Each decision that is made, along with its predicted outcome, should be an essential input to a management control system. I shall return to this point below.

3. Aggregation of decisions. Decisions with the same or largely overlapping informational requirements should be grouped together as a single manager's task. This will reduce the information a manager requires to do his job and is likely to increase his understanding of it. This may require a reorganization of the system. Even if such a reorganization cannot be implemented completely what can be done is likely to improve performance significantly and reduce the information loaded on managers.

4. Design of information processing. Now the procedure for collecting, storing, retrieving, and treating information can be designed. Since there is a voluminous literature on this subject I shall leave it at this except for one point. Such a system must only be able to answer questions addressed to it; it should also be able to answer quesetions that have not been asked by reporting any deviations from expectations. An extensive exception-reporting system is required.

5. Design of control of the control system. It must be assumed that the system that is being designed will be deficient in many and significant ways. Therefore it is necessary to identify the ways in which it may be deficient, to design procedures for detecting its deficiencies, and for correcting the system so as to remove or reduce them. Hence the system should be designed to be flexible and adaptive. This is little more than a platitude, but it has a not-so-obvious implication. No completely computerized system can be as flexible and adaptable as can a man-machine system. This is illustrated by a concluding example of a system that is being developed and is partially in operation. (See Figure 2.)

The company involved has its market divided into approximately two hundred marketing areas. A model for each has been constructed and is "in" the computer. On the basis of competitive intelligence supplied to the service marketing manager by marketing researchers and information specialists he and his staff make policy decisions for each area each month. Their tentative decisions are fed into the computer which yields a forecast of expected performance. Changes are made until the expectations match what is desired. In this way they arrive at "final" decisions. At the end of the month the computer compares the actual performance of each area with what was predicted. If a deviation exceeds what could be expected by chance, the company's OR Group then seeks the reason for the deviation, performing as much research as is required to find it. If the cause is found to be permanent the computerized model is adjusted appropriately. The result is an adaptive man-machine system whose precision and generality is continuously increasing with use.

Finally it should be noted that in carrying out the design steps enumerated above, three groups should collaborate: information system specialists, operations researchers, *and managers.* The participation of managers in the design of a system that is to serve them, assures their ability to evaluate its performance by comparing its output with what was predicted. Managers who are not willing to invest some of their time in this process are not likely to use a management control system well, and their system, in turn, is likely to abuse them.

Discussion Questions

1. What does Ackoff cite as the chief obstacle to efficient decision making? How can the filtration and condensation of information help? In what ways might an emphasis on the elimination of irrelevant information, rather than the supply of relevant information, affect the design of management information systems?
2. If, as Ackoff suggests, managers often do not know what information they need, who does? How can an MIS designer deal with the problem of deciding what information is useful to retain and what to eliminate as irrelevant? What will happen if an MIS designer's estimate of a manager's information needs differs from the manager's estimate?
3. Is the objective of an MIS to provide information or to improve decision making? If "better" information is provided and does not lead to better management decisions, is the information really better? If not, is the failure one of information or management? How can such a failure be prevented? If it occurs, how can it be detected and remedied?
4. Why does the design of an MIS require the collaboration of information systems specialists, operations researchers, and

Figure 2 Simplified diagram of a market-area control system

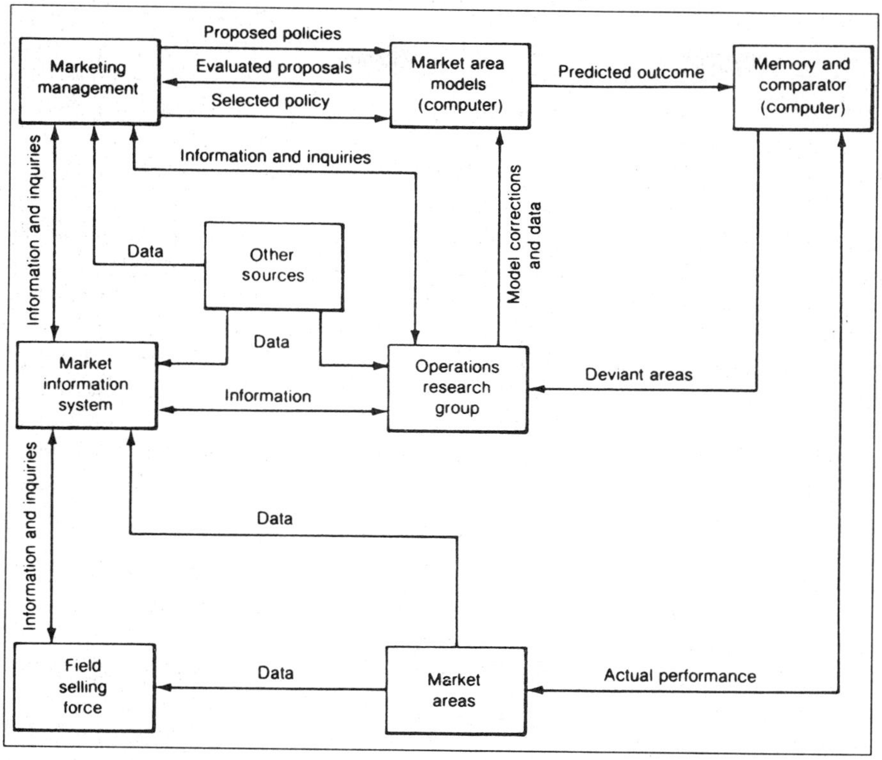

managers? What is the unique contribution of each group to the design process?

Footnotes

1. S. S. Sengupta and R. L. Ackoff, "Systems Theory from an Operations Research Point of View," *IEEE Transactions on Systems Science and Cybernetics*, vol. 1, November 1965, pp. 9-13.

READING 10

Management Misinformation Systems—Another Perspective

article by
ALFRED RAPPAPORT

An identification and critical examination of the assumptions made by designers of management information systems is particularly timely. Russell L. Ackoff attempted to do just that in his article, "Management Misinformation Systems" (*Management Science*, December 1967). He identified five common assumptions underlying management information systems design and proposed that these assumptions are unwarranted in many (if not most) cases and lead to major deficiencies in the resulting systems. The purpose of this letter is to examine briefly these assumptions (given in boldface) and the supporting illustrations presented in the Ackoff article.

Source: Reprinted by permission of Alfred Rappaport, "Management Misinformation Systems—Another Perspective," *Management Science*, Volume 15, Number 4, December 1968, pp. B133-B136. © 1968 The Institute of Management Sciences.

1. The critical deficiency under which most managers operate is the lack of relevant information. Ackoff contends that managers suffer more from an over-abundance of irrelevant information than they do from lack of relevant information. This is followed by the suggestion that information be filtered (evaluated) and condensed to reduce the information overload to which managers are subjected. In the face of seemingly endless pages of computer printouts, book-size requests for equal expenditures, and other forms that consume unnecessary hours of managers' time, suggestions leading to filtered and/or condensed information are likely to be greeted with enthusiasm. This does however raise another important issue: What are the useful limits to filtration and condensation?

Just as processing leading to information overload is not in the best interests of the organization, indiscriminate filtration and "over-condensation" can likewise lead to non-salutary results. For example, consider the case of major capital investment proposals originating from various divisions of a company. Assume that book-size capital expenditure proposals are not condensed for headquarters to a single listing of proposed projects (with brief descriptions) and ranked according to some criterion function such as internal rate of return. The headquarters group has two basic options available: (1) accept the divisional estimates; or (2) make a subjective adjustment to compensate for estimated divisional bias. Neither of these alternatives is very comforting since there is no compelling basis for choice except perhaps assessing past behavior which may be neither instructive nor relevant. Here then is clearly a case of "overcondensation" since the report received by headquarters cannot be used to make an intelligent appraisal of the proposals competing for scarce resources since information about the uncertainty underlying key market and cost variables is not available. "Over-condensation" can occur even if risk analysis techniques are actually employed in a company.

In brief, the undesirable state of "over-condensation" is reached when the decision maker no longer has a sound basis for judging the validity of transmittal information.

Filtration has potential as an effective adjustment in the face of information overload. The key question is: where in the system should "filtration decisions" be made? If these decisions were initiated largely at the lower levels of the organization one might question the limited perspective underlying the decisions. Filtration decisions made at the highest level of the organization, however, offer little or no relief from information overload. The relevant strategy then is a function of the confidence that executives have in the filtration decisions made by managers at lower levels.

To illustrate this in context of the capital expenditure analysis example, consider the set of projects enumerated by the divisons for review by the headquarters group. This set consists only of those projects proposed for adoption and excludes projects rejected at the divisional level. Hence, the information presented to headquarters was indeed filtered. If there are no serious conflicts between the way divisions and headquarters perceive organizational objectives and their attitudes toward risk are identical, then the filtered list of projects is in all probability justified. In the overwhelming majority of cases, where the ideal headquarters-divisional relationship does not exist, it would seem to be more appropriate to ask divisions to enumerate their total set of project opportunities with "accept: or "reject" recommendations for each. (Even in this situation divisional managers would undoubtedly filter certain projects, but the potential for filtering is decreased.)

In summary, while managers can often make reasonable adjustments to compensate for information overload, overfiltration and condensation tend to accentuate the biases of lower-level managers and provide the executive decision maker with an inadequate basis for making necessary adjustments. The relevant information for managers is somewhere on the continuum between over-filtration and condensation, and information overload. I contend that the basic assumption that "the critical deficiency under which most managers operate is the lack of relevant information" remains unchallenged.

2. The manager needs the information that he wants. Ackoff argues that the conditions for a manager to know what information he needs are rarely satisfied. The principal problem here is that the decision maker's own conception of an appropriate decision model to fit a specific situation is generally not well developed. I would fullly subscribe to Ackoff's subsequent plea for an active collaboration among information systems specialists, operations researchers, and managers in the various stages of system design as the best available strategy for overcoming this deficiency.

The respective roles of the operations researcher, information specialists, and manager can be illustrated in the context of the service station problem presented by Ackoff. I would envision the main thrust of the manager's responsibility to be, first, to recognize occasions for making decisions and, then, to frame appropriate questions in light of the decisions to be made. The manager in the major oil company, for example, finds it necessary to make decisions concerning locations of future service stations. An appropriate criterion may be sales or profit maximization subject to certain technological and management-imposed constraints. The manager clearly wants information about future sales potential for alternative service-station locations. *And the manager needs the information that he wants.*

While the task of enumerating relevant variables for forecasting equations should be conducted jointly by the operations researcher and manager, in most situations it would be reasonable to expect that model choice and refinements are largely the domain of the operations researcher. The choice of a statistical forecasting model in this case or any model in the more general case calls for the exercise of careful judgment on the part of the operations researcher. Problem type, relative importance of the problem, time available before decision must be made, and expected degree of utilization of model results by decision makers all qualify as strategic considerations in choosing among alternative models. Finally, the information specialists should present the results to the manager in an easily understood form, without resorting to either information overload or over-condensation.

3. If a manager has the information he needs his decision making will improve. Ackoff points out that because of the complexity of the decision process, managers oftentimes cannot use information well. To support this contention, Ackoff suggests that most managers furnished with an *initial* tableau of a typical mathematical programming, sequencing, or network problem are unlikely to come close to an optimal solution. While one certainly would not want to argue with the validity of this proposition, its relevance to the main argument must be questioned. Specifically, I would submit that to furnish a manager with an initial tableau *is to furnish him with data, not information.* (The distinction is explained by Adrian M. McDonough in his book, *Information Economics and Management Systems*: "The term 'data' is used here to represent messages that can be available to the individual but which have not as yet been evaluated for their worth in a specific situation....'Information' is used here as the label for *evaluated data* in a specific situation....A given message may remain constant in content and yet, under this approach change from data to information when it is put to use in making a decision.") The fact that managers cannot easily convert data to information underlies the very need and justification for developing management decision models. If managers could independently iterate from an initial to a final tableau, the simplex and other related algorithms would become redundant and unnecessary. In the Ackoff case, the manager is not provided information until the results appearing in the final tableau are communicated to him. At that juncture we can only hope that his decision making will improve.

In brief then, Ackoff's illustration fails to invalidate the assumption that if a manager has the information he needs his decision making will improve, because the decision maker was not provided with the *information* he needed. Perhaps, a more interesting and significant question to ask is: to what extent does the information the manager really needs (e.g., final tableaus) improve decision making?

4. Better communication between managers improves organizational performance. It is true that better communication between managers does not necessarily improve organizational performance. Ackoff's example imvolving a purchasing and a merchandising department store illustrates this point. I believe it is important to emphasize, however, that the origin of the problem described does not lie in the communication, but instead in the conflicting measures of performance used to judge the two departments. Ackoff thus has properly established that interdepartmental communication among departments with conflicting measures of performance may not only be of doubtful value, but may actually work counter to the best interests of the organization as a whole. However, the proposition that well-conceived interdepartmental communication enables managers to coordinate their decisions more effectively when appropriate, nonconflicting measures of performance are present was not invalidated.

5. A manager does not have to understand how an information system works, only how to use it. Ackoff's challenge to the notion that a manager need not understand how an information system works, only how to use it, is particularly significant. It is difficult to debate the merits of this assumption without a more detailed agreement concerning the degree of understanding Ackoff would require of managers. The best available evidence of intent can be gleaned from the case study presented.

A computerized production and inventory control system was discovered to be costing the company almost $150,000 per month more than the former manual system. Most of this was attributed to excess inventories. Apparently, a major cause of unreasonable inventory accumulation was a program error which confused the maximum allowable stock level and the reorder point. To suggest that the manager understand the information system to a point where he would detect the progrmaming error seems neither reasonable in an organizational plan nor an economical use of the manager's time. Indeed, to argue for understanding and analysis by managers at this level of detail is legitimate cause for cries of "information overload." A more constructive approach would suggest that a manager should have developed techniques and guidelines using exception reporting for discovering a situation where an "improved" system costs $150,000 more than its unglamorous predecessor. Perhaps even more importantly the manager would be well advised to develop a more reliable system for hiring better systems designers.

While I agree with Ackoff that "no management information system should ever be installed unless the managers for whom it is intended are trained to evaluate and hence control it rather than be controlled by it," my agreement is within the context explained above. To insist upon *detailed* systems design knowedge by managers as a prerequisite for new management information systems is tantamount to calling for an information systems moratorium or at a minimum a significant reduction in research and progress in the field.

Discussion Questions

1. Would Ackoff disagree with Rappaport's characterization of information as "evaluated data?" What is the difference between evaluated data and filtered/condensed data? When does filtration and condensation become overfiltration and overcondensation? Would this occur if the implementation strategy proposed in the last section of Ackoff's article was faithfully applied?
2. What arguments did Ackoff advance to support his contention that the information that managers ask for is not always the information they really need? Did Rappaport effectively refute these arguments?
3. Recall Ackoff's example in which two departments within the same company hinder each other's effectiveness because of conflicting measures of performance. Rappaport says of this example that "the origin of the problem described does not lie in the communication." If his contention is correct, will improved communication necessarily lead to improved performance? Has Ackoff's point been strengthened or weakened?
4. Can cost overruns, such as those described in the last section of Rappaport's article, occur if a manager really understands his/her system? Can they be prevented by a manager who understands how to use the system, but knows nothing about the way it works?

READING 11

MIS Is a Mirage

article by
JOHN DEARDEN

Some years ago I expressed the opinion that "of all the ridiculous things that have been foisted on the long-suffering executive in the name of science and progress, the real-time management information system is the silliest."[1]

I no longer believe this statement is true. We now have something even sillier: the current fad for "*the* management information system," whether it is called the Total System, the Total Management Information System, the Management Information System, or simply MIS.

I certainly do not mean to suggest that a company does not need good management information systems—nothing could be further from the truth. But the notion that a company can and ought to have an expert (or a group of experts) create for it a single, completely integrated super-system—an "MIS"—to help it govern every aspect of its activity is absurd.

For many businessmen, it is probably inconceivable that the lofty phrases and glittering promises surrounding the MIS conceal a completely unworkable concept. Yet this is exactly what I propose to demonstrate—that a company that pursues an MIS embarks on a wild-goose chase, a search for a will-o'-the-wisp.

Let me first try to explain what I understand by the "MIS concept" and examine its alleged advantages, and then show why the concept is unworkable. Then I shall be in a position to recommend some practical remedies for defective management information systems, which certainly constitute a real problem for executives today.

Confusion Between Terms

It is difficult even to describe the MIS in a satisfactory way, because this conceptual entity is

Source: Reprinted by permission of the *Harvard Business Review.* "MIS Is a Mirage," by John Dearden (January/February 1972), Volume 50, Number 1, pp. 90-99.

embedded in a mish-mash of fuzzy thinking and incomprehensible jargon. It is nearly impossible to obtain any agreement on how MIS problems are to be analyzed, what shape their solutions might take, or how these solutions are to be implemented. This confusion makes it very difficult to attack the concept, because no matter what assumptions a critic makes about the nature of the MIS approach, a proponent can always reply that *his* use of the term is different from others'.

But there is a common thread which runs through the various uses of the term, a thread that at once unifies but also subverts the MIS literature. This thread is the computer-based information system.

Computer-Based Activity...

Whever the MIS is discussed, it is almost invariably stated that a management information system does not necessarily require a computer and that many forms of management information are not computer-based.

Yet, if one looks at what is actually being discussed, he quickly discovers that the term "MIS" is used, essentially, to stand for "computer-based information systems." For example, a recent article in *Business Week* read as follows:

> [Some], concerned that systems analysts are...a "mixed bag" whose training and knowledge are a hit-or-miss proposition, are convinced that management information systems (MIS) is *the* emerging field in business administration. Both Wharton and MIT have tailored programs especially for systems specialists, but no school has gone further than the University of Minnesota, whose B-school now offers M.S. and Ph.D. degrees in management information systems and has launched an MIS research center. Since the center's opening three years ago, MIS Director Gordon B. Davis and his staff have worked to develop 12 new systems-related courses—from on-line, real-time systems to a seminar on software. In addition, the program's 50 M.S. and 22 Ph.D. candidates spend a good portion of their time alone and in teams at work on actual computer problems in industry.[2]

It seems evident to me that MIS education as described here is principally education in computer-based information systems.

It is vital to note, first of all, that the information generated by this kind of system does not include a great deal of the information that is most important to management—especially, important *qualitative* information. Second, a specialist group that develops such a system is usually responsible for implementing only one part of any of a company's individual management information systems—namely, that part that interfaces directly with the computer. For example, such a group has little (if anything) to do with specifying the nature of an accounting and financial control system, although it may be responsible for the computer programming this system employs.

My conclusion, therefore, is that such a group has little impact on most of the information supplied to management, particularly at upper levels. Consequently, it is ridiculous to say that it creates (or *can* create) a total management information system.

...vs. MIS

To the extent that MIS refers only to company information systems that use a computer base and to the extent that everyone understands this limitation, I have no serious quarrel with the trend to MIS; it is vital that management tightly control its computer-based information systems, and in general the so-called MIS groups seem designed to guarantee a tight rein to management.

In my experience, however, such a limited definition of MIS is *not* what advocates of this approach to information systems mean when they use the term. They intend something novel and far more global, some entity that can provide revolutionary benefits we cannot derive from the traditional approach. Walter Kenneron suggests this definition of the MIS:

> A management information system is an organized method of providing past, present and projection information relating to internal operations and external intelligence. It supports the planning, control and operational function of an organization by furnishing uniform information in the proper time-frame to assist the decision-maker.[3]

This is approximately what I perceive most people

to mean by MIS. And if this definition seems grandiose, I can only remark that "*the* management information system" describes a grandiose idea. If the definition werre less global in its scope, it would not measure up to the term. If, for example, one were to limit the definition to the context of a company's financial accounting programs, he would have to speak of the *financial* MIS of the company, rather than its general MIS.

However, in practice, no such limitations are intended. Kenneron's inclusive definition of the MIS approach is quite consistent with the nearly universal benefits claimed for it.

The MIS Approach

Given this inclusive definition, how is management to apply it? In other words, how should management think about the problem of setting up an MIS?

Fundamental Assumptions

First, it appears that if management wishes to subscribe to the theory of the MIS, it must make up its mind to accept two fundamental (if highly questionable) assumptions that are quite different from traditional ones made in this area:

1. Management information is a subject for study and specialization. That is, it is sufficiently homogeneous so that a set of principles and practices can be established for evaluating all management's information needs and satisfying them. In short, the MIS approach attacks all the problems of management information as a whole, rather than by individual areas, such as finance and marketing. This homogeneity is a necessary assumption, since without it there is no reason why general solutions to a management's information requirements can be found.
2. The systems approach can and should be used in analyzing management's information requirements. Proponents claim the systems approach is necessary for mastering the sprawl of requirements and for synthesizing the general MIS solution. (I shall have more to say about the systems approach later.)

Diagnosis and Development

Once management has accepted these two assumptions, it can begin to develop an MIS program. As the theory goes, there seem to be two techniques for setting to work:

- Management can hire an MIS expert to act as a superconsultant to the president of the company. This expert studies the types of problems that the president must solve, the decisions that he must make, and so forth, and recommends methods for satisfying the president's total information requirements. He then drops to lower levels of management and provides the same services there.

  In general, the expert depends on others to implement his recommendations. For example, the controller becomes responsible for changing the cost accounting system in the way the consultant recommends.
- Management can create a staff department that reports to the top. This group is responsible for the company's computer-based systems but also provides the same type of diagnoses and evaluations as the superconsultant.

The staff group, unlike the consultant, usually has responsibility for implementation.

Its Alleged Advantages. . .

Under this approach, then, either a single person or a group of persons is responsible for developing and overseeing the construction of the entire management information system. This concentration of authority and responsibility in the hands of systems experts supposedly creates a number of significant advantages:

- Experts schooled in the MIS "discipline" can analyze management's information needs more effectively than can the people traditionally responsible for satisfying them. Moreover, these experts can better determine which techniques will best meet these needs.

• Because the MIS is developed as a unified, single system, rather than as a number of separate systems, it is completely coordinated and completely consistent.

• Information needs are determined from the top down. Hence the top will be in better control; the frequent practice of letting lower management decide what information will pass upward is eliminated.

• The company reduces its direct information costs by eliminating systems. Also, the MIS itself is cheaper to run because it has been designed by information experts who know the most economical means for satisfying management's information needs.

• Since one expert or group is responsible for the system, management's desire that the system be kept up-to-date can readily be satisfied.

In short, the proponents promise, experts can design an MIS that is more effective, more efficient, more consistent, and more dynamic than the haphazard aggregate of individual systems a company would otherwise employ.

These are impressive advantages that any manager would enjoy, and doubtless this approach was developed to solve the real problems of poor information that have been plaguing management with increasing frequency. The growing complexity and the pace of change of modern business, expecially in the last ten years, have surely made many information systems obsolete and many more inadequate for present tasks.

Equally, the last ten years have seen the extensive development of information technology, managment science, and systems analysis—a development that has been accompanied by rapid growth in the number of experts working in information systems.

To some—that is, the proponents of MIS—it seemed logical to centralize the development and control of information systems in the hands of these experts. After all, the problems that beset information systems have been the result of change and growth, they reasoned; and these problems could perhaps be solved by using the new information technology that had been developing simultaneously.

Several companies have tried this approach, and many people currently advocate it. In spite of its apparent logic, however, I know of no company in which it has worked out. This fails to surprise me because, as I have already implied, I believe the whole MIS approach is fundamentally fallacious.

. . .And Its Real Fallacies

There are four fallacies and one serious misconception inherent in the MIS approach, as I have described it. The fallacies are these:

• Management information is sufficiently homogeneous so that it can be made an area of specialization for an expert.

• If the different information systems ordinarily used by a company are developed separately, the resulting management information system will necessarily be uncoordinated and therefore inefficient and unsatisfactory.

• The "systems" approach is a new boon to business administration.

• It is practicable to centralize the control over a company's entire management information system.

The misconception is this:

• The specialist expertise that creates a good logistics system for a company can extend its talents into the broad domain of general company activity and create a general management information system.

There is no reason to suppose an MIS group can actually do this—in fact, there is good reason to think it cannot.

Let me refute these errors one by one.

1. The true MIS expert does not and cannot exist. A complete management information system consists of such a huge assortment of different types of activities that no man can possess a broad enough set of special skills to apply to even a small proportion of them. Consider the skills required to build any one of these individual information systems.

The financial accounting and control system. This includes preparation of financial statements, development of budgets and long-range plans, analyses of capital investments, publication of product costs, and so forth.

Traditionally, the controller is responsible for all these financial subsystems; with respect to the financial information systems, he plays the role that the MIS expert is supposed to play in the general management information systems. In complementary fashion, the MIS expert must have a thorough understanding of the controller's sytems function.

The logistics information system. This system controls the flow of goods from the purchase of raw materials to the physical distribution of the finished products. Next to the financial control system, it is probably the most comprehensive information system in the typical manufacturing business.

A logistics system normally consists of several subsystems of varying degrees of independence. For example, there could be distinct systems for different product lines. Within each product line, furthermore, there could be subsystems for procurement, production scheduling, finished goods, inventory control, and so forth, and still others for plant utilization and expansion. Depending on its industry, a company has a larger or smaller number of complex, interrelated logistics information subsystems.

The critical point to note here is that the logistics information system is almost completely different from the financial information system. In point of fact, most of the skills needed to develop financial information systems are of no use in developing logistics information systems and vice versa. Even the user relationships are different. In building a financial information system, the controller develops a system that provides information for management outside the finance function, whereas logistics information is normally developed and used by the people directly concerned with logistics.

Furthermore, logistics subsystems frequently have little in common with each other, so that an expert in one type of subsystem might not be able to transfer his expertise to a different type. For example, there may be little or no similarity between a procurement information system and a finished-goods distribution system. Like the financial system, the logistics information system or subsystem is a job for a specialist.

The marketing information systems. Like the two systems just described, the marketing information system can also consist of a number of subsystems. A company may maintain separate subsystems for separate product lines; and within a product line, it may maintain further subsystems for advertising and sales promotion, short-term sales forecasting, long-term sales forecasting, product planning, and so forth.

Again, the critical point is this—a marketing information system is almost completely different from the other two systems. Consequently, expertise in either or both of the other systems would be of limited value in developing a marketing information system and vice versa.

Legal services, industrial relations, and public relations. One of the major purposes of each of these staff functions is to provide top management with specialized information different from that provided by any other staff office and different from that provided by the three information systems previously described.

R&D reporting. The information system management required in this area is distinct from all others, and expertise in these other areas offers limited help in developing an R&D information system.

In short, except in the small company (which probably needs only simple systems), there are several information systems that have very few similarities and many wide differences. Consequently, it makes no sense to regard the processes of developing and implementing these several management information systems as constituting a single and homogeneous activity.

I conclude that few, if any, individuals have the training to call themselves experts in management information systems. Indeed I believe it is much more practical to teach the new information technology to the functional experts than to teach information technologists functional specialties. After all, the man who could master all the functional specialities—the true MIS expert—would have to be an intellectual superman; and hence he does not and cannot exist except, perhaps, as a very rare exception.

If an MIS can be implemented at all, it can only be implemented by a staff group, and one of considerable size.

2. Coordinated systems for functional areas can be developed without a "total systems approach." "Unless you develop the MIS as a single, integrated system, all you will get is a bunch of unrelated, uncoordinated, ineffective systems." If I have heard this statement once, I have heard it a hundred times; and it still is not true.

I have seen many systems that have intricate interfaces with one another and that are still efficient and effective. In the automobile industry, for example, the development of a new model car involves many functions—styling, engineering, product planning, finance, facility planning, procurement, and production scheduling. Each functional unit develops its internal information system for controlling its part of the operation; in addition, at each interface, the functional units exchange the information necessary to maintain coordination between them.

If an information system is ineffective, the cause is very likely to be the incompetence of the people responsible for it, *not* the absense of the general MIS apporoach. In this connection I might quote William M. Zani:

> Most companies have not conceived and planned their management information system with any significant amount of attention to their intended function of supportintg the manager as he makes his decisions.[4]

Zani goes on to suggest a new approach to developing an MIS as a solution to this situation. My solution would be to make some personnel changes, because anyone who fails to design an information system for its users is incompetent.

Such incompetence is very prevalent. I have seen dozens of companies where management is not receiving half the relevant accounting information that could be made available if the financial information system had been properly designed in the first place. And although I am not sufficiently expert in other types of information systems to know whether the same situation exists there, I have no reason to believe accounting is worse than the others.

To assert that such problems as these result from the independent development of different information systems, rather than from sheer and ordinary incompetence, is simply ridiculous—and to recommend the "MIS cure" is even more ridiculous. To ensure that a company has efficient information systems which are well coordinated with one another, management need only bear down on the personnel in the various functional areas who are responsible.

3. "The systems approach" is merely an elaborate phrase for "good management." There are many definitions of the systems approach, but the following is representative:

> The systems approach to management is basically a way of thinking. The organization is viewed as an integrated complex of interdependent parts which are capable of sensitive and accurate interaction among themselves and with their environment.[5]

What does this mean? It took me some time to figure it out.

When the systems approach first appeared in the literature, I had a great deal of difficulty understanding the concept; and my confusion increased until I started asking people this question: "What would an executive do differently if he were to adopt the system approach in place of the traditional one?"

Without exception, the replies I received made assumptions about the traditional approach that simply are not valid. For example, some assumed that the executive perceives his organization as static; others, that he fails to consider the interaction of related variables. In other words, the replies were predicated on an incompetent, even a stupid, executive.

Thus I concluded that the alleged advantages of the systems approach really result from the difference between an adequate and an inadequate manager. If you doubt this, I invite you to ask the question I did the next time you hear someone champion the systems approach to management.

It is therefore not surprising that good managers follow the systems approach, because this approach is merely the ancient art of management. Would a competent business executive plan a major expansion program without considering the sources and timing of funds, the availability of people, the possible reactions of competitors, and so forth? Certainly not. And he would consider them in relation to one another.

My conclusion, then, is that the systems approach is precisely what every good manager has been using for centuries. The systems approach may be new to science and to weapons acquisition, but it is certainly not new to business administration.

At this point, let me summarize briefly. First, an MIS would have to be developed by a *group* composed of experts in the various types of information systems used by management. This must be so because the possibility that a single individual will be expert in *all* types of information is remote. Second, the approach taken by the MIS group would be approximately the same as that taken by any competent and expert manager working in one of the functional information systems.

How, then, does the MIS approach differ from the traditional approach to information systems?

The only difference I can see is that a company's management information system would be the responsibility of one centralized group; whereas, traditionally, the information systems experts have been located in the various functional areas. This brings me to the last fallacy—that such centralization is practicable.

4. Centralizing the control of a company's information systems in a staff group creates problems that are insoluble; therefore it is simply not feasible. It is theoretically possible to assemble a staff MIS group that is sufficiently large and diversified to have expertise in all the formal information systems described earlier—marketing, manufacturing (logistics), finance, and so forth. But to organize this group properly, the company should appoint an executive vice president for information to supervise the work of the group—that is to say, the systems of the staff vice presidents, the controller, the logistics information group, the marketing information group, and so forth. But what would this accomplish? Let me ignore the fact that no sane manufacturing or marketing executive would delegate the responsibility for his information system.

One result might be that this executive vice president for information would promote better coordination between functional areas. On the other hand, of course, the problems of coordination would drastically increase in the manufacturing and marketing areas because the responsibility for the information systems had been separated from the people who hold the line responsibility. And in any event, simply having all of the information groups, including the MIS group, report to a single executive would hardly change the *approach* to developing information systems. Thus the special value of the MIS approach is still obscure.

In short, it seems to me that if any of the MIS people are competent to tell the functional experts what to do, they should be in the functional area. I see no logical way to centralize the responsibility for all the management information systems.

Significant Misconception

If the MIS approach is as fallacious as I believe it to be, how has it been able to maintain even a superficial credibility?

The answer, as I have hinted earlier, is this: the early success of information technology in renovating logistics systems has been so great that there is a natural inclination to try the same methods on the company information systems as a whole.

This misconception has evolved in a natural enough way. Responsibility for a logistics system has traditionally been divided among several executives—e.g., in purchasing, in manufacturing, and in marketing. This divided responsibility has often resulted in poor coordination throughout the system. Furthermore, the people responsible for the system have often been old-fashioned in their methods and relatively unskilled in information techniques. Thus a vacuum has frequently existed with respect to the responsibility for a company's logistics information system into which the burgeoning information technology has moved easily and successfully.

However, as we have seen, there is no reason to suppose that the principles of information technology used so successfully in the logistics area can be generalized to apply to the other management information systems within a company or to the management information system considered as a whole.

Thus, when a group of experts has completed its overhaul of the logistics system, it will *not* be in a position to attack the financial, marketing, or any other system. First, the group will not have the specialist expertise required. Second, the type of problems the group may have found in the logistics area will almost certainly not exist in other areas if the staffs in these other areas are competent. Third, there will be no responsibility vacuum as in the logistics area; the MIS group will not be in a position to take over by default.

If you have any doubt about the validity of these statements, I suggest that you examine the kinds of things that any MIS group is doing. Outside of the routine computer systems, you will almost certainly find them concerned basically with parts of the *logistics* information system only.

Roots of Poor Information

So far this article has been quite negative. Now I should like to suggest some positive actions to mitigate the information crisis, if it can be called that. Before I propose these actions, however, it is appropriate to review the causes of management information problems.

As I have pointed out,the principal cause of pooor information systems is that we have put incompetent or ineffective people in charge of these systems.

The secondary causes are somewhat more complicated.

Growing Use of Computers

Computers and computer-related systems activities have been growing very rapidly, and currently the cost of these activities has become very significant in many companies. In spite of large expenditures, however, the quality of the information available to management appears unimproved.

One reason is, of course, that some computer installations are not run effectively. Another is that the computer-based information systems have been oversold; management has been led to expect much more than it has received. In other words, management's dissatisfaction with its information occurs, not from any deterioration in its information systems, but from its inflated expectations.

Interface Conditions

Individual systems change and improve at different rates, and this creates problems at the interfaces between them. For example, operations research techniques, used in modern logistics systems, require much more sophisticated cost accounting information than traditional cost accounting techniques can generate. Problems can also occur at the interface between production and marketing, because production-scheduling techniques are frequently much more sophisiticated than the techniques ordinarily used in market forecasting.

In general, the benefits of advanced techniques may be largely lost where they are dependent on primitive ones. (To some extent, of course, the problem of proper coordination at the interfaces reflects the competency of the staff involved. Other things being equal, only an incompetent would use an advanced technique whose effectiveness would be undermined by inadequate support.)

Rapidity of Change

Many companies are changing very rapidly, and it is necessary that their information systems keep pace. In some companies, information systems are *not* keeping pace. To some extent, this is caused by the inability of the staff personnel traditionally responsible for information systems to react to change. After all, many people who were once perfectly adequate in a relatively static situation become ineffective in a dynamic situation.

Greater Management Challenge

Management must always operate with insufficient information. And frequently, the more important the decision, the greater the uncertainty. In many areas the truth of these statements is becoming more salient because, while the role of management is becoming more complex, the new information technology is not helping significantly.

For example, I have spent many years working on control systems for decentralized companies.

The problems of control in such companies today are much more difficult than they were ten years ago—increases in size, complexity, and geographical dispersion have made control much more difficult. Yet the new information technology has been of little help in this area, simply because the problems of controlling decentralized divisions do not lend themselves to computerized or mathematical solutions.

Accordingly, it is important to realize that part of our information crisis results from the nature of the present business environment. We shall simply have to live with it. This does not mean, of course, that we should not continue trying to improve the situation.

Toward Real Solutions

Any company that believes it is facing genuine management information problems and wants to solve them should consider the following measures.

1. Place competent people in each of the formal information systems. To my mind there is no question that incompetency is the leading cause of problems in many management information systems. Hence the obvious answer is to retrain or replace the incompetents.

2. Examine the interfaces. This is best done in connection with system evaluation, and the examination should focus on these evaluative questions:

- Is there adequate communication between individual groups at all important interfaces? The executive might bear in mind formal techniques such as scheduled meetings and formal agreements.
- Does each group involved in an interface know enough about the other interfacing systems to do its job effectively?

This is a question of education. For example, cost accountants should know enough about company operations-research models to be sure these models are providing correct information; or, at the very least, they should be able to explain to the OR group the relevant limitations of the information their group can supply. On the other hand, the OR people should know enough about cost accounting to ask for the right type of data and to appreciate the limitations in the data they receive.

But although this is pricipally a matter of education, it may well be that some staff members are not intellectually capable of handling interface requirements, and they may have to be replaced.

3. Examine the logistics system. Originally many logistics systems were organized for manual data processing and have never been changed. Equally, the procurement, production, and distribution functions typically report to different executives, and consequently no one is formally responsible for the logistics information system. Since it is here that computers and information technology are most applicable, management should evaluate its logistics area and, where appropriate, reorganize it and make a staff unit, responsible for its logistics information system, report to the company officer who directs the logistics system itself.

4. Organize a central computer group for systems control. Computer use will continue to expand, and it is vital that management maintain central control over computers and computer-based information systems.[6] Such a group should be responsible for overseeing all computer-related work—for long-range planning, coordination, and control of all computer acquisitions and applications. In addition, it should be responsible for coordinating computer-based systems and might even undertake the systems and implementation work in a situation where several organization groups use the same data base.

Most companies already have such groups. Some are even called "MIS groups," although in reality, they have authority only over computer-related work.

5. Create an administration vice president, if one does not already exist. I recommend the creation of an office to which the following report:

- The controller
- The treasurer
- The computer and systems group
- The legal office
- The industrial relations office

• Other offices for company relations (that is, [both] public and governmental)
• Organization planning

The marketing, manufacturing, and R&D groups would continue to be independent.

Such an office has several advantages:

• It provides better control over the staff activities. The increasing number of staff operations, together with their increasing specialization, has made it nearly impossible for the president to exercise real control here. An administrative vice president can exercise much more effective control over the size and direction of these activities.
• It provides a practical alternative to locating the computer and systems group in the controller's office. An administrative vice president can provide effective supervision and, at the same time, maintain an objectivity that a controller often finds difficult because of his involvement with specific computer applications.
• It allows the company to handle miscellaneous projects easily—for example, an evaluation of a functional information system or an analysis of the formal information entering the president's office. To take care of nonrecurring or particularly pressing information systems problems, frequently the best arrangement is to organize temporary task forces that report to the administrative vice president.
• It simplifies the process of coordinating staff offices.

However, I would not make the administrative vice president or the offices reporting to him responsible for the entire information system. Marketing, manufacturing, and R&D would all be responsible for their own information systems. Also, the different activities reporting to his office would develop their information systems in relative independence except where interface communications are in question.

Questions for my Critics

Inevitably, I shall be accused of setting up a straw issue in this article and then demolishing it.

If the MIS approach really embraces only computer-based information systems or centralized logistics systems, then I *have* set up a straw issue. No harm has been done, however, because I have at least clarified the meaning of "MIS."

But I cannot believe the concept is meant to embrace only this. I have done my best to discover what the MIS approach really is, through talking with its proponents and studying its literature; and this article honestly represents my best understanding.

If I am correct in believing that the approach pretends to embrace more than computerized systems and logistics, then I have *not* set up a straw issue. And those who doubt my conclusions, negative as these may be, would be wise to ask themselves the following questions before they take up the pen of protest:

• Which information systems are to be included in the MIS?
• What kinds of experts are to be included in an MIS group, and what training shall they have?
• Where is this group to fit into the corporate organization? In particular, what will happen to the staff groups from the controller's office, the legal department, the marketing research department, and so forth?
• What authority is the MIS group to have? Is it to have authority to design and implement systems, or is it to serve in an advisory function only?
• What can this group accomplish that cannot be better accomplished by placing information specialists under functional groups?

Arguing the viability of the MIS approach is pointless unless answers to these questions are set forth clearly. And the clearer the answers, I believe, the more transparent the MIS mirage.

Discussion Questions

1. Is there really a difference in practice between computer-based activity and management information systems? Is all computer-based business activity related to MIS? Is all MIS activity computer-based? Has Dearden drawn the correct distinction between the two?

2. Are you convinced by Dearden's arguments against centralized control of the information system? Are the information requirements of functional areas like accounting, logistics, and marketing so different that expertise in one of these areas is of no use in another? Is there a body of specialized knowledge or techniques that can be successfully applied to all of them?
3. Do you agree with Dearden that the systems approach is nothing but good management technique? Does this argue for or against the systems approach?
4. Why would logistics be a particularly fruitful area for the application of information technology? Why, according to Dearden, would the same technology not be applicable to other areas? Do you agree?
5. Do you think (as Dearden anticipates that his critics will claim) that the issues raised in this article are "straw men"? Refer back to the "fundamental assumptions" stated early in the article. Has Dearden succeeded in establishing that these assumptions are necessary to the MIS approach? Has he shown that the assumptions are fallacious?

Footnotes

1. "Myth of Real-Time Management Information," *Harvard Business Review*, May-June 1966, p. 123.
2. June 5, 1971, p. 96.
3. "MIS Universe," *Data Management*, September 1970.
4. "Blue print for MIS," *Harvard Business Review*, November-December 1970, p. 95.
5. Spyros Makridakis, "The Whys and Wherefores of the Systems Approach," *European Business*, Summer 1971.
6. See Warren F. McFarlan, "Problems in Planning the Information System," *Harvard Business Review*, March-April 1971, p. 75.

READING 12

MIS: Mirage or Misconception?

article by
JAMES C. EMERY and
CHRISTOPHER R. SPRAGUE

Professor Dearden, in his article, *MIS Is a Mirage*, correctly anticipated that his critics would accuse him of setting up a straw issue and then demolishing it. We believe that he has done just that—and thereby marred some otherwise well-conceived advice to management. He quite correctly cautions against wild fancies of MIS advocates. He also raises some provocative questions that help to clarify important issues about information systems and their implementation.

Our quarrel with Dearden stems from his description of an MIS as perceived by practitioners in the field. Dearden states that MIS advocates take the view that the only acceptable MIS is a unified, single system that is completely coordinated and completely consistent. Such an MIS is indeed a mirage—but one created by Dearden's own misconceptions about the nature of an MIS.

Dearden gives us few clues as to the identity of those who still peddle the idea of the totally integrated system. Although such advocates exist, they are hardly worthy opponents: they are few in number and have had little influence on MIS practitioners since the early 1960s. They cannot be long-term practitioners themselves—Darwinian mortality takes its toll too soon for that.

Competent practitioners do not set out to design a totally integrated MIS. They rightly view the MIS—or whatever name one chooses to use—as composed of a collection of subsystems. In some cases a considerable degree of integration exists among these subsystems; but in most cases the subsystems are only loosely coupled or largely independent. The issue is one of degree. The choice in a particular case must take into account such factors as design and operating costs, available technology, system complexity, existing

Source: Reprinted by permission of the *Harvard Business Review*. "MIS: Mirage or Misconception?" by James E. Emery and Christopher R. Sprague (May/June 1972), Volume 50, Number 3, pp. 22-23.

organizational boundaries, management policies and style, and technical risk.

Integration among subsystems is achieved in various ways. An important form of integration is the sharing of data among subsystems—between the logistics and accounting subsystems, for example. To some extent the sharing is accomplished through access to common files; more often it involves the transfer of information from one subsystem to another in the temporary form of some machine-readable storage medium (commonly magnetic tape). Integration is also achieved through the sharing of the computer and other processing resources. The consolidation of functions—such as personnel and payroll functions—provides still another form of integration.

No system is completely integrated; there always exists some duplication of data and data collection, some dedicated processing resources, and a great deal of fragmentation of programs and functions. It is technically, economically, and operationally infeasible to design a completely integrated system. But it is perfectly legitimate, given today's technology and understanding of MIS, to speak of systems that move toward a higher degree of integration than was feasible before.

Thus, a well designed information system is likely to have the following characteristics:

1. It is based on one or more computers. Virtually any organization can profit from applying the computer to certain of its functions. The extent to which the computer is applied depends on the tradeoffs involved. For high-volume, routine information processing activities, the computer generally enjoys a great advantage. On the other hand, for infrequent, vague, and ill-defined problems of the sort often faced by high-level managers, the computer is unlikely to provide much direct assistance. However, as advances take place in the technology of decision models and computer science, the boundaries expand within which the computer can prove useful.

2. It offers a variety of decision aids. Some (relatively few) decisions are well enough defined to be almost completely programmed in the form of an optimizing model. Others can be partially formalized, and require close cooperation between a human decision maker and the computer (the man, for example, posing "what if..." questions, the computer responding—perhaps in real time—with a prediction based on a model of some sort). For still other decisions very little can be formalized; the computer is limted in this case to providing summarized information or perhaps no role at all. It may well be that this latter category includes some of the organization's most important decisions, but this in no way diminishes the attractiveness of applying the computer to functions for which it is very well suited.

3. The MIS thus cannot be characterized as either exclusively computer-based or all-encompassing. It should be viewed as a man-machine system, with tasks included according to the comparative advantages currently enjoyed by man and the computer. Its boundaries shift with changes in needs and advances in technology.

4. The system is composed of a collection of subsystems with varying degrees of integration among the parts. The extent of data and hardware sharing and the consolidation of functions should be determined through a tradeoff analysis of each specific case.

5. Implementation of the MIS involves both centralized and decentralized development of systems. Certain tasks will tend to be handled by a central group—such as hardware and software specification, organization-wide standards (dealing with documentation, for example), maintenance of specialized skills, and the development of systems that cross organizational boundaries or that are used by several departments. Tasks that are largely unique to a particular organizational unit will tend to be handled on a decentralized basis (but normally subject to overall guidelines and standards).

6. Implementation of the system proceeds over many years, and in fact continues indefinitely. A well designed system normally gives interim benefits sufficient to justify its cost. It is also designed with flexibility in mind so that it can be adapted to changes in the environment, management needs, and technology. Inevitably, some tradeoffs arise between short-range and long-range benefits.

In short, a good information system embodies a series of complex tradeoffs or compromises—in the extent to which functions are automated; the rapport between man and machine; the integration of files, hardware, and functions; the amount of centralization; and the effort devoted to long-range improvements. There is nothing very profound, radical, or controversial about this view of an MIS. Indeed, a broad majority of MIS practitioners would almost surely subscribe to these concepts.

If this prevailing conception of an MIS differs considerably from that of Prof. Dearden, the prevailing approach to successful implementation does not. Few MIS practitioners would argue against Dearden's guidelines: hire competent personnel, develop functional subsystems, take care of interfaces among subsystems, pay particular attention to the logistics subsystem (or analogous "mainline" functions in non-manufacturing organizations), handle certain functions on a centralized basis, and establish a senior executive in charge of administrative functions. These guidelines are completely compatible with the prevailing view of an MIS; they are, in fact, an essential requirement for its successful implementation.

Despite this seeming agreement between practitioners and Prof. Dearden, we suspect that in practice the approaches to implementation would differ rather substantially. Prof. Dearden emphasizes the dissimilarities that exist among various subystems of an MIS, while we prefer to focus on their similarities. This rather subtle distinction can lead to major differences in the way one tackles the tasks of implementation.

A person who dwells on dissimilarities often fails to exploit what commonness exists. He tends to rely on piecemeal implementation carried on in relative isolation. He relies primarily on persons with functional skills rather than persons having generalized MIS skills.

Those of us who take the other viewpoint look for ways to handle the interdependencies and commonness that exist among subsystems. An essential part of this is the development of an overall master plan to guide the development process. Such a plan should only sketch out the system in enough detail to identify (at least provisionally) the boundaries and interfaces of subsystems, their estimated costs and benefits, and the projected sequence of implementation. Planning of this sort generally requires only a few persons, but they must be extremely competent and well versed in the very set of skills that Prof. Dearden claims does not exist.

Our differences with Prof. Dearden hinge, then, on the issue of whether or not we can expect an MIS practitioner to acquire generalized skills that allow him to take a relatively global view of the system. Persons having these skills are not in plentiful supply, but they certainly exist—and in growing numbers. An MIS depends heavily, in our view, on an organization's ability to hire and retain at least a few practitioners with such skills.

A person meeting these requirements has a solid background in computer technology and systems design. He understands the nature of systems and how one can best design and implement them. He appreciates the difference between technical sophistication and cost-effectiveness—and opts for the latter if a conflict exists. He understands that a good MIS reflects all manner of tradeoffs. He has an overall view of the major functional areas of management, and is likely to have considerable knowledge of at least one of them. He is neither a superman or Renaissance man; he is simply a well-trained and well-seasoned professional who can deal effectively with the exceedingly complex systems that are now evolving.

Obviously, a great deal of other skills are required to implement a successful MIS. These include relatively narrow technical skills, as well as detailed knowledge and experience in each of the various management functions served by the MIS.

Prof. Dearden would not, we suspect, quarrel seriously with our assertion that the implementation of an MIS should be planned, and that competent computer professionals play an important role in such planning. (We make this point lest we, too, be accused of building straw men.) We do part company, however, on the question of the relative importance of the MIS professional versus the functional specialist.

We have been heavily committed over the past dozen years to educating future MIS practitioners. The Wharton School, where we now teach, offers an "information systems option" as part of its MBA program. A student takes four computer-related courses during his two-year stay; the rest of his work is devoted to traditional management subjects (including a major in one of the functional areas).

The four systems courses deal with computer technology and general MIS concepts.

With a strong formal background in both management and systems, our students have had no real difficulty in applying their education to a broad range of functional areas, types of organizations (e.g., manufacturing, insurance, public administration, etc.), and countries. We have seen ample evidence that such persons can very soon begin to make substantial contributions to an MIS project. In our own research and consulting we similarly find that lack of detailed knowledge of a particular industry or function rarely constitute a serious barrier to understanding an organization's information system. Indeed, too detailed a knowledge of, and day-to-day involvement with, a particular function is often a hindrance to such understanding.

We draw from this experience two basic conclusions. First, there exists a general body of knowledge about information systems that can be applied in virtually any organization (supplemented, to be sure, by more specialized skills). Second, this body of knowledge can be imparted to talented—but not necessarily brilliant—persons through a professional program of modest length (but, as in all professions, the formal education must be reinforced and extended through experience).

A great deal of nonsense has been written by both the MIS advocates and their debunkers. The issue has been made unnecessarily emotional. We have long ceased looking for that Holy Grail, the MIS Concept. Management Information System is simply a label that has been put on an activity that goes on in every organization—the formalized marshalling of information to support the decision-making process. Every functioning organization already has an MIS—good, bad, or indifferent. The MIS practitioner aims at improving the system in the most cost-effective way, subject to all of the constraints imposed by technology, organizational boundaries, limited resources, and the like. Success in doing this requires continued management support and great professional competence. The investment made in the MIS is likely to yield substantial but not overwhelming benefits; it is, in short, neither an extravagance nor a panacea.

Although a well designed MIS that exploits current technology is likely to differ in many ways from most existing MIS, it will certainly not be entirely computer-based, totally integrated, operating in real-time, and serving all levels of management with equal facility. It is highly misleading to imply that MIS practitioners aim at such gee-whiz systems; it only serves to reinforce the limited perspective of the hairy-chested school of managers who cannot see any significant role of the computer beyond routine data processing.

Discussion Questions

1. In what ways can independently developed specialized subsystems be integrated into a total MIS? Should the process be coordinated by a centralized MIS group? How can such a group acquire the special understanding of specific functional areas in order to develop information subsystems for those areas?
2. What aspects of the development of information systems can be usefully centralized? Which should be decentralized? How might Dearden answer these questions?
3. What are some of the similarities among different subsystems of an MIS? Do they outweigh the dissimilarities stressed by Dearden?
4. How much difference is there between the opinons expressed in this article and those of Dearden in the previous article? Have Emery and Sprague answered Dearden's "questions for my critics"? Which article do you find more convincing?

UNIT THREE

Managing Information Systems and Decision Support Systems

Today's manager must be prepared to successfully work with computerized information processing systems. He or she must understand and appreciate the broad impact computers have had, are having, and can be expected to have on managers and the environments in which they work. The emerging information technology can provide managers with many benefits, but it can also present them with significant difficulties if they are not prepared to cope with the problems of organizing and controlling the information resource. The problems of managing information systems and decision support systems are the subject of Unit Three. How an organization deals with these problems (or fails to deal with them) will, in large measure, determine the success or failure of the system.

Section Six (Planning) concerns methods of management planning for information systems activity. The key to effective MIS management is to view the MIS in its proper relation to the total operation of an organization. Managers must not allow themselves to be overawed by a computer's aura of mystery and the arcane jargon of technical staff. To make an effective contribution to a firm's operations, the information system must be subject to the same rigorous practices of justification, planning, monitoring, and control that are applied to any of the firm's other activities.

Section Seven (Development) addresses the many organizational issues involved in developing information systems. A set of principles has emerged in the information systems field to guide the development of these systems. The principles are organized around two areas: technical and developmental factors, and behavior and organization development factors.

Section Eight (Organizational Issues) examines the mutual interaction of an information system and the organization it serves. One central issue concerns the proper organizational location of systems activities within a firm. Should it be located in a department, such as finance or accounting, that makes extensive use of computers? In administration? Or should it be organized as an autonomous department reporting directly to top management? An allied issue is that of centralization versus decentralization, which appears in a number of different but related guises.

Section Nine (End-User Computing) focuses on the role of microcomputers within an organization and as a component of an information system. The acquisition and use of microcomputers that adheres to organizational policies and procedures is critical to their successful use by end-users.

Section Ten (Decision Support Systems) discusses the nature, scope, and content of decision support systems (DSS). The required technology, organizational strategy for the creation of a DSS, and roles of key people in the building and use of a DSS are explored.

Section Eleven (Artificial Intelligence and Expert Systems) discusses the development of computers that retain the present "memory" capabilities and also have the "brain" capabilities similar to that of humans; this is called artificial intelligence. Computers with these two human-like capabilities are called expert systems. This section discusses the potential organizational role of these computers.

Section Twelve (Data Management) turns to the design and management of the all-important data base. Difficult problems and challenges face data base designers, and many are working to create online data base systems that will cut across traditional departmental lines. This is commonly regarded as a subject for technical specialists; however, the efficiency of an information system depends critically on the active contribution of those who plan and design the data base and the managers who will use it.

SECTION SIX

Planning and Development

READING 13

Making Operational Long-Range Planning for Information Systems

article by
MARJORIE A. LYLES

Planning for information systems has traditionally consisted of analyzing the present system to determine needed equipment and new or continued projects, and then evaluating it on the basis of cost effectiveness. Missing have been systematic attempts to direct the information systems (IS) toward supporting the long-range goals of the organization. Development has been aimed primarily at appraising individual projects or proposals rather than assessing how these fit into the long-range image of the information system. Rarely have attempts been tried to incorporate creative and innovative changes in the information system that are aimed at making the information system more relevant and responsive in the long run.

Source: Reprinted by special permission of the *MIS Quarterly*, Volume 3, Number 2, June 1979, pp. 9-19.

Previous models for planning for information systems have focused on linking the information system to *current* organizational activities and decisions. Even decisions concerning the acquisition of equipment have been based more on a model of current activities rather than assessment of future organizational activities. What appears to be missing are efforts aimed at making the processes encompass the long-term development, alternatives, and opportunities of the organization.

Traditional Planning

A descriptive model of an organization's information system that will be used as a case example appears in Figure 1. It is a *Fortune 500* organization involved in the manufacturing of chemical products. The model provides a basis for discussing the topic of planning for information systems; it is *not* meant to depict a literal model of all information systems development planning. Nonetheless, this model is a

Figure 1 Descriptive Model of Information Systems Planning

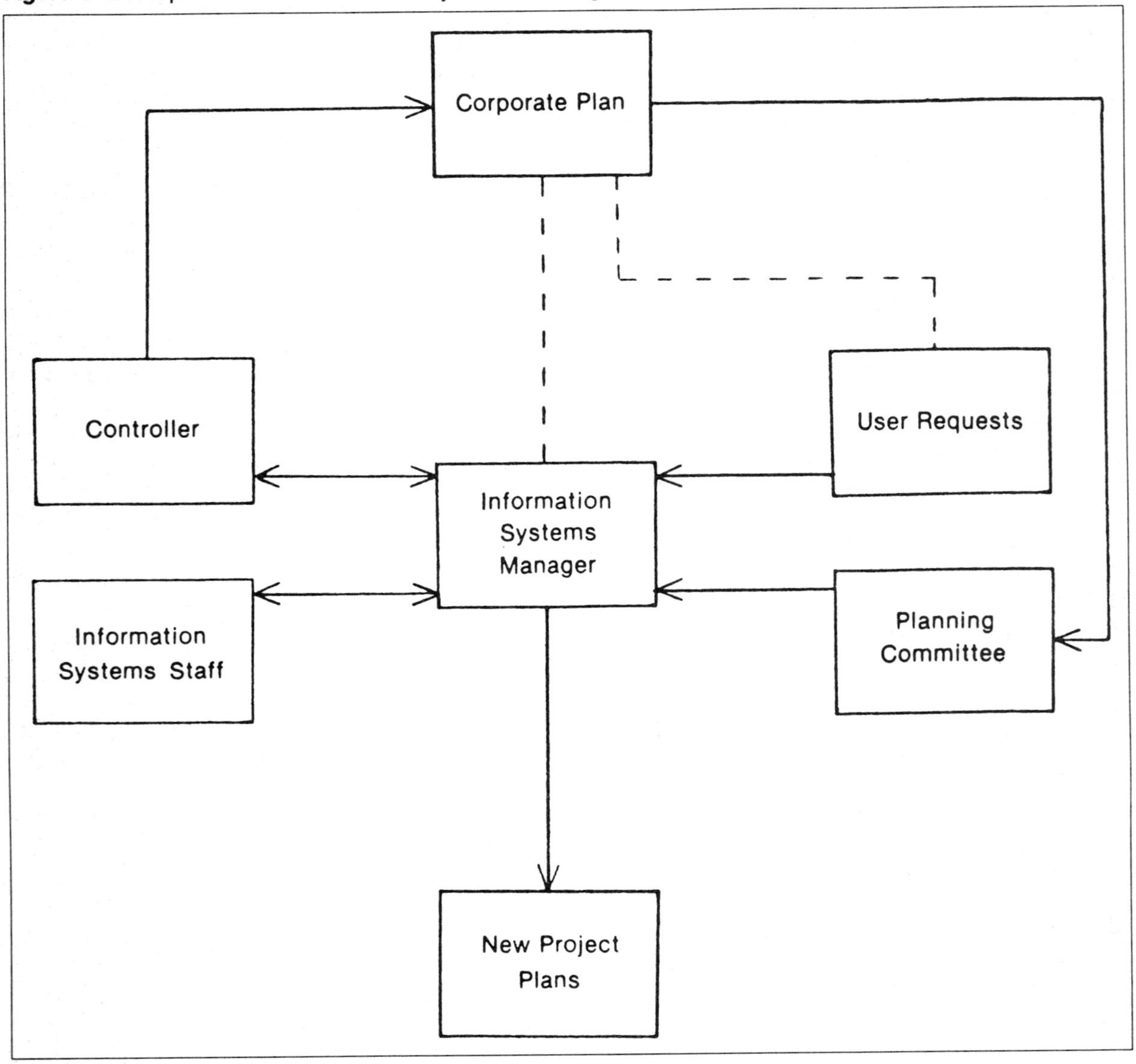

good starting point for describing some of the relationships and processes inherent in the information systems planning process.

The information systems manager is the hub of the process. All inputs into the planning process go through the IS manager, and the outputs or plans are a result of that manager's decisions. The manager has the primary role in the decision-making process but relies on inputs from the controller. These interactions keep the information system in line with the power structure of the organization and keep the power structure aware of information systems development.

Upper management's view of information system development is filtered through the comptroller. No direct communication link exists between the IS manager and top management, and thus the goals and the objectives of the organization are not directly communicated to the manager. The IS staff keeps the manager knowledgeable about trends in the field, user needs, and the status of current projects. Part of the staff activities are to gather information for strategic planning.

A review committee meets to discuss the strategic development of the information system. However, this committee does not have direct access to the corporate five-year plan. It is up to the manager, who must specially request a copy of this plan, to interpret the relevant portions to the committee. The planning committee is viewed by the manager as being parochial, short-sighted, and ineffective. He describes the individual members as primarily interested in subunit goals and objectives and without the context of organizational goals and objectives. The committee members operate in a time frame of about six months rather than five years or longer.

User requests are made to the information systems manager who is responsible for evaluating them and deciding on the priorities among them. In other organizations where information services are sold to organizational subunits, the manager may have little control over which projects are accepted, because it depends upon which departments have money to support the development of the project. In the ogranization studied, one technique used for determining the importance of a project is the requirement that the department provide a fulltime person to the project. Those departments unwilling to support a liaison person are thought to have little commitment to the project.

Hence, the direction of the MIS development is determined primarily by the information systems manager. The corporate plans are adhered to but appear to offer no risk-taking guidelines. User requests, the recommendations of the planning committee, and interactions with the controller and the systems staff are used by the manager in proposing plans.

As in this case and in the relevant literature, IS planning has focused on three primary activities: organization, system design, and evaluation.

Organization is the process of grouping people to do the MIS planning, *i.e.*, committees and task forces. This process involves planning the structure of the information systems group. *Systems design* encompasses the physical structuring of the information system, while *evaluation* is best described as the development of criteria for determining the effectiveness of the information system. The process of identifying the relationship of people and groups in order to make the information system more relevant to the company is a major task in planning, *i.e.*, the use of the committee in the prior example.

Organizing also involves the structure of the information systems group in order to provide flexibility and skills for solving the information problems throughout the organization. This emphasis on organizing is an important aspect of IS planning because of the weak communication links between system groups and other groups within the organization. Organizing provides more opportunities for direct communication and transfer of information about future needs. Project management techniques are used for designing and implementing particular projects, but organizing for the planning process is less defined. It appears that the responsibilities for planning fall primarily upon the information systems manager. A planning process that involves greater direct communication about future organizational information needs could reduce some of the uncertainty in assessing the future needs of the information system.

Evaluation techniques focus on evaluating and choosing among alternative information system designs. These techniques include simulations, the quantification of various factors, weighting methods, mathematical formulations, and the use of benchmarking. Turning this process back upon itself, *i.e.*, assessing the process of planning, is not a technique which has been addressed. Most evaluation techniques are inappropriate for evaluating information systems that are geared to long-range corporate developments. This weakness may be the result of using historical information and the *current* state of the system and decisions as a basis for evaluation. A better choice would be the acceptance of specifying objectives for the future of the IS which guide the selection among future projects. Missing from the current evaluation techniques has been a process for identifying "long-range" alternatives for the development of the IS.

Design as a process focuses on system configurations, equipment needs assessment, and software trends. Murdick and Ross [10] and King and Cleland [7] discuss design from an information analysis viewpoint. They suggest matching decisions and activities with information required to support these processes. Alternative information system designs are suggested, and the design process includes evaluating the alternatives and selecting the best design based on the criteria determined.

A methodology for making the design process future-oriented is not built into this process. Few attempts are documented which operationalize strategic planning for MIS. King [6], Murdick and Ross [10]. Ein-Dor and Segev [5], and Sporn [11] suggest improving communication, strengthening the connection between organizational decision-making and long-range goals with MIS planning, and assessing the organizational context as a means of improving the planning process. However, suggestions for implementing the process are not covered.

An examination of MIS planning processes suggests several major problems:

1. **the heavy reliance upon a single person in determining the direction of the MIS:** this works fine if there is a good manager but may lead to problems if there is a turnover,
2. **the lack of a strategic orientation:** the time horizon for planning is short-term and lacks orientation for long-term planning,
3. **the lack of systematic planning within the IS group itself:** there is no organized effort for planning within the group,
4. **planning is primarily for political and behavioral reasons, rather than for decision-making,** and
5. **plans evolve out of current projects rather than being developed with a long-term master plan in mind.**

These problems can play a dominant role in maintaining the current *state-of-the-art* for planning for MIS. However, if these problems are recognized and addressed, this increases the likelihood of a more successful planning process.

Table 1 Factors in Planning for Information Systems

CHARACTERISTIC	EXAMPLES
Organizing	Project Management Committee Top Down
Evaluating	Systems Analysis Cost Effectiveness Value of Information
Designing	Information Analysis Physical Development Feasibility

Attributes of Planning for MIS

This analysis suggests that every planning process can be characterized by a description of the attributes of that process. A summary of traditional attributes along with those suggested by the author are shown in Figure 2.

The *scope, philosophy,* and *image* of the planning process are highly interrelated. Planning has traditionally been reactive rather than proactive. It has been highly dependent upon user requests rather than active efforts to determine the information needs of the organization. Consequently, the scope of the planning process has been very project-oriented, with the future development of the information system determined by project suggestions. A futuristic approach suggests a more systematic approach in which a mission is defined for the information system. A mission is a statement defining what the information system *should* be in 10 to 15 years and provides a guideline for the development of the objectives and plans. Currently, particular projects provide the objectives and plans. Information systems planning literature emphasizes project planning and management rather than the importance of a mission for the development of the information system.

The image of the information system held by the people participating in the planning process is of great importance. A positive image of the MIS partially determines its success. Information systems have traditionally been viewed as data processing systems with some capabilities for statistical analysis and model-building. The futuristic view of the information system is a

Figure 2 Planning for Information Systems

ATTRIBUTES	TRADITIONAL	FUTURISTIC
Scope	Project-Oriented	Mission-Oriented
Philosophy	Reactive	Proactive
Image of IS	Data-Processing	Decision-Making
Time Horizon	Short (6 months +)	Long (10 years +)
Activities Supported	Operational Managerial	Operational Managerial Stragegic
Decisions Supported	Well-Defined	Well-Defined Ill-Defined
Innovativeness	Evolutionary	Opportunistic
Orientation	Parochial	Organizational
Criteria	Process	Decisions

decision-making system that can aid in the organization's decision-making activities as well as provide general information support.

The *time horizon* of the planning process is often short-term. Only in terms of equipment acquisition has the orientation been more long-term. The individuals involved have not been trained or rewarded for thinking ahead in the long-term and beyond the current projects. Organizations are more concerned with the "now" issues. Equipment acquisition decisions support current projects; new uses are developed later.

The *decisions* and *activities* that have traditionally been supported are operational and managerial, because the image of the information system is generally that of a data processing or report generating unit. These deal with well-defined information and programmable decisions. Another approach views the information system as supporting all managerial activities, including addressing ill-defined problems. McLean and Soden [9] support this view by suggesting a proactive approach relating the MIS to the organization as a whole. Although Mason [8] does not suggest how to implement such a system, he does mention that information systems should progress from information processing to decision supporting activities. Cleland and King [2] extend this framework by suggesting that the MIS can support strategic planning activities.

The acceptance of the information system as a supporting arm of these strategic activities may be a difficult concept because it means moving from a well-defined, existing, and established base into an area that is by nature ill-defined. It means that planning must move from an evolutionary process to one that is opportunistic. The overall plans must incorporate some plans that are *risk-taking* because information systems support activities that do not necessarily require well-defined information.

Instead, the required information needs to be wide in scope, aggregated, future-oriented, and largely external or environmental.

This also means a shift in orientation from a parochial perspective to an *organizational perspective*. This means forces the planning process to anticipate the implications of the organization's mission and long-range objectives and to attempt to develop an information system prepared for the future. The parochial orientation in information system planning develops the self-image of the department by increasing computer capabilities and projects that enhance its power within the organization. This parochial orientation must shift to an organizational orientation in which the system is developed in line with organizational needs.

The procedures and criteria for the planning process may differ with a more normative approach. The *criteria* for the planning process is traditionally the process itself. For example, planning is thought to be valuable because it gathers support for plans, has people participate in the decision process, and aids coordination. However, a more futuristic approach places the emphasis on the decisions and plans that are formulated, while at the same time maintaining emphasis on the importance of the process.

If the planning process emphasizes the decisions that are made, it takes some of the decision-making power away from the information system manager making the process truly participative. The *procedures* associated with the planning process shift from a routine development of plans and activities to a less routine, less defined procedure for decision-making.

Planning for Information Systems

The discussion above has identified several areas in which major changes in the planning for information systems development can take place. Three of these areas are listed below and are discussed in greater detail. These three areas appear to contribute most to successful MIS planning:

1. change in the image of information systems,
2. change toward a strategic orientation, and
3. development of an organized effort for planning within the information systems group.

Image

Information systems currently are described as a service which supports operational activities and provides information support to those who need it. Using Mason's model [8] as a vehicle for illustrating this concept, the image of the MIS is that of a data manipulator. The development of the concept of an intelligent MIS and the ability of computers to aid in decision-making makes it possible for the information system department to play a more active role in the management of the organization. Preceding this change, or at least simultaneous to it, must be a change in the image of the information system within the organization.

Two methods for changing this image can be outlined. First, pull the information systems group out from under the auspices of the comptroller and make the MIS manager report directly to one of the top management team. As long as the information systems department remains under the comptroller, it will be viewed as a super calculator rather than a vehicle that can be useful to the organization in the decision-making process. This organizational change is supported by Ein-Dor and Segev [4] who suggest that the responsibility for the MIS should be assigned to the highest possible person in the organization in order to increase the opportunities for success. A second method for changing the IS image requires the direct participation of the manager of the information systems group in the corporate planning process. This is imperative to enhance the image of the information systems group, to contribute to the long-range objectives of the organization, and to keep the MIS group informed about goals that will affect the development of the information systems. By including the information systems manager in the corporate planning process, the organization benefits by becoming more aware of the potential uses of the computer within their industry. This benefit can be seen clearly in the banking industry.

Strategic Orientation

The strategic orientation of the information systems group can be changed in several ways:

1. **Shift from project to organizational orientation.** The IS must shift its orientation away from merely responding to project proposals and user requests. It must move to a more proactive orientation for developing the information to support organizational activities. This involves tying the information system to future, long-term activities and also proposing new uses for the information systems group.
2. **Define a mission.** Shift to a strategic orientation; this relies on the change discussed in the first point above. Once the orientation supports organizational long-range activities, a new mission can be proposed for the information systems.

   OLD: The mission of the information systems group is to act as a service agency for the corporation and to supply the information needed to support the projects and decisions.

   NEW: The mission of the information systems group is to provide the information needed by the organization and to actively develop new uses for the information systems group to help the organization meet its long-range objectives.

   The difference in these two mission statements involves a change in the image both that the information system group has of itself and that it communicates to the rest of the organization. Another difference is the extent to which the group actively tries to anticipate long-range organizational objectives and develop new opportunities for the information services group. It also includes the notion that the information systems group helps the organization identify new opportunities.

   Often this mission statement or long-range purpose of the MIS is not explicitly defined by the organization [4]. Explicitly stating the MIS mission as seeking long-range opportunities helps to clearly identify the interrelations between corporate long-range objectives and the roles of the MIS.

3. **Top management support is imperative for the successful shift to a long-range orientation.** Resources must be available to the information systems group for planning and for the developing projects that may be more risk-taking. Using the banking industry as an example, some risks were initially involved when it switched to computerized customer services. Money and top management support had to be available for the development of these projects.

Development of An Organized Effort for Planning

The most important method for developing strategic planning for information systems is to create a planning process within the information systems group. An organized planning effort eliminates some of the problems that have been identified: heavy reliance upon a single individual, more emphasis on planning for decision-making, and an opportunistic orientation.

A framework for identifying the planning activities by the staff of the information systems group is presented in Figure 3. Although these activities are based on those usually incorporated into the corporate planning, they are still relevant for information systems planning. Several guiding questions developed by King [6] are helpful in directing the corporate planning process:

1. Where are we now?
2. What has been our mission?
3. What do we want to be?
4. What can be done to develop our proposed mission?

Extending this process one step further, Figure 4 illustrates some of the activities that can be performed to respond to these four questions. This figure represents an initial attempt to clarify a systematic approach to planning within the information systems group. Each of the activities

Figure 3 Formalized Planning for Information Systems

QUESTION	ACTIVITIES
Where are we now?	Analysis of Strengths and Weaknesses
	Image Analysis
What has our mission been?	Analysis of Current Projects
	Analysis of IS Role Within Organization
Where do we want to go?	Claimant Analysis
	Competitive Analysis
	Environmental Analysis
	Involvement in Corporate Planning Process
	Anticipating Future Requirements
How do we get there?	Mission, Objective, and Strategy Formulation
	Managing Planning Process

identified could be broken down into specific tasks and activities.

For example, environmental analysis could consist of determining the legal and governmental trends that would be affecting computer systems development as well as the trends within the computer industry in terms of hardware and software development. Competitive analysis could be aimed at identifying the competition of the information systems department, identifying the internal communications or reporting activities that a manager might use instead of using the information systems department. Figure 4 also illustrates which position might assume the major responsibility for this activity. All members of the group would participate in every activity but not necessarily equally.

The typical job classifications in the IS group are manager, information analyst, applications programmer, and computer operations specialist.

The IS manager, because of the nature of the job, takes on major responsibility for the linking role between the IS group and the organization's upper management. It is the manager's responsibility to analyze the strategic role of the MIS based on the overall policies and goals of the organization. At the same time, the manager introduces ideas for IS development to upper management. It is also the responsibility of the manager to plan for the planning process within the IS group to make sure that it meets the objectives, and to see that it operates effectively.

Among the roles defined is that of information analyst (IA). The definition of the IA role is based on the ACM Curriculum Committee Report [1] which suggests that information analysts have the

Figure 4 Formalized Planning for Information Systems

QUESTION	ACTIVITIES	PERSONNEL			
		MANAGER OF IS	INFO ANALYST	APPLICATION PROGRAMMERS	COMPUTER OPERATIONS SPECIALIST
Where are we now?	Analysis of Strengths and Weaknesses	B*	A*	*B	B
	Image Analysis	A	B	B	B
What has our mission been?	Analysis of Current Projects	B	B	A	B
	Analysis of IS Role Within Organization	A	B	B	B
Where do we want to go?	Claimant Analysis	B	A	B	B
	Competitive Analysis	B	A	B	B
	Environmental Analysis	B	B	B	A
	Involvement in Corporate Planning Process	A	B	B	B
	Forecasting Future	A	B	B	B
How do we get there?	Mission Objective and Strategy Formulation	A	B	B	B
	Managing Planning Process	A	B	B	B

*A = major responsibility
B = reporting and information gathering responsibilities

skills necessary to interface with the system's clients to determine their information needs. Individuals with these skills are particularly skilled in analyzing the strengths and weaknesses of the IS group, collecting information about the different claimants or stakeholders who have an interest in the development of the IS, and also in providing information about other means for obtaining needed information.

The last two roles are those of applications programmer and of computer operations specialist. Each of these roles has the responsibility for the analysis of current projects and the environment respectively.

Using this framework enables an information systems group to effectively utilize corporate planning concepts in preparing the long-range goals for the IS group. This process provides an effective analysis of the current role and image of the IS within the organization, a better understanding of its competition, and a purposeful approach to determining its role in the organization's future. It provides the information systems group with a process to collect the information, evaluate it, and to provide an opportunity for the members of the information systems group to participate in the process.

Conclusion

The planning process described in this article provides a means for addressing the three major problems identified in the development of a decision-oriented, futuristic and proactive information system. By changing the image of the information system and by developing a strategic orientation, the information systems group is a more valuable asset to the organization in meeting its long-range objectives.

If this methodology for the planning process is used, it provides a structured and systematic approach to strategic planning for the MIS. In addition, this methodology provides a process that requires the information systems group to be self-reflective and analytical in terms of its own development.

The planning process provides a basis for the development of the information system to reflect more accurately the needs of the organization. It does this by providing the IS group with a direct link into the corporate planning process so that there can be an exchange of information and ideas. This process can be highly beneficial to both the corporation and the IS group.

Discussion Questions

1. According to this article, what is "traditional" MIS planning?
2. Why is long-range planning for information systems not a part of "traditional" MIS planning?
3. How is long-range planning for information systems related to overall corporate strategy, corporate goals, and corporate objectives?
4. Describe three prerequisites for successful MIS planning.
5. Do the major responsibilities, presented in Figure 4, seem reasonable for each job title? If not, why not? If yes, explain the basis for each major responsibility.

References

[1] Ashenhurst, R. L. (ed.) "Curriculum Recommendations for Graduate Professional Programs in Information Systems: A Report of the ACM Curriculum Committee on Computer Education for Management," *Communications of the ACM*, Volume 15, Number 5, May 1972, pp. 363-398.

[2] Cleland, D. E. and King, W. R. "Competitive Business Intelligence Systems," *Business Horizons*, Volume 18, Number 6, December 1975, pp. 19-28.

[3] Couger, Daniel and Knapp, Robert. *System Analysis Techniques*, Wiley, New York, New York, 1974.

[4] Ein-Dor, P. and Segev, E. "Organizational Context and the Success of Management Information Systems," *Management Science*, Volume 24, Number 19, June 1978, pp. 1064-1077.

[5] Ein-Dor, P. and Segev, E. "Strategic Planning for Management Information Systems," Tel Aviv University, Working Paper 269/76, July 1976.

[6] King, W. R. "Strategic Planning for Management Information Systems," *MIS Quarterly*, Volume 2, Number 1, March 1978, pp. 27-37.

[7] King, W. R. and Cleland, D. I. "Design of Management Information Systems: An Information Analysis Approach," *Management Science*, Volume 22, Number 3, November 1975, pp. 286-297.

[8] Mason, R. O. "Basic Concepts for Designing Management Information Systems," Graduate School of Business, UCLA, AIS Research Paper Number 8, October 1969.

[9] McLean, E. R. and Soden, J. V. *Strategic Planning for MIS*, Wiley-Interscience, New York, New York, 1977.

[10] Murdick, R. G. and Ross, J. E. *Information Systems for Modern Management*, Prentice-Hall, Englewood Cliffs, New Jersey, 1977.

[11] Sporn, D. L. "Designing and ADP Planning Process," *Long Range Planning*, Volume 11, February 1978, pp. 43-46.

READING 14

Three Stage Model of MIS Planning

article by
BRENT BOWMAN, GORDON DAVIS
and JAMES WETHERBE

1. Introduction

The necessity for effective MIS planning is well documented [14,20,22-24,27, and 28]. The need to plan is clear; the process is less obvious. Differing methodologies have added to the confusion as to how to do MIS planning.

The objectives of this article are to clarify the process of MIS planning and to provide insight as to the value of various methodologies at different stages. The first objective is accomplished by reviewing the problems of MIS planning and proposing a three-stage model for the planning process. The second objective is met by reviewing several planning methodologies and placing them within the framework of the three stages. The article contains recommendations for applying the three-stage MIS planning model.

Source: Reprinted by permission of North-Holland Publishing Company from *Information & Management*, 6 (1983), pp. 11-25.

2. The Problems of MIS Planning

Through discussions with MIS executives and from a survey of the MIS literature we have identified four difficult processes in MIS planning:

1. Alignment of the MIS plan with the overall strategies and objectives of the organization.
2. Design of an information system structure or architecture for the organization as a framework within which applications are to be designed and developed.
3. Allocation of information system development and operations resources among competing applications.
4. Selection and use of methodologies for performing the first three processes.

2.1. Alignment of the MIS Plan with Organizational Plan

The first problem is making sure the MIS planning process identifies and selects information systems applications that fit the priorities established by needs and priorities of the organization. However, the organizational strategies and plans may not be written, or they may be formulated in terms that are not useful for information system planning. It is therefore often difficult to ascertain the strategies and goals to which the information system plan should be aligned, but without this alignment, the information system plan will not obtain long-term organizational support. If the selection and scheduling of information system projects is based only on proposals submitted by users, the projects will reflect existing computer-use biases in the organization, aggressiveness of some managers in submitting proposals, and various aspects of organizational power rather than reflecting the overall needs and priorities of the organization.

2.2. Design of an Information System Architecture

The term "information system architecture" refers to the overall structure of the information system. This structure consists of the applications for the various levels of the organization (operations, management control, and strategic planning) and applications oriented to various management activities such as planning, control, and decision making. The system structure or architecture also includes databases, model bases, and supporting software. An information system architecture for an organization should guide long range development but also allow response to diverse short range information system demands.

Selecting an information system architecture is difficult. The difficulty stems from two processes: the architecture selection (assuming a complete and correct understanding of requirements) and the eliciting of requirements. If organization information requirements are well specified, the number of alternative architectures can be fairly large. If requirements are fuzzy and poorly specified, the alternatives for information system architecture expand further. Even after introducing constrains such as limited vendor list, stable software, etc., the analysis of alternatives can yield recommendations that are subject to question.

The process of obtaining information requirements can, at best, result in a tentative set of fairly complete, reasonably correct requirements. At worst, the information requirements can be incomplete and incorrect. In the absence of well-defined processes for information requirements determination, it is difficult for an organizational unit or functional area to define completely its information requirements. The managers of the units are constrained in defining information needs by their bounded rationality. Many useful computer-based solutions are not considered. Also, perceived information needs are biased by human processing limitations that cause users to "fix" on recent problems as the most important and to draw unwarranted conclusions from a small number of occurrences of some event. These and other human limitations in defining information requirements mean that when managers are required to define their information needs without the aid of systematic information requirements determination processes, the result is a set of requirements that are probably not complete nor arranged in "real" priority order by the submitters (see [9] for further discussion).

2.3. Allocation of Development Resources

The rational, organizational-optimal allocation of development resources among competing units is difficult, especially if the portfolio of potential applications does not fit into an overall organizational plan and functional/organizational unit requirements do not fit into some orderly framework that establishes completeness and priority. Organizational dynamics such as relative power, aggressive advocacy, etc., may be used in place of some rational allocation.

2.4. Selection of Methodologies

The last major problem is the selection of one or more planning methodologies from the set of competing methodologies (especially methodologies for developing the application portfolio and allocating resources). In the literature, each of the methodologies tends to be presented as "the solution". Enthusiastic developers (and even some users) provide testimonials of the power of the methodologies in MIS planning processes. But, even though the techniques are competing, they are not directly equivalent. Presumably each methodology has a set of circumstances under which it is superior. There is very little guidance in the literature to make such a selection taking into account the contingencies an organization is facing. In fact, there is no overall framework for classifying methodologies.

The discussions of problems in MIS planning suggests a need for a comprehensive model of MIS planning, so that the process can be researched, explained, and applied.

3. Three-Stage MIS Planning Model

A basic, generic MIS planning model has been formulated based on observation of planning efforts, the literature, and an analysis of methodologies being used in the planning process. The basic MIS planning model depicted in Figure 1 consists of three major, generic activities: strategic MIS planning, information requirements analysis, and resource allocation. See Table 1 for a description of each of these activities.

Table 1

Major MIS Planning Activity	Description
Strategic MIS planning	Establishing the relationship between the overall organizational plan and the MIS plan.
Organizational information requirements analysis	Identifying broad, organizational information requirements to establish a strategic information architecture that can be used to direct specific application system development project.
Resource allocation	Allocation of both MIS application development resources and operational resources.

Most organizations engage in each of these stages, but involvement tends to be evolutionary and governed by problems as they occur rather than by a plan for engaging in each stage as appropriate. Planning methodologies often are chosen during these stages based on the persuasive power of methodology developers rather than on a reasoned choice of a methodology for a given stage of MIS planning. The basic MIS planning model presented here provides a framework for study and evaluation of the MIS planning process and for mapping methodologies to the basic activities.

The three-stage basic MIS planning model can be illustrated by a case study in which an organization followed the steps described by the model. A Fortune 100 company, based on recommendations from its external auditors, was upgrading its computing capabilities from predominantly batch, second generation systems. Major problems were being encountered in the accounting area in terms of processing speed and ability to integrate data. For example, processing was so slow in accounts payable that the company's credit rating was being affected. Therefore, the company made a *strategic* decision to upgrade its computing capabilities to an online, database environment with initial emphasis on improving accounting processing. Other applications were also to be reviewed. Although they did not use a formal approach, the organization had, at this point, gone through the strategic stage. The top management of the organization was strategically determining MIS objectives.

During the next six months the organization hired a new MIS management team and had them conduct analysis on the new system and look at overall information requirements. The MIS group used the BSP methodology (Business System Planning) to conduct a comprehensive study. This period of analysis can be characterized as an organizational information requirements analysis planning stage.

During the following 18 months several systems were implemented both in the accounting and operational areas. User management began to complain about two issues: they wanted more systems and they wanted faster responses for new systems. But MIS costs had proliferated during the past two years. Top management and consequently MIS management had become concerned about

Figure 1 Basic Three-Stage Model of MIS Planning

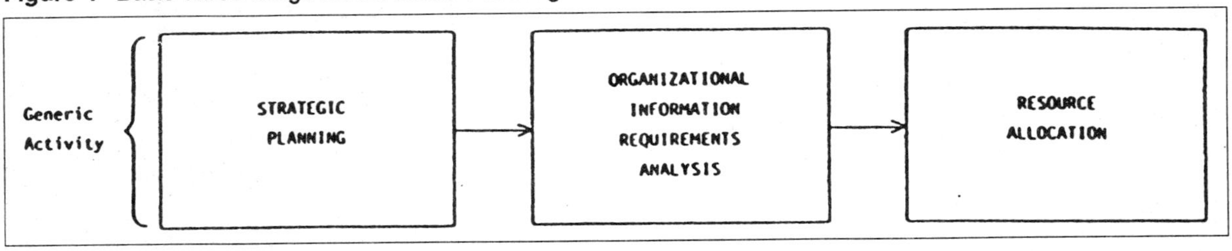

allocating limited resources to increasing demand. This put the organization in the resource allocation stage. They decided to install a chargeout system to allocate resources.

The case illustrates how, based on organizational requirements, MIS planning moves from one stage to another. It also illustrates how specific formal models may be selected for use in each of the three stages. In the case situation, the formal models were BSP in the organizational information requirements analysis stage and chargeout in the resource allocation stage. There was no use of a formal model in the strategic planning stage, but strategic MIS decisions were a function of overall company strategy.

4. Expanding the Planning Stages

The very general three-stage model presented in Figure 1 can be expanded to include major activities and outputs of the three stages as shown in Figure 2. By adding this detail, the model moves from a high level of abstraction to a more concrete formulation of MIS planning activities.

4.1 Strategic MIS Planning

During the strategic planning stage, it is critical to align MIS strategic planning with overall organizational planning. To accomplish this the organization must:

- Assess organizational objectives and strategies
- Set MIS mission
- Assess environment
- Set MIS policies, objectives, and strategies

The output from this process should be an accurate perception of the strategic aspirations and directions of the organization, a new or revised MIS charter, an assessment of the state of the MIS function, and a statement of policies, objectives, and strategies for the MIS effort.

4.2 Organizational Information Requirements Analysis

The first phase of the Organizational Information Requirements Analysis (OIRA) stage consists of assessing current and projected information needs to support decision making and operations of the organizations. This effort is not to be confused with or replace the detail information requirements analysis associated with application system specifications (e.g., report and terminal display layouts). Rather, this is a higher level of information requirements analysis aimed at developing an overall information architecture for the organization or a major sector of the organization.

The second phase of the OIRA stage consists of assembling a master development plan. This plan is derived from the information architecture and defines specific information system projects, ranking of projects, and a development schedule.

4.3. Resource Allocation

Resource allocation consists of developing hardware, software, data communications, facilities, personnel, and financial plans needed to execute the master development plan defined in the OIRA stage. This stage provides the framework for technology procurement, personnel planning, and budgeting to provide appropriate service levels to users.

Figure 2 Major Activities and Outputs in Three Stages of MIS Planning

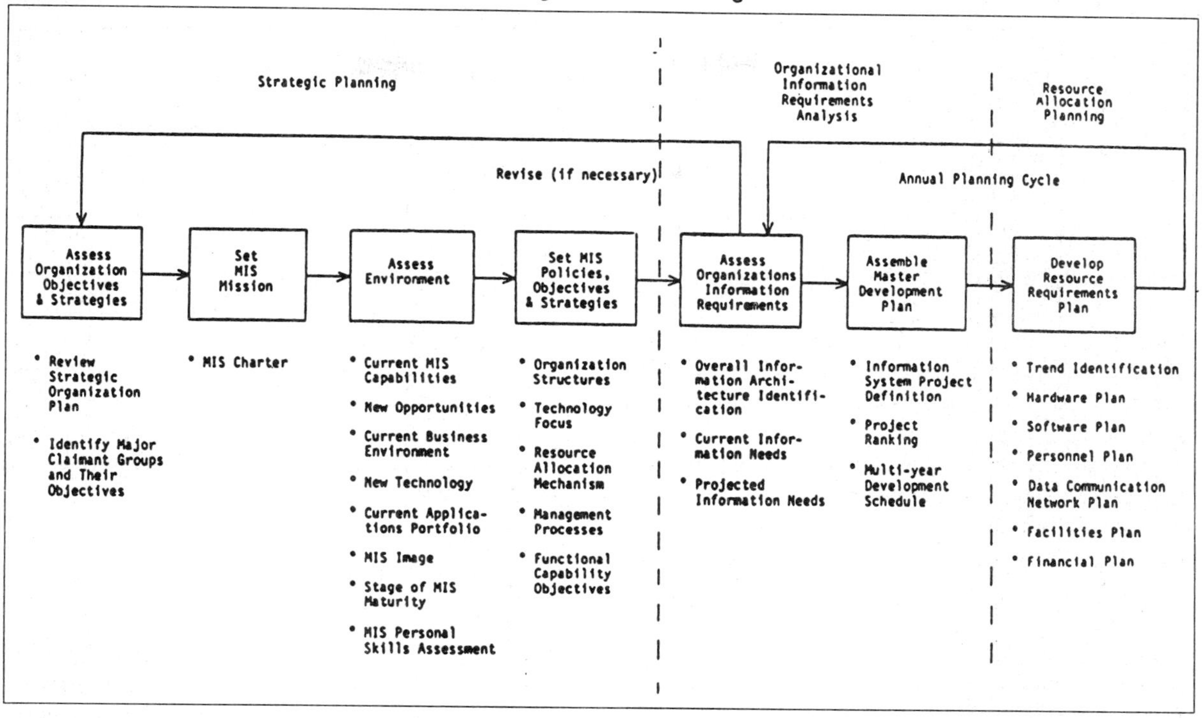

4.4. Staging of the Model

As depicted in Figure 2, the activities within stages and the stages themselves have a sequential flow starting with "assess organization objectives and strategies" and ending with "develop resource requirements plan." A complete execution of the model is not necessary at each planning effort. As Figure 2 portrays, the annual planning cycle may only consist of assessing organizational information requirements, assembling a master plan, and developing a resource allocation plan. The time interval between executing an entire model is a function of how rapidly the organization's overall objectives and strategies are changing in ways that impact MIS requirements. The interval between comprehensive planning cycles may be from one to five years.

5. Methodologies for Use in MIS Planning

The next issue is the relationship of the various planning methodologies to the three-stage planning model. Several of the most publicized planning methodologies are listed below:

• Strategy Set Transformation[21]
• Business System Planning (BSP) [19]
• Critical Success Factors (CSF) [30,42]
• Business Information Analysis and Integration Technique (BIAIT) [5,7,10]
• Ends/Means Analysis [39]
• Return on Investment
• Chargeout [14,18,24,28]
• Zero-Based Budgeting [29,38]

A brief description of each approach is presented together with a discussion of its relationship to the three major planning activities.

5.1. Strategy Set Transformation

King [21] proposes an approach to the strategic phase of MIS planning that he terms strategy set transformation. The overall organization strategy is viewed as an "information set" consisting of the mission, objectives, strategies, and other strategic variables (e.g., managerial sophistication, proclivity to accept change, important environmental constraints, etc.). Strategic MIS planning is the process of transforming the organizational strategy set into an "MIS strategy set" consisting of MIS system objectives, constraints, and design strategies.

Step one of this methodology is the identification and explication of the organizational strategy set. The obvious starting point in this activity is review of the organization's written strategic or long-range plan. If such a document does not exist or if it is deficient in providing purposeful guidelines for managerial choice, a strategy set may be constructed. King describes the strategy set construction process as:

1. delineating the claimant structure of the organization (i.e., owner, managers, employees, suppliers, customers, creditors, governmental agencies, local communities, competitors, etc.).
2. identifying goals for each claimant group.
3. identifying organizational purposes and strategy relative to each claimant group.

Once the tentative statement of the organizational strategy set has been developed it should be presented to top managers for review and comments.

The next major step involves transforming the organizational strategy set into an MIS strategy set consisting of system objectives, constraints, and design principles. The transformation process involves identification of the MIS strategic elements for each element within the organizational strategy set. Information analysts then construct alternative structures for the overall MIS architecture subject to the MIS objectives, strategies, and constraints enumerated as the MIS strategy set. The general alternatives are then presented to management.

As an example, a claimant group may be creditors. They have goals of protecting their assets and their relative priority for repayment plus making sound decisions on extending additional credit or enforcing repayment of existing debt. The organizational purposes and strategy of this claimant group include timely analysis of financial statements of the company to which they have extended credit to determine ability to repay the loans and to identify any impairment of security for the debt. One system objective of the company MIS is therefore to provide prompt information to all major creditors. The information should allow a creditor to reevaluate the decision to extend additional credit or to continue with existing credit. The alternative structures for achieving these MIS system objectives are to provide regular financial statements in the traditional format and to make these available to the creditors or to provide a special report for creditors that will present data in a form that is especially useful to creditors. This latter option might even include comparative industry data to show the credit worthiness of the company in context within its industry.

This methodology focuses exclusively on strategic MIS planning. To be successful, this approach requires accurate and concise articulation of organizational objectives and strategies. Identification of the organization's claimant structure offers a useful framework to define this information, but the activity is still somewhat unstructured and subjective. Assuming the organizational strategy set can be adequately defined, this technique can result in a strategic MIS plan with an appropriate long-range time horizon and a high level of integration with overall business strategy. Information analysts may be used to interpret or elicit the organizational strategy set and then to enumerate the MIS strategy set elements and develop alternative general designs for the overall MIS architecture. Because of the subjective nature of the process, there should be significant management and user input and review.

5.2. Business Systems Planning

Business Systems Planning (BSP) [19] is a comprehensive planning methodology developed by IBM. BSP was initially developed for IBM's internal use, but as IBM customers expressed interest in learning how they might better manage their MIS resources, BSP was released as a generalized methodology to assist in this task. It is supported by IBM manuals and training courses.

BSP basically involves a two-phase approach. It is conducted by a BSP planning team composed of both user and MIS personnel. Phase I focuses on developing a broad overall understanding of the organization, identifying how MIS currently supports the business, specification of the gross network of information systems required to support the business, and identification of the highest priority subsystems to be implemented within the network. Data is primarily gathered through interviews with numerous managers to determine their environment, objectives, key decisions and problems, and perceived information needs. The analysis concentrates on business processes without regard for organization structure.

The objective of Phase II is to develop a long-range plan for the design, development, and implementation of a network of information systems to support the business process identified in Phase I. The current information systems are assessed and weaknesses and deficiencies are noted. Processes and users that share data are identified and the potential for common information systems across organizational boundaries is determined. The output of Phase II is the Information Systems Plan. The plan describes the overall information systems architecture as well as defines the scheduled implementation of individual systems within the overall network. It serves as what Zani calls the "blueprint for development of an integrated MIS [42]."

BSP can also be described as an eliciting, analysis, and synthesis process. In this view, the primary activities are:

1. In the eliciting and discovery activities, the questions center on organizational functions performed, decisions made, and problems requiring information.
2. In the analysis activity, organizational processes are summarized and associated with information needs and data required.
3. The synthesis activity specifies applications to meet needs, data required in database to support applications, and priority for development.

The fundamental thrust of the BSP approach is toward identifying the information necessary to run the organization. It is suggested that the master development plan include resource requirements, but the principles and guidelines of the methodology are directed at information requirements analysis.

BSP utilizes a top-down approach to identification and definition of information requirements. Information concerning the organizational processes and associated information needs is obtained by the BSP study team via observation and interviews. This approach can be effective in identifying current requirements, but without explicit consideration of overall strategic plans and objectives the resulting plan could lack the proper long-range perspective. Another drawback of the interview approach is the significant personnel time required to collect and analyze information. A sizeable number of managers must be interviewed in order to develop the broad understanding of the organization's processes and the associated information requirements. Although IBM proposes a variety of useful matrices and other graphical techniques to assist the BSP team in collecting the data, analysis and synthesis of the rather large volume of data into a viable information system plan can be somewhat difficult.

5.3. Critical Success Factors

As suggested by Zani [42] and further developed by Rockart [30], the information needs of top managers are derived from critical success factors, i.e., the key areas for any organization in which performance must be satisfactory if the business is to survive and flourish. Critical Success Factors (CSFs) differ among industries and for individual firms within a particular industry.

As an example, Rockart cites the four industry-based CSFs of supermarkets as: having the right product mix available at each store, keeping it on the shelves, effective advertising to attract shoppers to the store, and correct pricing. As these areas of activity are major determinants of a supermarket chain's success, the status of performance in these areas should be continually measured and reported. The Rockart research team at MIT has identified the four primary sources of CSFs as:

1. Industry-based factors
2. Competitive strategy, industry position, and geographical location
3. Environmental factors
4. Temporal factors

The CSF approach involves a series of interviews (though not nearly so many as with BSP) conducted in two or three sessions. In the first session the manager is queried as to his or her goals and the CSFs that underlie those goals. Considerable discussion may be required to ensure that the analyst thoroughly understands the interrelationships between the goals and CSFs. Every effort is made to combine or eliminate similar CSFs and an initial set of performance measures are developed. The second session is a review of the first and primarily focuses on identification of specific performance measures and possible reports. Additional sessions are held as necessary to obtain agreement on the CSF measures and reports for tracking them. The reports and related information systems required to provide them are designed by the MIS group.

5.4. Business Information Analysis and Integration Technique

An interesting and innovative approach to information analysis and planning has been developed by Burnstine [5,7,20]. The technique called Business Information Analysis and Integration Technique (BIAIT) is a distinct demarcation from other approaches. Most planning approaches tend to use open-ended questions that elicit information from managers about their information requirements and the properties of those requirements. Open-ended questions such as—what information do you need to support your decision making?—allow managers complete freedom to articulate their requirements.

Burnstine, through extensive experimentation with over 400 items, has factored out seven close-ended questions that can be used to determine a normative set of information requirements. These questions require only a binary (yes or no) response from a manager. From the responses to these questions overall information requirements can theoretically be defined. This capability is independent of organizational or departmental size and is independent of the products or services provided.

The key focus of the seven classification questions is on orders and suppliers. Suppliers are persons, departments, or organizations that respond to orders. Orders are anything that require a response from a supplier. The entity ordered is either a thing, a place, or a skill. The key point is that if a supplier, be it an organization, department, or an individual, receives no orders, it has no reason for existing.

The seven questions of BIAIT are as follows:

1. Do you bill customers or accept cash?
2. Do you deliver products or services in the future or immediately?
3. Do you create and maintain profiles of customer's buying behavior or not?
4. Do you negotiate price or operate on a fixed price basis?
5. Do you rent or sell your products or services?
6. Do you perform product recall and update to the product or service you have offered?
7. Do you make to order or provide from stock the product or service that you supply?

These seven questions allow an analyst to classify an organization in terms of its systems and establish a generic model of the information handling activities necessary for it to operate.

The generic model is customized by the unique characteristics of the organization. A helpful by product of this process is that it defines who the data owners and data users should be. BIAIT is still in an experimental state but initial applications show promise.

5.5. Ends/Means Analysis

Ends/Means Analysis is a new planning technique developed by Wetherbe and Davis [39] at the MIS Research Center at the University of Minnesota. The technique can be used to determine information requirements at the organizational, departmental, or individual manager level.

Based upon general systems theory, the technique focuses first on the ends or outputs (goods, service, and information) generated by an organizational process. Next, the technique is used to define the means (inputs and processes) used to accomplish the ends.

The ends or output from one process, whether the process be viewed as an organizational, departmental or individual process, is the input to some other process. For example, the inventory process provides a part to the production process, the accounting process provides budget information for other organizational processes, and the marketing process provides products to customer processes.

End/Means Analysis is concerned with both the effectiveness and the efficiency of generating outputs from processes. Effectiveness pertains to how well the outputs from a process fill the input requirements of the other process. Efficiency pertains to resources required and the use of those resources to transform an input into an output.

A model of Ends/Means Analysis is provided in Figure 3. The model provides two types of information effectiveness and efficiency. Effectiveness information is based upon what constitutes effectiveness for outputs and what information or feedback is needed to evaluate effectiveness. Efficiency information is based upon what constitutes efficiency in an input and transformation process and what information or feedback is needed to evaluate efficiency.

As an example of the flow of questions in ends/means analysis, an inventory manager might specify the following:

1. Ends specification: The outputs or end result of the inventory management function is an inventory that is as low as possible but maintained at an acceptable level of availability.
2. Means specification: The inputs and processes to accomplish the ends are: Forecasts of future needs; amounts on hand and on order; items that are obsolete or in useable condition; safety stock policy; demand variations; cost of ordering and holding inventory; cost of items; stockouts.

Figure 3 Model of ENDS/MEANS Analysis

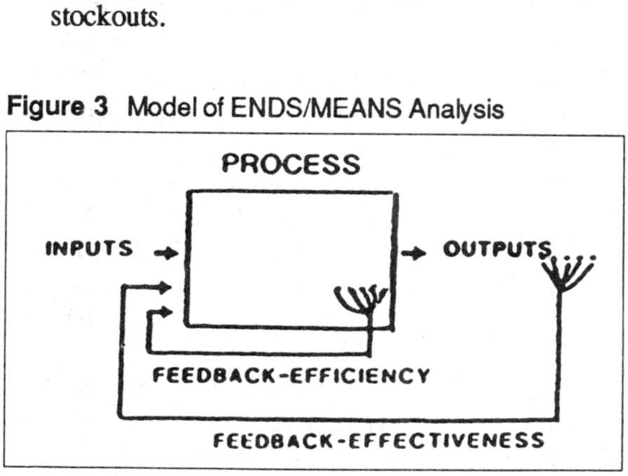

3. Efficiency measures for inventory management are number of orders placed, cost of holding inventory, and loss on disposal of obsolete or unuseable inventory.
4. Effectiveness measures are the level of inventory and number and seriousness of stockouts.

Ends/Means Analysis has been used in diverse industrial settings with positive results. Information requirements are determined that are usually more extensive than those generated using other techniques. The problem with most information planning tools is that they usually result in information systems that provide efficiency oriented information. However, managers agree it is more important to be effective than to be efficient. Ends/Means Analysis brings out effectiveness information requirements. Such requirements typically transcend departmental boundaries and therefore ends/means analysis is especially useful for a database planning effort.

5.6. Return on Investment (ROI)

ROI is a cost benefit analysis technique widely used in a variety of planning applications. Typically, projects are ranked in descending order by ROI and the highest ranked projects providing an acceptable rate of return are selected. Considerations other than ROI such as resource constraints, organizational priorities, or politics may alter the selection process.

Many organizations apply ROI analysis to MIS projects in an attempt to make them pass the same criteria as other organizational undertakings. To the extent cost and benefits are quantifiable, ROI is a useful planning tool. Unfortunately, MIS projects often do not lend themselves to easy quantification and estimation of costs and benefits. The costs and benefits of MIS projects are viable, complex, interrelated, and difficult to estimate. This often negates a meaningful ROI analysis.

5.7. Chargeout

Some form of chargeout system is frequently used as a basis for planning and controlling MIS

[14,18,24,28]. In large organizations, the MIS function is often organized as a service bureau charged with providing MIS services to all organizational sub-units. Fee schedules are developed for each unit of service (e.g., CPU seconds, DASD I/Os, lines printed, programming time, etc.) with the objective of recovering (or partially recovering) MIS expenditures (see Hootman [18] for detailed discussion of chargeout system design). Users are charged for those MIS services consumed. In theory, holding users responsible for the cost of their information systems fosters greater planning and control of those systems.

Chargeout-based planning systems are typical of the traditional approach to MIS planning. In addition to the chargeout system, this approach usually includes guidelines, procedures, and schedules to specifically direct planning efforts, but the focus is frequently towards justifying the costs of proposed new information systems relative to the benefits. Planning decision-making is decentralized to user departments. This can tend to limit the search for potentially beneficial new information systems, especially with respect to integrated systems affecting multiple departments and to applications areas with intangible benefits. Wetherbe and Dickson [38] identify a number of problems associated with chargeout-based planning including: high expense (in terms of both administrative and computer processing overhead), complexity, market imperfections, and difficulties with the development of integrated, multi-departmental systems.

The nature of chargeout-based planning systems varies across organizations. However, without specific procedures to the contrary, there are no systematic mechanisms linking information system planning based on chargeout to broader organizational strategy and objectives. This may result in strictly bottom-up development of information systems with short-range time horizons.

5.8. Zero Based Budgeting (ZBB)

ZBB is a highly structured planning technique developed by Peter Pyhrr as an alternative to incremental budgeting [29]. Its use has been fairly widespread by various governmental and private organizations.

Wetherbe and Dickson [38] suggest the use of ZBB as an MIS planning and control tool and as an alternative to chargeout-based systems. The first step in this process involves conceptually reducing all MIS activities to zero-base, i.e., no development or maintenance of information systems. Next, all potential information systems applications are identified and structured into sequentially dependent incremental service levels. Expected benefits and MIS resource support requirements are listed for each service level. The projects are combined into an applications portfolio and submitted to a steering committee (or some other resource allocation mechanism) for priorities to be established. The projects are listed in ranked order of priority and cumulative resource requirements are calculated. Whetherbe and Dickson [38] advocate the use of the Delphi [37] technique to conduct the ranking of projects. Selection of projects to be implemented becomes a function of the MIS funding level.

This technique is particularly useful in identifying applications that have out-lived their usefulness. It has a strong bottom-up orientation and the service level concept could conceivably result in a logical evolutionary design of the MIS. This methodology has a strong focus on resource allocation, but again, there is no explicit strategic planning cycle or direct link to the host organization's overall planning process. Compared with ROI, ZBB allows a more subjective analysis that does not require quantification of all cost and benefits. Compared with chargeout, using an MIS Steering Committee to establish priorities adds a centralized, high-level perspective to planning decision-making, but the lack of explicit consideration of strategic MIS planning may result in a planning process with a short-range time horizon.

The amount of personnel time required to utilize the ZBB approach can be significant. Information analysts must devote a considerable amount of time interacting with users in identifying information system projects and structuring proposed systems into incremental service levels. Also, preoccupation with service level definition may narrow the search for alternatives.

6. Relationship of Methodologies to MIS Planning Model

The methodologies that have been reviewed fit into the framework of the basic MIS planning model. Each may be classified as applying primarily to one of the three generic activities (see Figure 4):

1. Strategic planning
2. Organizational information requirements analysis
3. Resource allocation

Strategy set transformation is the only methodology described in this article that falls into the strategic planning category. In fact, it is the only methodology we are aware of that is designed to provide a direct link to overall organizational strategic planning.

BSP, CSF, BIAIT, and E/M analysis fall into the organizational information requirements analysis (OIRA) category. The four approaches differ in their method and comprehensiveness. BSP is the more comprehensive and labor intensive approach and generates a more extensive definition of total information requirements. CSF and E/M Analysis are less labor intensive and direct information requirements analysis at higher level management requirements. BIAIT is a highly structured engineering approach that appears to be efficient in arriving at a set of normative requirements. A concern is whether it is applicable to high-level decision making information requirements.

Chargeout, ROI, and ZBB fall into the resource allocation category. All three approaches are concerned with allocating resources; however, their orientations are quite different. Chargeout advocates decentralized "market place" decision making with cost recovery. ZBB advocates centralized planning committee decision making with MIS expenses carried as overhead. ROI can be used in either a centralized or a decentralized decision making process.

The ability to classify the various planning methodologies within the three-stage model adds validity to the model. Since each of the planning methodologies has been implemented in a number of organizations, this indicates that under certain circumstances, each of the planning methodologies performs a useful and needed function. The ability to map the planning methodologies into the taxonomy indicates that strategic planning, organizational information requirements analysis, and resource allocation are good generic definitions of stages of MIS planning.

7. Guidelines for MIS Planning Based on the Three-Stage Model

At the beginning of the article, the major problems of MIS planning were identified as:

Figure 4 Alternative MIS Planning Methodologies Classified by Stage of MIS Planning of Most Significant Impact

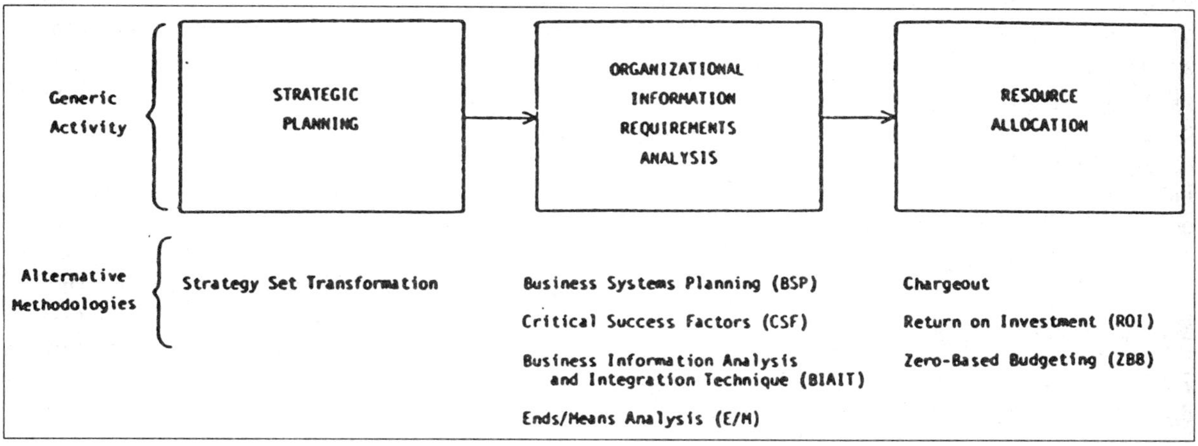

1. Alignment of MIS strategy with organizational strategy
2. Developing an information architecture
3. Resource allocation
4. Selecting a methodology for the above steps

These problems are addressed directly by the three-stage MIS planning model. The first three problems correspond to the three stages of the model. Given the framework of the model, the set of appropriate methodologies is specified for each stage. This aids in selecting a methodology for each stage.

Practical guidance for MIS planning can be gained from the model. It can aid in recognizing the nature of the MIS planning problems and in selecting the appropriate stage of planning. Too often, this is not done. For example, some organizations may view their MIS functions as making minimal contributions to organizational objectives. In seeking to resolve this problem, some organizations have installed a chargeout system (resource allocation planning) to make MIS pay its own way. Other organizations have conducted a BSP (OIRA planning) exercise to resolve the same problem. While these activities may result in improved MIS services, the MIS planning model suggests they are probably not the appropriate methodologies in this situation. If the MIS effort is not responsive to the organization, the three-stage MIS planning model indicates a strategic oriented planning effort should precede OIRA and resource allocation planning exercises.

To establish MIS planning, an organization should conduct a stage assessment to determine the extent to which each stage of MIS planning has been accomplished. This can be performed by analyzing the major activities and outputs of the three-stage planning model depicted in Figure 2. After the MIS planning needs at each stage have been established, appropriate methodologies can be selected.

7.1. Stage Assessments

The stage assessment is performed for each of the three stages of the MIS planning model. To conduct a strategic stage assessment an organization should ask the following questions:

1. Is there a clear definition of organizational objectives and strategies?
   Has the strategic organizational plan been reviewed?
   Are the major claimant groups and their objectives identified?
2. Is there an MIS mission expressed in an MIS charter?
3. Is there an assessment of the MIS environment?
   Are MIS capabilities adequately assessed?
   Are new opportunities identified?
   Is the current business environment understood?
   If the current applications portfolio defined and documented?
   Is the MIS image healthy?
   Is the stage of EDP growth understood?
   Are MIS personnel skills accurately inventoried?
4. Are MIS policies, objectives, and strategies established?
   Is the MIS organization appropriate to the overall organization?
   Is the MIS technology focus appropriate to the technology focus of the organization?
   Are the objectives for allocating MIS resources appropriate?
   Are the MIS management processes appropriate?
   Are the functional capability objectives appropriate?

If answers to these questions indicate a strategic stage weakness, a strategic planning exercise is in order. Strategy set transformation offers a formal methodology for conducting such an exercise. However, a formal methodology may not be necessary.

Before conducting an OIRA stage assessment an organization should ask the following questions:

1. Is there an adequate assessment of organizational information requirements?
   Is the overall organizational information architecture identified?
   Is there a good understanding of current

information needs of the organizations?
Is there a good understanding of projected information needs of the organization?
Are the major databases and their relationships defined?

2. Is there a master MIS development plan?
Are MIS projects defined?
Are projects ranked by priority?
Is there a multi-year development schedule?

If an organization does not have acceptable answsers to the OIRA stage questions, an OIRA planning exercise is in order. Examples of formal planning methodologies available to conduct such exercise are BSP, CSF, Ends/Means Analysis, and BIAIT.

To evaluate the current status prior to conducting a resource allocation stage assessment an organization should ask the following questions:

1. Does the organization have a resource requirements plan?
Are trends identified?
Is there a hardware plan?
Is there a software plan?
Is there a personnel plan?
Is there a data communications plan?
Is there a facilities plan?
Is there a financial plan?
2. Does the organization have an adequate procedure for resource allocation?

If an organization does not have acceptable answers to the resource allocation stage questions, a resource allocation planning exercise is in order. Formal planning methodologies available to conduct such an exercise are chargeout, ROI, and ZBB.

7.2. Selecting a Methodology

The three-stage planning model provides considerable insight into the MIS planning issues. This should reduce confusion among competing planning methodologies. For example, it can prevent an organization from using a resource allocation methodology when an OIRA or strategic methodology is appropriate. However, the planning model does not indicate which of several methodologies categorized within a planning stage should be used for that planning stage.

There has been almost no research to evaluate the comparative advantages of one technique or combination of techniques over another. The three-stage MIS planning model has clarified the need for such research and provided a basis for grouping the methodologies for comparison. The selection of methodologies for different planning stages is an issue of research currently being pursued by the MIS Research Center at the University of Minnesota.

8. Conclusion

The three-stage model of MIS planning provides a framework for addressing critical issues and problem areas of MIS planning. The first stage of the model—strategic planning—addresses the problem of alignment of the MIS effort with the overall strategic objectives of the organization. The second stage—organizational information requirements analysis—addresses the problem of development of a long range information architecture for the organization. And the third stage—resource allocation—addresses the allocation of information system development and operational resources among competing applications.

The three stage-model provides a framework in which competing and diverse planning methodologies can be categorized. The model can thus lead to better MIS planning and aid MIS planning research.

Discussion Questions

1. Compare the three-stage model of MIS planning with the long-range planning approach described in the previous article. Are the concepts expressed in each essentially the same? Explain.
2. What is an information system architecture? What are some useful techniques for analyzing, developing, and selecting an information system architecture? Can you think of other techniques which might also be useful?
3. How is the three-stage model of MIS planning related to overall corporate strategy, corporate goals, and corporate objectives?

4. How are critical success factors and ends/means analysis used in deriving information requirements?

References

[1] H. I. Ansoff. "State of Practice in Planning Systems," *Sloan Management Review*, Vol. 18, Winter, 1977, pp. 1-24.

[2] R. N. Anthony, *Planning and Control Systems: A Framework for Analysis*, Division of Research, Graduate School of Business, Harvard University, Boston, Mass., 1965.

[3] L. Beard, "Planning a MIS: Some Caveats and Comtemplations," *Financial Executive*, Vol. 45, May, 1977, pp. 34-39.

[4] B. Bowman, G. B. Davis, and J. C. Wetherbe, "Modeling for MIS," *Datamation*, July, 1980, pp. 155-162.

[5] D. C. Burnstine, *BIAIT An Emerging Management Discipline*, BIAIT: International, Inc., New York, 1980.

[6] R. L. Bush, and I. E. Knutsen, "Integration of Corporate and MIS Planning: Its Impact on Productivity," Proceedings of Ninth Annual Conference of the Society for Management Information Systems, Chicago, Ill., 1977.

[7] W. M. Carlson, "Business Information Analysis and Integration Technique (BIAIT)—The New Horizon," *Data Base*, Vol. 10, No. 4, Spring, 1979, pp. 3-9.

[8] G. B. Davis, *Management Information Systems: Conceptual Foundations Structure, and Development*, McGraw-Hill Book Co., New York, 1974.

[9] G. B. Davis, "Strategies for Information Requirements Determination," *IBM Systems Journal*, Vol. 22, No. 1, 1982, pp. 4-30.

[10] S. Diamond, "Contents of a Meaningful Plan," Proceedings of the Tenth Annual Conference of the Society for Management Information Systems, Chicago, Ill., 1979.

[11] P. F. Drucker, *Management: Tasks, Responsibilities Practices*, Harper and Row, New York, 1974.

[12] P. Ein-Dor, and E. Segev, "Strategic Planning for Management Information Systems," *Management Science*, Vol. 15, November, 1978, pp. 1631-1641.

[13] A. J. Forster, "Effective Strategies and Techniques for the Development of MIS Master-Plans for Top Management Approval," Proceedings of the Tenth Annual Conference of the Society for Management Information Systems, Chicago, Ill., 1978.

[14] D. G. Gibson, and R. L. Nolan, "Managing the Four Stages of EDP Growth," *Harvard Business Review*, January-February, 1974, pp. 76-88.

[15] E. Gurry and R. Bove, "Effective Data Processing Planning," *CPA Journal*, Vol. 47, August, 1977, pp. 46-47.

[16] R. V. Head, "Strategic Planning for Information Systems," *Information Systems*, Vol. 25, October, 1978, pp. 46-47.

[17] C. Holloway and W. R. King, "Evaluating Alternative Approaches to Strategic Planning," *Long-Range Planning*, Vol. 12, No. 4, August, 1979, pp. 74-78.

[18] J. T. Hootman, "Basic Considerations in Developing Computer Charging Mechanisms," *Data Base*, Vol. 8, No. 4, Spring, 1977, pp. 1-13.

[19] IBM Corporation, *Business Systems Planning—Information Systems Planning Guide*, Publication No. GE20-0527.

[20] D. V. Kerner, "Business Information Characterization Study," *Data Base*, Vol. 10, No. 4, Spring, 1979, pp. 10-17.

[21] W. R. King, "Strategic Planning for Management Information Systems," *MIS Quarterly*, Vol. 2, No. 1, March, 1978, pp. 27-37.

[22] M. A. Lyles, "Making Operational Long-Range Planning for Information Systems," *MIS Quarterly*, Vol. 3, No. 1, January, 1979, pp. 16-21.

[23] F. W. McFarlan, "Problems in Planning the Information Systems," *Harvard Business Review*, Vol. 49, March-April, 1971, pp. 74-89.

[24] E. R. McLean, and J. V. Soden (eds.), *Strategic Planning for MIS*, Wiley-Interscience, New York, 1977.

[25] D. E. Mulvihill and B. J. Cohen, "Strategy Formulation and Information Systems: Setting Objectives," in *The Information Systems Handbook*, F. W. McFarlan and R. L. Nolan (eds.). Dow Jones-Irwin, Inc., Chicago, Ill., 1975, pp. 19-31.

[26] M. C. Munro and B. R. Wheeler, "Planning,

Critical Success Factors, and Management Information Requirements," *MIS Quarterly*, Vol. 4, No. 4, December, 1980, pp. 27-38.

[27] R. L. Nolan, "Managing the Computer Resource: A Stage Hypothesis," *Communications of ACM*, Vol. 16, July, 1973, pp. 399-405.

[28] R. L. Nolan, "Managing the Crises in Data Processing," *Harvard Business Review*, Vol. 57, March-April, 1979, pp. 115-126.

[29] P. A. Pyhrr, "Zero-Base Budgeting," *Harvard Business Review*, Vol. 48, November-December, 1970, pp. 111-121.

[30] J. F. Rockart, "Chief Executives Define Their Own Data Needs," *Harvard Business Review*, March-April, 1979, pp. 81-93.

[31] R. L. Rush, "MIS Planning in Distributed Data Processing Systems," *Journal of Systems Management*, Vol. 30, No. 8, August, 1979, pp. 17-26.

[32] M. H. Schwartz, "MIS Planning," *Datamation*, Vol. 16, No. 10, September, 1970, pp. 28-31.

[33] J. G. Shidal, "Long-Range DP Planning," *Journal of Systems Management*, Vol. 29, April, 1978, pp. 40-45.

[34] J. Soden, "Pragmatic Guidelines for EDP Long Range Planning," *Data Management*, Vol. 13, September, 1975, pp. 8-13.

[35] J. Soden, and C. Tucker, "Long-Range MIS Planning," *Journal of Systems Management*, Vol. 27, July, 1976, pp. 28-33.

[36] G. A. Steiner and J. B. Miner, *Management Policy and Strategy*, MacMillan Publishing Co., New York, 1977.

[37] W. Wedley, "New Uses of Delphi in Strategy Formulation," *Long Range Planning*, Vol. 10, December, 1977, pp. 70-78.

[38] J. C. Wetherbe and G. W. Dickson, "Zero-Based Budgeting: An Alternative to Chargeout," *Information and Management*, Vol. 2, No. 5, November, 1979, pp. 203-213.

[39] J. C. Wetherbe, and G. B. Davis, "Strategic MIS Planning Through Ends/Means Analysis," MIS Research Center Working Paper, 1982.

[40] J. A. Zachman, "Control and Planning of Information Systems," *Journal of Systems Management*, Vol. 28, July, 1977, pp. 34-41.

[41] J. A. Zachman, "The Information Systems Management System: A Framework for Information Systems Planning," Proceedings for the Ninth Annual Conference on the Society for Management Information Systems, Chicago, Ill., 1977.

[42] W. M. Zani, "Blueprint for MIS," *Harvard Business Review*, November-December, 1970, pp. 95-100.

READING 15

Technology is Not Enough

article by
BRANDT ALLEN

This should be the best of times for computer departments: installed capacity is increasing at better than 30% per year in the U.S. and even more in the largest and most advanced companies.[1] Demand for new applications is rising even faster. Pressures for increased productivity in our manufacturing, distribution, services, and especially the office together with renewed emphasis on improved quality for American products can only place even greater demands on computing organizations in the future. Indeed, the overall picture reads like a technologist's dream: huge backlogs, increasing demand, increasing price-performance of computers, new technology including that for the office, the plant and probably the home promising even greater potential, and inflation enabling the justification of more and more applications. It sounds almost too good to be true—and it is! In spite of these glowing prospects, many businesses today face problems so serious in their use of our wonderful technology that they threaten to jeopardize not only the bright futures of many of those computer professionals, but also that of the firms which employ them. Matters are at a crisis point in computing for many corporations. Technology, by itself, is not enough. Businesses face a tough set of computer problems today and in the future where the solutions are largely managerial in nature, and most are beyond the scope of the executive charged with managing the computing function. Key to these solutions is the formulation of a comprehensive strategy for the deployment of information resources with the firm, something that can only be done by senior management. Unfortunately, many of these people do not understand the problem.

Source: Reproduced by permission of the author, Brandt Allen, The Colgate Darden Graduate School of Business Administration, University of Virginia.

The Biggest Problems

Computer users today face a common set of problems and challenges:

The economics of computing have turned around—total costs for an application are now rising. The costs of computing have dropped steadily since business use began some thirty years ago, driven primarily by the dramatic improvements in the performance/price of processors and memory. And continuing improvements in this technology on the order of 25% per year can be expected for the rest of this decade, but these changes are nowhere near great enough to offset the rising cost of people necessary to support it all. The total cost of most applications today, including hardware, communications, software maintenance, and operations support has stopped declining and is about to rise even without considering the cost of development. An historic turning point in computing has been reached: the biggest cost element for an application today, or all applications together for that matter, is for people. The cost of the hardware will continue to drop steadily as a percentage of total costs; but the increasing cost of people will raise total costs of an application almost as rapidly as the underlying rate of inflation!

The shortage of applications and systems programmers is the major constraint for computer users today—it will become more severe in the years to come. The enormous demand for computing, even at increasing cost levels, requires growing numbers of new, entry-level employees; for example the Department of Labor has forecast that the employment for new programmers and systems analysts will increase 20% in the U.S. throughout the 1980's (Occupational Outlook Handbook). Other forecasts from the Bureau of Labor Statistics place the estimated jobs for new entry-level computer programmers in 1990 43% higher than that in 1980. In spite of these rosy forecasts, the supply of such people will probably decline over this same time period due to changing demographics in the U.S. Between 1981 and 1988 the number of young people (aged 20) entering the workforce will fall 20% (U.S. Department of Commerce). Along with this decline one can also expect a serious and depressing drop in aptitude for computer programming and systems work, at least insofar as can be measured by standardized tests. For example, math SAT scores of college-bound high school seniors dropped from 493 to 467 from 1968/69 to 1978/79 (College Entrance Examinations Board). Verbal scores dropped even more, from 463 to 427 for the same years. Compounding the problems of the present shortage of people as well as the shortfall to come is the alarming dropout or loss rate of employees from computing. For whatever reason, and there are many theories, the exodus of gifted employees from the ranks of application and systems programmers and systems analysts is very high. The shortage of people, not money or equipment or demand, will be the biggest constraint for computer users in the decade.

The pace of technological change exceeds the ability of many organizations to keep up—many today are falling behind, some are technologically obsolete. That we live in an age of rapid change is without doubt; that computers, communications systems, and office automation technology are some of the fastest changing parts of the business is also unquestioned. However, many managers seem unaware of the costs and dangers of such rapid change. First, this fast pace is a threat to employees. Many computer system personnel and their managers live in fear of the technology passing them by; too many have already fallen behind. To keep up requires a degree of training and education that many organizations are unable or unwilling to provide. Second, not only are individuals falling behind, but entire companies do as well. Businesses and government agencies with obsolete computers, old and outdated applications, and antiquated management practices based on late 1960's and early 1970's environment risk the continued existence of the firm itself in certain industries. As time goes by the best people leave and they fall farther and farther behind to the point where they cannot benefit from technology without taking great risks. Increasingly, one's business cannot incorporate the most modern and efficient manufacturing technology without up-to-date computer systems in place. Those who let their DP organization fall behind risk losing the entire company as well.

Senior managers do not have confidence in their ability to manage information resources—and they do not have confidence in DP management either. The crisis in computer systems starts at the top. Of all the important functions of a business, information systems is the one area where senior management lacks real experience and understanding. There are several explanations: for many executives, the computer is still a new technology that has been always treated as a specialized function in which their participation was minimal. Even today, an assignment in information systems is not on the career paths of general managers in most firms. Technology has changed so fast that what little managers do learn is quickly absolete. Finally, few senior managers have come from the computing field. As a consequence, we find senior executives managing information resources either defensively (minimize budgets and risks, go slow, do not innovate, use strict controls) or by remote control (lots of consultants, heavy turnover of senior DP staff, frequent changes of direction), always looking for some piece of magic that will suddenly make all the problems go away. The situation is made worse by the lack of comprehensive measures of performance and results that typify most DP shops.

Backlogs of applications awaiting development are large and growing—trends in development productivity are disappointing. While there is little agreement as to what a three year backlog actually is or what it means, most companies think they have such a situation or worse, and for most it is a big problem. Today some firms claim their backlogs are measured in man-centuries! Businesses are creating and approving new computer projects at a rate faster than their ability to actually develop and install those applications. In many companies the delay in getting projects even begun is indeed measured in years, especially if the applications have to be programmed by conventional methods. If the problems caused by big backlogs and increasing demand were not enough they have been compounded by the dismal record of productivity improvements many companies have realized in programming. Indeed, too often there has been no improvement at all. Today medium-sized computers cost about as much per hour as does a programmer, tomorrow it will be the programmers alone causing the bottlenecks because we shall surely get increased productivity from the technology. If means cannot be found to dramatically improve development productivity, backlogs will grow and grow. This tends to drive users to outside vendors, service bureaus, and software packages, or they respond by pushing for their own systems or for higher priority on their own pet projects—thus, putting great pressure on the DP organization, computer-steering committees, or both. These alternatives to the traditional company developed and operated computer applications are not necessarily ill-advised, but often users turn to them for the wrong reasons. Sometimes users simply give up and blame their failure to meet their business plans on lack of computer support.

Applications and data collections prove inflexible and difficult to change—a large part of the "computer problem" in most organizations stems from the poor products developed in the past. "Every change request gets to be a giant project that takes forever to complete and costs a fortune," is a universal complaint. Some blame it on programming languages, other claim it is because of their database system or even the database concept itself, while others say it is due to the shortsightedness of the original users and designers. Whatever the reasons, there is general dissatisfaction with the adaptability of information systems to changing requirements. Yet it is just this flexibility that is the crucial element of information systems, especially when one considers their high cost, and long development time and economic life—typically ten years or more. "Overall, they're just not doing the job," is a common judgment one hears everywhere.

Many core systems now need replacement—at a time when all resources are needed to whittle away at the backlogs. On top of large and growing backlogs, a great many companies now find many of their most basic core applications sadly out of date and in need of replacement. The replacement projects, reflecting expanded requirements, more advanced technology, and more stringent controls, often are considerably larger than the applications they replace. These replacement projects now loom as big, costly, high risk endeavors which will further delay work on the backlogs of totally new projects, and yet will only marginally improve the results of delivered products as perceived by the users. The U.S. Social Security Administration is a good case in point. Their benefits payment system is quite old, primarily batch, with large tape files and programs mostly written in assembly language. Their rewrite will be five years in the planning, seven in development and conversion, and when completed will then be expected to last late into the 1990's. The effort will require thousands of man years. While few businesses face conversions and rewrites of this magnitude, countless firms will be surprised at the burdens and risks of these big replacement projects.

Instead of establishing administrative procedures and tactical systems to manage information resources, steering committees have been formed to fill the gap—and they are not working well in many companies. Steering committees of one kind or another are widely used to review computer projects, set priorities, allocate scarce resources, propose budgets, and coordinate planning activities. Too often these committees are failures. Membership on such committees is often the most frustrating and time consuming assignment the manager has. Usually these failures result from a committee being used as a substitute for much needed administration practices, managerial systems, an overall structure, and a comprehensive information resources strategy.

The related technologies of telecommunications, office automation, and computer controlled manufacturing technology pose integration challenges almost overwhelming to many firms. While a few businesses have made great strides toward integrating not only their plans for this technology, but major pieces of it as well, the majority of firms still have not sorted out what they should do or how to go about it. It is quite common, even in large businesses, for computing and information systems to be under one head, word processing and other office automation projects under another, voice and message communications under a third, and for there to be no thought given to how, if at all, the various computer controlled equipments and processes of manufacturing or distribution are to be related, even though those machines are all information collecting and processing devices.

DP managers themselves are in trouble. Many DP managers today hold classic "no-win" jobs. They are caught in a squeeze between users who want more and more computer services and senior management concerned with costs and control. Many are trying to fight off outside service bureaus, mini- and micro-computer vendors who are courting their users, and even inside managers wishing to establish their own information systems groups. Unhappy users are the norm; irate users are common. In spite of increased budgets for development and new development tools, backlogs keep growing. There seems to be an invisible backlog at least as large as the visible one. Purchased packages prove difficult to implement to the user's satisfaction. Even with continued improvements in price/performance of processing and memory and bigger budgets for equipment, capacity problems never go away. The squeeze is most apparent in the budget process: user budgets grow and flex with departmental and divisional requirements, but the DP or computer department budget is normally fixed or capped. Information resources becomes the battleground between growth-oriented users and defensive, reactive senior managers. Overriding all of these concerns is the realization on the part of many of the senior DP managers, if not the majority, that they are in dead-end jobs; there is no next, higher job for them in their company. As an example, the person to whom they report, Executive Vice President, Vice President Administration, or Chief Financial Officer almost always holds a position they are not equipped to assume.

The Need for Strategy

Each of these problems is serious in its own right. Taken together they present a challenge so great as to jeopardize not only the computer systems of many firms but increasingly the very existence of the business itself. The 1980's will witness businesses in many industries which go on to succeed over their competitors due largely to their ability to manage the new technology and develop information systems of strategic importance to the company. Competitors will suffer and decline because they lack this ability. Obvious examples of organizations where information resources will become the key strategic factor are American Express, Master Card, and Merrill Lynch, but there are a great many others where the products and services that the firm can design and produce, the quality and cost structures of those products and services, and speed and responsiveness to changing market conditions will depend in large part on the quality, creativity, and flexibility of their information systems.

If there was ever a time for senior executives to be closely involved with information systems this is it, yet too often we find such managers active with matters of secondary importance: approving new projects, allocating scarce budget dollars to competing departments, reviewing the status of development projects, selecting vendors, approving software packages and the like. No doubt these activities are important and need to be decided with care, but they are largely operational or tactical in nature and are not the most important issues for top management attention. These topics are frequently forced onto the agendas of steering committees because senior management has failed to perform its primary task: to establish an overall strategy for information resources. Senior executives should spend their time addressing just four key strategic questions:

- How should information resources be organized and deployed within the firm?
- Where and how are information resources to be controlled?
- What overall architecture should one have for applications and data?
- What overall architecture should one employ for technology?

Organization Design

The key strategic planning question for information systems today is: how should we be organized?

- How many data centers should there be and to whom should they report?
- How should the development groups be organized, where should they be located within the business?
- What role should the corporate information department play vis-a-vis the various users?
- Should computing be brought together with office systems and communications and in what type of structure?
- Should planning be an activity separate from development and operations?
- How should the traditional data processing and basic business systems be organized relative to information reporting systems and decision support activities?

None of these questions can be answered until the company sorts out what responsibility for information resources each organizational participant (user department, systems developer, data center, planner) is to assume. Each must have a clear and comprehensive statement of mission and responsibility. Few companies have such a strategy.

Almost all organizations must decentralize increasing amounts of responsibility for information systems than was necessary in the past. Computers and their related technologies have become so pervasive that the simple organizational solutions of the past are no longer practical. No central group can hope to manage all this technology in a large or even medium-sized business. Even companies that have decentralized computing to a divisional or group level now find that they must go even further. End-user facilities, Decision Support Systems, Information Centers, and many of the new non-procedural programming systems all require more decision responsibility to be given to users, yet to be successful they all depend upon databases and other centrally-managed technology for their effectiveness.

The key organizational question today for many large companies is that of segmentation: what information resources should be structured centrally, what should be located elsewhere but managed and designed centrally, what should be managed locally, and how and where should the activities be linked? Difficult tradeoffs are required to properly balance the advantages of integration with costs of that integration. The costs are typically those of flexibility, adaptability, and the money and time required to respond to change. For example:

Electronics Company—This large multi-national firm is organized in a traditional decentralized profit center fashion with several dozen divisions. Data collections at corporate include only those needed to support contracting, external financial reporting, and the legal function. Applications related to that information are the responsibility of the corporate information systems group. All other data collections and supporting applications are by division except for the order entry function which spans the divisions and performs the billing and collections. Their segmentation is on three levels: corporate, distributed (linking the divisions for order entry), and divisional.

Control

The second element of computer strategy is that of control: who is to control which aspects of information resources, how is control to be effected, and how is performance to be assessed, and by whom? Key issues include;

- Who approves applications and sets priority? According to what basis or criteria?
- Who selects and approves new technology and on what basis?
- How are budgets set and who determines spending levels and constraints?
- How are outside sourcing decisions (and all "make or buy" decisions) made and by whom?
- Where and how are costs collected and charges rendered?
- What financial control structure is used for the data centers and development group?
- How is performance measured?
- What is the role of audit?

The primary options or choices are illustrated in Figure 1 (Allen, 1981). As depicted in the first column, responsibility for applications, budgets, and priorities is typically either vested in the information services department or function; shared between that department and the end users, but coordinated by a steering committee or several committees; or a user responsibility, either departmental or divisional (but not information services). The key control question is simply: who is responsible for assuring that this company's information systems are effective? The answer tells a lot about a company. Many firms do not have an answer, or responsibilities are overlapping or conflicting.[2]

A few examples may help to illustrate these options. A DP manager of a large firm came up to me at a conference recently and said, "I don't know why everyone here is so anxious to have steering committees. I'm the Director of Information Systems in my company and the title means just what it says. I'm responsible for seeing that we have the information systems that we need, just as the Director of Accounting has that responsibility for accounting systems. He doesn't have a steering committee for accounting and I'll be damned if we're gonna have one in my department." This is obviously an example of centralized control. At the other end of the spectrum are those companies where that same manager is called Director of Information Services and operates what amounts to an internal service bureau. Responsibility for identifying potential applications, evaluating and justifying them, and then funding or budgeting these applications is strictly a user responsibility.

With decentralized control, corporate systems are simply the responsibility of some corporate department, the so-called system "owner." In this situation, the corporate information services organization is not responsible for these key decisions on applications, priorities, and budgeting; they are not application owners. And there are a wide variety of organizations falling somewhere in between (bureaucratic) where a centralized DP function shares responsibility with various users for these key decisions. Such an approach to control is typically effected through the use of steering committees.

As depicted in the second column, the approach to budgeting reflects another important control choice for information services. In many firms the information services budget, once approved, remains fixed for the year, while in others it is variable or flexible depending upon user demand. In the latter situation, information services management is delegated the authority to increase expenditures if demand increases over what was originally budgeted, and they must also cut back if the reverse is true, although this rarely happens today. For most businesses the key question is how fast capacity will grow. The type of budget employed is really a question of whether budgetary control for DP rests with a corporate information services function or the users.

An example of a company with a flexible DP budget is illustrated below:

Manufacturing Company—A large industrial

Figure 1 Elements of Control Strategy

	Decision Responsibility for Applications Budgets, and Priorities	Type of Budget	Financial Structure for Information Resources	Objective of Charge-Out	Use of Outside Services
Centralized	Information Services	Fixed	Cost Center	Cost Awareness	Decision of Information Services
Bureaucratic	Steering Committee		Service Center	Cost Allocation	Approval of Information Services
Decentralized	Divisional or Departmental User	Flexible	Profit Center	Pricing	Local Option

products company provides information products and services to both divisions and corporate departments from a central tele-computer center in New York. Each division is a profit center; corporate staff departments are cost centers. Tele-computer charges these users for services provided and has no upper limit on their gross or total DP expenditures. However, they do have a limit or cap on the net or unrecovered portion of their budget for those activities that cannot be charged out. In effect they have a flexible budget. Budgetary control over computing in this company is a function of the budgeting and decision activities of the divisions and corporate staffs.

Closely related to the type of budget is the type of management control or financial control structure used for information services. Centralized control is typically achieved by operating information services as a cost center with a fixed budget; in decentralized control structures it is more likely to be an internal profit center with a flexible budget. Charge-out practices are another key control device. The objective of charge-out under centralized control is to provide cost information to various parties short of actually charging out costs. There is either no charge-out at all for development or operations, or it is of the "memo-record" variety. Bureaucratic control structures typically use cost allocation charge-out mechanisms either by monthly charge-backs of costs incurred or by budgeting machine rates and collecting job accounting statistics for billing. Charge-out in a decentralized control structure is more often a type of transfer pricing accomplished either by adding a margin to costs or in some way reflecting standard costs or market prices. Pricing here is usually monitored or reviewed by some function other than computer services, such as the controller.

Lastly, another key control issue is that of sourcing: in centralized structures the decision to purchase outside or to provide services from within is made by information services or DP, in bureaucratic structures it is frequently a steering committee decision with advice or approval from DP, while in decentralized control forms it is a user's option, frequently within previously established guidelines or standards.

It is essential that these various options be selected consistently. Decentralized control over applications, budgets, and priority-setting is best accomplished when Information Services has budget flexibility, is run more like a profit center than a cost center, and has an advanced pricing-oriented charge-out system. It makes little sense and could lead to very serious problems if an organization were, for example, to delegate applications, budgeting, and priority decisions to users, but attempt to use a fixed budget for information services while trying to structure it as a cost center with a break-even charge-out system. The result would be chaos.

The Architecture of Applications and Data

Closely related to the issues of organization and control is the question of overall architecture for applications and data. Although the concept of a Total Information System or Total Database has been long ago dismissed and with good reason because most of those efforts bogged down in detail, the need for a master plan has never been greater. This grand design must answer these questions:

- What will be the major data collections?
- How, if at all, should they be related?
- What types of application systems will feed them and draw on them; how are these to be related?

Data flows and information requirements typically mirror the organizational structure of the firm. Most large American businesses are organized on a decentralized or divisional basis, yet corporate and often group, or strategic business unit staffs, are significant and growing in both size and involvement in both planning and coordination activities.[3] The grand design for applications and data is not merely an extension of the basic corporate structure and way of operating the business day-to-day, it must be a key element of the way in which the business structure is defined and operations proscribed.

The data architecture, for example, must address issues as whether plant data such as inventory, orders, scheduling, shipping, billing, and purchasing should be located at the plant, or grouped together with other plants at the division or group level, or be at corporate, or how much should be where, and how the major elements should be linked, and why it should be done that way. This architecture must specify the core data processing applications, how they should tie together, and how they are to be integrated with the data collections. Other key issues in planning the applications architecture include which functions to automate (or the scope of applications), the use of shared systems and the mix of traditional data processing, information reporting, and decision support applications. Another strategic issue exerting a strong influence on applications and data architecture is the determination of what to attempt inhouse through the use of traditional, custom-tailored programming, what to contract out, what to purchase in package form, and what to implement through information-center or non-traditional programming means.

Too often DP managers mistake their current applications portfolio and databases for the grand design which they attempt to guard jealously. Unfortunately such rigidity is often painful because the requirements for new applications and data change rapidly. Business segments change quickly as markets and products evolve, as organizational units change and as managers come and go. Indeed, many vital aspects of the firm change much faster than do information systems. It takes months to construct a database, or to redo a major core application, or to convert DP operations from one type of technology to another. It takes years to restructure the applications and data architecture of a business.

Two brief cases illustrate what is meant by strategic architectural planning:

The Bank Holding Company—This bank is expanding by acquiring during the 1980's. Each bank has been run as an autonomous profit center. In the past each banks's DP operations were distinct, although they frequently shared application packages when convenient. Such a decentralized approach had been quite satisfactory during the 1970's and was largely the outgrowth of the holding company's acquisition program and method of operation, but the strategy has now changed. In the future, operations of the banks will be consolidated so as to offer common services on a state-wide and probably a regional basis. What was once a customer of one of the member banks will in the future be a customer of the integrated bank company. As a consequence, the new architecture envisions central collections of integrated customer information, probably segmented by type of customer, and integrated applications, bank-wide, linking formerly quite separate applications such as the deposit accounting, consumer loans, and cash management services.

An Energy Company—The situation at one of the large energy companies is considerably different. In the past all major applications were planned to support company-wide needs, and all data collections were centrally managed and tightly integrated to avoid redundancies and to insure commonality and accuracy. But the business structure is changing and the firm, now organized into operating companies, finds their various business activities and information requirements increasingly diverse. As a consequence they have changed their architecture to one based upon operating company and divisional data collections for operational information leaving corporate systems and databases only to support staff and corporate office needs. In time, even such core systems as general accounting and payroll will be broken up along divisional lines.

As these examples illustrate, the applications and data architecture of a firm is the primary determiner of the firm's future information services and products. In the words of Tregoe and Zimmerman, it is "the driving force" for information systems planning (1980).

The Architecture for Technology

In the past most firms provided data processing services from a central site, primarily for reasons of economy of scale (for both computing technology and staff) and to maintain control. If the firm was quite large, or operations geographically dispersed, or the firm operationally decentralized, one often found multiple data centers again with large host machines centrally managed within a designated segment of the business. Technology planning was basically a process of determining the number of central sites, their size and how, if at all, they were to be linked together, usually through some collection of dial-up and leased telephone lines. Today we still face these same issues, but the technological options are so much richer and the scope of architectural planning so much broader that firms today face the same requirement for an overall architecture or grand design within which technology planning can occur, the integration of computing, communications, office automation technology, and process control, as they do for applications. Key issues today include:

- The general mixture of large host computers, minis and micro computers best for the firm. Everyone requires some mixture of this technology, the question is what mix is best?
- The geographical siting of the technology.
- The technological plan for office systems. Again there is a question of mix: how much office system should be done on computers, how much on traditional office machines, and how much on the new technology just emerging from the laboratories.
- The technological plan for manufacturing, distribution, and services with respect to computer controlled processes. The role of Computer-Aided Design and Manufacturing Technology.
- How and where processing devices should be linked, how many networks there will be, and the mix of company and public carrier networking facilities to be used.
- Which software concepts to employ for operating systems, communications, databases, and programming.

This type of architecture requires a level of planning without resort to the details and specifications of specific equipments, operating systems, or communication protocols. For example:

A University has decided to continue to operate three primary data centers (research and academic computing, administration, and hospital/medical center) each with its own separate network, with a fourth and also separate network for voice and electronic mail, based on Rolm technology, and finally a mixture of stand alone word processors, micros, and minis for certain designated types of applications. This strategy was conceived and approved without specifying vendors, machines, operating systems, or database packages; indeed, they really do not know what the specifics will be, but there is considerable confidence in the architecture itself.

A U.S. Government Agency is about to choose one of three options for a technological strategy: a single large multiprocessor host configuration with nation-wide communications network, several regional host machines with regional networks and a central switching center, and the third option based on dozens of localized minis and a hostless interlinking network, probably employing satellite-based data transmission.

Determinants of Strategy

As depicted in Figure 2, the determinants of strategy for the information resources function include not only the business strategy, goals and objectives, and basic organizational structure of the firm, but also the enviornment external to the firm, the technological environment, and certain key constraints. The determinants are different for each organization. Examples of factors in the technical environment that could be key to strategy and especially the architectural issues include satellite data transmission capability, the home computer/terminal, the growth of the software industry and the availability of software packages, mass storage technology including optical stores, mini and micro processor developments, networking systems, and advanced programming languages, to mention just a few. External environmental factors important to the development of strategy could be the changing business environment of the firm such as the predicted restructuring of the U.S. banking environment, deregulation of the airlines, or possibly the trucking industry and legislation governing transnational data flows and privacy. Internal environmental considerations might include the existing portfolio of applications and data structures, and the expertise and experience of users and user managers. Constraints could include financial considerations, personnel limitations, and availabilities, and corporate policies governing personnel management.

Summary

Computers and their related technology do indeed promise almost unlimited potential to businesses today, but only to those who learn to manage them. Information systems are in trouble because of inadequate management practices, attention, and direction. Many organizations lack a strategy for information resources that properly reflects their future business and technological environment. They will soon discover that computer problems have a way of quickly becoming tomorrow's business problems.

Discussion Questions

1. Does long-range or strategic MIS planning imply that the concept of total systems is a viable one? If yes, explain how the arguments against total systems can be overcome. If no, explain how long-range MIS planning is different from the total systems approach.
2. What is the danger of using chargeout as a resource allocation and cost control-cost recovery approach?
3. What are the environmental forces which pose problems and challenges for the management of information systems?
4. What are the organizational factors which pose problems and challenges for the management of information systems?
5. What is the best strategy that might be employed to control information systems costs?
6. In what way is technology "not enough"?

References

Allen, B. "Computer Strategy: A Philosophy for Managing Information Processing Resources," *The Economics of Information Processing*, Lorin and Goldberg edition, Wiley, forthcoming 1981.

College Entrance Examinations Board, *National Report, College Bound Seniors*, 1979.

Occupational Outlook Handbook, 1980-81 Edition, U.S. Department of Labor, Bureau of Statistic, Bulletin 2075.

"Population Estimates and Projections," *U.S. Department of Commerce, Bureau of the Census*, Series P-25, No. 870.

Figure 2 Determinents of Information Resources Strategy

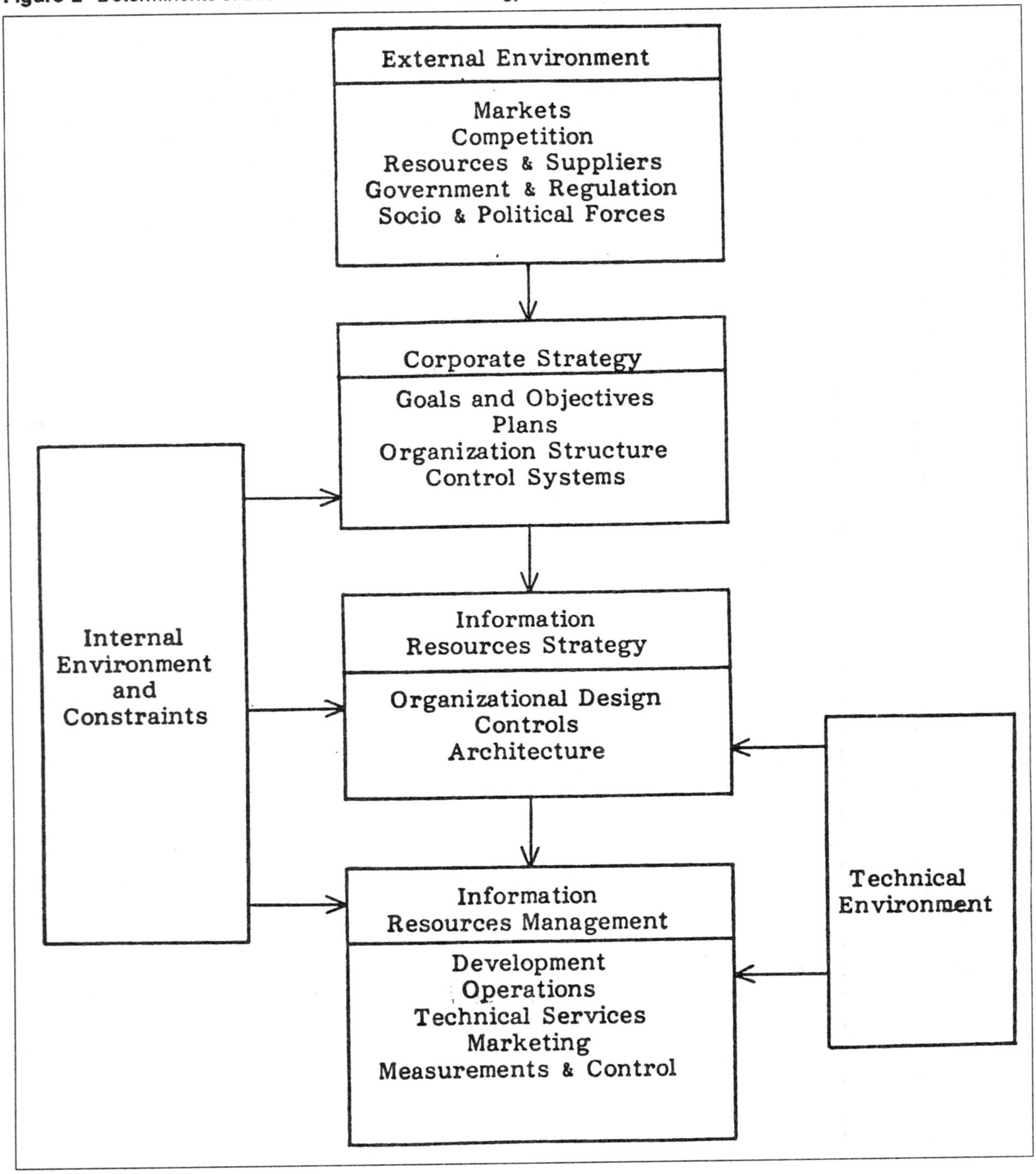

Tregoe, B. B. and Zimmerman, J. W. *Top Management Strategy: What It Is and How to Make It Work*, Simon and Schuster, New York, New York, 1980.

Footnotes

1. Throughout this paper the terms DP, computer, information resources, and information systems have been used interchangeably. "Information resources" is the more descriptive as it encompasses functions ranging from traditional data processing and information reporting to the technologies of office automation, networking, and process control in manufacturing as well as non-traditional applications such as Decision Support Systems and the Information Center concept.

2. For additional perspective on the issue of responsibility assignment for information resources, see Buchanan, J. R. and Linowes, R. G., "Understanding Distributed Data Processing," *Harvard Business Review*, July-August, 1980.

3. Richard Vancil in *Decentralization: Managerial Ambiguity by Design*, Dow Jones-Irwin, 1978, documents the apparent ambiguity of increasing decentralization of operational responsibility and increasing centralization of staff activities in large U.S. firms.

READING 16

Creating Competitive Weapons from Information Systems

article by
CHARLES WISEMAN and
IAN C. MACMILLAN

Metpath, a large clinical laboratory, competes in a tough commodity business where low differentiation of service has led to a lack of customer loyalty and frequent price discounting. Doctors send specimens to the labs for processing, and timely test results are often critical for diagnosis and treatment. Metpath has enhanced its customer service by installing computer terminals and linking them to its lab computers so that, for a small monthly fee, physicians can retrieve test results as soon as they are known.

From a purely technical point of view, this is an on-line database application. Strategically, however, Metpath is consciously using this information system as a competitive weapon in two ways: (1) to build barriers against new and existing competitors by raising the information system ante; (2) to gain advantage over other labs by differentiating an otherwise commodity service by keeping records of patient data on file and by offering financial processing services through billing and accounts payable applications. This differentiation is intended to secure the loyalty of physicians who normally have a tendency to switch from lab to lab in search of lower costs.

The Metpath system reflects a significant departure from the traditional purpose of information systems: to automate an organization's basic business processes like payroll, order entry, and accounts receivable or to satisfy the information needs of its managers and professionals for improved decision making.

Also far from traditional are the extended uses made by American Airlines and United Airlines of their computerized reservation systems, Sabre and Apollo, respectively. Developed in the mid-1970s at a cost of over $300 million, these information systems are no longer employed merely as neutral scheduling mechanisms to automate the seat

Source: Reprinted with permission from *Journal of Business Strategy*, Fall 1984, Volume 5, Number 2,

reservation process. Rather, they are used as weapons in the struggle for a competitive edge.

Sabre and Apollo give priority listing to American and United flights when travel agents request information on their computer terminals. An agent who uses the Sabre system and requests a listing of flights from New York to Los Angeles with stops in between knows that the first few screens may not show the most direct way, nor the least expensive way, but for sure they'll show the American way. In the computerized travel agency market, American and United dominate, with shares of 41 percent and 39 percent, respectively. (Over 80 percent of the nation's 20,000 travel agencies, accounting for more than 60 percent of airline ticket sales, are computerized.) In regions where the airline with the reservation system has numerous flights, the prioritization procedure can lead to as much as 20 percent additional business.

The two cases above involve *strategic information systems*—computerized information systems used to support an organization's competitive strategy, its strategy for gaining advantage over its competitors.

Emerging from the convergence of technological innovations in information processing (including telecommunications) and competitive forces reshaping industry landscapes, strategic information systems form a new variety of information system, radically different in organizational use from traditional management information systems and from the more recent decision support systems. As competition increases, information systems will become critical to gaining a competitive edge.

This article provides an instrument, called an "option generator," for identifying opportunities to gain a competitive edge, via use of modern information systems technology and, generally, by adding value to the products and services currently offered to clients.

Generating Strategic Options

The option generator helps vastly expand the search for strategic opportunities by asking planners to address the questions in Figure 1. Using this series of questions, a business unit can generate systematically more than 100 possibilities for using information systems to create a competitive edge. In the author's experience, not one company that has seriously attempted to find such an edge has failed to do so. This does not mean, however, that the advantage that is identified can be implemented without commitment of resources, particularly software development. But the option generator helps create a large number of possible opportunities to get the edge on competitors.

What is the Strategic Target?

The first and broadest set of options comes from the selection of a strategic target on which to focus the information systems advantage. Here a planner can pick one of three possible choices—the target can be a supplier, a customer, or a competitor. *Suppliers* include those who provide raw materials, capital, labor, or services. *Customers* include those who retail, wholesale, warehouse, distribute, or use the products sold. *Competitors* include those currently in the industry, possible new entrants, firms in other industries offering substitute products, or other organizations competing for scarce resources. The following examples illustrate strategic information systems targeted at the supplier, customer, and competitor arenas.

Supplier as Target

Equitable Life Assurance, the nation's third largest insurer, developed an on-line system to tie the firm's field offices with its seven regional offices, four warehouses, and corporate headquarters in New York. The warehouses stock all inventory items required by the company.

In the past, warehouse purchasing agents often lacked information to analyze vendor bids and determine the best buy. With the new inventory control and purchasing system, Equitable corporate purchases most of the inventory supplies from a distributor in New York and then offers them at a marked-up price to the warehouses. The warehouses are free to buy supplies from corporate or to go outside if they find a better deal. The information system gives them leverage during vendor negotiations, since they have on-line access to the

Figure 1 Major Options to Secure a Competitive Advantage

	Suppliers	*Customers*	*Competitors*
Differentiation			
Cost			
Innovation			

inventory database and can check the terms of all recent deals struck for items they want.

This is an example of a strategic information system targeted at a supplier group that has enabled Equitable to reduce the bargaining power of suppliers. The firm estimates that the system has saved it over $2 million a year, as well as increased the reliability and quality of deals it cuts with its suppliers.

Customer as Target

Wetterau, the fourth largest U.S. food wholesaler, has prospered by concentrating on small, independent supermarkets. Up to 1982, according to Ted Wetterau, the chairman, "the cornerstone of our whole business was that we would not service the chains."

But the slack economy of 1982 and a costly battle to defeat an unexpected takeover attempt in the fall of 1981 stalled the company's efforts to gain new business. Moreover, with the total number of independent grocers declining by 35 percent in 10 years (from 174,000 units in 1970 to 113,000 in 1980), Wetterau had to revise its strategy. For the first time, the St. Louis-based concern decided to offer its wide array of services and volume discounts to chains of 10 to 20 units.

The backbone of Wetterau's diversification move in its targeted retailer arena is its expertise and electronic check out scanners (point-of-sale terminals) and computerized inventory systems. Wetterau has more than 100 scanner-equipped stores on-line with its host computer, which updates prices, tracks reordering information, generates shelf labels, and performs many other functions (which supermarket executives are hesitant to reveal here because a competitive edge might be lost). In any case, this is the bait that the technologically undernourished chains might find too appetizing to resist; at least that's what the top management of Wetterau's seems to be betting on.

Competitor as Target

According to E. F. Hutton, packaged investment products accounted for 30 percent of its commission revenues last year, up from 4 percent five years ago. Packaged investments are bundled, often unique products targeted directly at the competitive offerings and designed to build customer loyalty and increase fee revenue. Financial service firms like Hutton use information systems as a "manufacturing process" to create tailored products.

The development of a recent CD fund gives a glimpse of the manufacturing process used to produce these new products. At 6 A.M., traders at a brokerage house called London to order sheafs of CDs from foreign banks, which often pay higher rates than their U.S. counterparts. By 11 A.M. they had accumulated $50 million of the paper. The next step in the fund-creation process depended on an information system that took the prices and rates, juggled them according to the firm's objectives and constraints embodied in its computer program, and arrived at management fees and commissions: Thirty-six hours after the start of this production run (job-shop style, to be sure) brokers were ready to start selling the fund.

Behind all the promotional hoopla surrounding

such new products in the financial services industry, there is generally an information system playing a critical role in product development, processing, or distribution. Shearson/American Express's managed commodity account, for example, has investments directed by a computerized portfolio management system. Merrill Lynch's Cash Management Account depends for its existence on database and laser technology.

Multiple Targets

Strategic information systems can be used to secure an edge with more than one target or to support activities in one arena so that advantage can be gained in another. The manager of General Electric's distribution center for large appliances in Kentucky uses an information system that helps GE keep down its substantial shipping costs so that its retailers can maintain competitive prices.

Xerox, Pratt & Whitney, General Motors, and others require their suppliers to provide computer-generated data on product quality, inventory levels, and the like for the items they supply. This is less an attempt to gain advantage over suppliers than a desire to produce more efficiently to meet competitive costs. But for the suppliers, the ability to respond to these new information systems-based demands from their customers might create a competitive advantage. As these large customers formulate supplier strategies in response to (especially international) competition, these strategies are often aimed at reducing the number of suppliers to a select few who can provide not only the desired components, but also valued-added services like quality-control reports. In this situation, a supplier's information system expertise can create a decisive edge in securing long-term contracts which would preempt the business from competitors.

What Strategic Thrust Can Be Used Against the Target?

Once a target has been selected, the option generator suggests three strategic thrusts: differentiation, cost, and innovation. This results in nine possible major options to secure a competitive advantage: a differentiation, cost, or innovation thrust targeted at suppliers, customers, or competitors (Figure 1). The aim of a *differentiation* thrust is to either (1) reduce the differentiation advantages that suppliers, customers, or competitors enjoy vis-a-vis your organization, or (2) increase the differentiation advantages you enjoy vis-a-vis your suppliers, customers, or competitors.

The aim of the *cost* thrust is to (1) reduce or avoid your costs vis-a-vis suppliers, customers, or competitors, (2) help your suppliers or customers reduce or avoid their costs so that you gain preferred treatment from these stakeholders, or (3) increase your competitors' costs.

The aim of the *innovation* thrust is to find new ways of doing business through the use of information systems. These new ways include, but certainly are not limited to, the use of information systems to transform steps on an existing industry (value-added) chain, diversify into new industries or markets, redefine the existing business, or create new businesses. Innovative strategic information system applications like the airline reservation systems developed by American and United, or the cash management account of Merrill Lynch, are preemptive strikes. They are major moves made ahead of the competitors, which allow the firms to secure advantageous positions from which they are difficult to dislodge because of advantages they have captured by being first movers [5].

The following examples illustrate uses of the three basic thrusts of differentiation, cost, and innovation.

Differentiation as the Thrust

The air traffic controller's strike illustrates the use of information systems to *reduce* the differentiation advantages of labor, in this case the controllers. Prior to striking, controllers were seen as highly trained specialists in short supply. The federal government's decision to dismiss the strikers was based in part on the availability of a new flow control information system.

According to labor relations expert Harley Shaiken of MIT, what doomed the strike was the "government's skillful use of a new weapon—information systems technology—to keep air traffic moving, gutting the strikers' leverage."

Soon after the walkout, 75 percent of the commercial flights were operating while 75 percent of the controllers were marching on the picket line.

By performing many of the controllers' tasks, the information system dramatically reduced the controllers' bargaining power, making the skill they had less valuable. Though air traffic control is *still* a skilled occupation, the pool of new applicants has been widened because the required level of expertise and training has been reduced. With reduced supplier differentiation advantages come lower buyer costs, so the price of controller labor has fallen.

This next example shows how Pacific Intermountain Express (PIE) *increased* its advantage through differentiation. PIE, a 63-year-old trucking firm based in California, competes in the newly deregulated, commodity-like trucking industry. To attract customers, PIE has developed an information system that allows shippers to call the computer to track the status of a shipment. This is important for misplaced or delayed shipments, emergencies, etc. Strategically, it created a way for PIE to differentiate its service from its competitors' and to attract shippers, thus increasing its profit opportunities. As W. D. Beatenbough, president of PIE, put it, "In trucking today, we all use the same highways and the same freight terminals. Our only competitive advantage is to stand out technologically."

Cost as the Thrust

To support a cost reduction thrust in the customer arena (in contrast to Equitable's cost reduction thrust described above in the supplier arena), the Hartford Insurance Company provides customers who have complex exposures and multiple claims with a computer-generated loss control analysis. Breaking out losses by location, time of day, type of accident, and so on, this information system pinpoints accident causes and, after preventive measures are taken, can lead to substantially lower premium costs for customers and, therefore, more business for Hartford.

Innovation as the Thrust

Toys "R" Us, the number one toy chain in the United States, has captured an impressive 11 percent share in the toy market. With over 165 stores, the company relies on a sophisticated information system to keep track of what's selling so that it can take quick markdowns to rid itself of slow movers. This information system is not the only reason for the chain's rapid rise to the top in this highly competitive industry: spacious parking lots, well-organized stores, and good management also count. But the information system is an essential ingredient.

Toys "R" Us selected the innovative thrust by using the information system's expertise and resources the company had developed in the toy market to support its diversification into the children's apparel market. When the spinoff Kids "R" Us was formed, response from the competition was immediate. "The new chain has upset everyone in the market," according to a spokesman from a group of 285 specialty and department stores nationwide. Clearly, Toys "R" Us is using the same information systems-based strategy it employed successfully in the toy market to enter the children's apparel sphere.

What Strategic Mode Can Be Used?

Once a strategic target and thrust have been selected, the next set of options is generated by asking which opportunities can be created by selecting a strategic mode: Are there opportunities to employ information systems *offensively* to increase an edge or *defensively* to reduce an edge now held by one of the targets? The following examples illustrate the offensive and defensive modes.

Offensive as the Mode

The offensive use of information systems against competitors is illustrated by some of the extensions of the airline reservation systems mentioned above. For example, the new cut-rate airlines contend that American and United overcharge them just to be listed. Airlines without their own system complain that the intricacies of Sabre and Apollo often stymie attempts to create innovative packages. As one rival put it, "If you're out of sync with their reservation system, then whatever you're doing won't exist." Finally, Braniff and Continental have argued that their recent cash flow problems are due in part to these automated reservation systems: When multiple carriers are involved, the first carrier in the itinerary is considered the ticketing airline, so it collects all the revenues, but repays the others only when the flight is over.

Defensive as the Mode

The previously cited case of the flow control system developed by the U.S. Department of Transportation illustrates the defensive mode of the differentiation thrust targeted at suppliers. Targeting customers instead, a Chicago law firm used its telephone information system, which monitors calling activity, to discover that it was substantially underbilling clients because its lawyers were careless about recording time spent on the telephone with clients.

What Direction of Thrust Can Be Used?

The involvement of both line and information systems executives is critical for the development of strategic information systems. In the selection of the information system direction, this is paramount. The direction indicates whether the strategic information system will be used by the organization or be provided by it as the output, and high expertise in information systems technology and resources is required to identify *usage* and *provision* opportunities. Note again that none of the options produced by the options generator is mutually exclusive (e.g., a strategic information system may be used by the firm *and* provided to stakeholders). The aim is merely to trigger ideas about options available: In fact, the more ideas the merrier. The following examples illustrate the usage and provision directions of strategic information systems.

Usage as the Direction

Scholastic Magazine, a 60-year-old publisher of elementary and secondary school materials and a subsidiary of Xerox, faces mounting pressures due to decreasing school enrollments and budgets. New product development and marketing skills are two key factors of success for *Scholastic* in the 1980s.

To meet its new challenges, the company maintains a marketing database with information on its product sales, 16,000 school districts, teachers and students who have bought its products, millions of U.S. households (i.e., census-derived demographic data), and so on. This marketing information system produces sales penetration ratios (e.g., sales/teacher, sales/student, etc.), district profiles, and the like.

Scholastic uses this information system to fine-tune the efforts of its 100 sales representatives. But the most critical use of this system is in direct mail, the major method it uses to reach the school market. *Scholastic* mails over 50 million items a year using its marketing information system as one would a telescopic lens on a rifle. Without it, like many of its competitors who lack such a system, *Scholastic* would be shooting in the dark. With it, they are able to define market segments exactly and to aim at their targets with a high degree of confidence.

Provision as the Direction

In 1977, Merrill Lynch announced its innovative Cash Management Account (CMA), an information system-based product that *provided* under one umbrella three appealing services to investors: credit through a standard margin account, cash withdrawal by check or Visa debit card, and automatic investment of cash, dividends, and the like, in a Merrill-managed money market fund. Without a 162-step (subsequently patented) computer program and the firm's resources in database and laser printing technology, the product would never have gotten off the ground.

Merrill sold the CMA through its brokers to investors with minimum balances of $20,000. The exponential growth of the CMA (180,000 accounts in 1980, 560,000 in 1981, and over 900,000 in 1982) was fueled by free-trip prizes to Hawaii and Puerto Rico that Merrill offered to the brokers who sold the most CMAs. These efforts brought in over 450,000 new accounts that had not been with Merrill previously. Merrill reaps over $60 million a year in fees for the more than $20 billion it manages in the three money market funds associated with the CMA product.

With this innovative information system-based product, Merrill preempted the market with a monopoly position for four years. Competition from other financial services organizations did not appear until 1981, and at the close of 1982. Merrill's closest rival, Dean Witter, had only 90,000 customers for its Active Asset Account. Only in 1983 did Merrill's premier position erode when banks and other financial service organizations finally entered the market with similar products and the information systems technology needed to develop them.

What Information System Skills Can We Use?

The last set of options by which to seek advantage lies in the choice of information system skills. Fundamentally, all information system applications require at least one of three generic skills: information processing, information storage, or information transmission. The competitive advantage must be created from an application of these skills. Note again, these options are not mutually exclusive. That is, a strategic information system can process *and* store, store *and* transmit, and so on. The following examples illustrate options that capitalize on processing, storage, or transmission skill.

Processing as the Skill Used

The information system-based product launched by National Decisions Systems is called "1980 U.S. Census." It consists of five volumes of statistical data derived from Census Bureau computer tapes that are sold at less than cost by the Bureau. National Decisions added value by developing programs to generate analyses and displays from the raw data. This new product is sold to those involved in market research, demographic analysis, and so on. In this marketplace, National Decisions enjoys first mover advantages.

Storage as the Skill Used

Ford Motor Company, working with AT&T's Information Systems division and its new digital network product, Net/1000, has developed an auto parts inventory system for its dealers. Data is stored on Net/1000 and made available to dealers who need auto parts for repairs. The system allows dealers who may have incompatible computers or terminals to search each other's inventories. The net effect is improvement in customer service and an increase in dealer loyalty, an important consideration for automobile manufacturers in this period of intense global competition.

Transmission as the Skill Used

Dun and Bradstreet, the information service and publishing conglomerate, has a new, valued-added product aimed at the Fortune 1000 market. It is a delivery system for the firm's on-line databases.

The product allows users to access all D&B databases with one standard procedure through its packet-switched network, DunsNet. It includes IBM personal computers, bundled with fourth generation languages and graphics software, and is targeted for financial departments. Many of these departments are customers of D&B's software subsidiary, McCormack and Dodge Corp., a supplier of general ledger, accounts receivable, and other financial software products.

Systematically Identifying Strategic Information Systems

Developing an effective information system is not done without effort. To achieve maximum benefit requires a joint effort on the part of line management and information systems managers. The best way to do this systematically is to have them *jointly* develop a competitive strategy for the business unit. As most planners are well aware, this process involves (1) assessing the current competitive strategy and position, (2) assessing environmental factors affecting the business, and (3) developing a strategy to meet the anticipated challenges over the planning period. What is less obvious is that substantial strategic information system opportunities can be uncovered at all stages in the process.

The competitive strategy process begins by establishing a working definition of the unit's business, which captures the current scope of its activities and shows how it differentiates itself across segments and from its competitors. By analyzing the unit's products and markets, one can pin down current scope: customer groups served, customer needs satisfied, and technologies employed to meet customer needs [1]. However, in this stage many opportunities to create information system advantages can be uncovered, and opportunities to identify strategic targets, thrust, and modes can be identified.

In the next stage, similar opportunities arise. After a working definition of the business has been formulated, the existing and potential competitors are identifed and comparisons made of the unit's performance to its principal competitors'. The purpose is to determine the extent of one's competitive advantages if they exist [2]. In this stage, opportunities to provide or use information systems, drawing on one's processing, storage, or transmission skill, can be identified—particularly if information system managers are participating in the process.

After an assessment of competitive strategy and position, a Porter-type [4] industry analysis of the competitive environment creates opportunities to identify possible innovative uses of information systems. Analysis of the $4 billion fragmented junkyard (i.e., automotive salvage) industry might reveal, for example, consolidation opportunities. The industry already uses computers to handle inventory, to aid in purchase decisions made at salvage auctions, and to prevent loss of sales because sales people don't know whether a part is in stock.

An entrepreneurial firm clearly has the opportunity to build a national service company to stock, locate, and deliver used parts to any U.S. city within 24 hours. Insurance adjusters who make 50 to 70 million requests a year for parts would certainly be eager customers for such a service, a service that could never become operational without an information systems-based service.

Attention paid to environmental variables (economic, social, demographic, and governmental) [3] should also stimulate the search for other strategic information system applications. A trend of increased governmental regulation might be the impetus for developing information systems to cut through the bureaucratic morass that slows down new product introductions.

In the stage of developing a competitive strategy for the business unit, after internal and external assessments have been made, an important step is to decide whether a redefinition of the business is called for. If so, an essential ingredient of this redefinition might be an information systems component, as it was for Reuters, the international news-gathering service based in London. Reuters redefined its business in the early 1970s by developing a computerized information and retrieval system targeted for banks, stock and commodity traders, and other businesses. The system provided the latest prices from stock, bond, money, oil, commodity, and other international markets. Additional economic services were added as the business evolved.

At the heart of the system is the Reuter's monitor, a video screen and keyboard that gives immediate access to financial and general news databases. Today, there are over 11,000 subscribers in over 60 countries. This information system-based service accounted in 1981 for over 85 percent of Reuter's sales ($254 million) and 100 percent of its profits ($30 million, pretax).

Alternatively, a firm could use its information systems capabilities for a corporate strategy of diversification-through-acquisition. The example of McKesson Corporation's entry into the embryonic distribution industry for personal computer software illustrates this opportunity. The current industry leader is Softsel Computer Products (1983 sales estimate: $75 million), followed by Micro D (1983 sales estimate: $28 million), and SKU Inc. (1983 sales estimate: $25 million). The market for personal computer software, now at $2.1 billion, is projected to reach $11.7 billion by 1988, with 25 percent handled by distributors. It is "the nation's fastest-growing distribution business," according to T. E. Drohan, president and chief executive officer of McKesson Corporation, a $4.08 billion distributor of drugs and health care products, alcoholic beverages, and industrial chemicals. McKesson has acquired SKU with the intent to expand the scope of its distribution business. This move is expected to transform the cottage industry of software distribution (with after-tax margins of at most 4 percent) into a larger, more profitable game. McKesson is using previously developed information systems as the synergistic fuel for its entry vehicle. The computerized order entry systems and other proprietary products it provides to over 16,000 mass merchandisers, supermarkets, and other outlets, will be tailored to this new marketplace. These information systems will not be used merely as aids to improve efficiency but as weapons to shape competitive strategy.

McKesson has proved to be an innovative user of information systems. Through the use of information systems, it has differentiated itself from its rivals and diversified successfully into adjacent industries. "The name of the game," says CEO Drohan, "has become adding value to distribution. Our primary goal is to set ourselves apart from the competition in dramatic enough ways that we become the first distributor a supplier thinks of. At the other end, by tying your customers to you as tightly as possible, you get more and more of his business as he grows."

If the past is prologue to the future, current and new participants in the software distribution industry can expect McKesson to use its information systems to increase its competitive advantage by:

- Establishing on-line links with software suppliers and retailers.
- Providing information to suppliers and retailers to help them better manage inventories, collect and analyze market data, and sales campaigns.
- Providing retailers with shelf management plans, price labels, inventory systems, and the like.
- Conducting computer-related technical seminars for suppliers and retailers.
- Joining with software suppliers to develop new products.
- Marketing associated services through its network.

In the process of developing a competitive strategy for one's business unit, one can equally well identify similar opportunities by systematic use of the key questions in Figure 2.

Figure 2 Option Generator

1. What is our strategic target?
   Suppliers Customers Competitors
2. What strategic thrust can be used against the target?
   Differentiation Cost Innovation
3. What strategic mode can be used?
   Offensive Defensive
4. What direction of thrust can be used?
   Usage Provision
5. What information system skills can we use?
   Processing Storage Transmission

Implications

In developing information system opportunities, there are several points to remember. First, the systematic search for strategic information systems opportunities should be conducted within the context of competitive strategy development. Only then can the business unit be sure that it has systematically and comprehensively explored all options.

Second, the active participation of information system professionals is necessary if the business unit is to identify all strategic information systems opportunities and to defend against strategic information systems' threats from its competitors. Creating information system advantages consumes resources, so it is best to actively involve the specialists as early and as intensively as possible—the rewards tend to exceed the costs.

Third, the role of the unit's information systems group, important as it is for identifying strategic information system opportunities, is critical for implementing any competitive strategy that must be supported by all but the most primitive information systems. Unless information systems planning is synchronized with the business unit's strategy, the unit will face misalignments of resource allocation, incorrect priority setting, and delays in system delivery that might well put its strategy in jeopardy. To ensure alignment of information systems development and the execution of the competitive strategy, full communication between line business managers and information systems managers must be ensured [6].

Finally, like the experimental physicists who discovered a new class of atomic particles with the aid of a formal framework for their search (in this case Dirac's theory of matter) and instruments designed from the theory, business and information systems managers now have a framework (competitive strategy) and an instrument (the options generator) to uncover new options for competitive advantage. Just as the physicists who scanned bubble-chamber photographs in search of the particles Dirac's theory had predicted knew what they were looking for and could search systematically for it, so too can a business unit search for information systems opportunities to gain a decisive edge. With more than 100 options to search for, it would be very surprising if a business unit did not find at least one.

Discussion Questions

1. From what perspective is this article written—the MIS executive or senior functional management?
2. What is the role of senior functional management in planning and developing corporate strategy? What is the appropriate role of the MIS executive?
3. What are some important prerequisites for creating competitive weapons from information systems?
4. What are the two key questions to consider in identifying strategic use of information systems?

References

1. Abell, D. *Defining the Business: The Starting Point of Strategic Planning.* Englewood Cliffs, N.J.: Prentice Hall, 1980.
2. Hax, A., and N. Majluf. "The Use of the Industry Attractiveness-Business Strength Matrix in Strategic Planning." Cambridge, Mass.: MIT, Sloan School of Management, 1982.
3. Hofer, C., and D. Schendel. *Strategy Formulation: Analytical Concepts.* St. Paul, Minn.: West Publishing, 1978.
4. MacMillan, I. "Preemptive Strategies," *Journal of Business Strategy*, Fall 1983, pp. 16-26.
5. Porter, M. *Competitive Strategy: Techniques for Analyzing Industries & Competitors.* New York: Free Press, 1980.
6. Wiseman, C. *Strategy and Computers: Information Systems as Competitive Weapons.* Homewood, Ill.: Dow Jones-Irwin, 1985.

READING 17

Information Systems For Competitive Advantage: Implementation of a Planning Process

article by
NICK RACKOFF, CHARLES WISEMAN and WALTER A. ULLRICH

Gaining Competitive Advantage

The principal role that information systems have performed in the past has been one of operational and management support. But recently companies have begun using information systems strategically to reap significant competitive advantage.

American Hospital Supply, being the first to install online order entry terminals in hospitals, now dominates the medical supply business. Merrill Lynch, with its Cash Management Account, dependent on database and laser printing technology, preempted the market with its innovative product. American and United Airlines, through their computerized reservation systems, Sabre and Apollo, established an edge that other air carriers have found impossible to overcome.

The significance of these computer-based products and services lies neither in their technological sophistication nor in the format of the reports they produce. Rather, it is found by examining the role they play in their firm's quest for competitive advantage. The cases just mentioned are instances of *strategic information systems* (SIS)—information systems used to support or shape an organization's competitive strategy, its plan for gaining and/or maintaining advantage.

American Hospital Supply's system yielded advantage by locking-in its customers. Sabre and Apollo gave priority listings to the two carriers when agents checked their screens for flights. The advantage has been so great that competitors have appealed to the government and the courts for relief. In addition, the systems have become vehicles for diversification and growth, propelling their developers into entirely new lines of business such as telemarketing. Merrill Lynch's Cash

Source: Reprinted by special permission of the *MIS Quarterly*, Volume 9, Number 4, December 1985, pp. 285-294.

Management Account, an innovative product made possible by an SIS alliance with the enterprising Banc One of Columbus, Ohio (that processes CMA debit card and check transactions), enabled the brokerage house to sign up over one million customers (10 times its nearest rival) and reap more than $60 million annually in fees.

Although the use of information systems may not always lead to industry domination, it can serve as an important weapon in a firm's strategic arsenal. Up to now, companies have uncovered SIS in an ad hoc fashion, without the benefit of a planning methodology designed specifically for the purpose. But as the pace of competition accelerates in the 80's, competitive leaders must develop a more systematic approach for identifying SIS opportunities.

This article presents the approach developed and implemented at GTE. It is a comprehensive method for generating a multitude of SIS ideas and selecting the most promising prospects for yielding substantial competitive advantage.

From the Conventional to the Strategic Perspective

The dominant view on information systems planning has for decades focused exclusively on the internal functions of the business. But this conventional perspective, powerful as it is for some purposes, cannot account for the SIS examples cited above in which information technology was used to gain competitive advantage. To understand why the conventional perspective is unsuited for identifying SIS, we need first to examine its theoretical underpinnings.

In the conventional view, the *targets* of information system applications are the organization's planning and control processes. These processes, described by Robert Anthony in his classic book, *Planning and Control Systems* [1], include: strategic planning (processes related to the organization's objectives, resource allocation policies, etc.); management control (processes related to assuring that strategic objectives are attained); and operational control (processes related to assuring that tasks are executed efficiently).

Anthony's model provides the foundation for identifying conventional information systems. The model was first applied in the information management field by Zani [17]. His work spotlighted areas in need of more penetrating analysis. In the 1970's and 80's, academics, and others working on conceptual frameworks for information systems, explored in greater depth topics merely mentioned in passing by Zani. Gorry and Scott Morton [2] and Keen and Scott Morton [4] focused on systems designed especially for managerial decision making. Nolan [7, 8, 9], IBM planners [3], King [5, 6], and Rockart [12, 13] concentrated on information systems planning topics. Rockart and Treacy [10, 11] specialized in systems targeted for top managers.

While the conventional perspective based on Anthony's model has served well to identify opportunities to improve internal business functions, it does not lead directly to the discovery of competitive uses of information technology. To uncover SIS opportunities, we need a new foundation for information systems planning, a foundation based in the world of competitive strategy, rather than in the arena of planning and control. This new foundation draws on some of the concepts developed by Porter in his book, *Competitive Strategy* [14].

Porter views business as being pressed by five competitive forces: the threat of new entrants, the intensity of rivalry among existing firms, the pressures from substitute products, the bargaining power of buyers, and the bargaining power of suppliers. He further proposes three generic strategies with which to combat these forces: differentiation (distinguish your company's products and services from others in all market segments), cost (become the low cost producer in all market segments), and focus (concentrate on a particular market segment and then either differentiate or become the low cost producer in that segment).

While Porter's model is helpful in thinking about the firm's competitive environment and the generic strategies a firm may follow, we have found it necessary to develop a more comprehensive framework, which we call *the theory of strategic thrusts*, for identifying SIS opportunities (see Figure 1).

Strategic thrusts are major competitive moves (offensive or defensive) made by the firm. It is our

Figure 1 Framework for Identifying SIS Opportunities

Strategic Target (columns) / **Strategic Thrust** (rows)

	Supplier	Customer	Competitor
Differentiation			
Cost			
Innovation			
Growth			
Alliance			

contention that the multitude of such moves reduce to five basic thrusts:

1. **Differentiation**—Achieve advantage by distinguishing your company's products and services from competitors, or by reducing the differentiation advantage of rivals.
2. **Cost**—Achieve advantage by reducing your firm's costs, supplier's costs, or customer's costs, or by raising the costs of your competitors.
3. **Innovation**—Achieve advantage by introducing a product or process change that results in a fundamental transformation in the way business is conducted in the industry.
4. **Growth**—Achieve advantage by volume or

geographical expansion, backward or forward integration, product-line or entry diversification.

5. **Alliance**—Achieve advantage by forging marketing agreements, forming joint ventures, or making acquisitions related to the thrusts of differentiation, cost, innovation, or growth.

Information technology can be used to support or shape the firm's competitive strategy by supporting or shaping strategic thrusts. Strategic thrusts, therefore, constitute the mechanisms for connecting business strategy and information technology. The theory of strategic thrusts is developed in detail in Wiseman's book, *Strategy and Computers: Information Systems as Competitive Weapons* [16].

These thrusts strike at three classes of *strategic targets*:

1. **Supplier targets**—Organizations providing what the firm needs to make its product, for example, those providing materials, capital, labor, services, and the like.
2. **Customer targets**—End users as well as organizations (e.g., middlemen, physical distributors, financial institutions, etc.) purchasing the firm's product for its own use or for sale to end users.
3. **Competitor targets**—Organizations selling (or potentially selling) products judged by customers to be the same as, similar to, or substitutable for the firm's products.

The SIS Planning Process at GTE

Description of GTE

GTE, a diversified, international telecommunications and electronics company with 185,000 employees and revenues over $14 billion, provides local telephone service in 31 states, two Canadian provinces, and the Dominican Republic. GTE Sprint operates the third largest long-distance telephone system in the U.S., and GTE Telenet runs a nationwide, packet-switched data communication network. In addition, GTE manufactures and markets a complete line of communication equipment, systems, and services, more than 6,000 types of Sylvania lamps and other lighting products, and precision metal, plastic, and ceramic materials used in electrical and electronic devices.

The largest business division, domestic telephone operations (TELOPS), contributes revenues of more than $9 billion, almost 90% of GTE's income. It consists of a corporate group, seven telephone companies, and a data services organization—GTE Data Services (GTEDS)—which provides information systems and services to the TELOPS units. Headquartered in Tampa, GTEDS has its own president who is also a TELOPS' corporate vice president. The methodology described below has been applied principally at TELOPS and the results discussed refer to this group. Preliminary efforts are underway to apply the SIS planning process at other GTE business units.

Overview of SIS Planning Process

GTEDS' information management (IM) planning staff realized the importance of the strategic perspective on information systems and took on the challenge of developing and implementing a planning process based on this point of view. They saw the task as two-fold:

1. Introduce management to this new perspective and secure its support
2. Create a mechanism for generating and evaluating SIS proposals.

To accomplish these ends, they designed a five-phase SIS planning process (see Table 1) that moved from an initial dissemination of SIS ideas and identification of opportunities to a final acceptance by members of the TELOPS' senior management team. The last step in the process resulted in a portfolio of SIS applications (not described here for reasons of confidentiality) earmarked for implementation.

SIS Planning Process

In phase A, the head of TELOPS' information management planning function introduced GTEDS' president to the SIS concept through a series of informal meetings and memoranda on the subject.

Table 1 SIS Planning Process

Phase	Activity	Content	Purpose
A	INTRODUCE IM CHIEF EXECUTIVE TO SIS CONCEPTS	Overview of SIS concepts; cases of SIS applications in other companies	Gain approval to proceed with SIS idea-generation meeting for IM group
B	CONDUCT SIS IDEA-GENERATION MEETING FOR IM MIDDLE MANAGEMENT	Execute SIS idea-generation methodology; evaluate SIS ideas	Test SIS idea-generation methodology; identify significant SIS ideas for executive consideration
C	CONDUCT SIS IDEA-GENERATION MEETING FOR IM EXECUTIVES	Execute SIS idea-generation methodology; evaluate SIS ideas	Identify SIS ideas and evaluate these together with ideas from previous meeting
D	INTRODUCE TOP BUSINESS EXECUTIVE TO SIS CONCEPT	Overview of SIS concept and some candidate SIS ideas for the business	Gain approval to proceed with SIS idea-generation meeting for business planners
E	CONDUCT SIS IDEA-GENERATION MEETING FOR CORP. BUSINESS PLANNERS	Execute SIS idea-generation methodology; evaluate SIS ideas	Identify SIS ideas and evaluate these together with ideas from previous meetings

The purpose here was to win top-level support for the project and approval for the next two phases.

In phases B and C, GTEDS' information management planning staff ran offsite idea-generation meetings aimed at developing the strategic perspective on information systems and identifying SIS opportunities. These sessions involved two groups of information systems professionals. In phase B, participants were drawn from the data processing company's cadre of middle managers; in phase C, attendees were the top information management executives within the local telephone companies and GTEDS.

The successful completion of phases A-C led to a meeting (in phase D) between GTEDS' president and TELOPS' top business executive. The latter was introduced to the SIS concept and told of the opportunities already discovered at the previous two brainstorming sessions. This meeting set the stage for phase E, an SIS idea-generation meeting with TELOPS' corporate business planners, those responsible for initiating the business' strategic thrusts.

The idea-generation meetings, which occurred at phases B, C, and E of the SIS planning process, consisted of seven explicit steps (see Table 2) designed to introduce the strategic perspective on information systems, stimulate the systematic search for SIS opportunities, and evaluate and select a set of projects expected to secure the greatest competitive advantage for the firm. A description of each of the steps follows.

Step 1. Present Tutorial on Competitive Strategy and SIS. The tutorial was led by a consultant expert on the theory of strategic information systems. The tutorial emphasized the concepts of strategic targets and strategic thrusts and

Table 2 SIS Idea-Generation Meeting Steps

Step	Activity	Purpose
1	PRESENT TUTORIAL ON COMPETITIVE STRATEGY AND SIS	Introduce the concepts of strategic thrusts, strategic targets, and competitive strategy
2	APPLY SIS CONCEPTS TO ACTUAL CASES	Raise consciousness about SIS possibilities and their strategic thrusts and targets
3	REVIEW COMPANY'S COMPETITIVE POSITION	Understand competitive position of the business and its strategies
4	BRAINSTORM FOR SIS OPPORTUNITIES	Generate SIS ideas in small groups
5	DISCUSS SIS OPPORTUNITIES	Eliminate duplication and condense SIS ideas
6	EVALUATE SIS OPPORTUNITIES	Evaluate competitive significance of SIS ideas
7	DETAIL SIS BLOCKBUSTERS	Detail each SIS blockbuster idea, its competitive advantage, and key implementation issues

covered the role of information systems in supporting or shaping the competitive strategy of the firm. More importantly, it provided attendees with an analytical framework with which they could identify SIS opportunities and threats.

Step 2. Apply SIS Concepts to Actual Cases. Following the tutorial, participants solidified their understanding of the concepts presented by analyzing a set of actual SIS microcases drawn from a variety of industries. Working through about 20 examples selected from a prepared list of 50, they learned how to identify strategic targets and thrusts.

Step 3. Review Company's Competitive Position. This step acquainted participants with the competitive realities facing the business. It was presented by the information management planning staff and covered such topics as markets, products, customers, suppliers, competitors, strengths, weaknesses, and business strategies. By understanding these elements, one is in a position to consider the question: "How can information technology be used to support or shape strategic thrusts aimed at the firm's strategic targets?"

Step 4. Brainstorm for SIS Opportunities. In this step the group divided into teams of 5-8 participants and each brainstormed for different kinds of SIS opportunities. Some teams focused on leveraging existing information management assets, while others explored the possibility of creating new assets. Some concentrated on opportunities related to *suppliers* (providers of raw materials, capital, or labor) by addressing such questions as:

1. Can we use information systems to gain leverage over our suppliers?
   Improve our bargaining power?
   Reduce the supplier's bargaining power?
2. Can we use information systems to reduce buying costs?
   Reduce our labor costs?
   Reduce our supplier's costs?
3. Can we use information systems to identify alternative sources?
   To locate substitute products and services?
   To make versus to buy?
4. Can we use information systems to improve the quality of products and services we receive from our suppliers?

Other teams looked for SIS opportunities related to *customers* (those who retail, wholesale, warehouse, distribute, or use the firm's products) by responding to such questions as:

1. Can we use information systems to reduce our customer's telecommunication's costs?
2. Can we use information systems to increase a customer's switching costs (make it difficult for the customer to change suppliers)?
3. Can we make our databases available to our customers?
4. Can we provide administrative support to our customers? (billing, collection, inventory management, etc.)
5. Can we use information systems to learn more about our customers and/or discover possible market niches?
6. Can we use information systems to help our customers increase their revenues?

And still other teams searched for SIS opportunities related to *competitors* by answering such questions as:

1. Can we use information systems to raise the entry cost of competitors into our markets?
2. Can we use information systems to differentiate our products and services?
3. Can we use information systems to make a preemptive strike (e.g., to offer something they can't because we have the data) against our competitors?
4. Can we use information systems to provide substitutes before the competition does?
5. Can we use information systems to improve or reduce distribution costs?
6. Can we use information systems to form joint ventures to allow entry into new markets?
7. Can we use information systems to match an existing competitor's offering?
8. Can we use a new information technology to establish a new market niche?
9. Can we use our knowledge of the information industry and markets to find new markets or better ways of doing business?

To aid in the development of an SIS idea, each team completed a short form describing the idea, the intended strategic target, the basic strategic thrust, and the specific competitive advantage. The ground rule in these SIS idea-generation sessions is that criticism or evaluation of ideas must be suppressed so that creativity is not inhibited or stifled in any way.

Step 5. Discuss SIS Opportunities. Each team reported its SIS ideas to the entire group and a scribe posted them on a flip chart for all to see. Group discussion encouraged clarification, elimination of duplicate proposals, and identification of overlapping suggestions. But again, as in the previous step, criticism was prohibited.

Step 6. Evaluate SIS Opportunities. The purpose here was to rate and rank each of the SIS proposals generated. Participants were to apply the following evaluative criteria when making their judgements:

- degree of competitive advantage,
- cost to develop and install,
- feasibility (from technical and resource points of view), and
- risk (understood as the probability of reaping and sustaining the competitive advantage promised by the SIS idea).

Applying these criteria, SIS proposals were classed into four categories:

1. blockbuster (potential for strategic dominance),
2. very high potential (but not blockbuster),
3. moderate potential (worthy of further consideration), or
4. low potential (not worthy of further consideration).

Step 7. Detail SIS Blockbusters. Here the group concentrated on refining and recording the SIS blockbuster ideas. This refinement details the technology employed, customer benefits, competitive advantage, responsibilities, and implementation concerns that aid in the process of transforming the idea into reality.

Meeting Dynamics. The SIS idea-generation meetings lasted for two full days. Each step took about two hours, with the exception of the tutorial and the exercise (Steps 1 and 2), which together needed about five hours from an outside consultant to convey the concepts. Step 4, the brainstorming session, unlike typical workshop breakouts whose effectiveness usually lasts between 45 and 90 minutes, required more time. In our meetings the teams of 5-8 were very lively and needed a solid two hours to develop their ideas.

Results

Identification of SIS Opportunities

Each of the three brainstorming meetings generated over 100 SIS ideas. At each meeting about 10 were considered real winners. Many proposals overlapped across meetings, and there was consensus on the blockbuster suggestions. This consensus was fortunate since it validated the top ideas and built support and commitment for them from a variety of constituencies: corporate management, information management, and local telephone companies. The SIS opportunities discovered by each group were combined after the final idea-generation meeting. Of the top 11 proposals, six were rated as blockbusters and five were classed as having very high potential. When one considers that most stories about the strategic use of information systems concern only one primary SIS idea, the process at GTE was prolific indeed. We would have scored our process a success had we uncovered one or two top ideas in this first pass, but instead we uncovered 11 worthy of implementation.

Impact on GTE

The development of a strategic perspective on information systems and the specific ideas generated in the SIS planning process resulted in several major managerial changes at TELOPS. For the first time, members of top management focused their attention on SIS opportunities. They now believe that information systems can play a critical role in shaping business strategy. Proof of this comes in management's immediate allocation of resources to implement the three best blockbuster ideas.

To insure that their new strategic vision about the role of information systems is made part of the fabric of the organization and not just a passing fancy, top management elevated the information management function in the corporate hierarchy. They created senior information systems positions at headquarters and at the telephone operating companies. These senior positions report directly to the chief operating officer of the unit instead of to the chief financial officer as they did in the past. (The positions are very much like the chief information officer function described by Synnott and Gruber [15]). Information management has finally become an equal partner in setting the strategic direction of the company.

Executives at GTE's local telephone companies agreed to implement similar SIS planning processes in their operating units. These will address the unique competitive environments, threats, and opportunities confronting each. The units also agreed to champion one of the original 11 SIS ideas.

To emphasize the importance of TELOPS attaches to the strategic perspective on information systems, TELOPS information management function formally added a new SIS strategy to its long-range plan, which previously focused only on operational improvements.

Impact on Other GTE Businesses

TELOPS, GTE's largest division was the first to implement the SIS planning process outlined above. Its success prompted other GTE units, in widely different competitive environments, to initiate similar projects.

Conclusion

The SIS planning process described above resulted in the identification of many ideas to provide GTE Telephone Operations with significant competitive advantage. Some SIS ideas require investment in new information-based assets, while others leverage existing information resources. The continued application of the SIS planning process within TELOPS will ensure that the idea pipeline is full and that quality ideas will be implemented. Beyond TELOPS, the methodology is being used by other GTE units to identify SIS opportunities. We believe the methodology can be used by other firms whose vision extends to using information systems as competitive weapons in their quest for advantage.

Discussion Questions

1. How are strategic information systems different from management information systems, decision support systems, and transaction processing systems?
2. How is this article related to the first three articles on MIS planning?
3. How is the theory of strategic thrusts related to overall corporate strategy, corporate goals, and corporate objectives?
4. What personnel are involved in the SIS planning and idea-generation processes? What are their roles?

References

[1] Anthony, R. N. *Planning and Control Systems: A Framework for Analysis*, Harvard University Press, Boston, Massachusetts, 1965.

[2] Gorry, A. and Scott Morton, M. "A Framework for Management Information Systems," *Sloan Management Review*, Volume 13, Number 1, Fall 1971, pp. 55-70.

[3] IBM *Information Systems Planning Guide: Business Systems Planning*, (4th Ed.), New York, New York, 1984.

[4] Keen, P. and Scott Morton, M. *Decision Support Systems: An Organizational Perspective*, Addison-Wesley, Reading, Massachusetts, 1978.

[5] King, W. "Achieving the Potential of Decision Support Systems," *Journal of Business Strategy*, Volume 3, Number 3, Winter 1983, pp. 84-91.

[6] King, W. "Strategic Planning for MIS," *MIS Quarterly*, Volume 2, Number 1, March 1978, pp. 27-37.

[7] Nolan, R. and Gibson, C. "Managing the Four Stages of EDP Growth," *Harvard Business Review*, Volume 52, Number 1, January-February 1974, pp. 76-88.

[8] Nolan, R. "Managing the Crises in Data Processing," *Harvard Business Review*, Volume 57, Number 2, March-April 1979, pp. 115-126.

[9] Nolan, R. "Plight of the EDP Manager," *Harvard Business Review*, Volume 51, Number 3, May-June 1973, pp. 143-152.

[10] Rockart, J. and Treacy, M. "Executive Information Systems," *Center for Information Systems Research*, CISR Working Paper Number 65, Massachusetts Institute of Technology, Cambridge, Massachusetts, 1981.

[11] Rockart, J. and Treacy, M. "The CEO Goes On-Line," *Harvard Business Review*, Volume 60, Number 1, January-February 1982, pp. 82-88.

[12] Rockart, J. and Bullen, C. "A Primer on Critical Success Factors," *Center for Information Systems Research*, CISR Working Paper Number 69, Massachusetts Institute of Technology, Cambridge, Massachusetts, 1981.

[13] Rockart, J. "Chief Executives Define Their Own Data Needs," *Harvard Business Review*, Volume 57, Number 2, March-April 1979, pp. 81-92.

[14] Porter, M. E. *Competitive Strategy: Techniques for Analyzing Industries and Competitors*, Free Press, New York, New York, 1980.

[15] Synnott, W. and Gruber, W. *Information Resource Management: Opportunities and*

Strategies for the 1980s, John Wiley & Sons, New York, New York, 1981.

[16] Wiseman, C. *Strategy and Computers: Information Systems as Competitive Weapons*, Dow Jones-Irwin, Homewood, Illinois, 1985.

[17] Zani, W. "Blueprint for MIS," *Harvard Business Review*, Volume 48, Number 6, November-December 1970, pp. 95-100.

SECTION SEVEN

Development

READING 18

Attributes of Information System Development

article by
HUGH F. JUERGENS

While numerous computer-based information systems have been developed and are in operation there is no unified or commonly accepted theory to guide the development process. If there were such a theory, I suspect that a higher proportion of these systems would be deemed successful [see 16, 20] and the systems would be more readily adaptable to change with a corresponding reduction in the high cost of maintenance.

This paper draws upon a variety of sources in an effort to integrate much of the current thinking on the information system development process. A general model of the development process is presented to provide increased understanding of the effect that this process has upon the characteristics of the resulting system. The concept of decoupling is introduced as a framework for guiding the development process toward achievement of the system's desired capabilities, while recognizing and planning for the accommodation of change.

Source: Reprinted by special permission of the *MIS Quarterly*, Volume 1, Number 2, June 1977, pp. 31-41.

Attributes of an Information System

The criteria by which the attributes of a system can be evaluated are presented first in order to provide a perspective from which the system development process can be evaluated. These criteria are user-oriented and fall into the broad categories of effectiveness and cost. The effectiveness attribute has to do with the ability of the system to satisfy the users' needs and gives an indication of the benefits or value provided by the system. Cost, on the other hand, constrains the development of the systems. Primary attention in this article will be directed toward the effectiveness with which the system satisfies users' needs. Ideally, desired attributes of the system are specified prior to the development of the system and become objectives that are used to guide the development process.

System Effectiveness

System effectiveness has three dimensions: capability, stability, and adaptability. [3] Capability refers to the ability of the existing system to satisfy the information needs of the operations and decision-making functions in the organization. As such, we can look at the outputs of the system and compare them with what is needed. Several aspects of capability include the ability of the system to perform its intended functions by providing the necessary output and the relevance of the output in satisfying the needs of the users. The fact that "well functioning" systems have unsatisfied users, as described by McKinsey and Company [16] and Powers and Dickson [20], gives rise to this distinction between the two similar views of capability. For example, in the absence of user participation when defining the content and format of reports, the development personnel may define the output in terms that may be difficult for the users to understand, even though all the necessary information may be present. Other aspects of capability include the accuracy and timeliness of the system's outputs.

Stability and adaptability refer to *future* capability and are intended to protect the organization's information system investment. Stability is the degree to which the capability of a system persists through changes in the system's non-user environment. In other words, if the capabilities of the system remain intact through variations in the workload, changes in the hardware and hard-software (e.g., operation system, compilers, data management systems, etc.), and changes or additions to other application programs and files, then the system may be said to be highly stable. Adaptability, on the other hand, is the degree to which adjustments to the system can be made as a result of changes in the user environment. An example is the ease with which changes in the information needs of the users can be incorporated into the system.

System Cost

The attribute of cost refers to the expenditure of resources during the development, operation, and maintenance of the system in order to provide the degree of desired effectiveness. The most visible resource, capital, is manifested in the information system organization through hardware, software, personnel, and supplies.

Theoretically, both the benefits and costs can be stated in terms of a single quantity, such as dollars, whose value is to be optimized. It is the responsibility of the development personnel to produce the optimum system. Unfortunately many of the benefits and costs cannot be quantified or measured *a priori*. It is not possible to determine meaningfully if a system will adequately meet user needs until after it is in use, given the present state of the art. Even then, placing a value on improved decision-making or increased customer goodwill is difficult, if not impossible. Benefits associated with the provisions for achieving stability and adaptability are not realized until the changes become imminent, and the danger still exists that the provisions are not adequate due to unforeseen circumstances. Yet, resources are expended to "ensure" the effectiveness of the system before its value is proven.

It is a risky venture to provide for the dimensions of capability, stability, and adaptability. This risk has two distinct, opposite sides: excessive costs are incurred both by providing capabilitities that are not needed or by failing to provide required capabilities. It is in the context of this uncertainty that the planning and development of an information system takes place.

Conflict exists between the objectives themselves and the means for achieving them. For example, there are several ways in which the cost of developing a system can be reduced. One alternative is to decrease one or more of the dimensions of effectiveness, *e.g.*, eliminating some of the desired capabilities or reducing the documentation effort. Such means of achieving a cost reduction may be unacceptable if the objectives for the system have already been set. They have often been used as a short-run measure to cut costs in a project and are symptomatic of inaccurate initial estimates and an inflexible project control system [20].

Development Process

Traditionally, the system development process within the system life cycle has been described as a series of chronological phases or stages [5, 18]. Different authors have diverse labels for the stages and have varying conceptions of what must be done in each stage. Each of these approaches has its own merits. A "new" series of stages, as such, is not presented in this paper. Viewing the development process at the system level as definition, design, and construction can draw these approaches together.

Definition

During the definition stage, the information system is placed into the organizational context. It is in this stage that the objectives or desired attributes of the system are defined and the boundaries for the system are delineated. The result of the analysis forms a set of *requirements* which include a definitinon of the overall functions to be performed, system inputs, system outputs, performance, and integrity.

Design

The design stage is concerned with translating the requirements for the system into *specifications* for providing the needed capabilities. One common practice associated with system design, especially when dealing with large-scale systems, is the factoring of the system into subsystems; each of these subsystems is in turn further factored into subsystems. In this manner, the amount of detail that must be analyzed, assimilated, and synthesized at any one point in time is reduced. The underlying logic of this approach is that each of the subsystems is easier to handle than the system of which it is a part, the subsystems can be handled somewhat independently, and ultimately the subsystems can be recombined or joined in a straightforward manner to form the complete system. [10, 12, 13, 15]

The design process for a system consists of understanding the context of the system with respect to its implications for the super-system of which it is a part:

- factoring the system into more manageable and somewhat independent subsystems,
- specifying the *requirements* to be accomplished by each subsystem, and
- specifying the interfaces between the subsystems.

Together with the interface specifications, the design stage results in the definition stage for each of the subsystems. Each of these subsystems becomes the system of concern when it goes through its design stage. The factoring process continues with increased refinement at each level and is increasingly aimed at the "mechanics" of how the system will function in the hardware and in manual procedures. It continues until the system's objectives are refined into a form that can be understood by the computer, whether in a higher level language, such as COBOL, or an assembly language. Figure 1 illustrates the decomposition process.

A production control system, for example, might begin with an overall objective of achieving better control over the costs of production and increased responsiveness to customer demand. As shown in Figure 2, it may be initially comprised of forecasting, production scheduling, purchasing, raw material inventory control, and finished goods inventory control subsystems. Each of these subsystems may be factored further into subsystems based upon differences in function or in the timing of inputs or outputs. Within each of these subsystems or processing cycles, programs may be identified for purposes such as input editing, file update, and reporting. Each of the programs is subdivided further according to functions performed such as input, output, and type of calculation. Modules are further factored and refined into submodules until subroutines are identified and finally the individual logic elements that eventually result in programming language statements are identified.

The arrows in Figures 1 and 2 identify the interfaces between subsystems and represent the flow of data. At the upper levels, this data will, for the most part, be contained in files although each arrow does not necessarily represent a single file. [13, 14] At the lower levels, data will be passed from one routine to another in central memory.

Construction

The construction stage is concerned with translating the system's specifications into the *means* for providing the identified capabilities. At each level in the hierarchical structure, construction consists of providing the interface between the subsystems and

Figure 1 Hierarchical Network Structure

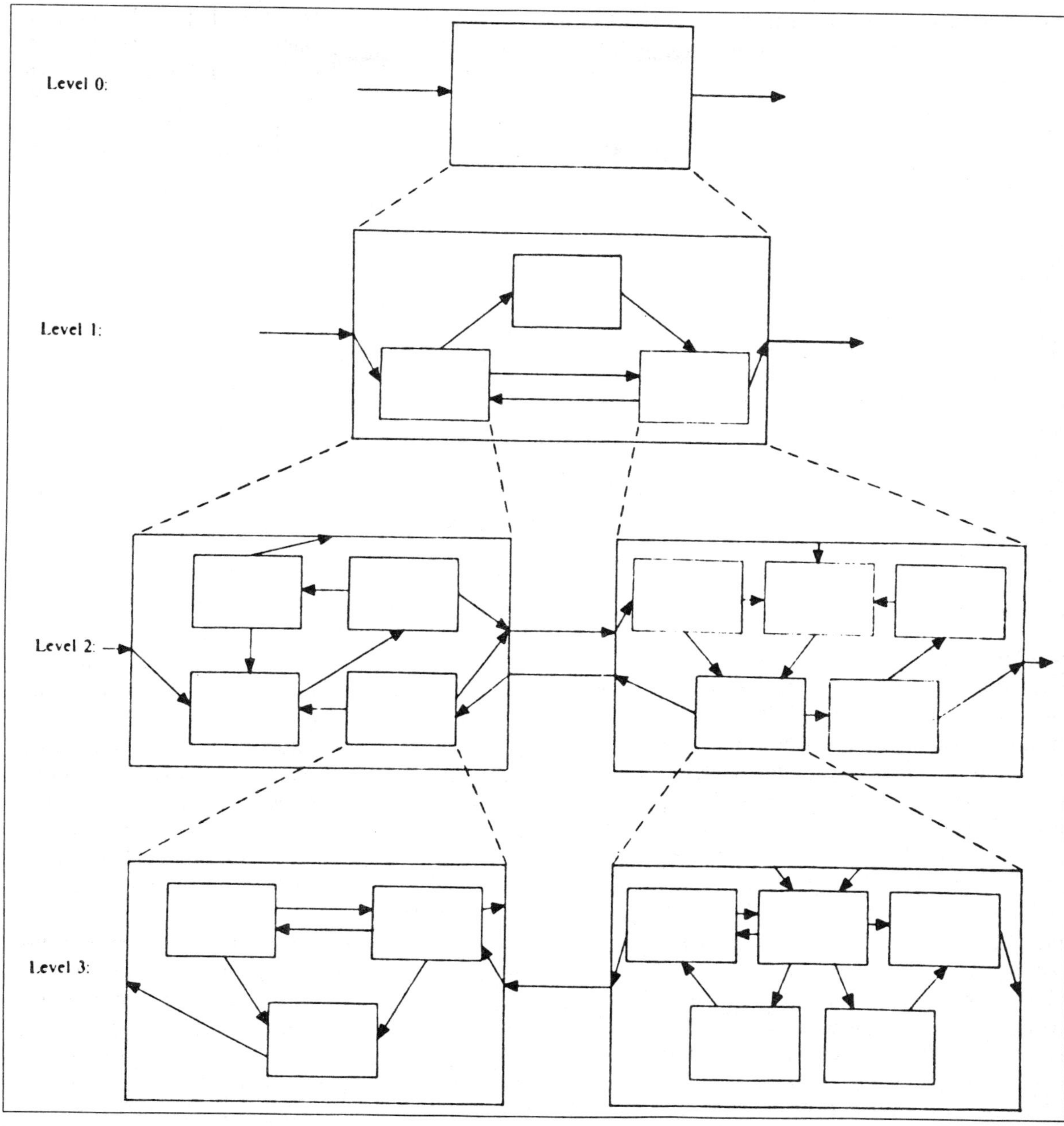

determining when each subsystem should be executed.

There are two schools of thought regarding how construction should be integrated with the design: top-down design with bottom-up construction, or top-down design with top-down construction. These two approaches are illustrated in Figures 3 and 4. In bottom-up construction, the lowest level subsystems are constructed first and tested. The next higher level is concerned with providing the necessary logic to coordinate their execution. This portion of the complete system constructed thus far

Figure 2 A Partial Example of the Hierarchical Network Structure for a Production Control System

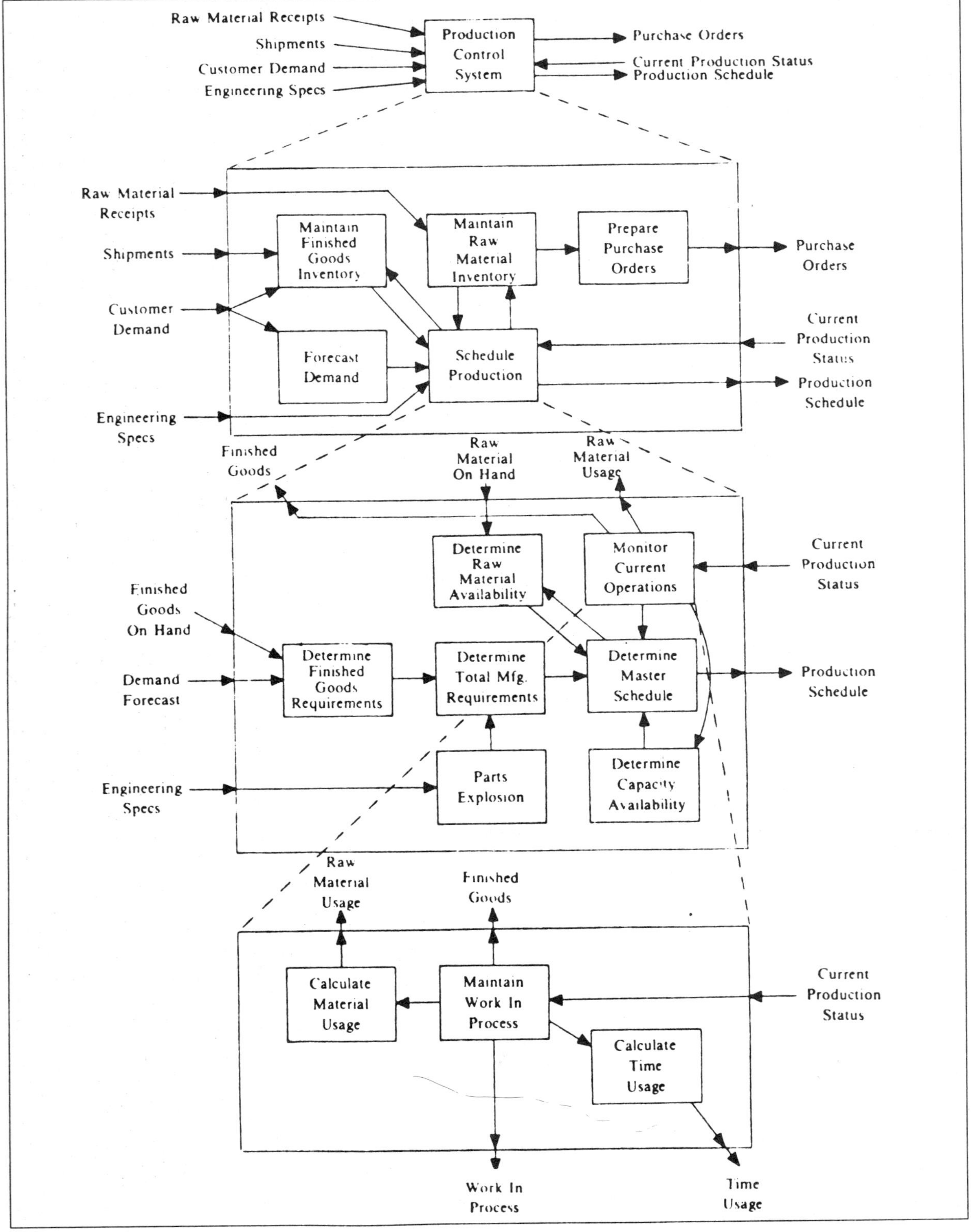

is then tested. Construction in this manner proceeds up through the hierarchy until the entire system has been completed. [2, 8, 19]

In top-down construction, the sequence of events is essentially reversed. Thus, at a given level in the hierarchy the subsystems are defined and the interfaces and coordination are constructed and tested before the subsystems themselves are designed and constructed. [2, 4, 19]

Attributes of the Development Structure

The structure of the system development process can be viewed both as a hierarchy and a network, as shown in Figure 1. There is a hierachical relationship between a system and its subsystems and there is a network relationship among the subsystems.

Figure 3 Top-Down Design With Bottom-Up Construction

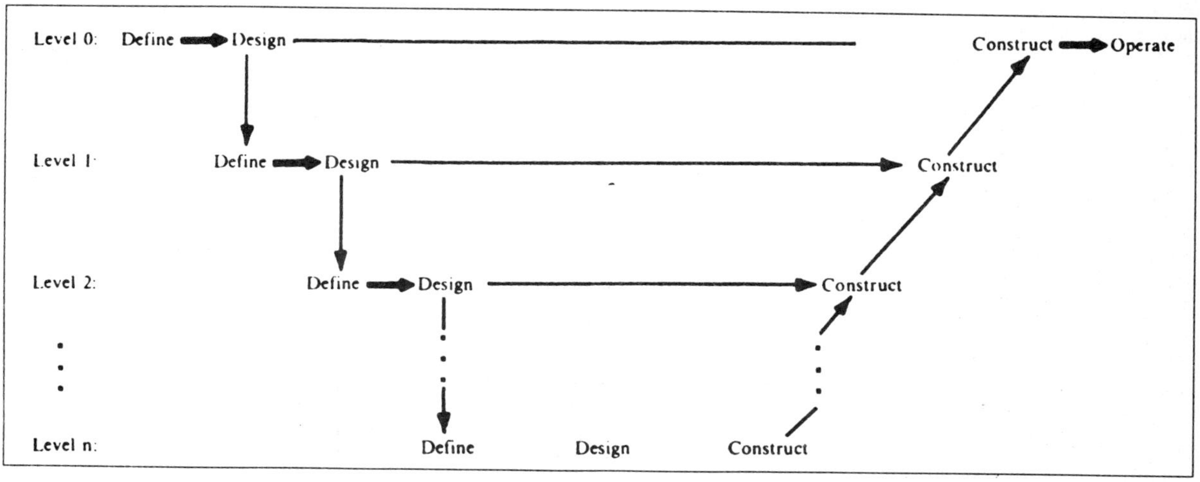

Figure 4 Top-Down Design With Top-Down Construction

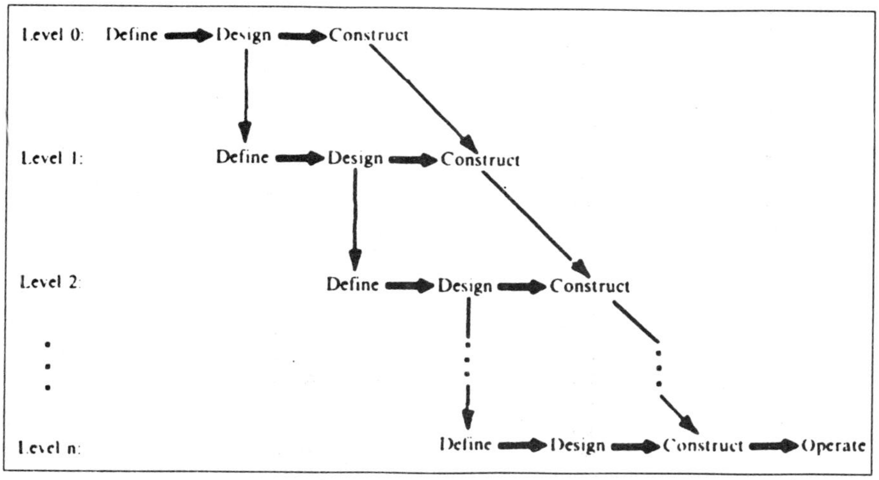

Vertical Decoupling

The hierarchical relationship between a system and its component subsystems may at times be clouded. For example, development personnel may be satisfied with an intuitive feeling regarding the objectives for a subsystem before proceeding down to another level in the hierarchy. If one proceeds in this manner, the link to the overall system objectives becomes nebulous and formalization of objectives and subsystem structure at the lower level becomes more difficult because of the greater amount of detail that must be assimilated.

If an effort on the other hand is made at each level in the hierarchy to formalize the objectives and the interface between the lower level subsystems, a clearer distinction will exist between successive levels. The extent to which this distinction exists is referrred to as the degree of *system/subsystem* or *vertical decoupling*. A high degree of vertical decoupling implies that there is a logical separation between subsystems at adjacent levels in the hierarchy from the standpoint that firm objectives are set forth for each subsystem prior to its development. Hence, the definition of objectives for a higher level system exerts a binding influence on the lower level subsystems. The capability of the system will be enhanced if the developmental efforts at each level are focused on the accomplishment of a unified purpose.

Tangible evidence of vertical decoupling in the development process takes the form of documentation and checkpoints. Periodically we stop to summarize what has been done and what will be done next. Checkpoints can be predefined: the development process can be viewed as a chronological series of phases or stages. [5] Other checkpoints may arise spontaneously: top-down program design or stepwise refinement can be used in program development. [2, 4, 24, 25]

System/subsystem decoupling does not imply that a system is independent of its subsystems. Quite the contrary, it is because of the dependence of a system's effectiveness upon the effectivenesss of its subsystems that this separation should occur. This allows development personnel to formulate explicitly the objectives for each subsystem. Such a formalization forms a basis for discussion with the users to confirm or revise the system objectives and provides a mechanism for recording the many details of the design. Additionally, control over the development process occurs through a comparison of the objectives for each subsystem with its design.

The definition of the lower-level subsystems, during the design of a higher-level subsystem, resembles the "black box" concept in which the inputs and outputs of a subsystem are defined, but the details for accomplishing the transformation are left undefined. We should concentrate on specifying realistic objectives for subsystems at succeeding levels and not become embroiled in the details of how the objectives will be accomplished. Decisions regarding the actual functioning of a system should be made only at the level in which the detail can be placed into perspective and can be understood and properly evaluated. In the previously mentioned production control example, if a variation of the classic economic order quantity formula [6] is used, we do not need to derive the specific formula until we design the module that will calculate it. Prior to this point, all that need be known is that the quantity will be determined by minimizing the appropriate costs.

It should be noted that no general guideline can be established for the number of levels in the system structure. The factoring process should result in a *tractable* set of subsystems for the development personnel. The tractability depends upon the skill and experience of development personnel and the scope and complexity of the system. Some insight into the problem of tractability for both the management of the development effort and for the actual development can be found in the literature. [2, 17, 33]

Horizontal Decoupling

A network structure, as shown in Figure 1, can be used to depict relationships among subsystems at a given level in the hierarchy. *Horizontal* or *subsystem/subsystem decoupling* refers to the degree of independence among subsystems in the network. The rationale for this form of decoupling is primarily to enhance the stability and adaptability of the resulting system by isolating the impact of potential sources of change upon the system.

This independence can be achieved in two ways. First, the *number of interconnections* among subsystems can be minimized. Hence, need for communication and coordination is reduced. This can be done by an appropriate choice of subsystem boundaries so that the number of interconnections is reduced, or by defining a special interface among subsystems or clusters of subsystems. An example of this latter approach is the use of database management systems. Data independence is the term used in the database management literature for decoupling. [1, 9, 11]

A second means of achieving horizontal decoupling is to minimize the *degree of interconnection*. The susbsystems should not make assumptions about the internal workings of other subsystems to achieve a high degree of independence. Even though certain assumptions may be valid at one time, changes to a subsystem can impact other related subsystems. This means if horizontal decoupling is aided partially by vertical decoupling and by specifying the functions to be performed by each subsystem and deferring the decisions regarding the means for accomplishing the intended functions. For example, Myers [19] has identified six degrees of interconnection between program modules ranging from content coupling (lowest or worst decoupling) whereby modules refer directly to the contents of other modules (*e.g.*, to modify a program statement) to data coupling (highest decoupling) whereby all data elements input and output of a module are passed as arguments and the arguments are not used to control execution (*e.g.*, flags).

Development Structure Overview

Besides enhancing the various dimensions of system effectiveness, horizontal and vertical decoupling are also of benefit in simplifying the development process and in providing greater flexibility in scheduling the development efforts. Simplification of the development is achieved by reducing the amount of detail that must be comprehended at any one point in time. Scheduling flexibility is achieved by permitting both concurrent development and implementation of subsystems so that partial capabilities within a long-term plan can be achieved.

Two problems associated with both vertical and horizontal decoupling are the cost of the decoupling mechanism itself (*e.g.*, documentation and database management systems) and the potential for suboptimization. The alternative to decoupling, however, is to stretch people's ability to perceive the masses of detail beyond their relatively narrow limits. We have to be content to tackle a large-scale problem a little at a time, until computers are used more effectively to automate the development process. [21, 22]

Factors to Consider in the Implementation of Decoupling

Viewing the development process in terms of the system life cycle may lead the reader to the conclusion that system development is sequential in nature. That is, first the system proceeds through the definition stage, then the design stage, and finally the construction stage. Chronologically, this may be true. However, recursion, parallelism, and iteration are inherent in the development process.

Recursion

Recursion in the development process is exemplified by the fact that at each level in the development hierarchy, the overall methodology is the same, although the orientation and details of implementing the methodology differ. For example, the upper levels in the hierarchy are directed more toward the overall problem to be solved and hence are oriented to the users and involve interpersonal skills. The lower levels are directed toward the computer and the physical realization of the system in hardware and software.

The development of a subsystem at any given level in the hierarchy is in general concerned with obtaining, understanding, translating, and communicating information. Information is obtained about the plans of higher levels in the hierarchy, because it is these plans that set the objectives for the subsystems. The technology available to the information system sets constraints with respect to what can be done. The environment, which may include other existing information systems, may also set constraints on the development. The people who will eventually be involved with the system, whether they are the users of the output or preparers of the input, add information that will help in further refining the system. Achieving an understanding through analysis goes hand-in-hand with obtaining the information; analysis of the information may point to the need for more information. Design consists of translating the results of the analysis into more detailed and specific plans which form the objectives for the lower level subsystems. These plans are then communicated to prior phases for review (feedback) and to subsequent phases for further development (feedforward).

This indicates that the system designer, in addition to addressing a current subsystem level, should think both up one level and down one level in the hierarchy. Looking at the higher level allows the system to viewed in its context within a broader perspective. The designer should think down one level because that is the object of his development efforts. Often, lower levels will set constraints upon the activities at a higher level, such as the capabilities of existing hardware.

Parallelism

Parallelism in the development process indicates that the subsystems, at any given point in time, may be in different stages of completion; some subsystems may be in the definition stage, others in the design stage, and yet others in construction. The parallelism adds scheduling flexibility to the development process so that partial capabilities within a long term plan can be provided. Alternatively, devoting resources to different subsystems concurrently may reduce development time. The degree of parallelism that can exist depends upon the degree of vertical and horizontal decoupling that is present.

Iteration

Iteration acknowledges the fact that the objectives of a system, and in turn the subsystem objectives, may not be completely defined and may even change during the development of the system. As we proceed further into development, insight on the part of the development personnel is gained into the properties of the system. Alternatives may be evaluated: inconsistencies, errors, omissions, and other desirable but unprovided capabilities. The users similarly through participation can be expected to gain increased awareness of (1) their information and decision making environment, and (2) the capabilities and limitations of computerized information processing. [20] These factors all indicate that it may be necessary to go back a level in the hierarchy to refine the plans for the lower level.

A high degree of vertical decoupling facilitates iteration between levels. Even though the objectives are subject to change, a clear statement of the objectives for each subsystem is necessary to track their evolution and signal any change. Otherwise there is a risk of having implicit objectives for each subsystem that reflect assumptions on the part of the development personnel rather than having explicit objectives formulated in the context of the overall system. On the other hand, having a well-documented but inflexible set of objectives can be just as dysfunctional as vague objectives. An unsatisfactory system may result by not taking advantage of the insight gained through the development efforts by the users and development personnel.

Some iteration is seen to be of a rather informal nature: *i.e.*, iteration that is carried out as the need arises. On the other hand, some may be of a formal nature: *i.e.*, iteration that is carried out as the need arises. On the other hand, some may be of a formal to either continue, revise, or discontinue the project. While it may seem desirable to have a number of these checkpoints to maintain close control, whatever parallelism exists in the development up to a checkpoint must halt and activities that lag behind must be allowed to catch up to the early finisher.

The preceding discussion focused on iteration between levels. Iteration is also experienced in the development efforts of each subsystem. For example, one must obtain information about the subsystem before it can be analyzed. However, this analysis may point to the need for additional information. Similarly, analysis of the subsystem precedes its design, but along with design comes increased understanding of the subsystem which may point to the need for further analysis; this, in turn, may require additional information, etc.

The amount of iteration experienced in system

development depends upon the degree to which the system fits into existing molds and the extent to which development personnel recognize and are able to take advantage of the correspondence. For example, developing a payroll system may involve little iteration whereas a system to furnish a manager with information needed to support decision-making activities may require extensive iteration.

Conclusion

Many current information systems are unsuccessful in that they do not adequately satisfy user needs and are inflexible when change is required. Part of this problem occurs because information system development is frequently viewed as strictly a technical activity, and as designers, we often are in too much of a hurry to delve into the details of the system and produce tangible evidence of our labor (*e.g.*, computer programs).

Computer science has recognized this problem for some time now. As a result, techniques such as structured programming, modular programming, top-down program design, and HIPO increasingly are being accepted and used. All these techniques for forcing disciplined creativity incorporate the concept of decoupling and are oriented more toward the lower levels in the development hierarchy. Reported benefits of these approaches include reduced development time and cost, increased quality of programs, and reduced maintenance. [2]

Recursion, as discussed in this article, suggests that decoupling is equally valid at the upper levels. The potential benefits, in fact, may be much greater given that we are trying to minimize the risk of developing wrong, inadequate, or inflexible systems as we venture into the vague area of improved decision support for management. Decoupling supports an iterative approach for determining the desired capabilities of the system by requiring a formalized, yet tentative, specification of objectives at each step of development for feedback to stimulate user involvement and to guide further development efforts. Thus, it helps to prevent design decisions that could yield unexpected and undesirable properties for the system. Further, decoupling recognizes the inevitability of change and in essence strives to minimize its adverse consequences by planning for change.

Discussion Questions

1. What is the relevance of general systems theory to decoupling?
2. What does decoupling mean in database management terms?
3. What does decoupling mean in terms of program and system design?

References

1. ANSI/X3/SPARC Study Group on Data Base Management Systems, "Interim Report," *EDT*, Vol. 7, no 2, (75-02-08), pp. 1-140.
2. Aron, Joel D. *The Program Development Process: The Individual Programmer,* Reading, Mass., Addison-Wesley, 1974.
3. Ashenburst, R. I., (ed.). "Curriculum Recommendations for Graduate Professional Programs in Information Systems," A report of the ACM Curriculum Committee on Computer Education for Management, *Communications of the ACM*, Vol. 15, No. 5 (May 1972), pp. 363-398.
4. Baker, F. Terry, "Chief Programmer Teams Management of Production Programming." *IBM Systems Journal*, Vol. 11, No. 1 (1972), pp. 56-73.
5. Benjamin, Robert I. *Control of the Information System Development Cycle*, New York, Wiley, 1971.
6. Buffa, Elwood S. *Operations Management: Problems and Models*, New York, Wiley. 1972.
7. Canning, Richard G. (ed.) "That Maintenance 'Iceberg'," *EDP Analyzer*, Vol. 10, No. 10 (October 1972).
8. Canning, Richard G. (ed.), "The Search for Software Reliability," *EDP Analyzer*, Vol. 12, No. 5 (May 1974).
9. CODASYL Systems Committee, *Feature Analysis of Generalized Data Base Management Systems*, New York, Association for Computing Machinery, May 1971.
10. Davis, Gordon B. *Management Information Systems: Conceptual Foundations, Structure, and Development*, New York, McGraw-Hill, 1974.

11. Everest, Gordon C. "Managing Corporate Data Resources: Objectives and a Conceptual Model of Database Management Systems," Unpublished Ph.D. dissertation, University of Pennsylvania, 1974.
12. Johnson, Richard A.; Kast, Fremont E.; and Rosenzweig, James E. *The Theory and Management of Systems*, 3rd edition, New York, McGraw-Hill, 1973.
13. Langefors, Borje, *Theoretical Analysis of Information Systems* (2 vol.), Lund, Sweden, Studentlitteratur, 1970.
14. Langefors, Borje and Sundgren, Bo. *Information Systems Architecture*, New York, Petrocelli, 1975.
15. Machol, Robert E. and Miles, Jr., Ralph F. *"The Engineering of Large-scale Systems,"* in *Systems Concepts: Lectures on Contemporary Approaches to Systems*, Ralph F. Miles, Jr. (ed.), New York, Wiley, 1973, pp. 33-50.
16. McKinsey & Comany, Inc., "Unlocking the Computers Profit Potential," *Computers and Automation*, April 1968.
17. Miller, George A. "The Magical Number Seven, Plus or Minus Two: Some Limits on our Capacity for Processing Information ," *The Psychology Review*, Vol., 63, No. 2 (March 1956), pp. 81-97.
18. Murdick Robert G. "MIS Development Procedures." *Journal of Systems Management*, vol. 21, No. 12 (December 1970).
19. Myers, Glenford, Jr. *Reliable Software Through Composite Design*, New York, Petrocelli/Charter, 1975.
20. Powers, Richard F. and Dickson, Gary W. "MIS Project Management: Myths, Opinions, and Reality," *California Management Review*, Vol, 15, No. 3 (Spring 1973), pp. 147-156.
21. Prywes, Noah S. "Automatic Generation of Software Systems," *Data Base*, Vol, 6, No. 2 (Summer 1974), pp. 7-17.
22. Teichroew, Daniel and Sayani, Hasan. "Automation of System Building," *Datamation*, Vol, 17, No. 16 (August 15, 1971), pp. 25-30.
23. Urwick, Lyndall F. "The Managers Span of Control" *Harvard Business Review*, Vol, 34, No. 3 (May-June 1956).
24. Wirth, Niklaus, "Program Development by Stepwise Refinement," *Communications of the ACM*, Vol. 14, No. 4 (April 1971), pp. 221-227.
25. Wirth, Niklaus, "On the Composition of Well-structured Programs," *Computing Surveys*, Vol. 6, No. 4 (December 1974), pp. 347-259.

READING 19

The Impact of Cognitive Styles on Information System Design

article by
IZAK BENBASAT and
RONALD N. TAYLOR

Introduction

The need to incorporate decision-maker characteristics into Management Information Systems (MIS) design has received increased attention in the past few years. MIS professionals attending the Founding Conference of The Society of Management Information Systems in 1969 when asked to rank various research projects, selected as crucial to MIS research needs:

- the development of methods for determining appropriate content of an information system, and
- investigating the characteristics of decision-makers which affect MIS design [19].

Source: Reprinted by special permission of the *MIS Quarterly*, Volume 2, Number 2, June 1978, pp. 43-54.

All of the conceptual frameworks for MIS design, however, which appeared before 1973 [29] neglected the human decision-maker's role in the system. The human decision-maker must be included in any complete analysis of MIS design since he is the user of the information or output of the system.

Some evidence suggests that both problem characteristics and user characteristics influence decision-making strategies and dictate information system design. Simon and Newell [37, p. 148] have argued that, "A few, and only a few, gross characteristics of the human information-processing system are invariant over task and problem solver." Although there is some disagreement regarding the relative impact of problem characteristics and problem-solver characteristics, the evidence emerging from experimental studies suggests that both problem and problem-solver characteristics influence problem-solving strategies[1] and, moreover, these two sets of characteristics may interact in exerting such influences. Several of the studies reviewed below exhibit this tendency.

The American Accounting Association Committee on Human Information Processing has suggested the following framework for incorporating decision-maker characteristics into information system design:

> *"The primary reason for accountants' interest in decision making is the potential for improving the quality of decisions. Three basic strategies exist for improving the quality of decisions:*
> *(1) The information set upon which such decisions are based may be altered. This alternative emphasizes information search and selection.*
> *(2) The ability of decision makers to use information may be improved. This alternative emphasizes education, training, and experience.*
> *(3) Formal models of human decision making may be constructed. Such models may be used to replace or supplement humans in various types of decision situations. This alternative emphasizes increased consistency of decisions." [3, pp. 1-2]*

Conceptual frameworks for MIS design presented by Chervany, *et al.* [16] and Mason and Mitroff [33] were the first to emphasize the importance of decision-maker characteristics. The developers of these frameworks, consistent with the first strategy stated above, suggested that information systems should be designed to suit the individual characteristics and capabilities of decision-makers. Incorporating behavioral variables representing decision-maker variables into MIS designs is far from complete, despite the encouraging trend in these frameworks. Mock [34] and Bariff and Lusk [6] presented useful classifications of behavioral variables which have potential relevance for MIS design. The Bariff and Lusk model for MIS design also suggests ways to evaluate the effects of behavioral variables and provides appropriate psychological tests to measure decision-maker characteristics. Their framework is similar to one devised by Chervany, *et al.* [16] in information systems characteristics and performance measures, but contains better development of user and organizational variables. Although the placement of some behavioral variables in the model is ambiguous, the treatment of cognitive style is quite relevant to the theme of this article and is developed in greater detail below.

The role of cognitive styles in MIS design must be considered in the overall context of MIS. The psychological characteristics of the information user are only a small subset of the many factors which influence MIS design. As Mason and Mitroff [33] asserted, factors such as the user's organizational context (strategic planning, management control, and operational control) and the type of decision problem (*e.g.*, structured or unstructured) the user faces are equally important in tailoring information systems to users.

Chervany, *et al.* [16] in this same vein have hypothesized the functional role (marketing, finance, production, *etc.*) of the information user to be an important determinant of MIS design. The importance of the managerial context on MIS design has been shown in empirical studies. Adams and Schroeder [2] conducted a survey which revealed that desired infomation characteristics such as accuracy, use, and summarization level, differed for different functional areas. Ghymn and King [25] also have shown that the importance attached to economic, social, and legal environmental data differed for top, middle, and lower level managers.

Cognitive styles represent only some of the characteristics of information system users which may influence MIS design. Characteristics such as intellectual ability, attitudes, demographics (age, education, *etc.*), and cultural background would also be expected to figure prominently in MIS design [38]. The MIS designer, therefore, must deal with a complex set of environmental, organizational, and behavioral variables in attempting to tailor the information system to the requirements of the user.

Cognitive styles, however, appear central to MIS design and have received considerable theoretical and research attention. Accordingly, they appear to be promising variables to explore in determining the impact of behavioral variables on information system design. Decision-makers, faced with the pervasive and well-documented problem of information overload [39], are attempting to bring order to their information-processing activities. The tendency is to act consistently despite informational variation. The literature suggests that a relatively fixed pattern for experiencing the world are learned by decision-makers; these patterns can be called cognitive styles [11]. Witkin, for example, who has done extensive research in this area has defined cognitive styles as ". . . characteristic modes of functioning that we show throughout our perceptive and intellectual activities in a highly consistent and pervasive way" [44, p. 2]. Essentially, a decision-maker is considered by cognitive theorists to learn strategies, programs, or other transformation processes which mediate behavior. Among the processes subsumed within cognitive styles are selective processes (filtering information), organizing processes (patterns or integrating selected information), moderating or controlling processes (*e.g.*, motives), and adapting processes (overcoming situational constraints of the task) [11].

More adequately incorporating cognitive styles into MIS models requires further attention to: 1) determining the nature of the cognitive styles construct and the psychometric properties of its measuring instruments, 2) strenthening research designs for investigating the impact of cognitive styles on information systems, and 3) developing ways to take knowledge of cognitive styles into account as information systems are designed and used. Items 1) and 3) are examined in this article as we critically evaluate the current state of cognitive styles research and explore its potential impact on MIS design. Research design considerations, item 2, will be briefly discussed in the concluding notes.[2]

Proposals for Clarifying the Nature of Cognitive Styles

The notion of styles of cognition implies that people have individual differences in cognitive processes and that such differences are relatively stable over time and situation. These stylistic variables must help us understand managerial information-processing and decision-making behaviors if they are to be relevant to MIS design and use. Having described briefly the general nature and function of cognitive styles, the following is a discussion of the types of cognitive styles which have been conceptualized in the literature.

Cognitive styles have beeen loosely defined and a number of approaches for measuring them have appeared in the research literature. This variety of operational definitions has led to confusion about the nature of the construct and has limited the generalizability of findings from studies using the different measures. The unresolved conceptual issues which plague research into cognitive styles are not unique to this variable [24]; they are common problems in attempting to conceptualize psychological constructs (*e.g.*, needs or motives). For example, there appears to be no simple answer to the question of how many cognitive styles must be described in an adequate conceptualization of personality. An isolated measure of a personality construct, not placed within the network of other personality constructs, is of limited value in understanding behavior.

Clarifying the nature of the cognitive styles constructs is essentially an empirical question which may be accomplished through factor analytic studies to identify the dimensionality of the constructs. Despite several attempts to determine the dimensionality of cognitive styles measures, the results are far from clear. There are several reasons for the inconclusiveness of these studies. The great number of measures proposed to reflect cognitive styles cannot all be included in a single factor-analytic study and the studies performed have each focused on a limited range of cognitive styles measures [13, 40, 41, 42]. Although such studies do not permit conclusions about the dimensions of cognitive styles in general, they do cast doubt upon the notion of a unitary cognitive styles construct (*i.e.*, a general cognitive styes trait). It is more likely that they measure different aspects of cognitive styles, but evidence regarding whether they also involve general intelligence, personality and/or interests is mixed. Vasarhelyi [41], for example, administered tests to a group of undergraduate students which were reported to measure the heuristic vs. analytic cognitive styles: the coin and pitcher tests developed by Huysmans [26], the Myers-Briggs Type Indicator [23], a heuristic-analytic questionnaire, and a self-evaluation instrument on which the subject rated himself as being analytic or heuristic. Factor analysis showed relatively independent factors tapped by the various tests; thus it is possible to be high on one measure of cognitive style and low on another measure of cognitive style. It is apparent that the various measures of cognitive style used in the literature are not interchangeable and, presumably, will differ considerably in their implications for MIS design.

The factor-analytic studies add little insight into the nature of cognitive styles variables, apart from indicating the multidimensionality of the cognitive styles construct. Logical classifications, however, of the measures reported to reflect cognitive styles may be helpful in understanding the construct. MIS models need to be refined to include various cognitive style constructs in order to effectively deal with them in information system design.

The cognitive styles which appear to have the greatest relevance for MIS design are: 1) cognitive complexity, 2) field independence-dependence, and 3) analytic-heuristic styles. These styles and their implications for information use are discussed briefly in the remainder of this section. It is hoped that the illustrations presented will clarify the nature of these cognitive styles and indicate their relevance for MIS design.

Cognitive complexity [18, 35, 46] involves the process of *differentiation* —number of dimensions extracted from the data, *articulation* — fineness of discrimination, and *integration* — complexity of the rules used to combine data. Cognitive complexity generally has been measured by the Sentence Completion Test [35], which identifies conceptual structures as either abstract or complex.

Such differences in conceptual structure have led to the development of the Decision Style Theory by Driver and Mock [22] to relate conceptual structure of decision-makers to both the amount of information they tend to use and the degree of focusing in the use of data they exhibit. A minimal user is the decision-maker who uses just enough data to make an adequate decision, on the "amount-of-information-used" dimension, sacrificing information use to gain time or results. The maximal user, in contrast, would tend to exhaust all relevant data before making a decision. The "one-solution" type on the focusing dimension would use all the data to arrive at one conclusion, showing rigid but consistent behavior. The opposite focusing type, multiple solution type, would put different interpretations to data at different times and try to support different solutions with it.

Witkin has conducted extensive research into a cognitive style which measures **field independence-dependence.** This classification has been used in two experiments which examined the relationship between cognitive styles and the acceptance of managerial reports [21, 30]. Witkin and his associates defined field independence-dependence as an analytical in contrast to a global, way of perceiving, and hypothesized that it entails a tendency to experience items as discrete from their backgrounds—*i.e.*, the ability to overcome the influence of an embedding context. The test frequently used to measure this cognitive style is the Embedded Figures Test [45], which requires subjects to perceive a simple figure within a larger complex figure.

Several research studies indicate that this cognitive style has strong implications for MIS design [21, 31, 43]. While both the high-analytic and low-analytic types may possess comparable abilities to differentiate and mentally structure a detailed report, only the high-analytic type perceives patterns of data inter-relatedness or wholeness. There are parallels between the field-dependence style, which is global in approach, and the heuristic style of Huysmans described below, which emphasizes looking at the totality of the situation. Similarities also exist for the analytic style which can distinguish the set of underlying causal functions in a problem situation and the field-dependent style which can separate parts from the totality of the context, but these relationships have not been empirically studied.

Huysmans developed a model of "ways of reasoning" for an experiment designed to test the impact of cognitive style on the acceptance of managerial recommendations [26]. Subjects in this model are classed as tending toward either **"analytic"** or **"heuristic"** reasoning types. Analytical reasoning refers to a tendency to reduce problem situations to a core set of underlying causal relationships. A more or less explicit model, often stated in quantitative terms, forms the basis for each decision. Heuristic reasoning refers to an emphasis on workable solutions to total problem situations. The search is for analogies with familiar solved problems rather than a system of underlying causal relationships. Common sense, intuition, and unqualified feelings about future developments play an important role to the extent that they are applied to the total situation. To measure cognitive style according to this model, Huysmans developed a test battery consisting of two mathematical puzzles, coin-and-pitcher tests, and a decision-making problem.

Suggestions for Assisting MIS Analysts in Incorporating Cognitive Styles into MIS Design and Use

The American Accounting Association framework [3] for incorporating decision-maker characteristics into information system design has implications for both the selection and training of information sytem users. The latter strategy is the focus of this article. The empirical evidence of cognitive styles impact upon MIS design is discussed in this section in terms of its influence on two key variables in information system design: 1) report format (*e.g.*, information presentation, content, aggregation, etc.), and 2) use of decision aids (*e.g.*, models and techniques).

Review of Cognitive Styles Research

Despite the theoretical and methodological difficulties evident in cognitive styles research, inferences concerning the significance of cognitive styles of MIS design can be drawn. Empirical evidence suggests that the use of decision aids or problem solving models is closely associated with the analytic (field-independent) - heuristic (field-dependent) dimensions of cognitive style. The analytic decision-maker is viewed as approaching problem analysis by developing a model of the situation. This would imply that the analytics would be more willing to use an information system which employed models or mathematical optimization techniques. Experimental results tend to support the above contentions. Analytics who were provided with various kinds of decision aids such as forecasting aids, order-point, or order-quantity models used less historical reports than heuristics who were also provided with decision aids [9], although no cost or performance difference between the two types was found. Still, a lower historical report usage would be preferred since this saves time for the decision-maker and reduces information overload. This shows that the value of such aids, or the desirability of their usage, is higher for analytics compared to heuristics. Other research studies [26, 30] showed that analytic types prefer reports which have formulas imbedded in the text and are quantitative, although some conflicting results on this point have emerged [21].

The fact that analytics prefer models or quantitative reports is not very surprising given the cognitive approach of analytic types. What is more important for the MIS designer is to find some kind of decision aid to help the problem solving task of the heuristic decision-maker. Keen [27] reports that an adaptive computer model developed by Botkin [12] had an appeal for and was used with equal effectiveness both by analytic and heuristic types. Botkin's model shown in Figure 1 had the following features necessary to provide adaptivity: 1) the user should be able to create an arbitrary order of processing in order to develop an approach at the time feedback from the problem environment is obtained, 2) the user should be able to explore scenarios to generate cues or test trial solutions, 3) the user should be able to shift between levels of detail and generality, 4) the user should be able to control the format of the output and have means for flexible inputs, such as commands for modifying the previous inputs by ± 5%.

The attraction of such an adaptive model for the heuristic users is its flexiblity; that is, it allows the users to impose their own processes on the model and not be restricted into a structured mode of response. Such a flexible model could also be helpful for the integrative types, described by Driver and Mock [22] as decision-makers characterized by their search for multiple solutions [22], though this point has yet to be experimentally tested.

In addition to designing decision aids, the second area of concern for the MIS designer is how to structure the data sources available to the decision-maker and how to filter this data to better suit his psychological profile. This area includes issues of summarization, aggregation, categorization, amount of information usage, and information load. Keen has developed a model of how decision makers differ in their *data gathering* modes and has classified people into receptives and preceptives [27]. Receptive user types have a desire to analyze and look at all the relevant raw or nontransformed data

Figure 1 Adaptive Modelling Flowchart

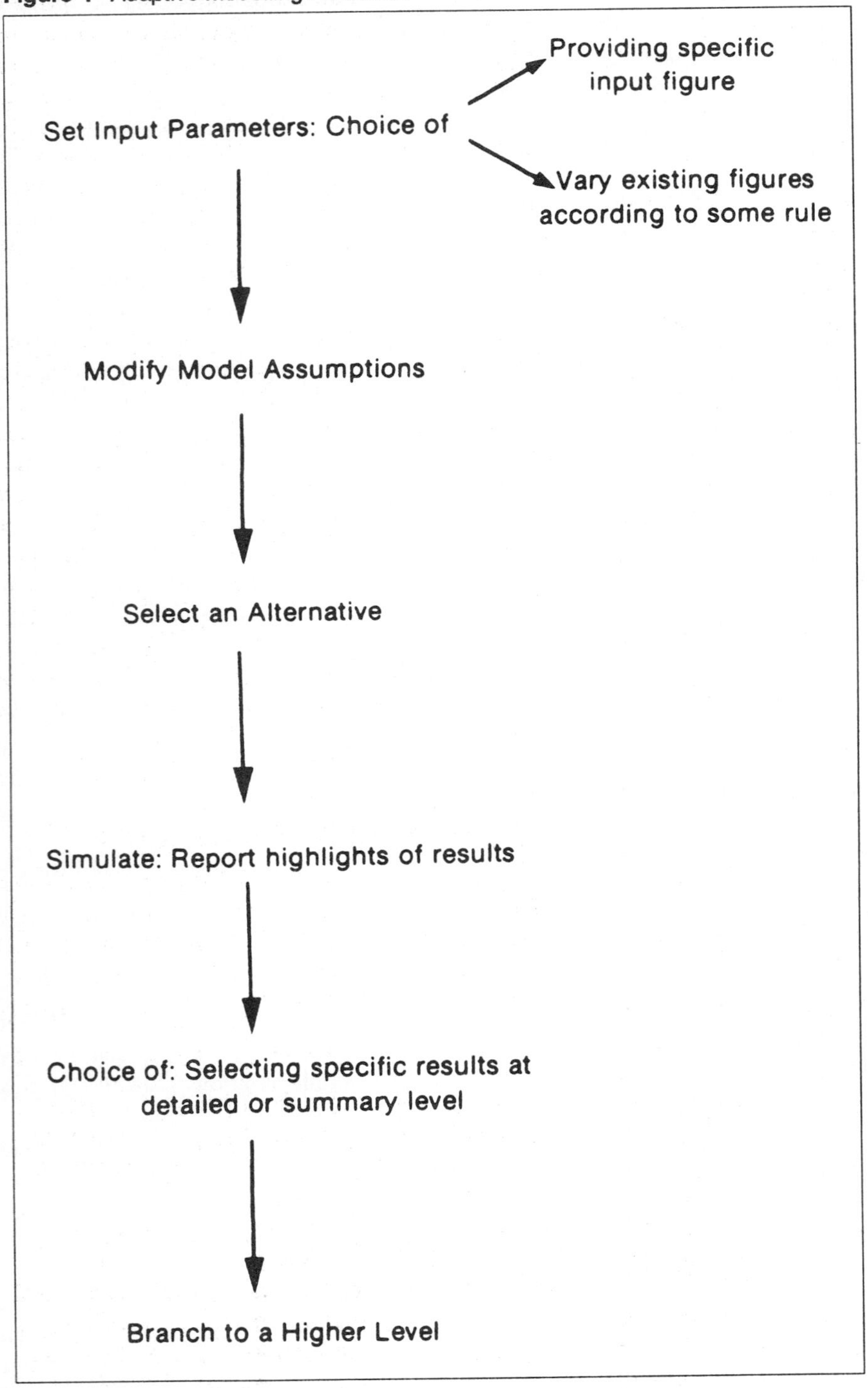

before making a decision. Such decision-makers desire access to a large database which carries extensive historical data, and a flexible and quick retrieval capability to this database. The preceptive types, who look for certain cues, deviations from or conformities with their expectations, prefer to work with a reporting system which has filtering capabilities on given parameters. These include exception reporting routines which filter out data falling outside given ranges; search routines for patterns such as increases or decreases of a certain parameter over a number of given periods; and categorization or summarization routines over time or over data attributes. Such a system may also be of interest to the minimal data users. All of these suggestions are again hypotheses which have to be tested experimentally.

One experimental study in the area of data use and summarization showed that analytics made more use of detail data reports, whereas heuristics were more interested in aggregate reports [8]. The results of this study conflict with other studies which showed that heuristic decision-makers exhibited higher data usage and preferred disaggregated reports [20, 28, pp. 73, 31]. For example, Lusk [31] presented users the same information content in four different report formats which were classified in increasing complexity as tabular raw data, percentage data, histogram, and an ogive report showing cumulative frequencies. He found the transformations of data, *i.e.*, increased data load, added perceived complexity and low analytic subjects' preferences were inversely related to increasing levels of complexity. Dickson and Barkin report that in an experimental production decision-making setting heuristic decision-makers selected more total data than did decision-makers exhibiting the analytic style [20]. They also found that heuristics selected more data *non-critical* to the decisions being made than did the analytics, therefore they infer that many data elements selected by decision-makers of differing cognitive styles were not the same and depended on cognitive style. The findings of these experiments seem to be more plausible if we consider the profile of a heuristic as one who prefers to look at the totality of the situation, tries to get feedback, and uses the trial and error approach. We would think that a heuristic would search for more data than an analytic who designs a solution approach in a more structured way and has a clearer understanding of how to proceed with the problem, assuming that the problem is amenable to analytical solutions. The conflicting results described above could be partially reconciled by another study which found that analytic decision-makers would use more historical reports than heuristics only if they were not provided with decision aids [9]. The above discussion shows that implications cannot be comfortably drawn from the experimental results. The data preferences of analytics or heuristics must be carefully discussed, considering their data gathering mode, *e.g.*, whether the individual is analytic-receptive or analytic-preceptive.

The conceptual structure of the decision-makers also has additional implications for the design of information systems. Extensive theoretical and experimental work by Schroeder and his associates [35] has shown that integratively more complex individuals can handle more conceptual data, derive more clues and search for more information than integratively simple individuals can. Therefore, reports provided to integrative simple decision-makers should be formatted so as to have hard facts, numbers, and objective data since these individuals would otherwise feel overloaded and their usage of the information system would consequently be reduced.

Conclusions from Cognitive Styles Research

The conclusions which may be drawn concerning the role of cognitive styles in MIS design are necessarily tentative because of the paucity and conflicting nature of the experimental results; however, the following generalizations appear appropriate:

1. Analytic decision-maker types tend to prefer decision aids and reporting systems which are quantitative in nature with results supported by mathematical formulas.
2. Heuristic decision-makers need to have more data search capabilities prior to reaching decisions. Since they rely on feedback and trial and error, an information system capability which can highlight trends and provide period by period comparisons would be suitable for them. The information system should give them capabilities to try alternative solutions and analyze the possible outcomes before they

decide on their final approach to solving the problem.

3. Decision-makers differ in their data gathering styles. The preceptives want a system which can organize and aggregate data into categories according to given parameters and exception reporting aids, whereas the receptives or maximal data users prefer an information system which has access to every piece of historical data.

Incorporating Cognitive Styles into MIS Design

Many of the researchers working on information systems design have reported their concern that system analysts, who are typically analytic types who like to rely on objective data, often try to design a system which will suit their cognitive style needs rather than the needs of the user. This approach may lead to the low usage or rejection of the information system by the heuristic user. The conclusions presented above may serve as a basis for improving the approaches the analyst uses in the design of systems and broaden his perspectives to better satisfy the psychological needs of the user-managers.

If the cognitive style of the manager is to be included as a parameter in the information structure, it has been proposed that the SA perform the following three steps:

1) development of cognitive style profiles,
2) design of report formats and implementation procedures, and
3) validation of system outputs.

Development of Cognitive Style Profiles

To develop an individual cognitive style profile the SA has options ranging from the subjective, such as asking the manager questions during an interview process to get an impression of his cognitive style, to the objective, such as using one or more of the tests mentioned earlier in this article. It can be argued that the interview method may be less threatening to the user than the testing approach would be in choosing betweeen the two approaches. However, it is important to keep in mind that the interview method, due to its unstructured format and differences between interviewers, tends to yield information of questionable reliability, and therefore, potentially questionable validity. Because of the generally unreliable nature of the interview, the people who do the interview should be carefully trained and provided with reasonably structured interview formats [36].

An important issue which arises here is the SA's skills in administering and interpreting psychological measures, such as the cognitive style measuring instruments. Both interviews and tests designed to measure cognitive styles should be performed by individuals trained in these skills. Schneider [36] strongly urges the use of qualified people in this area:

> "This is not a suggestion, it is a warning, and the warning applies not only to the development of such measures (which would obviously require trained persons), but to the administration, scoring and interpretation of the results of such tests as well" [36, p. 191].

Therefore, if the SA is not so trained, the design team should include a person with these skills.

Bariff and Lusk suggest that the use of psychological tests represents a step toward a more systematic basis of MIS design [7]. They have done some preliminary analysis to compare the time that would be involved in the interview versus the testing methods. Their preliminary conclusion is that the testing method, using a controlled mass testing of users, will result in a more cost efficient approach than the interview approach as the size of the user group increases. However, objective testing methods have a number of disadvantages. One problem is the difficulty in judging the quality in terms of reliability and validity of some of these instruments. Since some of the psychological tests discussed earlier in this article have only recently been applied to measuring cognitive styles as they impact MIS design, more testing and research is necessary to evaluate their quality. Also, if the SA decides to use more than one cognitive style dimension (*e.g.*, data collection and data evaluation styles), the number of tests which are used increases the cost and time spent in testing.

Another critical issue in the use of objective

testing is managerial acceptance and participation in the testing process. Considerable tact and ingenuity may be required to reduce managerial apprehension and resistance to being tested. An explanation of what the test measures and its use is important in eliminating such fears. The manager needs to understand that these tests do not measure the quality of managerial performance, but reflect information processing preferences which will assist in the designing of an information system that will be more useful to each manager. These users must be assured that users with different cognitive styles, using information systems compatible with their individual styles, can all reach similar levels of decision quality.

Design of Report Formats and Implementation Procedures

Once the managers' cognitive styles are determined, the SA has a range of options for matching the information system to their cognitive style profiles. Two approaches will be discussed, but in practice a strategy involving selected features from each of these approaches could be adopted. One approach involves a flexible system providing a variety of report structures and decision models suitable for all of the cognitive styles of the system's users; this is similar to Botkin's adapative model [12] discussed previously. A second approach would provide each user only those information system elements which the SA thinks will fit the user's cognitive style.

Davis favors the flexible approach:

> *"..Information systems to support decision making should be designed so that both types of individuals (analytic/heuristic) will be willing to use them. A likely means to this end is a system that allows the user to explore a wide set of alternatives but also provides a predetermined sequence of analysis for the individual who desires it. In other words, the decision model is available to structure the decision, but the manager may depart from the model to explore alternative approaches. Such a system may also teach the intuititve user to utilize the systematic approach by allowing for an intuitive learning process" [17, p. 15].*

The flexible approach assumes that each user will choose those reports or models which will suit his cognitive styles. Ghymn and King provide support for the flexible approach by suggesting that "the data base must reflect and, the system must provide, information which satisfies the *perceived* needs of its user-managers" [25, p. 197]. There is also research evidence to support the contentions that increased flexibility in the information system leads to increased confidence in decision making, even though it may not necessarily lead to improved performance [4, 15].

It should be considered, however, that the user faced with the option of choosing from a flexible information system may spend too much time trying to understand the different options. Similarly, one researcher discovered that the the user may be hesitant to choose only a subset of the available reports fearing the loss of important information [9].

In spite of the above criticisms. the flexible approach appears valuable. The SA has recognized the differing needs of the user by making available different information system options which provide for the demands of various cognitive styles. Also, the flexible system does not give the user the feeling of being constrained in his options, as the second approach we will next discuss may, and is likely to lead to higher decision confidence and user satisfaction.

The second approach the SA may use gives each user only those information system elements which fit the user's cognitive styles. This approach can be justified by extending Ackoff's argument which disagrees with the notion that "the managers know what information they need and want it" [1]. He contends that a flexible system, as discussed previously, may lead to the acquisition of unnecessary reports.

We do not wish to make a strong recommendation for the adoption of one approach versus another; both approaches have proponents in the literature. However, given the current difficultites in cognitive styles assessment, it may be feasible to use the second approach for users who are assessed to be at the extremes of the cognitive styles scale, where assessment is presumably more accurate, and resort to the flexible approach in providing reports to users in the midde range of the cognitive styles scale.

Validation of System Outputs

The SA and analysts must work together in system analysis and design projects after the initial system specification phase to make sure that the SA includes all the user needs and requirements in the system outputs. This important feedback process may take different forms and be conducted in various steps: 1) the user may look at sample outputs and analyze the description of system capabilities, 2) the user may be given a pilot system with which to work, or 3) the user may request changes after the system is in full operation [5].

Example of a Cognitive Style Design Application

To our knowledge there is only one published account of the use of cognitive styles in a design application. ,This is understandable since the suggestion that user characteristics should be considered in systems design is a relatively new concept in MIS literature. Bariff and Lusk report an application using cognitive styles assessment in the design phase of a "nursing evaluation information system" for a community nursing service in a large metropolitan eastern U.S. city [7]. The Witkin Embedded Figures Test [45] was used to measure cognitive styles. Designers found that all users were low in cognitive complexity. Since this was a first use of this approach, the designers used a partial validation process in which users were given sample reports with varying levels of aggregation. It was found that the users who were low in cognitive complexity preferred disaggregated reports with raw rather than transformed data; this is consistent with the research findings reported earlier in this article. The validation process was repeated after three months with similar findings.

To incorporate these findings into the system, the designers disaggregated the old information system report structure which had seventeen reports into a new system with sixty-nine separate reports. The reporting frequency was increased from quarterly to monthly for selected reports.

Concluding Notes

The wealth of psychological research and the variety of operational definitions of cognitive styles have made it difficult for both practitioners and researchers in the MIS area to get a clear understanding of the effects of cognitive styles. In addition, the limited amount of research which has explored cognitive style variables in the MIS area makes it difficult to draw conclusions on design issues. However, the following suggestions are intended to serve to improve the research in the conitive styles area:

1) give greater attention to the psychometric properties of the measuring instruments,
2) have provisions to insure the generalizability of research conclusions to populations of interest,
3) use controls—experimental and statistical—in experimental studies involving one or more "attribute" variables (measured rather than manipulated).

Psychometric properties, reliability and validity, must be determined and reported for measures of cognitive styles. Frequently this information, which is essential for determining the value of the measuring instruments, is not reported. Unfortunately, construct validation requires a well-developed theory to specify the placement of cognitive styles variables into a theoretical network of relationships; such a theory has not yet been formulated.

Sampling difficulties in cognitive styles research have been related to the type of subjects used in the experiments. Since the population of primary interest in MIS design is the user, typically the organizational manager, it is important to be able to generalize research conclusions to this population. If other subjects are used, such as business students, a central issue is whether these subjects are sufficiently similar to business managers in their information processing behaviors to justify generalizing findings from research conducted on them to managers. Caution must be exercised when managers, due to different experience, status, or motivations, tend to deal with information in ways which differ from processes typical of subjects who have not acquired these skills, status, or motives. An even more serious problem is the possibility that the differences in subject characteristics may interact with experimental treatments, thus threatening both internal and external validity [14].

Control difficulties also have plagued cognitive styles research. Experimental research typically uses control groups, with random assignment of subjects to experimental and control groups, to cancel out any influences which may spuriously distort the outcomes. One problem inherent in cognitive styles research is that cognitive styles are an attribute variable in the experimental design, *i.e.*, subjects are assigned on the basis of their cognitive styles, but the characteristic is not manipulated. As such, experimental designs for cognitive styles research fail to fully capitalize upon the ability of experiments to cancel out or control for alternative explanations by randomly assigning subjects to treatments. Since subjects cannot be randomly assigned to cognitive styles as they are to other treatments, it is always possible that other characterisitcs of the subjects which are systematically related to cognitive styles may remain an alternative explanation for the effects attributed to cognitive styles.

We hope that the literature presented and the issues raised in this article will lead to the consideration by practitioners of the cognitive style differences in design, and will interest researchers in conducting studies to further clarify the nature of cognitive styles and their relationship to information usage and decision-making.

Discussion Questions

1. Why might cognitive style be a relevant factor in the design of information systems?
2. As a practical matter, is it possible to develop information systems to support varying cognitive styles or other individual differences? Why or why not?
3. Is there an alternative to developing information systems to support individual differences without actually doing so? Explain.

References

[1] Ackoff, R.L. "Management Misinformation Ssytems," *Management Science*, Vol. 14, 1967, pp. 147-156.

[2] Adams, C.R. and Schroeder, R. "Managers and MIS: They Get What They Want," *Business Horizons*, Vol. 16. No. 8, December 1973, pp. 63-68.

[3] American Accounting Association, Report of the 1976-77 Committee on Human Information Processing, Working Paper, August 1977.

[4] Anderson, J.C., "Decision Maker Response to Probabilistic Information in the Capital Investment Decision Process," Ph.D. Thesis, Graduate School of Business Administration, University of Minnesota, Minneapolis, Minnesota, 1973.

[5] Bariff, Martin L. "Information Requirements Analysis: A Methodological Review," Working Paper 76-08-02, Decision Sciences Department, The Wharton School University of Pennsylvania, Philadelphia, Pennsylvania, 1977.

[6] Bariff, Martin L. and Lusk, Edward J. "A Study of the Utilization of Cognitive and Personality Tests for the Design of Management Information Systems," Working Paper 74-06-01, The Wharton School, University of Pennsylvania, Philadelphia, Pennsylvania, 1974.

[7] Bariff, Martin L. and Lusk, Edward J. "A Study of the Utilization of Cognitive Style and Personality Tests for the Design of Management Information Systems," *Management Science*, Vol. 23, No. 8, 1977, pp. 820-829.

[8] Barrett, M.J. "Information Processing Types and Simulated Production Decision Making," Management Information Systems Research Center, MISRC-WP-73-07, University of Minnesota, Minneapolis, Minnesota, 1973.

[9] Benbasat, I. "An Experimental Evaluation of the Effects of Information System and Decision Maker Characteristics on Decision Effectiveness," Ph.D. Thesis, University of Minnesota, Minneapolis, Minnesota, 1974.

[10] Benbasat, Izak and Taylor, Ronald N. "The Impact of Cognitive Styles on Information Systems Design," Working Paper No. 388. Faculty of Commerce and Business Administration, The University of British Columbia, Vancouver, B.C., Canada, May 1976.

[11] Bieri, J. "Cognitive Structures in Personality," in Schroder, H.M. and Suedfeld, P. (Eds.), *Personality Theory and Information Processing*, New York, Ronald Press, 1971, pp. 178-208.

[12] Botkin, J.W. "An Intuitive Computer System: A Cognitive Approach to the Management Learning Process," Doctoral dissertation, Harvard Business School, 1973.

[13] Broverman, D.M. "Dimensions of Cognitive Style," *Journal of Personality*, Vol. 28, 1960, pp. 167-185.

[14] Campbell, D.T. and Stanley, J.C. *Experimenal, and Quasi-Experimental Designs for Research,* Rand-McNally, Chicago, 1966.

[15] Chervany, N.L. and Dickson, G.W. "An Experimental Evaluation of Information Overload in a Production Environment," *Management Science*, Vol. 20, No. 10, June 1974, pp. 1335-1344.

[16] Chervany, N.L. Dickson, G.W., and Kozar, K.A. "An Experimental Gaming Framework for Investigating the Influence of Management Information Systems on Decision Effectiveness," Management Information Systems Research Center, MISRC WP-71-12, University of Minnesota, Minneapolis, Minnesota, 1972.

[17] Davis, G.B. *Management Information Systems: Conceptual Foundation, Structure and Development*, McGraw-Hill Series in Management Information Systems, 1974.

[18] Dermer, J. "Cognitive Characteristics and the Perceived Importance of Information," *Accounting Review*, Vol. 48, 1973, pp. 511-519.

[19] Dickson, G.W. "Management Information Systems: Definitions, Problems and Research," *SMIS Newsletter*, Vol. 1, 1971, pp. 6-12.

[20] Dickson, G.W. and Barkin, S.R., "An Investigation of Data Selection and Cognitive Style," MISRC-WP-76-08, Graduate School of Business Administration, University of Minnesota.

[21] Doktor, R.H. and Hamilton, W.T. "Cognitive Style and the Acceptance of Management Science Recommendations," *Management Science*, Vol. 19, No. 8, 1973.

[22] Driver, Michael and Mock, Theodore. "Human Information Processing, Decision Style Theory, and Accounting Information Systems," *The Accounting Review*, Vol. 1, No. 3, 1975, pp. 490-508.

[23] Educational Testing Service, *Manual for the Myers-Briggs Type Indicator*, Princeton, New Jersey, 1962.

[24] Fiske, D.W. "Can a Personality Construct Be Validated Empirically?" *Psychological Bulletin*, Vol. 80, 1973, pp. 89-92.

[25] Ghymn, K. and King, W.R. "Design of a Strategic Planning Information System," OMEGA, Vol. 4, No. 5, 1976, pp. 595-607.

[26] Huysmans, J.H.B.M. *The Implementation of Operations Research*, Wiley-Interscience, New York, 1970.

[27] Keen, P.W.G. "The Implications of Cognitive Style for Individual Decision Making," D.B.A. Thesis, Harvard University, 1973.

[28] Lucas, Henry C., Jr. *Why Information Systems Fail*, Columbia University Press, New York and London, 1975.

[29] Lucas, H.C., Jr., Clowes, K.W., and Kaplan, R.B. "Frameworks for Information Systems," *Infor*, Vol. 12, No. 2, 1974, pp. 245-260.

[30] Lusk, Edward J. "Cognitive Style Aspects of Annual Reports: Field Independence/Dependence," *Empirical Research in Accounting Selected Studies*, 1973.

[31] Lusk, Edward J. "Cognition: A Study of Its Effects on Abstraction of Decision Information," Wharton School Working Paper, University of Pennsylvania, 1973.

[32] MacCrimmon, K.R. and Taylor, R.N. "Problem Solving and Decision Making," in Dunnette, M.D. (Ed.), *Handbook of Industrial and Organizational Psychology*, Rand-McNally, Chicago, 1975, pp. 1397-1453.

[33] Mason, R.O, and Mitroff, J.J. " A Program for Research on Management Information Systems," *Management Science*, Vol. 19, No. 5, 1973, pp. 475-487.

[34] Mock, T.J. "A Longitudinal Study of Some Information Structure Alternatives," *Data Base*, Vol. 5, Nos. 2, 3, and 4, 1973, pp. 40-45.

[35] Schroder, H.M., Driver, M.J., and Streufert, S. *Human Information Processing*, Holt, Rinehart and Winston, Inc., New York, 1967.

[36] Schneider, Benjamin, *Staffing Organizations*, Goodyear Series in Management and Organizations, 1976, p. 199.

[37] Simon, Herbert A. and Newell, Allen. "Human Problem Solving: The State of the Theory in 1970," *American Psychologist*, Vol. 26, No. 2,

1971, pp. 145-159.
[38] Taylor, R.N., "Psychological Determinants of Bounded Rationality: Implications for Decision Making Strategies," *Decision Sciences*, Vol. 6, No. 3, July 1975, pp. 409-429.
[39] Taylor, R.N., "Perception of Problem Constraints," *Management Science*, Vol. 22, No. 1, 1975, pp. 22-29.
[40] Vannoy, J.S. "Generality of Cognitive Complexity—Simplicity as a Personality Construct" *Journal of Personality and Social Psychology*, Vol. 2, 1965, pp. 385-396.
[41] Vasarhelyi, M.A. "Man-Machine Planning Systems: A Behavioral Examination of Interactive Decision Making," Ph.D. Thesis, University of California at Los Angeles, June 1973.
[42] Vernon, P.E. "The Distinctiveness of Field Independence," *Journal of Personality*, Vol. 40, 1972, pp. 366-391.
[43] Wiggins, N. "Individual Differences in Human Judgments: A Multivariate Approach," in Rappaport, L. and Summers, D. (Eds.), *Human Judgment and Social Interaction*, Holt, Rinehart & Winston, New York, 1973, pp. 110-142.
[44] Witkin, H.A. *The Role of Cognitive Style in Academic Performance and in Teacher-Student Relations*, 1972.
[45] Witkin, H.A., Oltman, P.K., Rushkin, E., and Karp, S.A. *The Embedded Figures Test*, Consulting Psychologist Press, Inc., Palo Alto, California, 1971.
[46] Zajonc, R. "The Process of Cognitive Tuning in Communication," *Journal of Abnormal and Social Psychology*, Vol. 61, 1960, pp. 159-167.

Footnotes

1. While these researchers, such as Simon & Newell [37], have emphasized the influence of the decision problem on the solution strategies chosen, cognitive style research has stressed the importance of decision-maker characteristics in choice of solution strategy. See MacCrimmon and Taylor [32] for a review of decision-making strategies encompassing the influence of decision problem, decision environment, and decision-maker characteristics.
2. A more detailed treatment of this topic is found in [10].

READING 20

Implementation by Cultural Infusion: An Approach for Managing the Introduction of Information Technologies

article by
OMAR A. EL SAWY

Introduction

Information technologies are becoming increasingly useful as personal productivity aids to individuals at various levels of their organizations, whether they are workers, professionals, or managers. However, compounded with the usual implementation problems, managing the introduction of these information technologies brings to the foreground a new set of challenges for top management to deal with. On the one hand, there is a need to develop an implementation strategy for a rapidly increasing number of potential users covering the entire organizational hierarchy, and for computer-based technologies which are continuously multiplying and changing. On the other hand, there is a concurrent need to ensure that it is not taxing to organizational resources, and that it does not change the computing function into a "imperialist expansion."

The organizational context in which the above issue is addressed is the Hoover Institution, which is a research organization affiliated with Stanford University. It is involved with research in the social sciences and employs about 200 people. In late 1978 a computer committee was formed to investigate the use of computer-based technologies to enhance personal productivity in research activities and research administration. Initially, one individual was hired in early 1979 to develop and manage the effort. An implementation approach was devised to set up a low-overhead computer services function which could support a high growth of applications.

The implementation approach that was developed, and which is described in this article, evolved over time and learning took place over the course of four years. Although in hindsight the concepts might seem very orderly and generalizable,

Source: Reprinted by special permission of the *MIS Quarterly*, Volume 9, Number 2, June 1985, pp. 131-140.

they were developed and learned in a much more evolutionary and context-specific way. It is only in retrospect that we are able to articulate and prescribe a series of organized steps and conditions for the approach to work successfully in other organizations.

This approach was tried in small research organization and was launched in an entrepreneurial mode. However, by exposing the underlying concepts and prerequisites of the approach in a generalized way, the article attempts to facilitate the transfer of the experience to large business organizations which have a larger end user community and a more diverse application base.

The Organizational Context

The Hoover Institution was founded in 1919. It has evolved over the years from what was initially a specialized library and archival collection into an interdisciplinary research institution primarily concerned with research in the social sciences. The results of the research are disseminated through a variety of channels: seminars, conferences, books published by the Hoover and other presses, journal articles, lectures, and interviews and articles in the news media.

The top management of the Institution consists of the Director, the Deputy Director, two Associate Directors, and six senior scholars who manage the various research and publication programs. There are also about ten middle management positions. The balance consists of reserachers at various levels of seniority (about 100), and administrative staff. In addition, there are part-time staff and visiting scholars. The Institution's 83-84 budget was over $9 million.

The organizational climate can be described as being very much a "Theory Y" type, as is typical of most research environments. It is decentralized, but well-coordinated. There is a great deal of trust in delegating the allocation of resources and there is much more emphasis on output than on process, resulting in some informality. There is little bureaucracy and decisions can be made expediently.

Throughout most of the 1970s, external services from Stanford University's main computer center provided all the computer support for research and administration. The administrative support consisted mainly of accounting and payroll support. Some of the Hoover researchers accessed the data analysis services through a handful of leased hard-copy terminals. Voluminous printouts were printed remotely and delivered by mail. The fees for the data analysis services had topped $50,000 for the small number of researchers who were using it, the projected figure for the coming years was increasing precipitously, and the turnaround time was becoming problematic.

To alleviate the problem the Institution acquired the high-end minicomputer with seven hardcopy terminals and two CRT terminals. The computer was installed in late summer of 1978 with data analysis packages made available. By fall it became obvious that the system would not run by itself, even with the partial supervision of one of the knowledgeable researchers. Coupled with some disagreements with the vendor, support problems resulted in the computer eventually being switched off. A computer committee was formed, chaired by a senior scholar. It consisted of three senior scholars and an associate director. Its purpose was to examine the use of computer-based technologies for the enhancement of personal productivity in research activities and research, administration. In February 1979, one individual was hired to develop and manage the effort. His charter was to "make things work" and he was handed the key of the darkened computer room.

Organizing for Implementation by Cultural Infusion

In the months that followed, the manager of computer services set out to "make things work," in consultation with the chairman of the computer committee, and with approval from top management. Serveral critical issues surfaced:

• The data analysis application was the tip of the iceberg. Rapid advances in the capabilities and friendliness of information technologies provided the promise of an arsenal of productivity aids for research and research administration at all levels of the institution. There was a need to quickly get into office applications such as word processing.

- There was a need to position the institution for the long term such that it could continuously capitalize on advancing information technologies. There was a need to build a computer-literate constituency whether they were researchers, managers, or staff.
- Given the rapid growth of computer-based productivity applications there would have to be a major and increasing implementation effort, especially given the nontechnical user community and their advanced average age (about 25% were over fifty).
- All the above had to be accomplished without major investment in facilities or personnel. Top management was not prepared to fund a growing "computer empire," especially after the recent minicomputer purchase which had not reaped any benefits.

Taking into consideration the above issues, the following philosophy was adopted by the computer services function in its mode of operation:

- It would have to ensure that users were well supported in terms of learning assistance, but that they became self-sufficient eventually. The principal support person for a particular application would also be a member of that user group. This self-sustenance would also include an administrative component.
- The computer services function would have to ensure allocation of some resources to carefully and continuously track which advances in computer-based applications would be suitable for the Institution's needs.
- The management of the internal operations of the computer services function would only expend minimal resources, and no major investments in facilities would be made.

To enable a mode of operation with the above emphasis to be successful, the computer services function was visualized as having three components as shown in Figure 1, and as elaborated below.

Scanning and strategy: This component would involve scanning the external environment to keep up to date on state-of-the art hardware, software, and procedures (such as training methods, implementation approaches, chargeback practices). It also would involve investigating users' application needs, planning for new services and expansion, getting top management support, and revising strategic posture.

User services: This component would involve initiating users' awareness of computer-based applications, supporting them, taking responsibility for initial implementation and training, identifying principal support persons within the user groups, and coordinating them. To encourage a user self-sustenance mode, proper documention and training would be stressed and the appropriate cultural values towards technology would be instilled among the potential users. The technologies were to be perceived as coming to the user rather than vice versa, and intimately integrated into the user's activities. There would be no public terminal rooms, nor would there be a "computer center." All terminals would be in the users' offices. User support persons would be located among the users since they were part of the user group. The information technology would be infused within the user culture. It is from there that the notion of cultural infusion evolved.

Internal operations: This component would involve systems management of computers and networks, and include housekeeping, data backup, and software updating. In order to have minimal resources allocated to this component there would be no in-house program development, except for very minor modifications, and no programmers would be hired. Reliable technologies, already tested elsewhere, would be used. The computers and network would run unattended, and there would be no operator. The accounting scheme should be as simple as possible. Terminals and printers would be considered user devices, and should not be part of the responsibility of the computer services function, except in the selection process. Terminal allocation, terminal and printer acquisition and maintenance, supplies management, and office wiring would be taken care of by the office of the assistant director for operations who effectively functioned as the office manager.

Figure 1 The Computer Services Function

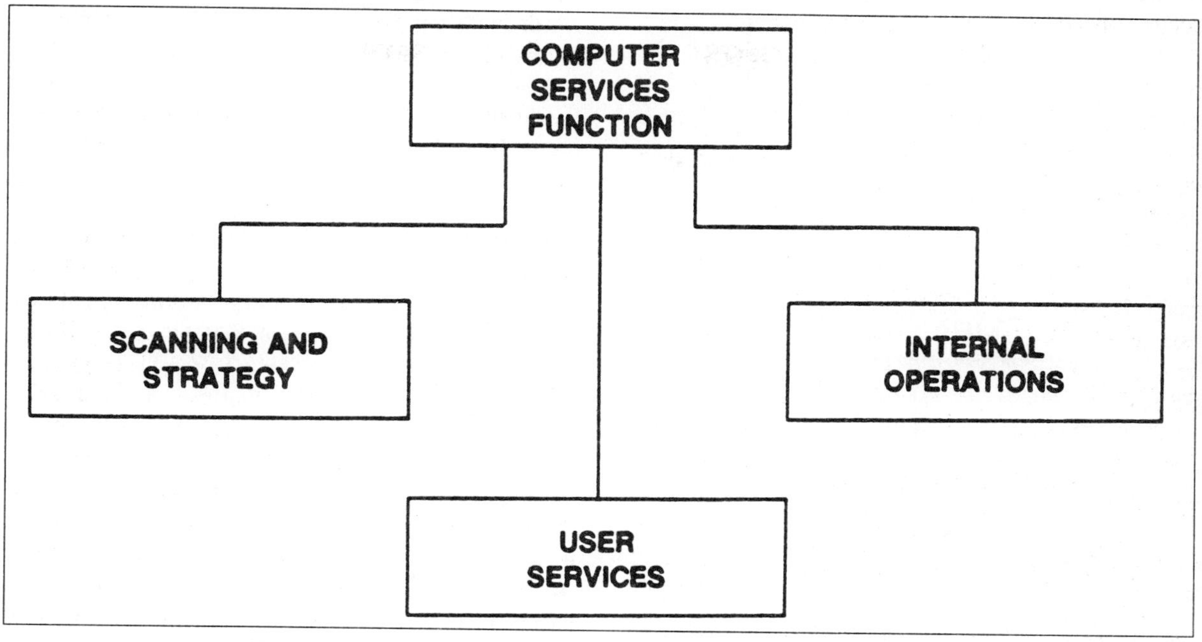

It was also determined that one other person, in addition to the manager of computer services, would be sufficient staffing while the number of user consultants would increase according to the increase in the number of applications. It was the manager's responsibility to also coordinate the three components.

Organizing the computer services function as such, put in place the infrastructural mechanisms that made it possible to develop and use the cultural infusion approach successfully.

Concepts and Dynamics of Implementation by Cultural Infusion

Although this section of the article draws on the Hoover Institution's experience, it describes the concepts and the dynamics of the implementation approach in generalized terms so they can be more easily translated to the context of different, and possibly larger organizations. Thus, for example, even though the computer services group at the Hoover Institution was staffed by only two people, we shall generalize to the case of a larger group in our description of the cultural infusion approach.

In generalized terms, the organization can be viewed as consisting of three sets of stakeholder groups: the computer services (CS) group, top management, and a variety of user groups. Membership in a user group is based on being a potential adopter of a specific computer-based application. Implementation by cultural infusion can be conceptualized as consisting of three stages (see Figure 2).

Stage 1: Matching

In this stage the CS group simultaneously scans the external technological environment and investigates potential user needs until a matched application is identified. This phase is continuous and several potential applications are at varying points of this stage at any one time. Some of these end up in a match; many of them do not.

A sizable amount of time is consciously allocated by all of the members of the CS group in scanning the external technological environment to keep up with the rapid changes in information

Figure 2 The Stages of Implementation by Cultural Infusion

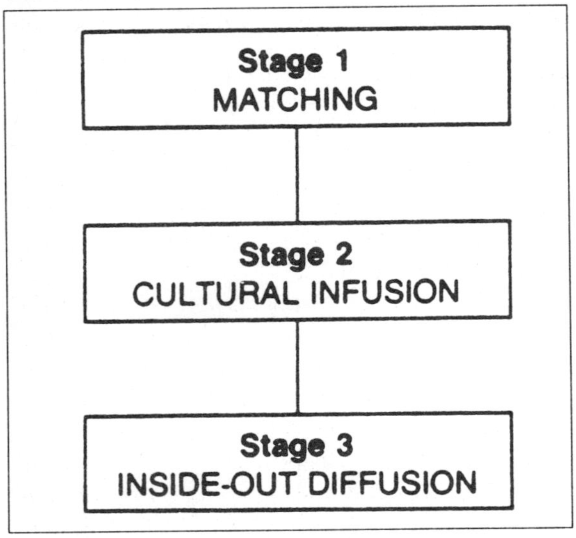

technologies and their applications, with a selective view as to how they might be useful for the organization. This involves subscription to, and regular scanning of trade publications concerned with computer and communication technologies, electronic office systems, and management information systems. This also involves regular participation in the local activities of computer user organizations in the different application areas (such as word processing, database management, accounting). The scanning is distributed among the members of the CS group. The user support persons are responsible for scanning topic areas which are related to the application area they are supporting.

Simultaneously, the CS group is continuously investigating potential user needs. This is mostly conducted on a direct face-to-face basis, and almost always in the user's office. It can best be described as a "sensing by walking about" approach. The CS group member becomes more familiar with the potential user's work activities, and through an unstructured conversation is usually able to tap some of the user needs and problems in terms of computer-based support. Very often the individual is a user of an existing application and is already a regular computer user. If the individual has never used a computer before, this informal talk can also be taken as an occasion to infuse some of the cultural values that facilitate effective use of information technologies (more on that in Stage 2).

The matching stage is thus a constant adaptation between the available technologies and the user needs until a match is made. For a match to occur several criteria must be satisfied. Apart from the expressed user need, the application must potentially be a high volume application such that it is economically feasible to support it. A quick informal feasibility study is done by the CS group to get an estimate of the initial costs and to determine whether it can be effectively supported. Another essential criterion is that there is an off-the-shelf package which can be quickly and easily installed such that minimal modifications are necessary. When the CS group senses that there is a matched application, top management is consulted to make sure that there is support for introducing the new application. If the support is there, the necessary software and hardware is purchased and the second stage of the process is started.

Although there is no system development activity in the traditional sense, the matching stage has some elements of participative design [9] in that the matching process puts prime value on user satisfaction. Responsibility for the design of a new work system is handed to the employees or managers who will eventually use it. This participation minimizes resistance to change, and helps set the level of user expectations. The matching stage is a collaborative and participative process, and can be used to build trust and credibility [6]. However, matching is not a broad-based organizational diagnosis, rather it is specific to a particular area of computer-based application.

Stage 2: Cultural Infusion

When a feasible match is identified a small subset of the targeted user group is chosen on the basis of the interactions in Stage 1. This core group consists of those individuals who are perceived by the CS group to have the most enthusiasm and need for the computer-based application, and whose work will most benefit from using it.

The core group must also include the individual who is most likely to be the support person. That individual is chosen preliminarily (again from interactions in Stage 1) on the basis of capacity and propensity to be a teacher and coach. But most important, this added part-time role must create incentives and represent some career advancement which is formally acknolwedged by top management. The final decision as to whether the person can fill the role is made during this stage.

There is no magical number for the size of the core user group. The number must be small enough for the CS group to be able to devote sufficient individual attention to each of the members. It must be large enough for there to be a shared camaraderie between the members, to be able to develop a viable subculture within the organization which promotes the implementation of the application. Thus, rather than there being an individual champion who is a strong opinon leader, there is an interested core group which is initially aided by the CS group. While we have no solid evidence to substantiate this, our limited experience suggests that core groups of less than three people will not sustain themselves.

Having selected the core group, the CS group starts the cultural infusion process. This process involves two simultaneous facets: infusing the application into the core group's work activities and using cultural values as a means of facilitating and sustaining the infusion. Thus, apart from educating the core group in the specifics of a particular software application and how to use it effectively in their work activities, the CS group has to create a facilitative cultural environment for sustaining effective use.

This approach capitalizes on the potency of strong cultural values in sustaining behaviors. Values form the core of any corporate culture, and strong values can be a powerful influence on behaviors [1]. In this stage, a subculture is created in the organization by instilling in the core group cultural values about the use of information technologies in general, and the use of the chosen application in particular. The matching in Stage 1 greatly lessens the chances of the subculture being a counterculture which is in conflict with the values of the rest of the organization [8].

Infusion is aided by ensuring that the information technology is adapted to the users' work activities. This is helped by having the users utilize the information technology from their own desks. For infusion to be effective it becomes essential that access to the technology be office based, rather than in shared public terminal rooms. This also requires answering users' questions in their offices, rather than in the CS group's offices.

There are many cultural values about the use of information technologies in general, which facilitate its effective infusion into work activities. The ones we have found most useful in our limited experience can be grouped into three sets: values which encourage continuous learning, values which clarify the respective roles of people and computers as they coexist in organizations, and values which break dysfunctional stereotypes of computer users. Examples of cultural values that encourage continuous learning are understanding that there is no way that users can keep all the instructions in their head, that user manuals are constant references, that it is acceptable to ask the same question more than once, and that user sophistication in the user of an application package is not a one-shot process. Examples of cultural values which clarify the coexistence of computers and people in organizations are understanding that computers are here to stay, that computers will help rather than hinder work if used properly, and that computers can help people get ahead in their job. Examples of cultural values which break dysfunctional stereotypes of computer users are understanding that older users can be very effective learners and doers, that using computers does not require a programming mind set, and that keyboarding is not a status-reducing activity.

Cultural values associated with the use of particular applications can be similarly infused. For example, in the case of word processing these might include values such as understanding that it is not necessarily a secretarial activity, that it has great benefit for idea processing, and that it does not mean that typewriters will be disposed of.

These cultural values, whether general or application-specific, can be infused directly or indirectly. Direct infusion can be achieved by telling people directly. Indirect infusion can be accomplished by demonstration. For example, if a user asks a question which is application-specific, the CS group member looks up the solution in the user manual in the presence of the user, even if he or she knows the answer, just to demonstrate the necessity of user manuals. All these values can be infused with the application specifics during the initial training period which can be one-to-one or group sessions. Simultaneously, the key support person is nurtured and encouraged to start taking a coaching role with the other core group members.

The evidence of cultural infusion is somewhat subtle. The most telling signs are changes in the user's vocabulary, how internalized the technology ownership has become ("our system" versus "your system"), and the willingness to try new things with the technology. Evaluation and corrective diagnosis is on-going in this stage, and it is still possible to abort if the application does not "take off" successfully with the core group. Also, the intensity of this stage will be much higher if it is the first computer-based application for the user.

This stage draws on the *social* change approach to implementaion [4, 5] in that the CS group is the active and responsible change agent which is trying to alter the user behaviors. However, our approach also includes a cultural change.

Stage 3: Inside-out Diffusion

The culture of the new application diffuses from the core group outwards to the secondary users, with the key support person assuming major responsibility. The CS group cuts itself loose from the application, gradually retiring to an advisory role. The key support person is responsible for diffusing the application to the rest of the organization and for training and supporting new users of the application.

Research has shown that interpersonal communication with near-peers who have experience with the innovation is the most important means by which an individual can evaluate and make the choice to adopt the innovation. Thus if Stage 2 is successful, in addition to the efforts of the key support person the core user group will also spread the new information technology to their peers. It is, therefore, very beneficial to have all the targeted levels of the organization represented in the core group.

Several mechanisms can be used to facilitate the core group—with the key support person as their teacher/coach—in becoming self-sustaining. After the CS group feels secure that the key support person can "hold their own," and that person agrees, a self-sustenance date can be announced to top management. The CS group can reassure the core group that they are always there in times of need, however, questions will only be dealt with after being channelled through the key support person. The application becomes self-sustaining and user-supported as far as the CS group is concerned. The CS group repeats the process with another application with another user group.

The elapsed time for each of these three stages will vary depending on contingencies such as the complexity of the application, available technologies, chracteristics of the user group, and the organization's previous experience with computer-based applications. In general, successive applications with the same user group will involve less time in each of the stages. It is difficult to pinpoint the exact time when the matching stage for a particular application starts because it is a continuous activity performed in parallel or multiple applications. In contrast, it is easier to recognize the point at which the match is made and the cultural infusion begins because a top management decision must be made. Sometimes, because of lead times for the acquisition of hardware and software, there may be an inactive period between the matching stage and the cultural infusion stage. The transition from the cultural infusion stage to the inside-out diffusion stage is fuzzy at first, as it involves a gradual withdrawal of the CS group. The selection of a self-sustenance date signals the point at which the direct support of the CS group ends.

Successes and Failures of the Approach

Having described above the concepts and dynamics of implementation by cultural infusion in generalized terms, this section describes examples of specific successes and failures in context of the Hoover Institution. The experience that we have had with this approach at the Hoover Institution has been very positive and, for the most part, the implementation has been judged as being very successful. However, we have also had some failures.

One example of a successful implementation was the word processing application. It has become so deeply ingrained into the work environment of the organization that it now involves a large part of the Institution and boasts users who are in their sixties. This was one of the early applications in 1979 when word processing needs were not as obvious as they are today. The matching phase lasted for three to four months. The manager of computer services scanned for suitable word processing software and talked to various potential users inside the organization about their writing needs. Several demonstration packages were brought in, and users gave opinions as to how suitable they were. Based on this feedback, one package was chosen and purchased and more CRT terminals were ordered for the core group. Top management was consulted for approval.

A core group of six people was chosen and the cultural infusion stage began. An introductory memo was passed out explaining how such a technology could be integrated into work activities and what the procedural and physical set up would be. This was reinforced and elaborated on by one-to-one interactions which involved infusing cultural values appropriate for the effective use of computer terminals for word processing. Subsequently, the software vendor gave a two day class in-house for 22 people. The key support person was chosen. She was a member of the office manager's administrative staff, and incentives were created such that this role would eventually occupy half her time. The cultural infusion and training continued to be done by the computer services manager. The key support person became self-supporting after three months, and successfully diffused the application to the rest of the Institution. She became responsible for all training, documentation, and support for the application, and the computer services group retired to a very minor role.

One application that failed was a database management system to keep track of the various researcher's publications, research interests, and professional activities. The matching stage was successful. A suitable database management package was identified, there was expressed need and involvement on the part of the manager and potential users in question, and there was top management support. The package was acquired, and the cultural infusion stage began. The core group was chosen, and a scaled-down version of the application worked well and was easy to use. However, the implementation failed in the later stages of Stage 2, and could never get to Stage 3. There was no key support person identified, and rather than the application being diffused to the rest of the organization, it dwindled. Thus, although the cultural infusion was executed properly with the core group, the implementation was unsuccessful because there was no key support person to sustain the implementation effort.

Assessing the Current Impacts

In terms of growth, starting from close to nothing in 1979 there are now a variety of personal productivity applications implemented. These include word processing, list processing, data bank access, data analysis software, database management, and electronic mail. Accounting, budgeting, and fund management applications are now being implemented. The Hoover Institution Press now interfaces with compositors via computer to speed up book production. There are two in-house multi-user computers, around 110 in-house CRT terminals hooked to them, and a local network is in place linking the Institution's three buildings. Every office in the complex is hard-wired for computer hook-up. Usage has grown steadily and rapidly and there are about 150 active user accounts.

In terms of overhead, the core staff of the computer services function is still two people, and exclusive of salaries, budgeted operating expenses for 1983-84 were only $66,000.

Top management has reported that the system has had pervasive impacts on productivity in both research and business management, and has transformed the way that research is conducted and disseminated. Several researchers who previously professed strong aversion to computers have become totally converted to the system as a result of discovering the gains in productivity they realize through its use.

The benefits of the adoption of these computer-based technologies are long term. The cultural environment of technology has been changed such that the Institution is always in a position to expediently and inexpensively implement new information technologies in the future.

Applicability to Other Settings

The cultural infusion approach to implementation evolved and was used at the Hoover Institution in response to the necessity for developing a high-growth, low-overhead computing services function with computer-based applications which pervaded all levels of the organization. The information technologies were culturally infused in the user work environment in order to make it easier for the users to become self-supporting. The approach was judged successful for this specific organization, but is it transferable to other settings?

The Hoover Institution situation has some unique features. It is a small organization which is fairly homogeneous and informal, and whose employees are all in the same geographical location. This facilitates interpersonal interaction between the computer services group and the user community. It is also a research organization where there is more emphasis on output than on process. Furthermore, information technologies are used as productivity aids and support tools and they do not have strategic significance, thus their use is discretionary. The applications selected are not complex or specialized; internal software development is not necessary.

In a larger organization the different stages of the implementation process will be different in terms of the mode of interaction between the computer services group, end users, and top management. In more formal environments the way that agreements are reached might be more demanding. Certainly, in manufacturing environments the types of computer-based applications will be different. Certainly, in strategic applications the user support will have to be more thorough and formalized. Certainly, in cases of mandatory use of technology, punitive mechanisms may have to be used. But in concept, there is no reason to believe that the cultural infusion approach is not transferable to other organizational settings, provided that the information technology management function is organized such that it allocates sufficient resources for the technology scanning and user services functions.

There is also reason to believe that many business organizations might find it attractive as an implementation approach. It is quite evident that most business organizations today are experiencing a tremendous growth in computer-based applications. Many of those applications are productivity aids which will eventually impact nearly all the employees, and which will have to be intimately integrated into the work environment. More and more applications are becoming user-driven, and the advantages of user-supported applications will become increasingly salient. A recent research study which polled leading information systems professionals on their views of key information systems issues in the 1980's [2] indicates the growing importance of managing end user computing. The results showed that facilitation and management of end user computing was regarded as the second ranked key issue in terms of importance among nineteen issues of key concern.

Research findings also reinforce the validity of the general concept of cultural infusion as a method for management of end user computing. An empirical study of end user computing in seven major organizations [10] indicated that a key area needing attention by information systems management was the development of a distributed organization structure for user support with more localized assistance. The conclusion was that, although the centralized information center approach has proven very effective in many organizations, it was only the first era of end user management. There was a desire and a need to move into the second era of distributed support. With respect to the importance of cultural change in implementation, a study of key recurrent issues in MIS implementation [4] indicated that commitment to change was a critical factor in differentiating between successful and unsuccessful implementation.

Conclusion

This experience has convinced us that introducing new information technologies using the cultural infusion approach makes it possible to sustain a high-growth, low-overhead computer services function, and to have effective implementation. Although the tactics may have to be different in other organizational settings, the essence of the approach appears to be transferable. It is hoped that more field reports on the use of this method in different settings will help refine the different tactical contingencies.

Acknowledgement

I would like to gratefully acknowledge the helpful comments of Bill Dutton in the formative stages of this article, the five SIM Paper Competition jury committee members, ana anonymous Associated Editor, and four anonymous reviewers.

Discussion Questions

1. What are the key activities of the computer services group in matching potential users' needs with technological solutions?
2. How is the "matching" process similar to participative design? How are they different?
3. Would cultural infusion be equally important to ensuring implementation success in all organizational contexts? Why or why not?
4. Describe in general terms the implementation "strategy" implied by this article.

References

[1] Deal, T.E. and Kennedy A. *Corporate Cultures*, Addison-Wesley Publishing Company, Reading, Massachusettts, 1982.

[2] Dickson, G.W., Leitheiser, R.L., Wetherbe, J.C., and Nechis, M. "Key Information Systems Issues for the 1980's," *MIS Quarterly*, Volume 8, Number 3, September 1984, pp. 135-159.

[3] El Sawy, O.A., and Hall, R.E. "Computer Services at the Hoover Institution," Internal Document, Stanford, California, 1981.

[4] Ginzberg, M.J. "Key Recurrent Issues in the MIS Implementation Process," *MIS Quarterly*, Volume 5, Number 2, June 1981, pp. 47-59.

[5] Keen, P.G.W. "Computer-Based Decision Aids: The Evaluation Problem," *Sloan Management Review*, Volume 16, Number 1, Spring 1975, pp. 12-31.

[6] Loftin, R.D., and Moosbruker, J.M. "Organization Development Methods in the Management of the Information Systems Function," *MIS Quarterly*, Volume 6, Number 3, September 1982, pp. 15-28.

[7] Lucas, H.C. *Implementation: The Key to Successful Information Systems*, Columbia University Press, New York, New York, 1981.

[8] Martin, J., and Siehl, C. "Organizational Culture and Counterculture: An Uneasy Symbiosis," *Organizational Dynamics*, Volume 12, Number 2, Autumn 1983, pp. 52-64.

[9] Mumford, E. "Participative Systems Design: Structure and Method," *Systems, Objectives, Solution*, Volume 1, Number 1, January 1981, pp. 5-19.

[10] Rockart, J.F., and Flannery, L. "The Management of End User Computing," *Communications of the ACM*, Volume 26, Number 10, October 1983, pp. 776-784.

[11] Rogers, E. "Once a System is Invented, How Do We Get it into Users' Hands," Paper presented at the Stanford University Symposium on Office Automation, Stanford, California, March 1980.

[12] Zmud, R.W. *Information Systems in Organizations*, Scott, Foresman and Co., Glenview, Illinois, 1983.

READING 21

Rituals In Information System Design

article by
DANIEL ROBEY and
M. LYNNE MARKUS

Introduction

It is commonly acknowledged that information systems (IS) impose both technical and social changes upon organizations. Understanding these changes requires an awareness of the values and assumptions built into systems during the design process. This awareness, however, is limited by the common assumption that is development is a rational process, directed toward the improvement of decision making and organizational effectiveness. This assumption ignores the possibility that IS design is a political process in which various actors stand to gain or lose power as a result of design decisions. In this article we examine several elements of system design from two perspectives, the rational and the political. From the first perspective, these design elements are viewed as logical features of a rational process. The political perspective treats these elements as rituals—symbolic behaviors that reinforce the prevailing belief system in an organization.

Recent literature on organizations demonstrates the usefulness of multiple perspectives or paradigms for analyzing organizational behavior [7]. In particular, organization theorists have become aware of a need to provide political interpretations of organizational events to supplement or replace rational interpretations. Recent books [31, 37] show a developing synthesis of material on power that balances more traditional treatments of the management process. Research which applies a political perspective reveals many new insights into the management area. For example, a case study by Borum [5] indicates far more support for a political interpretation of events in planned intervention than the more rational and humanistic assumptions normally made by organization development practitioners. In a similar fashion, Lund [22]

Source: Reprinted by special permission of the *MIS Quarterly*, Volume 8, Number 1, March 1984, pp. 5-15.

conducted a political analysis of the impact of worker participation on worker power. In both of these studies, the researchers gained insight by examining the political motives of actors and subgroups.

IS scholars have drawn sparingly from these developments in organization and management theory. Commmon frameworks for IS research do not include political variables to any significant extent [11, 20, 33]. However, some writers have recognized the value of political models for analyzing IS development. For exmaple, Argyris [1] provided early insight into the area, and Mason and Mitroff [27, p. 484] mentioned the relationship between information and power in their seminal article on IS research. The most thorough study of an IS-related decision process, Pettigrew's [36] analysis of a computer purchase decision, not only demonstrates the value of political analysis, but also shows how to do it well. More recently, a number of authors have offered both conceptual frameworks and empirical studies which substantiate the value of a political perspective [2, 3, 14, 16, 23, 25, 43, 44]. These works are consistent with the focus of this paper.

The Rationality of System Development

Characterizing a process as rational implies two things: first, that the process has an identifiable and agreed upon set of goals and, second, that it has been prescribed to achieve that goal. The systems development process is rational to the extent that two primary goals can be identified:

- to produce systems that enhance task performance and organizational effectiveness, and
- to produce systems that are accepted and used appropriately.

Two common features of the IS development process, the development life cycle and techniques for user involvement, are often prescribed to achieve these goals. In this section, we describe these activities and show how they support the view of systems development as a rational process. In the following section, we show how the same activities are consistent with a political view of systems development.

System Development Life Cycle

Virtually everyone in the system field is familiar with the concept of the system life cycle. The life cycle describes the stages through which a project develops as it becomes part of an organization's normal activities. These steps include project inception, a study of its feasibility, systems analysis, design, preparing specifications, programming, testing, training users, installing, and finally, operating the system. These activities are outlined in Table 1.

The life cycle is intended to ensure the translation of system objectives into operational systems within constraints of schedule and budget. It disciplines practitioners to respect technical prerequisites, for example, by delaying programming until file design and input/output requirements have been specified. Likewise, estimates of project costs should be made prior to investing many resources in systems analysis and design. In addtition to these technical requirements, the life cycle shows concern for human users and their needs. Thus, training is conducted prior to conversion and installation in order to reduce resistance that might accompany abrupt changes in the work environment.

The life cycle also delineates the responsibilities of various actors over the entire process. Systems development entails considerable skill specialization. Fundamental differences between analysts, programmers, hardware technicians, and computer operators necessitate a rather extensive division of responsibilities during the life cycle. By logically definining the steps involved, the life cycle shows where each group of specialists contributes. Significantly, the transition from one step to the next requires "handoffs:" or a formal "signoff" from one group of specialists to the next when work on one step is completed.

Techniques for User Involvement

Technically-sound systems completed on schedule and within budget are not always accepted, as many

Table 1 The Systems Life Cycle

- Inception
  - Preliminary survey
- Feasibility study
  - Existing procedures
  - Alternative systems
  - Cost estimates
- Systems analysis
  - Details of present procedures
  - Collection of data on volumes, input/output files
- Design
  - Ideal system unconstrained
  - Revisions to make ideal acceptable
- Specifications
  - Processing logic
  - File design
  - Input/output
  - Programming requirements
  - Manual procedures
- Programming
- Testing
  - Unit Tests
  - Combined module tests
  - Acceptance tests
- Training
- Conversion and installation
- Operations
  - Maintenance
  - Enhancements

Source: H.C. Lucas, Jr. *Information Systems Concepts for Management*, 2nd edition, McGraw-Hill Publishers, New York, New York, 1982, p. 292. Reprinted by permission.

studies have shown [17, 18, 41]. Frequently, these failures are attributed to a lack of user involvement throughout the life cycle. Consequently, Lucas [19] and many others have strongly advocated techniques for user involvement intended to achieve acceptance and appropriate use of systems.

In theory, user participation in systems design affords all parties the opportunity to confront important issues and resolve differences of opinion [12]. Various techniques have been used to involve users in systems design. Below, we review briefly the use of steering committees, information requirements analysis techniques, prototyping, and other behavioral approaches. This is by no means an exhaustive list, but rather a sampling of methods intended to improve the utility of computer systems for those who use them.

Steering Committees

One way to achieve the involvement of top management in system activities is to form a steering committee. The purpose of such a committee is to review proposed systems and to administer information system policy. Of 127 firms in a recent survey, 85% had corporate executive steering committees [35, p. 72]. Specific functions of these committees included setting direction, rationing resources, designing appropriate organization structures, staffing, and auditing performance. Conceptually, and empirically, considerable justification can be found for involving top managers on steering committees [38, 46]. Lack of support from upper management is often cited as the reason systems projects fail. The steering committee ideally supports worthwhile projects while disbanding less worthy projects before they go too far. In this way, information resources are conserved and directed only toward projects that meet the established strategic plan of the organization [15].

Information Requirements Analysis

Of the specific types of user involvement considered here, none has received more attention than Information Requirements Analysis (IRA) methods for determining what information managers need for effective decision making. In a review of 22 IRA techniques, Taggart and Tharp [45] found a heavy reliance on rational problem-solving approaches, as evidenced by the sequential structure of most methods. These methods typically lead users through several steps where management objectives are specified, existing jobs analyzed, improvements planned, and new information needs determined. This involves more than simply asking managers what they *want*. Rather, the techniques require either "bottom-up data analysis" or "top-down decision analysis" to determine what information is *needed* in making decisions [32].

Prototyping

Another approach to user involvement is the development of systems prototypes which users can operate experimentally before suggesting changes. Use of prototypes has been shown to improve significantly the likelihood of developing systems that users require and to shorten the overall life cycle [26]. Prototype methods, like the life cycle itself, use iterations to determine specifications. One methodology begins with "scenarios" constructed from sequences of display screens and proceeds through several iterations until the user agrees to an adequate first-level representation of the application [26]. Following this, issues such as screen-flow sequences, screen content, and layout are clarified with the user through further interactions with the prototype. Prototypes offer the user the advantages of hands-on trial and error in systems design. Ideally, the user and developer are brought together and communicate more accurately by referring to the physical prototype.

Behavioral Approaches

The three techniques of user involvement discussed above incorporate few explicit behavioral techniques for improving communication between users and developers. Mason and Carey do refer to the role of systems architect intended to bridge the communication gap between the user and developer, but say little about specific activities for this role. Several other authors report success in using specific behavioral exercises to create a climate of mutual respect and appreciation. Ward [47] describes the use of group training techniques to improve the likelihood of implementing quantitative models. Green [10] has used the nominal group technique, developed by Delbecq et al. [8], to aid design projects. Kaiser and Bostrom [13] have explored personality differences between users and developers within project teams and used that knowledge to improve project success. Also, Bostrom and Thomas [6] have used the PRECISION communication techniques [28] in a similar context to improve the accuracy of information requirements analysis. These behavioral approaches complement the more structured user involvement methods. They aim explicitly at the social and emotional factors inherent in human behavior and focus on the dynamics of planned change.

With this emphasis on human issues, the behavioral techniques exhibit a logic of their own. The main idea is to take a situation where there is potential for conflict and use it constructively. Advocates of constructive conflict see interdepartmental differences as necessary for successful performance of subtaskss, but ideally these differences are successfully integrated so that overall goals are also achieved [25, 39]. To some extent, the various behavioral approaches mentioned above strive for this integration by using third-party consultants or integrators, improving communication between parties, increasing the influence that each party perceives, and encouraging a consensus solution. Partial empirical support for this model of constructive conflict was reported by Robey and Farrow [40] and is implicit in much other research [39].

Evaluation

The systems life cycle concept and the techniques for user involvement discussed in this section can be defended as rational attempts to make systems better and to improve the effectiveness of the organization through more effective decision support. Systematic procedures assure proper sequences of development activities, producing higher quality systems. This structuring of the design process and interactions between users and developers eliminates redundancy and honors both technical and social requirements. The behavior approaches assume that conflict resolution results from maximum information exchange, awareness of superordinate goals, and shared power.

At the same time, these same activities can be described as elements of a political process. A political interpretation, as presented in the next section, does *not* imply that the above techniques are unnecessary or ineffective. Rather, systems development activities may well serve purposes beyond the rational goals of system quality and user acceptance.

System Development as a Political Process

Political Processes

For a process to be described as political there are two minimum requirements which may loosely be termed motive and opportunity. *Motive* refers to the presence of two or more actors, either individuals or groups, having differing objectives and interests. *Opportunity* refers to a situation involving the actors in which some may achieve their objectives to the absolute or relative disadvantage of the others. The systems development process satisfies both of these requirements because it almost always entails multiple actors with differing objectives, and brings them together in various forums. (Users of interactive or personal computing sometimes build systems for their own exclusive use, but this situation will not be considered in this paper.)

For the sake of simplicity, we shall consider only two types of actors: systems developers and users. While the specific motivations of developers and users vary among individuals, organizations, and situations, it is clear that developers and users rarely have identical or similar interests. Unlike users, developers are usually computer professionals who may even be employed by an external software house, consulting firm, or service bureau. Consequently, developers may differ from users in one or more of the following characteristics:

- cognitive style and personality differences which either influence an individual to select an occupation or which are reinforced by specialized occupational training.
- job characteristics which mold the evaluation criteria and reward mechanisms applied to the actors,
- location in the organizational structure, and
- organization affiliations which shape loyalties and perspectives.

Together, these differences in background and circumstance may produce different motives during systems design. For example, a user may prefer to keep computing costs low by purchasing software packages, using outside services, or using existing in-house computer hardware. A system-developer, on the other hand, may be motivated by the professional challenge of building a sophisticated system or by a personal concern to avoid career obsolescence. This interest could motivate the developer to suggest building the system in-house and running it on state-of-the-art computers and systems software.

In many cases of systems development, the picture is further complicated by the presence of multiple users and designers. This plurality of interest threatens one of the key assumptions of rationality, that is, a well-defined and accepted goal. In cases of conflicting interests, appeals to a superordinate goal may be ignored by parties seeking to achieve their own ends. Unlike the rational perspective, the political perspective makes no claim that actors will work toward the integration of their differences with other groups. As Keen [14] has observed, "while we all may try to act in the 'corporate' interest, we often have very different definitions of exactly what it is" (p. 28). Two examples illustrate the shortcomings in the rational view of systems development.

Illustrations

Markus [23] describes a financial information system developed for two different accounting units in a manufacturing firm. *Divisional* accountants reported to divisional general managers, who, in turn, were responsible for the profits and losses in their organizational units. *Corporate* accountants reported to the vice president of finance, who was concerned with the timely production of external financial statements to comply with SEC reporting requirements. Corporate accountants felt disadvantaged in their dealings with the divisional accountants by the lack of an information source other than divisional reports.

Consequently, when faced with the opportunity to develop a new accounting system, the two groups had very different objectives. The divisional accountants desired a system that would ease the burden of data entry and provide them with timely reports for managerial decision making. The corporate accountants desired a system that would produce consolidated financial statements, tax analyses, and independent audits of divisional performance. The objectives of these two user groups not only differed but were in direct conflict on the issue of who would control the creation of information about performance.

Rational analysis suggests that the differences between the corporate and divisional accountants could be resolved through user involvement and perhaps one or more structured techniques. Markus reports, however, that the corporate accountants systematically *excluded* the divisional accountants from the design process. The design team was composed entirely of people from corporate accounting and data processing. Two full years after the team's formation, divisional accountants were given their only role, to provide input data for the system, long after its main features had been determined. Divisional accountants were effectively forced to use a system which reduced their power by making division performance more transparent to corporate analysts. While divisonal users resisted the system, much of their protest came too late to prevent the shift of power to corporate personnel.

A second example demonstrates that different motives may exist *within* the functional specialities of "applications development" (business analyst, system analyst, programmer, maintenance programmer). In one company systems analysts were located in two different organizational units [24]. Those reporting directly to the user department were responsible for meeting user requirements; those reporting to the IS department were responsible for the technical aspects of systems design. Analysts in the user area, however, had been trained in IS and feared losing their technical skills. To remain technically current, they tried to perform the design activities of the technical group, but this tended to shortcut their requirements analysis duties. The technical systems analysts were determined to avoid such encroachment and responded by redoing the work performed by the user analysts. This conflict produced several systems which did not meet the users' needs and ultimately had to be reprogrammed or scrapped.

These examples illustrate both chracteristics of a political process: two or more actors with different interests and motivations, and an arena in which actors achieve objectives at the expense of others. Interestingly, these political activities occur within those processes previously described as rational elements of system design—the development life cycle and user involvement. .This presents a potential paradox because political actions seem to be at odds with the rational objectives of systems development. To help understand this dilemma, we must reanalyze the rational elements from the viewpoint of the political perspective.

Design Process Elements from the Political Perspective

System Life Cycle

From a political perspective, the life cycle of systems development creates the opportunity for parties with diverse interests to exert influence over one another. For example, in performing the feasibility study (see Table 1), systems professionals may strategically state "truths" about project costs and requirements. Their expert knowledge and position in the cycle allows them to represent data about user needs, implementation alternatives, and cost-benefit analyses in ways that may be advantageous for themselves and disadvantageous for users. The prescribed precedence of the feasibility study over later activities creates an inherent power advantage for those conducting it.

While the hand-offs, sign-offs, and approvals are designed to formalize and rationalize the interdependence between users and developers, they also encourage political behavior. "Upstream" errors may require major corrections at later stages, leading "downstream" parties to limit their liability for error correction by requiring a formal sign-off on obligations and responsibilities. Users, for instance, may sign off on specifications delivered to developers, promising, in effect, to accept the system if it meets those specifications. But users may also insist on the right of final approval, arguing that little would be gained by implementing a system that does not meet current needs. As a result, each of the hand-offs and subsequent approvals become opportunitites for covering one's position, blaming others, and escaping responsibility for poor performance. In short, the life cycle provides the opportunity to achieve one's own objectives at the expense of others.

Techniques for User Involvement

Each of the methods for user involvement contains potential for political behavior as well. For example, major issues in forming steering committees are their composition and leadership. As the committee members perform their function of project review, different coalitions may seek to head off or minimize each others' efforts to support private objectives. Clearly, steering committees may perpetuate disagreements about subgoals rather than directing computing resources toward superordinate goals.

Nolan, one of the strongest advocates of steering committees, notes that their importance increases as organizations progress through various growth "stages" to maturity [34]. Later stages imply the highest level of user involvement, with the end user and data processing becoming jointly accountable for systems design and data quality. However, a political perspective on computing growth would examine possible self-interests that underlie the voiced concern for user control. In this regard, Lucas and Sutton [21] present evidence that growth in data processing budgets was best predicted by the prior year's budget. Since budget size is a useful measure of organizational power, we can surmise that data processing power, rather than user control, motivates growth. Similar findings on budget growth have been reported to universities and explained with reference to political motives [42]. Lucas and Sutton noted that budget growth may occur in data processing departments that are not responsive to user needs, but instead concentrate on developing sophisticated hardware and software for its own sake [21].

With respect to information requirements analysis, most IRA methods have an inherent bias to preserve the status quo, a beneficial outcome for those who already possess power. Boland [4] argues that such a strategy is acceptable "only if the world is the best of all possible ones" (p. 266). He calls for more action-based approaches to IRA which would challenge the status quo by "opening issues, making assertions, posing questions, holding forums, developing agendas, and conducting debates" (p. 263). Taggart and Tharp [45] have also suggested extending IRA techniques to include "nonrational" methods for determining managers' information needs. Clearly, these radical changes would make IRA a more open, political process. The fact that few, if any, IRA methods come close to this challenge reveals the conservatism in the IRA process.

Finally, efforts to improve communications through the use of systems architects and behavioral techniques offer further opportunities to influence systems outcomes. Departmental affiliation of the faciliation or change agent is a crucial issue. For example, Mason and Carey [26, p. 349] recommend that systems architects be drawn from the systems development area because it ". . . is the one equipped to manage, train, and support the specialized professional skills embodied in this role." Clearly, their point is arguable. Whoever fills the facilitator role assumes power to guide the outcome of the systems development efforts. Despite the humanistic language used in most behavioral approaches, these methods also remain vulnerable to political influences.

Discussion and Conclusions

We have argued that IS design can fruitfully be explained as both a rational and a political process and have shown evidence to support this contention. The phases and handoffs of the systems development life cycle and the techniques of user participation that are the hallmarks of the rational perspective in IS design can also be viewed as rituals from the political perspective. From this viewpoint of rationality, systems design elements are instrumental to the achievement of organizational goals. As rituals, these same elements fulfill different, although equally important functions.

Rituals in systems development function to maintain the appearance of rationality in systems development and in organizational decision making. Regardless of whether it actually produces rational outcomes or not, systems development must *symbolize* rationality and *signify* that the actions taken are not arbitrary, but rather acceptable within the organization's ideology. As such, rituals help provide meaning to the actions taken within an organization.

By performing this function, systems design rituals uphold the myth, central to Western society, that organizations are rational entities serving social interests by pursuing their own goals. Myths are not necessarily false; their essential characteristic is that they are widely believed. Since a lore of rationality surrounds both computing and organizational decision making, it is completely understandable that the systems development process be regarded as rational also. The rituals help to ensure this perception.

Recent studies contribute to our awareness of myths, rituals, and ideologies in organizations. Meyer's [29, 30] studies of hospitals show that computing can play a key role as a symbol of an organization's rationality. For example, in one hospital, information technology signified a "corporate cybernetic" ideology. The language used reveals the significant role of the computer, capable of "interfacing our clinical and administrative data bases in real time" and having the potential to "revolutionize health care delivery" [30, p. 54]. In this case, computing assumed a symbolic value beyond its utility as a tool for administrative decision making. It signaled to employees, clients, and the outside world that the organization stood for progressive and efficient management.

Feldman and March [9] have further explored the symbolic use of information processing in organizations. They cite many instances where organizations collect (at great cost) information which is not used, but ignore relevant information that is available (at low or no cost). While such behavior does not seem rational, the information may have a symbolic value beyond its instrumental value. Thus, a computer-generated report may have little instrumental value for making a decision, especially if the total cost of producing the report is considered. However, a fat report resting on a manager's desk may be useful evidence that a decision was based on "hard information" rather than "soft intuition." In a society committed to intelligent choice, managers who want to look effective will demonstrate overt rationality by gathering and displaying such information.

Clearly, this need for rationality extends into the systems development process. The rituals of systems development perpetuate the prevailing ideology of rationality and provide an acceptable cover for unexpressible political motives in the dealings between users and designers. Overt conflict and manipulation are thereby controlled, lending stability and order to systems development. In effect, the rituals of systems development enable participants to act in their self interests without discrediting the organizations rational ideology.

Of course, the political perspective is also well-equipped to explain overt conflict where it does occur. Often systems fail to be developed to any party's satisfaction, or projects may be terminated in spite of apparent rational justification. Cases like these are more obvious evidence of political behavior. Our concern in this paper has been to make the less obvious point, i.e., that systems which appear to be rationally justified also serve political aims. Behind participants' skillful honoring of the appropriate rituals may lie self-interest and considerable negotiating power.

Some contend that a political perspective of IS development should be applied only under certain conditions. Kling [16], for example, argues that political analysis is more appropriate as the settings for systems design become more pluralistic and dynamic. Stable settings characterized by widely-shared values and consensus are likely to be more receptive to rational interventions. Rapidly changing environments with many actors, however, tend to produce conflict more readily than consensus. Thus, political behavior may not exist in some situations, and researchers may be unable to apply political analysis effectively [24]. By the same token, however, researchers and managers should not assume that politics is irrelevant simply because rational processes are used.

An alternative view suggests that rational and political views can both be applied to any situation. These perspectives simply provide different interpretations of the events which occur during systems development. The events themselves may be described objectively, but their interpretations may vary considerably depending on which perspective is used. In other words, rational and political perspectives are not mutually exclusive [39]. Each merely provides a different interpretation of the same events.

In conclusion, it seems important for systems designers, managers, and researchers to be aware of rituals in systems development and the important functions they perform. Because IS development can be both rational and political, it is essential for those engaged in the process to be aware of what is really going on. There is nothing inherently wrong with organizational politics. However, the naive actor who remains unaware of the differences between symbol and substance, or between ritual and reality, will be a less effective participant in the process.

Discussion Questions

1. How is the rational perspective of IS development different from the political perspective described in this article?
2. Give some specific examples of how system developers might differ from users. How are these differences relevant to the systems development process and successful implementation?
3. Give some examples (from your personal experience, if possible) of situations in which political motivations might underly ostensible rational motivations for a new information system.
4. How might formalized transitions between systems development stages (i.e., sign-offs by users) be interpreted as inherently political?

References

[1] Argyris, C. "Management Information Systems: The Challenge to Rationality and Emotionality," *Management Science*, Volume 17, Number 6, February 1971, pp. B275-B292.

[2] Bjorn-Andersen, N. and Eason, K.D. "Myths and Realities of Information Systems Contributing to Organizational Rationality," in A. Mowshowitz, ed., *Human Choice and Computers*, 2, North-Holland, Amsterdam, 1980, pp. 97-109.

[3] Bjorn-Andersen, N. and Pedersen, P.H. "Computer Facilitated Changes in the Management Power Structure," *Accounting Organizations and Society*, Volume 5, Number 2, 1980, pp. 203-216.

[4] Boland, R.J., Jr. "Control, Causality and Information System Requirements," *Accounting, Organizations and Society*, Volume 4, Number 4, 1979, pp. 259-272.

[5] Borum, F. "A Power-Strategy Alternative to Organization Development," *Organization Studies*, Volume 1, Number 2, 1970, pp. 123-146.

[6] Bostrom, R.P. and Thomas, B.D. "Getting the Requirements Right: A Communication Perspective, " Unpublished paper, 1982.

[7] Burrell, G. and Morgan, G. *Sociological Paradigms and Organizational Analysis*, Heinemann, London, England, 1979.

[8] Delbecq, A.L., Van de Ven, A.H., and Gustafson, D.J. *Group Techniques for Program Planning*, Scott-Foresman, Glenview, Illinois, 1975.

[9] Feldman, M.S. and March, J.G. "Information in Organizations as Signal and Symbol," *Administrative Science Quarterly*, Volume 26, Number 2, June 1981, pp. 171-186.

[10] Green, T.B. "Improving Modeller-User Interaction," *Operational Research Quarterly*, Volume 28, Number 3, September 1977, pp. 527-537.

[11] Ives, B., Hamilton, S., and Davis, B. "A Framework for Research in Computer-Based Management Information Systems," *Management Science*, Volume 26, Number 9, September 1980, pp. 910-934.

[12] Ives, B. and Olson, M.H. "User Involvement and MIS Success: A Review of Research," *Management Science*, in press.

[13] Kaiser, K.M. and Bostrom, R.P. "Personality Characteristics of MIS Project Teams: An Empirical Study and Action-Research Design," *MIS Quarterly*, Volume 6, Number 4, December 1982, pp. 43-60.

[14] Keen, P.G.W. "Information Systems and Organizational Change," *Communications of the ACM*, Volume 24, Number 1, January 1981, pp. 24-33.

[15] King, W.R. "Strategic Planning for Management Information Systems," *MIS Quarterly*, Volume 1, Number 2, June 1977, pp. 55-67.

[16] Kling, R. "Social Analyses of Computing: Theoretical Perspectives in Recent Empirical Research," *Computing Surveys*, Volume 12, Number 1, March 1980, pp. 61-110.

[17] Lucas, H.C., Jr. *Why Information Systems Fail*, Columbia University Press, New York, New York, 1975.

[18] Lucas, H.C., Jr. "Unsuccessful Implementation: The Case of a Computer-Based

Order Entry System," *Decision Sciences*, Volume 9, Number 1, January 1978, pp. 68-79.

[19] Lucas, H.C., Jr. *Information Systems Concepts for Management*, 2nd edition, McGraw-Hill, New York, New York, 1982.

[20] Lucas, H.C., Jr., Clowes, K.W., and Kaplan, R.B. "Frameworks for Information Systems, INFOR, Volume 12, Number 2, October 1974, pp. 245-260.

[21] Lucas, H.C., Jr. and Sutton, J.A. "The Stage Hypothesis and the S-Curve: Some Contradictory Evidence," *Communications of the ACM*, Volume 20, Number 4, April 1977, pp. 254-259.

[22] Lund, R. "Indirect Participation, Influence, and Power: Some Danish Experiences," *Organization Studies*, Volume 1, Number 2, 1980, pp. 147-160.

[23] Markus, M.L. "Power, Politics and MIS Implementaion," *Communications of the ACM*, Volume 26, Number 7, June 1983, pp. 430-444.

[24] Markus, M.L. *An Organizational Angle on Systems: Their Bugs and Features*, Pitman, Marshfield, Massachusetts, 1984.

[25] Markus, M.L. and Robey, D. "The Organizational Validity of Management Information Systems," *Human Relations*, Volume 36, Number 3, March 1983, pp. 203-225.

[26] Mason, R.E.A. and Carey, T.T. "Prototyping Interactive Information Systems," *Communications of the ACM*, Volume 26, Number 5, May 1983, pp. 347-354.

[27] Mason, R.O. and Mitroff, I.I. "A Program for Research on Management Information Systems," *Management Science*, Volume 19, Number 5, January 1973, pp. 475-487.

[28] McMaster, M. and Grinder, J. *PRECISION: A New Approach to Communication*, Precision Models, Beverly Hills, California 1980.

[29] Meyer, A.D. "Adapting to Environmental Jolts," *Administrative Science Quarterly*, Volume 27, Number 2, December 1982, pp. 515-537.

[30] Meyer, A.D. "How Ideologies Supplant Formal Structures and Shape Responses to Environments," *Journal of Management Studies*, Volume 19, Number 1, January 1982, pp. 45-61.

[31] Mintzberg, H. *Power In and Around Organizations*, Prentice-Hall, Englewood Cliffs, New Jersey, 1983.

[32] Munro, M.C. and Davis, G.B. "Determining Management Information Needs: A Comparison of Methods," *MIS Quarterly*, Volume 1, Number 2, June 1977, pp. 55-67.

[33] Nolan, R.L. and Wetherbe, J.C. "Toward a Comprehensive Framework for MIS Research," *MIS Quarterly*, Volume 4, Number 2, June 1978, pp. 1-19.

[34] Nolan, R.L. "Managing the Crises in Data Processing," *Harvard Business Review*, Volume 57, Number 2, March-April 1979, pp. 115-126.

[35] Nolan, R.L. "Managing Information Systems by Committee," *Harvard Business Review*, Volume 60, Number 4, July-August 1982, pp. 72-79.

[36] Pettigrew, A.M. *The Politics of Organizational Decision Making*, Tavistock, London, England, 1973.

[37] Pfeffer, J. *Power in Organizations*, Pitman, Marshfield, Massachusetts, 1981.

[38] Radnor, M. and Bean, A.S. "Top Management Support for Management Science," *Omega*, Volume 2, Number 1, 1974, pp. 63-75.

[39] Robey, D. "Conflict Models for Implementation Research," R.L. Schultz, ed., *Applications of Management Science*, JAI Press, 1984.

[40] Robey, D. and Farrow, D.L. "User Involvement in Information System Development: A Conflict Model and Empirical Test," *Management Science*, Volume 28, Number 1, January 1982, pp. 73-85.

[41] Robey, D. and Zeller, R.L. "Factors Affecting the Success and Failure of an Information System for Product Quality," *Interfaces*, Volume 8, Number 2, February 1978, pp. 70-75.

[42] Salancik, G.R. and Pfeffer, J. "The Bases and Use of Power in Organizational Decision Making: The Case of a University," *Administrative Science Quarterly*, Volume 19, Number 4, December 1974, pp. 453-473.

[43] Saunders, C.S. "Management Information Systems, Communications, and Departmental Power: An Integrative Model," *Academy of Management Review*, Volume 6, Number 3, July 1981, pp. 431-442.

[44] Shrivastava, P. "Decision Support Systems for Strategic Ill-Structured Problems," M. Ginzberg and C.A. Ross, eds., *Proceedings of the Third International Conference on Information Systems*, 1982, pp. 75-91.

[45] Taggart, W.M., Jr. and Tharp, M.O. "A

Survey of Information Requirements Analysis Techniques," *Computing Surveys*, Volume 9, Number 4, December 1977, pp. 76-88.

[46] Vanlommel, E. and Debrabander, B. "The Organization of Electronic Data Processing (EDP) Activities and Computer Use," *Journal of Business*, Volume 48, Number 3, 1975, pp. 391-410.

[47] Ward, R.A. "More Implementation Through an OR/Behavioral Science Partnership and Management Training," *Operational Research Quarterly*, Volume 25, Number 2, June 1974, pp. 209-218.

READING 22

Essential Principles of Information Systems Development

article by
JAMES A. SENN

The use of computer-based management information systems (MIS) to support managerial decision making has increased significantly since computers were introduced into the business community during the 1950's. The realization of a number of distinguishing characteristics of MIS has come with this increase in use and investigation of computer-based systems. These characteristics form the basis for an emerging set of very fundamental and basic principles of systems development for management information systems.

This discussion presents and examines some MIS development principles and characteristics as we know them today. Many are drawn from experiences that organizations have had developing and using these systems while others are based on research findings through both field studies and laboratory experiments. While this report draws together knowledge about MIS principles, it is hoped that the basic set will be expanded substantially as the field continues to grow and mature.

Source: Reprinted by special permission of the *MIS Quarterly*, Volume 2, Number 2, June 1978, pp. 17-26.

Background

One of the problems in dealing with the subject of management information systems is that in the past there has been no agreement on exactly what the term means. The Society for Management Information Systems has examined this problem in depth and has developed an extensive list of the various ways the term has been defined [16, 38].

The primary emphasis of MIS is that of providing decision support to management as contrasted with mere transaction processing to replicate clerical functions. Throughout this discussion the term MIS will be used when referring to decision-oriented activities and data processing or transaction processing systems will imply clerical activities. The important point to remember is that MIS is aimed at more than replication of clerical processing of data.

An information system is organized; it condenses and filters data until it becomes information for use in decision making at various levels of the organization. Ideally an MIS should provide outputs that are reliable, timely, and accurate to support making decisions. Today this frequently involves the use of computer systems. However, an information system does *not* presume computer processing. Instead, it requires a system that can deliver the necessary information for management in a timely fashion at a reasonable cost. In many instances, information may be produced by purely manual means and it may be transmitted as either an oral or written report. Some manual systems may produce information on a routine basis at fixed time intervals, perhaps monthly or quarterly, and sometimes the information may be produced on request as study results based on a special analysis.

The important point to recognize is that systems for clerical processing have quite different purposes from systems for providing information for management decision making, and that systems of either type need not involve computer processing. Despite the fact that important differences exist between the two, there is definitely a relationship. Efficient clerical systems are vital to the operation of large, highly complex organizations. Frequently these systems form the basis for organization information systems [23]. An organization may have many clerical systems, parts of which provide inputs to a management information system.

Based on these fundamental realizations, it is logical to conceive of a management information system as

> "...an organized method of providing past, present and projection information relating to internal operations and external intelligence. It supports the planning, control and operational functions of an organization by providing uniform information in the proper time-frame to assist the decision making process."[25]

We can begin to assemble technical and developmental, and behavioral factors from this common definition that should be guidelines for development and use of computer-based management information systems.

Technical and Developmental Factors

The technical and developmental factors associated with information systems focus on the structure of the components comprising the system. They also deal with the role of data and how it is managed within the system framework.

A Federation of Information Systems

The views of the MIS model in the literature and among practitioners in industry and government have generally taken one of two forms. The early view was one of MIS as a total, global system carefully integrated into all parts of the firm. The system was monolithic in form under this philosophy, where formal information networks were interrelated by conscious design *before* implementation. The underlying assumptions were that managers' information needs could be identified and or anticipated, as could the ways in which such information might be used. As a result, the total systems approach is based on the thought that it is appropriate to define explicitly the proper information flows to management and then to design a system that would assume the continual support of these flows.

One of the most disconcerting factors underlying the global concept was the fact that system expectations, requirements, and use change as the MIS exists over time. Hence what might be considered a total system today most likely will be only a partial system tomorrow. Similarly, it is somewhat naive to assume that it is possible for one person or one group of managers and experts to design a total or global MIS to develop effective boundaries and interfaces with the various organizational systems, and to integrate *the* system into the management stream.

Out of dissatisfaction with the global view came a more workable framework for MIS development. This view distinguishes an MIS as being dependent on lower level activities in the firm because it draws upon and integrates information from the several functional area information systems such as the marketing information system and the production information system, to provide a uniform body of details and knowledge for uncertainty reduction in decision making.

Speaking directly to this issue, Terrance Hanold, Past Chairman of the Executive Committee of The Pillsbury Company and an Honorary Founder of SMIS, indicates that,

> "As distinguished from an information system, I conceive of a management-information system to consist of a cluster of business information systems...MIS is a symbol rather than a descriptive name, which designates an integrated complex of information systems of such variety and sophistication and interrelationship as experience qualified by rational assessment determines to be essential or useful to the general or executive management of the business enterprise."[22]

Herbert Schwartz while at the U.S. Atomic Energy Commission used essentially the same framework and context for development of the MIS:

> "The management information system for an entire organization must be visualized as a supersystem of systems, as a federation of management information systems. Only the most monolithic of organizations can build and gain strength from a single total system...The federation should be structured as a set of systems, each system tightly integrated internally, but only loosely integrated when taken together."[34]

The same view is repeatedly expressed in the literature of the field.

This approach enables specialists to collect the information that they are best trained to gather. The accountant should be concerned with the collection of accounting information, the financial specialist should focus on the collection of financial knowledge, and so forth. Each has the training in a particular area of knowledge and should be more proficient in these activities than one with background in another area of the firm. Interchange of the information can then be accomplished to ensure that each functional area receives the information that it requires from other areas. We will focus on this aspect more in the following sections on management of data. But the principle of these systems is that *a management information system is a federation of functional area information systems.*

Data as the Center of MIS

The central resource in a management information system is data. Initial reaction to such a statement is often that it is an obvious fact that does not merit comment. However, past and present activities of some organizations involved with MIS seems to indicate that this principle is not always operationalized.

Data should be the central resources in an MIS since they provide the base from which processing takes place to develop the information needed for managerial decision making. Emphasis should be placed on data as opposed to hardware and software. We saw an era in which the attention of systems developers and users was focused on hardware and software during the early days of computer-based systems. The focus in many instances was on acquiring more and more computer power and larger machines. Much attention was also devoted to the development of a diversity of unique languages and software systems [32]. This was the day of the super-salesman, the glass enclosed computer palace, and the aura of "gee whiz" systems [39]. Data almost seemed to play a secondary role as everything revolved around the hardware and software.

As applications grew in sophistication, so too did a large portion of the users. Many persons came to realize that the data that these machines processed is the key to success. The data for business applications was recognized as a resource of the firm and thus came to be controlled and managed. As more and more users came into the information systems arena, they too placed their emphasis on data rather than on hardware or software. Data became the resource and hardware and software the tools—almost a complete reversal from the early days. Requirements for an improved level of technology came with the increased emphasis on data that allowed the users to gain the support they wanted without the need for large scale purchases of equipment or development of applications software.

Thus the new view of data's place in the organization led to such developments as minicomputers, networks and distributed processing, teleprocessing methods, and database management systems. All of these developments in effect de-emphasize hardware and software, even while they advanced the state of the art, and reinforce the central nature and importance of data. Manufacturers and vendors, however, do not always want us to view the world through these eyes; therefore, there are many camps that still do not pay proper respect to the role of data in computer-based information systems. We will see this more in the next section on databases. However, there is little question for the majority of persons involved with MIS that *data is the central resource in effective management information systems.*

The Database in MIS

The database is at the foundation of an MIS. It is the primary factor in a collection of information systems that enables integration of the various business information systems, thereby providing uniform knowledge to managers and decision makers throughout the organization. Since the basic underlying purpose of an MIS requires that the information be drawn from throughout the enterprise, it follows that the database should cut across organizational lines. A database, in other words, can be viewed as *more than* the ordinary collection of all data stored for one or more related computer-based application programs. It is visualized as a generalized, common, integrated collection which fulfills the data requirements of all application programs which must access it. Additionally, the data within this entity must be structured to model the natural data relationships that exist in an organization [33].

It should be pointed out, however, that the database does not contain all the data used in an organization. Various functional areas maintain files of data that are not needed by other parts of the enterprise. A record, however, should be maintained along with the database indicating where these "outside" files exist.

A high volume of data enters the database from throughout the organization. Each department or division provides data and information for storage and use by other parts of the company. A large number of forms for the data typically are found in the input stream, because of the diversity of data sources. Yet if the database truly is intended to serve to integrate and interface the various functional areas as well as to provide support to corporate-level management, a certain amount of control needs to be placed over entering data. Haphazard recording of facts will result in service to no one and to eventual degradation of the database to the extent that it is used by few persons. Incoming data should conform to a predetermined definition of form and should be stored according to precise rules. Data that does not match the definition should not be allowed to enter the database.

The issue of data exchange or data use is an important one in that it should be feasible through the database to provide uniform information across functional area lines. That is, two managers requesting information on sales volume, for example, should receive the the *same picture* of the state of sales, regardless of the area of the organization in which they are located. Further, although the form of the information may vary, *e.g.*, sales in dollars versus sales in product units, the picture portrayed through the data should remain constant.

Control of the database is an important aspect of MIS activities. An equally important factor, however, is the assurance that the data will be available when they are needed. It must be remembered that the database will change over time due to the nature of incoming facts and because of demands which users make on it. As this resource is in existence, users reliance will increase asssuming that it is properly designed, and they will expect more extensive support from it. Consequently, the database itself must be adaptable to the demands made on it. This capability is referred to as *evolvability* [20].

In general, the database plays a central role in management information systems. This is to say that *the database is at the foundation of an MIS and makes possible integration of the business information systems. It must be controlled and used as a management resource to ensure reliability, integrity, and evolvability.*

Data Independence

There needs to be a certain amount of independence between the way data is stored and the way different users intend to deal with it in a certain application. Conflicts frequently can arise between storage structures (the way the data is physically stored on devices and media) and data structures (the way each user views the data he or she needs). What may be the most efficient organization of data in stored form may not be best in terms of the data structures of the individual users. Yet the system should be able to accommodate user requirements while still physically dealing with the data in the most efficient manner. In addition, one user should be able to adjust his or her requirements without causing a change in the way data is stored. In turn, it should be possible to restructure the database when it is necessary because of new organization-wide requirements or because of improvements in computer-related technology. The restructuring efforts should not affect the users or their applications.

We do not yet have the means to accomplish all facets of his objective, but it is clear that *independence between the stored versions of the data and the requirements of each individual user should be sought whenever possible.*

Lifestream Systems

First, attention in MIS development needs to be given to the basic underlying system activities in the firm, *i.e.*, the "business of the firm." Establishment of systems to support these functions such as sales order processing, accounting, and purchasing, is important because of the sheer volume of activities in each of these areas, implying that potential cost savings can be realized if automation leads to more effective performance levels. In addition, the high level of understanding of the tasks performed in these areas usually means minimal difficulty in including them within the overall MIS framework.

Ease of conversion is not the only reason for giving priority to development of life stream systems. Organizations may experience cost savings and higher levels of profits or revenue by decreasing the time devoted to basic transaction-oriented systems, and coupling this with improved accuracy and increased volume [13]. However, it is also essential that transaction data from these activities be captured for inclusion in the database. The combination of cost savings, increased volume of processing, and improved data capture lead to the conclusion that *first attention in the development of management information systems should be given to the firm's basic lifestream systems.*

Information System Structure

Information system analysts and users typically have been concerned with what information should be provided to the user or decision maker and into which report it should be incorporated. It is, however, also necessary to focus on being able to provide information that is appropriate to the characteristics of both the decision maker and the decision task. Information system structure consists of characteristics of the person, the decision environment, and the information system, each of which has an impact on various measures of decision effectiveness [17]. Mason and Mitroff developed a similar framework which indicated a need to focus on the individual decision maker, the problem being examined, the organizational context, and a mode of presentation for the necessary information [28]. The information structure in both frameworks is believed to have an impact on various measures of performance and decision effectiveness.

A series of experiments. The Minnesota Experiments, were conducted to determine whether or not the above beliefs appear valid [9, 17, 35]. Each of the nine experiments in the series examined various aspects of the decision support problem. The evidence from these efforts strongly suggests that a relationship exists between information system structure and decision effectiveness. It appears that information requirements and related requirements may vary with changes in form or media of information, but performance levels may not necessarily be affected. The studies also appear to confirm Ackoff's previously published beliefs that more information need not lead to improved performance and that the manager may not need the information he or she wants [1, 31].

Consequently, system designers and users alike should pay close attention to the structure they adopt for management information system efforts. It appears that it is possible to improve information system efficiency without decreasing decision effectiveness: *the structure of a management information system significantly impacts managerial decision effectiveness.*

Behavior and Organization Development Factors

Too often in developing systems *the people* in the system are overlooked and an inordinate amount of attention is given to the technical factors. It is essential that systems people consider possible resistance to the system and the need for top management and user support.

Resistance to MIS

Introduction of MIS projects necessitates consideration of some of the behavioral aspects of change. A change may be ideal in both a technical and an economic sense, but this is no guarantee of its success. Unless persons want a change or the introduction of new techniques, it cannot significantly improve operating effectiveness or efficiency.

Management information systems frequently result in changes to the formal structure of an organization (e.g. adjustments in department boundaries, individual responsibilities, and communication channels), or to the informal structure (e.g., work relations, work group norms, or status). Such changes potentially affect many persons. However, the method by which they are introduced may be an overwhelming factor in determining its acceptance and its success. Also, resistance to the introduction should be anticipated and steps taken to prevent its occurrence.

When the information system specialist is faced with the problem of gaining system acceptance from operating managers and personnel, he or she is inclined to offer as evidence the same issues that were responsible for top management approval. The logic is relatively straight forward. If the project will result in reduced operating costs or increased profits, decreased decision time, job streamlining, or more accurate information on activities, it is often expected that managers will welcome such a system. The fallacy in this reasoning centers around the use of logic to change managers' attitudes about the job and the way it is performed. Attitudes may not be formed in a logical manner, as indicated repeatedly in the psychology literature, nor are they changed through the use of logic. Emotion and not logic is a key factor in attitude change [40]. The systems person is most illogical in attempting to use logic to affect attitude change. The result of improper handling of change is a form of resistance, which falls into the categories of:

> **Aggression** — Physical or nonphysical attack on the information system in an attempt to make it either inoperative or ineffective.
> **Projection** — A means by which persons can "energize" their resistance to the introduction of an information system (Blame the system).
> **Avoidance** — Withdrawing from or avoiding interaction with the information system, often as a result of frustration [18].

Problems such as these can easily develop if systems are not considered as major changes in various aspects of organizations. Acceptance of MIS activities cannot be based solely on the use of logic or measures of efficiency: *improved performance in organizations will not necessarily prevent resistance to the introduction of management information systems applications.*

Top Management Support

Successful development, implementation, and operation of an MIS requires the continued support and interaction with top corporate management. The importance of top management support for such systems has been noted often in the literature [3, 4, 14, 15, 19, 24], but in many instances the importance of involvement has been overlooked in application settings. The proper organizational philosophy and attitude as seen in managerial climate, for example, are necessary to assure that a change of the management of an MIS project will not be viewed unfavorably. If top management would, for example, indicate that it feels change is generally disruptive and an imposition on managers, then it is logical that MIS developments will not be favorably regarded by employees. Since change is a common phenomenon in busines and government today, particularly in the area of new procedures and managerial tools, management needs to communicate this to its people.

Top management support of MIS means more than just allocation of funds, although this is certainly an important factor. It also means assistance in establishing the chain of support needed in the various parts of the enterprise. Formal and informal structures may be altered because of MIS development. If top managers are involved in such developments through the establishment of systems goals and objectives along with operating procedures, support from operating and middle management levels should be more easily obtained. After all, if top management feels that an activity is important enough to devote valuable time and effort to it, perhaps the change is an important, significant, and necessary one which all persons should support. Although the mere involvement and support of top management is not sufficient to insure system success, it is necessary. Thus, we can state that a fundamental principle of computer-based information systems is that: *top management involvement, interaction, and support is a necessary but not sufficient factor for successful development and introduction of systems.*

User Interaction—The Project Team

It is necessary also, in addition to top management involvement in the MIS, to have user interaction. The logic here is that since an individual manager or employee will be using outputs from a system to do his or her work, he should be involved in the effort to develop the supporting system. The inputs of these individuals need to be heard directly.

It has been widely held in the past that establishment of clear objectives was a significant factor in achieving success with MIS project activities. Research indicates, however, that this is not quite accurate. Powers and Dickson [29] examined this factor in a field study on correlates of success with MIS projects. The results of this study, which involved firms in manufacturing, finance, marketing, transportation, and utilities, indicate that clarity of MIS project objectives is *not* related to user satisfaction, nor to any other criterion of success. There were some projects in those studied where the initial objectives were reportedly vague. However, through a gradual process of evolution where the users worked quite closely with the information systems staff, the users defined their objectives and information/decision-making environments. As a consequence, these projects resulted in products with which the users were highly pleased.

An additional aspect to user participation is that a *lack of correlation* was found between a successful project and utilization of a project team comprised of MIS staff and user personnel. The managers who eventually used the outputs created by the MIS project activities in several cases in the study, did not themselves participate on the teams. Rather, they delegated the team membership to staff personnel in their departments. Consequently, while there was user participation, the manager who later used the system and its outputs and rated it in terms of his own information requirements *did not* participate. Even though the assignment of user area staff personnel to project teams may be reasonable and effective for data processing or information systems developments where the primary requirement is for procedural expertise, this delegation by managers in an MIS environment appears detrimental in terms of the manager's satisfaction with the results of the project. Consequently, *successful management information systems efforts require the* ***direct involvement and participation*** *of the managers who will use the system outputs.*

Integration Upon Implementation

It follows that management information systems should be integrated into the decision system such that they are a *natural* part of daily activities, since they are designed to support managerial activities. These systems too often are somewhat extraneous to the managers when they are designed, and do not fit his or her normal way of operating. In other words, the systems are designed with the apparent underlying assumption that the manager will change to fit the system. Consequently, the systems are often perceived as "being in the way" and seem almost like an extra task for the manager rather than being of assistance.

When systems are developed and implemented, they should be integrated into the managerial process. However, the only way this can successfully come about is when the MIS project fills a *real need* or a hole in the information network. It does this either by providing information previously not readily available or by providing information already available with *less difficulty* and/or *greater reliability* than before. In either case, *an MIS project should be integrated into the organization upon its implementation. This is done by insuring that the system is designed to fill a real information need.*

Future Efforts

Knowledge about the use of management information systems has increased significantly in the last decade as evidenced by the fact that we can now begin formulation of principles such as those discussed here. However, the field remains relatively new and many important developments are still to be seen. An interesting question therefore is, "where do we go from here?" Some of the most important areas to examine are discussed here.

MIS Support For Planning

Most MIS activities today have focused on support of operating level decision making [12, 26, 27]. Although there is good reason for this, as was pointed out, more attention needs to be given to suport of planning, an area that is currently underdeveloped. The majority of the decision processes at this level of a company are relatively unstructured, require a long formulation period, involve large parts of the firm, and often result in long-term commitments of resources to a particular program [36].

We need to consider how information requirements will vary for unstructured tasks and for individuals performing these tasks. In addition, it is appropriate to determine what types of planning problems are suitable for on-line decision making support. The nature of the underlying database is a related factor that often is not fully considered in examining planning problems. Most MIS activities support operating level processes and the databases are thus designed for operating purposes. Does this mean that most databases are inadequate for planning support? If so, we need to determine what adjustments and changes generally are necessary to overcome this problem.

Analysis and Design Techniques

Analysis and design techniques need to be modified to make it possible to provide more individual tailoring of MIS activities. At the same time, tools must be found to advance the state of the art in analysis and design so that systems can be developed more efficiently had effectively. Modification, too, must be made possible without the long and expensive delays that are now customary. A great deal of work is continuing at the University of Michigan and elsewhere [36] concerning the automation of system building. This research is valuable and will offer long range benefits to the entire business community in the development of information system. However, we also need to develop tools which will assist managers and system users in identification of their information requirements and their decision processes. It is not clear how this can be accomplished [13], yet it is only this assumption that many of our systems activities are based today. We also need tools and techniques which will permit the evaluation of existing systems, to make changes to these systems, and to "run the system forward and backwards" to determine the impact of these changes. As you can see, substantial progress needs to be made in the area of systems analysis and design.

Data Management Techniques

A good deal of work has taken place in realizing the objectives of managing data, particularly in the database area. The concept of data independence has also been born as a means of attaining the objectives of evolvability; however, we do not yet have the necessary tools to fully reach this objective. Along with additional research in this area, we also need to formulate workable technology guidelines that provide systems people and database administrators with answers to such questions as when to restructure the database, or when to reorganize certain sections of it in response to new user requirements or advances in hardware and software. These are major research areas for the future, and they are areas where the payoffs will be significant.

Economic Evaluation of MIS

The importance of analyzing the benefits of implementing a particular MIS has been recognized for some time. Organizations, however, have done little in the way of adopting techniques for doing this. The traditional accounting methods for determining a rate of return, payback, and present value concepts which are frequently mentioned as a way of accomplishing this evaluation primarily measure cost displacement; they ignore the intangible benefits accruing to an MIS project.

Other approaches have been suggested to examine the issue of MIS benefits [5, 8, 10, 30]; they have centered around the use of information theory, simulation, and Bayesian statistics. Methods have been developed for evaluating sample information in decision situations, but these efforts have not been integrated into the problem of MIS benefit analysis.

Conclusions

The field of computer-based management information systems has developed dramatically since the first introduction of computers into business decision making. We can now begin statement of principles to guide others who are becoming involved with these systems. Much more research and development, however, is needed to answer the many questions being raised by theorists and practitioners alike.

Discussion Questions

1. Explain what is meant by the term "technical and developmental factors" then discuss the six factors that are guidelines for the development and use of computer-based management information systems.
2. Explain what is meant by the term "behavior and organization development factors." Discuss the four factors that are guidelines for the development and use of computer-based management information systems.
3. Discuss the four areas mentioned in the article which the author believed worthy of future examination.

References

[1] Ackoff, F.L. "Management Misinformation Systems," *Management Science*, Vol. 14, No. 4, December 1967.

[2] Anthony, R.N. *Planning and Control Systems: A Framework for Analysis*, Division of Research, Graduate School of Business Administration, Harvard University, Boston, 1965.

[3] Argyris, C. "Management Information Systems: The Challenge to Reality and Emotionality," *Management Science*, Vol. 17, No. 6, February 1971.

[4] Argyris, C. "Resistance To Rational Management Systems," *Innovation*, Issue 10, 1969.

[5] Bedford, N. and Onsi, M. "Measuring the Value of Information—An Information Theory Approach," *Management Service*, Vol. 13, No. 4, January-February 1966.

[6] Bennis W.G. *Organization Development: Its Nature, Origin and Prospects*, Addison-Wesley Publishing, Reading, Mass. 1969.

[7] Blumenthal, S. *Management Information Systems: A Framework for Planning and Development*, Prentice-Hall, Inc., Englewood Cliffs, N.J., 1969.

[8] Boyd, D. and Krasnow, H. "Economic Evaluation of Management Information Systems," *IBM Systems Journal*, Vol. 2, March 1968.

[9] Chervany, N.L. and Dickson, G.W. "An Experimental Evaluation of Information in A Production Environment," *Management Science*, Vol. 20, No. 10, June 1974.

[10] Chervany, N.L. and Dickson, G.W. "Economic Evaluation of Management Information Systems: An Analytical Framework," *Decision Sciences*, June-October, 1970.

[11] Churchill, N.C., Kempster, J.H., and Uretsky, M. *Computer-Based Information Systems For*

Management: A Survey, National ASsociation for Accountants, New York, 1969.
[12] Cougar, J.D. and Knapp, R.W. *Systems Analysis Techniques*, John Wiley and Sons, New York, 1974.
[13] Cougar, J.D. and Wergin, L.W. " Small Company MIS," *Infosystems*, Vol 21, No. 10, October 1974.
[14] Dean, N.J. "The Computer Comes of Age," *Harvard Business Review*, Vol. 46, No. 1, January-February, 1968.
[15] Dearden, J. "MIS" Is A Mirage," *Harvard Business Review*, Vol. 50, No. 1, January-February 1972.
[16] Dickson, G.W. "Management Information Systems: Definitions, Problems, and Research," *Society For Management Information Systems Newsletter*, July 1970.
[17] Dickson, G.W., Senn, J.A., and Chervany, N.L. "Research in MIS: The Minnesota Experiments," *Management Science*, Vol. 23, No. 9, May 1977.
[18] Dickson, G.W. and Simmons, J.K. "The Behavioral Side of MIS," *Business Horizons*, Vol. 13, August 1970.
[19] Diebold, J. "Bad Decisions On Computer Use," *Harvard Business Review*, Vol. 47, No. 1, January-February 1969.
[20] Everest, G.C., "Objectives of Database Management," *Information Systems: Proceedings of the Fourth International Symposium On Computers and Information Sciences* (COINS-72), December 1972, Plemum Press, New York, 1974.
[21] Gorry, G.A. and Scott Morton, M.S. "A Framework for Management Information Systems," *Sloan Management Review*, Vol. 13, No. 1, January 1971.
[22] Hanold, T. "The Executive View Of Management Information Systems," SMIS *Special Report*, The Society For Management Informaton Systems, Chicago, September 1972.
[23] Head, R.V. "Management Information Systems: A Critical Appraisal," *Datamation*, Vol. 13, No. 5, May 1967.
[24] Hertz, D.B. "Unlocking The Computer's Profit Potential," McKinsey and Company, New York, 1968.
[25] Kennevan, W. "MIS Universe," *Data Management*, September 1970.
[26] Lucas, H.C. Jr. "An Empirical Study of A Framework for Information Systems," *Decision Sciences*, Vol. 5, No. 1, January 1974.
[27] Lucas, H.C. Jr. *Toward Creative Systems Design*, Columbia University Press, New York, 1974.
[28] Mason, R.O. and Mitroff, I.I. "A Program For Research On Management Information Systems," *Management Science*, Vol. 19, No. 5, January 1973.
[29] Powers, R.F. and Dickson, G.W. "MIS Project Management: Myths, Opinions, and Reality," *California Management Review*, Vol. 15, Spring 1973.
[30] Pratt, J.W., Raiffa, H., and Schlaifer, R. *Introduction to Statistical Decision Theory*, John Wiley and Sons, New York, 1966.
[31] Rappaport, A "Management Misinformation Systems—Another Perspective," *Management Science*, December 1968.
[32] Schubert, P.F. "Directions in Data Base Management Technology," *Datamation*, Vol. 20, No. 9, September 1974.
[33] Schwartz, M.H. "MIS Planning," *Datamation*, Vol. 16, No. 17, September 1, 1970.
[34] Senn, J.A. and Dickson, G.W. "Information System Structure and Purchasing Decision Effectiveness," *Journal of Purchasing and Materials Management*, Vol. 10, No. 3, August 1974.
[35] Simon, H.A. *The New Science of Decision*, Harper Brothers Publishers, New York, 1960.
[36] Tiechrow, D. and Hershey, E.A. III "A Computer-Aided Technique for Structured Documentation," *Data Base*, Vol. 8, No. 1, Summer 1976, pp. 7-9.
[37] *What Is A Management Information System?* Research Report Number 1, The Society For Management Information Systems, Chicago, 1970.
[38] Williams, L.K. "the Human Side of Systems Change," *Systems and Procedure Journal*, July 1964.
[39] Withington, Frederic G. "Five Generations of Computers" *Harvard Business Review*, Vol. 52, No. 4, July-August 1974.
[40] Wolk S. "Resistance to EDP An Employee—Management Dilemma," *Data Management*, Vol. 6, No. 9, September 1968.

READING 23

Programming Without Tears

article by
DAVID H. FREEDMAN

Developments in computer software have given a productivity boost to nearly every profession. Clerical workers have word processing and electronic mail, managers have decision support systems and spreadsheets, engineers have computer-aided design tools. Ironically, the one calling that has managed to escape the trend to automation is computer programming. For the most part, software is still developed much the way it was 20 years ago. But that situation is changing, thanks to more productive programming languages and to software that helps write software. With these new tools, even nonprogrammers can create simple applications for their own use.

Until now, dependence on traditional programming techniques has slowed companies' efforts to use information technology. Well over 100,000 database management systems (DBMSs) of all types are in use worldwide—up from fewer than 300 in 1970, according to George Schussel, president of Digital Consulting Associates (Andover, Massachusettes). But data-processing departments are typically bogged down with three years' worth of requests to produce application programs that would make the data more meaningful and accessible to managers. Meanwhile, approximately 60 percent of the total yearly business expenditures on computers goes to fixing and updating aging programs written in COBOL—the most common business programming language—rather than to producing new ones, says Vaughan Merlyn, whose Atlanta-based firm, Merlyn Consulting, specializes in application development productivity.

Many corporations are mounting a three-pronged attack on this information bottleneck. They are acquiring fourth-generation programming languages that permit programmers to churn out applications

Source: Reprinted with permission, *High Technology* magazine, April 1986, pp. 34-35.

in record time—and that even let computer-illiterate users write simple programs. They are bringing in COBOL generators that automatically produce COBOL code under the direction of programmers. And they are equipping information systems staffs with intelligent, graphics-oriented workstations that could do for application program designers what computer-aided design work-stations have done for engineers.

Software Generations

The years between 1955 and 1965 were good ones for programmer productivity. Over that decade, the form in which computer instructions were written advanced two generations beyond first-generation machine language, which consists of rows of binary *0s* and *1s* that the machine can use directly. Assembly language, the second generation, essentially established English mnemonics for each machine language instruction, making the programming process much less onerous. Third-generation languages such as FORTRAN, COBOL, and PL/1 broke away from the one-to-one relationship between machine and assembly languages: A single statement in COBOL, for example, might generate several hundred machine-language instructions. These increases in the power of computer language statements resulted in a fiftyfold reduction in the time it took to write a typical program, Schussel estimates. Since then, however, progress has been slow.

Fourth-generation programming languages (4GLs) first appeared in 1973, but only recently has the market begun to assimilate and exploit them. These languages are closer to English than their predecessors, making them relatively easy to learn. If using the Nomad2 4GL, for example, a programmer who wanted to double the salary of all programmers in the company would write: "change all employee salary to employee salary x2 where skill contains programming." A COBOL program for the same purpose would require dozens of lines of code, all of it unintelligible to a nonprogrammer. Another salient feature of 4GLs is their nonprocedural format: Users need specify only what it is they want the program to do, as in the above example, and not how to do it. With COBOL, a decidedly procedural language, typically 80 percent of a program consists of commands that tell the computer which instruction to process next.

But beyond these basics, the term *fourth-generation language* has come to embrace such a wide variety of products that many experts recommend ignoring it altogether. "Fourth-generation languages are essentially a philosophy," maintains consultant Merlyn. A more concrete picture is given by an oft-quoted definition from James Martin, an independent consultant and a guru of information systems management: "A 4GL is a language whose basics can be learned in two days and that offers at least a 10-to-1 productivity gain over COBOL." In any case, these are some of the products that have been lumped under the 4GL umbrella:

End-User-Oriented Languages

These are the classic 4Gls, designed for use by computer novices and pros alike. They generally run on large mainframe computers and combine the features of a database management system and a programming language. They are also usually compatible with popular DBMSs such as Cullinet Software's IDMS, and, increasingly, with easier-to-use computer resources as efficiently as the third generation, these languages are best suited for developing simple analytical programs that don't repeatedly run large volumes of data. Three products have this category more or less to themselves: Focus from Information Builders (New York), Ramis II from Martin Marietta Data systems (Princeton, New Jersey), and Nomad2 from D&B Computing Services (Wilton, Connecticut). Prices range from $100,000 to $135,000.

DBMS-Oriented Languages

These products are designed to work with a specific DBMS offered separately by the same vendor. Though not always as easy to use as the Focus-type 4GLs, these languages provide larger and more detailed sets of commands and can be used to develop more complex, higher-volume applications. Best-sellers in this category (listed with their associated DBMSs) include Ideal (Datacom/DB)

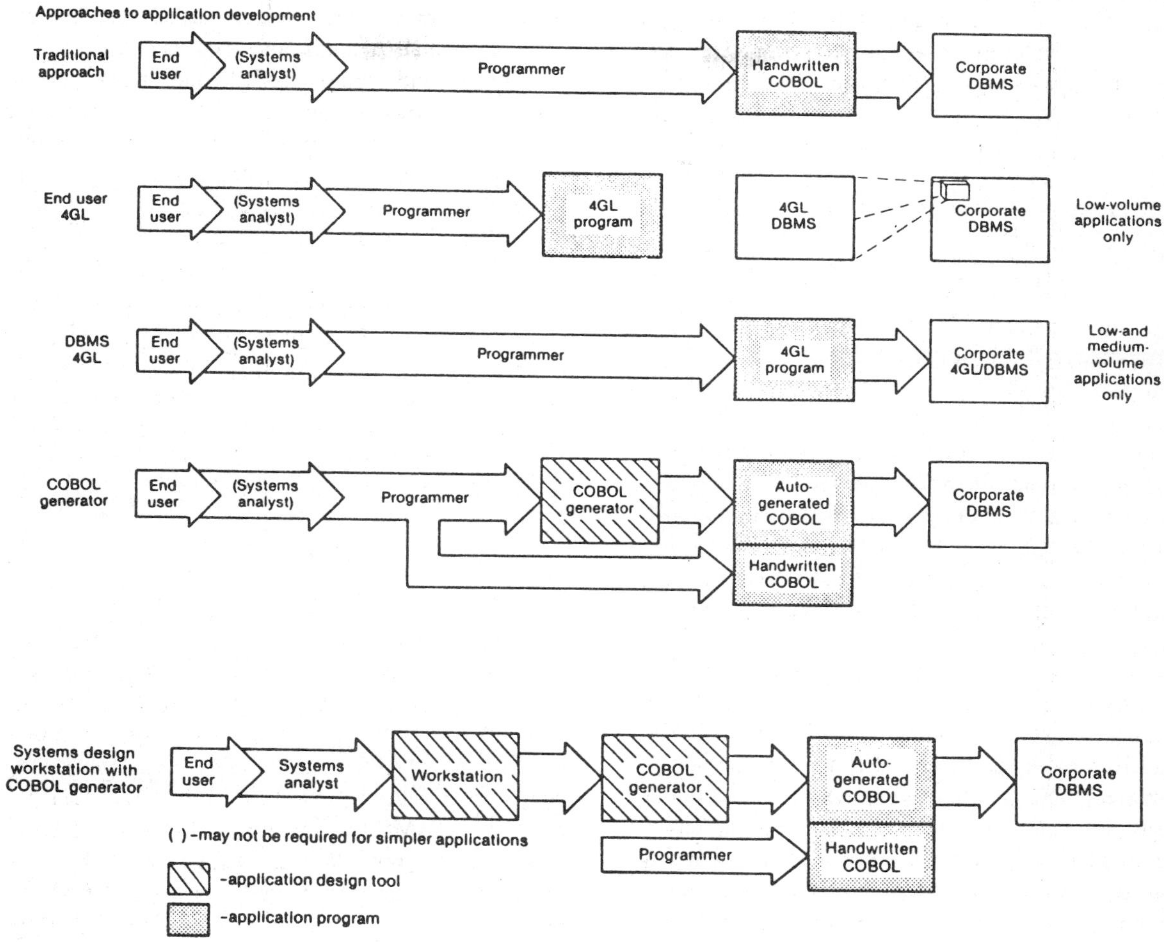

Users who need to obtain information from a corporate database traditionally work through systems designers (who define the overall application) and programmers (who write the necessary software). Fourth-generation languages (4GLs) can let users write their own programs and can increase the productivity of professional programmers as well. An end-user-oriented 4GL first interacts with its own internal database, which in turn accesses data from the full database. DBMS-oriented 4GLs generally work only with database management systems sold separately by the same vendor; they also give programmers more tools with which to build larger applications than the end-user 4GLs. The popular third-generation language COBOL is more flexible than the fourth-generation languages but also more difficult to learn and use. However, COBOL generators can automatically produce up to 80 percent of a program's code, leaving only 20 percent for a programmer to write manually. Systems-design workstations help analysts develop an application's overall design, and can be linked by software bridges directly into COBOL generators, which then produce programs based on the analyst's specifications.

from Applied Data Research in Princeton, New Jersey; Natural (Adabas) from Software AG in Reston, Virginia; and Inquire (Inquire) from Infodata Systems in Falls Church, Virginia. They typically cost from $50,000 to $80,000.

4GL-Like Tools

A Number of products can accomplish, within limits, what some of the above products do, even though they aren't really languages. Application generators like Gener/OL from Pansophic Systems (Oakbrook, Illinois) ease program development via menu options, simple commands, and "screen painting," with which the user creates an electonric mock-up of a paper document such as an insurance form. Another example is decision support development systems, such as one from Pilot Executive Software (Boston); these are application generators with integrated DBMSs geared to developing applications that provide summaries of corporate and competitive data along with "what if?" comparisons. And at the limit, some observers insist that Lotus® 1-2-3® and other integrated spreadsheet products are also 4GLs.

However 4GLs are defined, one indisputable benefit is that they let programmers program faster—although how much faster is a hotly debated question. Vendors have been known to promise one hundredfold increases in productivity, which may be true in some applications, but companies whose programmers achieve a seven-to-one improvement generally consider themselves ahead of the game. Richard Cobb, vice president of Martin Marietta Data Systems' Information Technology Division, calculates that a five-to-one productivity gain enables a programmer to generate enough extra applications to save a typical company nearly $1 million over a three-year period. Bank of America is a believer, having realized productivity improvements of about 10 to 1 when it started using Nomad2 10 years ago. Today 10,000 of the bank's employees—a third of them professional programmers—work primarily with that 4GL.

Fourth-generation languages could have an even greater impact on end users than on programmers. A novice can use the basic features of a 4GL with just two hours of training, says Nicholas Rawlings, director and senior technical adviser at D&B Computing Services. At 3M, 12,000 nonprogrammers use the System 1032 4GL from Software House (Cambridge, Massachusetts) to glean information from the company's database. "That's 123,000 users that don't have to go to the information systems department for answers," says Software House's technical marketing manager Paul Perkovic.

Programmer Resistance

COBOL fans needn't brace themselves for a 4GL takeover, however. Over 50 billion lines of COBOL are still knocking around inside corporate computers, and companies aren't about to rewrite them. But even when it comes to new applications, 4GLs meet stiff resistance from many programmers, who claim that they are blunt instruments incapable of producing finely tuned programs. Each successive language generation does in fact lose some of the flexibility of its predecessors. Because 4GLs generally lack such programming staples as loops, arrays, and string manipulations—a single statement in the newer languages is designed to encompass many funtions of the former—they offer less control over the results.

"If a fourth-generation language is like one of those nifty new automatic cameras, then COBOL is like a manual SLR (single-lens reflex camera]," assserts DCA president Schussel, who lectures extensively on 4GLs. "If you know how to operate the SLR, you can make it stand up and dance." but some suggest that programmers also belittle fourth-generation languages because they're concerned about maintaining the market for their hard-earned COBOL experience. "A 4GL can be 'deskilling,' robbing programmers of career and pay opportunities," says consultant Merlyn, noting that a top COBOL programmer can make $15,000 more per year than a Focus programmer.

Even programmers who embrace 4GLs have to be careful to accept the languages' limitations. While 4GLs work well when it comes to noncritical, internal applications that don't demand a lot of computer resources, they are too inefficient for most powerhouse applications like order processing or payroll. New Jersey motorists learned that lesson the hard way last September when the

Department of Motor Vehicles' Ideal-based vehicle registration system brought the department's computer to its knees, leaving a million drivers without registration. (Ideal vendor Applied Data Research claims it warned the system's developers that the languages might be unsuitable for the high-volume segments of the application.) To avoid such problems, some data-processing departments use 4GLs only to develop quick application prototypes; if the prototype works they rewrite the program in COBOL.

End users can run into difficulties too. Although they can learn to write working 4GL programs, getting current and accurate data sometimes requires additional knowledge about how the corporate database is set up. Some companies maintain information in more than one database, and the 4GL language may not be compatible with all of them. Also, the English-like aspects of a 4GL may mislead novice users into thinking that it will "understand" their needs, even if these aren't specified in detail. For example, a user who simply requests a report on yearly sales might get fiscal year figures when calendar year figures were desired. Or invoices for goods shipped might be confused with invoices for goods received. Another problem that novice 4GL users can face is that some information systems department provide access only to copies of the actual database. If the copies aren't updated every time the main database changes, the user may end up with old or ambiguous data.

Despite the problems, Schussel says 4GLs and 4GL-like tools can now be found at about half the 17,000 mainframe sites in the United States, and he expects penetration to hit 80 percent by 1990. By then, he adds, a large percentage of companies will have more than one 4GL.

The growth of 4GLs beyond 1990 may be tied in part to the spread of effective "natural language processing," which allows users to query databases in ordinary English. Although 4GLs are English-like, the user must still adhere to each language's vocabulary and syntax constraints. Natural language systems, on the other hand, employ rules of grammar and lexicons of commonly used words to translate English requests into a 4GL or some other database query language. With a good natural language system, a user can ask in a variety of ways for the same data, and the system will "understand" the common goal of each request.

The leader in this field is Artificial Intelligence Corp. (Waltham, Massaachusetts), whose Intellect software lets a user type in requests such as "Give me a pie chart showing the population for each state in the Midwest." The program interfaces with several software products and languages, including Focus, and is installed at about 350 sites. Martin Marietta offers English and French natural language modules of its Ramis II; the English version contains a dictionary of 5,000 root words and phrases, and, like Intellect, allows the user to build application- and user-specific dictionaries.

One problem with natural language tools is that because of the fuzzy syntax and semantics of real languages, they are liable to misunderstand a command. Unless the system can detect ambiguous statements and request clarification from the user, it may provide apparently correct, but inaccurate, data. "I advise people to use these languages to experiment, not to build strategic systems," warns DCA's Schussel.

Some companies are employing natural language interfaces for applications broader than simply querying databases. One example is an application development system from Exsys (New York), which holds an English question-and-answer session to gain information about the user's needs. The system takes this information and automatically builds an application that works with the system's proprietarty DBMS.

Other features likely to become common on 4GLs include layered interfaces that vary in complexity according to the sophisitication of the user, like those of Software House's System 1032; integrated office automation functions such as document processing and electronic mail, like those offered with Natural; and completely menu-driven interface options, like the one available with Ramis II. Also, PC links into mainframe-based 4GLs have become *de rigueur*. Information Builders has gone further than most in this regard with its PC/Focus, which lets users actually develop mainframe Focus applications on their PCs.

Cobol Generators

Those who like the rapid application development powers of 4GLs but insist on running COBOL can turn to COBOL generators. These mainframe-based software packages draw on their libraries to produce chunks of high-quality prefabricated COBOl code—as much as 80 percent of a typical program. Tying the chunks together and customizing the program—the other 20 percent—is left to a programmer.

COBOL generators can spew out as much as 2,000 lines of code a day, versus the 20 lines expected from the flesh-and-blood model, according to vendor Netron (Downsview, Ontario). Because of the time required to stick together and customize the canned code, the productivity increase is not actually 100 to 1, but it's comparable to that provided by a 4GL. And since the final program is in the efficient COBOL language, companies don't have to restrict the use of generators to low-volume applications, as they might with a 4GL. That's why some say COBOL generators are the best of both worlds.

Others say they are more like the worst of both worlds. After all, COBOL generators don't let programmers get at the language's high-precision tools; the resulting code, meanwhile, could require the kind of expensive maintenance that data-processing departments are trying to get away from. Indeed, modifying automatically generated COBOL presents some unique problems. For one thing, much of the code the programmer will have to modify won't be something he or she actually wrote. For another, every time a change is required, the programmer must decide whether to make the change by hand or to regenerate the entire application. In the latter case, all previous hand-made modifications will be lost, since the generator has no way of incorporating them.

COBOL generators are newer than 4GLs and not yet as popular. One of the most widely used generators, Pacbase from CGI Systems (Pearl River, New York), has an installed base of about 400, a fifth that of the more popular 4GLs. Also, the $100,000 to $200,000 price tags of most COBOL generators don't encourage experimentation. But vendors are adding impressive features that could eventually put COBOL generators on top. Netron, for example, offers a "frame-based" structure that it claims isolates automatically generated code from handwritten and modified code; that way, users can regenerate an application without losing previous customization efforts. Pacbase incorporates project management capabilities in its system, and Higher Order Software (Cambridge, Massachussetts) has endowed its "Use.it" generator with a graphics-oriented interface similar to that of the easy-to-use Apple Macintosh personal computer.

Systems Design

COBOL generators and 4GLs offer reasonable responses to the challenge of programmer productivity. But programming typically represents only 15 percent of the cost of the "application life cycle," as it is called by systems analysts, who are to programmers what engineers are to drafters. The life cycle consists of first determining the end users' requirements and then designing the application (ensuring, in part, that it works smoothly with any existing applications), writing the program, testing it, and maintaining it as bugs appear and users' requirements change.

There is a growing awareness among information systems managers that their departments may be tripping up in the critical design stage. "A fourth-generation language that offers a 10-to-1 improvement in programming productivity doesn't do you much good if you're using it to build the wrong application," notes Merlyn. "All it means is that you'll be able to rebuild it 10 times before you have a net loss in productivity."

If programmers have been trailing a bit in the productivity-through-automation revolution, then systems analysts—whose primary tools have consisted of pencil and paper—have been left in the dust. But now a new class of product is aiming to rectify this situation. Systems-design workstations bring to systems analysts the same type of capabilities that computer-aided design workstations have long offered engineers. And according to consultant Martin, such capabilities are sorely needed: "The design of the interlocking computer applications of a modern enterprise are not less complex than the design of a microchip or a jet aircraft."

The workstations usually based on powerful

PCs, provide sophisticated graphics-based design tools that help analysts create flowcharts. Multiple-screen windows, icon-based menus, and pointing devices speed editing and let users zoom in from a systemwide view to a detailed look at any element. Design-rule databases ensure that users' don't violate design conventions: A user who assigned two types of permissible data for an order entry system at the systemwide level and then tried to permit three types at a detailed, "zoomed-in" level would be reprimanded by the system. Encyclopedias" keep track of all objects, labels, and relationships, preventing inconsistent definitions and tracking the effects of changes throughout the system. Other modules offer project management features and complete application design documentation.

Perhaps most significant, many of these products can be networked. As a result, teams of developers can work independently on different parts of the same application, with a shared encyclopedia watching for conflicting entries among the users. This capability may ultimately be more important than how much the system helps individuals, says John Henderson, a professor of management science at MIT's Sloan School of Management. "The quality of the final product may have more to do with how the team works together."

Three similar workstation products are currently competing in this new market: Excelerator from InTech (Cambridge, Massachusetts), DesignAid from Nastec Corp. (Southfield, Michigan), and Information Engineering Workbench from Knowledgeware (Ann Arbor, Michigan). The software packages for each system sell for $5,000-$10,000, and all run on the IBM PC family and compatibles (Nastec and Knowledgeware also offer mainframe components). Excelerator and DesignAid have each had modest sales of a few thousand copies; Workbench was just introduced. A fourth vendor, Cadre Technologies (Providence, Rhode Island), offers a simlar product that runs on engineering workstations from Apollo and IBM. Such workstations cost about five times as much as an IBM PC/AT, but Cadre claims that the extra power lets its software handle larger and more complex projects.

Future versions of systems-design products promise what has become something of a holy grail in the software field: the capability to generate programs automatically when the system design is complete. Nastec is off to an early start, having announced in February a software bridge between its DesignAid product and the Gamma COBOL generator from Tarkenton Software (Atlanta). Although the bridge—which conveys system-level information to the COBOL generator—still requires a programmer to do some work directly with Gamma, Nastec claims that it will be fully automatic by year's end. Knowledgeware and InTech say they will soon announce similar bridges between their products and other COBOL generators.

While automatic bridges between systems-design workstations and COBOL generators are already appearing, it's not clear when, if ever, the COBOL generators themselves will be able to produce 100 percent of the necessary code with no programmer intervention. Smaller companies with simpler needs might be able to reach this goal within five years, estimates Paul Bassett, vice president of research at Netron. But the generators may never be able to meet all the programming requirements of Fortune 500 companies, he says, because of the size and compexity of their typical applications.

Meanwhile, the systems-design workstation vendors are exploring various components based on artificial intelligence—such as products that suggest application designs according to the user's needs and predict the performance of each design—and program generator modules that offer a choice of programming languages. Other products might automate database design so that information is stored in the most efficient and accessible fashion, and might be able to assist companies in evaluating and planning their corporate-wide information requirements.

Assuming these promises are met, the fifth generation of programming languages may not be a language at all. It could be a tightly meshed medley of tools that "discusses" information needs with systems analysts and end users, finds or constructs the appropriate databases, and then writes the required code in the language of choice.

Discussion Questions

1. How is a procedural programming language different from a non-procedural language?

2. What will be the impact of fourth-generation programming languages upon the use of COBOL in the next twenty years?
3. What will be the impact of fourth-generation programming languages and automated development tools upon the future job opportunities for MIS professionals?
4. Are fourth-generation languages a panacea for both systems developers and end users?
5. What is a natural language interface? Why are they useful? Why might they be a hindrance?

SECTION EIGHT

Organizational Issues

READING 24

Design Alternatives for Organizing Information Systems Activities

article by
ROBERT W. ZMUD

Introduction

Information systems activities (those tasks associated with acquiring, deploying, and managing information technologies) are in a considerable state of flux in many organizations. Recent articles have concluded that changes must occur in how information systems activities are *organized* in order to meet the challenges of an information society [1, 2, 3, 4, 17, 25].

Two major forces are behind much of this turmoil. First, a substantial increase in computing has occurred over the last decade because of the phenomenal advances achieved in computer hardware and software [3, 19]. As a consequence, individuals responsible for directing an organization's use of information resources face an expanding user base and an exploding portfolio of information services. Second, resource scarcities have led many organizations to stress the improvement of existing services rather than the provision of new services [2]. This, in turn, has led many end users to act independently of the centralized information systems authority in deciding when and how to exploit information technologies [17]. The recent availability of high quality, fourth-generation software products has heightened this trend. Managing information resources within such an environment is considerably more difficult than the environments of the 1960s and 1970s, where an intimidating, relatively inflexible, but generally stable, technology-base resulted in the centralized information systems authority maintaining a virtual monopoly as a provider of information services.

The main reaction of leading information systems organizations to these external and internal challenges has been to decentralize information systems responsibilities. Generally, this

Source: Reprinted by special permission of the *MIS Quarterly*, Volume 8, Number 2, June 1984, pp. 79-93.

decentralization has been limited to the acquisition and deployment of relatively simple, stand-alone applications. However, as information technologies become more deeply embedded within an organization's operational, tactical, and strategic activities, line managers will be increasingly motivated to gain authority over applications. For example, managers with bottom-line profit and loss responsibilities who depend on the availability of reliable, on-line transaction processing systems are increasingly demanding full control over the computer systems providing these services. Such authority transferals result in much more than simply changing the location of information processing activities. Significant changes are increasingly being observed in both the ownership of information resources and the stewardship of information systems activities.

It is the intent of this article to describe and discuss alternative designs for organizing information systems activities for the information resource environments expected throughout the 1980s and 1990s. Practitioners need to be actively considering their options for managing this transition period. A final objective of this article then, is to stimulate research programs that critically assess the viability of the options available to information systems managers.

Evolving Nature of Information Systems Activities

Throughout the 1960s and 1970s, information systems activities in most organizations were handled by a centralized information systems authority primarily serving a *manufacturing* role. This typically involved configuring and operating a production facility consisting of large-scale hardware and systems software as well as establishing and maintaining a sizeable in-house application software development group [17].

This central authority was most often organized with four information systems subfunctions [11, 14, 17, 26, 33]: systems development, operations, technical services, and administration. Table 1 provides a summary of the information systems activities included within each of these subunits. This strategy for partitioning an organization's information systems activities recognized that the task environments of each of these information systems activities would benefit from quite different management styles and practices. Large-scale application systems development, for example, involves a series of interdependent tasks, emphasizes organizational effectiveness, and benefits from a high degree of end user involvement. Operations involves a series of interdependent tasks, emphasizes efficiency and reliability, requires a moderate degree of end user interaction, and involves short time horizons. Technical services involve relatively independent tasks of a highly technical nature requiring minimal end user interaction. Finally, administration involves a wide variety of tasks primarily directed toward coordinating and controlling other information systems activities.

While this manufacturing role remains important today, two emerging roles—distribution and technology transfer—may soon account for a majority of information systems activities within most organizations [13, 17].

The distribution role arises in recognition of the multiple channels through which information services can be obtained. Application software, for example, can be acquired through an internal development group, the use of fourth-generation end user development tools, software package vendors, time-sharing services, systems houses, etc. Given the expense of in-house software development and the scarcity of talent for developing sophisticated applications software, it is usually advantageous to acquire externally-produced information products and services. However, locating available products and services and then assessing their quality and appropriateness can consume a significant amount of time unless the effort is effectively managed.

The technology transfer role is associated with organizational efforts to keep abreast of innovative information technologies by identifying and experimenting with new technologies, by developing a technical and social infrastructure such that appropriate technologies can be absorbed, and by managing the introduction of new technologies into the work units. Many organizations have recently established office automation and microcomputer subfunctions to develop plans, policies, and support services to facilitate the organizational diffusion of these technologies.

Table 1 Traditional Information System Roles

Subfunction	Activities
Operations	data preparation and data entry input and output controls machine operation file storage and control hardware maintenance job scheduling
Systems Development	feasibility studies systems analysis and design software development packaged software acquisition system conversions user training application software maintenance
Technical Services	systems software maintenance telecommunications support database support
Administration	capacity planning systems planning budgeting systems personnel management systems personnel training standards development

Table 2 suggests a partitioning of information systems activities that accounts for these new roles. Here, delivery systems and systems development represent the traditional manufacturing role of assuring that mainstream information systems are correctly implemented, efficiently operated, and effectively maintained. The support center and the information center represent a distribution role that serves to unite end users, end user development tools, and external products and services. Research and development, along with technology diffusion, represent the technology transfer roles concerned with, (1) ensuring that technological innovations are recognized and assessed with regard to their organizational relevance, and (2) facilitating the diffusion of appropriate technologies into the work units. Finally, planning, internal auditing, and administration represent an administrative function responsible for the overall planning, control, and coordination of information systems activities.

As the set of information system activities given in Table 2 also involve different task environments, they are likely to benefit from differing management styles and practices. Considerable variation exists with regard to issues such as efficiency versus effectiveness, reliability versus flexibility, pragmatics versus technical elegance, and dependability versus innovation. Furthermore, desired work behaviors within these subunits might, at times, be contradictory. Consider the following characteristics recently proposed for software development groups [24]: innovative, technologically current, adaptable, and highly productive while producing quality software products that are reliable, maintainable, and portable. Devising an organizational design that promotes such a demanding set of work behaviors is clearly not a simple, straightforward chore.

Organizational Design Alternatives

Organizational design involves specifying relationships between tasks and work groups such that work behaviors will be consistent with the

Table 2 Evolving Information System Roles

Subfunction	Activities
Delivery Systems	operations as described in Table 1 end user facility operations support database support telecommunications support maintenance (hardware, systems software and applications software) end user liaison and quality assurance for production systems capacity planning
Systems Development	system design and software development for production systems, for critical systems, for sensitive systems, for corporate-wide systems, and for software tools
Support Center	internal consulting service for organizational analyses, modeling, feasibility studies, and systems analysis broker for packaged software, external data services, word processors, and microcomputers end user and systems personnel training
Information Center	internal consulting service and support facilities for end user applications development via microcomputers, decision support systems, modeling languages, data inquiry systems, and automatic applications generators
Research and Development	monitor technological developments develop technical infrastructure technological forecasting
Technology Diffusion	develop organizational infrastructure investigate potential for applying new technologies within organizational areas plan and manage system implementations plan and manage pilot studies
Planning	overall information planning liaison with corporate strategic planning overall evaluation of organizational use of information systems establishing information policies
Internal Auditing	standards development evaluation of adherance to controls
Administration	budgeting personnel management document management

performance criteria characterizing that particular task environment (e.g., effectiveness, efficiency, reliability, flexibility, innovativeness, etc.). Efforts to arrive at an appropriate organizational design should attend to a variety of issues [6, 9]: selecting appropriate organizational structures and processes, establishing appropriate management and motivational systems, and facilitating required interpersonal interactions.

It would be extremely difficult to adequately cover all these organizational design issues within a single paper. This section will limit its focus to those issues relating to organizational form: the structures through which subunits are established, the processes through which subunits are directed, and the coordination mechanisms through which subunits are integrated.

Structural Forms

As any organization grows in size, a point is invariably reached where communication problems require that its activities be partitioned. The two most basic partitioning strategies are to form work groups on a functional or product basis. Each of these structures possesses certain advantages and disadvantages. A third form, the matrix organization, was devised to simultaneously capture the strengths of both the functional and product structures.

With the functional form, work groups are organized according to the nature of the tasks undertaken with concern primarily directed toward achieving economies of scale and work specialization. The objective is that of internal efficiency [7, 16, 30]: functional skill development is actively promoted, standards for performing activities are devised, and a long-term perspective is developed within work groups ('Let's discover the best way to perform this task'). As each functional work unit performs only a portion of the tasks associated with an organization's mission, tight hierarchical control is necessary to ensure overall work success. Performance problems often arise, nonetheless, because of incomplete or inaccurate information flows between work groups and the limited number of employees who hold a global understanding of the organization's mission.

The product form, on the other hand, finds subunits organized around end products or services. Because total mission responsibilities are given to the subunit, decisions can be made more quickly and with a more complete grasp of client/customer needs [7, 16, 30]. Attention is directed toward external effectiveness, local responses to problems are promoted, global perspectives are encouraged, and a medium-term perspective is developed within work groups ('Let's provide the best product/service we can'). Certain disadvantages accompany these advantages: economies of scale and skill specialization are not exploited, and work groups tend to act independent of the global organization.

With the matrix structure, employees are officially housed within functional subunits but are assigned to product work groups in performing their duties. The result—constantly shifting assignments, authority relationships, and interpersonal ties along with a project-oriented interweaving of reporting relationships—provides a very flexible organization able to adapt to changing work circumstances [6, 7, 10, 16, 23]. The informal communication flows and simple control relationship associated with the matrix structure make it particularly well suited for turbulent environments: personnel skills are broadened, adaption is promoted, compromise is encouraged, and a short-term perspective is developed ('Let's perform this task to the best of our abilities given the current situation'). Matrix forms are the most difficult structure to establish and nurture. A considerable investment in administrative overhead is usually required. The dual reporting structure can produce individual role ambiguity, job anxiety and stress, and the potential for work group conflicts and power struggles. Employees must develop political skills along with a sense of trust and a willingness to compromise.

Basic Process Forms

As used here, organization processes refer to the patterns of authority and responsibility that influence the behaviors of individual employees within subunits. A popular view of these issues locates work environments along an organic-mechanistic continuum. High levels of employee discretion and few work policies and procedures characterize organic processes. Low levels of employee discretion and many policies and procedures characterize mechanistic processes [5].

Individuals in organic work groups are allowed considerable discretion regarding the manner in which work is performed. As a result, behavioral reactions to evolving demands tend to be quick and well-targeted to client/customer needs. Mechanistic work groups, on the other hand, are generally very efficient and reliable through the tight control that results from routinization of work behaviors.

Basic Coordination Forms

It is impossible, when partitioning an organization into subunits, to allocate work such that a perfect fit occurs between work group responsibilities and required organizational activities. Many tasks must be passed between work groups, thus increasing task uncertainty. Coordination mechanisms are used to facilitate handling these joint assignments by establishing channels for information exchanges.

An indication of the wide variety of coordination mechanisms that can be applied is provided in Figure 1 [8, 16, 21]. Here, the mechanisms are roughly classified according to their capability to enable work units to cope with task uncertainties. While limited to the coordination of well-understood and routine activities, formal, static, and uni-directional mechanisms promote consistency and predictability. The more informal, dynamic, and multi-directional mechanisms, as they promote both behavioral flexibility and work group interaction, are especially useful when poorly understood or nonroutine activities predominate.

Summary of Basic Design Alternatives

Table 3 contrasts basic design alternatives by indicating the task environments that each is most suited for, as well as the major work behaviors each promotes. As a further means of illustrating these basic designs, Table 4 indicates those forms typically used in organizing the traditional information systems subunits given in Table 1. It should be recognized that most 'real' organizational designs are hybrid forms rather than pure representations of these basic forms.

Figure 1 Basic Coordination Mechanisms

Formal, Static, Uni-directional
direct supervision
formal rules and procedures
planning and control systems
committees, task forces, liaison roles
continual, interactive planning between work groups
physical work group rearrangements
manipulation of work group power relationships
Informal, Dynamic, Multi-directional

Organizational Designs For Evolving Information Systems Activities

While these basic organizational designs provide a useful starting point, they are not sufficient given the nature of the work objectives desired in today's information systems task environments. Certain information systems activities, particularly those associated with distributor and technology transfer roles, require considerable innovativeness and adaptability. Innovativeness refers to a work group's creativity in approaching problems and opportunities as well as the work group's willingness to experiment with new methods for performing work. Adaptability refers to a work group's ability to recognize the need for change and to successfully implement a change program.

Designs Promoting Innovativeness and Adaptability

Generally, innovativeness and adaptability can be enhanced by broadening the knowledge, perspectives, and interests of a work group's members. This can be achieved through increasing the diversity of the work group [22, 28], through organic processes [5, 28, 32], and through informal coordination mechanisms [9]. The willingness of a work group to adopt and accept change does not always follow these prescriptions, however [22, 32]. For example, the adoption of new work methodologies occurs most readily in mechanistic organizations, and acceptance of new work methodologies can be facilitated with either mechanistic or organic processes, depending on a work group's attitudes toward the new methods. This last point introduces the important notion that innovativeness and adaptability can be promoted through seemingly contradictory organizational designs.

Quite different organizational designs can adequately confront change depending on the nature of the change effort. When change is localized to a single subunit, or when a change effort can be incrementally pursued, designs that both isolate a work group and allow for considerable discretion in handling the change effort can be very effective [9,

Table 3 Major Distinctions Among the Basic Design Alternatives

Design Alternative	Task Environment	Work Behaviors
Structural		
functional	stable routine	efficiency consistency reliability
product	dynamic segmented market	effectiveness rapid response
matrix	turbulent	effectiveness flexibility
Process		
mechanistic	simple stable	efficiency dependability
organic	complex dynamic	effectiveness adaptability
Coordination		
formal	stable routine independent tasks	consistency reliability
informal	dynamic uncertainty interdependent tasks	adaptability rapid response cooperation

Table 4 Traditional Organizational Designs

Information Systems Subunit	Structure	Process	Coordination
Systems development	product	mechanistic	informal
Operations	functional	mechanistic	formal
Technical Services	functional	mechanistic	informal
Administration	functional	mechanistic	formal

29]. Such a strategy enables the work group to engage in continuous, improvised, highly-localized change actions without impacting other work groups or disrupting organization-wide operations. This approach may prove effective, for example, when introducing a stand-alone microcomputer into an organization's work units. Even here, however, individual work units cannot be allowed total discretion; some standards will have to be enforced regarding microcomputer acquisition in order to ensure a desired level of organization-wide compatibility regarding hardware, software, support, training, etc.

With radical or large-scale change, it might be best to blur rather than define work group boundaries [20]. Here, the simultaneous recognition of a need for change by multiple work groups, along with the inevitable boundary disputes between work groups, can encourage productive intergroup negotiations as well as collaborative problem-solving efforts. This strategy, then, is aimed at providing integrated solutions to global change events. Accordingly, it might very well be employed when implementing a corporate DSS to support an interactive planning process throughout an entire organization.

It is also necessary for most organizations to simultaneously demonstrate stability and flexibility in their work behaviors in order to exploit current and future opportunities [9, 29]. By effectively applying the notion of an organizational *overlay* [28], it becomes possible to employ a single organizational form characterized by both stability and flexibility. With an organizational overlay, a secondary organizational form is used along with a primary organizational form such that certain limitations of the dominant form are overcome. A recent study found that software groups that employed overlays were more innovative than software groups that did not employ overlays [32]. For example, mechanistic software groups that had established R & D subunits to identify and then introduce new software methods made greater use of these methods than mechanistic software groups without such R & D subunits. Similarly organic software groups that assigned their analysts and programmers to projects as fixed teams (through which new software methods could be channeled) made greater use of these methods than did organic software groups that assigned their analysts and programmers to projects on a more ad hoc basis.

This discussion, oriented toward promoting innovativeness and adaptability, suggests that any organizational designs facilitating information systems activities must themselves be flexible. The appropriateness of any given organizational form will vary, however, depending on the technology being applied, the organizational support being provided, the organizational unit being supported, and the activities currently being taken in applying the technology.

The Need for Multiple Forms. While the tasks involved might appear very similar, information systems activities, even within the same subunit, may required different organizational forms because of specific task environments. For example, software provided to maintain financial ledgers are quite distinct from that supporting on-line inquiry into customer files by clerical personnel [13, 15, 17]. Project team structures for these two applications are likely to be quite different in order that design criteria such as reliability, auditability, error control, ease-of-use, and 'natural' end user interactions can be reinforced. Technology transfer efforts (office automation, flexible manufacturing systems, programmer's workbench, end user development, etc.), can present a variety of task environments depending on the degree of change required within the target unit, the target unit's readiness to accept this change, and whether these uncertainties are technological or organizational in nature.

The Need for Dynamic Forms. Information system activities often consist of lengthy task sequences requiring different participants and different work orientations at each stage [12, 19, 23, 31, 34]. While such an activity might have a single project administration, organizational form is likely to vary with each successive stage. A critical design element here involves establishing coordination mechanisms that not only apply across a variety of organizational forms but also enable work to flow smoothly to each succeeding stage.

The Need for Disintegrating Forms. Three forces are at play that periodically require the destruction of information systems work groups. First, as software development and technology transfer efforts possess finite time horizons, work groups responsible for such activities undergo periodic restructuring as old projects are completed and new projects are begun. Second, given the dynamic nature of information technologies, the appropriateness of specific products, services, or technical skills lessens over time. As the organizational relevance of any work group erodes, the group itself should disband. Finally, much information systems activity involves organizational learning through the transfer of new technologies. For example, the intent of establishing a centralized information center might be to have similar units formed throughout the organization. If the staff of such an information center is successful in establishing spin-off centers serving local needs, the central staff may eventually erode the justification for its own existence. Together, these forces suggest that many information systems work groups should adopt a life cycle perspective in which a continual stream of work group births and deaths is viewed as one measure of information systems success. However, as Pettigrew [27] has pointed out through his analysis of influence shifts between programmers and systems analysts in Britain, it can prove very difficult to reduce, let alone remove, a work group's organizational role.

The Need for Umbrella Forms. Whenever organizational activities are dispersed throughout work units whose interrelations themselves evolve over time, the need emerges for a managerial superstructure that provides overall coordination, that sets directions, and that resolves the disputes that will invariably arise among subunits [20, 23, 25]. Devising suitable structural mechanisms (committees, task forces, review boards, planning groups, etc.) is clearly going to be a critically important task in organizing information systems activities.

Prototypal Designs

Building on the concepts which have been developed, Table 5 provides a prototypal collection of design alternatives for organizing the information systems function. An awareness of the changes occurring within many of today's information systems organizations, particularly those making innovative uses of information technologies, will indicate that these prescriptions are not simply idle speculation. Even so, it would be unusual to find these designs fully implemented as specified. Actual design efforts must necessarily consider a number of factors not brought out here, e.g., an organization's dominant structural form, leadership styles of key managers, organizational priorities and strategies, etc.

Delivery System. As it is likely that efficiency concerns will dominate other objectives, a mechanistic product structure based upon processing environments, such as batch, interactive, high security, etc., might be preferred. This product structure would be aligned with functional technical support groups responsible for services such as database management, telecommunications, and systems programming. Coordination mechanisms would likely differ with the degree of end user interaction encountered with particular processing environments.

Systems Development. This technical service subunit is primarily responsible for developing large, well-defined but complex information systems requiring disciplined behaviors to ensure adherance to end user specifications and to organization-wide software standards. Given such a task environment, a very tight organization stressing technical proficiency and high productivity might, in general, be preferred.

Support Center. As support center personnel act in a variety of roles, such as broker, consultant, advisor, or systems analyst, the preferred organizational form is likely to be a matrix structure

Table 5 Prototypal Organizational Designs

Information Systems Subunit	Structure	Process	Coordination	Other Issues
Delivery System	product some functional	mechanistic	informal some informal	
Systems Development	functional	mechanistic some organic	informal some formal	multiple dynamic
Support Center	matrix	organic	informal (external) formal (internal)	overlapped dynamic
Information Center	functional product	organic	informal	overlapped disintegrating
Research and Development	product	organic	informal	isolated
Technology Diffusion	matrix	organic	informal	dynamic disintegrating overlapped
Planning	functional some product	organic	informal (internal) formal (external)	dynamic overlapped umbrella disintegrating
Internal Auditing	functional	mechanistic	formal	overlapped
Administration	function	mechanistic	formal	umbrella

emphasizing specialized skills as well as knowledge of end user application areas. While mechanisms linking the support center to end users should be informal, internal coordination of the support center might benefit from more formal mechanisms to ensure consistency regarding project selection criteria, hardware/software acquisition, etc. One might also expect that as end users gained sufficient expertise they would begin to incorporate these activities within their own task domains with the support center eventually serving as a coordinating body for these local support centers.

Information Center. The pure consulting service provided by an information center might benefit from an organic hybrid form using both functional work groups skilled in the application of end user development tools and product work groups knowledgeable of specific end user areas. An organic climate is preferred because of the short life of many projects, the desirability of flexible internal relationships, and the benefits to be derived from adaptable end user relationships. Finally, a major aim of the information center should be to encourage networking among end users such that information center responsibilities could eventually be spun-off to end users.

Research and Development. This subunit primarily serves to maintain an organization's technical infrastructure by scanning the environment for new information technologies, assessing their appropriateness, and communicating this information to others. One might expect that an organic structure, isolated from other work units, might perform best. A product orientation, where personnel expertise was maintained along technological lines, would also seem desirable.

Technology Diffusion. As this subunit performs a range of activities requiring quite different skills, it would seem that a matrix form combining skill specialization along with end user familiarity under a project management umbrella would be preferred. Given that most projects would involve numerous stages, flexibility and adaptability regarding project structures, processes, and coordinating mechanisms would be mandatory.

Planning. The planning subunit might best be viewed as occurring at two distinct organizational levels—a senior level where organization-wide concerns are handled, and a lower level where specialized concerns are handled. While the senior-level activity might best be performed through a single umbrella-like executive steering committee [25], the lower-level work groups would be composed of dynamic, eventually disintegrating task forces formally reporting to the senior-level committee.

Internal Auditing. In order that it perform its responsibilities in a consistent and objective manner, this subunit should ideally have few linkages with other organizational work units. The rigorous, disciplined, and specialized nature of its task environment clearly suggests that a mechanistic, functional form might be preferred.

Administration. As this subunit serves a housekeeping role in providing and managing the resources necessary for all other information systems activities, the task environment should promote behaviors emphasizing efficiency, consistency, and reliability.

Implications

Movement toward the organizational forms just described will require substantial changes in the perspectives, activities, and styles of many information systems managers. Two critical issues in particular must be directly confronted: recognizing that information resources can be owned, operated, and managed by all of an organization's work units; and, recognizing that power losses will invariably be felt by the information systems function as this transition to end user computing unfolds.

As information technologies become embedded deep within the fabric of organizations, responsibility for information resources will increasingly be given to line and staff management. As a consequence, the manufacturing role of the information systems function is likely to take on a custodial or advisory nature. In order for their influence to be felt, information systems specialists and managers must demonstrate an organizational as well as technical expertise such that they are perceived as the catalysts behind the organization's innovative uses of information technologies.

Even if information systems specialists and managers actively support this democratization of organizational computing, the influence that information systems personnel exert in their organizations is likely to be initially reduced. The severity and tenacity of this power loss will follow one of two paths depending on the directions taken by information systems managers. If an effort is made to hold on to the manufacturing role, this power loss could very well be substantial and irreversable. If evolution toward the distributor and technology transfer roles occurs, however, a substantial increase in power could result.

The following anecdote illustrates how an information systems manager's long-term power position can actually be increased through end user computing [18]. The information systems director in a large consumer goods firm diffused office automation technologies through the use of joint (user and information systems personnel) pilot projects which, over time, became fully user managed. This director then established an umbrella organization, a Standards Review Board composed of information systems office technology specialists and key users, which now exerts a significant influence within the organization. By developing this business-dominated but technically competent organizational unit, the information systems director assumed a new and necessary organizational role. Information systems personnel should, if they can combine their understanding of information technologies with an understanding of organizational purpose, find their influence growing with any increase in an organization's reliance on information resources.

These fluctuations in the organizational influence maintained by information systems managers should be tempered by two additional thoughts. First, a broad understanding of information technologies may very well prove requisite for line management responsibility in those operating units where information resources are the primary vehicle through which organizational activities occur. Thus, information systems management experience might become a necessity for promotion into senior management positions. Second, information systems managers serving under line managers not technologically conversant may find themselves with considerable influence because of their ability to reduce organizational uncertainity regarding the technology.

Such scenarios are not common today for the simple reason that most organizations are just beginning their transition toward end user domination of information systems activities. While successfully managing through this transition period is likely to be a trying experience for *all* managers, it will prove especially difficult for the information systems manager, as the information systems function itself will be drastically reorganized. To ease this experience, information systems managers and researchers must commit themselves to undertake a number of important tasks for the redesigning of the information systems function.

Information Systems Manager Tasks

Redesigning the information systems function would require four actions. First, assess the current situation regarding the assignment of information systems responsibilities throughout the organization. How is the information systems function currently organized? To what extent are other organizational units responsible for information resources or activities? How are organization-wide information responsibilities being addressed?

Second, work with corporate planners in specifying short- as well as long-term scenarios depicting the manner with which information technologies will be applied to perform and support organizational activities. These scenarios are necessary as it is through them that one begins to envision the likely shifts regarding both information systems activities and organization-wide responsibilities.

Third, begin to evaluate the various organizational forms with regard to their capability to provide these activities and responsibilities. This effort should ultimately result in the development of a few future organizational designs along with the steps to be taken in implementing each.

Finally, experiment with the various organizational forms in order that their strengths and weaknesses become apparent. Such experimentation should mesh well with the pilot project or task force operations that often accompany the use of new information technologies.

Information Systems Researcher Tasks

Researchers can provide two extremely valuable services to those managers addressing the question of organizing for these new information systems activities and responsibilities. First, it seems clear that the appropriateness of a particular organization form for a specific information systems activity will be contingent upon a variety of factors. Exactly what these factors are and how they relate to particular organizational forms, however, have yet to be determined. Research projects aimed at developing a contingency theory for organizing information systems activities are strongly advocated. Second, it also seems clear that many impediments are likely to arise as organizational redesign programs are implemented. Research is needed that both identifies likely problems and prescribes strategies for managing around, or through, these problems.

Joint Manager-Researcher Tasks

A final set of tasks will be required that are likely to be accomplished only through the cooperative efforts of information systems managers and researchers via active research programs. If the notions behind the prescriptions given in Table 5 are accepted, it seems likely that information systems design will involve a mixed-bag of organizational thrusts. How exactly does one *manage* such an organization? Not only is it comprised of many different work groups, but these work groups are likely to be characterized by quite distinct cultures. What are effective management systems, e.g., planning, control, and evaluation processes, for such an organization? How are these units staffed? What type of career path can be established to provide for both skill development and personal advancement? As this type of organization does not exist today, conjectures regarding its nature are fraught with uncertainty. Research must take place along with the early experimentation by innovative information systems organizations.

Conclusion

These views on organizing the information systems function are primarily directed toward large, complex organizations making sophisticated use of information resources. Organizations of all sizes, nevertheless, might very well benefit from applying these notions in examining their own practices for organizing information systems activities. While it is unlike that the prescriptions offered here will ever by fully applied, the information systems function in most organizations must evolve if it is to remain a potent organizational force. An information systems function continuing to serve as primarily manufacturing role will eventually find its influence regarding information resources preempted by other organizational units. If these other organizational units do not have the expertise to successfully manage information technologies, the overall loss to the organization may be severe. It is hoped that the ideas expressed in this paper will encourage experimentation with different but appropriate organization forms such that this transition to the distributor and technology transfer roles not only occurs but transpires smoothly.

Discussion Questions

1. How is "operations" different from "systems development" in terms of structure? Give some examples of how the systems development subfunction is organized and compare and contrast this with the operations subfunction.
2. Why might software maintenance and "new" systems development be separate subfunctions of the MIS department?
3. Describe the basic structural design alternatives. Are these alternatives mutually exclusive? Why or why not? Give examples.
4. Why would some subfunctions require formal coordination mechanisms and other subfunctions less formal coordination mechanisms?
5. What is the impact of new technologies and increased interest in user developed systems upon the organizational structure of the MIS department?

Acknowledgement

This paper was initially prepared for the CIS/ORG seminar entitled "Information Systems and Organizational Structures: Implications for Complex Organization", TIMS/ORSA meeting. San Diego, October 24, 1982.

Support received from the Business Foundation of the School of Business at the University of North Carolina at Chapel Hill is greatly appreciated.

References

[1] Allen, B. "Computer Strategy: A Philosophy for Managing Information Processing Resources," in R. Goldberg and H. Lorin, eds., *The Economics of Information Processing,* Volume 1, Wiley-Interscience, New York, New York, 1982.

[2] Allen, B. "An Unmanaged Computer System Can Stop You Dead," *Harvard Business Review,*

Volume 60, Number 6, November-December 1982, pp. 76-87.

[3] Benjamin, R. I. "Information Technology in the 1990's: A Long Range Planning Scenario," *MIS Quarterly*, Volume 6, Number 2, June 1982, pp. 11-31.

[4] Buchanan, J. R. and Linowes, R. G. "Understanding Distributed Data Processing," *Harvard Business Review*, Volume 58, Number 4, July-August 1980, pp. 143-153.

[5] Burns, T. and Stalker, G. *The Management of Innovation*, Tavistock, London, England, 1961.

[6] Cleland, D. I. "The Human Side of Project Management," in A. J. Kelley, ed., *New Dimensions of Project Management*, Lexington Books, Lexington, Massachusetts, 1982.

[7] Daly, E. B. "Organizational Philosophies Used in Software Development," in R. Goldberg and H. Lorin, eds., *The Economics of Information Processing*, Volume 2, Wiley-Interscience, New York, New York, 1982.

[8] Galbraith, J. R. "Organization Design: An Information Processing View," *Interfaces*, Volume 4, Number 3, May 1974, pp. 28-36.

[9] Galbraith, J. R. "Designing the Innovating Organization," *Organizational Dynamics*, Volume 10, Number 3, Winter 1982, pp. 5-25.

[10] Hemsley, J. R. "Matrix Organizational Structures in Brazilian Organizations," in D. Soen, ed., *Industrial Development and Technology Transfer*, George Godwin Ltd., London, England, 1981.

[11] Jenkins, J. M. and Santos, R. F. "Centralization vs. Decentralization of Data Processing Functions," in R. Goldberg and H. Lorin, eds., *The Economics of Information Processing*, Volume 2, Wiley-Interscience, New York, New York, 1982.

[12] Keen, J. S. *Managing Systems Development*, John Wiley, Chichester, England, 1981.

[13] Lientz, B. P. *An Introduction to Distributed Systems*, Addison-Wesley, Reading, Massachusetts, 1981.

[14] Lucas, H. C., Jr. "Alternative Structures for the Management of Information Processing," in R. Goldberg and H. Lorin, eds., *The Economics of Information Processing*, Volume 2, Wiley-Interscience, New York, New York, 1982.

[15] Mantei, M. "The Effect of Programming Team Structures on Programming Tasks," *Communications of the ACM*, Volume 24, Number 3, March 1981, pp. 106-113.

[16] McCann, J. and Galbraith, J. R. "Interdepartmental Relations," in P. C. Nystrom and W. H. Starbuck, eds., *Handbook of Organizational Design*, Volume 2, Oxford University Press, Oxford, England, 1981.

[17] McFarlan, F. W. and McKenney, J. L. *Information Systems Management: A Senior Management Perspective*, Richard D. Irwin, Inc., Homewood, Illinois, 1982.

[18] McKenney, J. L. "User Domination Means DPer Must Know Business," *Information System News*, September 19, 1983, pp. 17, 20.

[19] McKenney, J. L. and McFarlan, F. W. "The Information Archipelago—Maps and Bridges," *Harvard Business Review*, Volume 60, Number 5, September-October 1982, pp. 109-119.

[20] Metcalf, L. "Designing Precarious Partnerships," in P. C. Nystrom and W. H. Starbuck, eds., *Handbook of Organizational Design*, Volume 2, Oxford University Press, Oxford, England, 1981.

[21] Mintzberg, H. "Structures in 5's: A Synthesis of the Research on Organization Design," *Management Science*, Volume 26, Number 3, March 1980, pp. 322-341.

[22] Moch, M. K. and Morse, E. V. "Size, Centralization and Organizational Adoption of Innovations," *American Sociological Review*, Volume 42, Number 5, 1977, pp. 716-725.

[23] Morris, P. W. G. "Project Organizations: Structures for Managing Change," in A. J. Kelley, ed., *New Dimensions of Project Management*, Lexington Books, Lexington, Massachusetts, 1982.

[24] Munson, J. B. and Yeh, R. T. "Report by the IEEE Software Engineering Productivity Workshop," Proceedings, 15th Hawaii International Conference on System Science, 1982, pp. 249-282.

[25] Nolan, R. L. "Managing Information Systems by Committee," *Harvard Business Review*, Volume 60, Number 4, July-August 1982, pp. 72-79.

[26] Olson, M. H. *Organization of Information Services: Alternative Approaches*, University Microfilms International, Ann Arbor, Michigan, 1980.

[27] Pettigrew, A. M. *The Politics of Organizational Decision Making*, Tavistock

Publications, London, England, 1973.
[28] Pierce, J. L. and Delbecq, A. L. "Organization Structure, Individual Attitudes and Innovation," *Academy of Management Review*, Volume 2, Number 1, January 1977, pp. 27-37.
[29] Weick, K. E. "The Management of Organizational Change Among Loosely Coupled Elements," in P. Goodman, ed., *Change in Organizations*, Jossey-Bass, San Francisco, California, 1982.
[30] Williamson, O. E. *Markets and Hierarchies*, Free Press, New York, New York, 1975.
[31] Zmud, R. W. "Management of Large Software Development Efforts," *MIS Quarterly*, Volume 4, Number 2, June 1980, pp. 45-56.
[32] Zmud, R. W. "Diffusion of Modern Software Practices: Influences of Centralization and Formalization," *Management Science*, Volume 28, Number 12, December 1982, pp. 1421-1431.
[33] Zmud, R. W. *Information Systems in Organizations*, Scott, Foresman & Co., Glenview, Illinois, 1983.
[34] Zmud, R. W. and Cox, J. F. "The Implementation Process: A Change Approach," *MIS Quarterly*, Volume 3, Number 2, June 1979, pp. 35-43.

READING 25

A Telecommuting Primer

article by
GERARDINE DESANCTIS

Although the popular media have given quite a bit of attention to telecommuting—the substitution of communications for travel so that all or part of a job can be performed at home—no one has much experience with it yet. Few companies have conducted experiments with home work and an even smaller number have committed themselves to the idea by establishing formal policies or programs. Where programs have been tried, they've generally been informal, involving small numbers of employees and little if any effort to formally measure results.

This makes it difficult to assess telecommuting's effects on productivity, motivation, and so forth. Still, numerous writers have speculated that it will result in reduced overhead for central work facilities, improved productivity, better morale, lower absenteeism and turnover, and more efficient use of computer resources. And there does exist a small body of experience with the practice; firms that have experimented with home work include Continental Illinois Bank, Investors Diversified Services, Control Data Corp., Interactive Systems Corp. and Mountain Bell Co.

It's possible, therefore, to examine some of the work that has been done to date and offer some initial guidelines for managers interested in implementing a work-at-home program. To that end, I interviewed eight organizations that have studied or experimented with telcommuting: a bank, a computer manufacturer, three computer service firms, two consulting firms, and one insurance company.

What kinds of jobs can be accomplished via telecommuting? Self-employed professionals, salespeople, college professors, and consultants all work in their homes; so do skilled workers who are paid on a contract or piece-rate basis. But if we focus on work currently done for an employing

Source: Reprinted with permission of *Datamation®* magazine, © Copyright 1983 by Cahners Publishing Company, Inc.

organization in a central office facility, the subset of jobs that can be profitably moved to a home setting narrows considerably.

A 1981 study by the Diebold Group, New York, suggests that jobs with the following characteristics are good candidates for relocation from the office to the home:

1. Performance of the job requires a minimal amount of equipment and space.
2. The job can be done with relatively little face-to-face contact with other people. When communication is required, it can be easily handled by telephone or "batched" during the time the employee is in the office.
3. The job requires concentration and large blocks of time when the employee works independently of others.
4. The job is project-oriented, with each project resulting in defined deliverables.
5. Projects can be completed with medium-term deadlines (approximately two weeks to four months).
6. There are defined milestones, or intermediate deadlines, that can be identified and measured.
7. The job can be performed without close supervision, and working conditions are not subject to union scrutiny.

To date, the practice of telecommuting has been applied primarily to structured work that contains a built-in method for communication between the office and a remote location. For many companies, computer programming and word processing appear to be the jobs best suited to home work. They are project oriented, can be performed independently, and allow telecommunications and computer technology to serve as the link between home and office. Although programmers may have to interact with other personnel, particularly if they do any systems analysis, they are good candidates for working at home because much of their communication can be done by telephone or conducted when they are in the office.

Telecommuting can be feasible for either part-time or full-time work; both have been tried. In either case, it is important that the work schedule be arranged so that the employee is in the office on a regular basis, anywhere from several hours every two weeks to two days every week. In this way, communication, supervision, and social contacts can be maintained.

Some employees are better candidates than others for participation in a telecommuting program. An employee must first of all want to be involved: participation in the program should be voluntary. Preference should be given to people who have experience in their jobs and are committed to the organization.

A telecommuter should be self-motivated, self-disciplined, and work well independently. If a person has a low need for social interaction, he's more likely to adjust to the home setting.

She or he should have good planning ability, be well organized, and efficient in managing time. Good communication skills—telephone and electronic mail—are important. The employee's manager must support the telecommuting project, as should the employee's family. They must be willing to respect the worker's need for quiet and isolation.

Until management of telecommuters becomes better understood, working at home should be reserved for those who have done their jobs well and are located in areas of the company that management has designated as suitable for home work.

In general, a project will be easier with exempt employees than with nonexempt employees, who by law must be paid overtime. For exempt employees, the firm can continue to use its current method for wage computation and hour tracking. Also, the employer may be able to negotiate part-year, annual, or project-based employment contracts. Conditions for nonexempt employees, who generally get overtime pay for working more than 40 hours in a week, are somewhat different. Policies must deal with computer or telecommunications "downtime." If a word processing specialist is paid according to number of lines typed, the incentive pay rate including downtime has to meet or exceed the hourly equivalent of the current minimum wage. In short, if nonexempt employees work at home, strict record-keeping is necessary.

Need for Pilot Testing

A company should regard its first experience with home work as a formal experiment or pilot test. Only a small number of employees should participate. The pilot is a chance to learn how to manage telcommuters in the context of that particular company and to discover some of the consequences, good and bad. Following completion of the experimental phase, the company can decide whether to establish a formal policy regarding telecommuting or conduct further study.

There should be a clear reason for experimenting with telecommuting in the first place. For example, the purpose of the project might be to improve utilization of computer resources during off hours, reduce absenteeism and turnover among technical personnel, improve employee morale, reduce work backlogs, or lower company overhead costs. If immediate benefits are not imporant, the company might study telecommuting because it anticipates a long-term need. In any case, the project should have a specific, stated purpose. The project objectives determine its design, the manner in which it is implemented, and the measures used to determine its success or failure.

When planning either a pilot or permanent telecommuting program, the organization should be prepared for the impact of the program in several areas. For example, how does productivity of the home worker compare to that of the office worker? Productivity data in work-at-home projects have been encouraging, though most measures have been subjective if reported at all. Employees tend to anticipate that their productivity will improve. Presumably the assumption is that distractions and interruptions will be fewer at home than at work, thus raising the quality or quantity of output. The organization should determine if these productivity expectations can in fact be realized, using objective measures if possible.

Another concern is that promotion of employees will be affected if they telecommute. Will the employee be forgotten or uninformed when openings occur? Does the employee have equitable access to developmental resources? Will the employee accept a promotion if his work-at-home status is affected?

A system to ensure adequate information may be needed (e.g., job postings through electronic mail). Also, the company may want to inform telecommuting employees of career path consequences prior to placing them in the home. In the long term it may be important to monitor the degree to which telecommuting is practiced by employees within protected classes (e.g., women, minorities, older employees). Stifling of promotional chances could be evidence of "adverse impact" upon these workers if a discrimination claim were ever filled. The firm should be able to show that promotion opportunities were present, advancement positions not suited to telecommuting were well supported through job analysis, this fact was understood by participants, and participants were free to return to the office.

A final area of concern is with employee acceptance of promotion opportunities. After employees become accustomed to the benefits of working at home, they may be unwilling to return to the office when a promotion opportunity becomes available. This may affect EEO/Affirmative Action programs and personnel planning in general.

Permitting certain employees to work at home may create resentment among the others. During the pilot stage, when only a small number of people are working at home and management treats telecommuting as experimental, employee jealousy and concerns of inequity should be minimal. If participation is expanded, however, a clear and equitable policy regarding employee selection will have to be developed. This is important since the point at which telecommuting will be worthwhile and feasible for large numbers of employees is probably in the distant future.

Before embarking on a telecommuting program, a company should make some effort to assess the attitudes of clients and customers. Several companies have reported negative reactions on the part of their clientele, although a positive response is certainly conceivable. This may be a concern should the telecommuting project be discussed in the popular media.

In some cases, a telecommuting project will enhance a company's image. The firm could be seen as being progressive in its willingness to experiment with a new work concept. The impact may be most pronounced if the purpose is to make more job opportunities available to elderly or handicapped citizens. In any event, since such programs are still a novelty, the company should be prepared for media attention.

Terms of Home Work

Several important issues should be stressed when a company plans for telecommuting, either on a permanent basis or as a pilot program. As part of the formal procedure of placing a worker in the home, a statement of the terms and conditions for employee participation in the project should be prepared. Responsibilities of the employee and the company should be outlined, along with conditions surrounding continuation or termination of the home work placement. It probably should be stressed that the company reserves the right to cancel the home work agreement at any time, given proper notice. The statement should be dated and signed by the employee and a representative of the company.

Security of Data. Remote access to corporate computer systems may create security problems, particularly if the firm has no prior experience with distant access. Controls should be established so that, once a home worker is connected to the central computing facilities, she can access only the system or files for which she is authorized. There are several ways to control initial entry into the system:

• Install dial-up capability. This is fairly inexpensive but somewhat risky because anyone who knows a correct phone number and account could conceivably access the system.
• Use a call-back procedure on dial-up. If done manually, this can be cumbersome to manage, especially if many users want to connect to the system simultaneously. A better alternative is to install an automatic call-back system. Call-back systems are somewhat more secure than dial-in procedures because only an authorized list of phone numbers can be dialed by the central facility.
• Equip the home-based user with a terminal that has ID acknowledgement capability. A central computer will communicate only with an authorized device.
• Equip the home-based user with a computer that must be keyed to start and that stores personal identification information about the authorized user.

Security of equipment. Because it is so difficult to develop a perfectly secure system, management should entrust terminal and other equipment only to trustworthy people. All equipment placed in an employee's home or other remote site should be registered and clearly marked as company property. The company is responsible for maintaining and insuring equipment, although the employee is responsible for reasonable care and protection of the goods and for reporting repair needs as they occur.

Zoning of residence. If the employee's home is treated as a secondary or alternate work location, no special permits, licenses, or approvals should be necessary. Should the employee decide to alter or add to his home, it is his responsibility to abide by any municipal property restrictions. The same rules apply to a worker whose housing is rented. If the work location is considered secondary, no problems should result. Deed or other rental agreement restrictions should be consulted if structural changes are made in the home.

Work site conditions and inspection. If an employee is to work at home on a regular basis, adequate space and a proper home environment are a necessity. If special furniture and equipment are to be installed, the employee may decide to convert a basement area into an office or to remodel some other part of the home so that it is suitable for work. In any case, the decision of where to locate the workstation is the employee's, and he or she is also responsible for absorbing any costs related to remodeling. The work place should be neat, quiet, and preferably used for no other purpose besides work. The company should make it clear to the employee that it reserves the right to improve and periodically inspect the work place. In conducting an inspection, the company is interested in assuring that its equipment is in a safe place and receiving proper care. In no case should it be assumed or implied that the employer is renting office space from the employee.

Compensation of participants. The opportunity to establish a lower wage rate for telecommuting employees has not been realized in practice. Control Data, Continental Illinois, and Investors Diversified Services all report that they have not reduced labor costs through telecommuting. Reducing salaries of current employees would prove difficult. The employee may experience a decline in clothing and travel costs, but home electricity, heating, and water costs may rise, and there may also be remodeling expenses. Telecommuters tend to desire wage equity with their labor market.

Termination of transfer conditions. The company needs to establish conditions and guidelines for equipment retrieval upon the termination or transfer of an employee. Because a telecommuter's immediate supervisor may switch jobs or leave the company, it is advisable that the employee have the approval and support of the next level of management.

Tax issues for employees. Contrary to popular belief, working at home does not necessarily constitute a rationale for an "office at home" tax deduction. It is up to the employee to decide what are fair and reasonable tax deductions, if any. The company may want to avoid advocating or counseling in tax issues for the employee.

Training considerations. The type and extent of training for home workers depends, of course, on the job and individuals selected for the program. The least desirable training situation in terms of cost and risk of failure would be the case of a nonprofessional with little or no experience in the job and no prior work record in the firm. Committed, professional, experienced employees are the best candidates for telecommuting. Training dealing with the job or the company is thus unnecessary.

Before a firm places people at home, however, they'll need some orientation regarding the purpose and objectives of the home work program. They should become familiar with the procedures, policies and expectations associated with home work, and they should receive advice on how to manage their time and activities. Also in order are suggestions on how to coordinate communications with other personnel and how to "block" work so that parts can be done in the office and parts can be done at home. Finally, they should be briefed on potential problems, such as interruptions or distractions while working, the family's reaction to the new situation, attitudes of neighbors, etc.

The employee's immediate manager should receive special instructions regarding the purpose and rules of the program, and in general should become familiar with all information given to the employee. Estimates regarding the cost of training are difficult to make until the exact nature and scope of the project are defined. In general, training costs should be minimal unless or until large numbers of employees are involved (say 15 or more) or inexperienced or new employees are permitted to work at home.

There are still many unresolved issues surrounding remote work and its impact on the organization, the employee, and the employee's manager and family. The ideas discussed here must be viewed as preliminary since additional knowledge will become available as telecommuting becomes more widely practiced. As more organizations experiment with home work and study its consequences, general management guidelines should evolve.

Discussion Questions

1. What are the forces that make telecommuting a viable alternative to working in an office?
2. Describe some of the negative aspects of telecommuting from the perspective of an employee faced with this option.
3. Describe the personnel issues a manager must consider when deciding whether employees should be allowed to work at home.
4. Is telecommuting a good alternative for all white-collar workers? Explain.

READING 26

Utilizing Information Technology: Guidelines for Managers

article by
HENRY C. LUCAS, JR.

THE COMPUTER AGE dawned for business in the 1950s, when a few firms acquired first-generation, vacuum-tube computers. The programming and operation of these machines were left to professionals—generally personnel who had previously worked with electronic accounting machinery and punched-card processing. Management and end users of computer systems had little contact with the specialists who were located in a data processing department.

The 1960s witnessed widespread disappointment with computers. The promise of "management information systems" was never fulfilled. Neither managers nor systems designers knew what information a manager needed nor how to provide it through computers, except in a few rate instances. The use of computers increased rapidly during this time, but the emphasis was on transactions processing and managerial control systems.

Advances like database and on-line systems, which had been introduced in the 1960s, flourished in the 1970s, thereby bringing users closer to computers. Users worked with computers directly, whether or not they influenced the design of systems. Older, batch-processing systems hid the computer from users and buffered them from it; that buffer was removed with on-line systems so that lapses in service became painfully obvious to users.

As we entered the 1980s, new problems in information processing in organizations became apparent. The information services department was seen, at best, as unresponsive to users and, at worst, as totally incompetent. The backlog for new applications was discouraging and was continually increasing in size. A user might be faced with a wait of two or three years before a new application was introduced, unless he or she could make a case that was strong enough to get the application moved

Source: Reprinted from Utilizing Information Technology: Guidelines for Managers, by Henry C. Lucas, Jr., *Sloan Management Review*, Fall 1986, pp. 39-47, by permission of the publisher.

to the front of the queue. Once the information services department started work on an application, it was likely to encounter large time and cost overruns, often ultimately delivering a product that did not meet the original specifications.

Lack of responsiveness was not confined to new applications; requests for maintenance and enhancements to existing systems were also put on hold, seemingly forever. To overcome some of these problems, firms established maintenance committees to set priorities on requests for changes. I heard one manager of an information services department, when pressed about when a request would be completed, respond, "It's up to the maintenance committee. If they put a high priority on it, we can do it next month. If it has a low priority, chances are it will never be done."

Trends in the Technology

Information technology has developed rapidly over the last five years; the technology itself offers some solutions for overcoming the problems described above, *if it is managed well.* Management must control this technology and its use in the organization; new developments have created a challenge to management that is even greater than any it faced in the early days of computers. Too many managers are now allowing the technology to drive decisions, rather than actively managing the technology.[1] The biggest danger is inaction; if left alone, trends in technology will result in management's loss of control over information processing. Today's inaction will prove costly in the future, when the firm wants to share hardware, software, and applications and when it is ready to develop an integrated communications network.

What are the trends in technology that should concern management? First, a number of firms are using information technology as a part of *corporate strategy.* Merrill Lynch gained a significant competitive advantage in the securities industry with its Cash Management Account, a product made possible by information technology. This innovation brought an estimated 450,000 new brokerage accounts to Merrill. The firm also gained $60 million in annual fees for managing the three liquid asset funds associated with the Cash Management Account.[2]

American Hospital Supply is another company that has used information technology to gain a competitive edge. In this case, AHS developed an order entry system, called ASAP, that features terminals in customer hospitals. The average order on this computer-based system is for 5.8 items, as compared with the industry average of 2.7 items per order. Three times more is spent by hospitals with ASAP than by those with the manual ordering system.[3]

The next major trend that should be of conern to management is the explosion of *end-user computing.* This term describes computing that is actually performed by the user of the technology rather than by a systems professional. The proliferation of microcomputers, for individual users, and of divisional and departmental minicomputers are examples of this trend. With powerful applications packages, users are developing systems and installing them more quickly than has been possible through the efforts of the traditional, centralized, information services department.

A third trend concerns the *options available for systems development.* There is no longer only one way to develop an application (i.e., classical, custom-developed systems). Now, we have prototyping, packages, and/or Fourth Generation Languages to ease applications development.

A prototype is a representation of a system under development. The prototype may correspond to some part of the system such as the input and output seen by the user. The prototype may be a miniature version of the entire application, developed on a microcomputer to test design before a system is programmed for a mainframe. A prototype may also grow to become the final application itself. This approach provides quick feedback to users who can see something concrete from the development effort early on in the design process.

Packages are used in a number of ways to speed applications development. A package is a program that is purchased from a third party for use in the organization. The first kind of package is general purpose; the user works with the package to solve a problem. A good example of this kind of package is Lotus 1-2-3. This micro spreadsheet program is intended for use in solving a wide variety of problems that can be cast into the format of a spreadsheet.

A dedicated package, on the other hand, represents a solution to a specific problem, such as processing accounts receivable, order entry, or controlling inventory, to nane a few. The package is the solution; the buyer usually has to modify company procedures or modify the package to employ it successfully. If changes can be kept to a minimum, a dedicated package provides debugged working code and should shorten applications development time. The demands on the user, however, may be greater than with custom development because installation is faster and more intensive.

Fourth Generation Languages are languages that are considered to be at a higher level than COBOL or FORTRAN. These are languages like FOCUS, NATURAL, RAMIS II, and NOMAD, which accomplish many tasks with one or two language statements. A single statement in one of the Fourth Generation Languages may take five or ten statements in COBOL. The higher level nature of the language hides the computer more than do COBOL-like languages. As a result many users have had success working with Fourth Generation Languages. Some firms are moving away from COBOL as their primary programming language and are using a Fourth Generation Language instead. The higher level of these languages allows for greater programmer productivity for professionals in the computer field, as well as for users.

We are close to the development of *managerial work stations*—systems that serve the manager in the same way that engineering work stations contribute to the productivity of technical personnel. The purpose of this system, constructed around one or more microcomputers, is to support the manager in whatever work must be performed. Some functions that may be included in a work station are:

1. Spreadsheet processing with a program like Lotus,
2. Word processing for preparing memos and reports,
3. Database management and file systems for setting up simple, personal applications,
4. Presentation graphics for meetings,
5. Electronic mail,
6. Access to external databases like D&B or Dow Jones, and
7. Connection with various networks to share data and programs.

Such a work station will become an increasingly valuable part of the knowledge worker's support system.

The use of computers has spread well beyond traditional business-information processing. *Computer-aided design and manufacturing* (CAD/CAM) are becoming more common as manufacturers struggle to meet competition. Engineers, factory managers, and others involved in factory operations are making decisions on the acquisition and installation of many different types of computer-based devices. These decisions involve expenditure of large amounts of capital and have significant implications for all of the information processing in the firm.

There is a trend toward *networking*—that is, tying many of a firm's computers together with communications links. What are the advantages of networking? One of the first uses of a network is distribution of mail and memos electronically. For example, DEC has an inter-company electronic mail network that incorporates over 6,000 nodes. The system has had a major impact on Digital, and its chairman has stated that it is difficult to imagine doing business without it.[4]

Another reason for networking is the sharing of data throughout a corporation. Users may also need the computational power, or a special program on a computer located at some other point on the network. A communications path through the network makes it possible to access the computer and/or its programs. Networks facilitate the sharing of devices. It is expensive to provide each managerial work station with a laser printer, but one printer shared by eight or ten work stations on a network would probably be more than adequate.

A final trend of interest to management is the *ever-decreasing cost of computation combined with an increase in the power of computers.* There will be more and more user-oriented software to take advantage of increased computer processing power. As these costs drop, it will be a rare organization whose entire budget for information processing does not increase because so much more processing is being done!

These trends in the technology have a number of implications for the firm. First, information processing will become even more pervasive; there is no end in sight to the increasing demand for computers and processing power. Firms will move toward better integration of their computers, forming networks of mainframes, minis, and microcomputers. Compatibility of hardware and software will be a major issue in building networks. More and more firms will seek ways to use information technology creatively to gain a competitive edge. Senior management will be more concerned with computers than ever before.

With the advent of packages and Fourth Generation Languages, there will be more applications, developed at a faster rate, than in the past. Although increased development speed will reduce user complaints, it means increasing demands for computer resources and a rapid pace of organizational change as new systems are implemented. And, as a result of more applications development and end-user computing, more managers and staff members at all levels in the organization will make hands-on use of computers.

We expect knowledge workers to embrace the concept of managerial work stations. These stations will become an integral part of the worker's job and will become as essential as a telephone.

All of these trends will create strong pressures for more user autonomy and control over processing. Unless constrained by management or company policy, the natural tendency will be for users to acquire hardware and software without any consideration of overall corporate goals.

Challenges for Managers

These trends and their implications present a major challenge to three groups of managers: senior management of the firm, divisional and departmental managers, and the manager of the information services department. This section presents a series of questions for each of the three groups. In a later section of this article (on recommendations), all of these questions are grouped into five categories of concerns in order to offer concrete suggestions for managerial action. The trends above lead directly to the questions raised here and the five categories into which the questions fall.

A major point of this article is that if these three groups do not actively control information processing and meet the management challenges of this new technology, the firm will be severely hindered in coming years. To do nothing is tantamount to admitting that management is incapable of controlling information processing. The results of such a policy, given the pace of technology, will be uncontrolled growth, leading in turn to an information processing environment that will be both chaotic and costly.

Senior management needs to answer the following questions:

1. How do we control information processing?
2. What is the best organizational structure for information processing?
3. How do we coordinate the acquisition of hardware and software?
4. How do we coordinate distributed users?
5. What role does information technology play in corporate strategy?
6. What are our communications needs?

In today's processing environment, *divisional and middle managers* are confronted with making decisions and supervising operations that used to be delegated to computer professionals. Now these managers must respond to the following questions:

1. How do we structure information processing in our organizational subunit?
2. How do we control the local acquisition of hardware and software?
3. How should we manage networks and distributed processing?
4. What must be done in order to develop hardware and software interfaces with other computers and among the division's computers?
5. What are the appropriate systems-development strategies for us?
6. Should we try to integrate voice, data, and video communications?
7. What are appropriate database strategies for access and query from various locations?

8. What kind of micro-to-mainframe links and networks are needed?

New technology has caught most *information services department (ISD) managers* in a vise-grip. The movement toward end-user computing clearly represents a loss of power and influence for this computer professional. Nolan describes a manufacturing plant that is probably typical of much of American industry.[5] In 1970 the manager of information services controlled 80 percent of the firm's budget for information processing. By 1980 he controlled only 36 percent of a much larger budget and, furthermore, his control extended over only 60 percent of the business use of computers.

The ISD manager recognizes the risks for the company of too much end-user control, but is almost powerless to stop it. This computer professional knows that the widespread proliferation of vendors of hardware and software will create immense support and integration problems when the firm decides to move toward a network environment. He or she also knows that most users do not bother with documentation or with careful testing and debugging of their applications; few show concern for data integrity.

The information services manager is often seen as unresponsive, based on a history of rather credible evidence. Discouraging end-user programming and the proliferation of computers appears to be an attempt to retain power. The ISD manager must figure out how to work with senior managers and users to help the firm control information processing. He or she must address the following questions:

1. What kind of information processing plan should the organization develop?
2. How do we organize the staff in the ISD to support end-user computing?
3. What type of architecture is appropriate for a corporate communications network?
4. How do we deal with heightened user expectations? If a micro application can be done so fast, why should a multiuser system on a mainframe take so long?
5. How can we educate end users about all aspects of information processing?
6. How do we advise, support, and control hardware and software acquisition?
7. What new technology and tools for systems development are best?
8. How can we control data integrity in a distributed, database enviornment?
9. Is the firm ready for office automation?

We will offer some suggestions for these three groups of managers after we discuss the key issue—control and coordination of information processing and how it interacts with the structure of the organization.

Control and Coordination

The most difficult management decision today, with respect to information processing, is how much control to give each of the three groups of managers above. Table 1 depicts three points on a continuum of processing control.

In a centralized environment, all control for information processing remains in a central information service department, including decisions about hardware and software acquisition and user support. In a decentralized environment, we find the opposite extreme: decisions are left to the user with no coordination by a central group. Users and divisional managers have total control.

Distributed processing is characterized, in theory, by shared control, but there is great potential for lack of control and ambiguity. Some standardization will be forced upon users because distributed processing implies a communications capability among various computers. However, there is still great latitude in how much control is given to local managers and in how much authority to coordinate is given to the ISD manager.

What is the role of senior management under these alternatives? Under centralized control, senior management can probably continue to ignore

Table 1 Control of Information Processing

Centralized	Distributed	Decentralized

information processing until the noise level from users becomes too high. Then managers will be forced to adjudicate between the central ISD group and users who want more freedom.

Under decentralized management, senior managers will also be able to ignore information processing, at least in the short run. Of course, it will be necessary to review budgets and to prevent a local manager from spending a a disproportionate amount on information systems but, in general, one can continue a laissez-faire approach to systems. In the long run, this strategy may lead to disaster. One major bank has equipment from forty-seven different vendors. Supporting this equipment and establishing a network are now formidable tasks that could have been simplified with prior planning and control.

Decentralized processing is probably the direction in which inertia will tend to take firms that do not make a conscious choice. Vendors are only too ready to sell hardware and software to anyone in the firm, and prices are low enough that it is easy to purchase substantial computing power without anyone noticing.

The Tradeoffs

What, then, is the best organizational structure for your firm? There is no single best structure for information processing. Right now, the majority of firms are distributed with respect to equipment, but the locus of control is not as clear. Table 2 presents some of the tradeoffs senior management should consider in structuring the information processing organization.

In a centralized environment, coordination is achieved through the authority of the ISD organization and requires little effort, except to police the local divisions. Service perceptions are likely to be poor and the ISD will have to market its support activities. There will be tight control over the technology.

In a decentralized mode, it is extremely hard to coordinate processing, even if management wishes to do so. Control is antithetical to the philosophy of decentralization. Evidence suggests that local control is associated with more favorable user perceptions of service, although it is quite likely that the local divisions will vary greatly in their adoption of technology. Some division managers will make good decisions while others will not.

With a "go-it-alone" approach, service will be perceived as good and users will have to provide their own support. Decentralized users may become complacent and fall behind in technology, or they may become fascinated with and adopt every costly advance.

Management can achieve distributed control and still provide local managers with a great deal of autonomy. The demands for coordination are heavy but the results, if managed carefully, should be highly favorable user perceptions of service and adequate corporate control over processing.

Recommendations

The challenges and questions for each group of managers can be grouped into five categories, each of which must be addressed by senior, divisional, and information service management.

The first task for management is strategic. Managers have to identify opportunities where the technology will provide a strategic advantage. It is also necessary to look for threats created by competitors who are using technology strategically.

Second, management must design a structure for information processing. While distributed is probably the most popular organizational form, it is not necessarily the best for every organization.

Third, the organization structure for information processing determines how management will control processing. A structure featuring a highly centralized computer staff has implications for control that are different from those of a decentralized structure. What are the variables that management should consider in controlling information processing?

It is easiest to manage when the policies and control exercised are seen to be in the best interest of those for whom the controls are intended. Keene and Woodman have presented an excellent example of this approach in describing one firm's control over microcomputers.[6] The authors argue that control should not be equated with prevention—something typically ascribed to the manager of the information service department.

Table 2 Organizational Structure Tradeoffs for ISD

	Structure		
	Centralized	**Distributed**	**Decentralized**
Control & Coordination	Little Effort	Heavy Demands	Extreme Demands
Service	Poor	Good	Good
Support	Market Services	Joint Effort	Users Alone
Technology	Tight Control	Policies Needed	Keep up with Technology?

The firm established a computer store and consulting services to help users and to control microcomputers in the organization. It was easier and more convenient for users to work with the store and consulting services than to look outside the organization. By keeping computers and software packages that the company was ready to support in the store, the firm influenced end users to make acquisitions that fit corporate plans.

This central issue of control involves setting policies for the acquisition of hardware and software, the coordination of requests for new applications, the coordination of distributed users, and approaches for supporting end users.

The fourth management concern is with communications and networking. Trends suggest that firms are moving toward a network environment. The organization needs to develop an architecture of hardware and software and plans for communications.

Finally, management must consider systems-development strategies. For example, a firm might require that at least three alternatives be considered for any suggested application: a custom-designed system, a package, or a simple system on a micro. Management may also encourage the use of Fourth Generation Languages as a replacement for COBOL in custom-developed systems where feasible.

Recommendations for Senior Managers

What should senior management do to address the five concerns above?

1. Look for strategic use of the technology. Firms are using technology more and more to gain a competitive edge, and senior management is responsible for corporate strategy.[7]
2. Define the organizational structure for information processing. Will the firm be centralized, decentralized, or distributed? If distributed, to what extent? How will the firm make decisions about information processing, e.g., through a corporate steering committee?
3. Work with the ISD staff to define an architecture for hardware, software, and communications. It is important to have one's future computer environment and network in mind in making today's decisions about hardware and software.
4. Determine how computer support will be provided, by whom, and how it will be charged. End users become easily frustrated when they encounter difficulties, and they need quick, easy access to help.
5. Determine the amount of coordination required over information processing. One policy might be to establish an approved list of hardware and software for purchase; no further approval is required if items on this list are to be acquired. Exceptions must be approved by the corporate vice president of information systems, who will respond within two weeks to a written request for an exception.
6. Establish a mechanism for the approval of suggested applications and look for common

systems. One policy might be to require that all applications other than those by a single end user for his or her own use must be sent for review to the corporate vice president of IS and/or a steering committee. The review will normally be completed within two weeks. The purpose of the review is to determine whether the firm already has such a system or whether there are other divisions working on one that is similar.

7. Establish coordination mechanisms. For example, all local information processing personnel are to meet every six months with the corporate vice president of IS and his or her staff to discuss common problems, new applications, and new technology. Encourage the local divisions to set up users' groups for popular software like Lotus 1-2-3.
8. Require that local budgets and plans for information processing be reviewed by the IS corporate vice president—not for approval, but to keep abreast of what will be happening in the divisions.

Table 3 shows how these recommendations may help senior managers meet the concerns described earlier.

Recommendations for Divisional Managers

Divisional managers must make decisions about information processing in their divisions. The following actions are recommended:

1. Look for opportunities for the strategic use of the technology at the divisional level.
2. Determine an organizational structure for processing in the division.
3. Following the guidelines above for senior management, establish policies for whatever degree of coordination and control is required at the local level.
4. Maintain involvement in systems analysis and design. Insist on alternatives for each application, attend review sessions, and agree on system logic.

Table 3 Senior Management Actions

	Areas of Concern				
	Strategy & Technology	**Organizational Structure**	**Control Coordination**	**Communication & Networks**	**Systems Development**
Actions	Seek Strategic Uses of Information Technology	Define Organizational Structure	Define Technical Architecture	Plan for Networks	Establish Applications Approval Mechanism
		Determine Coordination Required	Support End Users		
			Determine Coordination Required		
			Establish Coordination Mechanisms		
			Review Budget		

5. Encourage the use of new technologies to improve design like prototyping, the use of Fourth Generation Languages, etc.
6. Support end-user computing, experiment with work stations, and control micros through support.
7. Consistent with corporate policy, develop network and communications strategies, including links among various types of computers.

Table 4 shows how these recommendations help meet the challenges of technology for the divisional manager. The manager of local divisions will undoubtedly receive more responsibility for information processing in the future. Just as in any other aspect of the business, this technology can be managed if one is willing to spend time and to take action.

Recommendations for Information Services Managers

The ISD manager is in the middle of the revolution in computer technology. The role of this individual is changing, from that of a person with almost absolute control to that of one who consults with, educates, and trains users. I believe that most ISD managers will eventually find this a more appealing role than trying to satisfy users while being in complete control over information processing, something that has proven almost impossible to achieve.

For the computer professional, more end-user involvement is a mixed blessing. End users can help reduce maintenance and enhancement requirements and enhance productivity. However, computer professionals must teach users to be concerned about documentation, database integrity, compatibility, and the maintainability of the systems or programs they develop. The ISD manager can help the organization most by:

1. Designing systems development, operating procedures, and communications to support the type of organizational structure desired by senior and divisional management for information processing.
2. Encouraging the use of advanced technology like Fourth Generation Languages and managerial work stations.
3. Setting a policy that multiple alternatives will be considered for each new application, such as a dedicated package, a small system for a micro, a custom-developed application, etc.
4. Generating ideas for senior management on

Table 4 Divisional Manager Actions

	Areas of Concern				
	Strategy & Technology	**Organizational Structure**	**Control Coordination**	**Communication & Networks**	**Systems Development**
Actions	Seek Strategic Uses of Technology	Define Organizational Structure	Determine Coordination Required Encourage End-User Computing	Plan Networks	Encourage Involvement in Systems Analysis Encourage Use of New Technologies Encourage End-User Computing

ways that information processing technology might be used strategically in the firm.
5. Taking the lead in developing networks and hardware and software architectures for the future.
6. Recognizing the changing role of computer professionals as consultants and educators.
7. Performing the information processing coordination role for the corporation as a whole, as deemed appropriate by senior and divisional management.

Table 5 shows how these recommendations help meet the concerns for information services managers posed earlier.

There is no single best way to organize and manage information technology. Regardless of the organizational structure chosen, there is a need for management to control and coordinate information processing in the organization. Information technology offers opportunities that will be crucial to the success of firms throughout the 1980s and beyond. Management needs to put mechanisms in place today so that information processing will make its maximum contribution to the firm now and in the future. The recommendations above should help senior, divisional, and information services management meet the challenge of managing the revolution in information technology.

Discussion Questions

1. Describe the major trends in technology that should concern management. What is the bottom-line implication of these trends for utilization of the technology? Explain.
2. With respect to IS services, is a highly centralized control and coordination mechanism practical for most large organizations? Why or why not? Under what conditions might such a scheme work well?
3. How are the recommendations for senior managers and divisional managers different from those for the MIS executive?

References

1. H. C. Lucas, Jr., and J. A. Turner, "A Corporate Strategy for the Control of Information Processing," *Sloan Management Review*, Spring 1982, pp. 25-36.
2. C. Wiseman and I. C. MacMillan, "Creating Competitive Weapons from Information Systems," *Journal of Business Strategy*, Fall 1984, pp. 42-49.
3. "Index Systems, AHS: The ASAP System," in a *Casebook for Management Information Systems* 3d ed., ed. H. C. Lucas, Jr. (New York: McGraw-Hill, 1985).

Table 5 IS Manager Actions

	Areas of Concern				
	Strategy & Technology	**Organizational Structure**	**Control Coordination**	**Communication & Networks**	**Systems Development**
Actions	Generate Ideas for Strategic Use of Technology	Support Firm's Information-Processing Structure	Recognize Changing IS Staff Role	Develop Future Network and Computer Architectures	Encourage Use of New Technologies
			Coordinate Information Processing for the Organization		Provide Multiple Alternatives for Each Application

"American Hospital's Marketing Program Places Company atop Troubled Industry," *Wall Street Journal*, 25 August 1984.

"Systems That Slash Hospital Costs," *Business Week*, September 1980, pp. 76A-76E.

4. A. B. Crawford, "Corporate Electronic Mail—A Communications-Intensive Application of Information Technology," *MIS Quarterly*, September 1982, pp. 1-13.

5. R. Nolan, "Managing Information Systems by Committee," *Harvard Business Review*, July-August 1982, pp. 72-79.

6. P. Keene and L. Woodman, "What to Do with all Those Micros," *Harvard Business Review*, September-October 1984, pp. 142-150.

7. Wiseman and MacMillan (1984).

SECTION NINE

End-User Computing

READING 27

Establishing a Comprehensive Microcomputer Administration Policy

article by
KEN STONECIPHER

Without comprehensive management or control, acquiring a microcomputer can lead to frustration, confusion, and overspending. With constructive implementation, developed and monitored by key managers within an organization, the microcomputer can become an extremely valuable information resource.

General Policies and Responsibilities

The Illinois Department of Transportation (IDOT) hoped to develop, before purchase and installation, a strategic policy for implementing microcomputers. A policy report was designed to inform IDOT personnel of their responsibilities in microcomputer selection and operation. The policy also outlined the role of key managers in helping select the appropriate cost-effective microcomputer hardware and software as well as in developing the role of key staff in supporting microcomputer hardware, software, and documentation. Under this policy, these managers also are responsible for helping users identify problems after buying and installing microcomputers.

The goal of this microcomputer policy is to help managers become informed consumers; this requires the assistance of specific staff members because of rapid technological change, the number and variety of hardware and software vendors, and the price of inappropriate or uninformed decisions regarding hardware or software purchases. The technical support staff should also review a comprehensive policy of microcomputer integration with word processing equipment, data processing equipment, and other office automation support components.

To help managers and technical support assess

Source: Reprinted with permission from *Journal of Information Systems Management*, Winter 1986, Volume 4, Number 1.

microcomputer requests from various departments, an evaluation process should be instituted. It should include, but not be limited to, administration of microcomputers, hardware and software evaluation and documentation, training of new users, maintenance and support of microcomputers, informational support of users, and necessary customized applications software.

The most important considerations in developing a microcomputer policy are:

- Documenting the new organizational structure associated with the microcomputers
- Examining management's monitoring and control of the new information resource
- Determining the organization's information needs and what the available technology can provide

Management should recognize the microcomputer's potential in performing a variety of functions. One of its most productive capabilities is planning budgets, making cost projections, and developing financial forecasts and projection programs. These projections can also be interfaced with graphics programs so that visual presentations can be incorporated into reports. The microcomputer can also be used as a word processor to support office management functions, enabling managers to prepare memos and brief reports themselves. Information flow between microcomputers can enable managers to transmit information by electronic mail; short messages, memos, and documents usually sent via telephone can be transmitted between microcomputers within an organization or across the country. This function eliminates "telephone tag" with other administrators; such transmissions are completed without any operator intervention.

The affordability of microcomputers means that information processing that once could be performed only at certain terminals connected to a large mainframe computer can now be performed by any user at a much lower cost. This same affordability, however, may result in the purchase of many of these units before a comprehensive policy or plan is finalized. The impact of gross purchases without a strategic plan for implementation can have serious cost/performance consequences.

An important component of microcomputer policy is the establishment of a methodology for comprehensive evaluation and understanding of the microcomputer's primary and peripheral equipment and software. Although managers involved in implementing such a policy are not directly involved with the daily activities of microcomputer support, they must thoroughly understand the terminology and have a working knowledge of the equipment and software if they are to be effective in dealing with technical staff and vendors.

Administration

Typical administrative considerations in establishing a microcomputer policy include:

- The selection process
- Examination of lease, purchase, and maintenance agreements
- Review of the necessary consumable supplies to support the microcomputer project
- Examination of security aspects if applicable
- Inventory assignments
- A cost/benefit analysis of the microcomputers.

The Selection Process

Procedures must be established regarding how a microcomputer or group of microcomputers is requested for a particular area. Complete documentation of the request procedure is necessary to ensure the use of appropriate organizational channels.

To assist microcomputer users in the analysis and selection process, IDOT outlined steps for requesting microcomputer services. These procedures aided the IDOT staff in microcomputer selection and also outlined the integration of other DP and word processing services in specific applications when a microprocessor was inappropriate. The procedures were designed to maximize the resources of available staff and minimize the time and cost lost through inappropriate hardware/software selections (see box).

Procedures for Hardware and Software Selection

1. An individual requests automated services to a specific IDOT bureau. It should be noted that microcomputers were not initially deemed appropriate until an analysis of the user's needs was completed.
2. A form requesting DP services (not specifically microcomputers) is completed and transmitted to the DP manager within IDOT.
3. The form is reviewed by the DP manager and assigned priority in accordance with IDOT's information processing goals.
4. Notification of implementation is transmitted back to the individual requesting information services.
5. The DP manager then meets with the appropriate staff to assign personnel to the user requesting information services.
6. The assigned information processing personnel meet with the user to perform a definition of requirements.
7. On completion of the requirements and definition analysis, hardware and software requirements are specified by the analysis team.
8. Based on the data obtained through the functional requirements definition, a determination is made to review the equipment before purchase (if the requirements definition indicated that a microcomputer and appropriate software could fulfill these requirements). Supportive information (e.g., an evaluation) is completed with the assistance of the appropriate staff.
9. The user and the assigned analysis staff develop a request for a proposal and outline the minimal functional checklist for the equipment.
10. The user and the information processing analyst review vendor bid submissions.
11. A vendor is selected.
12. The information analysis team and appropriate personnel install equipment.
13. The user is trained off-site through IDOT's information processing section; training at the actual work site with the new equipment is phased in.
14. Maintenance and support are conducted on an ongoing basis by the appropriate personnel.

Throughout the request procedure, management judges the information processing request in light of the analysis of the user's needs and the technology that would best fulfill them, rather than in terms of the equipment that the user wants. Information processing requests may eventually evolve into combined services of a microcomputer, word processing equipment, minicomputers, and large host mainframes. Managers assigned to working with microcomputers must therefore confer with others as part of a committee on project requests and implementation, or they must report to senior management to avoid duplicating information services or selecting inappropriate equipment.

Lease, Purchase, and Maintenance Agreements

IDOT wanted a policy on leasing agreements for all its DP equipment, because current technology can become outdated quickly. Unfortunately, microcomputer costs are so low that many vendors do not have any lease agreements. Some retail stores do rent and lease equipment; the leasing agreements vary and therefore demand a knowledge of specific contractual requirements before any form of lease is entered.

A lease/purchase agreement (i.e., the actual contract) should be thoroughly reviewed before it is accepted. This is critical in terms of equipment replacement or service, especially when it is discovered after implementation that heavy use necessitates replacement or repair. A malfunctioning unit must be replaced in the least possible time. This can be accomplished in one of two ways:

- Because of the low cost, it is possible for the staff maintaining the microcomputers to have backup equipment at their disposal.
- A leasing agreement can provide for repair or replacement by the retailer within 24 hours.

The technical expertise of retailers varies greatly. The best approach is to direct an inhouse staff with a working knowledge of the equipment to perform light maintenance. Even minor maintenance, however, may void the vendor's maintenance agreement or replacement policy. It is important to review warranty provisions in purchase and lease agreements to ascertain how they specify user support as compared with retail-vendor support; this reduces the changes of voiding equipment warranty through in-house support.

Consumable Supplies

The managers's job regarding consumable supplies should not deviate from present organizational responsibilities of those in charge of ordering them. Initially, those staff members ordering consumable supplies should be assisted by the manager in the review of recommendations by the vendors. Consumable supplies include diskettes, paper for printers, mailing labels, print wheels if a letter-quality printer is used, and ribbon cartridges if either a dot-matrix or letter-quality printer is used.

It is important that the vendor-specified print wheels be used with the letter-quality printers calling for them. Using subquality print wheels with a letter-quality printer results in reduced print-wheel life (which cancels the cost-saving factor). In this case it is wise to consider the vendor's recommendations.

Security

Security requirements vary according to the organization and workstations within it. Managers should ensure the prevention of data theft and the establishment of backups of secure information on diskettes; however, the best security for such information is to place the diskettes in locked storage where they cannot be accessed by unauthorized personnel.

Some software vendors offer security software that can be used with diskettes; however, the user may fail to understand thoroughly how the security encryption scheme works. If a software maintenance problem points to damaged secure information on a diskette, recovering that information becomes difficult. Management must select a security policy that is as simple as possible for the users, is not time-consuming, does not necessitate a whole new organizational structure, and is easy to implement. Extensive security schemes may appear attractive because of their complexity, but they may also hinder the user in implementing the new equipment.

Inventory Assignments

Although inventory number assignments are necessary when the new equipment arrives, they should require no additional staff. A routine organizational structure for assigning numbers should be established. It may be necessary, however, to develop a policy regarding software inventory assignments. Because a great deal of software is maintained at individual user workstations rather than at a central repository, management must keep track of software lending between users. Another factor to be considered is the portability of microcomputers and the peripheral equipment, which makes them easy to steal. IDOT requires that any room containing microcomputers equipment be locked during designated hours. In addition, no equipment leaves the office without the signature of the appropriate manager.

Cost/Benefit Analysis

IDOT viewed its microcomputer implementation as a benefit because text and management support programs that had been run through a large mainframe computer using telecommunications and time-sharing options could now be operated in a standalone mode.

A more comprehensive analysis format is a cost-avoidance one; purchasing microcomputers is preferred to installing other terminals and enlarging the network tied into a large host computer. Microcomputers eliminate phone and telecommunications costs, CPU time costs, and vendor terminal costs. In addition, with the implementation of microcomputers as alternatives to word processors, the administrative support staff can be more efficiently used as a result of the time saved through the comprehensive software available to microcomputers; hiring additional staff because of the volume of administrative support work is unnecessary.

In the final analysis, a cost/benefit or cost-avoidance analysis is only as good as its developer. The best cost/benefit or cost-avoidance analysis can only give trends or indications of where some of those cost factors may lie. Management should remember that the analysis is only a support component of the overall justification for a microcomputer project.

Tackling Development and Training

A comprehensive development and training program for all individuals associated with microcomputers implementation, maintenance, and support should be incorporated into a microcomputer implementation policy. An educational plan specific to managers and to technical, professional, and clerical or support staff should be developed. Consideration should also be given to those with expertise in using microcomputers or DP equipment; their training can be in the form of self-instruction.

The objective of any development and training program is to acquaint the new users as quickly as possible with the appropriate hardware and software. IDOT recommended two-phased training. The first phase is training with the new equipment outside the user's normal work area. This gives individuals time to gain an in-depth understanding of their new equipment before using it. The later phase consists of training tailored to particular user work areas and applications. Management should also be sympathetic to the time that individuals must spend away from their desks during the training period. Training costs will be recovered, because the two-phased approach ensures better use of the equipment in less time.

The technical staff should have a more intensive training program than users. It should involve a thorough understanding of such areas as:

- Microprocessor systems, including RAM, ROM, I/O routines, memory-mapped I/O, chip architecture, and bus architecture
- Disk storage, including diskettes, Winchester disks, logic assemblies, and mechanical subassemblies
- Printers, including dot matrix and character imprint
- Modems
- Monitors/CRTs
- Operating systems
- Clock assemblies
- Installation procedures
- Application software
- Maintenance procedures

Education of the technical staff should be ongoing to increase knowledge in relation to the expanding technology. A plan of professional staff education should specify goals to be achieved through the training process. These goals should address how the new equipment is to be used under the supervision of their respective managers. Implementation should be codeveloped by the professional staff and the microcomputer team assigned to train users.

The initial phase is taught off-site in an area designed by the microcomputer training team; it is an intensive introduction to new hardware and software. The second phase involves the equipment at its permanent work site. The training program should satisfy the educational goals as specified in the development guidelines. The length of training for the professional staff depends on the needs of the trainees.

The training program for clerical and support users should also be specified in an educational plan, with specific goals for using the equipment in their area. All planning should be developed in accordance with the directive of the respective bureau, department, or office in which the support staff will be working. If it has been determined through an implementation plan that the microcomputer user has had sufficient experience with microcomputers or other DP equipment, the team should develop a self-training program.

The plan contains specific goals for the self-training program; these goals should address how the new equipment will be used. Anyone qualified for this program should also undergo the two-phase educational program.

Individuals requiring education and training through the assistance of the microcomputer training team are evaluated on completing the program. This evaluation provides the microcomputer training team with methods for improving the program. All evaluative data for participants in the microcomputer training program should remain confidential and be used only to help individuals use microcomputer hardware, software, and peripheral equipment.

The Importance of Maintenance and Support

Managers should consider two major areas in terms of maintenance and support of the on going microcomputer program: hardware support and software support. Hardware support involves staff directly responsible for:

- Speed calibration tests
- Read/write verification tests
- RAM and ROM tests
- Communications board tests
- Documentation
- Problem determination

The software maintenance and support areas include:

- Analysis of change at user request
- Change policy
- Backup and storage
- New software release applications
- Documentation
- Problem determination
- Custom-developed applications for users

Management should consider the maintenance and technical support team as necessary as the training team, because it is responsible for the upkeep of both hardware and software. It should also be able to troubleshoot users' problems. After new equipment is installed and a new user is being trained, the team is still responsible for that equipment. The most critical aspect of operating a microcomputer network is maintaining the equipment and troubleshooting. The maintenance and support areas encompass a wide range of preventive maintenance. The list continually evolves according to user needs and hardware and software performance.

Hardware

Hardware support should be focused directly on areas that involve the highest degree of product failure. Mechanical components are more likely to fail than electronic ones. The maintenance team must therefore perform preventive maintenance on such units as the diskette drives, which have movable assemblies. The maintenance team should also be able to diagnose some problems of printers, especially letter-quality printers.

The tests involved in diskette maintenance are for speed calibration and read/write verification; these two tests determine whether the motor is rotating at the proper revolutions per minute and whether the logic subassembly and read/write head are performing properly. The most common problem with diskette drives is input/output errors caused by inability to perform a read or write operation to translate the data from the diskette to main storage or from main storage to the diskette. These two tests must be performed by the technical support team to prevent such occurrences.

The next major area in hardware maintenance support is RAM and ROM tests, which involve software operations that are loaded into the microcomputer to test an operation in which storage is used from available RAM and ROM. The only option available when failures occur in this area is to have the malfunctioning unit replaced; this requires an individual with a knowledge of electronics to replace chips or boards within the microcomputer. Advantages of having a technical support team able to perform RAM and ROM tests are that the team can isolate problems and specify storage areas where the failure may be occurring. This will isolate chips that the electronic specialist or vendor can replace.

The maintenance and support team should be able to determine problems in the communications area by using software that performs testing operations on the communications board or the modem being used. Again, this only focuses on the particular problem area; the vendor must replace the unit specified.

One of the important functions of the maintenance and support team is documenting problems. Any problem that is discovered and resolved or is suspected to be ongoing should be so documented; if the problems recur, the actions taken to resolve them have already been specified. In addition, documentation can indicate chronic hardware and software weaknesses. With this data, the vendor can replace the units or software involved. Without proper documentation of problems, the maintenance and support team has no reliability record of implemented hardware and software.

Software

Software maintenance and support (as critical as hardware support) requires a staff capable of analyzing software changes requested by users. When changes are made to the existing software, management must develop a policy regarding change. This policy involves two considerations: whether the microcomputer software is protected and whether staff is available to resolve and debug a problem and reprogram, implement, and test a solution. Most software is flexible enough to incorporate many of the changes that users may request. If the software cannot accommodate a particular request or is copy-protected, management's only option is to contact the vendor about the change.

If the software is not copy-protected, programs can be changed as the user's request; this, however, involves personnel and time. Depending on the software, this can be as complicated as any major programming project. The change requested must be weighed against the amount of time and staff available to make the change and support it.

Backup and storage of software are other important maintenance functions. It becomes the responsibility of the maintenance and support team to maintain an adequate number of generations of backup and storage of program and diskettes.

Software problem determination and documentation are also critical. Again, to assess the true performance of the software, a format should be established to document problems. The documentation should also specify the method used to determine the problem and resolve it.

Information Support

Information support can prove very valuable in avoiding unreliable software or hardware currently on the market. It can indicate future hardware and software trends. A library of information on microcomputer publications and product evaluations should be established; this information can be tapped to provide managers with indices of product performance and evaluation before purchase.

Maximizing Microcomputer Potential

Key considerations of microcomputer implementation include the analysis of those products being considered, a working knowledge of the technical specifications of a microcomputer systems, an appropriate training and development program, and proper maintenance and support for the units once they have been installed.

The random purchase and installation of microcomputers without an analysis policy may spell disaster. Without consideration for organizational goals and objectives, cost overruns may result. A microcomputer policy can ensure that implementation and subsequent maintenance are comprehensive. Managers are making them valuable tools and creating an alternative to large mainframe computers for supporting specific organizational needs.

Discussion Questions

1. Discuss the potential problems of a microcomputer acquisition that takes place without an administrative policy. Are there potential problems with having a policy? Explain.
2. What are the typical administrative considerations in establishing a microcomputer policy?
3. Discuss security issues with respect to microcomputer use. Do you think these issues are exacerbated by the use of hard disks, local area networks, or other advanced technologies? Why or why not?

4. Compare the cost of acquiring a $70,000 mainframe-based decision support system with that of 100 users acquiring a microcomputer-based spreadsheet package at $700 each. Which do you think is the most cost-effective? Give the reasons for your answer. Be sure to consider issues such as training, utilization, capacity of hardware, flexibility of software, and so on.
5. What are some of the cost-benefit considerations when acquiring a local area network?

READING 28

Strategies for Effective Microcomputer Management

article by
EUGENE R. KLEINBERG

Microcomputer hardware and software technology has advanced to the point at which no organization can ignore the potential application of these systems in its business. The hardware is more powerful, portable, and affordable. Software is more reliable, sophisticated, and integrated as well as easier to use. End users are becoming more sophisticated and less dependent on central computing services. They are discovering that such applications as word processing, data base management, and business graphics are accessible and adaptable to their needs. In addition, vendors are introducing such new applications as electronic mail and providing integrated services that enhance data transfer as well as internal and external communication.

Source: Reprinted with permission from *Journal of Information Systems Management*, Winter 1986, Volume 4, Number 1.

Critical Areas Affected by Microcomputers

With each of these advances, however, organizations are exposed to greater data abuses. Management is especially challenged by computing systems that, by their very nature, defy central control. The following paragraphs describe the impact of microcomputers on various critical areas.

Security

Unlike mainframes, microcomputers are usually not physically controlled; they are, by design, accessible to many users. Diskettes, documentation, peripherals, expansion circuit boards, and even the microcomputer itself are highly transportable and easily stolen. Unauthorized users can copy, manipulate, or destroy diskettes without leaving an audit trail and can steal data diskettes containing confidential information, leaving no record of a security breach and thereby exposing the organization to business and legal liabilities. The unauthorized copying of program diskettes violates license agreements and thus subjects the organization to litigation.

Another security problem is that microcomputers can be used to gain unauthorized access to mainframes and minicomputers.

Data Integrity

Microcomputers that do not communicate with other computers must receive information from manually entered hard copies. Data entry errors are therefore common, and erroneous recordkeeping as well as software differences increase the probability that the data on the microcomputer will differ from that of the source system. Because printed computer reports are often regarded as more authoritative than reports generated by other means, management may not question the discrepancy, which could seriously affect the accuracy of its decisions.

Incompatibilities

Microcomputer systems comprise numerous components, including hardware, operating system, application software, programming language, and data communication capabilities. When any of these components are incompatible with other microcomputers in the organization, the sharing of data and applications becomes difficult or impossible. Such incompatibility can also render their microcomputer experience useless when employees are transferred to new positions.

Data Recoverability

Data can be lost or damaged as a result of data entry errors, software errors, mechanical failures, or such environmental hazards as fire and magnetic interference. Without backup provisions, data reconstruction is difficult. Although MIS professionals have learned, and now practice, data backup, many end users are unacquainted with the dangers of system failures.

Application Controls and Audit Trails

Most end users purchase software for their computer applications. Although there are many advantages to purchased software, it allows the user to implement only those security controls that the vendor provides. The vendor, of course, cannot meet the individual control needs of each customer. For example, providing an audit trail requires more disk space than the minimum configuration. The vendor therefore does not provide the audit trail because this feature reduces its base of potential customers. Even for custom-built applications, hardware and operating system limitations limit the controls and audit trails that can be implemented. Without such controls as edits and transaction files, applications may not be reliable or auditable.

Acquisition and Use

Inexperienced users are unacquainted with system development techniques, which can identify their requirements before they acquire hardware and software. Because end users are often unable to evaluate technical features, they are more susceptible than MIS professionals to vendor sales pressure. In addition, it is often difficult to thoroughly test the hardware and software before purchase. In fact, most software cannot be returned after the packaging seal is broken. Similarly, end users are often unfamiliar with proper techniques for using hardware and software and thus cannot properly evaluate the advantages of such controls as documentation and preventive maintenance.

Costs

Before acquiring mainframes and minicomputers, most organizations perform a formal cost/benefit analysis. Because microcomputers are relatively inexpensive, however, many users easily justify their acquisition without any formal review. Some users acquire microcomputers because it is the popular thing to do, bypassing formal qualification procedures by classifying the new equipment as a miscellaneous office expense. Microcomputers obtained in this way are usually underutilized or used for nonproductive purposes (e.g., games). Although the unit cost per computer is low, the total investment of the organization can be substantial.

Establishing Controls

The organization should establish a task force of end users, MIS personnel, and auditors to plan the control of microcomputer acquisition and use. Such related functions as the purchasing and finance departments should also be consulted, and task force recommendations should be consistent with organizational policy.

Planning Approaches

The task force can follow one of two planning approaches. In the first approach, a risk analysis should be performed to identify all exposures, calculate their probabilities of occurring, and estimate their cost. Controls that reduce the probability of the exposures occurring or mitigate their consequences should be identified. The projected benefits of these controls should be weighed against implementation and maintenance costs.

The objective of the second approach is to implement and maintain a reasonable level of control without unduly restricting end users. This level of control is reached by implementing cost-effective controls formulated through surveys, interviews, and brainstorming sessions. This approach is based on the recognition that although individual controls are insufficient to control the acquisition and use of microcomputers, controls are effective as an integrated unit.

The first approach should be considered when particular exposures need special attention. For example, an insurance company gave each of its agencies a microcomputer to process essential information. Such controls as reconciling that information between the host and microcomputers and educating the agents to properly use the computer were therefore critical and accorded highest control priority. The second approach can be used for organizations planning for general microcomputer applications.

Survey

The task force must first survey existing computing facilities to determine user experience and hardware and software constraints. Case studies of past computer implementations are particularly informative. If microcomputers are not currently used in the organization, pilot cases should be implemented. The costs and benefits of these tests should be evaluated before microcomputers are introduced on a large scale.

Responsibilities

A control plan must specify the responsibilities of each group contributing to the plan. The following sections describe the responsibilities of each group involved in the acquisition and use of microcomputers.

Task Force. The task force should develop the control plan, including policies and standards, and make recommendations to senior management. The task force must designate personnel to maintain recommended controls and a microcomputer coordinator whose full-time responsibility is to oversee the plan's execution. Task force members should recognize that a control plan changes with technological developments and user requirements.

Senior Management. Senior management must approve the control plan and ensure that the resources necessary to implement and maintain the plan are available. The plan cannot succeed unless senior management gives its commitment and support.

MIS. The MIS department or an independent microcomputer staff should provide end users with such technical services as installation, consulting, and training. The MIS staff should also monitor adherence to policies and standards and perform such administrative activities as a microcomputer acquisition.

One MIS employee should support users as a microcomputer coordinator or information center manager. This person may also evaluate all acquisition requests.

Auditor. The auditor should regularly review the control plan, including policies and procedures, while application controls are developed or maintained. The auditor should also periodically test the controls to ensure that the planned controls are enforced and effective.

Recommended Controls

Controls can be implemented generally so that they apply to all microcomputers and associated applications, or they can be implemented for isolated applications. The following sections address general controls.

Support Approaches

Adequate MIS support in acquiring, implementing, and using microcomputer systems can provide control in many critical areas. The MIS department can provide support in one or more of the following tasks.

Recommending Hardware and Software. The end user is faced with thousands of hardware and software options, many of which are incompatible with each other or with systems already in the organization. Selection from a list of approved hardware and software should therefore be required or, at least, recommended. This list should include market evaluations as well as products that are currently working well in the organization. The end user should be able to select quality products that are consistent with the rest of the organization; marginally acceptable products should be identified as such on the list. End users should be able to select unapproved products only after submitting written justification for their acquisition. The list of approved products should reflect the changing needs of the organization and technological advances.

Training and Consulting. Training and consulting services for recommended products are an attractive incentive for end users to choose from the approved list; they are also a tool for promoting optimum microcomputer use. This support can range from one consultant who answers occasional end-user questions to a full-time group that helps end users acquire products and formally trains them in productive uses of the new equipment. Support consultants can also help develop applications.

Large-scale training and consulting services should include refresher courses and a help hotline as well as initial training. Computer-based training and experienced end users working as instructors enhance the quality of the training program.

The level of training and consulting needed depends on such factors as end-user experience, the application's sophistication, and the resources of the organization. Although most organizations hesitate to create a large support staff at the beginning of the project, some training and consulting must be provided to guide end-user purchases and lend other basic support.

Newsletters. A newsletter (or newsletters) addressing general microcomputing concerns and security and control problems should be published regularly for all microcomputer users. The microcomputer coordinator can edit the newsletter, but the users should submit the articles. The newsletter should present case studies, disseminate general news and product announcements, offer product reviews, and recommend further reading.

Security and control articles do not create policy, but they develop security awareness and inform users of proper control practices. For example, a corporate policy requiring diskette backup copies would be explained in a newsletter article. When users understand policy rationale, they are more likely to adhere to its dictates.

User Groups. User groups complement the newsletters. Users should meet regularly to exchange information and make recommendations for improving support, products, and policies. Community user groups are helpful, but they attract a diverse audience and may not fulfill the specific needs of the organization. Internal user groups are therefore preferred.

Information Exchange Network. The microcomputer coordinator should maintain a catalog of all significant applications and products in the organization. End users should refer to this catalog and consult with other users and application authors because shared applications and experience reduces duplicated effort and costly mistakes.

Purchasing and Maintenance. Large organizations can usually negotiate significant hardware, software, and maintenance discounts with their purchasing power. The microcomputer coordinator should be responsible for negotiating these discounts with appropriate assistance from other departments (e.g., law, purchasing, or finance) for contracts, purchase orders, and leasing arrangements.

Extended purchasing services include acquiring products on loan for extended demonstration purposes. A company store, or information center, should be established in large organizations to allow end users to learn more about alternative products without being pressured by salespersons. Organizations unreservedly committed to microcomputer standardization can acquire all their systems in one major purchase.

Value-Added Services. Specific tools can be developed or acquired to improve the value of hardware and software products. For example, an interface that allows data from a mainframe application to be downloaded and reformatted into microcomputer applications for further processing is valuable to end users who manually enter data. If the interface is supported only for certain products, end users will have a strong incentive to follow the recommendations of the microcomputer coordinator.

Staffing Considerations. Although the microcomputer support staff needs technical expertise to evaluate hardware and software products properly, communications skills are even more important. The staff needs patience and compassion to help new end users. End users who have demonstrated microcomputer expertise are good candidates for the support staff. An education or consulting background is also helpful.

Policies and Procedures

The preceding controls address acquiring and using microcomputers without formal policies and procedures. Nevertheless, the organization must have sufficient controls to reasonably ensure that assets are being protected and applications are auditable. Although formal policies and procedures are needed to ensure this, they must not be unduly restrictive. The following paragraphs describe recommended policies and procedures.

Valid Applications. Some applications are inappropriate for the microcomputer. For larger organizations, financial applications that require extensive controls and audit trails should be run on the mainframe or minicomputer. In addition, data base systems for data shared among multiple departments do not belong on a microcomputer.

A strong policy states that all proposed end-user applications must be reviewed and approved. A slightly less stringent, but more practical, policy requires this review process for only significant financial applications and for applications that cross departmental lines.

The reviewer (usually from the MIS department) ensures that business needs are established and a cost/benefit analysis is performed before any products are acquired. The reviewer helps determine whether a microcomputer-based application is appropriate for satisfying business needs. For larger applications, a formal systems development life cycle should be followed.

Standard Products. A list of approved and required products ensures a reasonable degree of compatibility. For example, to facilitate the transfer and integration of information, the organization should establish a standard data communications protocol. Other products that can be standardized include hardware, operating systems, programming languages, and applications software.

Segregation of Duties. Although the traditional control of separating responsibilities in order to ensure that errors are detected and improper activities are deterred applies to microcomputers, segregation of duties is not possible when an end user also acts as a programmer and operator. In this case, supervisory reviews and periodic audits can be compensating controls. As in traditional MIS operations, a backup should be designated to support the applications if the primary user is not available. For sensitive applications, however, segregation of critical duties is mandatory.

Physical Environment. Some of the physical controls associated with mainframe and minicomputers may not be applicable to microcomputers. The following policies, however, should be considered:

- The microcomputer should be in an area that has limited traffic and can be secured during off hours.
- An inventory should be maintained of all hardware (including peripherals and expansion boards), software diskettes, and documentation. The records should be periodically compared with a physical inventory.
- The microcomputer should have antistatic protection and approved electrical service.
- Smoking, drinking, and eating should not be permitted near the microcomputer.
- Cleaning and general housekeeping should be performed on a regular basis.
- Data diskettes should be stored away from extreme temperatures, humidity, dust, magnets, CRT, telephones, and radios. They should be labeled with a felt tip pen, kept in their protective jackets when not in use, and stored in an upright position.

Data Security. Because it is so easy to copy and remove diskettes, measures should be taken to protect data from unauthorized users. Prohibiting the home use of company microcomputers may help, but an increasing number of users have computers at home. Data security becomes an even greater concern when a microcomputer can communicate with a host computer, in which case data can be manipulated or destroyed or copied from the host onto a diskette. The following measures can prevent unauthorized data access:

- Data diskettes should be kept in a secure location.
- Sensitive data on disks should be protected by password requirements or encrypted.
- The host computer should have a security system that allows access only by authorized microcomputer users.
- After access is granted to the host computer, a microcomputer user should be permitted access only to specific files with limited authorities (for inquiry, update, downloading, or uploading).
- The host computer should log all system accesses, and violations should be investigated.

Authorized users, however, must be trusted with their data unless the organization is willing to physically search them for diskettes.

Backup and Recovery. Cost-effective controls should be established to prevent the loss or damage of hardware, software, and data. If disaster does strike, a recovery plan should be in place to reduce the consequences of the disaster. The recovery plan should specify the following:

- Diskettes should be write-protected when they are not being updated.
- Diskettes and disks should be backed up after each update. The backups should be stored in a secure location away from the microcomputer.
- A backup microcomputer with an equivalent configuration should be available if the primary microcomputer cannot be used.

In addition, a maintenance agreement and insurance coverage should be considered.

Documentation. Frequently used microcomputer applications should be documented. Documentation is especially useful when the end user changes jobs. Documentation standards should be established, although the amount of documentation should vary based on the complexity of the application. Documentation should include:

- Clear labeling of all data diskettes and documentation
- A brief narrative of the application, including functions performed and major data elements used

- A listing of the source code
- Vendor-supplied documentation
- Such information as application author, software product used, and file names.

Software Integrity. Software applications should have adequate controls and audit trails, including edits, balancing totals, and exception reports. The extent of these controls depends on the type of application and potential exposures. In addition, all applications should have controls to ensure that the software is working as planned. These software integrity controls include ensuring that most current vendor software is used and extensive application testing.

Miscellaneous. Other controls that should be considered include:

- Proprietary software should not be copied except for archival purposes or to use a hard disk.
- Warranty cards should be completed.
- Microcomputers should not be used for nonbusiness purposes.

Why You Need a Control Plan

An organization using microcomputers must prepare a control plan for the acquisition and use of microcomputers. The control plan should assign responsibilities, determine how end users will be supported, and establish policies and procedures. Periodic audits should be performed to ensure that the control plan is working as anticipated. Finally, the control plan should be continually updated to keep it current with changing technologies and organizational objectives. The checklist provides the basis of a thorough program that can ensure that the organization's microcomputer investment is well protected.

Discussion Questions

1. What are the critical areas affected by microcomputer use?
2. Does this article describe additional security issues that the previous article overlooked? If so, what are they?
3. What general services can an MIS department provide to users that will make microcomputer use more effective?
4. What impact might a lack of standards have upon the effective use of microcomputers?

Controlling Microcomputers Checklist

	Yes	No	NA	Comments
Responsibilities				
Is there a microcomputer coordinator?				
Are end users responsible for controls?				
Support				
Does microcomputer support include:				
• Recommending hardware and software?				
• Training and consulting?				
• Information exchange network?				
• Purchasing and maintenance assistance?				
Microcomputer Applications				
Are valid microcomputer applications defined?				
Are proposed applications reviewed?				
Is a systems development life cycle used for larger applications?				
Standard Products				
Are there standards for:				
• Communications protocol?				
• Hardware?				
• Operating Systems?				
• Programming languages?				
• Applications software?				
Are the standards being followed?				
Segregation of Duties				
For sensitive applications, have critical duties been separated?				
Where separation of duties is inadequate, do compensating controls exist?				
Physical Environment				
Is the microcomputer in an area that has limited traffic and is secured during off hours?				
Is an inventory of all hardware, software, and documentation maintained?				
Are the inventory records periodically compared with a physical inventory?				
Does the microcomputer have antistatic protection and approved electrical service?				
Are smoking, drinking, and eating prohibited near the computer?				
Is preventive maintenance performed?				

Checklist (Cont)

	Yes	No	NA	Comments
Are data diskettes: • Stored away from extreme temperatures, humidity, magnets, telephones, and radios? • Labeled with a felt tip pen? • Handled carefully (no touching, folding, bending, or stapling)? • Stored in protective jackets in an upright position?				
Data Security Are data diskettes kept in a secure location? Is sensitive data on disks password-protected or encrypted? Does the host computer allow access by only authorized microcomputer users? Is microcomputer access permitted for only specific files? Are levels of authority (e.g., inquiry, update, downloading or uploading) restricted appropriately? Does the host computer log all system accesses? Are all security violations investigated?				
Backup and Recovery Are write-protection labels in place for all backup diskettes? Does each diskette and disk have a backup? Are backups as current as the working copies? Are backups stored in a secure location away from the microcomputer? Is a backup microcomputer with an equivalent configuration available? Is a maintenance agreement used? Is insurance coverage in force?				
Documentation Is there adequate documentation for each application? Does the documentation include: • Clear labeling of all data diskettes and documentation? • Brief application narrative including functions performed and major data elements? • Source code listing? • Vendor supplied documentation?				

Checklist (Cont)

	Yes	No	NA	Comments
• Such information as application author, software product used, and file names?				
Software Integrity				
Is the most current vendor software used?				
Are applications tested before they are productively used?				
Are application controls and audit trails adequate?				
Miscellaneous				
Is the copying of proprietary software prohibited except for archival purposes or to facilitate use on a disk?				
Are warranty cards completed promptly?				
Are the microcomputers used for only business purposes except when proper approval is given?				

READING 29

Service Support Levels: An Organized Approach to End-User Computing

article by
ROBERT L. LEITHEISER and
JAMES C. WETHERBE

Introduction

MIS departments are struggling to keep up with the demand for computing. The traditional methods for producing systems have been overwhelmed and long lead times have resulted. Promising computer applications are being deferred or dropped because of the delay. In a survey of user managers' computing needs, Alloway and Quillard [2] found that the number of desired, but not formally requested systems was 160% of the number of systems in development or in the development backlog. They concluded that even with dramatic improvements in development efficiency, MIS departments alone could not meet users' computing demands.

Source: Reprinted by special permission of the *MIS Quarterly*, Volume 10, Number 4, December 1986, pp. 337-349.

This unmet demand has combined with the fall of hardware costs and improvements in software design to increase the amount of computing being done by end users. Benjamin [3] estimated that for a typical large U.S. manufacturing firm, end-user computing had grown from virtually nothing in 1970 to 40% of computer processing capacity in 1980. He projects it to grow to 75% by 1990. Rockart and Flannery [11] found 50-90% annual growth in timeshare computing by end users as compared to 5-15% growth in traditional computing.

The rise of end-user computing has not gone unnoticed. In a survey of leading MIS executives, consultants, and researchers [8], the "facilitation and management" of end-user computing was ranked as the second most important MIS management issue for the 1980's. Only MIS planning was ranked higher. The need to effectively manage end-user computing is being widely felt.

This article reviews the opportunities and risks presented by end-user computing. It then presents an approach to managing end-user computing that uses the concept of service support levels. This approach offers organizations the opportunity to gain the benefits of end-user computing while minimizing its risks.

End-User Computing Opportunities and Risks

There is much discussion of end-user computing in the academic and popular press, but no generally agreed upon definition. In this article, end-user computing is defined as:

> "... the use and/or development of information systems by the principal users of the systems' outputs or by their staffs" [13, p. 3].

End-user computing has been motivated by the inability of the MIS department to meet computing needs. End users choose to do their own computing because [13]:

1. lead times on development requests are shorter,
2. end users have more control over system development and use,
3. services are not available from the MIS department,
4. MIS department procedures are not appropriate for small applications,
5. the MIS department is not perceived as being concerned about users' needs,
6. end users want to learn about computing,
7. end users gain more flexibility,
8. the information systems developed better meet users' needs, and
9. development costs are lower.

The rapid and continued growth in end-user computing is evidence that users believe the benefits from doing their own computing are substantial.

Besides the advantages for users, there are also benefits for the MIS department. First, the shortage of systems development personnel can be relieved. This allows MIS executives to use their expensive human resources on larger, more technical development projects. Second, if users know their requirements, they can implement them directly into a system. This allows users to avoid going through the time consuming and error-prone process of communicating requirements to an outside developer. Finally, system implementation becomes the responsibility of the users. Their ownership of the system is thereby insured and a major stumbling block to successful system implementation is removed. Taken together, these benefits to both users and the MIS department are substantial.

Unfortunately, end-user computing has a down side. The organization's hardware, software, and data are valuable resources which can be lost or diminished if not properly developed and protected. End users, acting independently, cannot always be expected to use these resources in ways that are optimum for the whole firm. Since end-user computing bypasses the monitoring and control mechanisms built into MIS department computing, there is no formal check on user behavior. To illustrate these risks, Davis [7] presents three scenarios where end-user computing leads to problems for an unwary firm.

A faulty corporate model leads to a disastrous acquisition which later forces the firm into bankruptcy.

Errors in retrieving data for an analysis cause a substantial underestimation of the cost of introducing a new employee benefit. The actual costs are so high the firm is forced to cancel the program with disastrous results for employee morale.

An employee who developed an important end-user application leaves a company to establish his own business. Since the system was not documented no one in the organization knows how to use or maintain it.

These scenarios appear to be hypothetical, but similar situations actually exist. In his survey of end-user computing, Benson [4] found problems with inadequate documentation, poor data backup procedures, and a lack of data security.

MIS executives might argue that they should not be held accountable for end-user mistakes and failures. And for certain kinds of computing and certain knowledgeable end users this position may be defensible. In the majority of cases, however, the expertise and experience of the MIS department make it the obvious organizational unit for protecting the computing resources of the firm.

Top management reasonably looks to the MIS department for leadership in computing, no matter who develops or uses the system.

The range of risks that result from end-user development is suggested by Davis [7]:

1. The elimination of the separate analyst functions of technical expert, independent reviewer of information requirements, and enforcer of standards and policies.
2. The inability of end users to completely and accurately specify system requirements without the tools, techniques and experience of the analyst.
3. A lack of end user knowledge about, and commitment to quality assurance in system development.
4. The development of continuously changing (unstable) systems, where stable systems are needed.
5. The encouragement of private information systems at the expense of shared corporate computing resources.
6. The expensive accumulation of unneeded information.

Most firms will find it too dangerous to ignore these risks. Clearly then, success in managing end-user computing requires the facilitation of beneficial computing, while minimizing risks to the firm.

Rockart and Flannery [11] present recommendations for both of these management goals. To facilitate end-user computing, they suggest: (1) establishing a distributed organizational support structure, (2) providing a range of software tools, (3) developing a broad educational program, and (4) establishing efficient procedures for locating and transferring data. Risk coordination recommendations include: (1) identifying critical applications, (2) controlling through user (not MIS) management, (3) using MIS experts to assist end users in making computing decisions, and (4) developing standards for hardware and software and creating incentives for following them. These recommendations provide valuable guidelines for MIS executives but they do not describe a systematic approach to end-user computing. Such an approach is important for achieving effective facilitation and coordination.

Before proposing an organized approach, it is useful to lay out four general responses that an MIS executive can take towards end-user computing [10]. These general responses represent the range of specific actions which are available to executives.

1. *Sink or swim:* Don't do anything—let the end user beware.
2. *Stick:* Establish policies and procedures to control end-user computing so that corporate risks are minimized.
3. *Carrot:* Create incentives to encourage certain end-user practices which reduce organizational risks.
4. *Support:* Develop services to aid end users in their computing activities.

Each of these responses presents the MIS executive with different opportunities for facilitation and coordination. The *sink or swim* response is the default action. It does nothing to increase the level of end-user computing or improve its quality. All of the risks mentioned above apply, while the benefits to end users and the MIS department are solely a function of end user efforts.

The restrictive, *stick* response forces coordination at the cost of some computing opportunities. Many of the risks associated with end-user computing could be reduced by effective policies, standards and procedures. These same policies, standards and procedures also are likely to reduce the incentives for end users to do their own computing; i.e., lead times are increased, user control and flexibility are reduced, and development costs are higher. A heavy reliance on standards/policies and their enforcement is a hallmark of an emphasis on coordination [e.g., [1]].

The *carrot* response motivates end user to reduce the risks to the firm associated with their computing. By allowing end users to retain their computing freedom, it maintains an important incentive for end-user computing but gives up some certainty about the reduction of computing risks. This response targets a specific benefit or risk, rather than providing a complete program of support.

The *support* response is designed to increase end-user computing through the provision of services. These services are carefully designed to increase beneficial computing and to foster coordination. As long as end users choose to use or not use services, they will retain control over their computing activities and will view services positively. This choice will provide a check on the MIS department because services that focus too much on coordination and not enough on facilitation will simply not be used.

Each type of response is appropriate in some situations, but a combination of responses is necessary for management on a broad scale. The next section describes an organized approach to defining these combinations.

Service Support Levels

An effective approach to managing end-user computing achieves both facilitation and coordination. Service support levels do this by (1) defining computing responsibilities, (2) providing a framework for designing support services, and (3) allowing end users to retain as much control as possible over their own computing.

Service support levels are formal divisions of computing responsibility between end users and the MIS department. These divisions are based on a small set of critical computing decisions that are made by end-user management. The way managers make these decisions commits them to accept certain responsibilities and allows them to turn over others to the MIS department. Since end-user management make the decisions they are free to choose the amount and kind of support they feel they need. This freedom to chose provides a check on the MIS department. If the MIS department is to meet its objectives of coordinating and facilitating end user computing it must develop and deliver support services to meet needs.

An approach based on service support levels offers several other advantages. First it reduces "finger pointing" by clearly specifying department responsibilities. When a microcomputer malfunctions everyone knows who is responsible for fixing it. Second, it provides a structure for the design and delivery of end-user services by the MIS department. This structure allows a range of support options to be provided from a common pool of services. For example, the same consultant can have clearly specified duties at each support level. Third, incentives are created for end users to improve their computing practices and thereby reduces the computing risks to the firm. By clearly stating what has to be done to qualify for better MIS service, end-user management are in a better position to make trade-offs in their computing decisions. Finally, it provides a means for the MIS department to coordinate end-user computing. The same staff that provides support services also monitor and report on end-user activities. Some end-user computing will remain outside of this coordination efforts, but those activities are recognized to be the responsibility of end-user managers.

Establishing service support levels requires four steps:

1. defining the levels,
2. dividing computing responsibility at each level,
3. designing services to meet MIS support level commitments at each level, and
4. implementing service support levels.

The process may be applied to each of the principal computing resources: hardware, software, and data.

A concrete illustration will highlight aspects of the approach. The purpose of the example is not to present a business case but to illustrate the definition process and give examples of its outputs. Due to unrelated business circumstances, the levels defined here have not yet been fully implemented and their success cannot, therefore, be reported. The authors know of several other companies that have used versions of the support levels approach, but this example best illustrates the main concepts. Some modifications have been made to the original level definitions to improve the clarity of the presentation.

Defining Service Support Levels

An important part of the process of instituting support levels is determining the critical decisions which will define the levels. These decisions must be few in number and generally perceived as affecting computing accountability. A small number of decisions insures that the requirements for obtaining levels is understandable and obvious to end users, top management, and MIS staff.

One obvious means of defining levels, and thereby dividing responsibility, is to base it on the relative amounts of control that departments have over the processes that affect a computing resource. For example, if the user manager purchases a piece of hardware then the responsibility for insuring that the equipment meets department and corporate needs should rest with that manager. Similarly, if the MIS department formally reviews and approves an application program, then the MIS department should be accountable for any subsequent quality problems. These indicators of control offer a fair means of assigning responsibility. Firms must consider their own unique computing environments when defining the qualifying decisions.

For example, if a company strives to integrate its application systems, then a decision emphasizing compatibility could be defined. Concerns regarding security, sharing of applications, and documentation could lead to other qualifying decisions. Many sets of qualifying decisions should be analyzed, but no set can be final until it is formally accepted by end-user, MIS, *and* top managements.

Control and compatibility are the basis for the qualifying decisions in the example firm. As Table 1 shows, separate decisions were defined for hardware, software, and data resources. Other firms may elect to establish support levels for only one or two types of resources (e.g., software only) or may combine two types of resources (e.g., software and data) and use one set of decisions. The qualifying decision sets given in Table 1 have general applicability and offer a good starting point for other firms.

Levels are defined by assigning outcomes to qualifying decisions. Figure 1 maps the example firm's decisions to specific support levels. Five levels are defined for each of the types of computing resources and range from almost complete MIS department responsibility (Level I) to almost no MIS department responsibility (Level V). Note that all possible combinations of decision outcomes need not be used. For example, at this firm all MIS department purchases of hardware and software for end users must be registered. This policy drops all combinations of purchase/develop? = "MIS" and registration? = "NO." Similar logical or policy restrictions apply to other combinations of decision outcomes so the number of possible levels is reduced. Notice also that qualifying decisions can be related. One data level qualifier in Figure 1 depends on decisions made for the software that processes the data.

In this example, the qualifying decisions were completely determined before the support levels were defined. In practice the process is iterative, with tentative decisions being suggested and tested for their ability to define useful levels. They may then be retained, modified, or discarded.

To be effective, the number of levels should be

Table 1 Qualifying Decisions for Service Support Levels

HARDWARE DECISIONS

1. What department will purchase or lease the equipment?
2. Will the hardware be formally registered with the MIS department?
3. Will the hardware be compatible with the MIS department's computing environment?

SOFTWARE DECISIONS

1. What department will purchase or develop the software?
2. Will the software be formally reviewed by the MIS department?
3. Will the software be formally registered by the MIS department?
4. Will the software be compatible with the MIS department's computing environment?

DATA DECISIONS

1. What department will provide the data?
2. What will be the support level of the software that processes the data? (see above)
3. Will the data be formally registered with the MIS department?

Figure 1 Support Levels for Hardware, Software, and Data

	HARDWARE SUPPORT LEVELS				
Qualifying Decisions	I	II	III	IV	V
1. Purchaser?	MIS	USER	USER	USER	USER
2. Register with MIS department?	YES	YES	NO	YES	NO
3. Compatible with MIS systems?	YES	YES	YES	NO	NO

	SOFTWARE SUPPORT LEVELS				
Qualifying Decisions	I	II	III	IV	V
1. Purchaser or developer?	MIS	USER	USER	USER	USER
2. Formal review by MIS?	YES	YES	NO	YES	NO
3. Register with MIS?	YES	YES	YES	YES	NO
4. Compatible with MIS systems?	YES	YES	YES	NO	YES/NO

	DATA SUPPORT LEVELS				
Qualifying Decisions	I	II	III	IV	V
1. Source of data?	MIS	USER	USER	USER	USER
2. Software support level?	—	I-II	III-IV	V	V
3. Register with MIS?	YES	YES	YES	YES	NO

"—" indicates that the cell does not apply at this level.

small (less than 10) while the qualifying decisions should be powerful, easily recognizable, and readily understandable. Review and modification are necessary to achieve a good balance among these factors. Once the levels have been defined and agreed upon, the specific responsibilities can be determined.

Dividing Computing Responsibilities

After defining support levels, the next step is to divide up specific responsibilities. This is a shared task for end users and MIS departments. One method for doing this is to first brainstorm a list of required computing activities. Make the list as long as possible before cutting it back to the 12 to 20 most important activities. These activities should then be defined as clearly as possible. This formal definition will avoid later questions about what was actually meant by the assignment of an activity. Table 2 lists the activities and definitions generated by the example firm.

Next, a two-dimensional matrix is created to link the decision defined levels with the required computing activities. Figure 2, 3, and 4 contain these matrices. For each activity and level an assignment of responsibility is made. In our example an "X" indicates that the MIS department has the major responsibility for that activity. The absence of an "X" means that the major responsibility is assigned to the end users. For example, the MIS department has major advising responsibility at all hardware levels, but major maintenance responsibility only at the Turnkey Level (Level I, see Figure 2).

Firms may elect to use a more finely partitioned system for assigning responsibility. For example, an "F" could indicate full responsibility, an "S" shared responsibility, an "L" limited responsibility, and an "N" no responsibility. A single level of hardware support may then include:

F — full MIS responsibility for hotline/debugging,
F — full MIS responsibility for purchasing,
S — shared MIS responsibility for training,
L — limited MIS responsibility for documentation, and

Table 2 Support Activities for End-User Computing

Support Activity		Definition
1.	Advising	Assist in analyzing needs, planning action, and selecting products or services.
2.	Backup	Provide duplicate hardware, software, or data.
3.	Compatibility	Insure compatibility of hardware, software or data.
4.	Development	Create or enhance a process, program, product or data set.
5.	Documentation	Provide descriptions of how to use a computing resource.
6.	Hotline/debugging	Isolate and correct system problems, perhaps through the use of a speical phone number.
7.	List resource	List the resource (hardware, software, or data) as available to other users.
8.	Maintenance	Keep the system in working order; including tests, measurements, replacements, repairs, and adjustments.
9.	Data transfer	Move data from one system to another.
10.	Newsletter	Produce and distribute a report on new products or services for users.
11.	Purchase assistance	Provide support for users who are buying their own systems.
12.	Recovery	Restore of hardware, software, or data after a failure.
13.	Research products	Investigate new products and services for possible use by end users.
14.	Training	Provide users with the knowledge needed to develop and/or use systems.

N — no MIS responsibility for backup.

The division of responsibility is more precise but the levels become more complicated to develop and administer.

The assignment of activities at a particular level involves many considerations. The first is that there should be a range of MIS support options. At one end of the range the MIS department should be assigned all or most of the activities, while at the other end all or most should be given to the end user departments. In the example the range goes from "Turnkey," where the user department limits its principal computing activities to just using the system, to "Advising," where the department assumes almost all responsibility and uses the MIS department only for advice.

Once the range is established, assignments in the middle levels can be made. Some activities are linked to qualifying decisions. For example, one of the qualifying decisions for hardware and software resources (Figures 2-3) concerns compatibility with MIS systems. The determination of this compatibility was defined in Table 2 as a support activity. The logical linkage between the decision and the activity was the basis for assigning the activity's responsibility. The linkage between the registration question with the list resource activity is less obvious but also exists and was used. Identifying such logical linkages is an important part of assigning activity responsibilities to support levels.

No division of activities will be optimal the first time. It is important for the MIS department to keep track of the support level choices being made by end users. More incentives may be needed to attract end users to higher levels of support. Since these higher levels also provide for better

Figure 2 Support Activities for Hardware Levels

	HARDWARE SUPPORT LEVELS				
Qualifying Decisions	I	II	III	IV	V
1. Purchaser?	MIS	USER	USER	USER	USER
2. Register with MIS department?	YES	YES	YES	NO	NO
3. Compatible with MIS systems?	YES	YES	NO	YES	NO
Support Activities	**Turnkey**	**Full Service**	**Partner-ship**	**Assis-tance**	**Advising**
1. Advising	X	X	X	X	X
2. Backup	X				
3. Compatibility	X	X		X	
4. Documentation	X				
5. Hotline/debugging	X	X		X	
6. List resource	X	X	X		
7. Maintenance	X				
8. Data transfer	X	X		X	
9. Newsletter	X	X		X	
10. Purchase assistance	X	X			
11. Recovery	X				
12. Research new products	X	X	X	X	
13. Training	X	X		X	

"X" indicates that the MIS department has major responsibility for the support activity.

coordination of computing it may be in the organization's best interests to shift support responsibilities in order to create those incentives. Any change must be approved by the MIS department, end users, and top management.

Designing Support Services

Once the responsibilities for computing activities have been determined, the MIS department can use them to design its support services. User departments can also use them to develop their own policies and procedures.

The services offered by the MIS department in our example include: (1) general consulting, (2) product support, (3) hotline/help desk, (4) technical support, (5) quality assurance, and (6) end-user training. These services are based on those suggested by Hammond [9]. Figure 5 shows a mapping between support activities and the six services.

All activities must be assigned. Notice that in doing a mapping it is allowable to assign multiple services to one activity. An activity is then broken up into logical parts so that responsibility can be clearly defined. For example, the development activity is shared by General Consulting, Product Support, and Quality Assurance. The first service is concerned with analysis, the second with design and implementation, and the third with testing and certification. Each of the six resulting services is described below.

The **general consulting service** is assigned advising, development, and purchasing assistance activities. Its focus is on problem definition and analysis. General consultants help end users define their requirements and steer them to the appropriate packages or development tools. They assist end users in making build vs. buy decisions, and provide guidance in planning end user development activities. The general consultants' responsibilities necessarily involve them in end-users' decisions about support levels. In these choices they may try

Figure 3 Support Activities for Software Levels

	SOFTWARE SUPPORT LEVELS				
Qualifying Decisions	**I**	**II**	**III**	**IV**	**V**
1. Purchaser or developer?	MIS	USER	USER	USER	USER
2. Formal review by MIS?	YES	YES	YES	NO	NO
3. Register with MIS?	YES	YES	YES	YES	NO
4. Compatible with MIS systems?	YES	YES	NO	YES	YES/NO
Support Activities	**Turnkey**	**Full Service**	**Partner-ship**	**Assis-tance**	**Advising**
1. Advising	X	X	X	X	X
2. Backup	X	X			
3. Compatibility	X	X		X	
4. Development	X				
5. Documentation	X	X	X		
6. Hotline/debugging	X	X	X		
7. List resource	X	X	X	X	
8. Maintenance	X	X?	X?		
9. Data transfer	X	X		X	
10. Newsletter	X	X	X	X	
11. Purchase assistance	X	X	X	X	
12. Recovery	X	X			
13. Research new products	X	X	X	X	
14. Training	X	X			

"X" indicates that the MIS department has major responsibility for the support activity.
"?" indicates that responsibilities are negotiable.

to influence the users, but they cannot make their decision. The general consultant's job is done when the building or installation of the application system is ready to begin. Then they refer end users to a product support staffer.

Product support personnel assist users with development, documentation, resource listing, and maintenance. They also do research into new products and the possible uses for them. Personnel specialize in particular high level development tools and/or in certain kinds of applications. After referral from the general consultant they become involved in the design, building, and maintenance of the application system. The degree of involvement depends on the support level selected by the end user. Most development needs can be met by these product specialists, but when difficult technical problems arise they can call in technical specialists.

Hotline/Help desk services support end users who have short, immediate problems. A hotline service uses a special phone number that end users call to get short answers to specific questions. Responses are immediate and callers do not have to leave their terminals or computers. The very nature of telephone communication, however, limits the kinds of problems that can be handled. Problems that can't be handled over the phone can be taken to a help desk. This service requires an MIS staff person to be at a particular location during particular times. The end user must go to the desk location, but once there can have a much richer and longer exchange of information. Program listings, for example, can be shared over a help desk but not over a phone. More time-consuming problems are referred to the technical or product support staffs.

Technical support includes backup, some

Figure 4 Support Activities for Data Levels

	DATA SUPPORT LEVELS				
Qualifying Decisions	I	II	III	IV	V
1. Source of data?	MIS	USER	USER	USER	USER
2. Software support level?	—	I-II	III-IV	V	V
3. Register with MIS?	YES	YES	YES	YES	NO
Support Activities	**Turnkey**	**Full Service**	**Partner-ship**	**Assis-tance**	**Advising**
1. Advising	X	X	X	X	X
2. Backup	X	X			
3. Compatibility	X	X			
4. Development	X				
5. Documentation	X	X			
6. Hotline/debugging	X	X			
7. List resource	X	X	X	X	
8. Maintenance	X				
9. Data transfer	X	X	X		
10. Newsletter	X	X	X		
11. Purchase assistance	X				
12. Recovery	X	X			
13. Research new products	X	X	X		
14. Training	X	X			

"X" indicates that the MIS department has major responsibility for the support activity.

Figure 5 Support Services Offered by MIS Department

Support Activities	General Consulting	Product Support	Hotline/ Help Desk	Technical Support	Quality Assurance	User Training
1. Advising	X					
2. Backup				X		
3. Compatibility					X	
4. Development	X	X			X	
5. Documentation		X			X	
6. Hotline/debugging			X			
7. List resource		X				
8. Maintenance		X		X		
9. Data transfer				X		
10. Newsletter						X
11. Purchase assistance	X					
12. Recovery				X		
13. Research new products		X				
14. Training						X

"X" indicates that the support activity is done as part of that particular MIS department service.

maintenance, data transfer, and recovery activities. These activities are aimed at specific technical problems which require specialized expertise. For example, communications specialists are needed to solve problems resulting from incompatible protocols. Database specialists are necessary for file conversions and database restructuring. Technical specialists are usually not contacted directly by end users, but are called in by product support or hotline/help desk personnel.

Quality assurance is involved with compatibility, development, and documentation activities. Implementing a quality assurance program requires designing a review process that reduces the risks while also considering the special needs of end-user computing. A process that is expensive and time consuming will defeat the very purpose of end-user computing. A balance between efficiency of service and risk reduction must be struck. Quality assurance efforts are especially important here because of the key role they play in determining support levels in the example.

End-user training is the final support service. This training ranges from establishing a general awareness about end-user computing to explaining the details of how a specific database query language works, including an explanation of support services and levels. The mechanisms available for training include classes, demonstrations, on-line training systems, user groups, and a newsletter. The demand for training in firms that support end-user computing has been tremendous so creating an effective program is essential.

Implementing Service Support Levels

For the MIS department, implementing support levels requires establishing a mechanism for officially assigning a computing resource to a support level, creating a process to maintain support level definition, and developing a means for delivering end user services. If the qualifying decisions have been properly selected, it should be easy to determine the level that a piece of hardware, a software package, or a particular database belongs to. Once the approach has been explained to the users they should be able to make their own determination about the applicable support level. An official assignment of a support level could be part of the registration process. This works for the example firm because any software or data that is not registered is automatically placed in the lowest support level. Only the two unregistered hardware levels would not be distinguished.

Since the definition of level qualifying decisions, the specification of computing activities, and the assignment of responsibilities are cooperative endeavors, so too must be their review and revision. A committee of MIS staff and users is an appropriate body for maintaining support levels. One of the first action items for this committee is to define procedures for submitting, reviewing, and gaining approval for any changes. The committee would also settle disagreements between the MIS and user departments.

The most obvious approach to delivering services is to use an information center. An information center is an organizational unit, usually part of the MIS department, whose principal function is to facilitate and coordinate end-user computing by offering support services. Large numbers of information centers already exist. In two different surveys, 60-70% of respondents claimed that their firms would have information centers by the end of 1984 [6, 13]. Empirical descriptions of existing information centers can be found in [5, 12, 13].

Most information centers are not large enough to justify separate full time personnel for each of the six defined service areas [13]. Therefore, individual staff members must be responsible for multiple services. General consulting and product support, for example, might be combined. Technical specialists are only needed for special problems so they may be shared with other MIS units. Whatever the arrangement, care must be taken to insure that the staff have the necessary combination of technical prowess, business sense, and interpersonal communication skills. The quality of the service staff is as important to success as the proper definition of service activities [5].

Selecting a Support Level

Crucial to the success of the support level approach is the ability of end-user managers to make appropriate decisions about levels of support. In making this choice, managers should consider the benefits of the support offered and the trade-offs of additional time and expense that result when MIS services are used. Beyond this cost/benefit assessment, end-user managers should ask themselves three questions.

1. Do I have the resources required to perform the set of activities not covered by MIS services?

The X's in Figures 2-4 indicate activities that are the major responsibility of the MIS department. It is the responsibility of the user department to perform the other activities. Different departments have different levels of computing expertise. Rockart and Flannery [11], for example, found knowledgeable end-users in many departments. To answer this question, managers of user areas must (1) know what their internal computing resources are, and (2) decide whether they want their own personnel spending substantial amounts of time doing support activities. Choosing a particular support level involves choosing a level of internal support activity.

2. How much risk is involved with this application and how much an I willing to assume?

Some computing applications are risker than others. If the risks are high it might be in the end-user manager's best interests to share some of these risks. Assessing the level of risk associated with a particular application is not always easy. End-user managers will want to consider:

- the size and complexity of the application,
- the number and sophistication of the users,
- the familiarity of end-user developers with this type of application, and
- the stability of the application environment.

The MIS department can help end-user managers by providing training and written procedures that can assist them in making the risk assessment.

3. Are other organizational units involved in this application? Should they be?

Rockart and Flannery [11] found a substantial number of end-user timesharing applications which extended beyond single departments. When different managers become involved with an application, coordination problems arise. Since the MIS department is concerned with meeting the overall needs of the firm, it is an obvious choice for coordinating multidepartmental computing. Selecting support levels with high MIS department involvement is recommended for interdepartmental systems.

Concluding Remarks

The growth of end-user computing offers MIS executives the opportunity to improve the performance of their firms. To do this requires a new attitude and a cooperative approach to working wih end users. No longer can the MIS department simply dictate which application systems are to be built and how they are to be developed and used. It must now compete for computing business with services that meet the needs of users. Given the right support services, MIS executives can take the lead in increasing the amount of beneficial computing done in their firms.

The growth of end-user computing also creates new risks for MIS executives. Until the new cooperative arrangement is structured, the MIS department will be open to every kind of claim by end-users who run into trouble while computing. Without a clear specification of responsibilities, top management will, rightly or wrongly, hold the MIS department accountable for these computing claims. MIS executives must reduce the risks of end-user computing to themselves and to their firms.

Obtaining the benefits of end-user computing, while minimizing its inherent risks, requires a clear delineation of responsibilities and an effective service program. This paper described an organized approach for doing this based on the establishment of service support levels. With end-user computing becoming the dominant kind of computing in this decade, MIS executives need such an approach for dealing with the demands of their new computing environment.

Discussion Questions

1. Why do end-users want to do their own computing? What are the risks associated with end-user computing?
2. In what ways is the support response to end-user computing superior to the carrot response? Under what circumstances would the carrot response be appropriate?
3. What risks are minimized by the partnership level of support? What risks are still present?
4. What approaches might an MIS department use to implement service support levels?

References

[1] Alavi, M. and Weiss, I. R. "Managing the Risks Associated with End-User Computing," *Journal of Management Information Systems*, Volume 2, Number 3, Winter 1985-86, pp. 5-20.

[2] Alloway, R. M. and Quillard, J. A. "User Managers' Systems Needs," *MIS Quarterly*, Volume 7, Number 2, June 1983, pp. 27-41.

[3] Benjamin, R. I. "Information Technology in the 1990's: A Long Range Planning Scenario," *MIS Quarterly*, Volume 6, Number 2, June 1982, pp. 11-31.

[4] Benson, D. H. "A Field Study of End User Computing: Findings and Issues," *MIS Quarterly*, Volume 7, Number 4, December 1983, pp. 35-45.

[5] Brancheau, J. C., Vogel, D. R. and Wetherbe, J. C. "An Investigation of the Information Center From the User's Perspective," *Database*, Volume 16, Number 1, Fall 1985, pp. 4-17.

[6] Computerworld, "Info Centers Gaining," *Computerworld*, February 27, 1984, p. 6.

[7] Davis, G. B. "Caution: User Developed Systems Can Be Dangerous to Your Organization," MISRC-WP-82-04, MIS Research Center, University of Minnesota, Minneapolis, Minnesota, 1984.

[8] Dickson, G. W., Leitheiser, R. L., Wetherbe, J. C. and Nechis, M. "Key Information Systems Issues for the 1980's," *MIS Quarterly*, Volume 8, Number 3, September 1984, pp. 135-154.

[9] Hammond, L. W. "Management Considerations for an Information Center," *IBM Systems Journal*, Volume 21, Number 2, 1982, pp. 131-161.

[10] Leitheiser, R. L. and Wetherbe, J. C. "Approaches to End-User Computing: Service May Spell Success," *Journal of Information Systems Management*, Volume 3, Number 1, Winter 1986, pp. 9-14.

[11] Rockart, J. F. and Flannery, L. S. "The Management of End User Computing," *Communications of the ACM*, Volume 26, Number 10, October 1983, pp. 776-784.

[12] Sumner, M. "Organizations and Management of the Information Center: Case Studies," ACM Proceedings of the Computer Personnel and Business Data Processing Research Conference, Minneapolis, Minnesota, May 2-3, 1985, pp. 38-49.

[13] Wetherbe, J. C. and Leitheiser, R. L. "Information Centers: A Survey of Services, Decisions, Problems, and Successes," *Journal of Information Systems Management*, Volume 2, Number 3, Summer 1985, pp. 3-10.

READING 30

Managing End-User Computing for Competitive Advantage

article by
JOHN C. HENDERSON and
MICHAEL E. TREACY

The creative use of computers by nondata processing experts, namely, "end users," is one of the most significant developments in corporate computing to have taken place in the past decade. In fact, it marks a major transformation of the nature of managerial work[1] and is of growing strategic importance to many corporations.[2] The challenge for information systems (IS) managers today is to satisfy the demands of these users while advancing an end-user computing strategy that will efficiently support the competitive position of the firm. In other words, IS managers are being called upon to strike a balance between end-user demands and an appropriate strategy that is somewhere between tight control and laissez-faire.

This balance is critical. While control may help to focus end-user resources on building systems in areas most critical to the business, it can also restrict learning and innovation, thereby creating general dissatisfaction among end users. On the other hand, a laissez-faire attitude holds no assurance that the most critical areas of the business will receive sufficient resources. This strategy can also result in a chaotic and expensive mixture of information technologies that impedes future progress.

The challenge for IS managers is further complicated by the phenomenal rate of end-user growth and change. Xerox Corporation, for example, estimates that in 1981, 25 percent of the company's computer resources were dedicated to end-user computing. By 1991, this percentage will triple.[3] Rockart and Flannery further report that end-user computing consumed between 40 and 50 percent of the computing resources in several

Source: Reprinted from "Managing End-User Computing for Competitive Advantage" by John C. Henderson and Michael E. Treacy, *SLOAN MANAGEMENT REVIEW*, Winter 1986, pp. 3-14, by permission of the publisher.

companies surveyed and that it is growing at a rate between 50 and 90 percent per year.[4] Similar results are reported by Benson.[5]

As a result of this rapid growth, end-user managers are confronted by difficult management questions. For instance, one of the main dilemmas facing managers is whether to implement hardware standards to facilitate machine to machine communication or to avoid standards altogether so that new and innovative technology can be more easily absorbed by the organization. Another question is how should companies address the need to manage data resources when an increasing portion of that data resides in end-user machines? Furthermore, how should end-user computing be justified and what are the support implications for the organization?

Four Fundamental Issues

A review of recent research on end-user computing suggests that there are at least four fundamental issues that IS managers need to address. In fact, effective management in this area depends upon managers' successfully addressing these issues in a timely fashion. Three of them deal with the infrastructures for technology, data, and support services that must be put in place to facilitate the effective use of information systems by end users. The last issue concerns the evaluation/justification and planning of end-user computing expenditures. These four issues characterize the difficulties that are at the core of the end-user computing dilemma.

1. Support Infrastructure. The issue of support infrastructure concerns education mechanisms, implementation, and leadership. Rockart and Flannery classify end users into six types: nonprogramming end users, command-level end users, programming-level end users, functional-support personnel, end-user computing support personnel, and data-processing programmers.[6] They observe that each type of end user needs different education and ongoing support, which is usually provided by one type of user to another. Thus, the diversity of end users and their interdependence on one another make it difficult to design an organizational infrastructure that supports end-user computing. Furthermore, a centralized information center or another structure for supporting end-user computing may not address the needs of all types of users and may be of only secondary importance to the informal support provided by other users.[7]

2. Technological Infrastructure. The technological infrastructure issue includes decisions about the appropriate hardware, software, and communications equipment to support office automation (OA) and decision support systems (DSS) in an end-user computing environment. In general, the diversity of equipment in use suggests that standards are a major issue. Such diversity not only makes communication between machines a difficult or an expensive technical task, but it also decreases the capability of standardizing software packages and applications. Overall, software standards would make it easier for users to share analyses, documents, and data and would also simplify the training and support process. Yet, standardized software could also prevent users from using the most suitable or desirable software, thereby reducing the quality of support for end users.

3. Data Infrastructure. The issue of data infrastructure includes questions about data standards, the need for subject databases, and security. The productivity of end users is also linked to the availability of data. Quillard, Rockart, Wilde, Vernon, and Mock found that less than 10 percent of the data used by personal computer-based end users was obtained directly from production or transaction-oriented information systems, while more than half the information was keyed in directly from computer-generated reports.[8] It is obvious that better access to data will be a key management issue.

4. Evaluation/Justification and Planning. Finally, another fundamental issue is the economic evaluation and justification of end-user computing. Although traditional cost-benefit frameworks for evaluation and justification may inhibit the use of these new technologies in innovative ways, the potential for end-user computing to affect the competitive positioning of a firm has been demonstrated.[9] For management to realize important improvements in organizational performance through end-user computing, it must be able to plan and maintain the financial and organizational impact of the investment in these systems.

An Evolving Management Framework

In light of these four issues, we propose an evolving management framework to help end-user managers move more smoothly from one critical issue to another. This framework is based on the proposition that (1) the relative importance of these four issues to end users changes over time and that (2) management must change its strategy to fit the shifting importance of these issues. As Greiner observes, in general, growing organizations that prove successful shift their management strategy to meet the changing needs of the organization.[10]

The same holds true for corporate end-user computing. As the end-user population in most organizations grows in size and in understanding of how to successfully use the technology, management must be able to align its strategy to the relative importance of a particular issue. In other words, management strategies must be able to evolve in order to successfully address the changing needs of end users.

The Growing End-User Population

The growth of the end-user population can be understood by looking at models of the diffusion of innovation in organizations and consumer markets.[11] Research characterizes the acceptance of any innovation over time as starting slowly, increasing rapidly as the innovation gains momentum, and trailing off gradually as saturation levels are reached. This pattern, known as the classic S-shaped curve, is analogous to the learning curve model used by McKenney and McFarlan to describe the absorption of innovative information systems technologies.[12] They note that organizations high on the learning curve for one type of technology must be careful to recognize that a new technology may instigate a new, separate learning curve phenomenon. Quillard et al. suggest that end-user computing is yet another technological learning curve that has just been initiated in most organizations.[13] Although different departments and divisions absorb end-user technology at different rates and at different times, most of them fall into a general pattern.

The General End-User Learning-Curve Pattern

Leading innovative end users initially are concerned with finding help in getting started. At a minimum, this requires some training and arranging to have a configuration of equipment and software installed. After this has been successfully completed, their concern shifts to gaining access to a broader group of people and a variety of data. Now training and technology are needed in much greater volumes, thereby making access to data an important issue. This is a critical stage, for without proper management, the increased need for access to data and technology can create innumerable problems. Therefore, management needs to address problems of technology standards and data management before further progress can be made. Finally, once an efficient end-user infrastructure has been created, attention turns to getting the value from the investment and meeting the long-term challenge of managing data.

Although this pattern is not followed in many instances, it generally holds true. As users learn about information systems, new issues and concerns are revealed and rise in importance; old issues fade as they are mastered. Figure 1 emphasizes the learning-curve aspect of end-user computing and illustrates the general pattern of change in relative importance to the various end-user issues.

A learning-curve model approach not only illustrates the need for a dynamic management strategy but also allows one to understand how the four major issues change over time. We will trace the importance of each issue over time and provide brief justifications for the proposed general relationships. We will then define alternative management strategies that respond to the changing importance of these issues.

Figure 1 Criticalness of Issues over Time

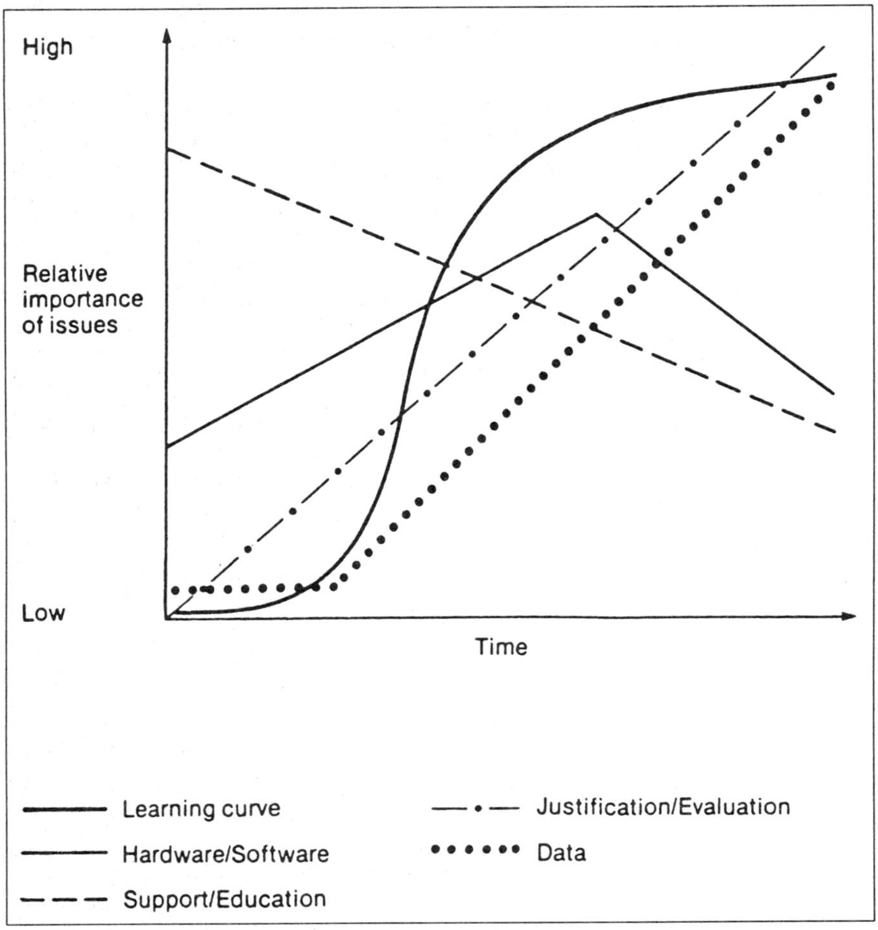

The Dynamics of These Issues

Creating a Supportive Environment

As shown in Figure 1, during the early phase of learning how to use end-user computing technology, effective organizational support and comprehensive education is a dominating issue. A rich tradition of change management[14] and innovation research[15] provides explicit methodologies for creating a supportive environment. These theories emphasize the role of individuals, the need to develop effective working coalitions among specialists, and the need to create and maintain an effective learning environment.

As an organization evolves, however, the relative importance of specialized organizational and educational support decreases. This results from both successful diffusion of basic skills and methods and pressures to attend to other issues that have developed out of rapid, uncontrolled growth. As these other issues grow in magnitude, the relative importance of support and education continues to decline. As shown in Figure 1, support and education of users always remain an issue of some importance. Yet, its relative importance diminishes over time.

Managing Technology

The term *technology infrastructure* refers to the

hardware, software, and communications technologies that make up the end-user computing environment. The importance of this issue as a management concern varies significantly over time. As Figure 1 illustrates, in the initial phase, the technology infrastructure is not a major managerial issue in that after the initial purchase, the cost of the technology in personal and financial terms drops below the threshold requiring a capital budget approval. Beyond avoiding the purchase of obviously poor technology, the major concern at this stage is how to arouse the interest and active involvement of the end users; the equipment and software end users utilize is a less important concern at this point.

However, Henderson and Schilling note that the technical complexity of end-user systems usually increases with the passage of time.[16] As the rapid growth of the number of end users begins to create higher interdependence among users, requirements for data sharing and transferring programs increase. Thus, the technological issue becomes increasingly important as this high growth peaks during the integration phase. The primary goal at this point should be to introduce policies and standards that allow infrastructure alternatives to be evaluated from an investment perspective. When this is accomplished, the importance of the technology issue declines. In this way, actions taken during the integration phase provide a basis for managing technology as a total investment in the mature stage.

Managing Data

Data management refers to the need to make data accessible, reliable, consistent, and secure. This issue has long been recognized by information systems professionals. Yet, during the initial phase of end-user computing, data is relatively unimportant. The Quillard et al. findings suggest that over 80 percent of the data used by end users is hand entered.[17] Moreover, since early applications tend to address specific problems of the end user, problems, other than data accessibility, are minimal. However, as rapid growth sets in, the need to coordinate the data and maintain reliability, consistency, and security increases. Further, the potential for economies of scale associated with electronically encoding a data element on a onetime basis becomes increasingly apparent. The importance of this issue continues to increase through the mature phase.

Ideally, during the mature phase, economic models for evaluating information would be developed. If this were the case, as it is with hardware and software, the relative importance of data management would then decrease. However, as shown in Figure 1, the proposed relationship does not decrease but instead continues to rise in importance. As of today, information cannot be treated effectively as an economic good. Current theories for measuring the value of information are not sufficiently robust or pragmatic enough to move the management of data into an investment framework. Thus, the importance of data management continues.

Evaluating and Justifying the Technology

The relative importance of a formal economic mechanism for managing end-user computing increases directly with the size of the investment over time. In the initial phase, justification of such an investment is not an issue. As the number of end users grows, however, the magnitude of the investment reaches a level requiring close attention. Ultimately, from a management perspective, the issue of evaluation and justification of corporate computing dominates. That is to say, at the point when an organization has truly absorbed a new technology, it will also have learned to manage the technology within the basic investment framework used to manage other organizational resources.

Implications of These Issues

There are two important implications that can be drawn from the dynamic nature of these issues. First, the changing importance of issues over time requires an evolving management strategy. For example, a managerial environment in which the issue of educational support dominates all other issues will require a significantly different approach from a situation in which issues of technology integration equal or exceed the need for support. Hence, in general, management techniques should be consistent and aligned with the issues facing that particular organizational environment.

Second, an evolving management framework provides the means to anticipate future management problems. In other words, this framework makes it possible for managers to deal with today's problems while developing the capacity to address the problems of tomorrow. For instance, while the issue of hardware and software is initially low in importance, it becomes a critical issue during the integration phase. Thus, the question is asked: How will management cope with the immediate problems of initiating and expanding the use of this technology, and yet deal successfully with the need to integrate a coherent corporate technological infrastructure?

Alternative Management Strategies

There are at least four basic management perspectives that can be used to contend with the ever-changing problems of end-user computing: implementation, marketing, operations, and economic.[18] Each perspective inherently places varying weight on each of the issues defined earlier. In this section, we will define each perspective and discuss how it affects an organization's strategy, structure, and control mechanisms. We will then illustrate the preferred sequence for adopting these perspectives and indicate how each addresses immediate problems while providing management with the means to smooth the transition between the various phases of the learning curve.

Implementation Perspective

Define Goals and Design Systems. Implementation can be viewed as organizational innovation that is achieved through the definition of goals and the design of systems to meet the requirements resulting from these goals. This view originates in the work of change management, the theoretical basis for most information systems implementation and organizational development strategies. It is consistent with research on innovation and, therefore, is a particularly appropriate perspective in terms of an organization's initial use of new technology.

Increase Usage and User Satisfaction. As shown in Table 1, the overall objective of the initial phase is to increase the use of information technology and enhance user satisfaction. This is achieved through a participatory management strategy, with heavy emphasis placed on individual and organizational education. The success of DSS, which relies heavily on an implementation approach, provides a clear model for successfully initiating the use of computers by nontechnical users. In essence, this strategy attempts to build an enthusiasm for change both through education and by providing effective facilitative roles (e.g., change agents).

Centralized Help Centers. The structural implications for this perspective call for *centralized* "help" centers and heavy use of roving consultants in a facilitating role (emphasis is placed on consultants rather than on computer experts). Such a role demands that a consultant have good interpersonal skills and an understanding of the user's business problem. Success is achieved through problem solving, not be providing technical sophistication. At this stage, the need is to provide an organizational structure that encourages usage and innovation by end users.

Innovation. Control mechanisms, which are minimal at this point, focus on end-user innovators. As indicated by the objective, performance measures are directed as usage and user satisfaction. Since measures of benefits are difficult, if not impossible, to obtain at this early stage, the control system emphasizes innovation and rewards effective over efficient behavior. Such an innovation orientation, often associated with R&D units, encourages experimentation and diversity, thereby discouraging extensive use of traditional control mechanisms such as a rigorous cost-benefit analysis.

Table 1 Different Perspectives for Managing End-User Computing

	Implementation	Marketing	Operations	Economic
Objective	Increase usage and user satisfaction	Market growth and market penetration	Integration and efficiency	Competitive advantage
Strategy	Opportunistic; supportive; educational	Value-added products and services; base building	Standards automation	Link IS plan to strategy; targeted investment
Structure	Centralized help centers; roving consultants	Local direct support group	Centralized formal planning; decentralized support	Distributed operations
Control mechanisms	Innovators	Departmental accountability	Centralized policies	Formal justification; organizational incentives

Marketing Perspective

Market Penetration and Market Share. The marketing perspective views end users as consumers and attempts to influence consumer choice (demand) through effective product design, advertising, and distribution management. The primary objectives are market penetration, often measured by market growth, and market share. As this perspective assumes that consumers (individual end users) are rational and evaluative, but perhaps underinformed, the strategy must provide for adding value to the products and services being offered in order to differentiate them from the alternatives. Educating consumers about the benefits of these products and appropriate distribution planning to maximize availability are also critical to the management strategy.

One may ask why market share is critical to this perspective. Of course, increase market share reflects the goal of diffusing this technology throughout the organization. But as we will discuss later, a dominant market share also permits the creation of a de facto standard. Thus, the need to move to a coherent infrastructure can be *effectively* addressed by implementing a coherent marketing strategy. As we will discuss later, this is a concept of business-driven standards rather than of technology-driven standards.

Departmentalized Help Centers. Here, management concentrates on both understanding the needs of the "market" for high payoff, value-added products and services, and shaping the demand to fit the available products. The education process is an attempt to influence choice as well as to transfer skills. At this point, the structural implications are to departmentalize or functionalize the help centers.

This perspective provides a transition from the implementation approach. The implementation structure creates departments that directly affect sales and services that are geared to the unique needs of each customer. In essence, these departments operate a small business. In the marketing perspective, a retail/distributor relationship is formed. Each departmental unit operates a "local" direct support group. The central group, which is established at the implementation stage, provides indirect support through these local groups by providing services, such as specialized training, enhanced products (e.g., software that allows uploading and downloading of data) and consulting to the local support units. In this way, the marketing perspective not only builds upon the efforts of the implementation perspective but also broadens the organization's understanding of the market and support distribution through the use of formal local support groups.

Expenditure Accountability. There are two key control mechanisms for this perspective. The first focuses on holding each department accountable for its expenditures. As in most marketing-oriented organizations, the ability to recognize and reward outstanding individual performance in support roles is critical. Control mechanisms should be consistent with this attitude and designed to maximize market share and market penetration.

Base Building. The second key control relates to the strategy of base building. In the implementation perspective, key individuals or innovators are the basis of control. In the marketing perspective, help centers should be directed to ensure an organization's strong market presence, that is, a clear competitive edge that can be the basis for expansion. Selection of appropriate bases upon which to build should also link directly to future opportunities to transform end-user computing into a competitive advantage. In this way, base building becomes a key leverage for both controlling and moving the organization toward a mature state.

Operations Perspective

Standardize the Technological Infrastructure. Operations is viewed as the ongoing management of equipment, software, personnel, and other information technology resources for the purpose of collecting, storing, analyzing, and distributing information. This perspective directly addresses the objective of integrating and managing information technology so as to maximize the efficient use of organizational resources. The key strategy is to integrate through high-level standards and policies across all aspects of the technological infrastructure—"high level" suggests a preference to develop standards that permit latitude at an operational level. For example, technological communications are integrated through standard protocols rather than through standardized hardware or specific application software packages. This standardization strategy translates into a formal information sytems planning process for end-user computing technology.

Centralized Planning and Policy Organization. The structure implied by this perspective is a centralized planning and policy organization, with a monitoring and advisory role concerning the operations of major end-user projects. This role does not attempt to force specific applications but ensures that established policies are adapted. Accountability for support services is distributed to the departmental level.

Traditional Cost-Benefit Analysis. As discussed earlier, evaluation/justification and data management also take on more importance at the integration stage. Key controls are centered on a traditional cost-benefit analysis that requires a solid business case to justify expenditures and to enforce data standards for a "core" group of corporate-related data elements. By the end of this stage, hardware and software policies should permit compatibility tradeoffs to be incorporated into a cost-benefit analysis, thereby providing the foundation for the next phase of development.

Economic Perspective

Maximize Return on Investment. The economic perspective views information as a corporate resource and thus strives to maximize an organization's return on investment in information technology. A key element in this perspective is the balance between regulating the "end-user" market and permitting a movement toward a free information market. Keen originally suggested that traditional data processing was largely based on supply constraints, hence there was a need for efficiency and a centralized resource allocation. However, he argues that the new technology has created multiple sources for information technology—this is, small building blocks that can be put together to construct custom systems.[19] Therefore, there is a new focus on demand constraints where issues of fast delivery and benefits provided far outweigh cost and efficiency considerations. This perspective addresses these trends in an attempt to manage how end users adopt a market, incentive-based approach.

The overall objective of this perspective is to translate investment in information technology into competitive advantage. Therefore, the key strategy is to link information systems planning to strategic business planning. An element inherent in this strategic plan is to target critical investment areas for regulation. Such targeted regulation extends the base-building process and ultimately provides the capital resources necessary to achieve competitive advantage. For example, the need to link the engineering CAD/CAM design environment to the manufacturing materials control systems requires increased regulation over both the technology used by the different functional areas and the data flow. Therefore, the need to regulate or control the data flow becomes particularly important.

Self-sustaining Organizational Units. The structure for this perspective is similar to that of operations. However, the monitoring role is relaxed in the nonregulated target areas: the emphasis is on self-sustaining organizational units. Thus, while operational units have clear policy direction from the IS strategic planning unit, they also have significant degrees of freedom to innovate and evolve.

Monitoring/Advisory Controls. The control structure remains focused on evaluation/justification and data management. However, the incentives introduced by the control mechanism are based on the organization's return on investment. The targeted regulated areas reflect critical growth or base-building efforts and receive a close monitoring/advisory control structure.

The Sequence of Perspectives

The perspective strategy proposed herein applies each perspective at a time when its strengths match the requirements of the most critical issues. Thus, the strategy calls for a sequence of perspectives: (1) implementation, (2) marketing, (3) operations, and finally (4) economic. In this section, we will discuss the appropriate sequence and show how each stage prepares the organization for transition to the next.

Initiation Stage

The *implementation perspective* clearly places emphasis on organizational support and education. There is a solid, pragmatic knowledge base suggesting tactics for participatory management—a skill requirement for internal consultants or change agents—and methods for identifying key innovators.[20]

While these management tactics provide the means to initiate the end-user evolution effectively, they also provide an organization with a very strong foundation in order that it may make the transition to the marketing perspective. Effective internal consultants learn about their clients' needs, which become the basis for value-added products and services. Equally important is educating the "consumer" so that he or she will have the confidence to make a rational choice when selecting an end-user system. A clear, targeted strategy for identifying key innovators and high payoff, low-risk initial projects also establishes a solid base-building effort.

If the end-user systems are part of a strategic thrust at the outset, the base building begun at this point should focus on strategically important functions. For example, the service function is becoming increasingly important for many organizations and offers significant opportunities for the use of end-user computing.

Currently, the use of information help centers has evolved into the framework of an implementation perspective. In fact, demand for such services has grown significantly, for they have become known to be effective in supporting the initial phase. However, such demand is currently outweighing help centers' capability to meet it. Thus, at this point, it is necessary to build on the information centers' initial success by beginning the transition into the marketing perspective.

Eventually, the growth stage upward trend in implementing hardware and software suggests that the initial phase is fading. In fact, many organizations may adopt the implementation and marketing perspectives simultaneously. The danger in such undirected evolution, however, is that the marketplace and base-building knowledge required to move effectively to a marketing perspective may be lacking, which may result in a difficult transition. Further, establishing an effective, credible centralized help center is a key component of the marketing phase. Without a central center to serve as the "source" for technology and expert advice, each departmental center will have to provide redundant specialized services, which may prevent it from attending to the business perspective, the key component in spurring growth.

In the *marketing phase*, centralized IS support decreases as management pushes responsibility and accountability down to the departmental units. Therefore, data management becomes more important as the number of end users increases. This increase creates demands for data sharing, security problems, and accuracy/integrity problems. Feasible service strategies are required to limit the range of hardware and software.

Creating limits is achieved by introducing value-added products and services. Rather than dictating standards at this point, the main objective should be to market particular packages of hardware and software to the organization. Traditionally, this is the means by which standards and technologies are established. The key here is to translate knowledge acquired during the implementation phase into value-added products and services and to further initial base-building efforts.

Integration Stage

Again, these activities provide the foundation necessary to make the next transition. As discussed earlier, a key strategy in the upcoming *operation perspective* is standardization. Through a value-added approach, management introduces the priorities and standards and lets the consumer, the end user, choose the first phase of standards. In this way, as the value of increased communication and functionality is learned, the business case for corporate technology policy is established simultaneously.

As the organization moves into the integration stage, standardizing information technology and formal planning activities increases. The information systems professional plays a key role at this stage as he or she has gained a technical expertise concerning standards. This technical perspective is combined with the knowledge of the market gained in the previous stage to create effective standards. The more formal a planning process is, the better it can cope with traditional issues such as capacity, security, space, and data integrity. Such a process also allows for increased emphasis on justification and evaluation in a manner analogous to well-established business and investment planning processes.

This stage accomplishes two goals that are vital to effective transition into the next stage, the mature phase. First, through standardization, alternative information technologies can be viewed as an economic good. That is, a variety of equipment can be obtained so long as it meets reasonable corporate standards such as compatibility with communication protocols. Thus, market pressures begin to ensure appropriate pricing.

Second, the organization learns how to fold end-user computing into a formal planning process. Appropriate terminology, assumptions, and benchmarks are established. The difficulty of this exercise is probably related to the current acceptance and quality fo the existing strategic information systems planning process.

The Mature Stage

The stage is now set for transition into the final phase of evolution, the mature stage. The capability to link the strategic business plan with an existing strategic end-user computing plan has been established. Thus, at this point, targeted regulation results since projects directed toward competitive advantage may require specialized service or resource commitment. As the end-user organization has fully absorbed the technology, it now can manage both the technology and the human resource issues that accompany this technology. Thus, at this stage, the organization seeks to convert this newly acquired management knowledge into action that continuously improves its company's competitive position.

The Implications of an Evolving Management Strategy

A Vision

An evolving management strategy has many implications. First, this approach assumes that the decision to promote end-user computing is based on a vision of how this technology will contribute to the competitive positioning of the firm. The management strategy proposed here is a means to achieve this vision. Such a vision holds the basis to evaluate alternative base-building strategies, to select strategically value-added products and services, and to postulate standards and policies. The lack of such a vision reduces the ability to provide a smooth transition from one management strategy to the next.

In addition, this vision may indicate a change in the relative criticalness of the issues described in Figure 1. For example, if the vision of end-user computing involves direct communication to geographically dispersed users, the implementation strategy may call for a preemptive action by the IS professional with respect to adopting certain communications standards. In essence, the relative importance of the technology issue may increase during the early stages.

The most likely scenarios are ones in which the primary role of the IS professional during the initial and growth phases is architectural, not visionary, in nature. Nonetheless, properly defining either a technological architecture or a data resource architecture is a complex and lengthy exercise. Such an effort, which could be going on simultaneously with attempts to diffuse end-user computing, would complement efforts to define appropriate value-added products or services and critical base-building efforts.

Emerging End-User Technology Group

A second implication is the need for an Emerging End-User Technology Group within the IS function. This framework calls for a team that offers value-added products and services that test and develop standards and policies. This value-based standards process can be achieved through either "make" or "buy" acquisitions; that is, the firm can either develop the products internally or acquire the products from an external market. Since many of the value-added products are intended to test options for standards, investment in these products should be closely monitored. Building upon emerging end-user technology to pilot test new products is one way to control the investment and still provide a timely response to users' needs. In this role, the Emerging Technology Group would function as both a technology-scanning group and a product R&D group. Such a group would position the central IS function for a future role as the technical support for departmental end-user groups.

Innovations

A third implication concerns the nature of the support role for the IS function. Early on, the support role, which is assumed by local end-user groups, is responsible for transferring skills. However, later on, a new role centering on the need to transfer end-user developed systems to the technological infrastructure will likely emerge. In this respect, end-user computing can be viewed as mass prototyping. Each prototype represents a potential organization system for which a functional statement of information requirements exist (though perhaps incomplete from an organizational perspective). Thus, a major challenge for the IS function in the future will be to facilitate the transfer of these local innovations to organizational systems. From this perspective, the organizational role for IS may not decrease.

Conclusions

In summary, three general conclusions appear justified. First, if the assumption is accepted that the criticalness of information issues is dynamic, our framework offers a comprehensive management plan for coping with this dynamic process. Therefore, management should take action as early as the initiation stage, which is directed toward smooth transition into the integration stage and ultimately into the mature stage. In essence, such a framework provides a pragmatic road map for the organization through the end-user computing learning process.

Second, we postulate that skipping a phase will increase organizational conflict and reduce effectiveness and productivity. For instance, the operations perspective is the one most often embraced by current information management. However, there is a tendency to impose this perspective on the organization too early. The result is that the IS manager usually loses credibility and is ultimately bypassed. Consequently, his or her experience and advice, which are critical at the integration stage, may be missing. Further, key decision-shaping standards in early stages may be made without effective consultation with the IS professional. For this reason, the framework suggests a macrostrategy that permits organizational growth, yet maintains the important role of the information systems professional.

Third, the framework suggests two important research issues for the future. Given the view that end-user computing represents an organizational commitment to DSS, the current inability to evaluate the impact of DSS or to justify DSS efforts may well limit the organization's usage of this technology. As indicated in the framework, evaluation and justification take on increasing importance over time. The research community must, therefore, respond to this trend by providing the *means* to carry out evaluation and justification activities.

In addition, the inability to reduce the relative importance of data management during the last stage is significant. As we do not have the theoretical means to treat data as an economic resource, we are limited in our ability to manage information from an economic perspective. A future research issue should focus on developing techniques that can determine the value of data in order to provide the key building block for management of data resources.

Discussion Questions

1. In what way is the learning curve relevant to providing support for end-users?
2. How is this article different from the Leitheiser and Wetherbe article?
3. Why is an evolving management strategy required in managing end-user computing?
4. What is the relevance of this article to corporate strategy?

Footnotes

1. S. Zuboff, "Psychological and Organizational Implications of Computer-Mediated Work" (Cambridge, Mass.: MIT Center for Information Systems Research, CISR Working Paper #71, 1981).
2. See G. L. Parsons, "Information Technology: A New Competitive Weapon," *Sloan Management Review*, Fall 1983, pp. 3-14; J. F. Rockart and M. S. Scott Morton, "Implications of Changes in Information Technology on Corporate Strategy," *Interfaces*, January-February 1984, pp. 84-95.
3. R. I. Benjamin, "Information Technology in the 1990's: A Long Range Planning Scenario," *MIS Quarterly* 6, no. 2 (June 1982), pp. 11-31.
4. J. F. Rockart and L. Flannery, "The Management of End User Computing," *Communications of the ACM* 26 (October 1983), pp. 776-84.
5. D. H. Benson, "A Field Study of End User Computing: Findings and Issues," *MIS Quarterly* 7, no. 4 (December 1983), pp. 33-45.
6. Rockart and Flannery, "The Management of End User Computing."
7. L. W. Hammond, "Management Considerations for an Information Center," *IBM Systems Journal* 21 (1982), pp. 131-61.
8. J. Quillard, J. F. Rockart, E. Wilde, M. Vernon, and G. Mock, "A Study of the Corporate Use of Personal Computers" (Cambridge, Mass.: MIT Center for Informational Systems Research, CISR Working Paper #109, 1983).
9. J. I. Cash, Jr., and P. L. McLeod, "Managing the Introduction of Strategic Information Systems Technology" (Boston Harvard University Graduate School of Business, HBS Working Paper, 1984).
10. L. E. Greiner, "Evolution and Revolution as Organizations Grow," *Harvard Business Review*, July-August 1972, pp. 37-46.
11. V. Majahan and E. Muller, "Innovation Diffusion and New Product Growth Models in

Marketing," *Journal of Marketing* 43 (1979), pp. 55-68.
12. J. L. McKenney and W. E. McFarlan, "Merging the Islands of Information Service," *Proceedings of International Conference on Information Systems*, ed. C. Ross (Cambridge, Mass.: Society for Information Management, 1982).
13. Quillard et al., "A Study of the Corporate Use of Personal Computers."
14. See D. A. Kolb and A. L. Frohman, "An Organization Development Approach to Consulting," *Sloan Management Review*, Fall 1970, pp. 51-65; E. H. Schein, "Management Development as a Process of Influence," *Industrial Management Review* (now *Sloan Management Review*), May 1961, pp. 59-77.
15. See T. J. Allen, *Managing the Flow of Technology* (Cambridge, Mass.: MIT Press, 1977); M. L. Tushman and R. Katz, "External Communication and Project Performance: An Investigation into the Role of Gatekeepers," *Management Science* 26 (November 1980), pp. 1071-85.
16. J. C. Henderson and D. A. Schilling, "Design and Implementations of Decision Support Systems in the Public Sector," *MIS Quarterly* 9, no. 2 (June 1985), pp. 157-69.
17. Quillard et al., "A Study of the Corporate Use of Personal Computers."
18. Many books have been written about each of these managerial perspectives. The definitions provided herein are only intended to illustrate the framework and the evolutionary nature of the overall managerial strategy.
19. P. G. W. Keen, "Decision Support Systems: Lessons for the 80's" (Cambridge, Mass.: MIT Center for Information Systems Research, CISR Working Paper #70, June 1981).
20. Allen, *Managining the Flow of Technology.*

SECTION TEN

Decision Support Systems

READING 31

A Framework for the Development of Decision Support Systems

article by
RALPH H. SPRAGUE, JR.

Introduction

We seem to be on the verge of another "era" in the relentless advancement of computer based information systems in organizations. Designated by the term Decision Support Systems (DSS), these systems are receiving reactions ranging from "a major breakthrough" to "just another 'buzz word'."

One view is that the natural evolutionary advancement of information technology and its use in the organizational context has led from EDP to MIS to the current DSS thrust. In this view, the DSS picks up where MIS leaves off. A contrary view portrays DSS as an important subset of what MIS has been and will continue to be. Still another view recognizes a type of system that has been developing for several years and "now we have a name for it." Meanwhile, the skeptics suspect that DSS is just another "buzz word" to justify the next round of visits from the vendors.

The purpose of this article is to briefly examine these alternative views of DSS, and present a framework that proves valuable in reconciling them. The framework articulates and integrates major concerns of several "stakeholders" in the development of DSS: executives and professionals who use them, the MIS managers who manage the process of developing and installing them, the information specialists who build and develop them, the system designers who create and assemble the technology on which they are based, and the researchers who study the DSS subject and process.

Definition, Examples, Characteristics

The concepts involved in DSS were first articulated in the early '70's by Michael S. Scott Morton under

Source: Reprinted by special permission of the *MIS Quarterly*, Volume 4, Number 4, December 1980, pp. 1-26.

the term "management decision systems" [32]. A few firms and scholars began to develop and research DSS, which became characterized as *interactive* computer based systems, which *help* decision makers utilize data and *models* to solve *unstructured* problems. The unique contribution of DSS resulted from these key words. That definition proved restrictive enough that few actual systems completely satisfied it. Some authors recently extended the definition of DSS to include any system that makes some contribution to decision making; in this way the term can be applied to all but transaction processing. A serious definitional problem is that the words have a certain "intuitive validity;" any system that supports a decision, in any way, is a "Decision Support System."

Unfortunately, neither the restrictive nor the broad definition helps much, because they do not provide guidance for understanding the value, the technical requirements, or the approach for developing a DSS. A complicating factor is that people from different backgrounds and contexts view a DSS quite differently. A manager and computer scientist seldom see things in the same way.

Another way to get a feeling for a complex subject like a DSS is to consider examples. Several specific examples were discussed in The Society for Management Information Systems (SMIS) Workshop on DSS in 1979 [35]. Alter examined fifty-six systems which might have some claim to the DSS label, and used this sample to develop a set of abstractions describing their characteristics [1, 2]. More recently, Keen has designated about thirty examples of what he feels are DSS and compares their characteristics [26].

The "characteristics" approach seems to hold more promise than either definitions or collections of examples in understanding a DSS and its potential. More specifically, a DSS may be defined by its capabilities in several critical areas—capabilities which are required to accomplish the objectives which are pursued by the development and use of a DSS. Observed characteristics of a DSS which have evolved from the work of Alter, Keen, and others include:

- they tend to be aimed at the less well structured, underspecified problems that upper level managers typically face;
- they attempt to combine the use of models or analytic techniques with traditional data access and retrieval functions;
- they specifically focus on features which make them easy to use by noncomputer people in an interactive mode; and
- they emphasize flexibility and adaptability to accommodate changes in the environment and the decision making approach of the user.

A serious question remains. Are the definitions, examples, and characteristics of a DSS sufficiently different to justify the use of a new term and the inference of a new era in information systems for organizations, or are the skeptics right? Is it just another "buzz word" to replace the fading appeal of MIS?

DSS Versus MIS

Much of the difficulty and controversy with terms like "DSS" and "MIS" can be traced to the difference between an academic or theoretical definition and "connotational" definition. The former is carefully articulated by people who write textbooks and articles in journals. The latter evolves from what actually is developed and used in practice, and is heavily influenced by the personal experiences that the user of the term has had with the subject. It is this connotational definition of EDP/MIS/DSS that is used in justifying the assertion that a DSS is an evolutionary advancement beyond MIS.

This view can be expressed using Figure 1, a simple organizational chart, as a model of an organization. EDP was first applied to the lower operational levels of the organization to automate the paperwork. Its basic characteristics include:

- a focus on data, storage, processing, and flows at the operational level;
- efficient transaction processing;
- scheduled and optimized computer runs;
- integrated files for related jobs; and
- summary reports for management.

In recent years, the EDP level of activity in many firms has become a well-oiled and efficient production facility for transactions processing.

Figure 1 The Connotational View

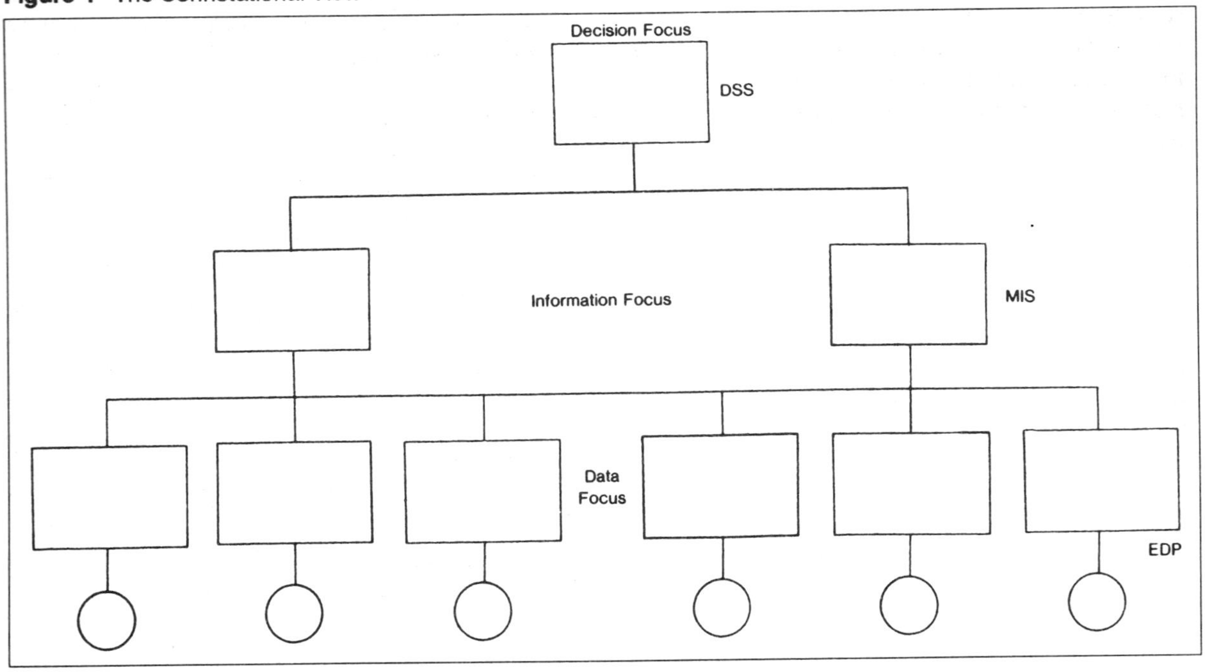

The MIS approach elevated the focus of information systems activities, with additional emphasis on integration and planning of the information systems function. In *practice*, the characteristics of MIS include:

- an information focus, aimed at the middle managers;
- structured information flow;
- an integration of EDP jobs by business function, such as production MIS, marketing MIS, personnel MIS, *etc.*; and
- inquiry and report generation, usually with a database.

The MIS era contributed a new level of information to serve management needs, but was still very much oriented to, and built upon, information flows and data files.

According to this connotational view, a DSS is focused still higher in the organization with an emphasis on the following characteristics:

- decision focused, aimed at top managers and executive decision makers;
- emphasis on flexibility, adaptability, and quick response;
- user initiated and controlled; and
- support for the personal decision making styles of individual managers.

This connotational and evolutionary view has some credence because it roughly corresponds to developments in practice over time. A recent study found MIS managers able to distinguish the level of advancement of their application systems using criteria similar to those above [27]. Many installations with MIS type applications planned to develop applications with DSS type characteristics. However, the "connotational" view has some serious deficiencies, and is definitely misleading in the further development of a DSS.

- It implies that *decision support* is needed only at the top levels. In fact, *decision support* is required at all levels of management in the organization.
- The decision making which occurs at several levels frequently must be coordinated. Therefore, an important dimension of *decision support* is the communication and coordination between decision

makers across organizational levels, as well as at the same level.

• It implies that *decision support* is the only thing top managers need from the information system. In fact, decision making is only one of the activities of managers that benefits from information systems support.

There is also the problem that many information systems professionals, especially those in SMIS, are not willing to accept the narrow connotational view of the term "MIS." To us, MIS refers to the entire set of systems and activities required to manage, process, and use information as a resource in the organization.

The Threoretical View

To consider the appropriate role of a DSS in this overall context of information systems, the broad charter and objectives of the information systems function in the organization is characterized:

> *Dedicated to improving the performance of knowledge workers in organizations through the application of information technology.*

• Improving the performance is the ultimate objective of information systems—not the storage of data, the production of reports, or even "getting the right information to the right person at the right time." The ultimate objective must be viewed in terms of the ability of information systems to support the improved performance of people in organizations.

• Knowledge workers are the clientele. This group includes managers, professionals, staff analysts, and clerical workers whose primary job responsibility is the handling of information in some form.

• Organizations are the context. The focus is on information handling in goal seeking organizations of all kinds.

• The application of information technology is the challenge and opportunity facing the information systems professional for the purposes and in the contexts given above.

A triangle was used by Robert Head in the late '60's as a visual model to characterize MIS in this broad comprehensive sense [22]. It has become a classic way to view the dimensions of an information system. The vertical dimension represented the levels of management, and the horizontal dimension represented the main functional areas of the business organization. Later authors added transactional processing as a base on which the entire system rested. The result was a two dimensional model of an MIS in the broad sense—the total activities which comprise the information system in an organization. Figure 2 is a further extension of the basic triangle to help describe the concept of the potential role of a DSS. The depth dimension shows the major technology "subsystems" which provide support for the activities of knowledge workers.

Three major thrusts are shown here, but there could be more. The structured reporting system includes the reports required for the management and control of the organization, and for satisfying the information needs of external parties. It has been evolving from efforts in EDP and MIS, in the narrow sense, for several years. Systems to support the communication needs of the organization are evolving rapidly from advances in telecommunications with a strong impetus from office automation and word processing. DSS seems to be evolving from the coalescence of information technology and operations research/management science approaches in the form of interactive modeling.

To summarize this introductory section, a DSS is not merely an evolutionary advancement of EDP and MIS, and it will certainly not replace either. Nor is it merely a type of information system aimed exclusively at top management, where other information systems seem to have failed. A DSS is a class of information system that draws on transaction processing systems and interacts with the other parts of the overall information system to support the decision making activities of managers and other knowledge workers in the organizations. However, there are some subtle but significant differences between a DSS and traditional EDP or so-called MIS approaches. Moreover, these systems require a new combination of information systems technology to satisfy a set of heretofore unmet

Figure 2 The Complete View

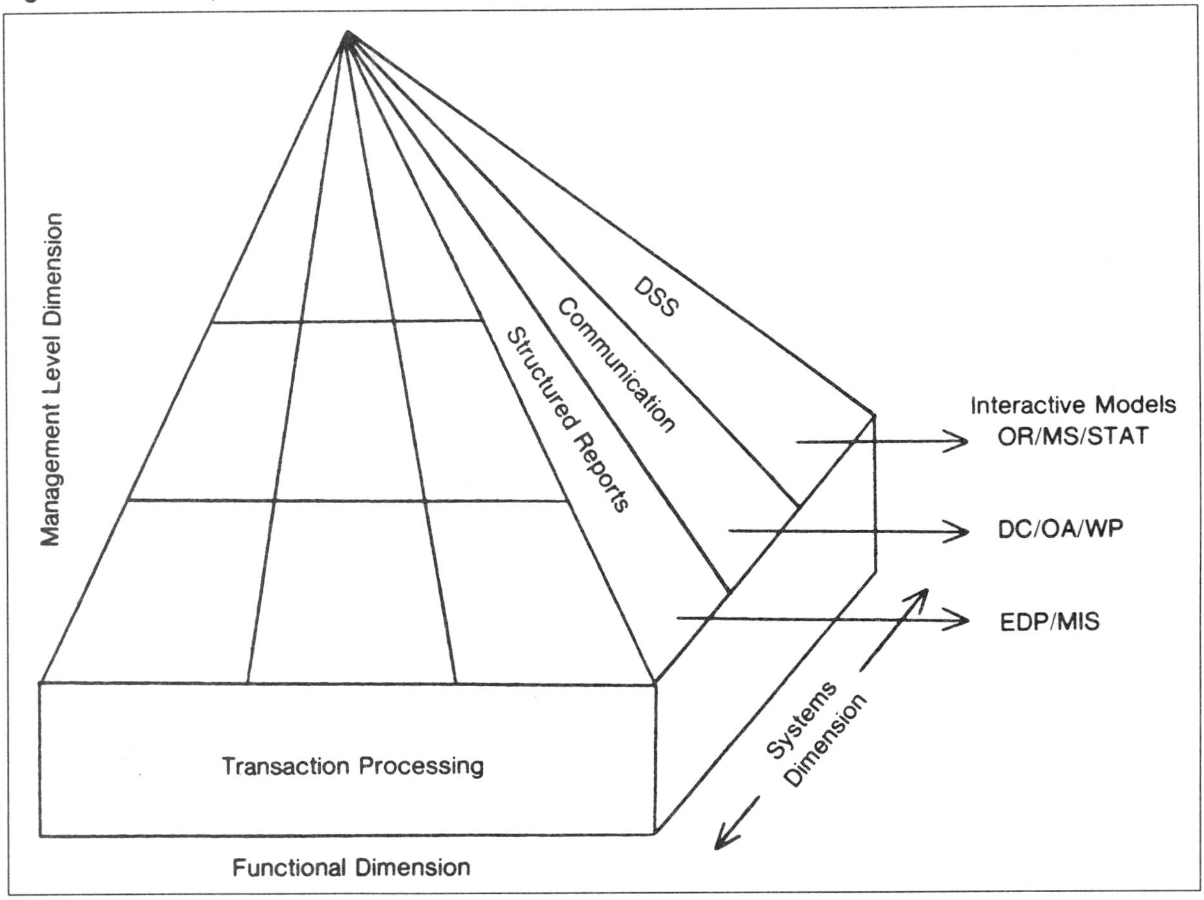

needs. It is not yet clear exactly how these technologies fit together, or which important problems need to be solved. Indeed, that is a large part of the purpose of this article. It is apparent, however, that a DSS has the potential to become another powerful weapon in the arsenal of the information systems professional to help improve the effectiveness of the people in organizations.

The Framework

The remainder of this article is devoted to an exploration of the nature of this "thrust" in information systems called "DSS." The mechanism for this exploration is another of the often maligned but repeatedly used "frameworks."

A framework, in the absence of theory, is helpful in organizing a complex subject, identifying the relationships between the parts, and revealing the areas in which further developments will be required. The framework represented here has evolved over the past two years in discussions with many different groups of people.[1] It is organized in two major parts. The first part considers: (a) three levels of technology, all of which have been designated as a DSS, with considerable confusion; (b) the developmental approach that is evolving for the creation of a DSS; and (c) the roles of several key types of people in the building and use of a DSS. The second part of the framework develops a descriptive model to assess the performance objectives and the capabilities of a DSS as viewed by three of the major stakeholders in their continued development and use.

Three Technology Levels

It is helpful to identify three levels of hardware/software which have been included in the label "DSS." They are used by people with different levels of technical capability, and vary in the nature and scope of task to which they can be applied.

Specific DSS. The system which actually accomplishes the work might be called the *Specific DSS*. It is an information systems "application," but with characteristics that make it significantly different from a typical data processing application. It is the hardware/software that allows a specific decision maker or group of decision makers to deal with a specific set of related problems. An early example is the portfolio management system [20] also described in the first major DSS book by Keen and Scott Morton [23]. Another example is the police beat allocation system used on an experimental basis by the City of San Jose, California [9]. The latter system allowed a police officer to display a map outline and call up data by geographical zone, showing police calls for service, activity levels, service time, *etc*. The interactive graphic capability of the system enabled the officer to manipulate the maps, zones, and data to try a variety of police beat alternatives quickly and easily. In effect, the system provided tools to *amplify* a manager's judgment. Incidentally, a later experiment attempted to apply a traditional linear programming model to the problem. The solution was less satisfactory than the one designed by the police officer.

DSS Generator. The second technology level might be called a *DSS Generator*. This is a "package" of related hardware and software which provides a set of capabilities to quickly and easily build a Specific DSS. For example, the police beat system described above was built from the Geodata Analysis and Display System (GADS), an experimental system developed at the IBM Research Laboratory in San Jose [8]. By loading different maps, data, menu choices, and procedures or command strings, GADS was later used to build a Specific DSS to support the routing of IBM copier repairmen [42]. The development of this new "application" required less than one month.

Another example of a *DSS Generator* is the Executive Information System (EIS) marketed by Boeing Computer Services [6]. EIS is an integrated set of capabilities which includes report preparation, inquiry capability, a modeling language, graphic display commands, and a set of financial and statistical analysis subroutines. These capabilities have all been available individually for some time. The unique contribution of EIS is that these capabilities are available through a common command language which acts on a common set of data. The result is that EIS can be used as a DSS Generator, especially for a Specific DSS to help in financial decision making situations.

Evolutionary growth toward DSS Generators has come from special purpose languages. In fact, most of the software systems that might be used as Generators are evolving from enhanced planning languages or modeling languages, perhaps with report preparation and graphic display capabilities added. The Interactive Financial Planning System (IFPS) marketed by Execucom Systems of Austin, Texas [18], and EXPRESS available from TYMSHARE [44], are good examples.

DSS Tools. The third and most fundamental level of technology applied to the development of a DSS might be called *DSS Tools*. These are hardware or software elements which facilitate the development of a specific DSS or a DSS Generator. This category of technology has seen the greatest amount of recent development, including new special purpose languages, improvements in operating systems to support conversational approaches, color graphics hardware and supporting software, *etc*. For example, the GADS system described above was written in FORTRAN using an experimental graphics subroutine package as the primary dialogue handling software, a laboratory enhanced raster-scan color monitor, and a powerful interactive data extraction/database management system.

Relationships. The relationships between these three levels of technology and types of DSS are illustrated by Figure 3. The DSS Tools can be used to develop a Specific DSS application directly as shown on the left half of the diagram. This is the same approach used to develop most traditional applications with tools such as a general purpose language, data access software, subroutine packages, *etc.* The difficulty with this approach for developing DSS applications is the constant change and flexibility which characterize them. A DSS changes character not only in response to changes in the environment, but to changes in the way managers want to approach the problem. Therefore, a serious complicating factor in the use of basic tools is the need to involve the user directly in the change and modification of the Specific DSS.

APL was heavily used in the development of Specific DSS because it proved to be cheap and easy for APL programmers, especially the APL enthusiasts, to produce "throw-away" code which could be easily revised or discarded as the nature of the application changed. However, except for the few users who became members of the APL fan club, that language *did not* help capture the involvement of users in the building and modification of the DSS. The development and use of DSS Generators promises to create a "platform" or staging area from which Specific DSS can be constantly developed and modified with the cooperation of the user, and without heavy consumption of time and effort.

Evolving Roles in DSS

All three levels of technology will probably be used over time in the development and operation of a DSS. Some interesting developments are occurring, however, in the roles that managers and technicians will play.

Figure 4 repeats part of the earlier diagram with a spectrum of five roles spread across the three levels.

• The *manager or user* is the person faced with the problem or decision—the one that must take action and be responsible for the consequences.
• The *intermediary* is the peson who helps the user, perhaps merely as a clerical assistant to push the buttons of the terminal, or perhaps as a more substantial "staff assistant" to interact and make suggestions.
• The *DSS builder* or facilitator assembles the necessary capabilities from the DSS Generator to "configure" the specific DSS with which the user/intermediary interacts directly. This person must have some familiarity with the problem area and also be comfortable with the information system technology components and capabilities.
• The *technical supporter* develops additional information system capabilities or components when they are needed as part of the Generator. New databases, new analysis models, and additional data display formats will be developed by the person filling this role. It requires a strong familiarity with technology, and a minor acquaintance with the problem or application area.
• The *toolsmith* develops new technology, new languages, new hardware and software, improves the efficiency of linkages between subsystems, *etc.*

Two observations about this spectrum of roles are appropriate. First, it is clear that they do not necessarily align with individuals on a one-to-one basis. One person may assume several roles, or more than one person may be required to fill a role. The appropriate role assignment will generally depend on:

• the nature of the problem, particularly how narrow or broad;
• the nature of the person, particularly how comfortable the individual is with the computer equipment, language and concepts; and
• the strength of the technology, particularly how user oriented it is.

Some managers do not need or want an intermediary. There are even a few chief executives who take the terminal home on weekends to write programs, thereby assuming the upper three or four roles. In fact, a recent survey of the users of IFPS shows that more than one third of them are middle and top level managers [45]. Decisions which require group consensus or systems design (builder) teams are examples of multiple persons per role.

Secondly, these roles appear similar to those present in traditional systems development, but there are subtle differences. The top two are familiar

Figure 3 Three Levels of DSS Technology

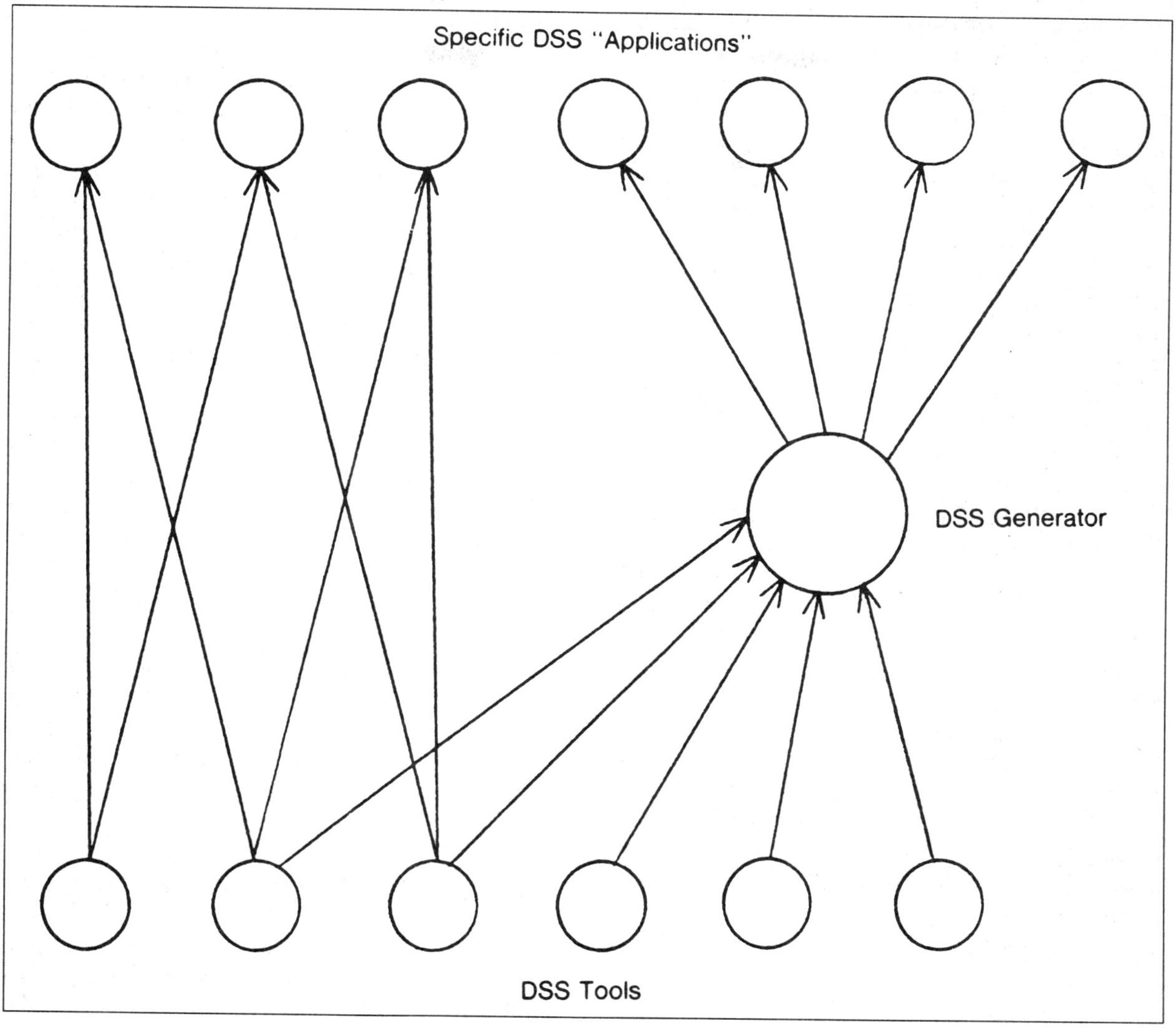

even in name for the development of many interactive or online systems. It is common practice in some systems to combine them into one "virtual" user for convenience. The user of the DSS, however, will play a much more active and controlling role in the design and development of the system than has been true in the past. The builder/technical supporter dichotomy is relatively close to the information specialist/system designer dichotomy discussed in the ACM curriculum recommendations [3]. Increasingly, however, the DSS builder resides in the functional area and not in the MIS department. The toolsmith is similar to a systems programmer, software designer, or computer scientist, but is increasingly employed by a hardware or software vendor, and not by the user's organization. The net result is less direct involvement in the DSS process by the information systems professional in the EDP/MIS department. (Some implications of this trend are discussed later.) Moreover, the interplay between these roles is evolving into a unique development approach for a DSS.

Figure 4 Three Levels of DSS with Five Associated Roles for Managers and Technicians

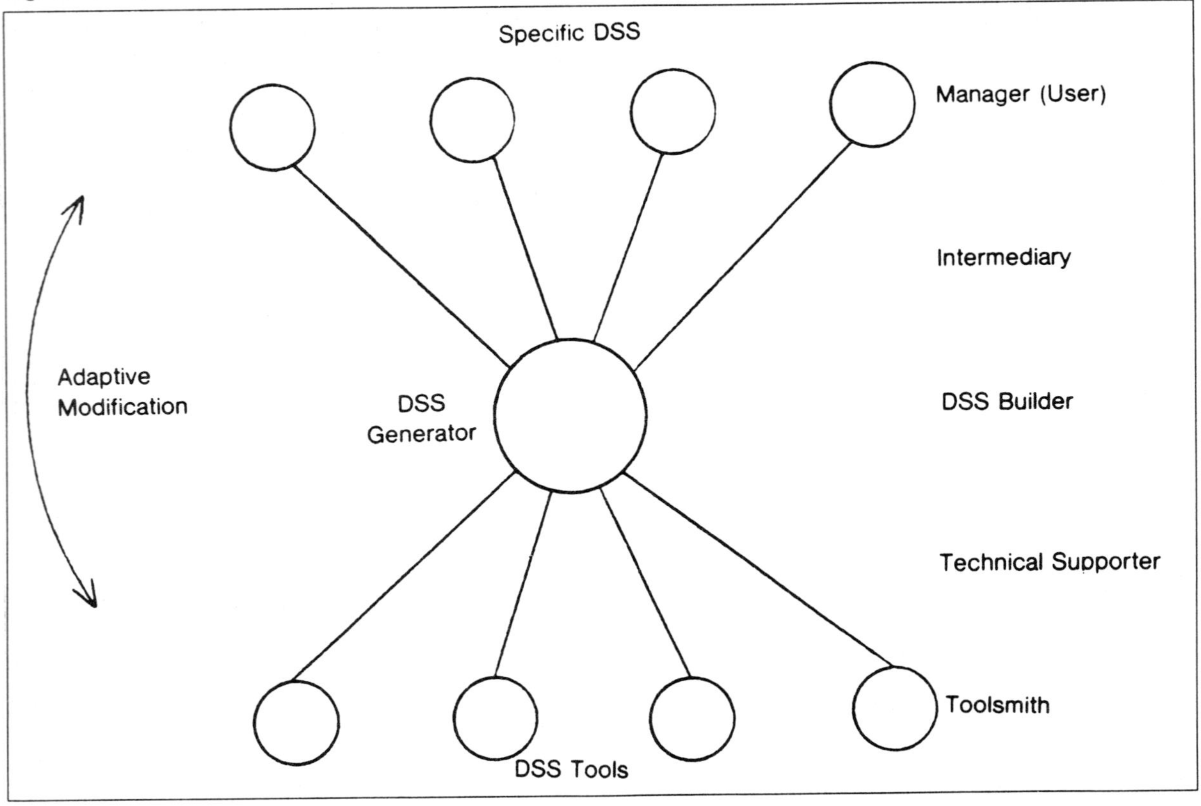

The Development Approach for DSS

The very nature of a DSS requires a different design technique from traditional batch, or online, transaction processing systems. The traditional approaches for analysis and design have proven inadequate because there is no single comprehensive theory of decision making, and because of the rapidity of change in the conditions which decision makers face. Designers literally "cannot get to first base" because no one, least of all the decision maker or user, can define in advance what the functional requirements of the system should be. A DSS needs to be built with short, rapid feedback from users to ensure that development is proceeding correctly. It must be developed to permit change quickly and easily.

Iterative Design. The result is that the most important four steps in the typical systems development process—analysis, design, construction, implementation— are combined into a single step which is iteratively repeated. Several names are evolving to describe this process including breadboarding [31], L'Approache Evolutive [14], and "middle out" [30]. The essence of the approach is that the manager and builder agree on a small but significant subproblem, then design and develop an initial system to support the decision making which it requires. After a short period of use, for instance, a few weeks, the system is evaluated, modified, and incrementally expanded. This cycle is repeated three to six times over the course of a few months until a *relatively* stable system is evolved which supports decision making for a cluster of tasks. The word "relatively" is important, because although the frequency and extent of change will decrease, it will never be stable. The system will always be changing, not as a necessary evil in response to imposed environmental changes, but as a conscious strategy on the part of the user and builder.

In terms of the three level model presented earlier, this process can be viewed as the iterative cycling between the DSS Generator and the Specific DSS as shown in Figure 4. With each cycle, capabilities are added to, or deleted from, the Specific DSS from those available in the DSS Generator. Keen depicts the expansion and growth of the system in terms of adding verbs which represent actions managers require [24]. Carlson adds more dimension by focusing on representations, operations, control, and memories as the elements of expansion and modification [11]. In another paper, Keen deals substantively with the interaction between the user, the builder, and the technology in this iterative, adaptive design process [25].

Note that this approach requires an unusual level of management involvement or management participation in the design. The manager is actually the iterative designer of the system; the systems analyst is merely the catalyst between the manager and the system, implementing the required changes and modifications.

Note also that this is different from the concept of "prototyping"; the initial system is real, live, and usable, not just a pilot test. The iterative process does not *merely* lead to a good understanding of the systems performance requirements, which are then frozen. The iterative changeability is actually *built into* the DSS as it is used over time. In fact, the development approach *becomes the system*. Rather than developing a system which is then "run" as a traditional EDP system, the DSS development approach results in the installation of an adaptive process in which a decision maker and a set of information system "capabilities" interact to confront problems while responding to changes from a variety of sources.

The Adaptive System. In the broad sense, the DSS is an adaptive system which consists of all three levels of technology in place and operating with the participants (roles), and the technology adapting to changes over time. Thus, the development of a DSS is actually the development and installation of this adaptive system. Simon describes such a system as one that adapts to changes of several kinds over three time horizons [34]. In the short run, the system allows a *search* for answers within a relatively narrow scope. In the intermediate time horizon, the system *learns* by modifying its capabilities and activities, *i.e.*, the scope or domain changes. In the long run, the system evolves to accommodate much different behavior styles and capabilities.

The three level model of a DSS is analogous to Simon's adaptive system. The Specific DSS gives the manager the capabilities and flexibility to *search*, explore, and experiment with the problem area, within certain boundaries. Over time, as changes occur in a task, the environment, and the user's behavior, the Specific DSS must *learn* to accommodate these changes through the reconfiguration of the elements in the DSS generator, with the aid of the DSS builder. Over a longer period of time, the basic tools evolve to provide the technology for changing the capabilities of the Generators out of which the Specific DSS is constructed, through the efforts of the toolsmith.

The ideas expressed above are not particularly new. Rapid feedback between the systems analyst and the client has been pursued for years. In the long run, most computer systems *are* adaptive systems. They are changed and modified during the normal system life cycle, and they evolve through major enhancements and extensions as the life cycle is repeated. However, when the length of that life cycle is shortened from three to five years to three to five months, or even weeks, there are significant implications. The resulting changes in the development approach and the traditional view of the systems life cycle promises to be one of the important impacts of the growing use of a DSS.

Performance Objectives and Capabilities

Most of the foregoing discussion has dealt with some aspects of the technological and organizational contexts within which a DSS will be built and operated. The second part of the framework deals with what a DSS must accomplish, and what capabilities or characteristics it must have. The three levels of hardware/software technology and the corresponding three major "stakeholders" or interested parties in the development and use of a DSS can be used to identify the characteristics and attributes of a DSS.

At the top level are the *managers or users* who are primarily concerned with what the Specific DSS can do for them. Their focus is the problem solving or decision making task they face, and the organizational environment in which they operate. They will access a DSS in terms of the assistance they receive in pursuing these tasks. At the level of the DSS Generator, the *builders* or designers must use the capabilities of the generator to configure a Specific DSS to meet the manager's needs. They will be concerned with the capabilities the Generator offers, and how these capabilities can be assembled to create the specific DSS. At the DSS tool level, the "*toolsmiths*" are concerned with the development of basic technology components, and how they can be integrated to form a DSS Generator which has the necessary capabilities.

The attributes and characteristics of a DSS as viewed from each level must be examined. From the manager's view, six general performance objectives for the Specific DSS can be identified. They are not the only six that could be identified, but as a group they represent the overall performance of a DSS that seems to be expected and desirable from a managerial viewpoint. The characteristics of the DSS Generator from the viewpoint of the builder are described by a conceptual model which identifies performance characteristics in three categories: dialogue handling or the man-machine interface, database and database management capability, and modeling and analytic capability. The same three part model is used to depict the viewpoint of the "toolsmith," but from the aspect of the technology, tactics, and architecture required to produce those capabilities required by the builders.

Manager's View: Performance Objectives

The following performance requirements are phrased using the normative word "should." It is likely that no Specific DSS will be required to satisfy all six of the performance requirements given here. In fact, it is important to recall that the performance criteria for any Specific DSS will depend entirely on the task, the organizational environment, and the decision maker(s) involved. Nevertheless, the following objectives collectively represent a set of capabilities which characterize the full value of the DSS concept from the manager/user point of view. The first three pertain to the type of decision making task which managers and professionals face. The latter three related to the type of support which is needed.

1. *A DSS should provide support for decision making, but with emphasis on semi-structured and unstructured decisions.* These are the types of decisions that have had little or no support from EDP, MIS, or management science/operations research (MS/OR) in the past. It might be better to refer to "hard" or underspecified problems, because the concept of "structure" in decision making is heavily dependent on the cognitive style and approach to problem solving of the decision maker. It is clear from their expressed concerns however, that managers need additional support for certain kinds of problems.
2. *A DSS should provide decision making support for managers at all levels, assisting in integration between the levels whenever appropriate.* This requirement evolves from the realization that managers at *all* organizational levels face "tough" problems as described in the first objective above. Moreover, a major need articulated by managers, is the integration and coordination of decision making by several managers dealing with related parts of a larger problem.
3. *A DSS should support decisions which are interdependent as well as those that are independent.* Much of the early DSS work inferred that a decision maker would sit at a terminal, use a system, and develop a decision *alone*. DSS development experience has shown that a DSS must accommodate decisions which are made by groups or made in part by several people in sequence. Keen and Hackathorn [24] explore three decision types as:

• *Independent.* A decision maker has full responsibility and authority to make a complete inplementable decision.

• *Sequential Interdependent.* A decision maker makes part of a decision which is passed on to someone else.
• *Pooled Interdependent.* The decision must result from negotiation and interaction among decision makers.

Different capabilities will be required to support each type of decision—personal support, organizational support, and group support respectively.

4. *A DSS should support all phases of the decision making process.* A popular model of the decision making process is given in the work of Herbert Simon [33]. He characterized three main steps in the process as follows:

• *Intelligence.* Searching the environment for conditions calling for decisions. Raw data is obtained, processed, and examined for clues that may identify problems.
• *Design.* Inventing, developing, and analyzing possible courses of action. This involves processes to understand the problem, generate solutions, and test solutions for feasibility.
• *Choice.* Selecting a particular course of action from those available. A choice is made and implemented.

Although the third phase includes implementation, many authors feel that it is significant enough to be shown separately. It has been added to Figure 5 to show the relationships between the steps. Simon's model also illustrates the contribution of MIS/EDP and MS/OR to decision making. From the definition of the three stages given above, it is clear that EDP and MIS, in the narrow sense, have made major contributions to the intelligence phase, while MS/OR has been primarily useful at the choice phase. There has been no substantial support for the design phase, which seems to be one of the primary potential contributions of a DSS. There also has been very little support from traditional systems for the implementation phase, but some early experience has shown that a DSS can make a major contribution here also [42].

5. *A DSS should support a variety of decision making processes, but not be dependent on any one.* Simon's model, though widely accepted, is only one model of how decisions are actually made. In fact, there is no universally accepted model of the decision making process, and there is no promise of such a general theory in the foreseeable future. There are too many variables, too many different types of decisions, and too much variety in the characteristics of decision makers. Consequently, a very important characteristic of a DSS is that it provide the decision maker with a set of capabilities to apply in a sequence and form that fits each individual cognitive style. In short, a DSS should be process independent, and user driven or controlled.
6. *Finally, a DSS should be easy to use.* A variety of terms have been used to describe this characteristic including flexibility, user friendly, nonthreatening, *etc.* The importance of this characteristic is underscored by the discretionary latitude of a DSS's clientele. Although some systems which require heavy organizational support or group support may limit the discretion somewhat, the user of a DSS has much more latitude to ignore or circumvent the system than the user of a more traditional transaction system or required reporting system. Therefore, a DSS must "earn" its users' allegiance by being valuable and convenient.

The Builder's View: Technical Capabilities

The DSS Builder has the responsibility of drawing on computer based tools and techniques to provide the decision support required by the manager. DSS Tools can be used directly, but it is generally more efficient and effective to use a DSS Generator for this task. The Generator must have a set of capabilities which facilitate the quick and easy configuration of a Specific DSS and modification in response to changes in the manager's requirements, environment, tasks, and thinking approaches. A conceptual model can be used to organize these capabilities, both for the builders and for the "toolsmith" who will develop the technology to provide these capabilities.

Figure 5 Phases of Decision Making

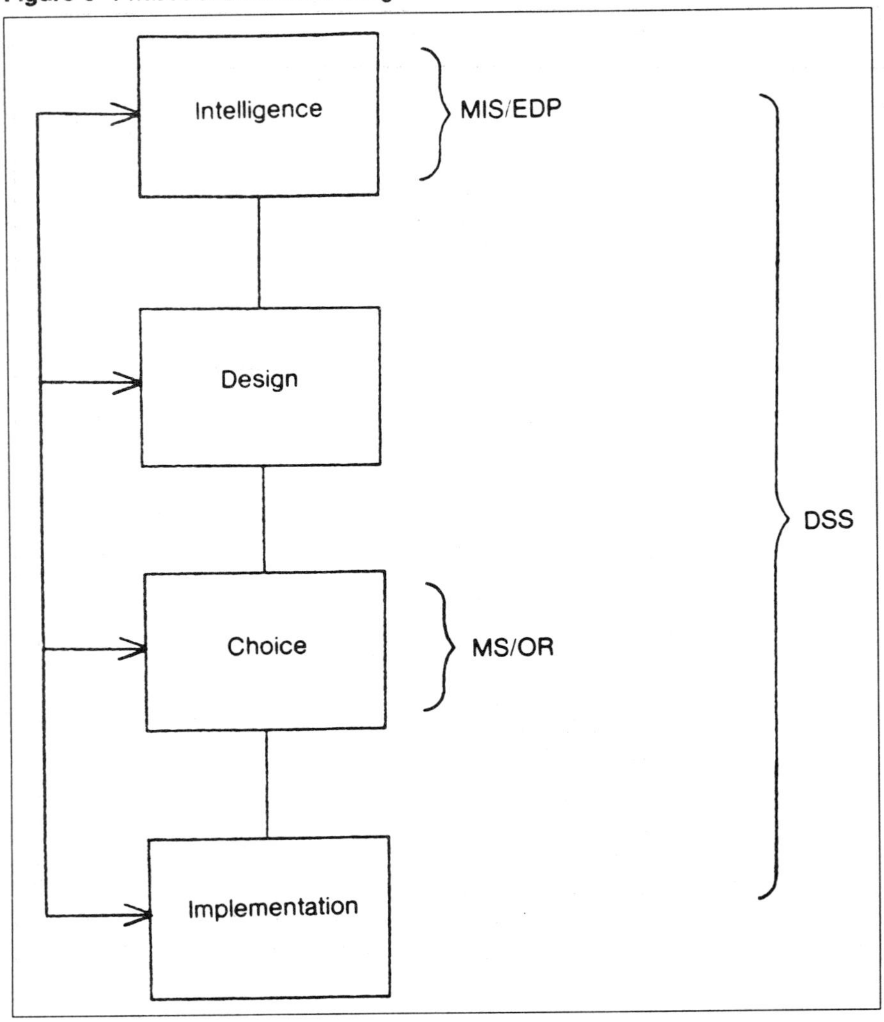

The old "black box" approach is helpful here, starting with the view of the system as a black box, successively "opening" the boxes to understand the subsystems and how they are interconnected. Although the DSS is treated as the black box here, it is important to recall that the overall system is the decision *making* system, consisting of a manager/user who uses a DSS to confront a task in an organizational environment.

Opening the large DSS box reveals a database; a model base, and a complex software system for linking the user to each of them as shown in Figure 6. Opening each of these boxes reveals that the database and model base have some interrelated components, and that the software system is comprised of three sets of capabilities: database management software (DBMS), model base management software (MBMS), and the software for managing the interface between the user and the system, which might be called the dialogue generation and management software (DGMS). These three major subsystems provide a convenient scheme for identifying the technical capability which a DSS must have. The key aspects in each category that are critical to a DSS from the Builder's point of view, and a list of capabilities which will be required in each category must now be considered.

Figure 6 Components of the DSS

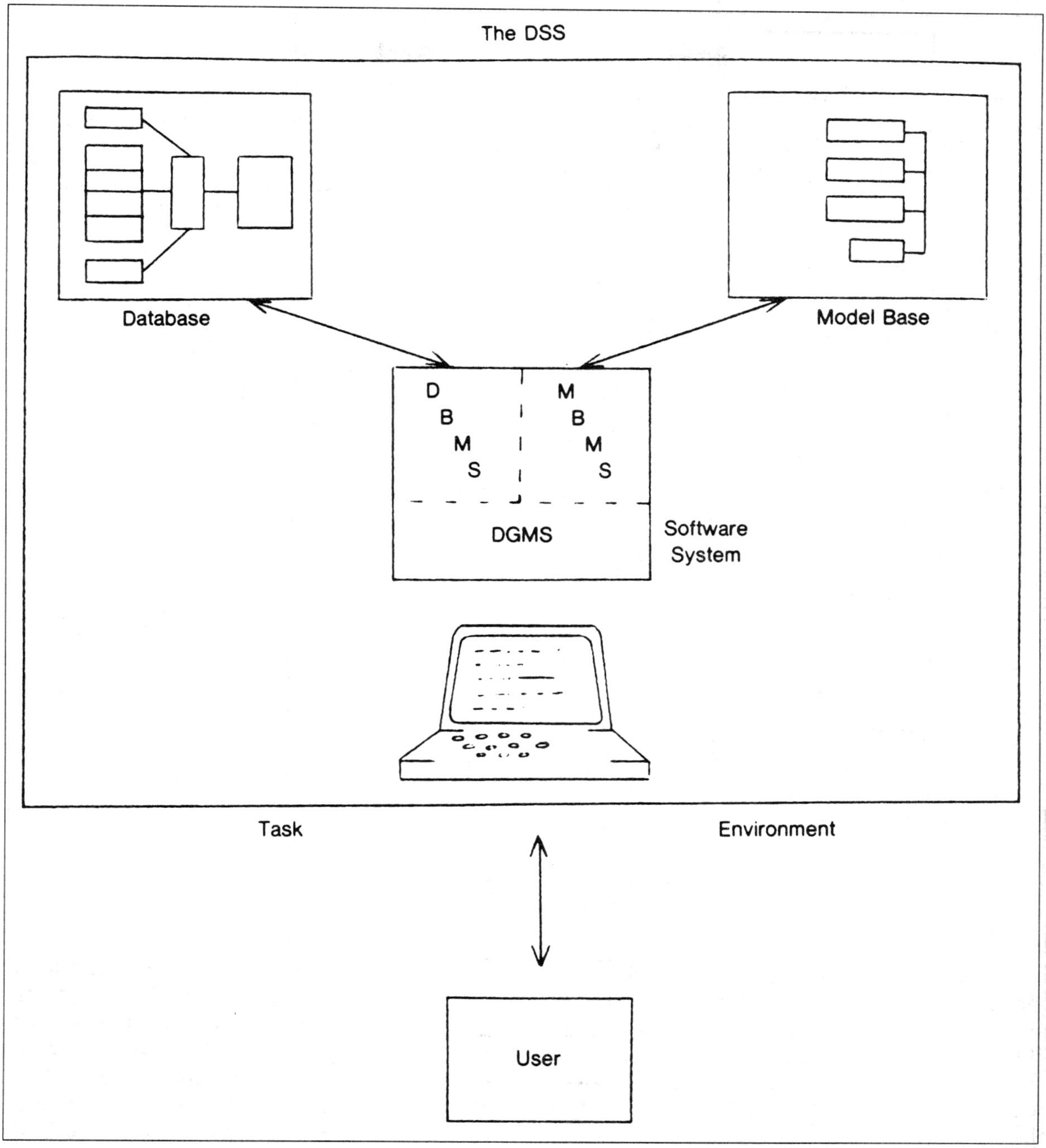

The Data Subsystem

The data subsystem is thought to be a well understood set of capabilities because of the rapidly maturing technology related to databases and their management. The typical advantages of the database approach, and the powerful functions of the DBMS, are also important to the development and use of a

DSS. There are, however, some significant differences between the Database/Data Communication approach for traditional systems, and those applicable for a DSS. Opening the Database box summarizes these key characteristics as shown in Figure 7.

First is the importance of a much richer set of data sources than are usually found in typical non-DSS applications. Data must come from external as well as internal sources, since decision making, especially in the upper management levels, is heavily dependent on external data sources. In addition, the typical accounting oriented transaction data must be supplemented with non-transactional, non-accounting data, some of which has not been computerized in the past.

Another significant difference is the importance of the data capture and extraction process from this wider set of data sources. The nature of a DSS requires that the extraction process, and the DBMS which manages it, be flexible enough to allow rapid additions and changes in response to unanticipated user requests. Finally, most successful DSS's have found it necessary to create a DSS database which is logically separate from other operational databases. A partial set of capabilities required in the database area can be summarized by the following:

- the ability to combine a variety of data sources through a data capture and extraction process;
- the ability to add and delete data sources quickly and easily;
- the ability to portray logical data structures in user terms so the user understands what is available and can specify needed additions and deletions;
- the ability to handle personal and unofficial data so the user can experiment with alternatives based on personal judgment; and
- the ability to manage this wide variety of data with a full range of data management functions.

Figure 7 The Data Subsystem

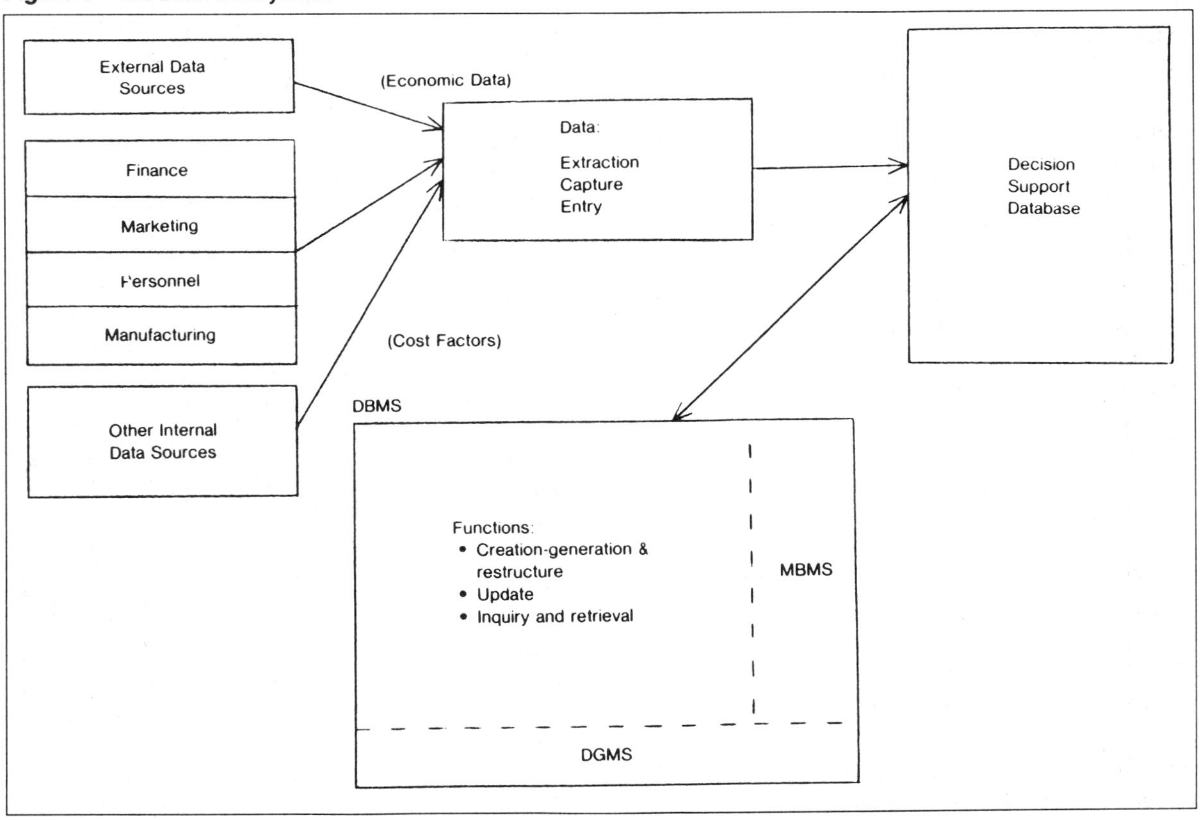

The Model Subsystem

A very promising aspect of a DSS is its ability to integrate data access and decision models. It does so by imbedding the decision models in an information system which uses the database as the integration and communication mechanism between models. This characteristic unifies the strength of data retrieval and reporting from the EDP field and the significant developments in management science in a way the manager can use and trust.

The misuse and disuse of models have been widely discussed [21, 28, 36, 39]. One major problem has been that model builders were frequently preoccupied with the structure of the model. The existence of the correct input data and the proper delivery of the output to the user was assumed. In addition to these heroic assumptions, models tended to suffer from inadequacy because of the difficulty of developing an integrated model to handle a realistic set of interrelated decisions. The solution was a collection of separate models, each of which dealt with a distinct part of the problem. Communication between these related models was left to the decision maker as a manual and intellectual process.

A more enlightened view of models suggests that they be imbedded in an information system with the database as the integration and communication mechanism between them. Figure 8 summarizes the components of the model base "box." The model creation process must be flexible, with a strong modeling language and a set of building blocks, much like subroutines, which can be assembled to assist the modeling process. In fact, there are a set of model management functions, very much analogous to data management functions. The key capabilities for a DSS in the model subsystems include:

- the ability to create new models quickly and easily;
- the ability to catalog and maintain a wide range of models, supporting all levels of management;
- the ability to interrelate these models with appropriate linkages through the database;
- the ability to access and integrate model "building blocks;" and
- the ability to manage the model base with management functions analogous to database management (*e.g.*, mechanisms for storing, cataloging, linking, and accessing models).

For a more detailed discussion of the model base and its management see [37, 38, 46].

The User System Interface. Much of the power, flexibility, and usability characteristics of a DSS are derived from capabilities in the user system interface. Bennett identifies the user, terminal, and software system as the components of the interface subsystem [5]. He then divides the dialogue, or interface experience itself into three parts as shown in Figure 9:

1. *The action language*—what the user *can do* in communicating with the system. It includes such options as the availability of a regular keyboard, function keys, touch panels, joy stick, voice command, *etc.*
2. *The display or presentation language*—what the user *sees*. The display language includes options such as character or line printer, display screen, graphics, color, plotters, audio output, *etc.*
3. *The knowledge base*—what the user *must know*. The knowledge base consists of what the user needs to bring to the session with the system in order to effectively use it. The knowledge may be in the user's head, on a reference card or instruction sheet, in a user's manual, in a series of "help" commands available upon request, *etc.*

The "richness" of the interface will depend on the strength of capabilities in each of these areas.

Another dimension of the user system interface is the concept of "dialogue style." Examples include the questions/answer approach, command languages, menus, and "fill in the blanks." Each style has pro's and con's depending on the type of user, task, and decision situation. For a more detailed discussion of dialogue styles see [13].

Although this just scratches the surface in this important area, a partial set of desirable capabilities for a DSS generator to support the user/system interface includes:

- the ability to handle a variety of dialogue styles,

Figure 8 The Models Subsystem

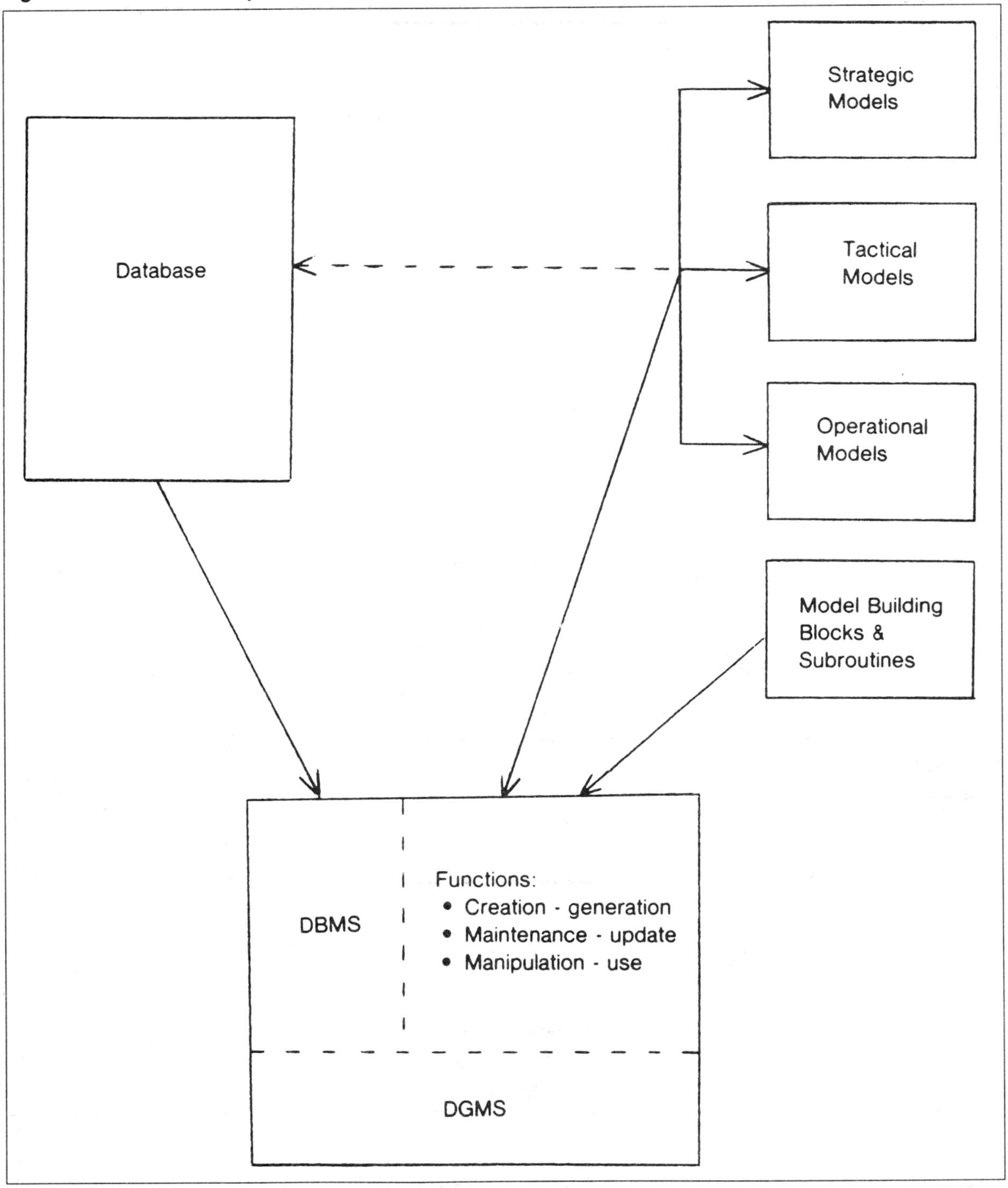

perhaps with the ability to shift among them at the users's choice;

• the ability to accommodate user actions in a variety of media;

Figure 9 The User System Interface

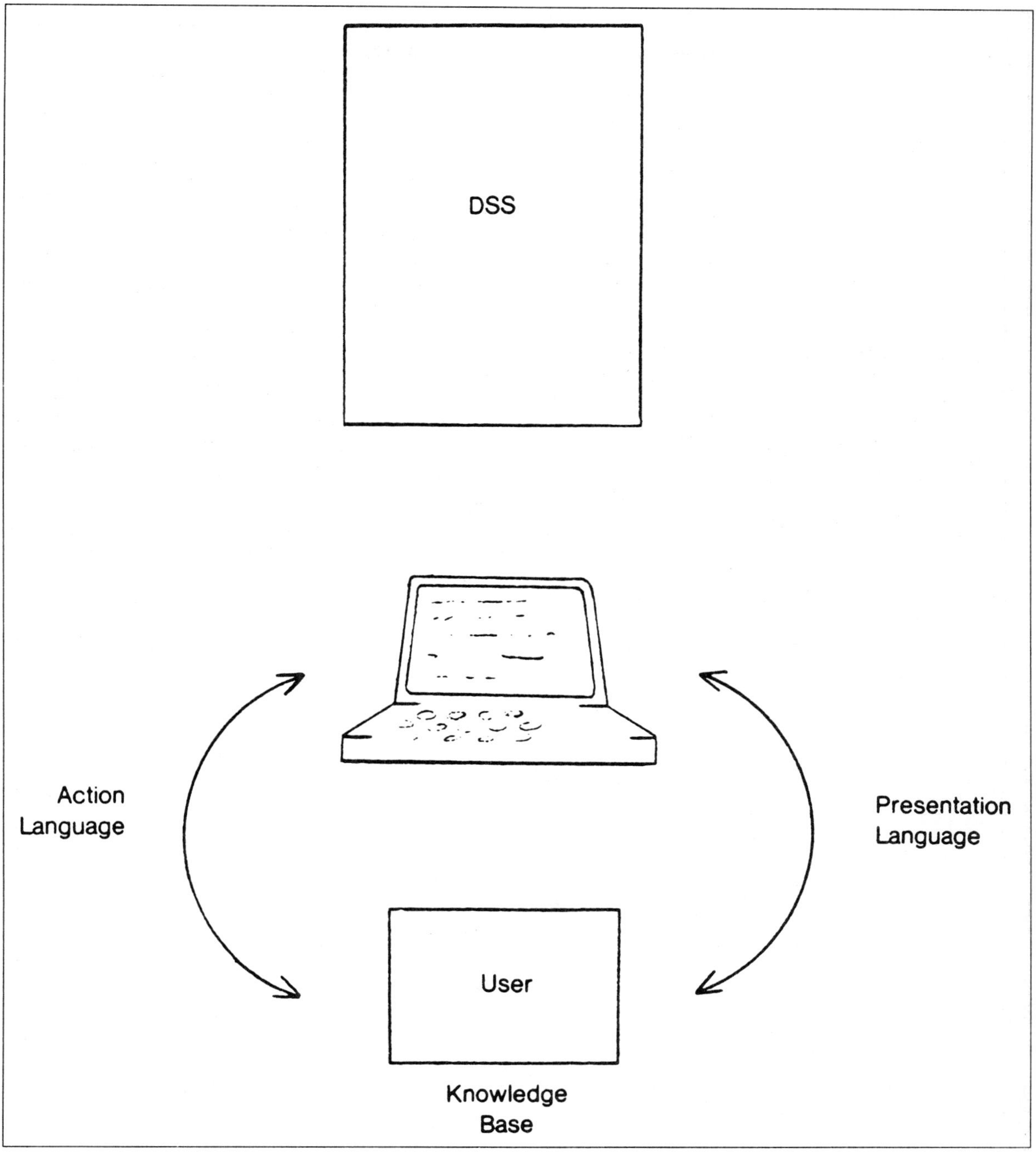

• the ability to present data in a variety of formats and media; and
• the ability to provide flexible support for the users' knowledge base.

The Toolsmith View: The Underlying Technology

The toolsmith is concerned with the science

involved in creating the information technology to support a DSS, and the architecture for combining the basic tools into a coherent system. The same three part model can be used to describe the toolsmith's concerns because the tools must be designed and combined to provide the three sets of capabilities.

Each of the three areas—dialogue, data handling, and model handling—has received a fair amount of attention from toolsmiths in the past. The topic of DSS and the requirements it imposes has put these efforts in a new perspective revealing how they can be interrelated to increase their collective effectiveness. Moreover, the DSS requirements have revealed some missing elements in existing efforts, indicating valuable potential areas for development.

Dialogue Management. There has been a great deal of theoretical and some empirical work on systems requirements for good man/machine interface. Many of these studies are based on watching users' behavior in using terminals, or surveying users or programmers to ascertain what they want in interactive systems [10, 16]. A recent study examines a series of interactive applications, many of which are DSS's, to assess the *type* of software capabilities required by the applications [43]. This study led directly to some creative work on the software architecture for dialogue generation and management systems (DGMS) as characterized in the model of the previous section [12]. This research uses a relation as the data structure for storing each picture or "frame" used in the system, and a decision table for storing the control mechanism for representing the potential users' option in branching from one frame to another.

Data Management. Most of the significant work in the database management area during the past several years is aimed at transaction processing against large databases. Large DBMS's generally have inquiry/retrieval and flexible report preparation capabilities, but their largest contribution has been in the reduction of program maintenance costs through the separation of application programs and data definitions. On the other hand, DBMS work has generally had a rather naive view of the user and the user's requirements. A DSS user will not be satisfied merely with the capability to issue a set of retrieval commands which select items from the database, or even to display those selected items in a report with the flexible definition of format and headings. A DSS user needs to interact repeatedly and creatively with a relatively small set of data. The user may only need 40-100 data variables, but they must be the *right ones*; and what is right may change from day to day and week to week. Required data will probably include time series data which are not handled comprehensively by typical DBMS's. Better ways are needed to handle and coordinate time series data as well as mechanisms for capturing, processing, and tagging judgmental and probabilistic data. Better ways are also needed for extracting data from existing files and capturing data from previously non-computerized sources. The critical area of data extraction with fast response, which allows additions and deletions to the DSS database from the large transaction database was a major contribution of the GADS work [8, 29]. In short, the significant development in database technology needs to be focused and extended in some key areas in order to directly serve the needs of a DSS.

Model Management. The area of model creation and handling may have the greatest potential contribution to a DSS. So far, the analytic capability provided by systems has evolved from statistical or financial analysis subroutines which can be called from a common command language. More recently, modeling languages provide a way of formulating interrelationships between variables in a way that permits the creation of simulation or "what if" models. A we noted earlier, many of the currently viable DSS Generators have evolved from these efforts. Early forms of "model management" seem to be evolving from enhancements to some modeling languages, which permit a model of this type to be used for sensitivity testing or goal seeking by specifying target and flexibility variables.

The model management area also has the potential for bringing some of the contributions of artificial intelligence (AI) to bear on a DSS. MYCIN, a system to support medical diagnosis, is based on "production rules," in the AI sense, which play the role of models in performing analytic and decision guidance functions [15]. A more general characterization of "knowledge management" as a way of handling models and data has also been tentatively explored [7]. More recent work proposes the use of a version of semantic networks for model representation [17]. Though this latter work is promising. AI research has shown the semantic network approach to be relatively inefficient with today's technology. Usable capabilities in model management in the near future are more likely to evolve from modeling languages, expanded subroutine approaches, and in some cases, AI production rules.

Issues for the Future

At this stage in the development of the DSS area, issues, problems, and fruitful directions for further research/development are plentiful. At a "task force" meeting this summer, thirty researchers from twelve countries gathered to discuss the nature of DSS's and to identify issues for the future. Their list, developed in group discussions over several days, was quite long [19]. The issues given here, phrased as difficult questions, seem to be the ones that must be dealt with quickly, lest the promise and potential benefits of DSS's be diluted or seriously delayed.

What's a DSS?

Earlier it was noted that some skeptics regard DSS as "just another buzz word." This article has shown that there is a significant amount of content behind the label. The danger remains, however, that the bandwagon effect will outrun our ability to define and develop potential contributions of a DSS. The market imperatives of the multi-billion dollar information systems industry tend to generate pressures to create simple labels for intuitively good ideas. It happened in many cases, but not all, of course, with MIS. Some companies are still trying to live down the aftereffects of the overpromise/under-undelivery/disenchantment sequence from the MIS bandwagon of the late '60's. Eventually, a set of minimal capabilities or characteristics which characterize a DSS should evolve. In the short range, a partial solution is education—supply managers with intellectual ammunition they can use in dealing with vendors. Managers should and must ask sharp, critical questions about the capabilities of any purported DSS, matching them against what is really needed.

What is Really Needed?

After nearly two decades of advancements in information technology, the real needs of managers from an information system are not well understood. The issue is further complicated by the realization that managers need and the needs of other "knowledge workers" with which they interact, are heavily interdependent. The DSS philosophy and approach has already shed some light on this issue by emphasizing "capabilities"—the ability for a manager to do things with an information system—rather than just "information needs" which too often infer data items and totals on a report.

Nevertheless, it is tempting to call for a hesitation in the development of DSS's until decision making and related managerial activities are fully understood. Though logically appealing, such a strategy is not practical. Neither the managers who face increasingly complex tasks, nor the information systems industry which has increasingly strong technology to offer, will be denied. They point out that a truly comprehensive theory of decision making has been pursued for years with minimum success.

A potential resolution of this problem is to develop and use a DSS in a way that reveals what managers can and should receive from an information system. For example, one of Scott Morton's early suggestions was that the system be designed to capture and track the steps taken by managers in the process of making key decisions, both as an aid to the analysis of the process, and as a potential training device for new managers.

The counterpart of the "needs" issue is the extent to which the system meets those needs, and the value of the performance increase that results. Evaluation of a DSS will be just as difficult, and important, as the evaluation of MIS has been. The direct and constant involvement of users, the ones in the best position to evaluate the systems, provides a glimmer of hope on this tough problem. Pursuit of these two tasks together may yield progress on both fronts with the kind of synergistic effect often sought from systems efforts. The iterative design approach and the three levels of technology afford the opportunity, if such a strategy is developed from the beginning.

Who Will Do It?

A series of organizational issues will revolve around the roles and organizational placement of the people who will take the principle responsibility for the development of DSS's. Initiative and guidance for DSS development efforts frequently come from the user area, not from the EDP/MIS area. Yet current technology still requires technical support from the information systems professional. The DSS builder may work for the vice president of finance, but the technical support role is still played by someone in the MIS department. To some extent, the demand for a DSS supports the more general trend to distribute systems development efforts out of the MIS department into the user department. The difference is that many DDS software systems, or generators, specifically attempt to directly reach the end user without involvement of the MIS group. The enlightened MIS administrator considers this a healthy trend, and willingly supplies the required technical support and coordination. Less enlightened DP administrators often see it as a threat. Some companies have set up a group specifically charged with developing DSS type applications. This strategy creates a team of "DSS Builders" who can develop the necessary skills in dealing with users, become familiar with the available technology, and define the steps in the developmental approach for DSS's.

How Should It Be Done?

One of the pillars on which the success of DSS rests, is the iterative development of adaptive design approach. The traditional five to seven stage system development process and the system life cycle concept have been the backbone of systems analysis for years. Most project management systems and approaches are based on it. The adaptive design approach, because it combines all the stages into one quick step which is repeated, will require a redefinition of system development milestones and a major modification of project management mechanisms. Since many traditional systems will not be susceptible to the iterative approach, a way is also needed for deciding when an application should be developed in the new way instead of the traditional way. The outline of the approach described earlier is conceptionally straightforward for applications that require only personal support. It becomes more complicated for group or organizational support when there are multiple users. In short, DSS builders will need to develop a set of milestones, checkpoints, documentation strategies, and project management procedures for DSS applications, and recognize when they should be used.

How Much Can Be Done?

The final issue is a caveat dealing with the limitations of technical solutions to the complexity faced by managers and decision makers. As information systems professionals, we must be careful not to feel, or even allow others to feel, that we can develop or devise a technological solution to all the problems of management. Managers will always "deal with complexity in a state of perplexity"—it is the nature of the job. Information technology can, and is, making a major contribution to improving the effectiveness of people in this situation, but the solution will never be total. With traditional systems, we continually narrow the scope and definition of the system until we know it will do the job it is required to do. If the specification/design/ construction/implementation process is done right, the system is a success, measured against its original objectives. With a DSS, the user and his systems capabilities are constantly pursuing the problem, but the underspecified nature of the problem insures that there will never be a complete solution. Systems analysts have always had a little trouble with humility, but the DSS process requires a healthy dose of modesty with respect to the ability of technology to solve all the problems of managers in organizations.

Conclusion

The "Framework for Development" described above attempts to show the dimensions and scope of DSS in a way that will promote the further *development* of this highly promising type of information system.

1. The relationships between EDP, MIS, and DSS show that DSS is only one of several important technology subsystems for improving organizational performance, and that DSS development efforts must carefully integrate with these other systems.
2. The three levels of technology and the interrelationships between people that use them provide a context for organizing the development effort.
3. The iterative design approach shows that the ultimate goal of the DSS development effort is the installation of an *adaptive system* consisting of all three levels of technology and their users operating and adapting to changes over time.
4. The performance objectives show the types of decision making to be served by, and the types of support which should be built into, a DSS as it is developed.
5. The three technical capabilities illustrate that development efforts must provide the DSS with capabilities in dialogue management, data management, and model management.
6. The issues discussed at the end of the article identify some potential roadblocks that must be recognized and confronted to permit the continued development of DSS.

In closing, it should now be clear that DSS is more than just a "buzz word," but caution must be used in announcing a new "era" in information systems. Perhaps the best term is a "DSS Movement" as user organizations, information systems vendors, and researchers become aware of the field, its potential, and the many unanswered questions. Events and mechanisms in the DSS Movement include systems development experience in organizations, hardware/software developments by vendors, publishing activities to report experience and research, and conferences to provide a forum for the exchange of ideas among interested parties.

It is clear that the momentum of the DSS Movement is building. With appropriate care and reasonable restraint, the coordinated efforts of managers, builders, toolsmiths, and researchers can converge in the development of a significant set of information systems to help improve the effectiveness of organizations and the people who work in them.

Discussion Questions

1. According to Sprague, how is a DSS different from an MIS? Are they really different concepts, or merely different buzzwords for the same concept?
2. How are transaction processing systems, decision support systems, and the levels of management related?
3. How is the development of a decision support system different from that of a transaction processing system?
4. Describe the components of a DSS. Which components are distinctly unique and uncommon in other types of information systems?

References

[1] Alter, S. "A Taxonomy of Decision Support Systems," *Sloan Management Review*, Volume 19, Number 1, Fall 1977, pp. 39-56.

[2] Alter, S. *Decision Support Systems: Current Practice and Continuing Challenges*, Addison-Wesley Publishing Co., Reading, Massachusetts, 1980.

[3] Ashenhurst, R. L. "Curriculum Recommendations for Graduate Professional Programs in Information Systems," *ACM Communications*, Volume 15, Number 5, May 1972, pp. 363-398.

[4] Barbosa, L. C. and Hirko, R. G. "Integration of Algorithmic Aids into Decision Support Systems," *MIS Quarterly*, Volume 4, Number 1, March 1980, pp. 1-12.

[5] Bennett, J. "User-Oriented Graphics, Systems

for Decision Support in Unstructured Tasks," in *User-Oriented Design of Interactive Graphics Systems*, in S. Treu (ed.), Association for Computing Machinery, New York, New York, 1977, pp. 3-11.

[6] Boeing Computer Services, c/o Mr. Park Thoreson, P. O. Box 24346, Seattle, Washington, 98124.

[7] Bonezek, H., Hosapple, C. W., and Whinston, A. "Evolving Roles of Models in Decision Support Systems," *Decision Sciences*, Volume 11, Number 2, April 1980, pp. 337-356.

[8] Carlson, E. D., Bennett, J., Giddings, G., and Mantey, P. "The Design and Evaluation of an Interactive Geo-Data Analysis and Display System," *Information Processing-74*, North Holland Publishing Co., Amsterdam, Holland, 1974.

[9] Carlson, E. D., and Sutton, J. A. "A Case Study of Non-Programmer Interactive Problem Solving, *IBM Research Report RJ1382*, San Jose, California, 1974.

[10] Carlson, E. D., Grace, B. F. and Sutton, J. A. "Case Studies of End User Requirements for Interactive Problem-Solving Systems," *MIS Quarterly*, Volume 1, Number 1, March 1977, pp. 51-63.

[11] Carlson, E. D. "An Approach for Designing Decision Support Systems," *Proceedings*, 11th Hawaii International Conference on Systems Sciences, Western Periodicals Co., North Hollywood, California, 1978, pp. 76-96.

[12] Carlson, E. D. and Metz, W. "Integrating Dialog Management and Data Management," *IBM Research Report RJ2738*, February 1, 1980, San Jose, California.

[13] Carlson, E. D. "The User-Interface for Decision Support Systems," unpublished working paper, IBM Research Laboratory, San Jose, California.

[14] Courbon, J., Drageof, J., and Jose, T. "L'Approache Evolutive," *Information Et Gestion No. 103*, Institute d' Administration des Enterprises, Grenoble, France, January-February 1979, pp. 51-59.

[15] Davis, R. "A DSS for Diagnosis and Therapy," *DataBase*, Volume 8, Number 3, Winter 1977, pp. 58-72.

[16] Dzida, W., Herda, S., and Itzfeldt, W. D. "User-Perceived Quality of Software Interactive Systems," *Proceedings*, Third Annual Conference on Engineering (IEEE) Computer Society, Long Beach, California, 1978, pp. 188-195.

[17] Elam, J., Henderson, J., and Miller, L. "Model Management Systems: An Approach to Decision Support in Complex Organizations," *Proceedings*, Conference on Information Systems, The Society for Management Information Systems, Philadelphia, Pennsylvania, December 1980.

[18] Execucom Systems Corporation, P. O. Box 9758, Austin, Texas, 78766.

[19] Fick, G. and Sprague, R. H., Jr., (eds). *Decision Support Systems: Issues and Challenges*, Pergamon Press, Oxford, England, forthcoming in 1981.

[20] Gerrity, T. P., Jr. "Design of Man-Machine Decision Systems: An Application to Portfolio Management," *Sloan Management Review* 12, Volume 12, Number 2, Winter 1971, pp. 59-75.

[21] Hayes, R. H. and Noland, R. L. "What Kind of Corporate Modeling Functions Best?" *Harvard Business Review*, Volume 52, May-June 1974, pp. 102-112.

[22] Head, R. "Management Information Systems: A Critical Appraisal," *Datamation*, Volume 13, Number 5, May 1967, pp. 22-28.

[23] Keen, P. G. W. and Scott Morton, M. S. *Decision Support Systems: An Organizational Perspective*, Addison-Wesley Publishing Company, Reading, Massachusetts, 1978.

[24] Keen, P. G. W. and Hackathorn, R. D. "Decision Support Systems and Personal Computing," Department of Decision Sciences, The Wharton School, The University of Pennsylvania, Working Paper 79-01-03, Philadelphia, Pennsylvania, April 3, 1979.

[25] Keen, P. G. W. "Adaptive Design for DSS," *Database*, Volume 12, Numbers 1 and 2, Fall 1980, pp. 15-25.

[26] Keen, P. G. W. "Decision Support Systems: A Research Perspective," in *Decision Support Systems: Issues and Challenges*, Pergamon Press, Oxford, England, 1981.

[27] Kroeber, H. W., Watson, H. J., and Sprague, R. H., Jr. "An Empirical Investigation and Analysis of the Current State of Information Systems Evolution," *Journal of Information and Management*, Volume 3, Number 1, February 1980, pp. 35-43.

[28] Little, J. D. C. "Models and Managers: The Concept of a Decision Calculus," *Management Science*, Volume 16, Number 8, April 1970, pp. B466-485.

[29] Mantey, P. E. and Carlson, E. D. "Integrated Geographic Data Bases: The GADS Experience," IBM Research Division, *IBM Research Report RJ2702*, San Jose, California, December 3, 1979.

[30] Ness, D. N. "Decision Support Systems: Theories of Design," presented at the Wharton Office of Naval Research Conference on Decision Support Systems, Philadelphia, Pennsylvania, November 4-7, 1975.

[31] Scott, J. H. "The Management Science Opportunity: A Systems Development Management Viewpoint," *MIS Quarterly*, Volume 2, Number 4, December 1978, pp. 59-61.

[32] Scott Morton, M. S. *Management Decision Systems: Computer Based Support for Decision Making*, Division of Research, Harvard University, Cambridge, Massachusetts, 1971.

[33] Simon, H. *The New Science of Management Decision*, Harper and Row, New York, New York, 1960.

[34] Simon, H. "Cognitive Science: The Newest Science of the Artificial," *Cognitive Science*, Volume 4, 1980, pp. 33-46.

[35] Society for Management Information Systems, *Proceedings of the Eleventh Annual Conference*, Chicago, Illinois, September 10-13, 1979, pp. 45-56.

[36] Sprague, R. H. and Watson, H. J. "MIS Concepts Part I," *Journal of Systems Management*, Volume 26, Number 1, January 1975, pp. 34-37.

[37] Sprague, R. H. and Watson, H. J. "Model Management in MIS," *Proceedings, 7th National AIDS*, Cincinnati, Ohio, November 5, 1975, pp. 213-215.

[38] Sprague, R. H. and Watson, H. "A Decision Support System for Banks," *Omega—The International Journal of Management Science*, Volume 4, Number 6, 1976, pp. 657-671.

[39] Sprague, R. H. and Watson, H. J. "Bit by Bit: Toward Decision Support Systems," *California Management Review*, Volume XXII, Number 1, Fall 1979, pp. 60-68.

[40] Sprague, R. H. "Decision Support Systems—Implications for the Systems Analysts," *Systems Analysis and Design: A Foundation for the 1980';s*, Elsevier-North Holland, New York, New York, 1980, in press.

[41] Sprague, R. H. "A Framework for Research on Decision Support Systems," in *Decision Support Systems: ; Issues and Challenges*, Fick, G. and Sprague, R. H. (eds.), Pergamon Press, Oxford, England 1981, in press.

[42] Sutton, J. "Evaluation of a Decision Support System: A Case Study with the Office Products Division of IBM," San Jose, California: *IBM Research Report FJ2214*, 1978.

[43] Sutton, J. A. and Sprague, R. H. "A Study of Display Generation and Management in Interactive Business Applications," *IBM Research Report No. RJ2392*, IBM Research Division, San Jose, California, November 9, 1978.

[44] TYMSHARE. 20705 Valley Green Driver, Cupertino, California, 95014.

[45] Wagner, G. R. "DSS: Hypotheses and Inferences," Internal Report, EXECUCOM Systems Corporation, Austin, Texas, 1980.

[46] Will, Hart J. "Model Management Systems," in *Information Systems and Organizational Structure*, E. Grochla and H. Szyperski (eds.), Walter de Gruyter, New York, New York, 1975, pp. 467-483.

READING 32

Organizational Strategies For Personal Computing In Decision Support Systems

article by
RICHARD D. HACKATHORN
and PETER G. W. KEEN

Phenomenon of Personal Computing

Decision Support Systems (DSS) are interactive computer based aids designed to assist managers in complex tasks requiring human judgment. The aim of such systems is to support and improve a decision process.

Early implementations of DSS were constructed using interactive timesharing on large-scale computer systems [13]. These developments were largely stimulated by MIT's Project MAC, which provided the individual user access to computing power for the first time. The technique of timesharing pointed toward a human-machine symbiosis that promised vast increases in our ability to handle complex problems [10].

More recently, small-scale "personal computer systems," such as the APPLE II computer, have been used directly by both technical and nontechnical individuals for a wide variety of information processing activities. With these small-scale systems, the user can exercise direct, personal control over all aspects of the technology [5]. These aspects include: equipment selection, software selection, software development, customization of applications, and data management. The emphasis is on the end user of the technology, acting as programmer, analyst, *etc.*—without role differentiation.

With the advent of personal computing, a different relationship is forming between the user and the technology. These differences occur both in the system usage and in the system development process. The growing body of conceptual and empirical work in the DSS area is relevant to understanding the impacts caused by personal

Source: Reprinted by special permission of the *MIS Quarterly*, Volume 5, Number 3, September 1981, pp. 21-26.

computing. This article explores these differences by starting with the concepts of Decision Support that address issues of how individuals can make effective use of computer technology.

Using Personal Computing for Decision Support

A coherent conceptual framework for Decision Support is emerging [8, 14]. Practitioners are extending the conceptual work of researchers by building innovative systems to support a range of managerial tasks. There are many case studies of DSS usage in organizations [1, 9].

Most of the conceptual literature on DSS has emphasized the individual manager. Its theoretical base comes from cognitive psychology; its focus is on human problem solving rather than organizational decision making. Common phrases in DSS literature tend to be: cognitive style, individual differences, information overload, heuristic problem solving, *etc.* Terms such as information flows and organizational environments are usually absent. On the other hand, it is clear that practitioners are far more concerned with organizational issues. The systems that they need are built around activities that involve planning and coordination. Therefore, while DSS theory prescribes a system to support a manager's budget *decision*, the DSS practitioner is building a system to support the organization's budget *process*.

Another issue is the requirement for a detailed understanding of the manager's decision making process prior to building the DSS. Unlike Operations Research, Management Science, and most of traditional Management Information Systems, Decision Support is based on descriptive paradigms of decision making, rather than prescriptive or rationalistic ones. An axiom of Decision Support has been that a DSS builder cannot improve the decision making of the manager unless the builder has a detailed understanding of that decision making. However, Personal Computing provides the opportunity for a manager to *directly use* the technology for Decision Support in a natural way, not dependent on another's notions of the decision making process.

The Challenge of Personal Computing

At its simplest level, Personal Computing can be viewed as a hobby [7, 12]. It is true that a significant percentage of sales of small-scale computers are to individuals rather than corporations, for entertainment rather than to perform some utilitarian function. Another portion is also to individuals but is used for performing a specific task, much in the same mode as a pocket calculator. These individuals could be performing tasks within the home or within a self-employed situation. In all of these cases, the use of Personal Computing has been very successful, especially when analyzed from a cost/performance standpoint.

Personal Computing has been driven by technological developments, and hence, has lacked a clear direction in its evolution. Decision Support can make several contributions to strengthening the directions of Personal Computing:

1. **Application**—What to do with the technology? Decision Support research contributes a clear distinction between automation and support that eliminates much of the users' resistance to the idea of using computer technology.
2. **Development**—How to apply the technology? Decision Support research contributes an adaptive or evolutionary approach to system development, emphasis on dialogue as the interface between the user and system, and attention to the learning processes of the user about the problem domain.
3. **Integration**—How to combine with other kinds of support technology? Decision Support research has made progress in merging concepts from MS/OR and traditional MIS, such as the use of data *plus* model management.

The challenge of using Personal Computing comes when it is used within an organizational context. On the positive side, Personal Computing can produce increases in productivity. It is an effective technology to aid thinking and communication. There are commercially available software packages, such as VisiCalc from Personal Software, Inc., that can be used as very effective

DSS tools. Personal Computing has started to integrate and enhance many existing technologies to aid thinking—such as the telephone for communications, adding machine for calculation, dictionary for standards, and copier for memory.

On the negative side of using Personal Computing in organizations are several management control issues within the organizational context. First, there is the data integrity of the "corporate" data. Secondly, there is the certification of reports produced by personal systems as to whether they are based on valid corporate data. Thirdly, there is the coordination of information sources and uses.

Dependencies Among Tasks

To understand the role of Personal Computing, let us extend a frequently cited framework for DSS described by Gorry and Scott Morton [4]. This framework combines Simon's dimension of task structuredness (*i.e.*, structured, semi-structured, and unstructured) with Anthony's classification of managerial activities (*i.e.*, operational control, management control, and strategic planning). The framework does not accommodate notions of interactions among persons within an organizational context.

This article suggests that a third dimension—*task interdependency*—be added to the Gorry and Scott Morton framework. This new framework is illustrated in Figure 1. The dimension of task interdependency is best described by J. D. Thompson [15] in which he differentiates among three types of interdependencies:

1. **Independent**—A task is independent if a person can perform the task without interaction with other persons.
2. **Pooled**—A task is pooled if two or more people must interact in order to perform their respective tasks.
3. **Sequential**—A task is sequential if several people can only perform their respective tasks in a certain sequence in which the outputs of one task must be used as the inputs to another task.

Note that this classification forms three levels of increasing task interdependence in terms of flexibility of interaction. In other words, independent tasks have more flexibility than pooled tasks, and pooled tasks have more flexibility than sequential tasks.

Using the Thompson dimension, the nature of Decision Support can be separated into three distinct, but interrelated, components:

1. **Personal Support** focuses on a user or class of users in a discrete task or decision (*e.g.*, setting a price, selecting a stock) that is relatively independent of other tasks.
2. **Group Support** focuses on a group of individuals, each of whom are engaged in separate, but highly interrelated, tasks (*e.g.*, office activities).
3. **Organizational Support** focuses on an organizational task or activity involving a sequence of operations and actors (*e.g.*, developing a divisional marketing plan, capital budgeting).

When the task is independent, the problem solving activities do not involve interdependencies and the manager can reach a decision through private analysis, though when the choice has been made, it must be communicated to others. In this situation, Personal Support (PS) may improve the quality of the decision by a system designed for direct and individual use by the manager.

Pooled interdependency requires face-to-face negotiations and discussions. No single unit can carry out its work without interaction with others. This suggests an additional type of support—Group Support (GS). This allows users to develop joint plans through a system that provides fast response, easy exploration of alternatives, and explanation of analysis.

When the task involves sequential interdependencies, each individual's activities must mesh closely with other people's. Any computer based aid will be used as much for a vehicle for communication and coordination as for problem solving. For example, Organizational Support (OS) for budgeting will need to provide facilities for storing disaggregated, detailed budgets at the department level, then allowing these to be

Figure 1 DSS Framework with Task Interdependency

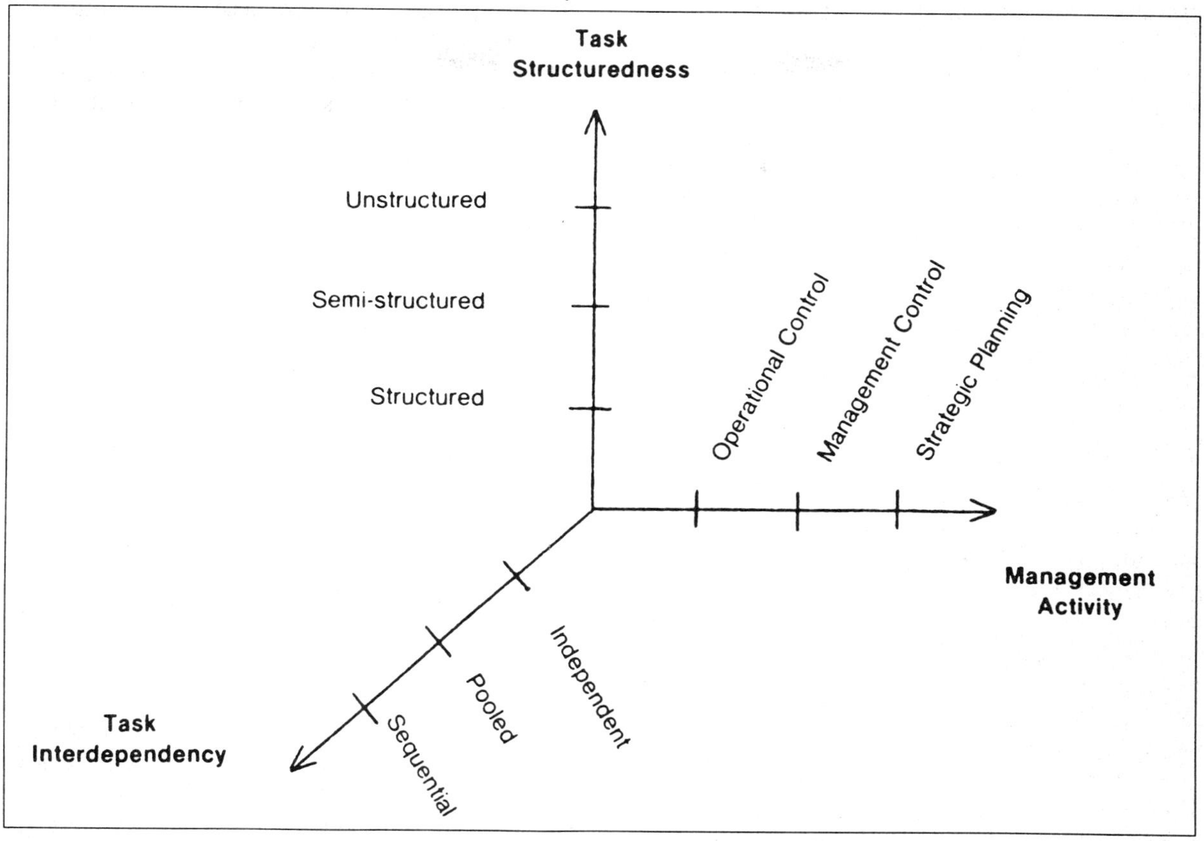

integrated first by division and finally for the company as a whole.

The benefit of the above distinctions among Personal Support, Group Support, and Organizational Support is the focus on interactions among persons based on tasks. The point is that these interactions generate dependencies or constraints on outcomes of the decision making process. Thus, the dimension of task interdependency has important implications for the application and development of DSS, as discussed in the next section.

Implications for Personal Support

Task interdependency has several implications for using technology to support decision making. There are many successful implementations of DSS that have assisted managers as effective tools for personal problem solving. An obvious characteristic of these implementations is that the user was able to make the complete decision without much interdependencies with other actors or units. Examples of this situation are the cases of BRANDAID [11] and PROJECTOR as described in Keen and Scott Morton [9]. By contrast, several DSS have been recently developed to support the planning activities of large organizations. For example, the EIS by Berger and Edelman [2] dealt with decision support of personnel information across an entire division of RCA.

Personal Support may be used within an Organizational Support context. For example, each manager may use a small-scale system to help set the department's marketing budget, and the divisional staff can then coordinate and integrate these budgets using Organizational Support. In both cases the aim of the system is to support the user's decision making; the key difference is that Personal Support focuses on a person, while the emphasis of Organizational Support is on an organizational process.

While the conceptual literature on DSS emphasizes Personal Support, several of the most successful applications of Decision Support involve Group Support, and more recently, Organizational Support. For example, the DSS built by Scott Morton [13] which facilitated marketing and production planning provides Group Support. It allowed managers from two departments to come together and use the system as a means of making tradeoffs, sharing ideas, and reaching a consensus.

There are at least a few DSS, designed for Personal Support, that have been difficult to institutionalize because the broader task actually involved sequential interdependency. For example, BRANDAID is a system that in one company substantially facilitated the development of marketing plans by individual brand managers [9]. Their plans are integrated at the next level of the organization. This requires a different process of analysis. In particular, the problem of "cannibalization," *i.e.*, the plan for an individual brand results in sales being gained at the expense of another of the company's products, had to be addressed. In addition, the managers responsible for integrating the plans required brand decisions to be presented in a format that was not directly compatible with the outputs from BRANDAID. This whole process needs Organizational Support in addition to, or in place of, this Personal Support. Clearly, current DSS research needs a much stronger exploration of organizational, rather than cognitive, issues [6].

This concept of different support types seems important, and not only in relation to DSS. For instance, Office Automation (OA) is a packaging of some differentiated technical building blocks similar to DSS. The conceptual literature on OA emphasizes Personal Support, such as text-editing, document preparation, and electronic mail. There are tools that assist and appeal to professional "knowledge workers." Practitioners are, however, far more concerned with Organizational Support. They wish to use OA to streamline order entry operations, coordinate decentralized activities, and improve the efficiency of large-scale administrative functions. The literature on OA does not seem to acknowledge the differences in priority and focus.

In summary, a DSS relies on a careful selection of application, descriptive understanding of use, and dèfinition of improved effectiveness. The type of DSS to be built depends on the clear identification of the task interdependencies involved. A successful DSS is a personal tool for stimulating creativity. It may not, however, lead to "more effective" decisions if these decisions are determined through a process that goes beyond the individual, and if the DSS is designed to provide only Personal Support.

Organizational Strategies

Personal Support, in and of itself, is only valid if the tasks involved are discrete and independent of other tasks. In other words, Personal Support may be inappropriate as a component of organizational tasks because of the issues of managerial control and data integrity. The mixture of Personal Support and Organizational Support is possible if an explicit management policy of the acquisition and usage of personal computing technology is adopted.

First, standardization is needed for the personal use of *data*. For instance, direct update to the corporate database by personal systems should not be allowed. The usual organizational transaction processing should maintain the corporate database. Also, personal databases should remain personal. Corporate reports should be certified as being valid. Extracts from the corporate database should be controlled on a "need to know" basis. See Clemons [3] for elaboration on data management for decision support.

Secondly, Personal Support tools should be facilitated in a systematic manner. In particular, the economic aspects of personal support tools, such as microcomputers versus timesharing, should be analyzed. Important and generic tasks that are oriented toward individuals and are discrete should be identified. Further, the purchasing of the Personal Support technology should be controlled uniformly based on appropriate consideration of duplication, servicing, *etc.*

Thirdly, good "end user" software packages should be disseminated throughout the organization.

An example is the VisiCalc package from Personal Software, Inc. for simple financial calculations. Other software packages should include application generators and flexible database managers. Leverage for the individual manager should be achieved through the technical staff.

Conclusions

This article presents the challenge that Personal Computing poses to developing Decision Support Systems in organizations. The potential for using Personal Computing for Personal Support within organizations is great, but serious problems with managerial control may result if Personal Computing becomes involved in Organizational Support activities.

This difficulty is best understood in terms of task interdependency that makes clear distinctions among Personal Support, Group Support, and Organizational Support. Organizational Support, if it is to be consistent and effective to the organization, depends on managerial control in ways that Personal Support does not. These concerns should not impede efforts to apply Personal Computing to Personal Support as long as the boundaries of this Personal Support are explicitly delimited.

Discussion Questions

1. How does this article further clarify the distinction between an MIS and DSS?
2. Why is end-user computing (or personal computing) particularly critical to the effective use of DSS in decision making?
3. Describe the Gorry and Scott Morton framework. Why is it useful?
4. What dimension does Hackathorn and Keen add to the Gorry and Scott Morton framework?
5. What is the implication of the new framework for various types of DSS support?

References

[1] Alter, S. A. *Decision Support Systems: Current Practices and Future Challenges*, Addison-Wesley, Reading, Massachusetts, 1979.

[2] Berger, P. and Edelman, F. "IRIS: A Transactions-Based DSS for Human Resources Management," Proceedings of the Conference on Decision Support Systems, *Database*, Volume 8, Number 3, Winter 1977, pp. 22-29.

[3] Clemons, E. K. "Data Base Design for Decision Support," *Proceedings of the International Hawaii Conference on System Sciences*, January 1981, pp. 580-588.

[4] Gorry, G. A. and Scott Morton, M. "A Framework for Management Information Systems," *Sloan Management Review*, Volume 13, Number 1, Fall 1971, pp. 55-77.

[5] Hackathorn, R. D. "Research Issues in Personal Computing," *Proceedings of the National ACM Conference*, Washington D.C., December 1978, pp. 547-551.

[6] Huber, G. P. "The Nature of Organizational Decision Making and the Design of Decision Support Systems," *MIS Quarterly*, Volume 5, Number 2, June 1981, pp. 1-10.

[7] Isaacson, P., Gammill, R. C., Heiser, R. S., Osborne, A., Tesler, L., and Warren J. C. "The Oregon Report: Personal Computing," *IEEE Computer*, Volume 11, Number 9, September 1978, pp. 86-97.

[8] Keen, P. G. W. "Adaptive Design for Decision Support Systems," *Database*, Volume 12, Number 1/2, Fall 1980, p. 15-25.

[9] Keen, P. G. W. and Scott Morton, M. *Decision Support Systems*, Addison-Wesley, New York, New York, 1978.

[10] Licklider, J. C. R. *Libraries of the Future*, M.I.T. Press, Cambridge, Massachusetts, 1965.

[11] Little, J. D. C. "BRANDAID," *Operations Research*, Volume 23, Number 4, May 1975, pp. 628-673.

[12] Niles, J. M., Gray, P., Carlson, F. R., and Hayes, J. "The Personal Computer and Society: A Technology Assessment," Presented at the National Computer Conference, Anaheim, California, June 1978.

[13] Scott Morton, M. *Management Decision Systems: Computer Based Support for Decision Making*, Division of Research, Cambridge, Massachusetts, 1971.

[14] Sprague, R. H. "A Framework for the

Development of Decision Support Systems," *MIS Quarterly*, Volume 4, Number 4, December 1980, pp. 1-26.

[15] Thompson, J. D. *Organizations in Action*, McGraw-Hill, New York, New York, 1967.

READING 33

A Contingency Model For User Involvement in DSS Development

article by
ROBERT I. MANN and
HUGH J. WATSON

A Contingency Model For User Involvement in DSS Development

Decision support systems (DSS) are one of the most recent and interesting developments on the computer-based information systems scene. They are used by marketing managers to support brand decision making [14], by bank officers for financial planning and controlling purposes [20], by physicians for diagnosis and therapy [6], by academic administrators for academic planning [8], and for a growing number of other applications. While there is no universally accepted definition for DSS, the following one is used here:

Source: Reprinted by special permission of the *MIS Quarterly*, Volume 8, Number 1, March 1984, pp. 27-37.

> *A decision support system is an interactive system that provides the user with easy access to decision models and data in order to support semistructured and unstructured decision-making tasks.*

This definition is compatible with those suggested by others [14, 22].

While definitions are useful, they often fail to "tell the whole story." Such is the case with DSS and explains why some scholars prefer to discuss DSS characteristics rather than definitions. For example, Sprague has suggested that a DSS [21]:

- tends to be aimed at the less well structured, underspecified problems that upper managers typically face;
- attempts to combine the use of models or analytic techniques with traditional data access and retrieval functions;
- focuses on features which make them easy to use by noncomputer people in an interactive mode; and

- emphasizes flexibility and adaptability to accommodate changes in the environment and the decision making approach of the user.

These characteristics enhance understanding of the DSS term as it is used in this article.

A number of practitioners and scholars have stressed that a DSS requires a somewhat unique development approach. Names such as heuristic [4], iterative [21], adaptive [11], and L'Approache Evolutive (evolutionary) [5] have been suggested. Advocates of these development approaches point out the difficulty, if not impossibility, of establishing DSS specifications without a trial-and-error process. Unlike transaction-oriented applications which are relatively well defined and not subject to rapid environmental changes, decision support systems often serve users who are, at least initially, unsure of their specific information needs. Furthermore, these needs may change over time as the environment changes. Consequently, the user tends to be more involved throughout the DSS development process than with most other systems.

Adding to the attention given to these new development approaches has been the emergence of DSS generators such as IFPS, EIS, XSIM and EMPIRE. These software packages have aided the development of decision support systems in many organizations. In some cases they have made it feasible for the user to develop his or her own DSS with little or no outside assistance.

It has been pointed out that as a given field in management matures, universal principles develop into contingency approaches. Schonberger has suggested that this is true of MIS design [18]. Based on our observations of systems which satisfy the DSS definition and characteristics given earlier, the same applies to DSS design. Our purpose is to provide a broader perspective of the role of the user in DSS development by providing a contingency model which describes the variations in the systems which we have observed.

The contingency model will be developed in the following way. First, the organizational personnel who may become involved in the creation of a DSS and their potential roles will be reviewed. Then, three DSS case studies which illustrate the range of potential user involvement in the development of a DSS will be presented.[1] Next, a tentative contingency model suggested by the MIS and DSS literature will be given. Finally, a refined contingency model which accurately describes the role of the user in the three DSS case studies will be presented and discussed.

Organizational Personnel and Roles

A variety of organizational personnel can become involved in the development of a DSS. Sprague has described them as the user, intermediary, DSS builder, technical supporter and toolsmith [21]. For our purposes, it is more efficient to describe the organizational personnel as user, intermediary and technician. Each category is differentiated by characteristics such as who they are, their potential DSS role, their knowledge and skills, and their location in the organization's structure.

Users

A user can be either a manager or a staff specialist (e.g., corporate planner, marketing researcher, or production planner). This is the person who benefits from the output provided by the DSS. Users can vary from managers with little knowledge and/or interest in computer technology to staff specialists with extensive computer training. Consequently, some users build and operate their own DSS while others have no hands-on contact with the DSS. A common denominator is that users are organizationally located where the decisions are made.

Intermediaries

Many organizations employ personnel with data processing, management science, and functional area skills to serve as information analysts. Often such personnel are MBA graduates with a Management Information System (MIS) specialization. They frequently serve as a liaison between the data processing group and a functional area or as an in-house consultant to a functional area. Their role in a DSS may be to build and/or to operate it for a user. Most commonly, an intermediary is organizationally located in a functional area, but some organizations are creating separate DSS groups and an intermediary may be housed there [22]. Sometimes a DSS is created by a consultant who may also be categorized as an intermediary.

Technicians

Data processing (e.g., programmers, systems analysts, and database administrators) and MS/OR personnel may become involved in the creation of a DSS. At one extreme they may assume the primary responsibility for building the DSS. At the other extreme, they may play only a minimal role (e.g., placing a DSS generator on a computer system). Technicians tend to have highly specialized skills in areas such as computer science, statistics, and mathematics. They are organizationally housed in units such as data processing and management science.

Three DSS Case Studies

The roles of users, intermediaries and technicians in developing a DSS can vary considerably. This can be seen in the three following case studies of decision support systems developed at Southern Railway, LTV, and General Dynamics.

Computer-Assisted Dispatching at Southern Railway

In 1976 Southern Railway began development of a computer-assisted dispatching system which became operational in 1980. The system contains two subsystems which are oriented toward slightly different functions. The dispatch management system handles the traditional dispatching activities of the rail system. It shows the current status of trains on a CRT, performs record keeping on train activity, and accepts "switch" and "signal" setting decisions from the train dispatcher. The meet-pass system provides the decision support capabilities of the system. Using data from the dispatch management system and a sophisticated branch and bound model, the system suggests dispatching plans designed to minimize train delay time. The dispatcher can either accept the suggested plan or explore other alternatives through the system's "what if" capabilities.

The computer-assisted dispatching system was developed by the management science group at Southern Railway. Specifications for the system changed relatively little during its development. At points in the development process, future users of the system were brought in to test a prototype of the system and to make suggestions for change. The length of the development process was substantial, requiring 10 man-years and encompassing a time span of 4 years. The system was configured using DSS tools rather than with a DSS generator. Existing DSS generators were not considered appropriate for this application.

The computer-assisted dispatching system is used by several organizational levels of the operations group at Southern Railway. Train dispatchers use the system continuously as part of their job of determining the dispatching plan for trains in the system. The chief dispatcher monitors the system continuously to insure that trains are dispatched effectively. The superintendent of operations employs the system for status reporting and reviews of previous operations. The system also generates summary reports on train and dispatching operations for middle management.

The Like Center Model at LTV

In 1981 the LTV Corporation was trying to decide whether or not to sell the Like Center, which is one of the largest downtown office buildings in Dallas, Texas. Because of the large number of variables, interactions among variables, possible conditions, and limited time in which to perform an analysis and arrive at a decision, management decided to construct a model to assess the building's future value and to support the decision making process.

The model was developed by the upper-level manager responsible for exploring the sale decision and by a financial analyst. The manager worked closely with the analyst in defining the model and the analyst created the model using Interactive Financial Planning System (IFPS), a DSS generator. Three weeks were required to develop the final model. The model allowed the manager to explore "what if" questions about the future value of the building and to "goal seek" conditions which would be necessary in order for a specified objective to be realized.

The model was used by the analyst under the direction of the manager or by the manager directly from 5 to 20 times per week while the sale decision was being considered. Based on the analysis performed by the model, a recommendation to sell the building was made, and was accepted by upper management.

Price Analysis at General Dynamics

In 1979 the corporate pricing department at General Dynamics developed a price analysis system. A major use of the system is to support the evaluation and approval of all proposals relating to pricing. This occurs in both the evaluation of prices to be paid for individual and component parts by General Dynamics, and for the sale of finished products by General Dynamics. The price analysis system provides answers to "what if" questions about the impact of price changes and decisions, uses linear programming to suggest optimal pricing decisions, and has a goal-seeking capability which identifies the price required to realize a prescribed goal.

The price analysis system was developed in the corporate pricing department with no external assistance. Development of the system required only one week, but occasional modifications continue to be made. The system was developed using Executive Information Services (EIS), a DSS generator, which is available on the Boeing Computer Services (BCS) timesharing network. Leading the development effort was the head manager of pricing who was the driving force in terms of both concept and hands-on development.

The price analysis system is used by all managers and staff analysts in the corporate pricing department. When information is needed quickly, a manager can operate the system personally, or can delegate the task to a staff analyst. The system is used on a daily basis.

Comments

These case studies illustrate the dramatically different degrees of user involvement in the development of a DSS. In the case of the computer-assisted dispatching system at Southern Railway, technicians were almost wholly responsible for its development. Users only made suggestions for change based upon experiences with a prototype. In the Like Center model at LTV, an intermediary with guidance from the user built the DSS. Finally, the price analysis model at General Dynamics was developed by users without outside assistance. These three cases actually illustrate three points along a continuum. All points along the continuum require some degree of user involvement, but this can vary from low to moderate to high.

It should be noted that we are primarily concerned with the user involvement dimension. A more detailed study might investigate various points in a three dimensional space with user involvement as one axis, intermediary involvement the second axis, the technician involvement the third axis. With this schema one could investigate the situation where the development of the DSS is largely the responsibility of technicians and intermediaries with little to moderate involvement by the users. This might be the case where an organization's database management system (requiring the technician's skills) and a DSS generator (requiring the intermediary's skills) are needed or used in the creation of a DSS. Such a situation would correspond to point A in Figure 1. Another situation, corresponding to point B in Figure 1, is where the user and intermediary work as a team creating the DSS with no technician involvement.

Utilizing the three dimensional schema, points 1, 2, and 3 in Figure 1 represent the projection to the user axis of the points representing Southern Railway, LTV, and General Dynamics, respectively.

A Tentative Contingency Model

For each of the cases discussed earlier the users considered their DSS to be successful. No attempt was made to empirically measure success. For that reason we consider this proposed model to be descriptive in nature, rather than normative. Nevertheless, the development of a descriptive model may be considered a first step toward the ultimate development of a prescriptive model.

Figure 1 Personnel Involvement Space for DSS Development

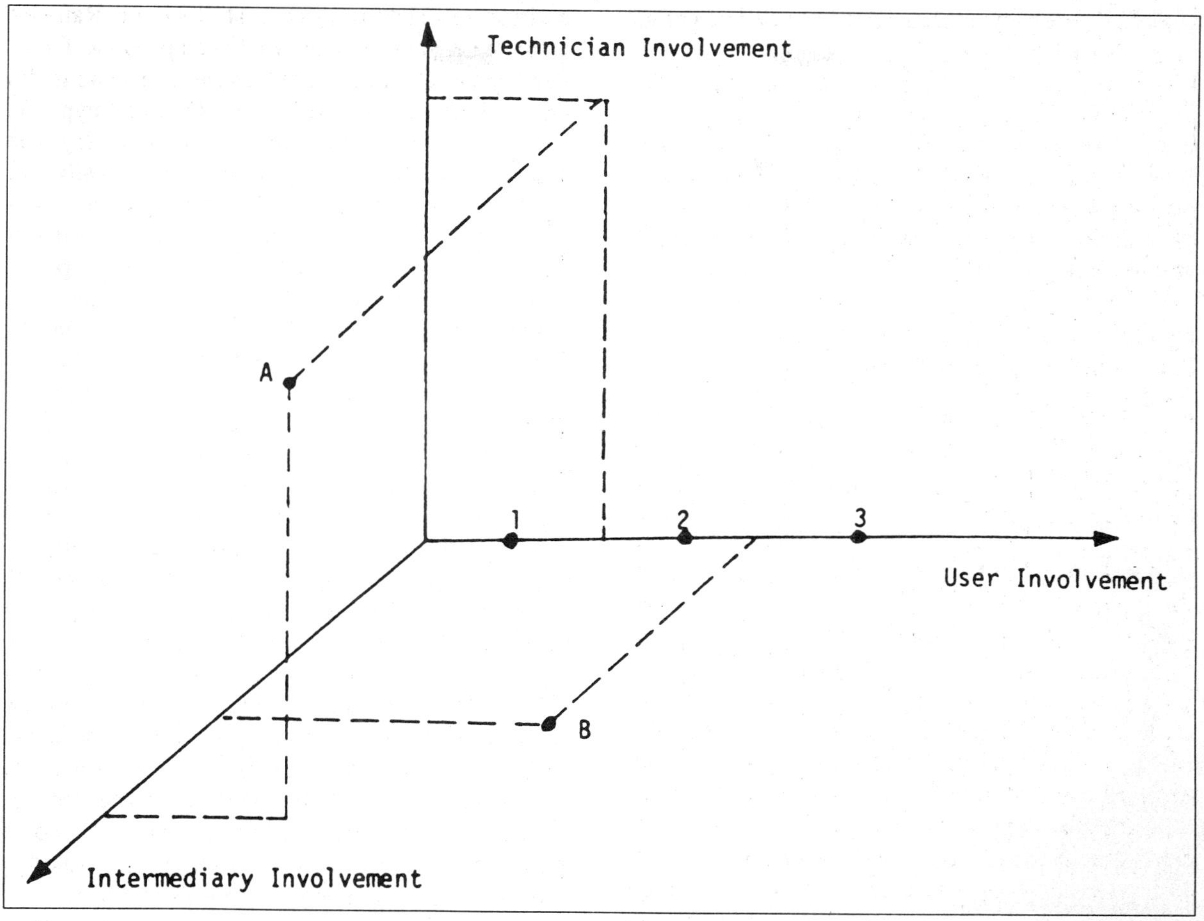

Consider the model

$$U = f(T_1, T_2, T_3, T_4, S_1, D_1) \quad (1)$$

where U is the extent of user involvement in the development of a specific DSS and

T_1 is the nominal level of management activity;
T_2 is the nominal level of task structuredness;
T_3 is the nominal level of task interdependence;
T_4 is the nominal level of task repetitiveness;
S_1 is the nominal level of user cognitive style;
D_1 is the nominal level of available DSS technology.

Note that T_i represents task technology factors, S_i represents social factors, and D_i represents DSS technology factors.

Task Technology Factors

Schonberger [18] has recommended a contingency approach to MIS design in which the desired level of user involvement depends on Anthony's [1] levels of management activities and Simon's [19] classification of decision structure. The Schonberger contingency model is an extension of the Gorry and Scott Morton [9] framework which hypothesizes that the attributes of the information needed by the decision maker depend upon the level of management activity and the degree of structure inherent in the decision process.

This hypothesis is partially supported by the findings of MacIntosh and Daft [17] in which evidence is submitted showing that task understanding and task variety are related to information attributes. Since task understanding and task variety are directly related to the degree of task repetitiveness, this model is extended to include task repetitiveness in order to differentiate between the *ad hoc* and institutional decision support systems described by Donovan and Madnick [7].

Finally, we include Thompson's [23] classification of task interdependence as suggested by Hackathorn and Keen's [10] and Sprague's [21] extensions of the Gorry and Scott Morton model. Table 1 illustrates the dimensions of task technology.

With the exception of Schonberger, each of the cited authors has focused on the impact of task technology variables on the information requirements. Our contingency model, and, implicitly, Schonberger's model, requires an additional link; one between a system's information requirements and the involvement of users in the development of that system.

To the best of our knowledge, no empirical work has been done to establish this link. However, its presence was certainly recognized by Gorry and Scott Morton when they stated that "these (decision support) systems may best be built by people other than those currently involved in the operational control systems area. The requisite skills are those of model building based on close interation with management, structuring and formalizing the procedures employed by managers, and segregating those aspects of the decision process which can be automated" [9, p. 65].

Table 1 Dimensions of Task Technology

Dimension	Categories
Management Activities	Operational Control Management Control Strategic Planning
Task Structuredness	Unstructured Semistructured Structured
Task Repetitiveness	*ad hoc* Institutional
Task Interdependence	Independent Pooled Interdependent Sequential Interdependent

The linkage is illustrated in Figure 2. With respect to equation (1), we would specify the following relationships.

$$U = g(R), \qquad (2)$$
$$R = h(C),$$

thus

$$U = gh(C) = f(C)$$

where

U is, as before, the extent of user involvement;
R is the set of required information attributes;
C is the set of contingency variables specified in (1).

Social Factors

If we hypothesize a link between the level of user involvement and information attributes, we must include problem-solver characteristics in our model. Lucas [16], Benbasat and Taylor [3], and Barriff and Lusk [2], among others, have investigated the relationship between information attributes and the decision maker's cognitive style. The results of these investigations have been mixed; nevertheless we include the user's cognitive style in our tentative model.

DSS Technology Factors

Finally, it seems reasonable to suggest that a direct relationship exists between the level of available DSS technology and the extent of user involvement in the development of the system. Here we refer to the taxonomy suggested by Sprague [21] as DSS tools, DSS generators, and specific DSS's. The specific DSS is the end product of the design process. We are more concerned with the nature of the software available to create this end product.

DSS generators are user-friendly software

Figure 2 Causal Linkage Determining User Involvement in DSS Development Process

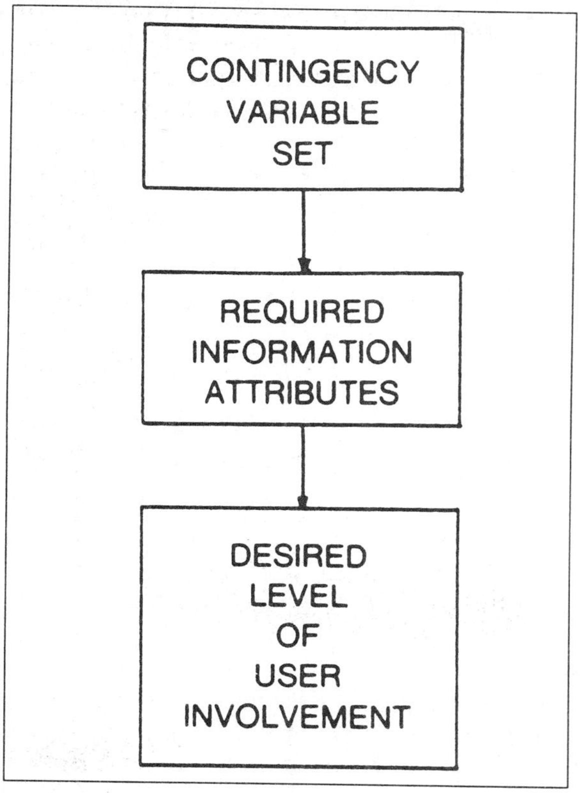

packages that combine a set of capabilities which facilitate the development of a specific DSS. Since these generators require minimal user training, we would expect to see greater user involvement in the system development process when one or more DSS generators are available.

DSS tools, on the other hand, are the basic software elements typically used by trained systems personnel to develop traditional management information systems, DSS generators, and specific decision support systems. These tools include programming languages, statistical analysis packages, mathematical programming packages, and database management systems. Their use requires extensive specialized training, and thus we would expect to see a relatively smaller ratio of user involvement in the design process where only the basic tools are available.

A Revised Contingency Model

The contingency model can be revised using observations from the three case studies. Table 2 gives a summary of the DSS case studies in terms of these development factors.

The Southern Railway system was developed by an operations research group using DSS tools, and with a minimum of end user involvement. The system is used on an ongoing basis for operational control by line operations personnel and by low and middle level managers. Each end user generally utilizes the system independently of other users and is held responsible for the outcome of decisions which are made. Only occasionally are pooled interdependent decisions made by a dispatcher working with a superior.

The LTV application was developed by an intermediary with the active involvement of the upper level manager responsible for making a single, strategic disposition decision. The intermediary used a DSS generator to build the system, and the manager used the system and reached a decision independent of other management.

The General Dynamics system was developed entirely by end-users utilizing a DSS generator. The system is used on an ongoing basis for management control by staff specialists and by middle and upper level managers. Decisions are frequently made on a group basis after evaluating the output of the system.

The three cases discussed illustrate the range of user involvement in DSS design approaches. While the sample is limited, some tentative observations may be made concerning the predictive ability of the contingency variables on the degree of user involvement in the creation of a DSS.

Schonberger [18] claims that the level of user involvement increases directly with the level of management activity. Although the involvement of upper level management in the creation of the LTV Corporation DSS was considerable, it was less than the involvement experienced with the General Dynamics DSS. The summary data presented in Table 2 suggest that task interdependence and task repetitiveness have entered the picture. One might also suspect that upper levels of management would have less time to devote to system development than would middle level management. It would

Table 2 Summary of DSS Case Studies

Development Factor	**Southern Railway: Computer-Assisted Dispatching**	**LTV Corporation: Like Center Model**	**General Dynamics Price Analysis**
management activity	operational control	strategic planning	management control
task structuredness	semistructured	semistructured	semistructured
task interdependence	independent	independent	pooled interdependent
task repetitiveness	institutional	*ad hoc*	institutional
user cognitive style	unspecified	unspecified	unspecified
DSS technology	tools	generator	generator
user involvement	low	moderate	high

make more sense for intermediaries to play a larger role. It would also appear that higher levels of task interdependence encourage higher levels of user involvement. Tasks that are highly interrelated have less well defined information needs initially, and tend to evolve over time.

Our example of a system developed with a relatively low level of user involvement was also the sole example of a system developed using DSS tools. Since the skills required to build a specific DSS without the use of a DSS generator are primarily possessed by technicians and intermediaries, user involvement relative to the other two categories of personnel can be expected to be less. This should not be construed to mean that significant user involvement is not or should not be presented.

Finally, we observe that three of the contingency variables originally considered appear to lack significance in our limited sample. Task structuredness, in each case, lies between the extremes of structured and unstructured. Since most DSS's fall within these extremes, it may be that this important MIS contingency variable has little explanatory power for DSS.

Task repetitiveness appears to have no consistent relationship to user involvement, with institutional systems occurring at both ends of the involvement spectrum. The cognitive style of the user was not explicitly measured. Since DSS's emphasize flexibility and adaptability to the decision making approach of the user, and since researchers have yet to conclusively establish a relationship between cognitive style and information attributes, we will disregard this variable in the revised model.

The proposed model of user involvement in the development of a specific DSS is presented in Figure 3 and in the following equation:

$$U = f(T_1, T_3, D_1) \quad (3)$$

where U, T_1, T_3, and D_1 are defined as in equation (1).

We suggest that this parsimonious model helps to describe user involvement in the decision support systems described earlier and may indeed be an adequate paradigm for DSS in general.

Conclusion

Decision support systems are currently being used in a wide variety of organizations for a diverse set of applications. The number of decision support systems will undoubtedly grow as decision makers seek support for the difficult decisions they face. This growth will be stimulated as the computer industry provides concepts (e.g., the information center) and products (e.g., DSS tools and generators,

Figure 3 Contingency Model for DSS Development

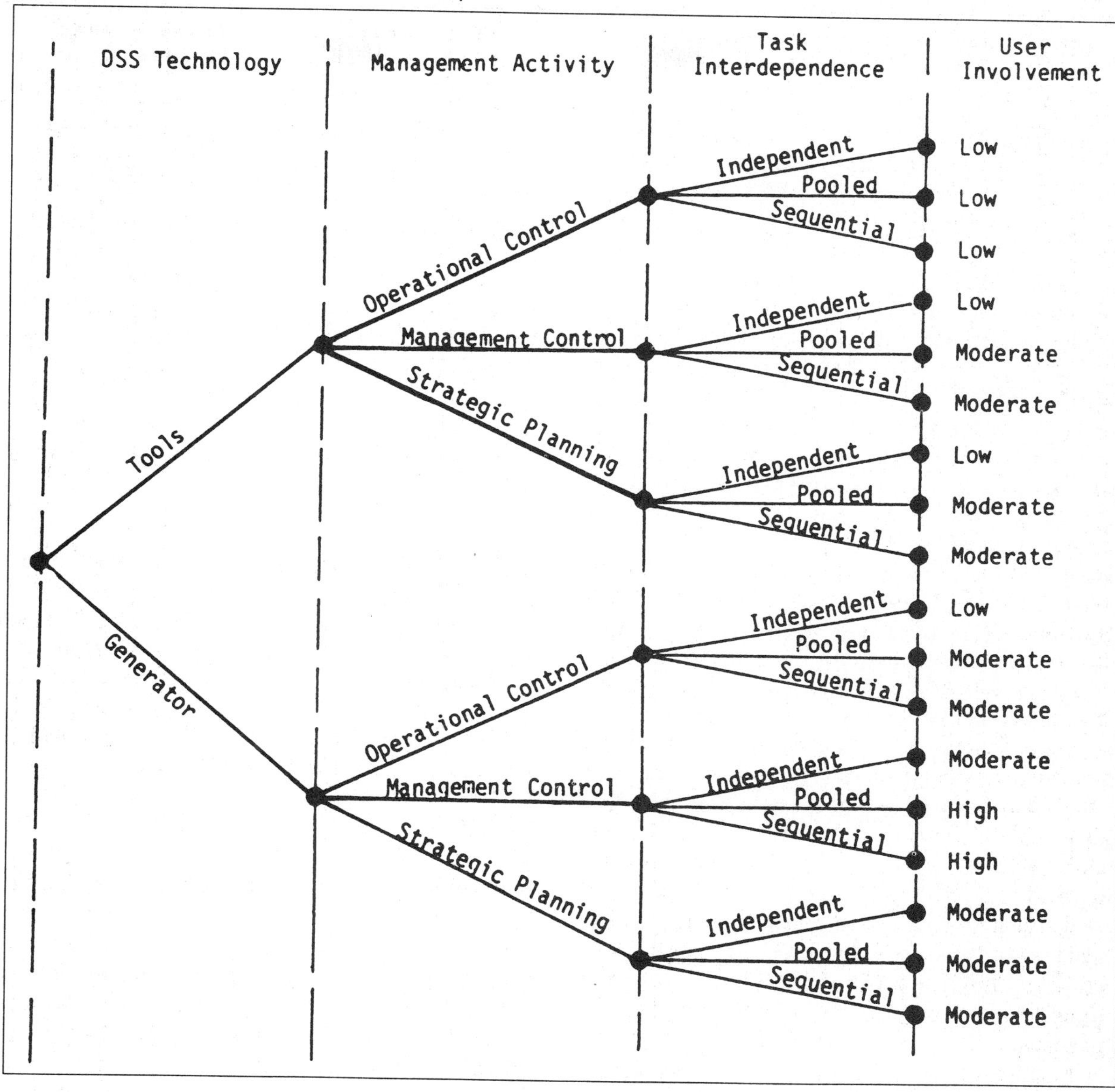

personal computers) that facilitate the development of decision support systems. These trends increase the importance of understanding the factors which affect the level of user involvement in the creation of a DSS.

Practitioners and scholars have suggested that decision support systems require a unique development approach. High levels of user involvement are commonly mentioned as being important to this approach. However, as the cases described in this article indicate, the level of user involvement can vary widely. A review of the literature and these cases suggest that the DSS technology (DSS tools and generators), the management activity (operational control, management control and strategic planning), and the nature of task interdependence (independent, pool interdependent and sequential interdependent) all interact to affect the level of user involvement.

The literature suggests that a user's cognitive style might be an important consideration when designing a DSS. If this is true, it might also be a factor which influences the level of user involvement in the creation of a DSS. None of the case studies presented in this article shed any light on this possibility. However, it is the authors' experiences that in most instances the user's cognitive style is not an item which is given much consideration when a DSS is designed. This is especially true when a DSS generator is used. DSS generators tend to accommodate the cognitive style of the users through the software system employed. Furthermore, this accommodation is growing as new and enhanced versions of DSS generators are released.

Our contingency model describes user involvement only as it relates to building a DSS. While this is an important focus, it should be recognized that there are other types of user involvement. In the case of a DSS which already exists, a user can become involved either through formal training or self-training. These types of involvement become increasingly important as an organization's decision support systems age and succeeding generations of users seek decision support.

A number of issues are left for future investigations. This study raised issues concerning the nature of the factors that may be important to the different types of user involvement. Earlier we discussed a three-dimensional model that included intermediary involvement and technician involvement as well as user involvement. What factors influence the involvement of intermediaries and technicians? Finally, and most importantly, we identified the descriptive nature of our model. How then, is involvement related to DSS success? Such questions suggest profitable directions for future research.

Discussion Questions

1. What are the three factors that determine the level of user involvement in the development of decision support systems?
2. How is this article related to the article by Hackathorn and Keen? What is different about this article?
3. Under what conditions would user involvement in the development of a DSS be high?

Footnotes

1. The authors would like to thank Jack T. Hogue at the University of Texas at Arlington for his help in documenting these case studies.

References

[1] Anthony, R. *Planning and Control Systems: A Framework for Analysis*, Division of Research, Graduate School of Business Administration, Harvard University, Boston, Massachusetts, 1965.

[2] Bariff, M. L. and Lusk, E. J. "Cognitive and Personality Tests for the Design of Management Information Systems," *Management Science*, Volume 23, Number 8, April 1977, pp. 820-829.

[3] Benbasat, I. and Taylor, R. N. "The Impact of Cognitive Styles on Information Systems Design" *MIS Quarterly*, Volume 2, Number 2, June 1978, pp. 43-54.

[4] Berrisford, T. and Wetherbe, J. "Heuristic Development: A Redesign of Systems Design," *MIS Quarterly*, Volume 3, Number 2, March 1979, pp. 11-19.

[5] Courbon, J., Drageof, J. and Jose, T. "L'Approache Evolutive," *Information El Gestion No. 103*, Institute d'Administration des Enterprises, Grenoble, France, January-February 1979, pp. 51-59.

[6] Davis, R. "A DSS for Diagnosis and Therapy," *DataBase*, Volume 8, Number 3, Winter 1977, pp. 58-72.

[7] Donovan, J. and Madnick, S. "Institutional and Ad Hoc DSS and Their Effective Use," *Data Base*, Volume 8, Number 3, Winter 1977, pp. 79-88.

[8] Dyer, J. S. and Mulvey, J. M. "An Integrated Optimization/Information System for Academic Departmental Planning," *Management Science*, Volume 22, Number 12, 1976, pp. 1332-1341.

[9] Gorry, G. A. and Scott Morton, M. S. "A Framework for Management Information Systems," *Sloan Management Review*, Volume 13, Number 1, Fall 1971, pp. 55-70.

[10] Hackathorn, R. D. and Keen, P. G. W. "Organizational Strategies for Personal Computing in Decision Support Systems," *MIS Quarterly*, Volume 5, Number 3, September 1981, pp. 21-27.

[11] Keen, P. G. W. "Adaptive Design for DSS," *Database*, Volume 12, Numbers 1 and 2, Fall 1980, pp. 15-25.

[12] Keen, P. G. W. and Scott Morton, M. S. *Decision Support Systems: An Organizational Perspective*, Addison-Wesley, Reading, Massachusetts, 1978.

[13] Kriebel, C. H. "The Future of MIS," *Infosystems*, Volume 19, Number 6, June 1972, pp. 18-19, 42ff.

[14] Little, J. D. C. "Decision Support Systems for Marketing Managers," *Journal of Marketing*, Volume 43, Number 3, Summer 1979, pp. 9-26.

[15] Lucas, H. C., Jr. *Toward Creative Systems Design*, Columbia University Press, New York, New York, 1974.

[16] Lucas, H. C., Jr. "Performance and the Use of an Information System," *Management Science*, Volume 21, Number 8, April 1975, pp. 908-919.

[17] MacIntosh, N. B. and Daft, R. L. "User Department Technology and Information Design," *Information and Management*, Volume 1, Number 3, 1978, pp. 123-131.

[18] Schonberger, R. J. "MIS Design: A Contingency Approach," *MIS Quarterly*, Volume 4, Number 1, March 1980, pp. 13-20.

[19] Simon, H. *The Shape of Automation for Men and Management*, Harper and Row, New York, New York, 1965.

[20] Sprague, R. H., Jr. and Olson, R. L. "The Financial Planning System at the Louisiana National Bank," *MIS Quarterly*, Volume 3, Number 3, September 1979, pp. 35-46.

[21] Sprague, R. H., Jr. "A Framework for the Development of Decision Support Systems," *MIS Quarterly*, Volume 6, Number 4, December 1980, pp. 1-26.

[22] Sprague, R. H., Jr. and Carlson, E. D. *Building Effective Decision Support Systems*, Prentice-Hall, Englewood Cliffs, New Jersey, 1982.

[23] Thompson, J. D. *Organizations in Action*, McGraw-Hill, New York, New York, 1967.

READING 34

Group Decision Support Systems: A New Frontier

article by
GERARDINE DESANCTIS
and BRENT GALLUPE

An exciting new concept is emerging in the area of decision support. This involves the development of computer-based systems for use by groups of people who are jointly responsible for making decisions. Known as "Group Decision Support Systems" (GDSS) they can be useful to committees, review panels, executive board meetings, task forces, and groups of managers who work together on either a regular or one-time basis. The precise design of a GDSS will vary depending on the proximity of group members to one another and the duration of the decision-making session. This paper presents an overview of the GDSS concept and explores issues related to the design, implementation, and study of these systems.

Source: Gerardine DeSanctis is with the Department of Management Sciences, University of Minnesota, Minneapolis, Minnesota and Brent Gallupe is with the School of Commerce, Queens University, Kingston, Ontario, Canada. This paper was supported by a research grant from the Association for Computing Machinery Special Interest Group in Business Data Processing and appeared in the Winter 1985 issue of *DATA BASE*.

Introduction

During the past decade, much attention has been given to the area of decision support systems by both industry and academia. The concept of a DSS as originally articulated by Gerrity (1971) involves "an effective blend of human intelligence, information technology and software which interact closely to solve complex problems." In theory this means that either an individual or a group of decision makers might benefit from a DSS. In practice, however, most systems have been designed for use by single decision makers. Although a DSS operating in a mainframe or micro computer environment might be available to many users simultaneously, the software itself accommodates the individual user faced with a particular decision for which he or she is responsible. Support of the individual decision maker undoubtedly is important for effective managerial functioning, but many organizational decisions are made by groups of people, particularly at the strategic or executive level. Moreoever, as organizations become increasingly complex, fewer decisions are made by single individuals (Gannon, 1979). Responsibility for organizational actions becomes diffused, resulting in more decision making that involves input from two or more individuals. These group decisions may also benefit from support by a computer-based information system.

A few researchers have acknowledged the need for a group-level focus in DSS (e.g., Hackathorn & Keen, 1981; Keen, 1984; Turoff & Hiltz, 1982). Huber (1984) recently presented some ideas regarding the design of information systems to support electronic meetings. But additional thought must be given to this perspective, particularly with regard to the definition of group decision support and issues related to the design and implementation of computer-based systems for use by groups. The purpose of this paper is to present a conceptual foundation for research and development of decision support systems for group-level decision making. We begin by defining the concept of group decision support systems (GDSS) and outlining the characteristics of these systems. Fundamental features of GDSS technology, including both hardware and software aspects, are described. Four "scenarios," or types of group DSS environments, are proposed. Finally, some specific questions in need of investigation by researchers are identified.

What Is a GDSS?

The concept of a "decision support system" has been widely discussed in the MIS literature. Although various definitions have been proposed, there appears to be general agreement that a DSS is an interactive computer-based system which facilitates solution of unstructured problems (Bonczek, Holsapple & Whinston, 1970; Neumann & Hadass, 1980; Sprague, 1980; Vazsonyi, 1978). The concept of "group decision support" builds on the now well-known idea of a DSS. A group decision support system (GDSS) is an interactive computer-based system which facilitates solution of unstructured problems by a set of decision makers working together as a group. Components of a GDSS include hardware, software, people and procedures. These components are arranged to support a group of people, usually in the context of a decision-related meeting (Huber, 1984). Important characteristics of a GDSS can be summarized as follows:

1. The GDSS is a specially designed system, not merely a configuration of already-existing system components.
2. A GDSS is designed with the goal of supporting groups of decision-makers in their work. As such, the GDSS should improve the decision making process and/or decision outcomes of groups over that which would occur if the GDSS were not present.
3. A GDSS is easy to learn and easy to use. It accommodates users with varying levels of knowledge regarding computing and decision support.
4. The GDSS may be "specific" (designed for one type, or class, of problems) or "general" (designed for a variety of group-level organizational decisions).
5. The GDSS contains built-in mechanisms which discourage development of negative group behaviors, such as destructive conflict, miscommunication, or "groupthink".

The definition of GDSS is quite broad and, therefore, can apply to a variety of group decision situations, including committees, review panels, task forces, executive/board meetings, remote workers, and so forth. Appropriate settings for a GDSS range from an executive group meeting which occurs in a single location for the purpose of considering a specific problem (such as a merger/acquisition decision), to a sales managers' meeting held via telecommunications channels for the purpose of considering a variety of problems (such as hiring of sales representatives, product offerings, and sales call schedules). Because the contexts of group decision making vary so greatly, it is useful to think of a GDSS in terms of the common "group" activities which it supports. The basic activities which occur in any group and which, therefore, are in need of computer-based support are: information retrieval, information sharing, and information use (Huber, 1984). *Information retrieval* includes selection of data values from an existing database, as well as simple retrieval of information (including attitudes, opinions, and informal observations) from other group members. *Information sharing* refers to the display of data to the total group on a viewing screen, or sending of data to selected group members' terminal sites for viewing. *Information use* involves the application of software technology (such as modeling packages for specific application programs), procedures, and group problem-solving techniques to data for the purpose of reaching a group decision.

The Technology of GDSS

A pictorial representative of a typical GDSS is shown in Figure 1. In this generalized model, a group of decision makers has access to a data base, a model base, and GDSS applications software during the course of a decision-related meeting. There is at least one computer processor, one input/output device, and one viewing screen. A "group facilitator" coordinates the group's use of the technology, and there is a flexible, friendly user-interface language available for use by the facilitator or each group member. As we shall see later, many different configurations of a GDSS are possible. However, the basic components of any GDSS include hardware, software, people and procedures. Each of these components is now considered in some detail.

Hardware

Regardless of the specific decision situation, the group as a whole, or each member, must be able to access a computer processor and display information. The minimal hardware requirements of the system include: an input/output device, a processor, a communication line between the I/O device and the processor, and either a common viewing screen or individual monitors for use in displaying information to the group. More sophisticated systems may contain I/O terminals or desktop computers for each group member, several central processors, long-distance communications equipment, and several large viewing screens. A design which allows each participant to work independently of the others, to publicly demonstrate personal work, and to see the work of other individuals and the group as a whole is preferred. Since "keyboarding" is a skill not totally accepted by managerial personnel in organizations, touch-sensitive screens or a facility to input handwritten communication (such as a graphics tablet) or voice communication may be desirable. Preferably, the viewing screen or monitors should be capable of displaying graphics and text, and should have color as well. Graphics can be used to summarize data or to display voting information in the group; color can be used to add attention value to the visuals or text which are displayed (Tullis, 1981). If a public viewing screen is used, it should be large enough to be seen by all members of the group. The screen would facilitate group discussion and take the place of flipchart or blackboard. It also could be used for video conferencing between subgroups in dispersed locations.

The amount of processing power necessary to support group decision making depends on the software being used, the number of members in the group, and the extent to which networking or teleconferencing are used. If the group members have microcomputers or workstations, then central processing can be used to manage communication among them and to store common databases, model bases, or applications software. With regard to communications, the requirements vary according to the setting in which the GDSS is used. In the confines of the traditional meeting room, hardwire links between an I/O device, a central processor, and display monitors or the public screen may be all that is necessary; more elaborate configurations might link microcomputers with one another and perhaps a central processor. For dispersed groups, a local area network, telephone lines, satellite, or microwave relay may be required to allow group members to communicate with one another. Electronic mail, computer conferencing, audio and video conferencing might also be integrated into the GDSS environment.

Software

The software components of the GDSS include a database, a model base, specialized application

Figure 1 A Model of a GDSS

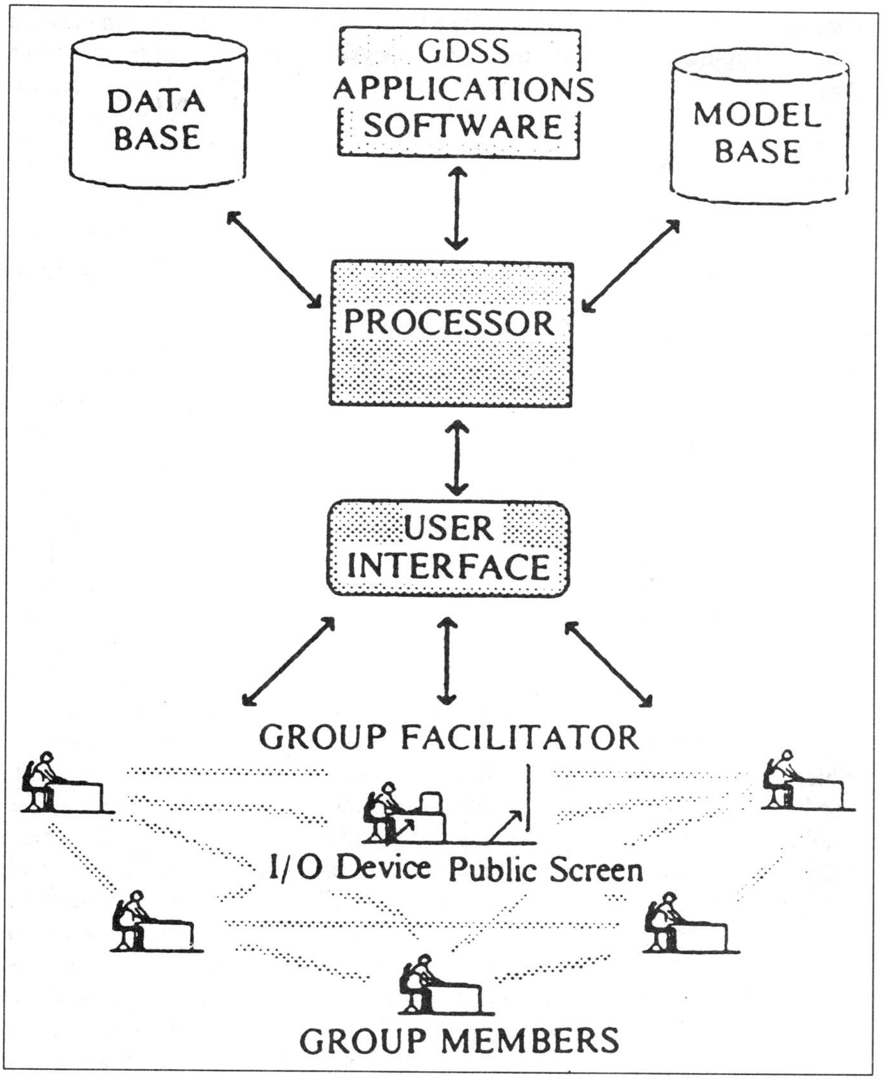

program(s) to be used by the group, and an easy-to-use, flexible user interface. Some highly specific GDSS systems may not require a database; for example, those that merely collect, organize, and communicate members' opinions about a problem. However, most sophisticated systems will include databases, along with model bases, very high-level languages for program writing, and interfaces with standard-managerial-level software (graphics, statistical/OR packages, spreadsheets, etc.). The GDSS software may or may not interface with individual DSS software.

The most distinguishing technological component of the GDSS is specially-developed applications software that supports the group in the decision process. The precise features of this software will vary extensively but may include the following:

Basic Features

• Text and data file creation, modification, and storage for group members

- Word processing for text editing and formatting
- Learning facilities for naive GDSS users
- On-line "help"facilities
- Worksheets, spreadsheets, decision trees, and other means of graphically displaying numbers and text
- State-of-the-art database management which can handle queries from all participants, create subschemas as necessary for each participant, control access to public, or corporate, database, etc.

Group Features

- Numerical and graphical summarization of group members' ideas and votes
- Menus which prompt for input of text, data, or votes by group members
- Program(s) for specialized group procedures, such as calculation of weights for decision alternatives; anonymous recording of ideas; formal selection of a group leader; progressive rounds of voting toward concensus-building; or elimination of redundant input during brainstorming
- Method of analyzing prior group interactions and judgments
- Text and data transmission among the group members, between the group members and the facilitator, and between the group members and a central computer processor

The GDSS software may be designed to support a specific decision or a class of decisions. In some cases the software will be built around a particular decision-making technique, while in other cases it will be more generalized. At the present time few GDSS software products are available. A great deal of development effort is needed before organizations will have a choice of systems for use in group decision making.

People

The "people" component of the GDSS includes the group members and a "group facilitator" who is responsible for the smooth operation of the GDSS technology when it is in use. The facilitator's role is a flexible one. He or she may be present at all group meetings and serve as the group's "chauffeur," operating the GDSS hardware and software and displaying requested information to the group as needed. On the other hand, the facilitator may be physically located in the MIS department or information center and act only on an on-call basis when the group experiences difficulties in using the technology. When the GDSS is first installed this person can be expected to be relied upon quite heavily to coordinate the group's activities and serve as the interface between the group and the technology. As group members become familiar with the technology and its use in their work, the facilitator's responsibilities may diminish, or even be eliminated.

Procedures

The final component of the GDSS consists of procedures which enable ease of operation and effective use of the technology by group members. These procedures may apply only to the operation of the hardware and software, or they may extend to include rules regarding verbal discussion among members and the flow of events during a group meeting. In the latter case, the GDSS may be designed to accommodate a specific group decision-making technique, such as the nominal group technique (Delbecq & Van de Ven, 1974), brainstorming (Osborn, 1957), the Delphi method (Dalkey, 1972), or social judgment analysis (Cook & Hammond, 1982).

Categories of GDSS: 4 Scenarios

An overview of the types of support systems which are needed for group decision making in organizations is presented in Figure 2. This framework emphasizes that the purpose and configuration of a GDSS will vary according to the duration of the decision-making session and the degree of physical proximity of group members. The cells that are shown should *not* be considered as independent of one another but as ends of two continua.

Scenario 1—Decision Room. The first scenario is similar to Gray's "Decision Room" (1981) and may be thought of as the electronic equivalent to the traditional meeting. The organization sets up a room (much like a

Figure 2 Framework: Group Decision Support

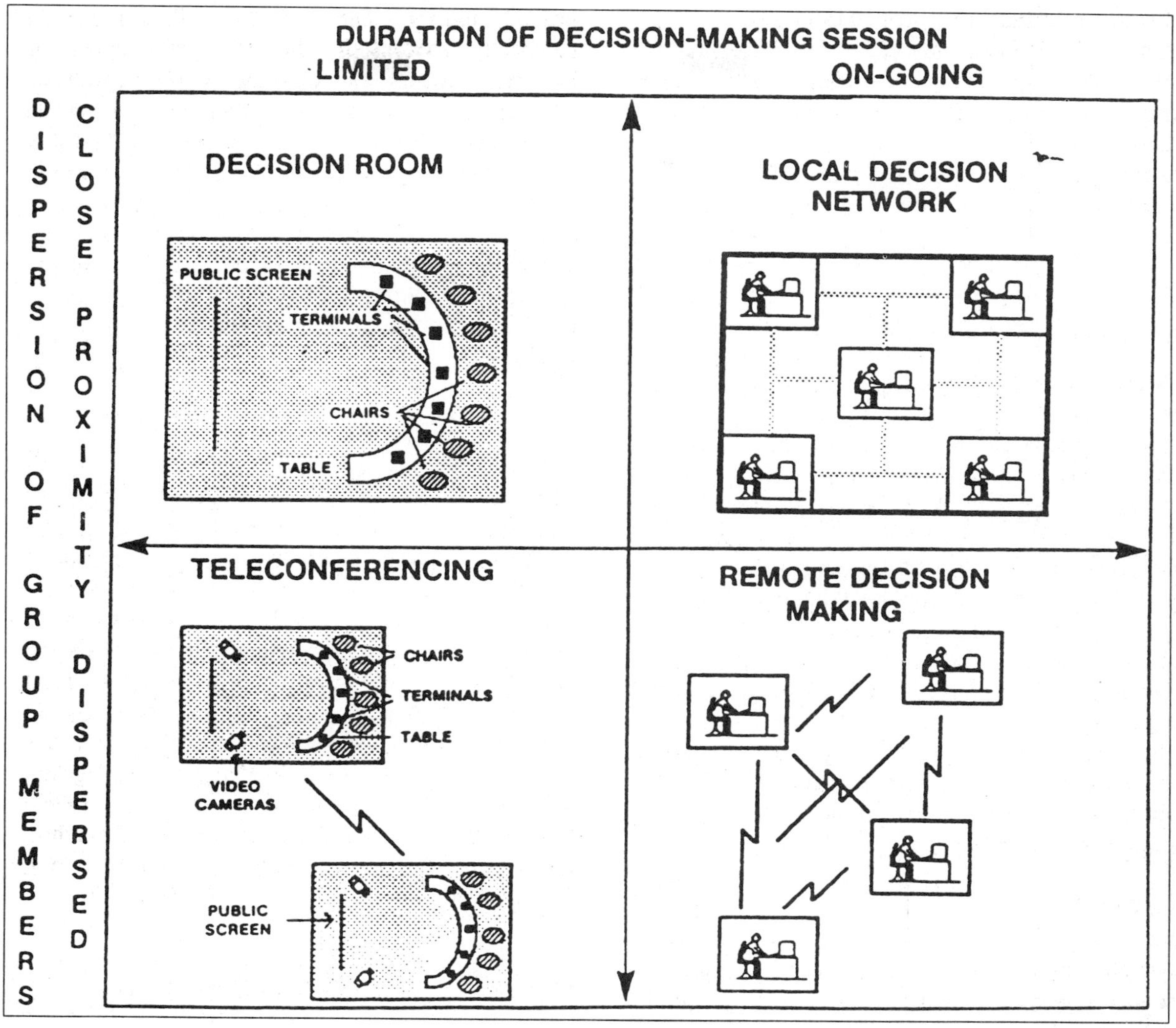

boardroom) with special facilities to support group decision making. Each participant is seated around a horseshoe-shaped desk facing a large screen. In a very simple configuration of a GDSS, only the group facilitator would directly interact with the computer. A more typical design would have a display monitor and terminal in front of each participant. Communications may be transmitted verbally or via computer messaging. The public display screen is used to enumerate ideas and to summarize and analyze data. Face-to-face verbal interaction combines with technology-imposed formalization to make the decision meeting more effective and efficient.

To illustrate this type of GDSS, consider a group of high-level managers who must decide on a marketing mix for the coming year. A variety of decision making approaches could be used, such as ordinary group process or Nominal Group Technique, but essentially the process would involve using the GDSS to show the decision makers the current situation in terms of markets and finances, etc., and to facilitate the generation and evaluation of ideas. There is continual interaction among group members, both verbally and through the communication network. Modeling software is used which is capable of being changed to adapt to the group's view of the problem. A number of alternative marketing mix strategies are tested via models and discussed before a specific strategy is selected.

Scenario 2—Local Decision Network. The GDSS may take on a somewhat different configuration in a setting in which a fixed group of decision makers, who work in close proximity to one another, must deal with certain problems on a regular basis. Rather than establishing a permanent "decision room" for group meetings, a "Local Decision Network" (LDN) could be developed to support group members as they work in their individual offices. Each decision maker would have a workstation, or what Dickson (1982) refers to as a "managerial support facility," located on their desk or worktable. A central processor would store common GDSS software and databases, and a local area network would provide member-to-member and member-to-central-processor communication. In the LDN environment group participants communicate via electronic messaging on the local area network. They can access common and private databases or DSS software as required, and view a "public screen" on their own CRT as needed. Decision makers engage in their day-to-day work and set up "group meetings" or conferences as needed. The approach offers greater flexibility in that the one-place/one-time constraint of Scenario 1 is removed. There is the disadvantage of removing face-to-face communication, but face-to-face meetings could be held when necessary.

As an example, consider a scenario found at the head offices of a large insurance company where decisions regarding corporate investments must be made on an ongoing basis. Financial managers, investment managers, and analysts are linked together in a local network that enables them to jointly make decisions in an interactive mode. GDSS software enables the group to analyze investments through the use of in-house investment models. The interactive nature of this "local decision network" provides group members with information on what the others are doing.

Scenario 3—Teleconferencing. A third type of GDSS is needed for groups whose members are geographically distant from one another but who nevertheless must come together for the purpose of making a decision. In this case two or more decision rooms are connected together by visual and/or communication facilities. For example, suppose that Company X, a large computer vendor with offices throughout the world, has decision rooms located in several major cities. Using teleconferencing technology, meetings could be arranged so that decision making could occur without all of the participants having to be in a single location. The approach is essentially the same as in Scenario 1 except that teleconferencing is used to supplement the communication component of the GDSS. Reduced travel costs (time, money, productivity loss), and flexibility in terms of time and duration of holding a meeting are advantages.

Scenario 4—Remote Decision Making. The fourth scenario is not yet commonplace but offers possibilities for the near future. Here there is uninterrupted communication between remote "decision stations" in a geographically dispersed organization which has a fixed group of people who must regularly make joint decisions. Part of the problem with scenario 3 is that meetings must be scheduled and coordinated in order to take place. This scenario, along with scenario 2, removes the constraint of meeting location and addresses the needs of decision makers who must work together on a regular basis.

An example of this scenario is a project development team of, say, 5 members which is dispersed in many parts of the country due to facilities at each location (or for whatever reasons that make it inappropriate to bring them all together in one place). Suppose that any changes made by one member will affect others members, and that a group decision is necessary before changes are made. In a remote decision making network, one group member could send a message to the CRT or workstation screens of the other members noting that a decision session is scheduled in, say, 10 minutes. All members are then informed of the problem and decisions to be made. A structured decision technique can be used by the group or a special GDSS application program may aid in the group decision. A long distance communication system, using telephone, microwave or satellite transmission, would provide communication among the group participants. Eventually, a decision is made by some voting scheme and each member notes the changes that must be made to his or her part of the project.

Summary

This section has presented a framework for categorizing group decision support systems. The precise configuration of a GDSS will vary considerably depending on the type of problem to be solved and the organizational context in which the problem is addressed. Nevertheless, there are design and implementation issues which are common to all categories of GDSS. Several of these are considered in the next section.

Design and Implementation Issues

Existing research on the dynamics of group decision making (Thibaut & Kelley, 1959; Cartwright & Zander, 1968; Bennis & Shepard, 1963; Hackman & Morris, 1975; Shaw, 1971; Guzzo, 1982) has several implications for the design and use of GDSS. Three design implications drawn from the group dynamics literature are first discussed, followed by a summary of implementation options available for GDSS.

First, *an objective of GDSS should be to encourage the active participation of all group members.* An overwhelming amount of research on groups indicates that the major barrier to effective group decision making is any condition which prevents the free expression of ideas in a group (Janis, 1972; Kolasa, 1975; Van de Ven & Delbecq, 1974). A number of events may lead to this problem. For example, group members may feel a strong pressure to conform, thus stifling the input of non-conforming ideas to the decision process, or certain members may regard other members as more competent or higher in status than they are (Hoffman, 1965). The extent to which group members are active in the group is also affected by the group's initial evaluation of the contributions of various members. People whose ideas are initially accepted by the group are likely to increase their participation, while those whose suggestions are rejected may withdraw from the discussion (Oakes et al., 1960; Pepinsky et al., 1958). The implication here is that a computer-based information system be configured to facilitate group members communication while reducing bias and prejudice, to enhance participation of all group members. An important feature of a GDSS may be the facility of allowing anonymous input and evaluation of ideas. In addition, GDSS software might have features that actively encourage group members to voice dissident opinions or play a "devil's advocate" role before a critical decision is made.

Second, *special accommodations are needed for groups who have no prior experience working together.* In groups that have never worked together before, members may feel uncertain about the exact goals of the group or their individual responsibilities and expectations. Newly-formed groups usually lack cohesion and a structure for operating (Klein & Ritti, 1980). The GDSS should support the group during the initial phases of group formation. For example, the group meeting room can be set up so that members are in a circle or semi-circle, facing one another. Terminals or other hardware should not obstruct their view or ability to easily interact verbally with one another. Special software might be used to query members on their expectations of how the group should function, and to feedback points of agreement and disagreement among members.

Third, *a useful feature of a GDSS would be to aid high-level management in selecting people to serve as group members for a given decision or problem.* All other things being equal, the quality of a decision made by a group is a function of the skills, abilities, and organizational status of the individual group members (Hoffman, 1965). Data from a human resource information system, or other similar source, could be used along with an appropriate model or selection criteria, to help structure the task of choosing people to serve on committees, boards, panels, or task forces.

Extensive developmental work is needed before decision support systems for groups become widely available and useful to organizations. At the present time only a handful of systems have been developed for in-house use by organizations or are available for purchase (Kraemer & King, 1984). Because of their relative novelty, the importance of careful pilot testing of these systems cannot be overemphasized.

Systems which fail to provide useful, easy-to-use facilities will quickly result in negative attitudes toward GDSS on the part of users. The role of attitudes in determining system success has been well documented (DeSanctis, 1984; Lucas, 1975; Robey, 1979; Swanson, 1974). We can anticipate that unrealistic expectations or frustrating experiences with GDSS on the part of even a few individuals could result in negative attitudes and poor use of these systems by decision-making groups.

With regard to installation, three options are possible (Huber, 1984): (1) install the system permanently at the user site; (2) rent the system on an on-call basis from the vendor; and (3) access the system remotely from the vendor site. Option 3 may be the best alternative today since option 1 is very costly and option 2 can be impractical. In years to come, however, option 1 may be the installation method of choice as GDSS systems become more sophisticated, more reliable, and less costly to organizations.

Research Issues

Because of the newness of the GDSS concept and the fact that so few systems have been implemented, the area is wide open in terms of theory development and empirical study. In this section we summarize what we see as the major research issues related to GDSS. Listed below are five major categories of questions which are in need of study.

I. GDSS Design

Gray (1981), Turoff and Hiltz (1982), Huber (1984), and the present authors have presented general guidelines regarding needed components, features, and configurations for GDSS. But many design issues remain unresolved for example:

- What human factors considerations are critical in the design of GDSS? (e.g., spatial arrangement of group members, size and location of public screens, accommodation of "informal" as well as "formal" communication between group members)
- What GDSS configurations are possible within each of the four major categories of GDSS (i.e., what are our choices)?
- What should be the differences in design between a "general" and "specific" GDSS?
- What is the best database design for group decision-making applications?
- What considerations are important in the design of a user interface for GDSS?
- How can a GDSS be interfaced with a DSS?
- What procedures should an organization follow when developing a GDSS in-house?

II. Appropriateness of GDSS

The framework for GDSS presented in this paper suggests that four types of systems are possible, depending on the proximity of group members and the duration of the decision-making session. Beyond these dimensions, what other factors are relevant in selecting an overall GDSS design?

- Given a group decision, are there situations or problems which cannot be expected to benefit from computer-based support? When should a GDSS not be used?
- What types of problems or settings are more appropriate for DSS as opposed to GDSS?
- How can an organization select a particular GDSS design?

III. Determinants of GDSS Success

Much of the research on DSS, and management information systems in general, has been devoted to identifying factors related to system success, where "success" is defined in many different ways. In the case of GDSS, some special measures of success may be required, such as: reduction in group conflict, degree of consensus, type of group norms which develop, and so forth. Important research questions include:

- What is a "successful" GDSS? What criteria are relevant here?
- What factors determine the success of a GDSS? Hardware configuration? Software design? Users' motivation? Top management support? etc.

• Will some types of GDSS be more successful than others?

IV. Impacts of GDSS

Our primary concern in decision support is to increase the efficiency or effectiveness of decision making (Keen & Scott Morton, 1978). But other outcomes may be of interest to organizations, such as the effects of GDSS on interpersonal communication patterns, decision confidence, or the cost of conducting meetings in the firm.

• How will use of GDSS technology affect group performance, particularly decision speed and decision quality?
• Will use of GDSS decrease the total number of meetings required to reach a decision in a group?
• Will there be more consensus in decision making following use of GDSS?
• Can use of GDSS improve a group's confidence in their decisions?
• How satisfied will users be with group decision support systems?
• Will GDSS make group decision-making less expensive for the organization?
• Will use of GDSS improve organizational communication and coordination?

V. Management of GDSS in the Organization

A final topic in need of study relates to the management of GDSS technology in the organization. When decision support systems first entered the corporate world, many firms created a subfunction within the information systems area which became responsible for development, implementation, and support of the systems. What will be the support requirements for GDSS?

• Who should be responsible for GDSS technolgoy?
• What are the planning needs for GDSS development and installation?
• What sort of training, maintenance, and other support will be needed for GDSS technology within the organization?

Conclusion

Computers are increasingly being used in organizations for group communication, and all indications are that this trend will continue (Hiltz & Turoff, 1978). With increasing pressure to use the group as a decision-making body in organizations, there is a need for development and study of computer-based systems to support group decision-making. The introduction of decision support technology for groups probably will not occur on a wide scale for quite some time. In this sense, GDSS may be an idea whose time has not yet come. But many of the components of such systems are available currently, and a few GDSS products have been produced. Systems developers and researchers should begin now to consider exactly how much systems can be designed, how they might be used in organizations, and what their impacts will be.

Discussion Questions

1. How does a GDSS differ from an MIS? from a DSS? from an expert system?
2. Describe the four general categories of GDSS presented in this article. Using your imagination, knowledge, and experience, list examples of potential situations in each of these categories.
3. Will GDSS eliminate the need for face-to-face meetings? Why or why not? Under what behavioral, managerial, and organizational conditions would a GDSS be suitable? Can you think of any potential disadvantages to using a GDSS?

References

Bennis, W. G., & Shepard, H. A., A theory of group development. *Human Relations*, 1963, (Summer), 415-457.

Bonczek, R. H., Holsapple, C. W., & Whinston, A. B., Computer-based support of organizational decision making. *Decision Sciences*, 1979, 10, 268-291.

Cartwright, D., & Zander, A. (Eds.), *Group Dynamics* (3rd Ed.) Evanston, Ill.: Row, Peterson, 1968.

Cook, R. L., & Hammond, K. R., Interpersonal learning and interpersonal conflict reduction in decision-making groups. In R. A. Guzzo (Ed.), *Improving group decision making*. New York: Academic Press, 1982, pp. 13-72.

Dalkey, N. C., *Studies in the quality of life: Delphi and decision making*. Lexington, Mass.: Lexington Books, 1972.

DeSanctis, G., A micro perspective of implementation. In R. Schultz & M. Ginzberg, *Implementing management science*. Greenwich, CT: JAI Press, 1984.

Dickson, G. W., Requisite functions for a management support facility. In J. G. Sol (Ed.), *Processes and tools for decision support*. North Holland, 1983.

Gannon, M. J., *Organizational behavior: A managerial and organizational perspective*. Boston: Little, Brown, & Co., 1979.

Gerrity, T. P., Design of man-machine decision systems: An application to portfolio management. *Sloan Management Review*, 1971 (Winter), 59.

Gray, P., et al. The SMU decision room project. *Transactions on the First International Conference on Decision Support Systems*, Atlanta, June 1981, pp. 122-129.

Guzzo, R. A. (Ed.), *Improving group decision making*. New York: Academic Press, 1982, pp. 13-72.

Hackathorn, R. D., & Keen, P. G. W., Organizational strategies for personal computing in decision support systems. *MIS Quarterly*, 1981, 5(3), 21-27.

Hackman, J. R., & Morris, C. G., Group tasks, group interaction process, and group performance effectiveness: A review and proposed integration. In L. Berkowitz (ed.g), *Advances in experimental social psychology*, Vol. 8. New York: Academic Press, 1975.

Hoffman, L. R., Group problem solving. In L. Berkowitz (Ed.), *Advances in experimental social psychology* (Vol. 2), New York: Academic Press, 1965, pp. 99-132.

Huber, G. P., Issues in the design of group decision support systems. *MIS Quarterly*, 1984, in press.

Janis, I. L., *Victims of groupthink: A psychological study of foreign policy decisions and fiascoes*. Boston: Houghton-Mifflin, 1972.

Keen, P. G. W., DSS & DP: Powerful partners. *Office Automation: Computerworld*, 1984, 19(07A), 13-15.

Keen, P. G. W., & Scott Morton, M. S., *Decision support systems: An organizational perspective*. Reading, Mass.: Addison-Wesley, 1978.

Klein, S. M., & Ritti, R. R., *Understanding organizational behavior*. Boston, Mass.: Kent Publishing, 1980.

Kolasa, B. J., Social influence of groups. In R. M. Steers & L. W. Porter, (eds.), *Motivation and work behavior*. New York: McGraw-Hill, 1975.

Kraemer, K. L., & King, J. L., Computer-based systems for group decision support. Unpublished Paper, University of California, Irvine, August 1984.

Lucas, H. C., Jr., Performance and the use of an information system, *Management Science*, 1975, 20, 908-919.

Neumann, S. & Hadass, M., DSS and strategic decisions. *California Management Review*, 1980, 22(2), 77-84.

Oakes, W. F., Droge, A. E., & August, B., Reinforcement effects on participation in group discussions. *Psychological Reports*, 1960, 7, 503-514.

Osborn, A. F., *Applied imagination*. New York: Scribner's 1957.

Pepinsky, R., Hemphill, J. K., & Shevitz, R. N., Attempts to lead, group productivity, and morale under conditions of acceptance and rejection. *Journal of Abnormal Social Psychology*, 1958, 57, 47-54.

Robey, D., User attitudes and MIS use. *Academy of Management Journal*, 1979, 22, 527-538.

Shaw, M., *Group dynamics*. New York: McGraw-Hill, 1971.

Sprague, R. H., A framework for the development of decision support systems. *MIS Quarterly*, 1980, 4(4), 1-26.

Swanson, E. B., Management information systems: Appreciation and involvement. *Management Science,* 1974, 21, 178-188.

Thibaut, J., & Kelley, H., *The social psychology of groups.* New York: Wiley, 1959.

Tullis, T. S., An evaluation of alphanumeric, graphic, and color information displays. *Human Factors,* 1981, 23(5), 541-550.

Turoff, M., & Hiltz, S. R., Computer support for group versus individual decisions. *IEEE Transactions on communications,* 1982, Vol. Com-30(1), 82-90.

Van de Ven, A. H., & Delbecq, A. L., The effectiveness of nominal, delphi, and interacting group decision making processes. *Academy of Management Journal,* 1974, 17, 605-621.

Vazsonyi, A., Information systems in management science. *Interfaces,* 1978, 9(1), 72-77.

SECTION ELEVEN

Artificial Intelligence and Expert Systems

READING 35

Expert Systems: The Promise of a Smart Machine

article by
HARVEY P. NEWQUIST III

Expert systems—computer programs that use human traits like logic to solve problems—will serve as the vanguard for the advance of artificial intelligence into the office. They are the first of AIs new-wave technologies that MIS managers must meet head on.

These systems, which sort and crunch knowledge much as traditional computers sort and crunch numbers, are better suited to office use and are further along in development than any other artificial intelligence technique.

Whether or not they are far enough along to bring most organizations strategic benefits remains open to question.

On one hand, about half of the companies in the Fortune 500 actively pursue expert system development, many with the hope of gaining an edge against competitors. Their interest gives the technology quite a bit of credence. Lockheed Corp., Digital Equipment Corp., General Electric Company, General Motors Corporation, and Boeing Computer Services Co., for example, all have either begun in-house development or invested in expert system companies. Very few firms in this league ignore the technology altogether.

On the other hand, few expert system success stories have come to the business community's attention. And, frankly, there aren't too many success stories out there.

Most large-scale expert system development remains just that—development. For the most part, innovators in the field are currently finishing up on prototype systems; they still face great obstacles on the road to full implementation. Whether or not expert systems will work their way into corporations on a narrower scale is not open to doubt. They will, and MIS managers must prepare themselves.

Generally, MIS departments are not taking the

lead in expert system development. Most shops are holding out until vendors can offer a link between the symbolic environment preferred for expert system development and the standard DP environments preferred for day-to-day business processing.

But while MIS waits for this missing link, users and top management will forge ahead with their own experiments in expert system use. DP professionals must keep abreast both of developments in technology and of action within their own organizations, so they can integrate expert systems into mainstream computing environments when the tools that allow this merger come to market.

Users will clamor for expert systems soon—and with good reason. Because expert systems accumulate, assimilate and analyze information with incredible speed, these tools can help managers make better decisions.

Given their attractiveness to users, expert systems will infiltrate most organizations department by department, much as personal computers did before them. The onslaught will begin early this year as packaged expert system applications come to market.

These applications are to expert systems what Lotus Development Corporation's VisiCalc® and Micropro International Corp.'s WordStar® were to business micros: They are task-specific tools that let end users exploit a technology on their own, without much help from programmers.

Another aspect of expert systems—their proficiency at solving narrow rather than broad problems—indicates that these tools will enter organizations haphazardly rather than following a centralized, controlled plan.

Initially, most organizations will develop expert systems as individual fringe projects, usually within a single department or division. These systems, built to perform well-focused tasks like oil exploration or aircraft engine analysis, will have little relation to the data base management sytems and financial reports generated within the MIS department.

Therefore, they will stay, for the time being, outside the umbrella of corporate DP.

Yet MIS managers must prepare to take part in the utilization of expert systems. As these systems become more prolific and take on tasks such as asset management and intelligent text retrieval that do affect the corporate host, MIS departments will need to assume control.

Right now, MIS managers would be well advised to learn all they can about expert systems. A keen understanding of what an expert system can and cannot do will help them identify appropriate trial applications; knowledge of expert system development methods and tools will help them carry out initial projects with success.

MIS managers must also keep watch for key technical advances in hardware, software, and communications. These developments will signal that the time to act with greater urgency has arrived.

Abilities and Limitations

An expert system embodies the traits that most people associate with artificial intelligence. It involves, for example, the use of logic (a decidedly human trait, though not one of which all humans seem capable) instead of relying on pattern matching and recognition (of which even insects are capable).

An expert system can respond to an operator's query about how to solve a problem and can give explanations for its answers. In addition, it can offer suggestions for alternative ways to solve the problem. The expert system operates by interpreting the query and comparing it against facts and rules that reside in a knowledge base—a collection of information gleaned from one or more experts in a given field and from supporting texts.

These abilities lend themselves to solving most business problems, but only if the problem's subject is tightly defined. As incident from expert system history illustrates the point. Some of the pioneers of artificial intelligence envisioned an expert system that would rival human chess masters. They succeeded in creating the system, but it could do one thing and one thing only—play chess. Human chess masters, of course, possess a broader range of skills.

Later, expert system developers brought forward more practical applications (see following chart). Even the most recent developments, however, share one trait with their early predecessor: Expert systems excel only at solving specific problems within specific areas of knowledge.

A Sampling of Real-World Expert Systems

Medicine

Mycin diagnoses and prescribes treatments for meningitis and bacteremia infections. The Stanford University Medical Experimental Computer Facility developed it in the mid-1970s.

Training

Steamer teaches naval officers, through simulation, the techniques needed to run a steam propulsion plant similar to those used in many ships. The U.S. Navy Personal Research and Development Center developed it in cooperation with Bolt, Baranek and Newman, Inc.

Computer Systems

Xcon configures VAX-11/780 computers on a daily basis for Digital Equipment Corp. DEC and Carnegie-Mellon University developed it and implemented it in June 1971.

Chemistry

Dendral estimates the molecular structures of unknown compounds by analyzing mass spectrographic, nuclear magnetic resonance and other data. Stanford University developed the system.

Engineering

Delta uses diagnostic strategies to identify and help maintenance workers correct malfunctions in diesel electric locomotives. The research and development center of General Electric Co. developed Delta.

Geology

Dipmeter Advisor estimates the subsurface geological structure of an area by analyzing dipmeter logs and other pertinent geological data. Schlumberger-Doll Research developed the program.

Expert systems have been developed here in the United States for many applications. The above list is a representative selection of those systems.

They perform with their highest degree of certainty and success in areas like aircraft engine analysis or medical diagnosis, where faults and failures can be traced to a defined origin. For example, an engine fails because of a hairline turbine fracture, and a stomach pain arises from a bleeding ulcer.

An expert system well suited to its task can even

outperform people. DEC's Xcon system, which the vendor designed to configure VAX machines for customers, operates with an average degree of success greater than 90 percent; human operators' success rates for the task average about 70 percent.

However, in broad, subjective problem solving, expert systems cannot compete. No expert system, for example, could offer suggestions on how to change a business' corporate culture, an endeavor governed by no criteria other than individuals' likes and dislikes. The solution for this kind of problem follows no universal pattern of logic; no expert system can discern it.

Clearly, it is important that companies choose appropriate areas for expert system development. Additionally, they must have the right reasons for going with expert systems in the first place (see Figure 1). Any organization that develops an expert system solely for the sake of bringing artificial intelligence in-house develops the system for the worst of reasons.

Successful systems usually center on an immediate need. The impending retirement of a corporation's sole expert in a given field, for instance, brings on the immediate need to preserve that person's expertise. An expert system can capture the individual's skill for continued and future use by the company or for training less skilled people who aspire to the individual's position.

A corporation may also employ an expert system to fulfill a perceived need to disseminate expertise from its highest echelons down to the level of junior employees. If the firm finds it unfeasible to spare the manpower to educate its junior members, an expert system may come in handy.

In such a case, the expert system will aid and assist experts and novices alike.

Once an organization identifies an application for its initial foray into expert system use, managers must take great pains to plan development efforts. Expert system projects have been known to fail, but proper planning ensures a better outcome.

Managers must take into consideration the huge amounts of time and money that a development project often entails. Before a project gets rolling, managers should make sure it will not run out of steam until it is completed. Technical and psychological factors determine whether an expert system development project will proceed to its envisioned end or whether it will fall apart midway.

Figure 1 Why Develop an Expert System?

√	To preserve knowledge that might be lost through the retirement, resignation or death of a company's acknowledged expert in any field.
√	To "clone" an expert mechanicaly so his knowledge can be disseminated.
√	To store information in an active form — a knowledge base — rather than a passive one — as textbook or manual.
√	To give novices an aid that will help them think the way more experienced professionals do.
√	To create a mechanism that is not subject to human failings like fatique and can hold up in positions where information must flow constantly.

No organization should develop an expert system merely to bring artificial intelligence in-house.

On the technical side, managers must make sure that an expert system—a computer program—can solve the problem at hand. Most problems are more complex than they seem on the surface. Overly complex problems lead to overly complicated programs, programs too cumbersome to run day to day.

On the psychological side, managers must see that every potential user feels comfortable with the idea of working with a computerized assistant (or even a mechanized peer). The fear that expert systems arouse in white-collar workers rivals that which robots stir in blue-collar workers. Generally, the interface between man and machine makes all the difference. A good interface encourages use—not annoyance or disdain.

System Shapes and Forms

Expert system development efforts follow one of three routes:

- A custom development route, whereby an organization starts from scratch, using AI development languages and highly skilled AI professionals to build a system to its specific needs.
- A semi-custom-development route, in which the organization starts with a commercially available expert system shell and fits that generic program to its specific needs by building a base of knowledge around the shell.
- A packaged route, whereby the organization installs a prewritten application and makes minor adjustments to fit its exact needs.

Resource constraints typically determine what route any one firm can follow. Custom-developed systems require the greatest amount of time, money, and professional expertise; systems that rely on packaged applications require the least. Expert systems developed around shells travel a middle ground.

Custom Expert Systems

To follow this route—the road most traveled by innovators in expert system use—an organization needs access to one of two pools of resources: a talented staff of AI professionals or a consulting firm with experience in knowledge engineering and development.

Once the organization secures the resources it will require and identifies a target application, it must follow a prescribed set of steps.

First, the development team must identify the expert or experts whose knowledge it wants to tap; next, team members must secure the expert's cooperation. Gaining this cooperation is not as easy as it may seem. The expert must agree to give of his time and his knowledge, both precious commodities.

In addition, top management must be willing to commit the expert's time to the project. This commitment is difficult because the person best suited for the project is usually the person the organization can spare the least in its daily operations. Management must view the sacrifice as a long-term benefit.

Once the development team secures both a willing expert and the support of top management, it sets out to codify the expert's knowledge. A specially trained professional known as a knowledge engineer carries out this step. The knowledge engineer begins by studying texts and otherwise immersing himself in the expert's domain. He then conducts one interview after another with the expert to try to determine how this skilled professional makes his decisions.

This process tends to fatigue both the knowledge engineer and the expert because most experts have trouble explaining why and how they make decisions. Yet, if the project is to succeed, they must articulate the subconscious rules of thumb, acquired instincts and gut feelings that the expert follows in his work. The expert and the knowledge engineer must overcome frustrations and mental blocks to create a comprehensive and tangible outline of what comprises expertise.

After the two professionals create the outline, the knowledge engineer translates it into computer code, usually in LISP. The knowledge engineer can, however, use any language—from BASIC to C—with which he is comfortable. The knowledge engineer then builds a structure known as the inference engine, which can correlate the outline's general rules to more specific pieces of knowledge that will get added to the system later.

In the next step, the knowledge engineer interviews the expert to uncover these specific pieces of information. He then enters the information into the system as a collection of facts, referred to as the system's knowledge base.

Combined, the inference engine and the knowledge base form the complete expert system. Once the two parts are in place, the expert and the knowledge engineer refine the system by running tests under hypothetical and actual conditions. They then compare the expert system's solutions with those that the expert comes up with on his own.

Elapsed time from the beginning of a custom development project to the implementation of the expert system often tops two years. Combined costs for knowledge engineering, software development, and hardware range from a few hundred thousand dollars to upward of $3 million.

Expert System Shells

The time and money an organization must spend on custom development pay off handsomely for solving business problems marked by either complexity or sensitivity. An organization that needs to solve a one-of-a-kind problem or keep its advances secret, in fact, has little choice but to build from scratch.

But very few people outside university laboratories and AI-specific companies are capable of creating expert systems from scratch, and many firms cannot justify the expense of hiring an outside consultant to do the work. Fortunately, vendors offer expert system development tools that allow businesses to test the waters without investing hundreds of thousands of dollars in custom development.

These tools—variously known as shells, inference engines, frameworks and structures—can cut system development time by one third to one half. They typically cost between $10,000 and $80,000.

All shells operate on the same time-saving principle: They pre-package an expert system's inference engine, freeing the knowledge engineer from the burden of creating this structure from raw code. To develop a complete expert system, the knowledge engineer need only add a specific knowledge base to the generic shell structure.

The process is much like that of adding a specific liquid to an empty cup. Once the liquid pours in, the cup becomes a new entity—a cup of coffee, perhaps, or a cup of tea.

By the same token, when developers fill an expert system shell with a specific base of knowledge, the shell becomes a new entity—a tax adviser expert system or a fuel tank maintenance expert system, for example.

Most shells are designed for implementation under a LISP environment on specialized hardware from DEC, Symbolics, Inc., Xerox Corporation, Texas Instruments, Incorporated, Lisp Machine, Inc., and other players in the AI market. The following are the top development tools for these machines:

- The Knowledge Engineering Environment from Intellicorp.
- The Automated Reasoning Tool (ART) from Inference Corp.
- S.1 from Teknowledge, Inc.
- The Knowledge Engineering Systems (KES) from Software Architecture and Engineering, better known as Software A & E.
- Knowledge Craft from Carnegie Group, Inc.

Other vendors offer shells that run under general-purpose DP architectures. Their various offerings bring expert system development capability to almost every popular machine—from DEC's Microvax to IBM's Personal Computer.

Different shells require varying levels of programming ability, but the most simple are quite easy to use. After just a few hours of experimentation, novices can get results out of most microcomputer shells.

Expert System Application Packages

In the last quarter of 1985, the artificial intelligence industry gave birth to a new market, one that will go even further than the shell market has gone toward enticing businesses to develop expert systems. That market is one of expert system application packages—off-the-shelf expert systems that are, quite literally, ready to run.

Expert system application packages will attract business users because of the great savings in development costs and time that they make possible. Outside of an initial purchase cost, these applications require almost nothing of a firm's DP management—neither time nor money.

End users merely define some parameters, and the programs are ready to run. An organization's programmers need not get involved at all; vendors typically provide all necessary maintenance and support. The end user must make sure, however, to input new parameters as the business environment changes. Otherwise, the system will not stay up-to-date.

The market for mainstream expert system application packages took a major leap a few months ago with the introduction of two new projects: Planpower, from Applied Expert Systems, Inc., and the Financial Advisor from Palladian Software, Inc.

Both packages are complete expert systems that help companies plan and control finances. Both are impressive in their scope, but their initial cost may drive prospective users away.

Planpower, designed as an assistant for financial planners, sells for $45,000. That price includes software and a Xerox 1186 workstation on which to run it. The program is written in LISP. Financial Advisor, aimed at corporate controllers, costs $46,000 without hardware. (Prices for multiple copies are substantially lower.) Like Planpower, it runs on LISP machines.

Other vendors sell expert system applications within niche markets:

- Fountain Hills Software, Inc. sells Fair Cost, a cost-modeling program for semiconductor components.
- Sterling Wentworth Corp. offers Planman, a financial planning expert system targeted at tax advisers.
- Ion Technology Services, Inc. markets Diagnostic Troubleshooter, an expert system for the maintenance of specialized semiconductor production equipment.

The niche applications listed above run on microcomputers and cost between $495 and $20,000. Persoft, Inc., another player in the expert system niche market, sells a mainframe-based application. Persoft's More, an expert system that qualifies names on mailing lists for direct mail campaigns, costs $375,000.

Eventually, expert system applications will provide organizations with all sorts of expertise that they cannot find in-house—everything from financial planning to factory scheduling. Certainly, companies that are not equipped to invest heavily in knowledge engineering will find these packages very attractive.

Eye on the Future

Today, the expert system market is worth approximately $75 million. Government and research efforts at custom design account for most of the figure, as much as two thirds. Fortune 500 companies' development efforts make up most of the remaining one third, and these companies primarily use shells. The applications market is too new to generate figures that indicate market penetrations.

The greatest obstacle to more widespread use of expert systems lies in the initial development environment. A huge percentage of expert system work proceeds under LISP, but very little traditional computing gets done in this language.

The jump from LISP to a central computing environment is not an easy one; at times, it is impossible. Usually, organizations must take the expert systems they develop under LISP and rewrite them in a language that is either more portable or more efficient.

For now, many companies employ their LISP machines for both development and delivery. But the expense of running developed systems on LISP machines makes this approach a burden. Most LISP machines cost between $55,000 and $85,000.

They are cost-effective as engineering workstations but not as general business machines.

To make matters easier for users, a number of AI vendors are now porting their products to C or offering interfaces that were designed to allow finished expert systems to run on microcomputers.

The vendors' efforts vary in scope and are at different states of readiness.

1. Lucid, Inc. is working to establish standard language protocols that allow LISP programs to run on different machines.

The firm currently offers Common LISP for a variety of hardware, including machines from Apollo Computer, Inc., Sun Microsystems, Inc., and Prime Computer, Inc.

2. Intellicorp and Gold Hill Computers, Inc. are developing networks that link LISP machines to machines with other architectures.

Last August, Intellicorp introduced PC-Host, which takes programs developed on LISP machines and downloads them for execution on IBM Personal Computers.

In November, Gold Hill began marketing GC-LISP Network, an Ethernet setup that connects IBM Personal Computers and Personal Computer ATs to each other and to Symbolics LISP machines. With it, users are able to develop systems on the LISP machines and then refine and run them on the microcomputers.

3. Software A & E, Teknowledge, and Inference are bringing C versions of expert system shells to market right now.

Software A & E has announced a C version of KES, and Teknowledge has announced C versions of both S.1 and M.1. (a micro-based shell). Inference expects to offer a C version of ART this summer.

Other vendors, notably Texas Instruments and Symbolics, are developing LISP chips, processors that can be embedded in standard computers so users can run LISP programs side-by-side with business applications on their corporate hosts. These chips should come to market sometime in 1987.

Problem Unsolved

The problem of connecting corporate computing environments with developed expert systems—those currently in the prototype stage at innovative Fotune 500 firms—remains unsolved. Any vendor that finally succeeds in making development environments compatible with IBM, DEC, Data General Corp., and other real-world machines will find itself incredibly successful.

So what now? Throughout 1986, innovative businesses will bring up expert systems, both as products of in-house development and as results of AI applications packages. And, despite the snail-paced implementation of expert systems into mainstream computing, the future looks quite bright.

Corporate commitment to artificial intelligence seems to be showing genuine results, especially in companies like Hewlett-Packard Company, Sperry Corporation, Boeing, and Lockheed that have invested in small AI companies in addition to creating in-house artificial intelligence facilities.

Although these large players may enter the AI business as vendors sometime down the road, their current efforts all focus on using expert systems to achieve a competitive edge in existing business concerns.

Managers in second-tier organizations would do well to watch the progress being made by firms on the cutting edge, keeping an eye, especially, on advancements that give expert systems immediate practicality.

In time, as the technology blossoms and more corporations try their hands at development, strategic benefits will arise for those who proceed wisely.

Discussion Questions

1. Why are expert systems currently outside of the umbrella of corporate MIS departments?
2. What is an expert system? How is the concept related to artificial intelligence?
3. Why would an organization develop an expert system?
4. How are expert systems developed?
5. What is the limitation of expert systems in solving business problems?

READING 36

Integrating Expert Systems and Decision Support Systems

article by
EFRAIM TURBAN
and PAUL R. WATKINS

Introduction

Expert systems represent one of the most exciting new developments in information technology. Emerging as a practical application of research in artificial intelligence (AI), expert systems combine knowledge of a particular application area with an inference capability, to enable the system to reach a level of decision making performance comparable to (or even exceeding) that of human experts in some specialized areas.

From applications in medical diagnosis, mineral exploration, and the configuration of computer hardware, expert systems (ES) are beginning to extend into business applications (e.g., [18, 28]). Prototype systems are now in use around the world. Major efforts are underway in industry, government, and science to exploit AI technology for practical use.

Although ES should be regarded as being in an embryonic phase, reports of successful commercial applications are increasing. The evolving ES industry, with several dozen competing companies, is projected to become a multi-billion dollar market before the end of the decade.[1]

One of the most interesting questions underlying this development is how to integrate ES programs into an existing (or evolving) management information system, and specifically into a decision support system (DSS), in order to create even more powerful and useful computer-based systems.

The objective of this article is to describe and discuss some issues of DSS/ES integration. Attaining this goal will be difficult for the following reasons. First, there is no consensus on what an ES is, and what constitutes a DSS [8]. Second, there are varying opinions regarding the

Source: Reprinted by special permission of the *MIS Quarterly*, Volume 10, Number 2, June 1986, pp. 121-136.

potential for integration of these technologies. This paper will summarize the current state of DSS/ES integration, and present two frameworks for integration; ES integration into the conventional DSS components, and ES as an additional component of DSS. Technical, behavioral and design issues of the integration will also be discussed.

Is an Expert System a Decision Support System?

A DSS is an interactive, computer-based information system that utilizes decision rules and models, coupled with a comprehensive database. In comparison, an ES is a computer program that includes a knowledge base containing an expert's knowledge for a particular problem domain, and a reasoning mechanism for propogating inferences over the knowledge base. In addition, an ES contains an explanation and justification mechanism which provides the user of the ES with some detail of the reasoning process.

Most existing expert systems are being used as *independent* computerized systems, advising users on a specific problem area. As such, they are considered by many to be intelligent DSSs (e.g., [6]). Further, ESs nicely fit the generic DSS framework, as developed by Bonczek, *et al.*, [4]. According to this framework, DSSs exhibit three major characteristics, all of which are present in ES. First, DSS aids a decision maker in solving unstructured (or semistructured) problems. Second, it possesses an interactive query facility. Finally, it uses an English-like dialogue language.

Additional support for this point of view can be found in Alter's [1] classification of DSS's into six major categories:

1. Retrieving a single item of information.
2. Providing a mechanism for *ad hoc* data analysis.
3. Providing prespecified aggregation of data in the form of reports.
4. Estimating the consequences of proposed decisions.
5. Proposing decisions.
6. Making decisions.

In contrast to this view of ES as an intelligent DSS, one can cite several fundamental differences between the two. Table 1 summarizes what we envision as the major differences between DSS and ES.

Specifically, the *objectives* of the system are different. The DSS supports the human who makes decisions; the ES operates as an advisor. DSS provides, in many cases, *institutional support* (e.g., when it is used for supporting long range planning), while ES acts as an advisor to an individual (or a group) in a narrow area.

The problem area attacked by DSS is broad and complex, while at least in the short run, ES is restricted to a much more structured and narrow domain. As a result, DSS is more suitable for dealing with ad hoc and unique situations, while ES is more suitable for providing advice on repetitive problem areas (such as diagnosis of malfunctions).

The database of DSS contains facts while its counterpart in ES, the knowledge base, contains, in addition to facts, also procedures for how to solve problems. ES, by definition, exhibits reasoning capability (e.g., deduction); while this capability is still limited, it is slowly being improved. DSS does not possess such a capability at all. Finally, some DSS provide limited explanation capabilities (e.g., *how* a solution is derived); ES, on the other hand, can also explain why a certain solution is recommended. Thus, ES has more powerful explanatory capabilities.

Additionally, ES typically involves a closed-system assumption, that is, the problem domain is circumscribed and the system's functions are confined to boundaries. In DSS contexts, the world is open. A DSS *must* be flexible and adaptive to meet the changing conditions in the environment and the evolving needs of the user [24].

The point to be made here is that even if an ES can be qualified as a DSS, it is certainly a special class of DSS with unique characteristics. Therefore, an ES can be a candidate for integration with a "traditional" DSS.

The Logic and Benefits of the Integration

Most existing ES and DSS are not integrated. ES

Table 1 Differences Between ES and DSS

Attributes	DSS	ES
Objectives	Assist human decision maker	Replicate a human advisor and replace him/her
Who makes the recommendations (decisions)?	The human and/or the system	The system
Major orientation	Decision making	Transfer of expertise (human-machine-human) and rendering of advice
Major query direction	Human queries the machine	Machine queries the human
Nature of support	Personal, groups, and institutional	Personal and groups
Data manipulation method	Numerical	Symbolic
Characteristics of problem area	Complex, broad	Narrow domain
Type of problems treated	Ad-hoc, unique	Repetitive
Content of Database	Factual knowledge	Procedural and factual knowledge
Reasoning capability	No	Yes, limited
Explanation capability	Limited	Yes

operate as independent expert consultation systems while DSS operate as support devices to decision makers. However, this situation is beginning to change. There is evidence (some of which will be presented later) that DSS/ES integrated systems are being developed and implemented at an increasing rate.

The benefits of the DSS/ES integration can be realized along several dimensions: ES contribution, DSS contribution, and the synergetic resulting from the DSS/ES combination. These benefits are summarized in Table 2, according to four specific areas: database, models, interfaces, and overall capabilities. The table also refers to research done in each area. Note that the benefits can be further classified into those that are achieved during the *development* of the system vs. those achieved during the system's *operation*.

The Synergy Between DSS and ES

In certain problem domains both ES and DSS may have distinct advantages that, when combined, can yield synergetic results. DSS typically gives full control to the decision maker regarding information acquisition, information evaluation, and the final decision. As research has shown, human judgemental biases may be present in complex decisions that are supported by a DSS (for a comprehensive review, see [13]). An ES, on the other hand, is free from acquisition, evaluation and judgemental biases, at least in the human sense (*if* the knowledge of the expert(s) is properly represented in the ES and *if* the ES is properly designed). The ES would serve to provide intelligence for a particular domain and would make a tentative decision. The decision maker could also utilize the DSS in the traditional sense and arrive at a tentative decision. The results of the ES and DSS could then be reconciled and evaluated, with a likelihood that the joint effort could produce better results than either approach independently. This approach is not necessarily constrained by the narrowness of the domain of the ES, since an operational DSS can also be domain specific, for

Table 2 Summary of Integration Benefits

	ES Contribution	DSS Contribution
Database and Database Management Systems (DBMS)	• Improves construction, operation and maintenance of DBMS [14] • Improves accessibility to large databases • Improves DBMS capabilities [14] • Permits symbolic representation of data	• Database provides to ES [14]
Models and Model base Management System	• Improves model management [2] • Helps in selecting models [9, 10] • Provides judgemental elements to models • Improves sensitivity analysis [9] • Generates alternative solutions [19] • Provides heuristics [12] • Simplifies building simulation models • Makes the problem structure incrementally modifiable • Speeds up trial-and-error simulation	• Provides initial problem structure [15] • Provides standard models and computatioins • Provides facts (data) to models • Stores specialized models constructed by experts in the model base
Interface	• Enables friendlier interface [11, 14, 27] • Provides explanations [15] • Provides terms familiar to user [12, 15] • Acts as a tutor [9] • Provides interactive, dynamic visual problem solving capability [3]	• Provide presentations to match individual cognitive styles
System Capabilities (Synergy)	• Provides intelligent advice (faster and cheaper than human) to the DSS or its user [20] • Adds explanation capability [12] • Expands computerization of the decision making process [9, 17]	• Provides experience in data collection • Provides experience in implementation [12] • Provides individualized advice to users to match their decision styles

example, DSS for routing vehicles in a textile company, or DSS for determining the allocation of IBM customer engineers to geographic territories.

While typical DSS support quantitative, mathematical, and computational reasoning, DSS should also be developed to support qualitative analysis based on methodologies such as analogical reasoning, pattern recognition, and content analysis. ES are particularly well suited for these types of methodologies, and thus may provide an important link to the DSS for providing more balance in supporting various types of decision processes.

ES Integration Into DSS Components

A DSS is composed of four basic components: a database, a model base, an interface and a user. Theoretically, one can add an ES (or several ES) to each component. The proposed integration diagrammed in Figure 1 is usually considered a one way integration; in other words, the ES supports the DSS. However, this connection can sometimes work in reverse.

ES #1. Expert System's Interaction with Database Management Systems. According to a study performed by Jarke and Vassiliou [14], ES can interface with DBMS in two ways. First, the ES can be used to improve the construction, operation, and maintenance of the DBMS. Second, the DSS can provide the expert system with essential business data.

DBMS usually offer some basic capabilities—for example, summarization or categorization of data.

Figure 1 Integration of ES Into All DSS Components

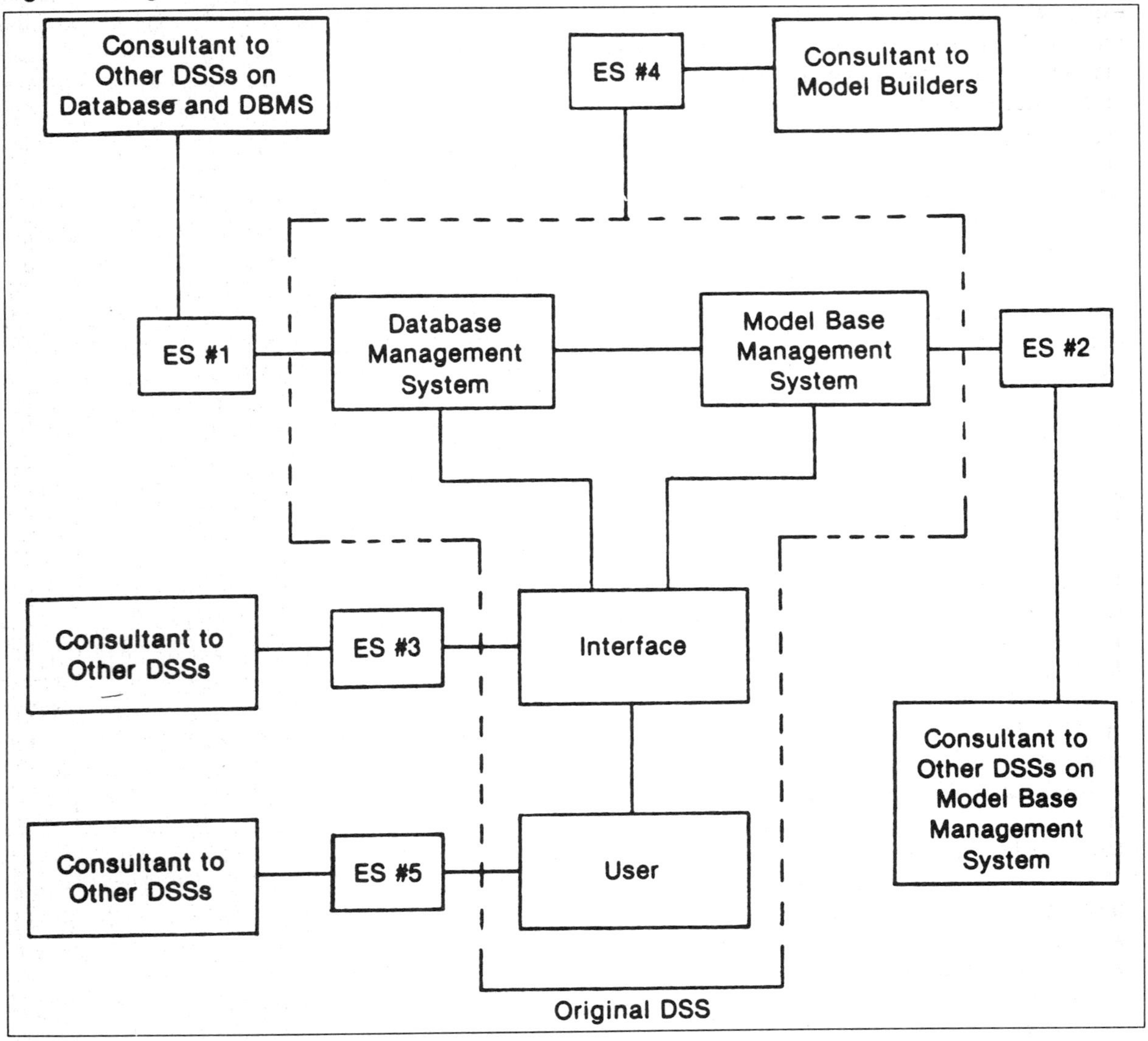

However, the user would often like more sophisticated capabilities, such as the ability to perform some reasoning operations on the data. The high level of semantic knowledge and deductive capabilities provided by ES could make the DBMS more user-friendly and more efficient to operate and maintain.

A human expert frequently uses databases. It is reasonable to assume that a computerized expert would need to do the same. Therefore, the ES should be able to access the DSS database to obtain factual knowledge. Another possible coupling would be the inclusion of judgemental data obtained from experts in a DSS database.

Jarke and Vassiliou [14] describe the process of coupling an ES with a DBMS in the system of a life insurance firm, a prototype project which is being developed at NYU.

ES #2. Expert System's Interaction with the Model Base. Human experts often use quantitative models to support their experience and expertise. For example, an expert may need to forecast the sales of a certain product or to estimate the future cash flow using a corporate planning model. Such a model can stand alone (meaning the expert can run the model on a computer as needed), or can be part of the DSS system used by several decision makers and experts. In the latter case, the model can be used by the ES (e.g., when certain IF-THEN rules call for it).

ES contribution in the area of models and model management can be demonstrated by examining the work of a consultant. A consultant is involved in the following steps:

1. Discussing with the manager (user) the nature of the problem,
2. Identifying and classifying the problem,
3. Constructing a mathematical model of the problem,
4. Solving the model,
5. Conducting sensitivity analysis with the model,
6. Recommending a specific solution, and
7. Assisting in implementing the solution.

In this process, the system involves a decision maker, a consultant and a computer.

If we can codify the knowledge of the consultant in an ES, we can build a DSS/ES capable of the same process. Unfortunately, at this time relatively little is known about the nature of the cognitive skills that consultants use. However, interesting work is being done at Oregon State University, where Goul, *et al.*, [9] have developed a DSS/ES system that attempts to replicate the manager-consultant-computer system. In this system:

1. The computer queries the manager to determine the general category of the problem (e.g., an allocation problem vs. inventory management),
2. The computer queries the manager to determine the *exact nature* of the problem (e.g., what kind of allocation problem), then
3. The computer suggests which management science model to use (e.g., dynamic programming vs. linear programming).

The manager can ask the system to define terminology to justify the recommendation made by the machine, and to explain the model used. The decision maker then can formulate the problem using the model, conduct "what-if" analysis, or use an alternative model. The ES, in this case, helps in identifying and classifying the managerial problem, acting as a tutor, providing illustrative examples and selecting the model(s) to be used.

Lehner and Donnel [15] claim there is a natural synergy between the prescriptive problem structuring techniques used in the DSS model base and the rule-based program architectures used in ES. In particular, the modeling procedures of the model base are suitable for *initial* problem structuring. Whereas, ES program architectures are suitable for (1) making the problem structure incrementally modifiable, and (2) developing a user interface that uses terms familiar to users.

Expert systems can be used as an *interface* between the user and the model base. Such an integration is demonstrated by BUMP, a statistical ES [10]. Large numbers of statistical packages are available on the market. These packages are being used both in industry and in educational institutions to support managerial decision making and research. They contain statistical tests and models that are included in the model base of a DSS. A major dilemma faced by a nonexpert user is to determine what statistical model to use for what purpose. This is where BUMP is brought into action. This ES selects the appropriate statistical procedure, and also guides the novice user in using the not-so-friendly statistical packages (such as MULTIVARIANCE and SPSS) that usually require a trained statistition for their operation.

Other ES/DSS connections that relate to models and their management include:

- ES that can provide heuristics to the DSS.
- ES that can ease the task of building simulation models [21].
- ES that can improve the DSS model management [2].
- ES that can improve sensitivity analyses [9].
- ES that can provide judgemental elements which are needed in using certain models. For example, a forecasting decomposition time-series model requires several judgemental decisions (e.g., which data to exclude when the seasonal component is computed). Such decisions are made only after the data are

collected and analyzed. ES can be used as a consultant to determine what to do in specific cases.
• A DSS model base that could include specialized models obtained from experts.

ES #3. Expert System Interaction with the Interface. Making the interface friendlier is a major objective of any DSS. Expert systems and other AI technologies (such as speech recognition and natural language processors) have made a significant contribution in this area.

A critical obstacle to the use of DSS is the mismatch between the needs of end users and their ability to communicate these needs to the computer. The development of interfaces such as the spreadsheet and menu systems used on desktop computers are important steps toward the improvement of the manager-computer interface. For many problems, however, greater capabilities, flexibility and control are needed.

One of the most interesting applications of artificial intelligence is the *natural language interface.* Its major objective is to enable non-technical people to access complex databases. Natural language interface can be integrated into DSS and/or ES to considerably improve the interaction between managers and computers. In order to visualize the potential contribution of such a language, let us examine Figure 2.

The inverted triangle represents the number of people in each language category and their required training. The computer languages are listed on the right side. DSS languages are in the middle of the triangle, ranging from PL/1 and APL to RAMIS II and FOCUS (fourth generation computer languages). The natural language interface is aimed at users who do not know (or do not want to know) formal computer languages but still want to use the computer. Typical users in this category are managers, doctors, lawyers, and other professionals. It should be noted, however, that only a few existing ES have natural language interfaces as front ends. Since natural language front-end systems, such as INTELLECT and CLOUT have been successfully applied to accessing complex databases it seems reasonable to assume that they will become an integral part of many DSS, ES and DSS/ES combined systems.

Another area where AI technology can make a significant contribution to DSS is the area of *interactive visual modelling* [1]. This technology enables the user to visually arrange models of certain management systems (e.g., factory layout) and determine all the necessary configurations. Then the user can observe the results (in terms of measures of performance) of different configurations. Furthermore, the configuration-results relationship can be observed in dynamic situations (e.g., one can see how a waiting line shrinks when the service rate increases). Such systems can support design and layout decisions, inventory, and scheduling, just to mention a few. A prototype of such a system is being developed by Intellicorp of Palo Alto, California.

Other possible areas of integration related to the man-machine interface include:

• ES that can add the explanation capability to the DSS to allow the user to follow the reasoning behind certain recommendations.
• ES that can manipulate symbolic information, thus making friendlier interfaces possible [27].
• ES that can provide terms which are familiar to the user.
• ES that can provide tutoring to the user [9].

ES #4. Expert System as a Consultant to the Model Builder. In addition to advice on constructing the various components of the DSS, one can visualize an ES which will give advice on how to structure a DSS, how to glue the various parts together, how to conduct a feasibility study, and how to execute the many activities which are involved in the construction of a DSS (as described by Sprague and Carlson [24]).

The same system may be used to advise the builder (or the user) how to change the DSS to fit the needs of the environment, or the specific scenario that the DSS describes.

ES #5. Expert Systems Integration with the User. The user who is considered a component of a DSS may solicit the advice of an expert for complex issues such as the nature of the problem, the environmental conditions, or the

Figure 2 Market for Natural Language

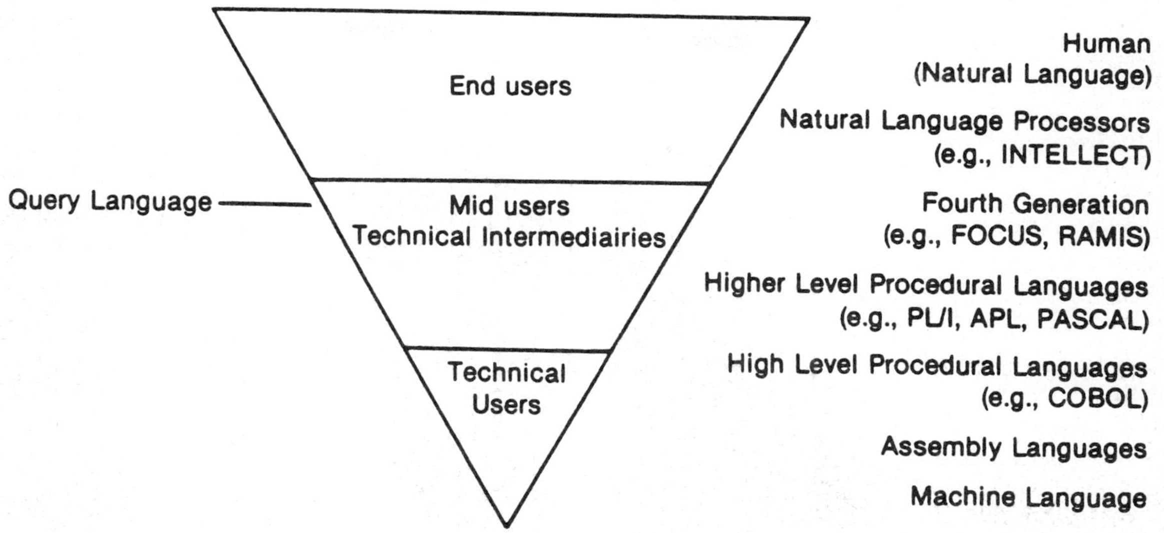

Adapted from Harris, L. R. "Natural Language Front Ends," *The AI Business*, The MIT Press, 1984.

possible implementation problems. For example, in a DSS designed to examine various proposals for reorganization, the user may ask an expert how the new structure will affect certain groups of employees. Instead of consulting an expert, the user may consult an ES. A user also may want an ES which will guide him (or her) how to use the DSS and its output. Another possible situation is for the user to seek advice on which specific DSS to use (if several are available).

ES as a Separate Component in the DSS

As the reader may recall, a DSS is composed of four basic parts. It has been proposed [23] that ES, and possibly other AI technologies, be added as a separate fifth component (see Figure 3). There are several possibilities for such integration.

ES Output as Input to a DSS. DSS users may direct the ES output to the DSS. For example, the ES can be used during the intelligence phase of problem solving to determine the importance of the problem or project and to identify the problem. Then the problem is transferred to a DSS for possible solution.

DSS Output as ES Input. In many cases the results of a computerized quantitative analysis provided by a DSS are forwarded to an individual or group of experts for the purpose of evaluation. Therefore, it would make sense to direct the output of a DSS into an ES which would perform the same function as an expert whenever it is cheaper and/or faster to do so (especially if the quality of the advice is also superior).

Sharing in the Decision Making Process. According to this approach, ES can complement DSS in one or more of the steps in the decision making process. An example for such an approach is proposed by Meador, *et al.*, [17]. Decision making is viewed as an eight-step process consisting of:

1. Specification of objectives, parameters, probabilities.
2. Retrieval and management of data.

Figure 3 ES as a Component of DSS

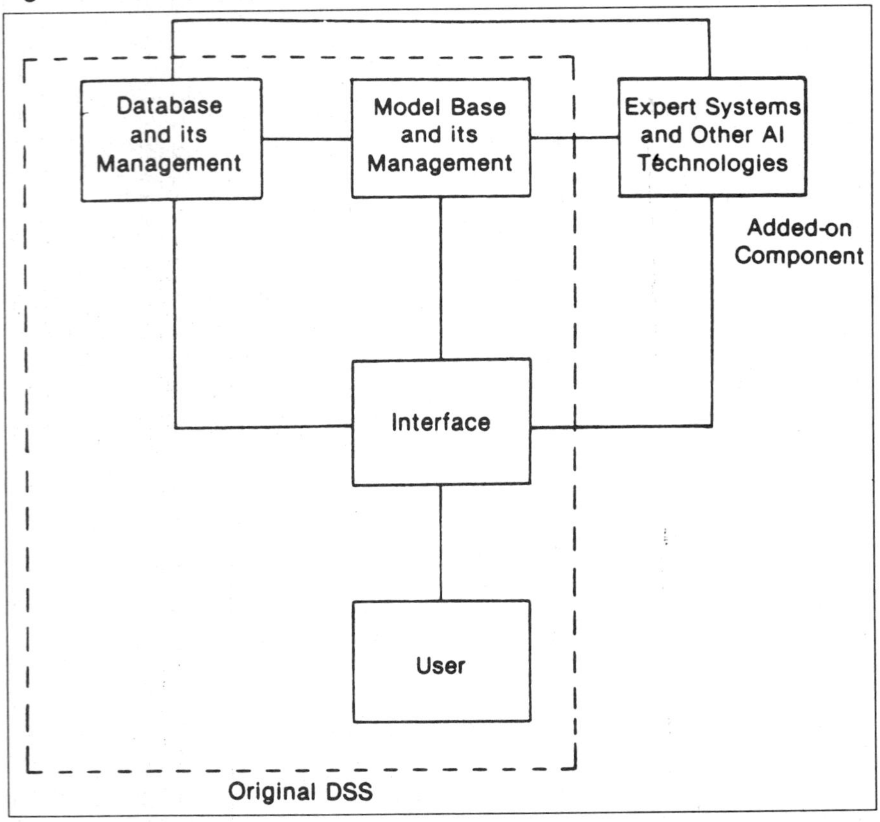

3. Generation of decision alternatives.
4. Inference of consequences of decision alternatives.
5. Assimilation of verbal, numerical, and graphical information.
6. Evaluation of sets of consequences.
7. Explanation and implementation of decisions.
8. Strategy formulation.

The first seven are typical DSS functions, while the last one, which requires judgement and creativity, can be done by an ES. Meador, *et al.*, suggest that ES might supplement the DSS by using a built-in associative memory with knowledge of business and inferential rules.

Such an integration may be visualized as follows: The user works with the DSS following the first seven DSS steps. Upon reaching the strategy formulation phase he/she calls upon the ES, which will be a completely separate system although it may share the database and perhaps use some of the capabilities of the model base. To better understand this type of integration, we assume that the ES plays the role of a human expert which the user can call upon when in need of expertise in strategy formulation. The expert may give an answer immediately, or may conduct some analysis (e.g., forecasting). Such analysis can be accomplished by using the DSS database and its forecasting model.

The Goul, Shane and Tonge Approach [9]. This approach views ES as an expert component in a DSS. The appropriate use of such a combination is in the intelligence or *problem-finding* phase of the strategic decision making process. The ES leads the decision maker to pertinent modes of reasoning. Therefore, it could offer conclusions with supportive justifications. This can also aid the decision maker in identifying objectives, diagnosing problems, and formulating models for analysis. The task of fathering data improves as the decision maker's scope is focused or expanded by the expert subsystem's requests for information. An additional outcome of this approach is that repeated use of the ES could reinforce effective decision making habits and teach new models of reasoning. It is logical to assume that the non-expert who repeatedly uses the expertise of an ES will learn and improve his decision making capabilities.[2]

Generating Alternative Solutions. Reitman [19] points out that most current DSSs help users evaluate and choose among potential courses of action (the choice phase of decision making). However, unlike a staff assistant these DSSs cannot suggest the alternative courses of action which should be considered (the design phase). He contends that this deficiency in existing DSS might be met by applying concepts and techniques taken from artificial intelligence.

Reitman describes an AI system that plays the game of Go. This system is able to work with non-numeric data to develop alternative game strategies, evaluate them, and select the best alternative. He provides a detailed description of the strategies employed by the system to find or develop courses of action:

—use of a network of experts at various levels of complexity of the game,
—successive refinement of problems from general to specific,
—assignment of priorities to situations, and
—use of an "expert and critic" structure.

Reitman demonstrates how the system tests alternatives, and how it limits a search in order to keep the solution to a manageable task.

After describing the Go system, Reitman considers how AI-based DSS might be transferred to systems in a business context. For example, decisions regarding trading futures of commodities appear to be roughly of the same order of complexity as existing AI applications, and therefore appear to be a promising place to begin exploring the practical use of AI-based DSS.

Problems and Issues in Integration

Technical Issues

Integration will require compatibility of hardware and software. For example, if an existing ES runs on a Lisp type machine, and the DSS on a micro we may face some technical problems, such as the need to use different programming languages. Additionally, if we use generators, shells and other building blocks there could be problems finding skilled programmers for developing and combining the different parts. Such technical problems may be lessened in the future as both hardware and software containing DSS/ES capabilities continue to be developed.

Behavioral Issues

Behavioral issues in DSS include consideration of the personal characteristics of decision makers, environmental or task characteristics, and related organizational issues. Behavioral research attempts to: (1) enhance the usefulness of information to the decision maker, (2) identify decision makers' information processing tendencies in order to tailor the database underlying the DSS to specific information processing styles, and (3) to provide insights into environmental and task characteristics that influence the decision. Since ES tend to draw conclusions and make recommendations, mimicking a human advisor, then certain aspects of the ES decision process do not directly benefit from much of the behavioral research accomplished to date in DSS. One reason for this is that ES focus on cognitive processes underlying the notion of expertise. These cognitive processes center on the long-term memory of the expert, and include perception, representation, retrieval, and reasoning [22]. In contrast, MIS and DSS behavioral research has tended to emphasize personality and abilities.

As discussed earlier, a desirable feature of ES is that it provides an explanation or justification for the decision reached. In practice, explanations of how ES arrive at their conclusions are not very convincing. One possible reason is that the explanations may not be tailored to specific individual users. The DSS behavioral literature concerning individual differences and the tailoring of information supplied by the DSS to individual decision makers could have relevance in tailoring the justification mechanism of ES. This is only one example for suggested research in this area.

Design Issues

Several approaches to the design process for DSS can be borrowed from the construction of ES and vice versa. For example, the iterative DSS design approach [1, 24] is also most suitable for ES construction. According to this approach, one uses a step-by-step dynamic approach to system development, as opposed to the systems life cycle approach commonly used in MIS system development.

Other design issues for expert systems or subsystem pertain to limitations of current ES. One limitation is the fact that constructing an expert system may require several man-years of effort from an expert in ES design, while ES designers are currently in short supply. The expertise required on the part of the designer is: (1) knowledge of cognitive processes and the appropriate methodologies needed for extracting expertise from expert(s), and (2) programming skills in appropriate languages such as LISP, PROLOG, and/or the specialty dialects such as frame representation, natural language processors, and assembly languages. Note that these skills need not be provided by a single individual—a team approach is usually used. Typical DSS builders, including programmers and database experts, do not have the level of expertise necessary for building ES.

Thus, the construction time of a DSS, even when constructed with the aid of a DSS generator, can be stretched to an unacceptable length, if an ES component is added. Commercially available "inference engines" and shells can reduce this problem by significantly decreasing the design and development time. Another possible relief to the problem is adding on "ready-made" expert systems to a specific DSS for advising in a general area of expertise.

Despite these (and possibly other) integration difficulties, there is evidence that DSS/ES integrated systems are being developed. Representative examples are given in the next section.

Existing and Developing Integrated Systems

There are a growing number of integrated systems, as well as tools for integrated systems. Representative examples are presented below.

IBM's Integrated manufacturing system [26]—A system called Logistics Management System (LMS) was developed by IBM for operations management. The system combines ES, simulation, traditional DSS and computer-based information systems. In addition, the system includes computer aided manufacturing (CAM) and distributed data processing subsystems. It provides IBM's Burlington plant manufacturing management a tool to assist in resolving crises and in planning. A similar system is used at IBM by financial analysts to simulate long range financial planning, where an ES provides judgemental information and other pertinent factors.

DSS/Decision Simulation (DSIM) [25]—DSIM is the outcome of combining traditional DSS, statistics, operations research, database management, query languages, and artificial intelligence. AI, especially natural language interfaces and expert systems, provides three things to DSIM:

1. Ease of communication of pertinent information to the computational algorithm or display unit.
2. Assistance in finding the appropriate model, computational algorithm, or data set.
3. A solution to a problem where the computational algorithm(s) alone is not sufficient to solve the problem, a computational algorithm is not appropriate or applicable, and/or the AI creates the computational algorithm.

Promoter—This ES analyzes the effects of promotions and advertisements on sales in the packaged goods industry. It was developed by Management Decision Systems Inc. and it must be used together with their mainframe EXPRESS DSS generator.

Engineering ES/DSS

This integrated system was designed to boost engineers' productivity. The DSS portion, called STRUDL (Structural Design Language), is essentially a passive tool thats effectiveness depends on the user's abilities. By supplying the proper data into the formula or the graphic modelling application, a design engineer can gain insight into his design prototype's potential. Unfortunately, STRUDL cannot help him decide what questions to ask or what data to key in, nor can it give any hints about further actions to take based on the results of an analysis. However, an expert system that assumes the role of teacher/partner was added on to do all this.

Statistical ES/DSS

IFPS Optimum includes a logic component which identifies the nature of the problem. For example, in an allocation problem the package will identify if this is a linear or a nonlinear programming problem.

Financial Services

A large financial services company already has a system which is close to being a working DSS/ES [20]. The company uses the system to match its various services with individual customers' needs (e.g. placing customers' assets into optimal investment packages).

Similar applications are being actively developed by large international accounting firms for combining analytical methods and judgement in auditing, and by other business entities for credit evaluation, strategic planning and related applications. General Dynamic Corp., for example, is using ES to support project management analysis.

REVEAL is a DSS generator with a strong modelling language designed mainly for financial and corporate planning (by Decision Products Inc.). It includes several typical ES capabilities. One important feature is *approximate reasoning* which is based on the mathematical theory of fuzzy sets. This capability enables representation of words such as "profitable," and "fairly good" and "reasonably strong" which are frequently used by decision makers. In fact, creative decision making processes are unstructured, playful, and rambling. Fuzzy thinking can improve DSS by providing flexibility, and freeing the imagination.

Developmental Tools

At the present time the developmental tools of DSS and ES are completely independent. However, there are some indications that such tools can be combined. Some ES developmental tools already possess DSS capabilities. For example, the Knowledge Workbench (from Silogic Corporation, Los Angeles) includes a universal database and a natural language interface. The M.1. (from Teknowledge, Inc., Palo Alto) includes a database interface. GURU, (from Micro Data Base Systems, Inc.), combines an expert system's shell with a database management system, a spreadsheet, graphics, communications, and a word processing package. Finally, KEE (from Intellicorp, Menlo Park) includes models for various computations and a system's simulation (regular and visual).

Joint Hardware

Lisp Machines, Inc. produces a computer that can serve a DSS user and an expert system user (and possibly some additional users) simultaneously. Called "Lambda 2 x 2 Plus," this sytem is equipped with a Lisp processor, a Unix processor, and the capability of adding a Prolog processor. Several other vendors are developing similar machines.

The Fifth Generation Project (FGP)

Bonczek, *et al.*, [5] cite the recent efforts of the Fifth Generation project as an example of the movement toward integrated DSS and ES. Figure 4 represents the conceptual diagram of the software system envisioned by the Japanese. As shown there, the key elements of the system are the knowledge base and its management system, which would incorporate the database, model base and the DBMS of current DSSs. The problem solving-inference system would be the ES aspect, and the intelligent interface system would encompass a natural language interface. In addition, intelligent systemization and utility systems would be developed. The basic application system would then interface with the rest of the components, much like current DSS.

Conclusions

ES can make DSS a more active, and potentially more valuable participant in the decision process. Presently DSS is often used to answer the question "what if?" DSS/ES will also be able to answer the question "why?"

Scott Morton, who pioneered the concept of DSS, made the following remarks regarding the DSS/ES integration:

> "DSS as we know them may even become obsolete in the foreseeable future. They are being supplanted by expert decision support systems—EDSS. This next generation of DSS

Figure 4 Conceptual Diagram of the Next Generation Computer Software System

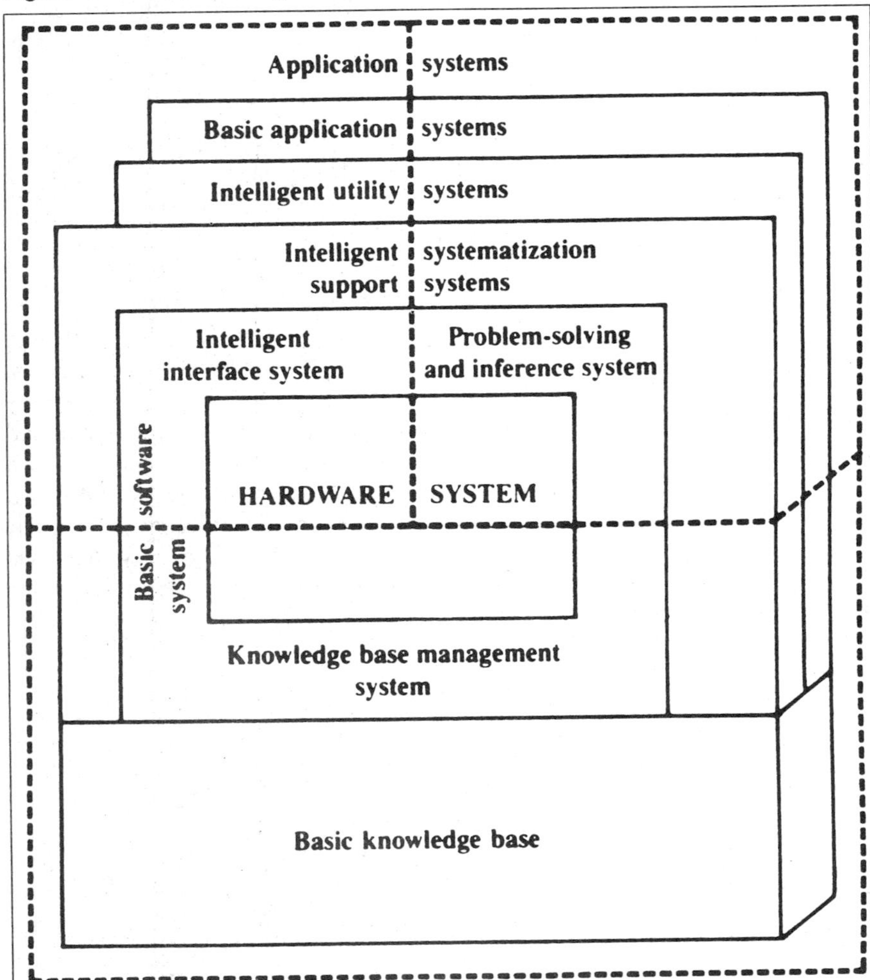

Source: Japan Information Processing Development Center
Reprinted by permission from the *1982 Proceedings of the Arthur Young Professor Roundtable*, Arthur Young & Company, New, New York, 1982.

> will combine existing DSS technology with the capabilities of AI . . . The languages users input and the computer's response will virtually duplicate everyday human conversation, and the EDSS will be able to supply a variety of alternative solutions to problems ("if that doesn't work, try this. . . ."). EDSS will even warn users when they are proceeding under faulty assumptions ("Are you sure your figures for FY 1988 are accurate?") or supplying incomplete information (if the user inputs, "Give me the sales figures for Kansas City," the system will quickly reply, "Do you mean Kansas City, Missouri, or Kansas City, Kansas?")" [20, p. 12].

Despite the great potential of integration, one should not conclude that all future systems will be integrated. On the contrary, most DSSs (especially the small ones for personal use) will remain independent, at best sharing certain AI concepts and technologies with ES. Similarly, many ES will operate as independent systems, advising users on specific issues which are completely unrelated to any DSS.

There are several reasons why we believe that model 1 (ES integration into DSS components) will be most prevalent. First, there is evidence (which will be presented later) that some current design efforts are using this approach and several systems already are structured in this fashion. Second, an ES is usually applied to a narrow domain, while a DSS is usually broader in scope; therefore, it logically follows that several ES may be needed to fully support one DSS. This seems to be a very expensive arrangement. However, an expert system that specializes in one area (e.g., in a model base) could advise several DSS builders on model base issues (such as selection of a model), thus reducing the cost through sharing. Finally, recent developments in ES software tools (see Kinnucan [19]) could make the construction of a simple ES, in a very narrow domain, an inexpensive and rapid undertaking, i.e., it would be economically feasible to have several small ES exclusively serving one large, even ad hoc DSS.

While evaluating the potential integration of DSS and ES, one should not forget the potential difficulties of such integration and the many limitations of ES. As we described earlier, DSS have the flexibility to support the solution of a wide range of semi-structured and unstructured problems. ES are developed for very narrow domains. Thus the integration of a general problem support system (DSS) and a specific, narrow problem support system (ES) poses some difficulties. It is not clear that the expertise in ES is transferable across problem domains such as those potentially supported by a DSS, and thus research needs to be undertaken in this area. Also, today's ES fall short of the goal of performing at high levels of general intelligent behavior [11, 16]. Additional technical, behavioral, and design limitations and issues could provide a fertile ground for DSS/ES integration research. These limitations are spurring development of smarter systems, systems able to reason from what is called "deep knowledge." But it may take several years before such systems are fully developed.

All of which is not to suggest that companies should refrain from integrating DSS and ES to wait until a trouble-free DSS/ES combination is available. Some experts contend that a state-of-the-art DSS could be upgraded today into an intelligent DSS with existing ES technology.

Recent studies from both the Boston-based Yankee Group and International Data Corporation in Farmingham, Massachusetts [20] show that decision support systems are currently being used by only two to three percent of non-DP/MIS executives and managers in U.S. companies. When the DSS/ES combination attain their full potential, and when executives are able to communicate with the computer by using their voice, these systems will be used by almost all managers and executives.

Discussion Questions

1. Distinguish the differences between an expert system, decision support system, and management information system.
2. Why is the integration of expert systems and decision support systems desirable?
3. How is this article related to the Sprague article on DSS?
4. Describe the various possible interfaces between an expert system and DSS.

Footnotes

1. According to *AI Trends 84*, a report complied by DM Data of Arizona, the U.S. market will reach $2.8 billion by 1990 [7]. Arthur D. Little Inc. estimates a market of more than $10 billion by the mid 1990s.
2. At the present time, there is little empirical confirmation for this assertion. However private communication with ES users at Digital Equipment and AMOCO strongly supports this assumption. In addition, there is some evidence (e.g., Hayes-Roth *et al.* [12] that experts themselves improve their expertise in the process of developing expert systems.

References

[1] Alter, L. *Decision Support Systems: Current Practices and Continuing Challenges*, Addison-Wesley Publishing Company, Reading Massachusetts, 1980.
[2] Basa, A. and Dutta, A. "AI-Based Model Management in DSS," Paper presented at ORSA/TIMS meeting, Dallas, Nov. 1984.
[3] Bell, P. C., Parker, D. C. and Kirkpatrick, P. "Visual Interactive Problem Solving—A New Look at Management Problems," *Business Quarterly*, Spring 1984, pp. 14-18.
[4] Bonczek, R. H., Holsapple, C. and Whinston, A. *Foundations of Decision Support Systems*, Academic Press, New York, New York, 1981.
[5] Bonczek, R. H., Holsapple, C. and Whinston, A. *Developments in DSS*. Research Report 1ST-8108519, MIS Research Center, Krannert Graduate School of Management, Purdue University, 1984.
[6] Davis, R. "A DSS for Diagnosis and Therapy," *Data Base*, Winter 1977.
[7] Dicken, H. K. and Newquist, H. P. *AI Trends 85*, DM Data Inc. Publishing, Scottsdale, Arizona, 1985.
[8] Ginzberg, M. J. and Stohr, E. "Decision Support Systems—An Overview," in *Decision Support Systems*, M. J. Ginzberg, W. Rertman and E. Stohr (eds.), North Holland Publishing, Amsterdam, Holland, 1982.
[9] Goul, M., Shane, B., and Tonge, F. "Designing the Expert Component of a Decision Support System," Paper delivered at the ORSA/TIMS meeting, San Francisco, May 1984.
[10] Hand, D. J. "Statistical Expert Systems: Design," *The Statistician*, Volume 33, Number 10, October 1984, pp. 351-369.
[11] Harris, L. R. "Natural Language Front Ends," in *The AI Business*, P. H. Winston and K. A. Prendergast (eds.), The MIT Press, Cambridge, Massachusetts, 1984.
[12] Hayes-Roth, F., Waterman, D. and Lenat, D. *Building Expert Systems*, Addison-Wesley, Reading, Massachusetts, 1983.
[13] Hogarth, R. M. and Makridakis, S. "Forecasting and Planning: An Evaluation," *Management Science*, Volume 27, Number 2, February 1981, pp. 115-138.
[14] Jarke, M. and Vassiliou, Y. "Coupling Expert Systems with Database Management Systems," in *Artificial Intelligence Applications for Business*, W. Reitman (ed.), APLEX Publishing Corporation, Norwood, New Jersey, 1984.
[15] Lehner, P. E. and Donnel, M. L. "Building Decision Aids: Exploiting the Synergy Between Decision Analysis and Artificial Intelligence," paper presented at the TIMS/ORSA National Meeting, San Francisco, California, May 1984.
[16] Martins, G. R. "The Overselling of Expert Systems," *Datamation*, Volume 30, Number 18, November 1, 1984, pp. 76-80.
[17] Meador, C. L., Keen, P. G. W. and Guyote, M. J. "Personal Computer and Distributed Decision Support," *Computerworld*, Volume 18, Number 19, May 7, 1984, pp. ID7-ID16.
[18] Michaelson, R. and Michie, D. "Expert Systems in Business," *Datamation*, Volume 29, Number 11, November 1983, pp. 240-246.
[19] Reitman, W. "Applying Artificial Intelligence to Decision Support," in *Decision Support Systems*, M. J. Ginzberg, W. Reitman and E. Stohr (eds.), North Holland Publishing Co., Amsterdam Holland, 1982.
[20] Scott Morton, M. "Expert Decision Support Systems," a paper presented at the special DSS conference, Planning Executive Institute and Information Technology Institute, New York, New York, May 21-22, 1984.
[21] Shannon, R. E. "Expert Systems and Simulation," *Simulation*, June 1985.
[22] Simon, H. *The New Science of Management*

Decisions, Harper & Row, Publishing, New York, New York, 1960.

[23] Sprague, R. "The Role of Expert Systems in DSS," A paper presented at ORSA/TIMS Meeting, Dallas, Texas, November 1984.

[24] Sprague, Jr., R. H. and Carlson, E. D. *Building Effective Decision Support Systems*, Prentice Hall, Englewood Cliffs, New Jersey, 1982.

[25] Sullivan, G. and Fordyce, K. *Decision Simulation, One Outcome of Combining AI and DSS*, working paper #42-395, IBM Corporation, Poughkeepsie, New York, 1984.

[26] Sullivan, G. and Fordyce, K. "The Role of Artificial Intelligence in Decision Support Systems," paper delivered at the International meeting of TIMS in Copenhagen, Denmark, June 17-21, 1984.

[27] Waltz, D. "Artificial Intelligence: An Assessment of the State-of-the-Art and Recommendations for Future Directions," *The AI Magazine*, Volume 4, Number 4, Fall 1983, pp. 118-133.

[28] Winston, P. H. and Predergast, K. A. (ed.) *The AI Business*, MIT Press, Cambridge, Massachusetts, 1984.

SECTION TWELVE

Data Management

READING 37

The Ten Commandments of Data Base

article by
GERALD F. PRICE

I. **Identify Data Elements**
II. **Define File Requirements**
III. **Design General System**
IV. **Evaluate Justification Criteria**
V. **Project Planning and Control**
VI. **Data Management and Control**
VII. **Develop, Test, and Document**
VIII. **Plan Security Protection**
IX. **Educate and Implement**
X. **Audit and Evaluate Results**

If you were among those who converted from second to third generation hardware, you can recall the pain of changing data files, programming languages, and the subsequent testing of those revised programs. It was a bitter experience at the time; however, the data processing industry focused its view on some basic inadequacies in documentation, standards, and technique uniformity within an installation.

As we look back, we can be thankful for the lesson gained through the conversion experience. Thankful, expecially, because this lesson was learned prior to the era of integrated systems and data base technology. Today, we have applied these experiences to avoid the need for future conversion efforts. We now enjoy freedom from hardware, software, and data bases. Our programs are independent, dealing strictly at an applications problem level. Our analysts now concentrate on application problems and technology is left to software specialists. We have taken advantage of the painful conversion experience. Or have we?

If you look back to the number of programs operating in your installation at the time of the conversion effort, you will find that today you operate two to three times as many programs. Would another conversion today be twice as

Source: From *Data Management Magazine*, Volume 10, Number 5, May 1972, pp. 14-23. Reprint permission granted. Data Processing Management Association.

difficult? Three times? We, of the data processing industry, must insure our firm's system investment by avoiding the need for reprograming efforts. Problem level languages and hardware, software, and data independence is one way to avoid future costly conversions. It can be done.

Defining a Data Base

Before looking at how one develops a data base, a definition is required of what a data base is. A data base is an orderly collection of business facts stored to serve information requirements. Data bases are frequently stored on direct access devices to provide rapid information retrieval. A dynamic business environment dictates that data bases be adaptable to change. The information storage technique must accommodate data entry, maintenance, and retrieval.

The ideal data base would contain all information required in the process of conducting your business. This ideal data base would contain current, historical and forecast information which would be stored in a logical manner and available for retrieval as need demanded. Ideally the data base would provide only the information necessary to satisfy each request, however cost considerations frequently rule out maintaining a data base at this ideal level. Information stored is limited to the more practical level of *active* data. If the cost of insurance (*storage*) exceeds the cost of the accident (*usage*), it may not be practical. A data base can be scaled to a practical level to contain the significant information while omitting information which can be stored more economically in a different manner.

In the days of second generation hardware, each application operated with its own independent set of data files. There were two choices in moving to third generation equipment. The first, *conversion* on an immediate basis, the most costly, was rarely selected. The second choice, *evolution*, provided the user an opportunity to convert one application at a time while he continued to operate his new third generation machine as if it were second generation. Evoluation worked the last time, but under an integrated data base, it may never work again. How would you convert one application at a time when your entire company data is stored in an integrated data base? With a large number of programs depending on the data base, development efforts must avoid unnecessary conversions. Advancements in data processing technology and hardware occur regularly. To take advantage requires an ability to adapt rapidly with minimum effort. There are basic steps which can help us avoid future conversion problems. The "Ten Commandments of Data Base" identify some significant considerations in data base development.

Identify Data Elements

Close examination reveals that most business decisions are based upon a relatively small collection of data elements. These elements must first be recognized. A data dictionary to define standard elements can be developed with uniform data names and field characteristics (Figure I-1). These elements are combined to form information in input documents, stored file records, and information retrievals. All data elements identified in the dictionary can be cross-referenced through a data directory to provide a data usage record (Figure I-2).

The process of identifying the data elements requires an examination of existing transactions, files, and reports. Document these elements in a dictionary in this basic identification step. A matrix can then be established to relate the identified elements to transactions, files, and reports. These study documents provide a basis for the data directory (Figures I-3, I-4, and I-5).

After examining the use of significant data elements in existing systems, data inconsistency and redundancy identification is common. Variation in field lengths, edit rules, and data interpretation contribute to the inconsistency between the independent files on non-data-base systems. Information stored in multiple files requires redundant maintenance. Early recognition of data element conflicts provides added intelligence for data base planning.

A review of the evaluation results with pertinent-using-organizations provides additional intelligence for defining control responsibility over each data element (e.g., grade assignment = faculty responsibility). Additional data elements and future control needs are identified in these reviews.

Figure I-1 Data Dictionary

ELEMENT	DATA NAME	CHARACTERISTICS
Accumulated Average	Accum-Av	3 Numeric XX.X%
Accumulated Credits	Accum-Cr	3 Numeric
Assignment Grade	Assign-Grade	3 Numeric XX.X%
Birth Date	Birth	6 Numeric XX-XX-XX
Class Days	Class-Days	5 Alpha MTWTF
Class Link	Class-Link	3 Numeric Storage Address
Class Year	Class-Yr	4 Numeric 19XX
Course Code	Course-No	3 Numeric
Course Name	Course-Name	10 Alpha
Days Absent	Days-Abs	2 Numeric
Faculty Member	Faculty-Name	15 Alpha
Final Grade	Final-Grade	3 Numeric XX.X%
First Name	First-Name	8 Alpha
Next Class	Next-Class	3 Numeric Storage Address
Next Student	Next-Student	3 Numeric Storage Address
Number Credits	No-Credits	1 Numeric
Registration Number	Reg-No	3 Numeric
Room Number	Room	3 Numeric
Sex	Sex	1 Alpha
Student Link	Student-Link	3 Numeric Storage Address
Surname	Surname	15 Alpha
Test Grade	Test-Grade	3 Numeric XX.X%
Time of Class	Class-Time	4 Numeric HR-MN

Figure I-2 Data Directory

ELEMENT	USAGE	T	F	R
Class-Yr	Student Application	X		
	Student Master		X	
	Grade Report			X
	Transcript			X
Course-No	Schedule & History		X	
	Course Master		X	
	Grade Report			X
	Transcript			X
	Course Definition	X		
Course-Name	Course Master		X	
	Transcript			X
	Course Definition	X		
	Grade Report			X

Define File Requirements

The three most significant elements which influence files are record size, quantity of records, and retrieval requirements. Retrieval influences the data management technique and will be examined later. This phase considers file content and size as criteria for planning and economic evaluation.

Figure I-3 Data Evaluation Array—Transaction to Data Element

TRANSACTION \ DATA ELEMENT	ACCUM-AV	ACCUM-CR	ASSIGN-GRADE	BIRTH	CLASS-DAYS	CLASS-LINK	CLASS-YR	COURSE-NO	COURSE-NAME	DAYS-ABS	FACULTY NAME	FINAL GRADE	FIRST-NAME	NEXT CLASS	ETC
FACULTY ASSIGNMENT					X			X	X		X				X
STUDENT APPLICATION	X	X		X			X						X		
CLASS ASSIGNMENT					X			X	X				X		X
TRANSFER REQUEST	X	X		X			X						X		X

Figure I-4 Data Evaluation Array—File to Data Element

FILE \ DATA ELEMENT	ACCUM-AV	ACCUM-CR	ASSIGN-GRADE	BIRTH	CLASS-DAYS	CLASS-LINK	CLASS-YR	COURSE-NO	COURSE-NAME	DAYS-ABS	FACULTY NAME	FINAL GRADE	FIRST-NAME	NEXT CLASS	ETC
STUDENT MASTER	X	X		X		X	X						X		X
SCHEDULE & HISTORY			X					X		X		X			X
COURSE MASTER					X			X	X		X				
FACULTY MASTER			X							X	X		X		X

Figure I-5 Data Evaluation Array—Retrieval Document to Data Element

RETRIEVAL \ DATA ELEMENT	ACCUM-AV	ACCUM-CR	ASSIGN-GRADE	BIRTH	CLASS-DAYS	CLASS-LINK	CLASS-YR	COURSE-NO	COURSE-NAME	DAYS-ABS	FACULTY NAME	FINAL GRADE	FIRST-NAME	NEXT CLASS	ETC
GRADE REPORT			X		X		X	X	X	X	X	X	X		X
TRANSCRIPT	X	X		X			X	X	X		X	X	X		X
COURSE SCHEDULE					X			X	X		X		X		X
CLASS ROSTER	X	X		X	X		X	X	X		X		X		X

A master file is organized through use of a key data element which identifies the record and provides storage control. Master file information relates to this key data element in a static sense. Maintenance activity in a master file consists mainly of record adds and deletes.

A subordinate file provides opportunity to extend a master file by a variable number of detail records. These detail records increase the available intelligence known about the key element at minimum storage cost. (Figure II-1).

The student master record contains information which applies to each student. This information does not change throughout the school year.

Figure II-1

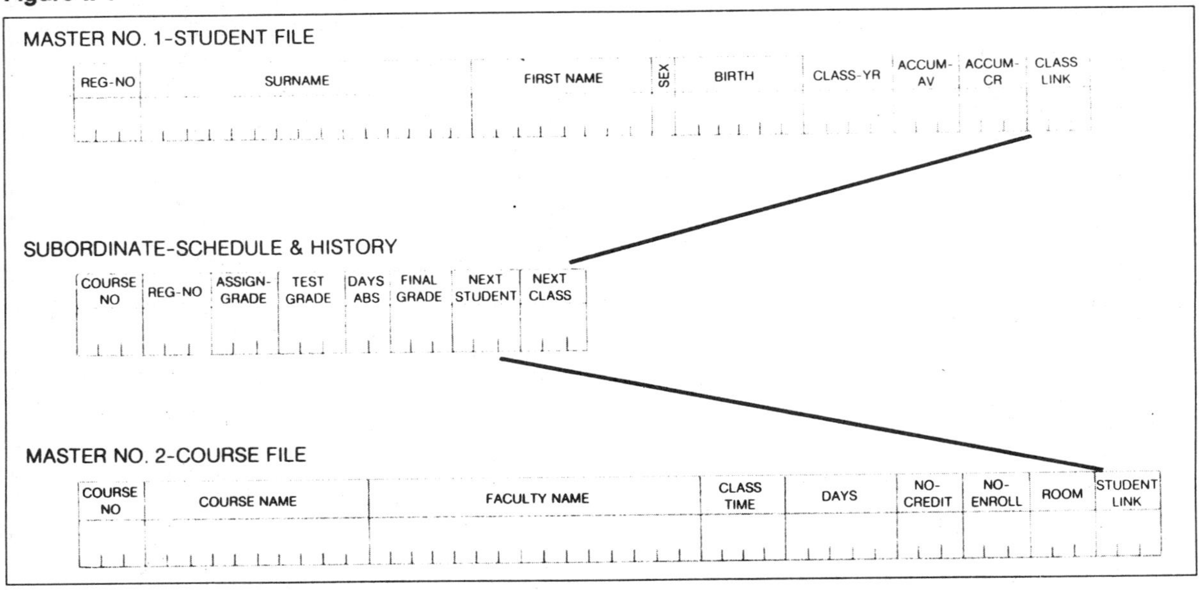

Limited updating is performed on an annual basis. The subordinate record provides opportunity to record a student's current schedule and prior course completions. The number of records per student depends on his class year and current schedule. The example shows a subordinate file supporting two masters.

Each data element is a candidate for either master or subordinate file storage. Basic identification of each data element by file type provides a basis for an initial file layout. This layout is preliminary and will be changed as specifications are solidified.

Once the file content is available, review with the system-using-organizations is required. This review initiates a communication with the system user which must continue through the entire development cycle. The user is best qualified to estimate the number of master and subordinate records by type. A requirement to document this estimate frequently improves the estimate' validity. Modifications in record content are identified through these user communication meetings.

Completion of this phase has provided a knowledge of what we are dealing with (data elements), how the elements are structured (file definitions), and storage requirements (volume estimates).

Design General System

Boundaries of an information system extend far beyond computer processing. They encompass the entire information flow from the condition which triggers initial action through the final result. It includes actions and responsibilities of all organization areas affected by the system. The basic design defines primary procedural flows, responsibilities, processing requirements, and controls. Economics of the system have not been examined. Documentation of the general design provides a basis for economic review and development effort of approved projects. System complexity controls logical limits of resource expenditure in this phase.

System objectives are fundamental to design. What end will the system accomplish? Objectives are defined as a shared user and development group responsibility. Systems developed without user participation are viewed as "ivory tower" logic by users and frequently fail. The user must be equally committed to the result. Documentation of objectives can be narrative. They must identify data usage, frequency, and volume (Figure III-1).

Flowcharting provides a simple means of information flow display. The flowchart

Figure III-1 Objectives—Student Record System

1. Provide a grade record for each student containing current and historical course information. Maintain accumulated credits and grade average.
2. Maintain course grade records for assignment grades, test grades, and final grade. Include absentee record by course.
3. Maintain record of course to faculty member assignments.
4. Provide course record of students enrolled, class days, time and room number.

communicates the means of producing results to satisfy the objectives. The flowchart provides understanding of procedural requirements and organization responsibilities. Changes in responsibilities can be considered in terms of manpower requirements and logic. (Figure III-2).

Processing logic and controls are documented through use of decision tables. Decision tables contain identification of variable conditions and corresponding actions. The decision tables of the general design are not adequately detailed for development programming. They are intended only to document the primary logic considerations. (Figure III-3).

Working with the user, the general design must further identify development responsibility. There are three data associations in an information system: data gathering, purification, and use. Gathering refers to the initial file creation action and subsequent file expansion. Purification provides maintenance capability to improve data accuracy. Usage is application of data in achievement of the objectives. Data base system logic incorporates control disciplines. Information failing to satisfy the logic disciplines is rejected. The using organization has responsibility for rejection response during and following the file creation and implementation effort. A data audit performed by the user during the development elapsed time may reduce file load rejections.

Evaluate Justification Criteria

Are the objectives of the new system currently being accomplished? If not, the development and operating costs of the new system will be added operating expense. If a current method of achieving the objectives exists, it must be either operating at greater cost or producing unsatisfactory results. Unless the proposed system reduces cost or increases benefits, why expend the development effort? The justification for development and future operating costs must be supported by improved results and/or cost reductions.

System operating costs are the direct result of resource expenditure. The resource is either labor or equipment. Clerical effort to get the job done today and equipment including non-data-processing machines which have maintenance, rental, and service contracts are primary cost considerations. The cost evaluation should consider all major elements associated with the system.

A similar cost evaluation should be developed in support of the system proposed. Clerical efforts and equipment requirements should be estimated and included. Development costs of the new system fall mainly in the category of manpower and equipment expenditures. The manpower portion must consider analytical progrmaming and clerical tasks required to satisfy systems objectives. Include the effort required by user personnel during development. One-time charges for forms design, freight, and building modifications should be identified. Equipment costs for programming and data conversion are additional cost considerations.

Elimination of one hour per day of a person's time does not reduce operating costs. True savings must result in a reduction of operating costs. Cancellation of a rental or maintenance contract is a true saving. Elimination of an existing position or the need to increase headcount are true savings. Such reductions of operating costs are tangible benefits. Associated with new systems are many intangible benefits which can be documented. The system user may not be able to identify the precise dollar value of intangible benefits for information control, accuracy, or timeliness. If the development effort is a business expense, a user estimate of intangible benefits is required to adequately identify the system value.

Development and operating costs, including one-time charges, can be calendarized over the life span of the proposed system. Experience tells us that this should not exceed five years' duration in most

Figure III-2 Enrollment Decision Logic

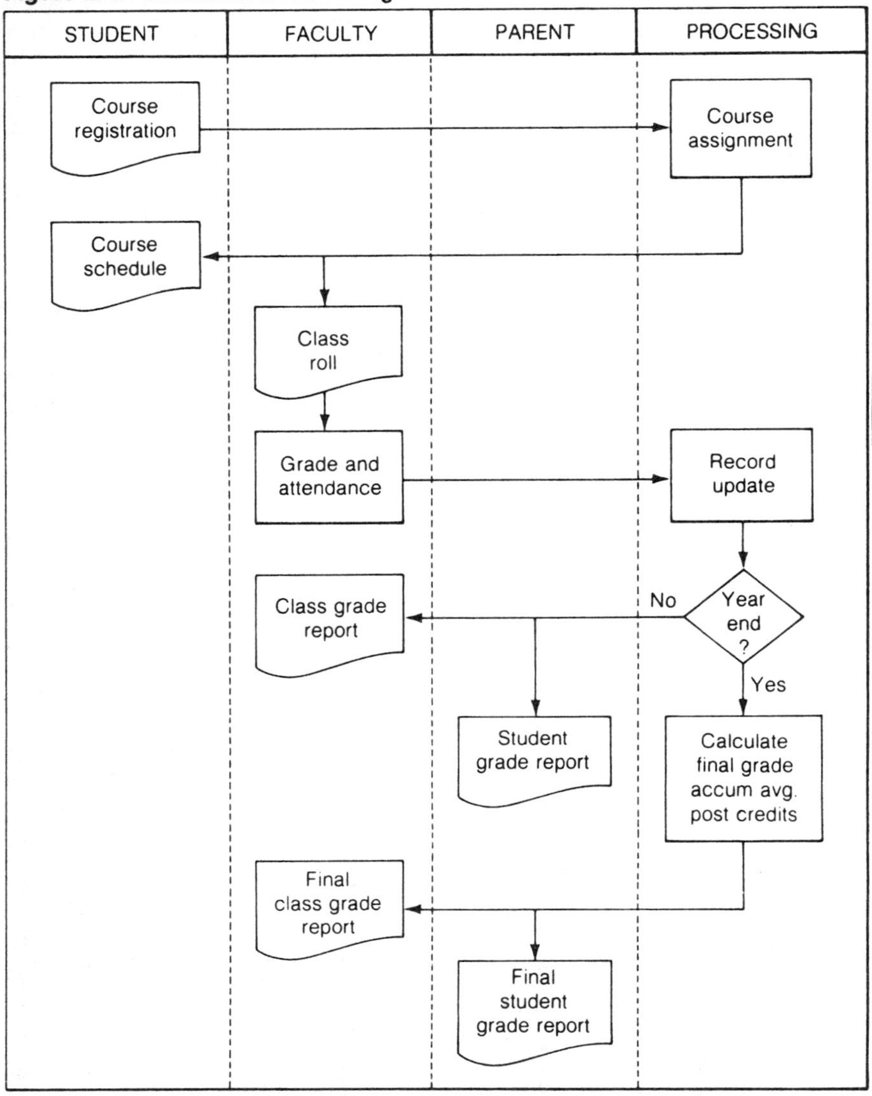

justifications. Identified savings can be spread over the system cycle in a similar manner. (Figure IV-1).

Knowledge of the cost versus savings criteria identifies the cash flows to calculate economic justification. Systems justified without a detailed approach frequently provide inadequate or unrecognized benefits. The expenditure for data processing equipment and manpower will contribute most to an organization which requires that each project developed contribute through reduced operating costs.

Project Planning and Control

Many projects developed have critical implementation dates established by fiscal or annual considerations. Elimination of project planning is commonly considered as a development time

Figure III-3 Student Record System Flowchart

CONDITION	1	2	3	4	5
Applied this course	N	Y	Y	Y	Y
Prerequisites satisfied		N	Y	Y	Y
Credit already earned			Y	N	N
Vacancy available				N	Y
ACTION					
Reject application	X	X	X	X	
Enroll					X
Notify faculty representative					X

reduction. If the result supports the development endeavor, planning is the insurance of result achievement and quality. The elements of planning are essential to success. Satisfaction of the design objectives requires achievement of all system aspects. Planning identifies the elements and provides a record of project status. Early recognition of project delay provides for corrective actions. Failure to plan results in overlooked considerations which may result in system failure.

A development network diagram identifies project tasks and task relationships. (Figure V-1). The network provides documentation of the project efforts and highlights critical activities. It includes all tasks required from project approval to completion.

Project work programs provide specification details relative to specific assignments in the project (Figure V-2). They show the timing schedule, available information and required activities. The work program identifies responsibilities of both the development and user personnel. Documentation of a system is not an afterthought. The work program identifies specific documentation requirements provided from each work step.

The combination of the network diagram and work program provide progress measurement tools. Completed activities can be noted on the network diagram for achievement recording. Project managers can inspect and approve satisfaction of each activity, including documentation required. These documents provide the ability to measure actual time expended versus plan. Since planning is an estimating process, knowledge of the deviation provides a basis for refining the estimating technique. Most significant, however, is the control it provides over resource utilization. The project

Figure IV-1 Cash Evaluation and Flow

			JUN	JUL	AUG	SEPT	OCT	NOV	DEC	JAN	FEB	MAR	APR	MAY	JUN	JUL
I. Development cost																
A. Programming/analysis	160 hrs/$10	$1600	(800)	(800)												
B. User participation																
1. Supervision	60 hrs/$10	$ 600	(200)	(400)												
2. Clerical	90 hrs/$4	$ 360		(180)	(180)											
C. COMPUTER COSTS																
1. Compilation and test	6 hrs/$50	$ 300	(100)	(200)												
2. File conversion	8 hrs/$50			(100)	(300)											
D. Total development cost		$3260	(1100)	(1680)	(480)											
II. Operating cost																
A. Computer cost	12 hrs/$50	$ 600				(100)	(50)	(50)	(50)	(100)	(50)	(50)	(50)	(100)	(50)	(50)
B. Keypunch/verification	30 hrs/$4	$ 120				(20)	(10)	(10)	(10)	(20)	(10)	(10)	(10)	(20)	(10)	(10)
C. Program maintenance	2 hrs/$10	$ 20							(10)				(10)			
D. Total operating cost		$ 740				(120)	(60)	(60)	(70)	(120)	(60)	(60)	(70)	(120)	(60)	(60)
III. Savings																
A. Part-time typist	$250/mo	$3000	250	250	250	250	250	250	250	250	250	250	250	250	250	250
B. Rental typewriter	$ 30/mo	$ 360	30	30	30	30	30	30	30	30	30	30	30	30	30	30
C. Transcript copies	$.20/copy	$ 200			20	20	20	20	20	20	20	20	20	20	20	20
D. Total savings		$3560	280	280	300	300	300	300	300	300	300	300	300	300	300	300
IV. Cash flow			(820)	(1400)	(180)	180	240	240	230	180	240	240	230	180	240	240
V. Cumulative flow			(820)	(2220)	(2400)	(2280)	(1980)	(1740)	(1510)	(1330)	(1090)	(850)	(620)	(440)	(200)	(40)

Figure V-1 Student Record System Development Plan

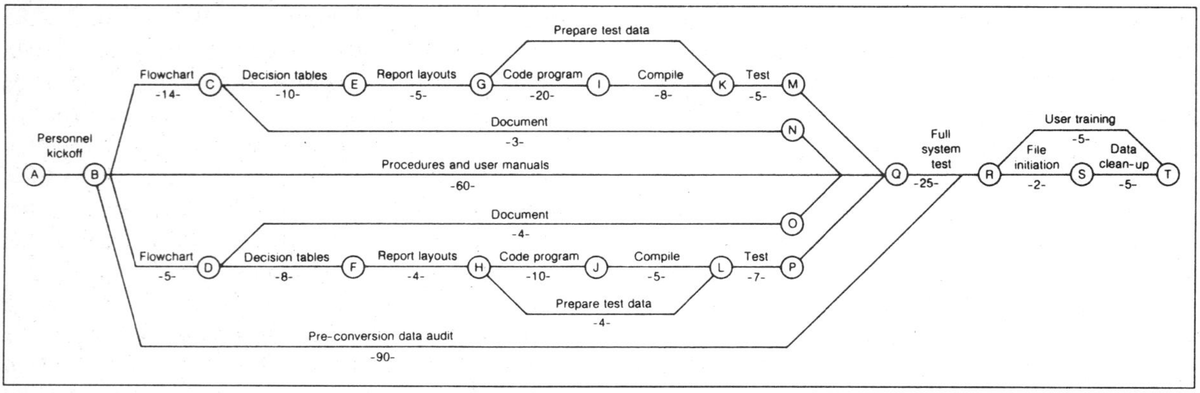

was justified on the basis of economic feasibility. Lack of control can delay development, fail to recognize realignment of assignments and thus hide true project costs.

The general design was the basis of estimating. Modifications to the design specifications must be evaluated and documented. Significant changes may require review of the economic factors and plan revisions.

Data Management Control

Data management is the process of disk data-base control. The Data Management Routine (D.M.R.) initializes files and provides record add, delete, retrieval, and update functions. The principle of data management promotes independence between application programs and file management technology. (Figure VI-1). The D.M.R. can be measured in terms of performance on retrieval efficiency, storage utilization, file restructuring conversion time, and contributions to simplification of application programming. Application of data management concepts promotes standard conventions and control over applications programming which reduce programming costs.

The D.M.R. may be identified in simple terms as a data base input/output control program. Information is stored on direct access files by a sequential or random access method included in the D.M.R. The problem program communicates with

Figure V-2 Development Project Work Program

DEVELOPMENT PROJECT WORK PROGRAM

Project description: Course assignment—student record system Start date: June 1 Completion date: July 31

Estimated project time: Development 56 hrs. User: 17 hrs.

A. **Information provided**

1. Basic logic flowchart
2. Basic logic decision tables
3. Internal control rules
4. File data layouts
5. Data dictionary/directory
6. Data management standards

B. **Development activities**	Develop hours	Used hours	Document created
1. Develop logic routine flowcharts	14	0	X
2. Prepare logic decision tables	6	4	X
3. Prepare report layouts	3	2	X
4. Code program	20	0	
5. Prepare test data	0	8	
6. Compile and omit diagnostics	8	0	X
7. Test and desk check (3 tests)	3	2	
8. Finalize documentation	2	1	X
TOTAL	56	17	5

the D.M.R. through modular programming linkage techniques. The application-programmer regards the management routine as a tool to achieve a system objective. Data management packages are available from equipment suppliers, software companies, or can be independently developed.

The D.M.R. responds to system requirements for action and control relating to file organization, access, and maintenance. A data base by definition is a collection of information. This information includes multiple master and subordinate files and maintain file relationship linkage.

Master files are sequentially or randomly organized. A specific record is located through a key data element. Subordinate master files are loaded by a controlled load through the D.M.R. Record availability and usage control must be recognized by the D.M.R.

A random access record has four segments: file address, key, data, and linkage. Data includes all stored information including the key. The key also serves as record identity and access control. File address is the physical device storage location for the record. Linkage provides a path from a master to a subordinate record. Subordinate files are stored by the D.M.R. and require no external key. Instead, accuracy verification controls are required. (Figure VI-2).

In the example, the STUDENT FILE is sequentially organized by SURNAME. The COURSE FILE is sequentially organized by COURSE-NAME. Follow the student CLASS-LINK path to trace academic history or course schedule. Now, follow the COURSE MASTER STUDENT LINK to obtain class enrollment. Other master files (i.e., FACULTY-MASTER) can be linked through additional subordinate files.

An application program requests a collection of data by field name from the D.M.R. The D.M.R.

Figure VI-1

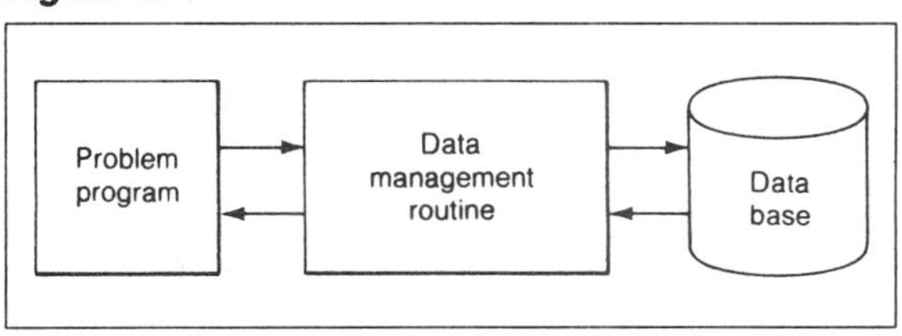

responds with the data only and need not provide address or linkage information. It communicates at a data element level rather than record level. Modifications to the file organization or record sizes do not affect the existing application programs. This provides data independence. Additional independence is possible through development of a standard interface to handle ALL input/output functions. This routine resides between the application program and the D.M.R. (Figure VI-3).

Fundamental COBOL without input/output is similar between all equipment manufacturers. The standard interface routine provides hardware and software independence. It provides conversion capability to accept new advancements in our industry with minimum application program change.

Data management is a tool. Use of this tool requires a skilled "craftsman" and brings a new specialist to our data processing scene. This man, the data base administrator, must achieve efficient response and maximum throughput through his technical skills. He must understand all tools of his trade including D.M.R.'s, access methods, and storage devices. His function relieves application programmers from storage technology and frees them to concentrate on the application problems.

Develop, Test, and Document

Throughout the preceding phases of our project development, personnel were involved with other assignments. Other projects were being evaluated simultaneously. We have defined the objectives, prepared a plan, identified justification, and employed a data base administrator to satisfy our technical needs. We are now ready to deal face-to-face with our system. Personnel assignment is step one on our project network. Where does this project relate in priority to other application projects? Who in the organization has authority to make this decision?

It is a decision which requires judgment and communication. An Information Services Steering Committee comprised of executive representatives can direct the development priorities based upon need and operating-cost/return-on-investment factors. Economics may justify staff expansion or use of

Figure VI-2 Loaded Data Base

MASTER NO. 1—STUDENT FILE

ADDR	REG-NO	SURNAME	FIRST-NAME	SEX	BIRTH	CLASS-YR	ACCUM-AV	ACCUM-CR	CLASS-LINK
18	452	ANDREWS	THOMAS	M	052757	1975	000	000	080
19	453	ATKINS	SHIRLEY	F	062056	1974	886	004	084
20	454	BAKER	SALLY	F	031757	1975	000	000	092
21	455	BROWN	ROBERT	M	112057	1975	000	000	096
ADDR	KEY	KEY	DATA						LINK

SUBORDINATE—SCHEDULE & HISTORY

ADDR	COURSE-NO	REG-NO	ASSIGN-GRADE	TEST-GRADE	DAYS-ABS	FINAL-GRADE	NEXT-STUDENT	NEXT-CLASS
80	M26	452	000	000	00	000	084	081
81	S01	452	000	000	00	000	091	082
82	E01	452	000	000	00	000	095	083
83	FR1	452	000	000	00	000	097	END
84	M26	453	950	934	02	932	087	085
ADDR	CONTROL		DATA				LINK	

MASTER NO. 2—COURSE FILE

ADDR	COURSE-NO	COURSE-NAME	FACULTY-NAME	CLASS-TIME	DAYS	NO-CREDITS	NO-ENROLL	ROOM	DATA
31	M26	ALGEBRA I	MR NOLAN	0830	MTWT	1	27	126	080
32	S01	BIOLOGY	MRS PIERCE	0930	M WTF	1	24	218	081
33	S04	CHEMISTRY	MR ADAMS	1030	M W F	1	28	222	090
ADDR	DATA	KEY	DATA						LINK

external services to achieve project objectives. Activities of prior phases have provided defined specifications for external quotations.

The user-development relationship is already a reality and now our project priority warrants personnel assignment. From here to implementation the two units become a single team. Too often, we see systems representatives resort to "walking the halls" in pairs following implementation of a system. Coordination and teamwork at this time is the best assurance a system has for success.

Case no. 1—after implementation without coordination. User: "Your system fails to recognize this condition; fix it!"

Case no. 2—after implementation with coordination. User: "I failed to recognize this condition. How do we change our system to include it?"

It may not be quite that easy, but it definitely helps. All members of the development team have responsibility for the result. The user has

Figure VI-3

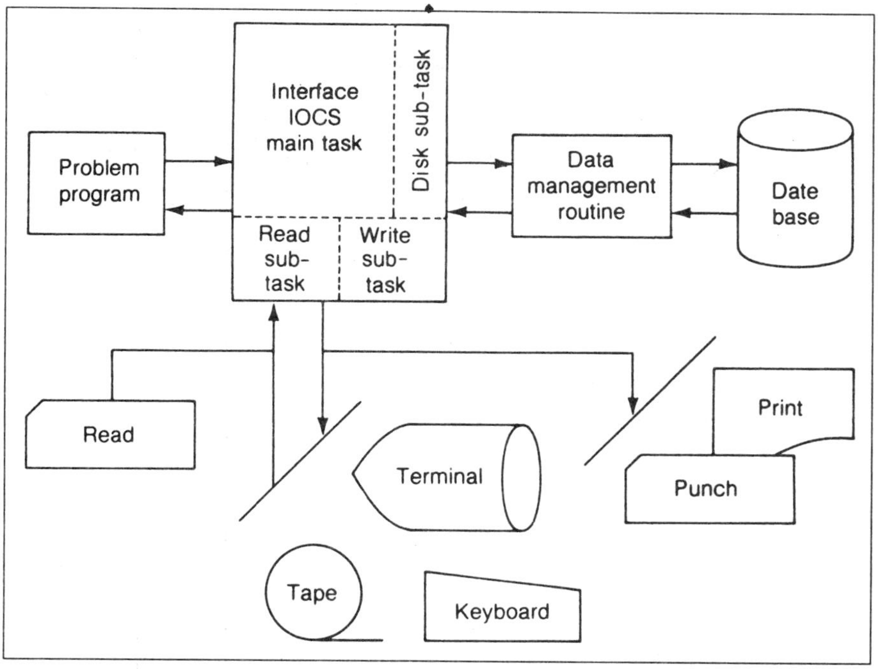

participated in logic, testing, and preparation. At implementation time he is aware of what the system does, how it does it, and the expected results. He lacks this knowledge if he sits back with an attitude of "call me when you're done."

What is job achievement? How do we recognize when we are ready for implementation? The Computer Standards Manual must define the required criteria to be satisfied to classify a project as complete. It must include documentation, test satisfaction, and mutual user/development agreement of achieved objectives.

The phase of development, test, and document is a roll-up-the sleeves working "party." It is the springboard to achievement. This phase frequently extends over a prolonged elapsed period if inadequate preparation preceded start-up. The efforts are more efficient if performed in an organized manner. Each step we have performed is essential to success and is required either before or during development.

Plan Security Protection

The Pentagon fire, university and industrial vandalism, and unauthorized time-share data access were given front-page coverage in business and data processing tabloids. Unfortunately, need for data processing security can be recognized too late. Data security is an insurance which protects the system investment, assures continued processing of data, and permits data processing managers a few extra hours of restful sleep.

Protection needs include equipment, data, programs, and documentation. Unintentional accidents occur from program and operator errors, floods, power failures, and equipment malfunctions. Economic justifications reveal the cost of system development and operation. They fail to identify the effect a prolonged operational failure has on operating costs. Imagine your organization's reaction to a prolonged operational failure. Redevelopment of a data base or procurement of replacement hardware could exceed several weeks. Security is a primary responsibility of information services management.

Major security considerations include confidentiality, data recovery, equipment protection, and program/system agreements, restricted computer-room access, and back-up. Back-up equipment elimination of glass computer rooms protect hardware. This development phase addresses the other aspects of data base security.

Confidential security restricts dissemination of the information captured by a system to persons authorized access to the information. Data bases may store available and restricted information in a single file or bank of files. Remote terminal access requires computer control over information dissemination in addition to prior administrative controls. Basic control by terminal identification can be incorporated in the interface sub-task to restrict confidential responses to authorized terminals. Key or password access can also be incorporated to restrict access to an authorized individual. (Figure VIII-1).

Data security implies the ability to recover from data destruction without loss of information validity. Cause of data destruction is not important when the data base is destroyed. Concentration rests on recovery and the ability to react. Previous tape systems provided the natural generation back-up procedure. Protection of data bases requires periodic capture of the file images on tape or disk packs. Back-up frequency is determined by considering the recovery duration and the effect on organization operations.

The file image changes in a data base system as a result of transaction processing. Reconstruction of a data base following destruction is a process of restoring the most current back-up and reprocessing the interim transactions. It is necessary therefore, to retain the processed transactions between back-ups for accurate recovery. A multi-level security procedure for a data base can be initiated. In this procedure, each back-up level may require higher organization authorization to initiate restore action. (Figure VIII-2).

Programs and software require similar protection. A system requires both data and programs to satisfy its objectives. Security protection requires librarian controls over program decks, listings, and documentation. Recording procedures to identify program modification details aid in debugging and protection.

System documentation is a volume of hand-written, computer generated, and correspondence papers accumulated from the initial specification

Figure VIII-1 Confidential Security Decision Logic

CONDITION	1	2	3	4	5
Data restricted	N	Y	Y	Y	Y
Terminal authorized		Y	N	N	N
Proper key			Y	N	N
Proper password				Y	N
ACTION					
Serve request	X	X	X	X	
Reject request					X
Log unauthorized request					X

through actual implementation. Much is using unnecessary drawer space. Some is valuable reference material which requires protection. Microfilm is a compact means of duplication and storing documentation at relatively low cost.

Computer management realizes the importance of security. They are responsible for its success and must enforce compliance with security standards. Unrecoverable loss of a data base would be difficult to explain to operating management.

Educate and Implement

Implementation is an elapsed period rather than a point in time. Implementation tools are information flow procedures and system user manuals. Preparation of these documents has been accomplished during the development cycle.

Procedures are written, published, distributed, and maintained by the development group. The procedures identify organization responsibilities and manual controls as information flows between organization units. "Playscript" method is a brief, simple method of procedure writing which identifies actions by responsible area.

The user manual documents detailed actions within a single organization unit. The user manual contains system flow diagrams and decision tables.

Figure VIII-2 Data Base Back-Up Procedure

File number 1262 Name Back-up

Frequency Daily Retention 4 generations

Transaction file identification No. 286 daily batch

Generation	File location	Transaction location	Rotation instrument	Authority to use
1	Tape library	Computer room	Move to Gen. No. 2	Shift supervisor
2	File vault	Tape library	Move to Gen. No. 3	Data base administrator
3	Payroll vault	File vault	Move to Gen. No. 4	Data processing manager
4	Bank vault	Payroll vault	Scratch	Director information services

Written action steps can also be written in playscript style. The user manual is an extension of the procedure and shows step-by-step actions to satisfy procedural information flows.

The user area representatives can be assigned responsibility for publishing their segments of user manuals. Writing assistance may be required from the procedures analyst; however, he should not write the manuals independent of the user.

Prior to implementation, procedures and user manuals must be presented to and discussed with persons who will work with the new system. These sessions are intended to clarify the responsibilities, actions, and objectives of the system. Both development and user representatives should participate in these presentations. If multiple sessions are necessary, all should be presented by the same individuals. Be prepared to repeat training following system start-up as required.

Programs, procedures, and education are completed. The system start-up can begin. The development representatives must be available to assist the user through retraining and answering questions. He must physically locate within the user area to be available to all user personnel. As system flows operate smoothly, and questions reduce, he can withdraw and return to his home area. A random sample of transactions should be traced to assure accurate data base results. Rejections must be examined and controlled. Rejection logs must verify that response and corrective actions have occurred. The development department is responsible to inform the user of any program modifications which affect the data rules. The stored data must never be altered without user control and participation.

The user is responsible for information accuracy. Data base information is the result of gathering data from multiple sources. The establishment of a data base can reveal past data inaccuracy which requires corrective action. Post-implementation clean-up must be a user responsibility.

Proper planning and adherence to the steps outlined in phases I through VIII pave the road for implementation. The approach outlined avoids undesirable surprises since adequate planning, coordination, testing, and education have preceded implementation. The combined participation of system and functional skills, sharing accountability for the result, leads a system to achievement of its objectives.

Audit and Evaluate Results

The system audit is a post-implementation review

of operating costs, savings, and investment security. The audit will be conducted by a person or group other than the development project leader or user. Large organizations may identify a system audit function. Others may assign this responsibility to a financial or data processing manager. The auditor has the economic study documents, development costs, and operating records as basis of his review.

A comparison of the economic evaluation to actual costs requires a comprehensive review. Transaction volumes, file sizes, computer operating costs in addition to user responsibilities must be examined. Projected savings, both tangible and intangible, must be reviewed for achievement. Additional costs or savings should be included in this audit study.

The audit report should be a brief narrative which describes the findings. It should be supported by an evaluation and cash flow similar to the economic study document (Figure IV-1) plus a comparison of plan to actual. Project audit and evaluation reports should be submitted to the Information Services Steering Committee.

Each organization has its own attitudes and opinions to ward systems responsibilities. These "Ten Commandments of Data Base" provide a procedure for systems development. They identify ten fundamental steps to follow in the development of data base systems. These steps may be applied to any information system design. A data base stores all organization information in a single, multi-phase system. The importance of the data base to organization operations places greater emphasis on design planning and control. These guidelines reduce the risk of failure, provide security recovery, reduce development time, failure, provide security recovery, reduce development time, provide project controls, assure investment justification, and achieve system objectives.

Through this ten-phase method we can enjoy freedom from hardware, software, and data bases. Our analyst will deal at a problem level and new technology may enhance but shall never restrict our development endeavors.

Discussion Questions

1. Why is it important to analyze the usage of data elements before attempting to define file structures and estimate storage requirements? In what ways can failure to perform such analyses affect the performance and cost of the resulting system?
2. Should project development plans be based on justification criteria or vice versa? Or should both be developed concurrently. How can oversights or misjudgments in one area affect the validity of the other?
3. What are the implications of the "integrated data base" form of system structure for problems of data security? What procedures can be built into the data management software to aid in maintaining security of the data base?
4. Why is adequate documentation of a system so important? Why is it often neglected in pratice? What may be the undesirable consequences of such neglect?

READING 38

Database Administration: Organization and Functions

article by
GORDON C. EVEREST

The database administrator (DBA) plays a key role in achieving the database management objectives of data availability and the maintenance of data integrity. The database administrator is the external human agent who is responsible for the control and use of an organization's data resources as represented in the database.

As the sharing of data becomes more widespread, there is a growing awareness of the need for both coordination and conflict resolution among those who share the data. The responsibility for various administrative functions must be centralized to achieve coordination and mediation of conflicting demands and to achieve a greater measure of global optimization. For example, in determining the content and structure of the database, it is necessary to make design choices based upon all the needs in the organization, both present and foreseen, to resolve any conflicting differences, and to balance the needs against the available resources. Recent literature suggests that the role of database administrator has become widely accepted today, in theory, if not in practice. Nevertheless, considerable diversity of opinion exists concerning the functions to be performed in that role and how the role should be incorporated into the organization.

Source: Reprinted with permission of McGraw Hill Book Company from *Database Management*, 1986, pp. 576-621.

Database Administration Within the Organization

Discussion of database administration involves its position within the overall organizational structure, and the internal structure of the database administration unit. In discussing database administration within the overall organization, it is initially assumed that the DBA functions are centralized into a single organizational unit.

Once an organization gives formal recognition to

the existence of data which is common across applications, functions, or organizational units, the next necessary step is to appoint an agent to be responsible for the creation and maintenance of this common resource. Such an agent is called the database administrator, or information resource manager. The role of database administrator is an ambivalent one.

On the one hand, the DBA is subservient to and works for using organization units, while on the other hand, the DBA has authority over several using organizational units. This is not unlike the personnel manager who serves other units in the organization but is directly responsible to top management. Should any conflict arise in the performance of the personnel or the database management function, it is up to top management to resolve it.

Sharing, Conflict, Mediation, and Compromise

Consider the chain of events:

SHARING
produces CONFLICT
necessitating MEDIATION
resulting in COMPROMISE
for one.
but yielding GLOBAL
OPTIMA for all.

Sharing produces conflict, for example:

• Users may disagree in the choice of data item names and the naming conventions used.

• A shared data file will necessarily contain the superset of data needed by all users. A user needing only some of the data may be burdened by having to view all the data (unless the system offers a user schema capability) and by having to wait for all the data to be transferred when it is being read from the disk.

• The major user of a database may experience degradation of performance when secondary indexes and pointers (which have to be maintained) are added to satisfy the needs of other users.

• Some users may require more extensive quality control measures (validation, etc.) than others, resulting in slower operation and greater "nuisance" for those other users. For example, data entry in the receiving and inspection department may be subject to strict validation controls which are required by users responsible for inventory control and order entry.

• Allowing concurrent update to common files places a burden and additional discipline on all users of the data.

Database administration is fundamentally a people-oriented function. The key responsibility of the database administrator is to coordinate and resolve conflicting needs and desires of users in their diverse application areas as they relate to the data resources. Furthermore, there must be a mechanism whereby each of the affected users will be bound to a mediated decision. While not necessarily having direct authority over the using organizational units, the DBA must be able to appeal to the authority of a manager who does. Similarly, whether the database administrator's decision is arrived at democratically or autocratically, a user must have the right to appeal to a higher authority for a review of the decision.

By centralizing the database management function, the database administrator can seek a globally optimal solution to such things as the logical and physical design of the database and the related efficiency of the applications accessing and maintaining the database. Furthermore, these decisions can be made and revised, based upon the changing needs and patterns of usage in the using environment.

Organizational Evolution of Database Administration

The early appearance of a separate database administration function grew out of systems development (see Figure 1). As development projects began to overlap in the data used, organizations recognized the need to coordinate the definition and use of common data files across application systems. Someone had to resolve conflicts in use and maintain common data resources. That necessitated giving up some autonomy in systems development.

Figure 1 Database Administration Serving Systems Development

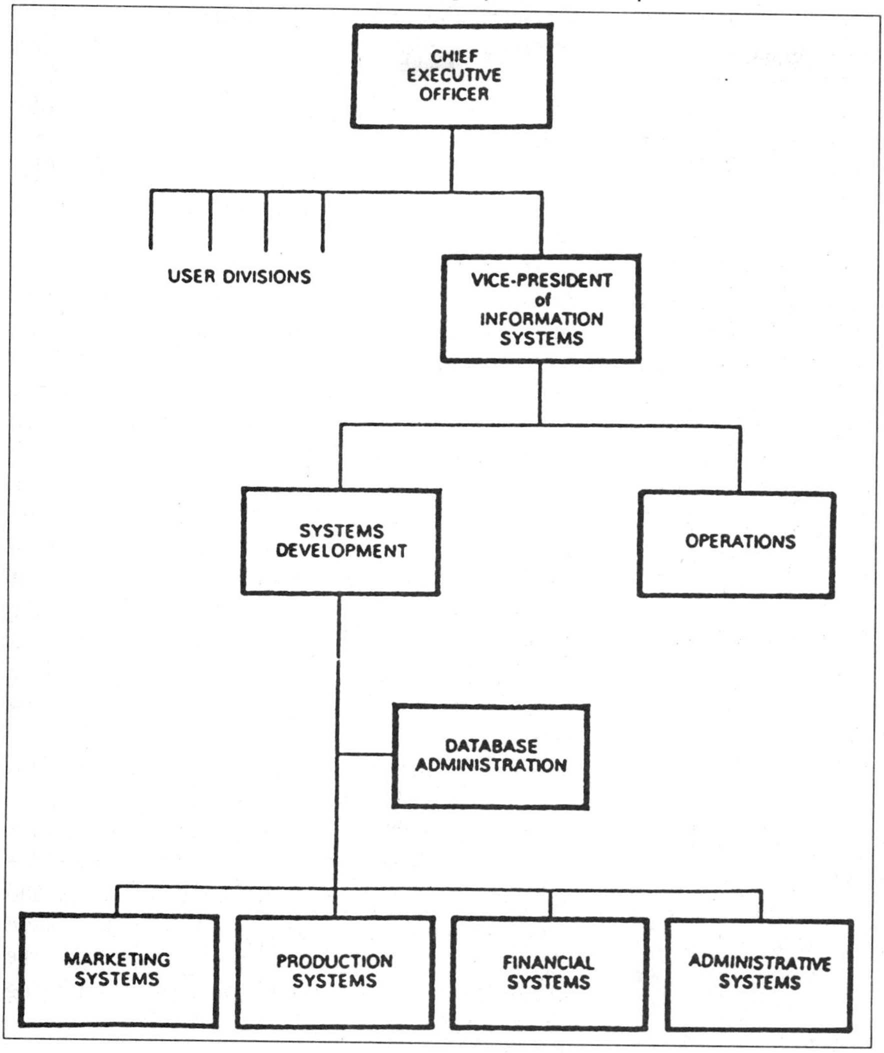

It was further discovered that the DBMS tool could assist developers in becoming more productive in building information systems. Since a DBMS can be very complex, difficult to select from those available, and require substantial training to use effectively, developers began to look to those who had mastered the use of DBMS for assistance in building systems.

In some organizations, database administration is placed along with other technical support functions under operations. Such a position tends to emphasize control over the physical and operational aspects of databases.

As database administration matures, the need for coordination and control extends beyond systems development into operations and directly to end users in other parts of the organization. This calls for raising the level within the information systems organization to report directly to the chief information officer, independently of development and operations (see Figure 2). It may be placed alongside other support functions such as planning, communications, and quantitative methods.

The position of database administrator should not be imposed on users. Users must first see the need for such a position. This may require a series of

Figure 2 Mature Database Administration within the Organization

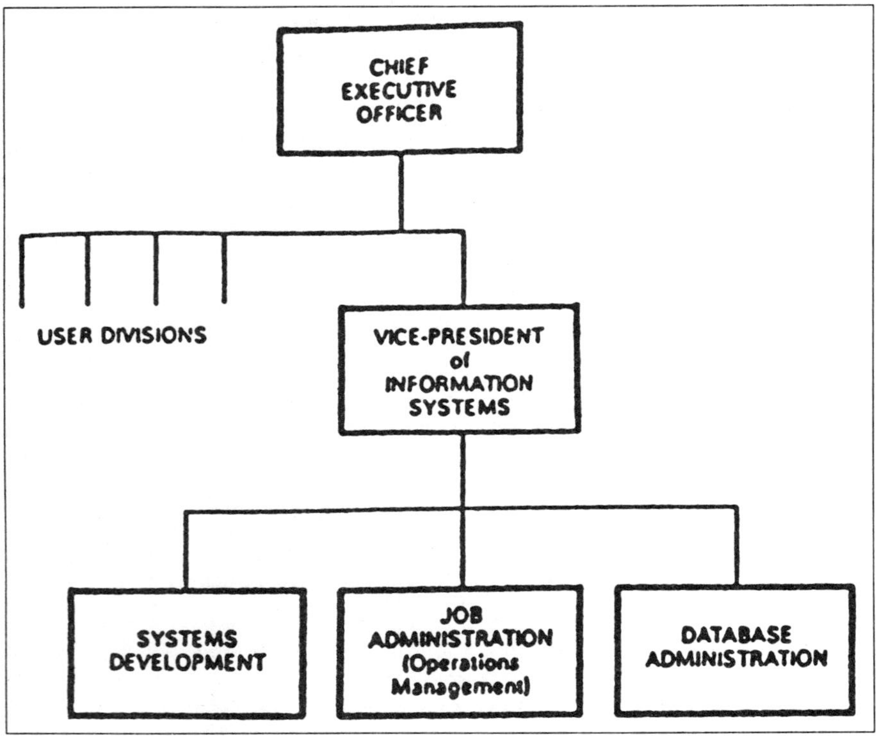

meetings and orientation sessions. When the position is established, users need to encounter a positive and helpful attitude, and experience some beneficial results when interacting with the database administrator. This reinforces their new roles and helps prevent the users from reverting back to their old behavior patterns, thereby undermining the DBA's authority and responsibilities.

Varying degrees of interaction between data and programs or between the database administrator and the job or system administrator are found in the following activities:

- Creating and maintaining a cross reference table showing what data elements are referenced by what programs and how (read, create, or modify data values).
- Approving user schemas (that is, the definition of the data as the program expects to view it) to ensure compatibility with the defined database.
- Providing a testbed of data for use in debugging programs.
- Authorizing programs to act on parts of the database after they have been thoroughly tested and debugged.
- Servicing requests for data access received from jobs in execution.
- Mounting and demounting offline files.
- Authorizing programs from the standpoint of data privacy to reference certain parts of the database.
- Monitoring program-data interaction and providing a record in the form of an audit trail.
- Providing for backup to the database in the event of destruction.
- Restarting the system after a breakdown. This involves restoring both the data and the programs before jobs can be restarted.

To clarify organizational roles, a definite assignment of responsibilities must be made relative to each of these activities.

An interface exists between database administration and system development. System development includes the planning, analysis, design, and implementation of application processes. The database administrator would participate in the design effort and determine technical and economic feasibility in seeking to satisfy the data requirements of the application processes. The data requirements of new systems may be satisfied by using data already collected and stored, or by extending the definition of the database to include new data requirements.

One of the more difficult tasks facing the DBA is to get the systems development personnel to use the new DBMS tools in building application systems. Tremendous inertia exists in favor of the old familiar system-building tools, such as COBOL, even if augmented with the (low-level) data manipulation language of a DBMS.

With the higher-level tools of a comprehensive DBMS:

- Developers can be much more productive in building application systems.
- A new approach can be taken in the development cycle of application system development.
- Users are more likely to get a system which better satisfies their needs.

In this new environment, database administration is not doing the systems development work. They are responsible for providing the tools, for training developers (which may be the end users themselves) and encouraging them to use these tools, for providing assistance and support in the use of these tools, and for establishing conventions and controls in the use of these tools.

Although responsible for the content and structure of the database, for making it available, and for controlling its integrity, the database administrator's responsibilities can be properly executed only through communication with the relevant users. In cooperation with users, the database administrator seeks to determine what data to collect and store and the criteria used in validating input data and stored data. It has been suggested that the correctness of data is the responsibility of the user, while the protection of data is the responsibility of the database administrator. Such a separation of responsibility is feasible only if a single user is associated with or has any interest in the database or a given part of the database. When multiple users share any part of the database, and sharing is assumed to be the normal case, they must agree on who will have the responsibility for its correctness. It could be the primary using organization, but if there are any other using organizations they would tend to receive second priority consideration. If the data collection activity is within an organization unit different from the primary using organization, database administrator, with the requisite level of authority, may be the best one to have responsibility for the availability and integrity of the database. Where a database administrator does not exist in an organization, the appointment of "prime responsible authorities" may be a good *interim* solution.

The datbase administrator in the key link is establishing and maintaining management and user confidence in the database and in the system facilities which make it available and control its integrity. They have a person to receive both requests and complaints. As with any organization, the degree of confidence is determined by the extent to which the database administrator and the DBA staff listen and are responsive to management and users.

Data Administration Versus Database Administration

Some authors have made a distintion between data administration and database administration, perhaps based upon IBM's distinction between data management and database management, the latter being the lower-level, more technical function within a computer system. The following table, adapted from Durell [1985, page 6] contrasts these two roles:

	DATA ADMINISTRATION	DATABASE ADMINISTRATION
PRIMARY ORIENTATION	Administrative	Technical
PRIMARY LIASON	Management	Programmers, analysts
HORIZON	Long-term data planning	Short-term database development and use
SCOPE OF DATA	All databases, both mechanized and nonmechanized	Database specific
DATA DESIGN	Logical information architecture	Physical design and implementation
FOCUS OF WORK	Metadata Data Dictionary Data Analysis DBMS independent	Data Database Data design DBMS specific

In many organizations, the person with the technical orientation is probably easy to identify—the management oriented role may not even exist yet. In this text, the term "database administration" encompasses both positions described in the preceding table.

Some larger organizations have established two places for the database administration function. One provides a direct interface with users in determining their information needs, development of user schemas, and global database design and long-range planning to meet collective user needs. The other unit is responsible for actual implementation in the DBMS, the formal definition and creation of databases, monitoring and fine tuning performance, and providing specific technical support.

Functions of Database Administration

Although the role of database administrator is often associated with generalized DBMS, most of the functions are relevant whether or not such a system is available in the organization. For example, it is still necessary to control the definition and (future) redefinition of shared files. The emergence of DBMS technology simply brings to light more of the problems of database management and, hopefully, offers some help in their solution.

The natural set of responsibilities of any manager includes the personnel, policies and procedures which relate to his or her own organization. To the extent that these are not uniqe to database administration, they are not discussed.

The unique functions of database administration are:

- Defining, creating, refining, and retiring data
- Making the database available to the using environment.
- Informing and assisting users.
- Maintaining database integrity.
- Monitoring operations and performance.

Each is discussed in the following subsections with a focus on functions rather than on activities.

Define, Create, Redefine, and Retire Data

The data resources in an organization constitute the central responsibility of database administration. The scope of responsibility may be limited to mechanized data resources, or further limited to the data defined with the DBMS tool(s). Ensuring that needed data is available to users may involve getting data into a mechanized form using a conversion utility or writing a special conversion program, and perhaps establishing a communication link between two computers if the data currently resides on a different machine.

The process of data definition begins in response to stated data requirements from the using environment. New data may be needed to satisfy a request from top management or from a user organization or to satisfy the data requirements of a new application under development.

The first step in the definition process is to design the logical data structure, incorporating as much as possible of the natural structure inherent in the data. In a sense, the logical data structure should model the real world of interest. The design should not have a "runs" or process orientation but instead should model selected aspects of the oeprations and entities as they really exist. When a data structure already exists in an organization the new data must be incorporated into existing databases in a way that is compatible with the logical structure of the existing data.

Once the logical data structure is developed, it is formalized in the data definition language (DDL) of the particular database management system being used in the organization. Since every system has a permissible class of data structures which can be defined, it is generally necessary to modify the "natural" data structure so that it will be acceptable to the system. For example, some systems permit the definition of tree structures with only two levels in the hierarchy. If the inherent relationships in the data suggest more levels, the natural hierarchy must be partially collapsed or modified in some way to arrive at a database structure acceptable to the system.

The data structure, in addition to being formally defined to system, should be fully documented in a master catalogue for the use of people in the organization. This suggests a form of graphical representation for easier comprehension.

Since the data described in the logical data structure will eventually be stored physically within the computer system, the system usually needs some guidance in how to linearize and partition the logical structure. The process of linearization and partitioning produces physical blocks which can be conveniently mapped onto and transferred to and from the storage devices. This definition of a storage structure may include the specification of block size, storage devices, data compression, access strategies, indexes, and orderings. Some and perhaps of all these features may be selected by default within a particular DBMS. The fewer choices that are made available within a system, the less the database administrator is able to give effect to tradeoffs in satisfying differing requirements. Such choices can have a direct impact on the responsiveness and efficiency of the system.

Whether the design activity is conducted by the database administrator or by a user, the resulting formal data definition and user-oriented documentation must be approved by the database administrator before the data becomes a part of the corporate database. The design process generally entails substantial interaction between the database administrator and the various user organizations who have an interest in the data being defined.

Having defined some data to the system, the next step is to set up the mechanisms to acquire the new data and to bring it into the system. The creation process refers to capturing data and storing it within the system according to the logical and physical structures previously defined. The creation process is often accompanied by extensive editing and validation of the incoming data.

The tasks of definition and redefinition go together. Modification of an existing data structure may be motivated by such factors as new data needs or changes in the current pattern of usage. When a logical data structure is modified, it necessitates a reorganization of the storage structure and notification of the using community, and it may involve a recompiling and perhaps rewriting some application programs. With a cross-reference listing of programs and data, the database administrator should ideally be able to predict the effect of a proposed change in the data structure. The DBA needs to be able to detect those programs (or rather user schemas) rendered inefficient or inoperative by a change in the data structure. Since it is probably impossible to predict all effects, some sort of checking mechanism would have to be invoked during the initial phases of program execution.

Finally, the last step in this process is to execute management policies regarding data retention. The value of data diminishes over time so it is desirable to aggregate older data, store the detail in offline archival files, and eventually retire all the old data to archival files.

Provide Availability Tools

To achieve the objective of availability, the database administrator provides the facilities and tools with which the users can query and update the database in a manner suitable to their needs. Meeting this responsibility involves acquiring (or developing) appropriate database management tools. Such tools can be extended and augmented to further enhance the facilities in response to increased diversity of requirements. The DBA should strive to acquire and make available common generalized functions. Pooling top talent to develop functional tools can often result in better use of human resources and the development of better software and systems for database use. When new system software tools are developed they must be validated by the database administrator and approved for use in production.

Availability tools are not only needed for the end users (query, report generation, update) but also for the system developers. They need to be able to develop tailored screen definitions for both retrieval and data entry/update, tailored menus for the end user, and set up predefined processes which interact with the store database. DBMSs with these enhanced capabilities for the system developer are sometimes called tools.

Inform and Assist Users

The database administration function is fundamentally a service function within the organization. The central part of a database administrator's responsibility is to relate to the people who use the data resources and the database management system tools. The DBA is the servant and agent of the persons who make up the diverse user community. The DBA informs and services people in user departments, top management, and programmers and analysts in other parts of the information systems division. Often the DBA offers assistance to a user who is in the process of attempting to solve problems and develop applications.

The database administrator has the responsibility to keep the users fully informed regarding many aspects of the database environment. First, the database adminstrator must maintain up-to-date documentation on the structure and contents of the database itself. Such documentation describes what data is kept in the database, what it means and how it is to be interpreted (not simply a listing of the codes that can be stored for a data item), how to access it, a dictionary of data names with cross references to similar or related data elements, a pictorial representation of the data structure intended for human understanding, and the more detailed and precise definition needed to accurately reference the database. The database documentation would be made available to users on demand, assuming no privacy restrictions and that they had a need to know. The appropriate users also need to be automatically notified when any changes are made to the database definition.

The database administrator is responsible for making available reference manuals and user manuals on how to use the facilities and languages of the database management tools such as retrieval, report generation, and update. The DBA may also conduct special training sessions based upon these manuals and on the proper application of these tools to solving particular problems. When a new database management tool is developed or otherwise acquired, it should be placed in the program library for general use and the users informed about its existence and how to use it.

Users need to be informed of potential or actual loss of integrity of the database, for instance, when an update process goes out of control or data is lost or destroyed. When data is found to be in error, the using community needs to be notified in case prior actions were taken based upon the erroneous data. For example, the price for a particular product may have been wrong, causing billings to be sent to customers with the wrong figures. The error is now beyond the control of the system, and the only recourse is to send out correction notices. The database administrator could go back to the audit records to find out when the wrong price was entered and notify the users, particularly those who might have used the price data.

Maintain Database Integrity

The goal of implementing integrity procedures is reduction in the incidence of degradation or failure, and reduction in the cost of recovering from or repairing a loss of integrity. Complete integrity protection is never possible, but if it is deemed important enough (and the level of importance can usually be reflectd in cost consequences), substantial resources can be applied to enhance and maintain a high level of integrity.

There are several procedures or controls which can be used in maintaining database integrity. Some or all of them can be implemented to varying degrees depending upon the expected benefit to be derived, or more accurately, depending upon the expected cost of not implementing them. What is actually done in any given situation will depend upon the requirements of the using environment and upon the results of a cost-benefit analysis.

Integrity protection measures involve both *preventative* and *curative* aspects. The actual establishment of any control procedure requires setting up certain information, *definitions*, or parameters. For example, to validate data requires, first, an explicit expression of what constitutes valid or "right" data. This provides some standard against which to compare existing data. The preventative aspects of a control procedure involve *monitoring* and *regulation* to ensure that defined integrity measures are being enforced or carried out, and to detect and report any deviations. The curative aspects relate to the *recovery* or corrective action taken in response to detected errors or deviations.

Existence Control seeks to ensure the physical existence and well-being of the database. This can be accomplished by instituting a wide variety of security measures including isolation of facilities and control over such physical conditions as temperature and humidity. Such measures are preventative and are usually externally administered, that is, administered outside of a DBMS.

The curative aspects of existence control are generally referred to as *backup* and *recovery*. Backup refers to the regular storage of parts of the database redundantly, and preferably, remotely. This is usually done by *logging* incoming transactions or before and after images of changes to the database, or by periodically *dumping* all or part of the database. Recovery is the process of using the backup data to re-create a lost or destroyed portion of the database. Besides safeguarding the existence of data, the backup mechanism can be used to recover from loss of integrity due to faulty update or a decline in data quality.

Definition Control seeks to ensure that data always conforms to its definition. This applies especially after any update action and after any form of redefinition or reorganization of the data. In reality, this must be a mandatory integrity procedure. The database adminstrator must seek to ensure that no database management system software would ever destroy the correspondence between the database and its definition as it accesses either one. Definition control is actually the most primitive form of quality control or validation.

Quality Control seeks to detect and correct errors in data and to maintain and improve the quality of data in the database. Data quality refers to the accuracy, completeness, and consistency of data. Analysis of recurring patterns of reduced data quality can lead to improvement in the processes which input, store, process, and retrieve data.

The scope of a data quality control program depends on the sensitivity of the value of data to varying levels of quality. For example, data pertaining to bank accounts, payroll and accounts receivable generally demands a high level of quality. On the other hand, marketing intelligence data may be fragmentary and based on hearsay. It may still be very meaningful, but its value is not very sensitive to level of quality. As with other integrity control measures, the extent of implementation should be determined by a cost-benefit analysis.

It is important to note that if the system does not perform quality control checks and they are important, then the checks must be done by the users, written into their procedures. It is a responsibility of the DBA to ensure that such quality control procedures are enforced.

Update Control seeks to ensure that a user who requests an update to the database has received prior authorization to do so. The same regulartory mechanism used in access control can be used for update control. There are two forms of update which imply two levels of authorization. The first involves adding data to the database without changing any data that already exists. The second form of update involves the modification or deletion of existing data. In some situations it may be desirable to distinguish these two forms of update and impose tighter control on modification and deletion.

The database administrator, in approving system or application software for regular production use, may want to set stronger program testing requirements for programs that add or modify the database. Certifying that software is "correct" and properly handles all possible input conditions is a major technical problem. It is one thing to establish that software will do what it is supposed to do. It is even more difficult to prove that it does not do what it is not supposed to do.

Concurrently Control seeks to control the concurrent execution of programs which update* the database thus protecting the integrity of the update action and the resultant database. While some systems employ a lockout mechanism at the level of files, record types, or file partitions, this cannot be considered a satisfactory long-run solution. Ideally, lockout should occur at the level of individual record instances. Most DBMS's provide no control over the method used to control concurrent updates. In some systems, the method is very obscure, if concurrent update is permitted at all. Furthermore, it may be practically impossible for users to know how to function correctly in a given concurrent update environment. All this points to the need for the database administrator to carefully evaluate any candidate DBMS to ensure that concurrent updates are adequately controlled and that the documentation makes it clear what the users must do in that environment.

*If the concurrent programs are all retrieving or only one of them is updating, there is no threat to the integrity of the database. However, there is a threat to the integrity of any one of the retrieval programs. That is, there is a threat to process integrity but not to data integrity. Also notice that the output resulting from a retrieval program may give the appearance of database integrity loss when in fact that may not be the case.

Access Control seeks to protect data from inadvertent or unauthorized disclosure to unauthorized persons or for unauthorized purposes. Some access control is realized in the use of physical security measures. Some form of restricted access is usually required since all data cannot be considered completely open to outsiders or even to all persons inside the organization. There is often a need to protect individual and corporate privacy and to control the interpretation of certain data.

The mechanism for access control requires the database administrator to set and periodically reset access authorizations on both users and objects of data to be controlled (sometimes called privacy locks and keys). At the time of an access request, the system can seek to identify requesters and check their authorization (which has been previously defined to the system) against their request. The system can monitor unsatisfied requests in an attempt to detect a potential breach of security. In addition, a record or audit trail may be kept of all accesses to the database to permit a followup investigation in case of a suspected breach, perhaps by an authorized person but for an unauthorized purpose. Another procedure for access control is encryption or the encoding of confidential data before it is stored or transmitted.

Monitor Operations

Finally, as a fifth function, the database administrator is generally responsible for the data-related aspects of operations. This includes:

- Keeping things in operation
- Controlling operations related to the database
- Striving to obtain maximum efficiency in operations against the database.
- Keeping a recorded history of data-related events which can be reviewed when problems arise.

The database administrator needs to monitor the usage of the database and gather performance statistics to periodically assess the appropriateness of the existing database to the current population of users. The information gathered can serve as the basis for changing the logical or physical structure of the database in response to changing patterns of usage. The database administrator constantly seeks to optimally serve the using environment, which means constantly seeking to balance the changing needs of the individual users. For each user or application, the volume of data and frequency of usage can change. When it does change, and sometimes the change is gradual, the database adminstrator must monitor operations to be aware of the changing pattern of usage and then attempt to respond to it.

Summary

Acquiring a DBMS is not sufficient for successful data management. The role of database administrator provides the human focus of responsibility to make it all happen. The DBA role may be filled by one person or several persons.

Whenever people share the use of a common resource such as data, the potential for conflict exists. The database administrator role is fundamentally a people-oriented function—to mediate the conflicts and seek compromise for the global good of the organization.

Within an organization, database administration generally begins as a support function within the systems development unit. Sometimes it is in a technical support unit associated with operations. Eventually, it should be separate from both development and operations, residing a collection of support functions reporting directly to the director of information systems. Such a position has some stature, some independence, and can work directly with users to capture their data requirements. Database administration works with development, operations, and users to coordinate the response to data needs. The database administrator is the key link in establishing and maintaining management and user confidence in the database and in the system facilities which make it available and control its integrity.

While the 'doing' of database system design and development can be decentralized to several development projects in the Data Processing Department or the user organizations, planning and control of database development should be centralized. In this way an organization can provide more consistent and coherent information to successively higher levels of management.

The functions associated with the role of database administration include:

- Definition, creation, revision, and retirement of data formally collected and stored within a shared corporate database.
- Making the database available to the using environment through tools such as a DBMS and related query languages and report writers.
- Informing and advising users on the data resources currently available, the proper interpretation of the data, and the use of the availability tools. This includes educational materials, training sessions, participation on projects, and special assistance.
- Maintaining database integrity including existence control (backup and recovery), definition control, quality control, update control, concurrency control, and access control.
- Monitor and improve operations and performance, and maintain an audit trail of database activities.

Discussion Questions

1. Distinguish the differences between data administration and database administration. How are their orientation and scope different?
2. How is the organizational location of a "mature" database administration function different from that of an "immature" database administration function?
3. Describe the unique functions of database administration.
4. Name the users that a database administration function serves.

READING 39

The Importance of Data Administration in Information Management

article by
MADELINE M. HENDERSON

Today, in the mid- to late-1980s, the process of information resources management (IRM) is maturing and finding its rightful place in the ranks of corporate objectives. This development admittedly is uneven and in many instances slower than might have been predicted. However, progress is unmistakable, and the only real question is "when"," not "why."

The developing technologies that affect IRM have been converging and interfacing to form systems at once more effective and more difficult to control. Networking, including local area networking, the proliferation of external data resources of interest to many organizations, and the remarkable spurt in the use of personal computers are providing information managers with greater opportunities and more complex responsibilities. These factors have necessarily confronted managers with the costs and problems associated with their organization's use of information and data. Data can be redundant, obsolete, unevaluated or of poor quality, and difficult to access. Manual systems and automated systems can operate independently within the organization, processing related data essential for executive decisions.

To ensure effective and efficient progress in information resources management, all possible aspects of good information management must be applied. One such aspect, often overlooked and in many cases misunderstood, is data administration.

The purpose of this discussion is to remind readers of the importance of data adminstration as a component of the overall IRM picture. Data administration can be perceived as a precursor to other, more familiar, IRM activities that can be enhanced by effective data adminstration.

Source: Madeline M. Henderson, "The Importance of Data Administration in Information Management," *Information Management Review*, Spring 1987. Reprinted with permission of Aspen Publishers, Inc. © 1987.

Functions of Data Administration

Data administration encompasses responsibility for managing one organizational resource and providing a broad perspective on the use of information and data in support of the organization's business. One must recognize that a clear distinction exists between data administration and database administration.

Management of an Organizational Resource

Data administration parallels the management of an organization's other resources: finances, personnel, and property. Like the financial, personnel, and administrative offices, the data administrator uses appropriate tools and procedures to determine the status of the organization's data: what are available, what have been used, and what are needed. Unlike other, relatively stable resources, the information and data resource is dynamic and not easily inventoried and is the only resource that can be shared by all divisions of the organization at one time. It is also the only resource used to manage and contrtol all the other resources, although it often is not itself managed. As a result, the data resource is apt to consist of myriad nonstandard application systems, with nonstandard data elements, designed for specific problems or users.

To manage the data resource effectively, the data adminstrator must learn about the use of data in the organization and how they must be collected, maintained, and made available to maximum advantage. Goals should include providing for use of shareable and available information by new systems as they are built, providing data that are standard, consistent, and accurate, and ensuring the independence of data from specific applications, so that the data can be used for many purposes and functions.

Broad Perspective on Data Usage

The role of data administration has been, until recently, too narrow and focused on solving immediate problems with current technology. However, the emergence of newer technologies and convergence of existing capabilities has caused management to take a longer look at planning for future organization needs. Central management of an organization's data and information files requires a mix of technical and administrative viewpoints. When the two processes of strategic systems planning and logical database design are successful, top management and the data administrator each have a clear picture of what the organization's business is, what data it needs, and what data it has.

One must recognize, however, that not all an organization's data should be available to everyone. Some data must be sheltered and protected from unauthorized or inappropriate access because the data are sensitive, proprietary, or protected by privacy law provisions.

Data Administration is Not Database Administration

Data administration (DA) is not the same as database administration (DBA), a function perhaps more familiar and of longer standing among data-processing professions. Database administrators are responsible for the technical implementation of automated systems that organize, locate, process, and format data into files and databases for use by application programs. The data administrator, on the other hand, is concerned with all of an organization's data, whether they reside in files, database management systems, or manual processing systems.

Thus the data administrator manages the development of standards and guidelines for data planning, analysis, and modeling and for mapping database designs against the organization's strategic plans. The database administrator, however, manages the development of standards and guidelines for implementation in the database and assists in the performance, monitoring, and tuning of database environments.

Organizational Environment for Data Administration

The DA function needs top management's commitment to the organizational goal of effective data and information management. DA also must be understood and supported by other operations within the IRM function and by middle management and technical staff who are affected by those data management goals. Policies such as support for the development of, and adherence to, data standards and to strategic data planning are essential to the effective functioning of an organization's DA office.

Management Commitment

In today's organization, policies must not only recognize that data are a corporate resource but must also provide for continual management of that resource. One estimate shows that at least 15 percent of an organization's revenues are spent on handling information. Most organizations spending such a percentage of budget on a specific resource "have someone at the top managing these resources, but they ahve not been doing it for information/data resources."[1]

Thus effective DA requires an adequately supported, technically competent staff whose responsibilities are clearly defined. The DA program must be an integral part of the overall management of the organization's programs.

Top management must recognize that the DA function will evolve over time and provide continuing support through the development stages. This evolution will move the data administrator from a staff function to line responsibilities and probably to a hybrid staff-line position. Top management must accept and support this evolution, with its requirement for larger budgets and increased authorities.

Relationships Within and Among Organizations

In addition to top management commitment, support from middle managers at all functional levels is necessary. These people are more concerned with day-to-day problems than with adherence to long-range plans. They must be involved, educated, and persuaded that good data management benefits their areas of responsibility as well as the organization as a whole.

The complexity of the data administration function results partly from the proliferation of microcomputers directly supporting end-user computing and partly from the myriad database management systems, word processing and electronic message systems, and other processing systems that magnify data management problems. DA functions thus must cut across program and application boundaries.

One of the organizational areas the data administrator will support is the information center function: DA can help end users locate information and data through the data dictionary and inventory. The normal information center procedure is to solve each problem as it is presented: data administration and its tools should be viewed as a source of data iand information already collected and paid for by the organization, available for further use at considerable cost savings.

The federal government program of IRM was formalized through the Paperwork Reduction Act of 1980, (Pub.L.No. 96-511). The law provided that each agency should appoint a single senior IRM official, who must report directly to the agency head. Such a central management focal point should provide coordinated and consolidated IRM activities within the agency and between agencies. In practice, the concept of IRM "has not been pursued as aggressively as originally predicted"[2] at the time of passage of Pub.L.No. 96-511.

A major responsibility of the program is to reduce the costs of collecting data and information for federal government needs. One approach is for agencies to share existing data whenever applicable and appropriate. The Federal Information Locator System (FILS), for example, was established to help agencies share data collected from the public. Agencies are required to file with the Office of Management and Budget (OMB) data about the data they collect in pursuit of their responsibilities. The FILS file contains metadata (data about data collection forms but not actual data collected).

The data on file with OMB was reviewed in order to discover possible modifications to FILS. The computer system, the hardware of FILS, was reported to be functioning well and to be suited to operational requirements. However, the data being entered into and processed by the computer system was unevaluated, redundant, nonstandardized, and difficult to access. Individual agencies operate independently in determining how to comply with the FILS requirements; with no source for standard data elements, greater variations in record content are found. As a result, agencies checking the FILS for shareable data are hampered in finding data matching their requests. A strong commitment to effective data administration, applied across agency and program lines, would go far toward improving the utility of the FILS.

Supporting Policies

Questions about the data an organization processes should focus on data acquisition or creation (identification of the sources of the resource). In addition, once the data are in the organization's hands, the data's ownerhsip must be clarified. Usually data in specific files were considered the property of those files, but managers increasingly recognize that some data are common to many needs within the organization and must be made available. At the same time, all data must be protected from inappropriate use or even misuse. Management policies for ownership, availability, and security must be explicitly formulated. Data administration assists in the identification and formulation of such policies and is primarily responsible for seeing that the policies are understood and followed throughout the organization.

Standards governing the processing and representation of information help control the complexity of the organization's IRM process. Data management standards include data dictionary/directory systems, generalized database management systems for varied applications, and data representation standards. Data standards contribute to effective operation of computer resources, improved data availability and access for users, and extended data and systems transferability.

An organization that initiates a program of DA must also implement an effective strategic planning process. The planning should include provisions for meeting the information needs associated with growth of the organization, diversification of services, the processes of organization, and results of broad changes in the organization's activities.

Tools of Data Administration

DA tools include systems for recording data elements in a dictionary with definition and rules for usage and in a directory with instructions for locating data. Standards are an important component of data dictionary/directory systems: compiling information about data leads to standardization of the data across systems and applications. Standard data elements enhance effective use of data processing facilities and data sharing among many applications.

Data Dictionary/Directory Systems

To manage its data effectively, an organization must document its data, including systems, procedures, and functional responsibilities. This process results in data about its data (metadata). The primary tool supporting administration and control of metadata is the data dictionary/directory system (DD/DS). The DD/DS is a computer software system that records, stores and processes descriptions of an organization's data resources.

The term "data dictionary" was used in early applications, which were simply catalogs with definitions of data elements. That term is no longer appropriate or descriptive of the contents and functions of the tools being used and for which standards are being developed, hence the current designation DD/DS.

Dictionary metadata describe what the data in the organization's data bank are, what they mean, and what exists (i.e., descriptions of pertinent entities such as individual data elements, data groups, data collection forms, records, files, databases, user procedures, and users). Dictionary descriptions include characteristics, relationships, and usage. Directory metadata describe where the data are located and how they can be accessed.

The DD/DS, therefore, is an information system about all of an organization's data and data-processing entities. An individual DD/DS entry contains important information about a named entity (e.g., a bibliographic data element such as "author's name") but does not contain actual instances of that element (i.e., an actual name). The actual instances would be data values stored in a database of bibliographic records.

Most DD/DS are based on specification of entities, relationships, and attributes. An entity describes a concept, person, event, or quantity. A relationship expresses an association between two entities. An attribute represents a property of an entity or relationship. An entity description entered into the DD/DS names the entity, identifies its type, and gives value for applicable attributes. For example, an entity might be "customer name," whose type is "data element," and whose attributes include "restricted to seven characters" and "entered as ANNNNNN."[3] Other entities might be "mailing address" and "zip code": a relationship between the two may show that the mailing address contains the zip code, and an attribute of the zip code may be its length, the value of which in current popular usage is five characters, expressed as NNNNN.

Entities might also include documents (e.g., "employment application form") or files (e.g., "personnel file"). Possible relationships include "contains" (illustrated by the zip code example above), "responsible for" (e.g., the personnel department is responsible for the personnel file), or "derived from" (e.g., lists of zip codes can be derived from mailing addresses).

The first step in building a data dictionary is to identify and define all the information and data in existing applications and databases, defining classes of entities such as data elements, people and organizational units, events, and processes. The next step is to identify and record the relationships between entities, and specify the attributes of both entities and relationships—not only logical attributes but also those associated with physical location of the entities. The dictionary entries must be recorded in a standard format and with comprehensible codes for ease of access by end users.

Ideally, a DD/DS should be introduced as a first step in data management: all of the data within the environment and the systems that use the data should be carefully documented and defined and entered in the DD/DS. Then appropriate databases to support the various information systems in the organization can be built. Thus the DD/DS can provide assessment and definition of the organization's data before the start of a new project, as well as a mechanism to control the development of new systems.

The benefits of an active DD/DS include better control of the organization's data resources, improved transportability of data and software between systems, and increased security and access control. A DD/DS is, in addition, a valuable documentation tool: as applications are designed and programs written, the pertinent entity descriptions can be introduced into the dictionary and documentation produced concurrently with development. By the same token, consistent and rigorous use of the DD/DS can help eliminate documentation problems during system conversions, whether from manual or conventional files to a database environment or from one database management system to another.

Standard Dictionary System

The National Bureau of Standards, Institute for Computer Sciences and Technology (NBS/ICST) and the American National Standards Institute (ANSI) Technical Committee X3H4 are jointly developing a generalized dictionary system proposed as a Federal Information Processing Standard (FIPS) and as an ANSI national standard.[4] The Information Resource Dictionary System (IRDS) is a software system that follows a modular approach and is designed to support a variety of user environments and to be portable. The IRDS will also support an organization's defined data element standardization program.

The IRDS design objectives include flexibility in implementations and use and adaptability to micros, minis, and mainframe computers. It will contain the most commonly used capabilities of existing dictionary systems, thus representing an outgrowth of them rather than an entirely new approach. For example, the draft IRDS is specified in terms of the familiar entities, relationships, and attributes of most dictionary systems in use today.

The system is composed of a core and optional modules, which interface with the core but are independent of each other. The system can be used by nontechnical and technical staff through a command language interface for more experienced users and a panel interface with screens and menus for the less experienced. An implementation of the IRDS must include either one or both of the user interfaces. Thus individuals will be able to use different implementations without significant retraining. In addition, an IRDS-IRDS interface provides a standard method for transferring data from one system to another. One organization, for example, can extract data from a specialized dictionary and add them to a centralized dictionary for organizationwide use.

Data Element Standardization

The NBS/ICST has been engaged in data management and software standards development for some times.[5] Much of the activity has been in data element representations and data interchange standards, but the program is now expanding to other aspects of data administration. The advantages of software standards are being recognized, for example, as was the value of earlier computer communications standards.

Data element standards define basic elements of information and how those units are stored in databases. Data elements are generic in nature; for example, "date" is a basic element and "date of birth of employee" is a particular application assigned to a personnel records database. The actual date, as noted earlier, is a value stored in a record in a particular file.

In the NBS/ICST program, 16 standards have been promulgated for widely used data elements and representations, mainly in the area of geographic locations, calendar dates, and time and time zone elements. The NBS/ICST maintains registers of data elements and codes to minimize individual development efforts and to facilitate the interchange of data among federal agencies.

Not only are federal and national programs, including NBS/ICST efforts, developing and implementing data standards; individual organizations and agencies also undertake standardization. For example, the federal reports-processing agencies have standardized the data elements used in their joint processing efforts and will continue to examine elements used in their individual systems for further standardization.

Some years ago a preliminary review of the documentation available for the four systems (National Technical Information Service, Department of Energy Office of Scientific and Technical Information, Defense Technical Information Center, and NASA Scientific and Technical Information Facility) revealed some differences in their handling of data elements common to all four systems and enumerated the advantages in development of further standards or update of the standards already in place. A project was started to compile a data element dictionary (DED) encompassing all the bibliographic data elements then used by the four agencies and the comparable elements used in similar processing by the Government Printing Office. A major purpose of the DED was to provide the reports-processing agencies with a detailed and current listing of their data elements as a guide for consideration of possible further standardization to achieve greater compatibilities and improved cooperative processing.[6]

The DED describes the meaning, contents, and rules for use of the elements specific to the individual processing systems.[7] The dictionary catalogs and defines the data elements; it does not locate the data within the agencies' computer system or process information about data entities and associated processing functions. Thus the DED is a more narrowly defined management tool than the DD/DS.[8]

The four agencies used the DED to examine the differences among their systems, to define ways to reduce redundant data collection, and to determine the effect of proposed changes in their operational environments. The DED was particularly helpful in documenting data element usage so that standards acceptable to all the agencies could be developed with minimal confusion.[9]

The study of the FILS, described earlier, is another example of data element standardization, or rather, the lack of it. The file contains data elements with little or no meaning for searches and misspellings or variations in spelling of the same data element that lead to false search results. Effective data administration should include compilation of a data dictionary, with groupings of related entities ad selection of appropriate standard elements for agency guidance. Emphasis should be placed on the data elements of most value when agencies seek evidence that wanted data already exist in federal agency databases.

The Future for Data Administration

As has been suggested throughout this discussion, DA is emerging as an integral part of IRM, an essential precursor to other management tools and techniques. DA is gaining acceptance as a distinctive point on the spectrum of IRM activities, one that requires its own commitment of staff, budget, and facilities. Managers must place more emphasis on information policies for the organization and explicitly promulgate and implement those policies. Reacting to immediate problems only, rather than developing long-range plans and programs, will overburden information management resources and endanger productivity.

The IRM efforts must also place more emphasis on the management of information content to catch up with the current attention to management of information technologies. Content management starts with efficient application of DA techniques and will probably involve interorganizational and interagency cooprative projects. For example, the four reports-processing agencies whose DED work is described above are now collaboring on review of their respective subject headings and keywords lists with the aim of standardizing the expression of common terminology. The FILS review suggested use of an existing thesaurus as a source of standard terminology individual agency use on input and search.

All in all, DA as a management principle has demonstrated its utility wherever it has been strongly supported. Given the combination of today's technology, current budgetary constraints, and increasing demands for effective information management, additional and widespread implementations are destined to appear.

Discussion Questions

1. Is Everest's distinction between data administration and database administration different from that expressed in this article? Explain.
2. Why is data administration required in addition to database administration?
3. Construct an argument for the organizational location of a data administrator. (Consider the arguments made by Everest for the organizational location of database administration in your discussion.)
4. How do data administration and database administration individually contribute to the management of the information resource?

References

1. Holland, R.H. "Data Administration in the Information Age." In *Data Administration Workshop Proceedings*, edited by F.E. Spielman. NBSIR 86-3324. Washington, D.C.: U.S. Department of Commerce, National Bureau of Standards, 1986, p. 4.

2. Levitan, K.B., and Dineen, J. "Integrative Aspects of Federal IRM." *Information Management Review* 1, no. 4 (Spring 1986): 66.

3. Applications Systems Division, Institue for Computer Sciences and Technology. *Prospectus for Data Dictionary System Standard.* NBSIR 80-2115. Washington, D.C.: U.S. Department of Commerce, National Bureau of Standards, 1980, p. 4.

4. Goldfine, A., and Konig, P. *A Technical Overview of the Information Resource Dictionary System.* NBSIR 85-3164. Washington, D.C.: U.S. Department of Commerce, National Bureau of Standards, 1985, p. 1.

5. Wood, H.M. "National and Federal Standards Effort." In *Data Administration Workshop Proceedings*, edited by F.E. Spielman. NBSIR 86-3324. Washington, D.C.: U.S. Department of Commerce, National Bureau of Standards, 1986, p. 176.

6. Henderson, M.M. "The Data Element Dictionary: Developments in Technical Reports Processing." *Government Publications Review* 13 (1986): 581-90.

7. Henderson, M.M. *Data Element Dictionary (DED): Contains All Public Data Elements Used in the Major Systems for Handling Federal Government Scientific and Technical Reports. Draft Report.* PB83-215723. Washington, D.C.: U.S. Department of Commerce, National Technical Information Service, 1982.

8. Henderson, M.M. "Compilation of Bibliographic Data Element Dictionaries." In

Proceedings of the NBS FIPS Software Documentation Workshop, edited by A.J. Neumann. NBS Special Publication 500-94. Washington, D.C.: U.S. Department of Commerce, National Bureau of Standards, 1982, p. 209.

9. Commerce, Energy, NASA, Defense Information (CENDI) Cataloging Committee. *Guidelines for Descriptive Cataloging of Reports. A Revision of COSATI Standard for Descriptive Cataloging of Government Scientific and Technical Reports.* Washington, D.C.: Defense Technical Information Center, 1985.

UNIT FOUR

MIS and People

The focus of Unit Four is on people. A management information system must operate in a human environment; its effectiveness depends critically on the acceptance and support of the people who use it and interact with it on a day-to-day basis. Experience has shown that neglect of "people problems" in the planning and design of an MIS can have disastrous results for the success of the project.

Section Thirteen (The Role of Top Management) concentrates on high-level managers and the part they must play in eliciting support and cooperation from employees toward the new system. Managers must take the lead and involve themselves actively in all phases of a system's design and implementation: their attitudes can strongly influence the success or failure of the MIS effort. Managers must be prepared for this role and the changes in their own decision-making methods that a new MIS is certain to bring.

In Section Fourteen (Behavioral Issues) we consider the reactions of an organization's members to the introduction of an MIS. These reactions may be surprising and sometimes destructive. The fears and anxieties associated with the introduction of a computer may undermine the success of the entire system. Managers must learn what behavioral effects they are likely to encounter and how to deal with them constructively.

SECTION THIRTEEN

The Role of Top Management

READING 40

Management's Newest Star: Meet the Chief Information Officer

article by
GORDON BOCK, KIMBERLEY,
and JO ELLEN DAVIS

There's a new breed of manager surfacing in the executive suite. As countless chief executives come to grasp the importance of information to their businesses, they're seeking people like Burden and assigning them a high-stakes mission: figuring out how to fashion a confusing array of often-incompatible computer and communications equipment into a cudgel that can clobber the competition. Some members of this new information elite sit behind such recognizable nameplates as senior vice-president, vice-president for information services, or information resources manager. Others are beginning to get a higher-sounding title to reflect their new status: chief information officer, or CIO.

However it's listed in the company directory, the job requires executives equipped to straddle the historic gulf between the nontechnical people in the boardroom and the traditional directors of management information systems (MIS) down on the data-processing floor, who often lack a broad sense of their company's overall business mission. Much more than just cheerleaders for new technology, CIOs look for ways to harness the power of new information technologies to slash costs, boost productivity, create new products, improve sales and marketing, and help set a company's strategic direction. The concept is still evolving, and today's CIOs are as different as the corporate cultures that spawn them. But most perform three basic functions:

- They oversee all the company's technology, including data processing, office systems, and telecommunications.
- They report directly to a high-ranking executive such as the chief executive officer or chairman.

Source: Reprinted from October 13, 1986 issue of *Business Week* by special permission, © 1986 by McGraw Hill, Inc.

• They concentrate on long-term strategy and planning while leaving the day-to-day operations of the computer room to subordinates.

"The job calls for a Renaissance man," says Eugene F. Bedell, vice-president for information services at First Boston Corp. in New York. "You have to provide technical leadership while you also talk strategy." Adds Leon Jackson, an Arthur D. Little Inc. consultant: "You have be part missionary, part salesman, and part consensus-builder."

New Guard

Typical of the new guard is Max D. Hopper, a senior vice-president of American Airlines Inc., who just returned to the airline after a 3 1/2-year stint as executive vice-president at Bank of America. Hopper, 50 is in charge of about 4,000 people and a budget of $400 million, including the airline's computer expenditures. But he is also responsible for selling American's Sabre computerized reservations system to other airlines, making it a marketing tool instead of just another data base. Such sales contributed 6% of American's revenues last year—and 28% of profits. "Our technology is a key aspect of our ability to expand," says the jovial Hopper, who meets with Chairman Robert L. Crandall for an hour or two each week. "Without it we wouldn't keep growing the way we have and offering the services we do."

So far, most chief information officers are in America's biggest corporations. In a recent survey of 120 of the nation's 500 largest service and industrial companies, the Big Eight accounting firm of Arthur Andersen & Co. found that 40% have one. While other surveys have produced lower estimates, the experts agree on one thing: CIOs are likely to proliferate in the next few years, especially in banking, financial services, airlines, and insurance—the most information-dependent businesses. "Once the CEO recognizes that he's got to do something to harness the strategic use of information, he's not going to do it himself," says Melvyn E. Bergstein, an Andersen managing director. "He's going to change the organization."

There are some who worry about the trend. Big corporations do not create new executive titles every day, and the growing presence of the CIO moniker causes Thomas J. Peters, co-author of *In Search of Excellence*, to fret that some companies are adding them in "fad-like fashion" by pinning a higher salary and fancier title on the MIS director. Those who disagree argue that even if the title itself evaporates, Corporate America has recognized the crucial role of computers and information. Companies will need senior-level people, they say, to handle the CIO job.

'Snow-Proof'

The advent of the CIO mirrors what happened when senior accountants blossomed into chief financial officers in the 1960s. "The accountant kept track of what we spent," says Eleanor M. Luce, director of management information systems for MCI Inc. in Rye Brook, N.Y. "Then we said we're going to have a CFO to worry about the financial health of the company."

Most of the people filling the new CIO jobs aren't computer types. Fewer than half have extensive technical experience, according to a recent survey by John Diebold & Associates, a consulting firm. They should speak enough computerese to be "snow-proof" with subordinates who watch over the equipment, says Professor James C. Wetherbe, director of the University of Minnesota's Management Information Systems Research Center. But the CIO's job, which brings a heftier salary, larger staff, and broader responsibilities than the old information-services manager, "is not for the classic computer jock or machine-room honcho," says Michael A. Weiner, a Diebold vice-president. "Chief information officers will know technology but must know business. They're more interested in what works than how it works."

Good Training

That's not to say that managers who grew up on the technical side can't make the transition into a CIO's shoes. Many are doing so. Robert C. Forney, 40, director of information systems at Akron-based GenCorp Inc., is studying for an MBA at Kent State

University to supplement his undergraduate degree in computer science and build his credibility with line managers at the diversified manufacturer. Robert M. Rubin, who ran the marketing department at Sun Co. for four years before joining Pennwalt Corp. as director of information systems in 1984, suggests that experience in line management is an even better recipe for success. "Running a profit-and-loss center is the best training a future CIO can get," he says. "You start to understand what businessmen do."

As their roles expand, the first priority of most CIOs is to squeeze the most out of their company's computer budget, holding down costs while making more effective use of what the company already has. When John M. Hammitt became vice-president for information management at Pillsbury Co. in 1983, one of his first acts was to put all computer spending on hold for a year while he reassessed what the company really needed. He used the time to develop a strategic, company-wide blueprint for technology use.

Hammitt hasn't been the only one reassessing his resources. From 1982 to 1984 corporations raised their computer spending by an average of about 18% a year, estimates International Data Corp., a Framingham (Mass.) market research firm. That binge left many senior managements feeling that their information-processing budgets were out of control. As a result, many corporations have started a period of digestion that has helped cause the computer industry's most prolonged slump in recent memory. The rate of annual spending growth has skidded to 9% in the past two years.

Scoring Points

Now CIOs are looking to use what they have in more strategic ways. They want to cut operating costs for line managers and make an impact on the company's bottom line. At Air Products & Chemicals Inc., workers who helped produce natural gas at 80 U.S. plants once had to read meters, write reports on the condition of the equipment, keep inventory, and then mail everything to headquarters in Allentown, Pa. But Peter W. C. Mather, a vice-president for management information services at the $1.8 billion company, saw a way to save time by having computers take over many of those tasks. Mather spearheaded the creation of a $30 million system that ties computers in the plants into a central computer at headquarters.

By controlling production levels, watching for and adjusting patterns of energy consumption in the plants, and even alerting engineers when the equipment needs upgrading, the system has increased the energy efficiency of the company's gas production by 14%, saving $25 million a year. By cutting operating costs, "information services has been recognized as a viable profession at Air Products," Mather says.

As CIOs win points with such projects, their chief executives are handing them operations that range far afield of the data processing floor. Edward A. Schefer, vice-president for information management at General Foods Corp., also supervises the company's critical function of market research. As vice-president for corporate administration at Aetna Life & Casualty Co., Irwin J. Sitkin oversees everything from computer systems to the print shop, mail room, and corporate art gallery. And Darwin A. John, an engineer by training who started out with Scott Paper Co. as MIS director in 1979, now serves as chief planning development officer as well as chief information officer. His goal: to "posture information as part of overall strategy."

For many CIOs, showing management how computers can help create new products is an increasingly important part of the job. In 1985, brokers for Boston's Fidelity Investments wanted to be first to come up with a way to guarantee customers the price of a select mutual fund at the hour they bought or sold it, rather than the price at the day's close. That way, customers who acted quickly on news affecting the market would not suffer full-day declines.

Biology Teacher

They turned to Michael Simmons, a former high school biology teacher and International Business Machines Corp. systems engineer who functions as Fidelity's chief information officer. One of 15 presidents of Fidelity's patent company, FMR Corp., Simmons came up with a way for Fidelity's computers to take a feed of proprietary data from another brokerage house, pull out those trades that affected the price of stocks and bonds in Fidelity's 32 select funds, and let Fidelity become the only U.S. seller of mutual funds to offer hourly pricing. No longer does management regard the computer operation "as some kind of giant calculator," says Simmons. He reports directly to Chairman Edward C. Johnson III.

CIOs are enjoying their most dramatic impact by honing the way their companies sell and market products. The group sales force at Northwestern National Life Insurance Co. has been isolated from headquarters in Minneapolis because 435 salespeople and support staff have used stand-alone personal computers in 25 regional offices. But David W. Haskin, a senior vice-president for corporate resources whose previous job experience was in personnel and general management, is currently having those offices connected to the company's IBM 3090 mainframe with midsize computers. That way salespeople can find out rates and deliver proposals immediately instead of waiting two weeks. The "gut feeling" of R. Michael Conley, Northwestern's vice-president for group sales, is that Haskin's move will spark sales.

Ross C. Ahntholz has a similar goal at Olin Corp., the Stamford (Conn.)-based chemical maker. He installed an IBM PC/AT at one facility where a major customer stores bulk chemicals delivered by Olin. The customer used to have to call Olin when something went wrong there—if, for instance, the temperature was dropping enough to affect the quality of the product. Now the computer monitors the process and automatically alerts Olin's headquarters of problems. Olin often responds before the customer even knows that there is a problem.

By next year, Ahntholz, who started his business career in marketing and sales before coming to Olin as director of information services in 1980, hopes to give customers access to a system showing where Olin's tank cars are at any given time and when they're likely to arrive at the customer's door. "Traditionally, we have been storekeepers of data and information," Ahntholz says. "The role is changing from storekeeping to facilitating change with technology."

The impetus to launch such change often starts in the executive suite, where chief information officers are fast becoming high-ranking advisers to senior management. At Aetna, Sitkin sits on the management committee. At Wells Fargo Bank, Executive Vice-President Jack L. Hancock, who is responsible for computer systems, strategic planning, and personnel, talks often with the bank's chairman. This kind of access allows Hancock to play a leading role in the most important decisions affecting his company, as he did in helping chart Wells Fargo acquisition of Crocker National Bank earlier this year.

Having the ear of the chief executive or chairman is one of the keys to success as a CIO. That has certainly been the case at Enron Corp., the $10 billion Houston energy concern that used to be called HNG/InterNorth Inc. Chairman Kenneth L. Lay recognized that information systems had become more important to Enron since deregulation and increased competition rocked the natural gas industry. So he named J. Ronald Knorpp chief information officer in 1985 and made it clear that the job was at the same level as the chief financial officer and chief legal officer. When Knorpp gave a presentation of 30 line managers, Lay was there. "The typical MIS director couldn't begin to ask the chairman to attend his meeting," Knorpp says. "Because I'm working for the chairman, this is his charge, and everyone knows it."

Not all of Knorpp's counterparts at other companies face such smooth sailing. Some run smack into fellow managers who fear the idea of one person controlling the flow of data in a big corporation. When Pennwalt's Rubin arrived at the company, a vice-president told him: "You seem like a really nice guy, but we'll have nothing to do with you because we don't need central guidance." After Rubin upgraded computer systems throughout the company, the same fellow "said he'd like to chat with me," Rubin recalls. "Within six months we were working well together."

'Show-Me Attitude'

Other CIOs bump up against line managers who feel that an information czar represents another layer of management separating them from the chief executive. "It isn't always easy to persuade line bosses that somebody working a computer knows what is best for the operation," says Firestone's Burden, who gained substantial credibility after he installed a point-of-sale network of sales terminals at the company's 1,500 retail automotive centers to improve the control of parts and inventory. "Middle management has a show-me attitude and a skepticism that is understandable. You really have to make the case."

GenCorp's Forney found the same thing when he moved up from manager of computer services to director of information systems at his company, which makes everything from tires to tennis balls. "Some view it as interference, an extra level of approval, or somebody looking over their shoulder," he says.

Getting involved in the affairs of line managers is a sea change from the way information managers acted in the past. The old-line technocrats weren't concerned with holding down line costs while they performed such back-office tasks as calculating the payroll and balancing the books in the glass-enclosed, air-conditioned computer rooms known as "glass houses." Because those functions weren't seen as strategically important, information managers reported to the chief financial officer. "We were more in tune with the computer industry than with the businesses we were supporting," notes Thomas J. English, director of information resource management at Federal-Mogul Corp., a Southfield (Mich.) maker of automobile parts.

Computers haven't ceased doing the corporate grunt work, of course, and such old-style information executives still exist. But more and more, they are becoming just one among the many managers reporting to CIOs, whose functions and responsibilities are getting broader. That has led to some jealousy because the old-line contingent is less than thrilled with being relegated to nuts-and-bolts work in the computer room while chief information officers with better business credentials whiz by on their way to high-visibility jobs with salaries of $250,000 and up.

Forced Out

The threat of trouble can be real. In one case, an MIS director of a Los Angeles-area real-estate developer was forced out when a new CIO judged him to be someone "who did not understand management's needs for information." In general, though, MIS directors aren't in danger of becoming extinct. "While the chief information officer is the captain of the ship, there's a need for a person in charge of the engine room," says A. D. Little's Jackson.

The trend toward CIOs hasn't hit most of Corporate America yet. Many chief executives, having long confined computer technology to the backwaters of the back office, are still not convinced that computers can be used to gain a competitive advantage.

But when just one rival makes that happen, they often feel driven to catch up. "People resist change," says the University of Minnesota's Wetherbe. "But that is being preempted by fear for survival." So it's a safe bet that there'll be more chief information officers on the scene in years ahead. Whether they'll be as influential as Firestone's Laurance Burden depends on what kind of information—and results—they deliver.

Discussion Questions

1. How is the concept of a chief information officer different from that of a traditional concept of the MIS/DP manager?
2. Describe the typical educational and skill requirements of a chief information officer.

READING 41

Manager or Technician? The Nature of the Information Systems Manager's Job*

article by
BLAKE IVES and
MARGRETHE H. OLSON

Abstract

The role of the information systems manager has evolved in twenty years from that of a technician managing a relatively unimportant service function into that of a vice presidential-level, general manager whose department can substantially impact the entire organization. In this article, we trace, by example, the historical evolution of the job, and through an observational study of six information systems managers, examine the position today. The analysis includes the daily activities of the managers, the nature of the oral contacts that constitute 76% of their day, and other notable observations. The information systems manager's role is depicted as one of coordinator, motivator, and planner, with a cadre of experts, both internal and external, who provide technical expertise.

Keywords: Managing computing, observing managers, information resource management, administration of computer centers

ACM Categories: 2.40

*The authors gratefully acknowledge the cooperation of the six participating managers as well as the Center for Research on Information Systems at New York University, and the Management Information Systems Research Center at the University of Minnesota, which assisted in contacting some of the subjects.

Source: Reprinted by special permission of the *MIS Quarterly*, Volume 5, Number 4, December 1981, pp. 49-62.

Introduction

How has the role of the information systems manager evolved with the changing needs of business organizations for data processing? A fictional account of one individual's rise through the ranks of information systems management will serve to illustrate a "typical" case.

Our manager's name is Ralph. In 1958, armed with a bachelor of arts degree, Ralph landed his first job as a draftsman. Shortly thereafter he transferred to data processing where he designed card-based systems, wired boards, and occasionally ran the tab card equipment.

By the mid-1960's Ralph was Manager of Data Processing, supervising a small staff of programmers, operators, and keypunch personnel. Even in those days the job was a difficult challenge. People with systems skills had to be trained internally, technology changed constantly, and potential new DP applications far exceeded the available resources. Late night telephone calls from harried operators and emergency trips to the office to fix system "crashes" were the rule.

In 1972 Ralph changed jobs. He inherited a new title—Manager of MIS—and a new set of problems. (Not that the problems from the 1960's had gone away!) During this period the manager of MIS was exhorted, at least in the trade press, to strive for effectiveness as well as efficiency, to focus on consistent, dependable user service as much as technological advancement, and to take a broader, bottom-line view of the data processing organization.

Ralph heeded some of the advice; he recognized that he needed a broader base of knowledge and at 35 enrolled in an evening MBA program. His nights were now dedicated to courses, case studies, and of course, late night telephone calls.

In 1975 Ralph's career had a setback. A major system exceeded time and cost estimates and failed to meet the information requirements of its highest level user. That, coupled with a lengthening queue of maintenance jobs and less than satisfactory response times on some online systems, led to predictable results. Ralph was unceremoniously fired.

Although he considered the dismissal unfair, Ralph was not surprised. As Nolan [15] had warned, MIS managers were mistreated guys from time to time:

> *...top management mishandles this key individual in many ways: it fails to recognize the fact that he needs to be at least as much a manager as a technician; it usually regards his job as a dead end from which no promotion is possible; it tends to use him as a scapegoat when things go awry...*

Dismissals among MIS managers were common [15, 16, 18]. In one study it was found that over 50% of 180 companies surveyed had replaced top systems executives within the previous eighteen months [18].

Ralph, nevertheless, did some soul searching. He had attempted to take a broader perspective in this job but it was difficult to escape the day-to-day problems of deadlines, cost overruns, and new system releases. Ralph was not alone. A survey [11] of over 300 information systems managers showed that, even in large information systems departments, MIS managers tended to list as their primary objectives those related to measures of system efficiency rather than effectiveness (*e.g.*, meeting deadlines, minimizing costs, minimizing turnarounds).

The next job would be different! Fortunately, with the demand for experienced information systems managers far exceeding the supply, the next job came quickly. Ralph accepted a position as MIS manager in a larger firm at a respectable increase in pay. In the new job he carefully developed an organizational structure and management control system that fostered a more organizationally integrated information systems function.

Now, six years later, Ralph has another new job, a new title, and a new list of problems. Our hero, now sporting Vice President of Information Resource Management on the door of his paneled, carpeted, corner office, finds text, image, and voice appended to previous responsibilities for corporate data. A sophisticated distributed processing network, minicomputers, and a very high level programming language have all contributed to giving users potential and even some real control over their own data. Meanwhile, however, competing voices call for organization-wide management of the newly discovered "data resource." Vice President Ralph's phone no longer rings at night, which makes him rather nervous every morning.

Ralph, though a fictional character, illustrates the

evolution of this complex management role. It is a role that requires balancing the inherent conflicts of development versus operations, effectiveness versus efficiency, user service versus technological advancement, and user control versus a central data resource. In the remainder of this article we describe this critical role as we have found it carried out in six organizations today.

Our research is motivated by several underlying concerns. The article's title identifies the most important: what are the relative contributions of technical and managerial expertise required of the information systems manager? A second issue is more pragmatic: what does this person do all day? Who does the information systems manager see? What subjects are discussed? Though perhaps mundane, these questions have implications for performance evaluation, management training, career planning, and the application of electronic office technologies.

A third issue focuses on the role of the information systems manager as a communications link with the rest of the organization (*e.g.*, users, top management) and with other organizations (*e.g.*, vendors). Finally, we sought to identify a set of problems facing information systems management that could benefit from future research.

Previous Research on Management of MIS

Although numerous prescriptions for the MIS manager's role exist [2, 3, 7, 8, 9, 10, 14, 16, 17, 19], little empirical research has been conducted. As noted previously, surveys have been employed to examine MIS manager turnover [18] and perceived job objectives [11]. Couger, *et al.* [6], also used survey techniques to examine motivation levels for information systems managers at three management levels. They found that these managers exhibited lower social needs than other management personnel and hypothesized that this may interfere with communications with subordinates and peers in other parts of the organization.

Nolan [16] interviewed eighteen MIS executives and found two extreme managerial styles. One, described as the "architect," draws a sharp line between technical data processing responsibilities and nontechnical user responsibilities. This manager maintains a highly defined organizational structure and a sophisticated management control system. A manager characterized by the second style, the "insider," maintains a fuzzy line between the technical and user components of the job. This manager attempts to infiltrate user areas with systems people and has less sophisticated control systems than the "architect."

Wetherbe and Whitehead [22] provide an interesting, though non-empirical, study of the MIS executive. They emphasize the strong distinction between the two primary suborganizations within the information systems function—operations and development—and the often conflicting managerial styles required in each. Operations is characterized as a closed/stable/mechanistic environment requiring the use of formal polices and procedures. Development is viewed as a relatively open/adaptive/organic environment, requiring a management philosophy emphasizing flexibility, decentralized decision making, and autonomy.

Perhaps the most rigorous examination of the MIS manager's role was conducted by Taggart and Sibley [21]. One of them served as director of a university computer center for six months and collected critical incidents related to his job. These incidents support a management style described as "balanced" between a "user community" orientation and another orientation labeled "systems professional."

Methodologies for Studying Management

Hundreds of studies have looked at issues related to leadership and management, but few focus on what managers actually do. McCall [12] found only forty reports of studies on behaviors exhibited by practicing managers. Many of these relied on diary self-reports, a methodology of dubious validity [13, 20]. Taggart and Sibley employed a "participant as observer" strategy [4] to examine a single MIS executive at work. An alternative strategy, "complete observation" [4], was utilized in the study reported here. This approach, in which an observer almost constantly accompanies the manager, had not previously been employed with MIS managers, and because of its high cost is infrequently used in studies of management.

"Complete observation" avoids some of the problems inherent in diary studies. However, the method is so labor-intensive that it is not practical over long periods of time. It is thus difficult to collect a truly representative sample of days at work. It is also difficult to avoid observer biases or changes in work style caused by the observer's presence. (See [12] for a comparison of the two approaches.) Nonetheless, the methodology of complete observation provides a particularly rich view of the information systems manager's job.

An Observational Study of MIS Managers

Six information systems managers were asked to participate in the project. The managers met the following criteria:

1. They were responsible for both information systems development and operations.
2. They were responsible for a department of thirty or more employees.
3. The information systems component constituted at least 75% of their management responsibilities.
4. They had been employed in their current position for at least six months.

The purpose of setting these criteria was to provide some consistency across the sample. The result of these criteria, particularly the first one, was that in the organizations selected this manager was at a relatively high level in the organization, usually two levels below the president. Of course, one overriding consideration was whether the manager was willing to be observed.

The six participating organizations are categorized in Table 1. All subject managers were male. Four, like Ralph, had come up through the ranks of data processing. Of these, two had been promoted into their present positions and two, like Ralph, had been hired into their positions from outside the company. Two others had been moved into the systems department from a different area of the company.

Each manager was accompanied by an observer (one of the authors) for three to four days. The dates were selected several weeks in advance based on the manager's judgment that these would probably be "typical days" (*e.g.*, no all-day meetings or vendor seminars). The observer stayed with the manager throughout the day, usually in an inconspicuous corner of the manager's office. When the manager left the office he was accompanied by the observer. In a few situations the observer was not permitted to attend a meeting (*e.g.*, a performance appraisal with the manager's superior). In those cases the nature and substance of the meeting were summarized for the observer at its conclusion.

Results

The observers collected data on a variety of dimensions of the manager's job. Some objective data was collected (*e.g.*, the amount of time spent on the telephone); in other cases, the measures were subjective, susceptible to varying degrees of observer bias. We report, first, the objective results and then subjective data that must be interpreted more cautiously.

Classification of Management Activities

Each management activity was classified into one of the following five categories that have been established as representative of managerial work in Mintzberg's study of chief executive officers [13]. They are the following:

1. **Desk Work** — Managers working alone in their offices, normally at their desks.
2. **Telephone Calls** — All incoming and outgoing telephone calls. Data was collected for both completed and uncompleted calls.
3. **Scheduled Meetings** — Meetings that had been prearranged. In many cases the meeting was arranged only minutes before.
4. **Unscheduled Meetings** — Meetings that were not prearranged. These included informal and unplanned contacts in the hall, lunchroom, or manager's or other's office.
5. **Tours** — Occasions when the manager left his office to walk about the premises. These tours often included one or more unscheduled meetings. Times for these meetings were

Table 1 Characteristics of Participating Organizations

DP Employees (range)		30-300
Organizational Level	Corporate	5
	Division	1
Industry Type	Manufacturing	3
	Utility	1
	Finance	1
	Service	1
Reporting Level (from CEO)	One	1
	Two	3
	Three	2

subtracted from the total time recorded for the tour.

A small number of activities could not be classified using this scheme. Primarily, these were instances when the manager spoke briefly to the observer, made a personal call, or disappeared too quickly for the observer to follow. These were classified as "off the record" and were not analyzed further.

Table 2 represents the occurrences of each activity type for an average day, the mean duration of each type of activity, and the proportion of total time spent on that type of activity. Numbers in parentheses here, and in the remainder of the article, are ranges for the six managers.

The total number of activities per day, excluding incomplete telephone calls and secretarial contacts, averaged 41 (28-63) for the six information systems managers. Previous research has shown that lower level managers are involved in more activities per day, each of shorter duration, than managers in positions of greater authority. First level supervisors have been shown to participate in about 200 activities per day [12], while Mintzberg [13] found that chief executive officers daily engage in nineteen to thirty-two activities. The number of activities performed by the information systems managers appears consistent with their management level.

Activities are generally short. Seventy percent (54-76) lasted less then nine months with only two percent (0-6) lasting more than one hour. Telephone calls and unscheduled meetings were common but constituted a relatively small percentage of the day. Though few in number, scheduled meetings accounted for over half the working day.

Nature of Oral Contacts

Information systems managers spend on an average 76 percent (64-91) of their day in oral contacts. Table 3 categorizes these contacts in terms of medium employed, location of the contact, and who initiated the contact. Table 4 breaks down scheduled or unscheduled meetings by the number of people participating. Contacts were most commonly held in the manager's office, attended by one other person, and initiated by the manager much of the time.

Table 5 presents a breakdown of the types of people with whom the information systems manager had oral contacts. Contacts with users constitute a fairly small percentage of the total contact time. Contacts with users were short, with

Table 2 Activities Per Day for Information Systems Managers

Activity	Number Per Day	Average Duration (in minutes)	Proportion of Time
Desk work	9 (6-17)	9 (5-13)	19% (9-36)
Phone calls	9 (6-14)	4 (2-7)	9% (6-14)
Incomplete calls	5 (2-10)	1[1]	1%
Scheduled Meetings	5 (2-10)	40 (22-103)	48% (30-67)
Unscheduled Meeting[2]	16 (8-28)	5 (4-10)	20% (11-29)
Tours	2 (0-3)	6 (0-11)	2% (0-6)

[1] estimated

[2] secretarial contacts not included

(Numbers in parentheses are ranges for the six managers.)

Table 3 The Nature of Information Systems Managers' Oral Contacts

	Percent of Contacts	Percent of Time
Media		
Telephone Calls	31% (27-36)	13% (7-21)
Scheduled Meeting	17% (7-26)	57% (44-73)
Unscheduled Meeting	53% (48-59)	30% (14-35)
Location		
Manager's Office	69% (50-80)	58% (25-94)
Other's Office	13% (4-23)	7% (4-12)
Hall	9% (2-15)	2% (1-6)
Conference Room	8% (0-31)	26% (0-51)
Other	2% (1-9)	6% (1-16)
Initiated By:		
Manager	54% (35-65)	
Other Party	38% (27-58)	
Clock	4% (2-7)	
Chance	4% (1-6)	

Table 4 Number of Participants in Oral Contacts

Size of Meeting	Scheduled Meetings	Unscheduled Meetings
Two People	53% (0-70)	90% (78-96)
Three People	15% (0-62)	8% (3-20)
Four People	5% (0-28)	1% (0-2)
More than Four People	27% (0-75)	1% (0-4)

two of every three initiated by the user. Frequently these were operations-related requests for follow-up (*e.g.*, a master file had been improperly updated twice and needed to be corrected). Interestingly the managers spent, on the average, slightly more time with vendors than with users.

Purpose of Oral Contacts

In his study of chief executive officers, Mintzberg [13] developed a classification scheme to categorize "the nature of managerial work." Although Mintzberg's categories have been shown to have questionable interrater reliability [5], they do provide additional insights into the information systems manager's job. Table 6 shows Mintzberg's categories of activities and the percent of contacts accounted for by each category. The researchers coded these categories as the *primary* purpose of each oral contact.

Classification of Message Units Within Oral Contacts

The categories shown in Table 6 represent only one classification of the primary purpose of each oral contact. Since a meeting or telephone call may result in several outcomes the single classification does not present a complete picture of the contact.

To provide additional insight into each contact the researchers collected data at a finer level of detail. It was generally possible to record, in abbreviated

Table 5 Types of People with Whom the Information Systems Manager Had Contacts

Person	Percent of Contacts	Percent of Time
Superiors	4% (0-7)	7% (0-10)
Immediate Subordinates	36% (22-45)	38% (23-60)
Lower Level Subordinates	24% (16-40)	23% (17-32)
Users	10% (3-20)	8% (1-33)
Corporate Service Groups (*e.g.*, personnel, maint.)	11% (6-22)	8% (5-18)
Vendors	6% (0-30)	9% (3-27)
Others	9% (3-9)	7% (1-16)

Table 6 Primary Purpose of Each Oral Contact

Category	Definition	Percent of Contacts	Percent of Time
Scheduling	Brief contacts for purposes of scheduling future contacts.	12% (8-20)	2% (1-4)
Receiving Information	Manager receiving information from others. Includes briefings and instant communications.	24% (13-47)	18% (6-36)
Giving Information	Contacts in which manager passes information to others.	12% (7-21)	8% (4-13)
Action Requests	Requests for managerial action by others. Includes requests by subordinates for authorization, requests for the manager to provide information, and requests by users and superiors to initiate something.	8% (0-19)	2% (0-7)
Manager Request	Managers requesting others—for information, to follow up on a previous delegation, or to delegate a new task.	15% (6-20)	5% (4-7)
Strategy	Contacts preparatory to major decisions. These included long range planning and budgeting meetings.	4% (0-11)	21% (0-70)
Review	Usually rather long meetings dealing with a number of issues. In some cases these were general "catch up" meetings with immediate subordinates. In other cases they were project review meetings.	14% (5-31)	28% (9-36)

form, "message units" representing distinct separate communications within a particular oral contact. For instance, the operations manager drops in to report that the hardware problems from the night before have been fixed (message unit 1) and describes the nature of the problem and its solution (message unit 2). The information systems manager inquires how far behind they are (message unit 3). The operations manager responds (message unit 4) and informs of his plans to catch up (message unit 5).

Coding message units involved assignment of a verb to indicate action (*e.g.*, request, inform, acknowledge, make, delegate) and a noun to signify the object of the action (*e.g.*, fact, status, plan, decision, action, opinion, suggestion). The source of the contact was recorded as were two codes indicating the content of the message unit. The first code indicated whether the content of the message was technical or nontechnical. Technical message units were those felt to be difficult for a person with no technical expertise (*i.e.*, related to information systems) to understand. In the above example, message unit 2 was classified as technical, the others as nontechnical.

The second code categorized the subject matter of the message unit, and was selected from the following categories:

1. operations,
2. new hardware,
3. maintenance/modification,
4. new applications,
5. new systems software,
6. new management control software, and
7. general administrative (e.g., budgeting, staffing, scheduling).

Coded message units for the contact between the operations manager and the information systems manager, described below, are shown in Table 7.

Coding message units presented some problems. When many people were talking it was difficult to record all relevant information. Furthermore, coding was susceptible to observer bias. Nevertheless, the message units provide an illuminating view of the information systems manager's job.

Analysis of the 7459 message units, an average of 392 per day, revealed that only 120 (3%) of the information systems managers' message units and 196 (5%) of the other participants' message units were technical. Figure 1 shows the breakdown by subject discussed. Forty-three percent were related to general administrative subjects; this compares to Taggart and Sibley's findings [21] that 70% of the critical incidents recorded by a single information systems manager were of an administrative nature.

The verb/noun categories present the information systems manager's role from a different perspective. These categories represent the managerial nature of the communication independent of its content. In Table 8 fourteen verb/noun categories are displayed, out of 68 combinations used, that in total accounted for 88% of the total message units. These are divided into three categories. In the first column are verb/noun combinations most frequently attributed to the information systems manager. The second column contains those used approximately equally for the information systems managers and the people to whom they spoke. The third are categories most frequently attributed to the other party in the oral contacts.

The results for the verb/noun categories suggest that information systems managers collect hard facts, status information, and information about problems from others; they pass on formal, future plans and less formal intentions. These results hold up well when managers rated by one observer are compared to those rated by the other, which suggests that the rating scales are not greatly impacted by rater bias and that these communication patterns are relatively robust.

Some Notable Observations

Categorization by activities, purpose of contact, or message units tells only part of the story. Through observation we learned some revealing aspects of the nature of the job and the environment of the information systems manager. These are described below.

Computer Based Management Support

Mintzberg [13] found that chief executive officers placed little reliance on formal information sources. The results reported here, ten years later, suggest a

Table 7 Sample Message Unit Coding

Message Unit #	Verb	Noun	Source	Technical	Subject
1	Inform	Status	Op Mgr	No	Operations
2	Inform	Background	Op Mgr	Yes	Operations
3	Request	Status	Manager	No	Operations
4	Inform	Status	Op Mgr	No	Operations
5	Inform	Plans	Op Mgr	No	Operations

Figure 1 Subject of Message Units

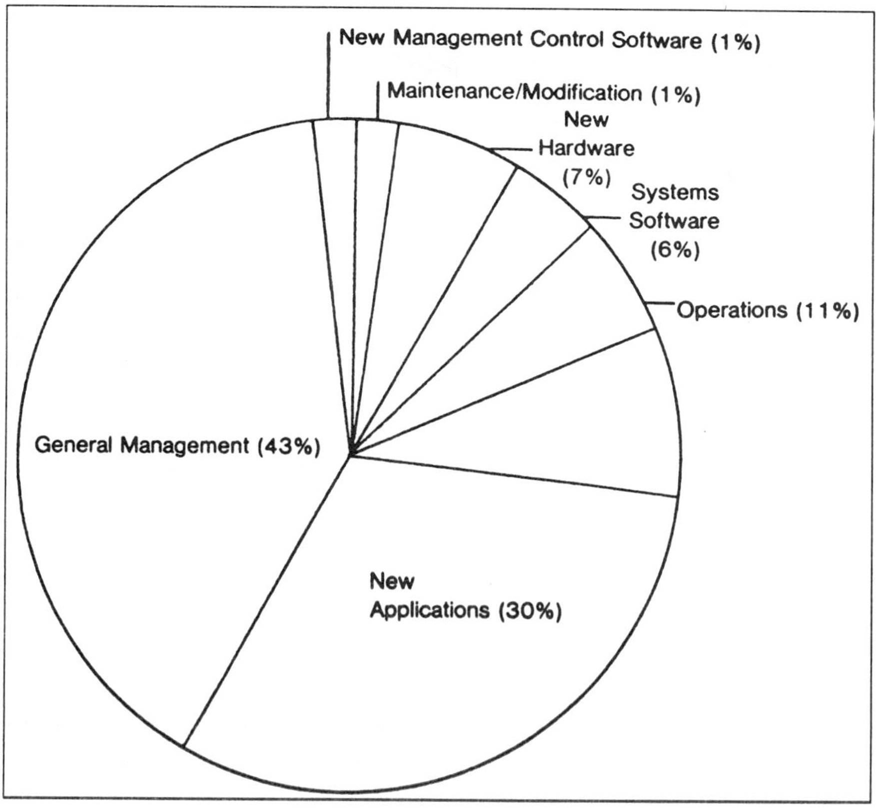

quite similar phenomenon for information systems managers. These managers rarely referred to computer based information systems. When they did, it was usually to reference reports generated from systems developed for other functional areas of the organization (*e.g.*, accounting, personnel). There were few computer-generated reports related to information systems activities and even fewer signs of the so-called "decision support systems" currently in vogue. Like the shoemaker's children, information systems managers seem to be among the last to directly benefit from the technology they purvey.

There were also few signs of office automation technology in the managers' own departments. Although word processing was common, only two managers had terminals in their offices; these were used infrequently and primarily for purposes of demonstration. Electronic mail systems were not utilized; one manager, however, used a voice store-and-forward message system to communicate with his subordinates. Clearly, all the managers relied heavily on face-to-face contacts as shown in Table 3 (*i.e.*, only thirteen percent of total time was spent on telephone calls). In addition, the vast majority of message units, as shown in Table 8, communicated "soft" information rather than facts. The efficacy of electronic mail for these managers is certainly not obvious from the date.

Keeping Current on Technological Trends

Although the managers all subscribed to trade publications, they generally spent little time reading them. These, and general business newspapers and magazines, were usually skimmed. Sometimes advertisements and articles were torn out and forwarded to others. Generally, managers relied on subordinates for specific technical expertise.

Table 8 Verb/Noun Categories Commonly Employed in Oral Contacts

Used More Frequently by IS Manager	Used About the Same by Both[1]	Used More Frequently by Other Parties
Delegate Action (3/93/7)[2]	Inform Concerns (4/51/49)	Inform Fact (9/38/62)
Inform Plans (2/64/36)	Inform Opinion (21/43/57)	Inform Prob. (4/39/61)
Inform Intentions[3] (6/60/40)	Give Sugg/Advice (6/47/53)	Inform Status (4/34/66)
Request Facts (5/67/33)	Request Clarification[3] (5/52/48)	
Request Opinion (3/74/26)	Inform Background (8/43/57)	
Request Status (3/66/34)		

[1] Classified as "about the same" if 41-59% of the message units were attributed to the IS manager and the other party.

[2] % of total message units/ % attributed to IS manager/ % attributed to the other party.

[3] Results for these verb/noun combinations are inconsistent between the two sets of managers rated by the two observers.

In several of the organizations, vendors played important roles as information disseminators. Although the vendor was selling a particular product, sales presentations were frequently treated by the managers as opportunities to learn about current technologies and to diffuse that knowledge throughout their organizations. In several instances presentations were given where it was clear beforehand that a sale was impossible. Typically, presentations were unskillfully executed by vendor personnel, who often targeted at the wrong audience. On the manager's side, there was little attempt to match a presentation with an appropriate audience. In some cases a dozen or more people spent an hour or more at a presentation of relevance to only two or three attendees.

In all six organizations users had begun to acquire their own minicomputers. In at least one organization this was happening without formal approval of the MIS group. This was viewed with alarm by the information systems manager who was concerned with the long term maintainability of systems developed for this equipment. On the other hand, in three of the organizations this proliferation had been anticipated. Acquisition of minicomputers and stand-alone systems was even encouraged under guidelines provided by the information systems group. Thus some centralized control over this proliferation was retained in at least some of the organizations.

Managing During an Economic Downturn

One of the organizations studied was undergoing business contractions during the study period. Budget cuts were the rule and every department was expected to share equitably in the cuts. This presented a difficult situation for the information systems manager. Few cuts were possible in the heavily equipment dominated operations budget. The development budget was difficult to reduce as the remainder of the organization turned now to data processing as a way to cut costs and even to assist in the development of a new microprocessor based product.

Acquiring and Retaining Employees

As shown in Table 5, the vast majority of contacts (60%) and total time (61%) were spent with first and second level subordinates. What is less obvious from the data is how much time managers spent in acquiring and retaining qualified personnel. Some of this time was spent studying resumes or considering alternatives for filling available positions. This time was generally classified as "desk work." The managers also interviewed potential employees (classified as "other" in Table 5). Many of their contacts with "corporate service" groups were with personnel and were related to hiring.

In terms of current employees, the managers were concerned with motivation, training, and career potential of their employees and spent more time maintaining healthy subordinate relationships than they did, for instance, with users. The researchers have no comparable data for other levels or types of managers. However, given the current market for qualified data processing specialists, it is not at all surprising that hiring and retaining personnel was a major preoccupation of the managers in our sample.

Discussion

The classic parable tells of the blind men who picturesquely describe an elephant on the basis of their separate physical contacts with various parts of the beast's anatomy. Similarly our analysis presents the information systems manager from several disparate perspectives.

Nature of the Work

Activity analysis shows a similarity to other managers. Work is fragmented, of short duration, frequently interrupted, and consists primarily of oral contacts—many of them unplanned. Scheduled meetings are few in number but are usually quite long; unscheduled meetings and telephone calls, though common, constitute a smaller portion of the day. Managers spend much of their time in their own offices, frequently in one-on-one discussions with immediate subordinates. Not surprisingly, contacts with superiors are infrequent. More surprisingly, however, is the finding that managers initiated few contacts with users.

The classification of purpose of contact as defined by Mintzberg shows the information systems manager to be heavily involved in activities related to strategic planning and management control, and to spend little time on activities of an operational control nature [1]. They spend the greatest amount of their time in either reviews or strategy sessions. The greatest percentage of their contacts are for the purpose of receiving information. Not surprisingly, they spend less time in negotiation or ceremony than the chief executive officers in Mintzberg's study [13].

The analysis of message units illuminates other aspects of the job. The manager is exposed to little technical jargon and responds with less. The majority of discussions are of a general administrative nature (*e.g.*, budgeting, training, recruiting, hiring, evaluating). Those that are related to information systems primarily deal with system development issues. Operations and maintenance/modification represent only 12% of the message units transmitted.

The information systems manager is shown by analysis of verb/noun categories, to be actively seeking others' opinions, information about existing projects (status checking), and facts required to perform the job. At the same time the information systems manager passes along organizational plans and future intentions. A relatively smaller number of message units concerns actual delegation of work.

Information systems managers use few formal written information sources. Subordinates and vendors keep the manager technologically current, with heavy reliance on subordinates for technical expertise.

Cautions in Interpreting Results

How accurate is the picture we portray? Naturally, it is based on a small, self-selected sample of managers that may not be representative of the broader population. Similarly, these managers probably behaved somewhat differently during the observation period. Finally, observer bias could have affected the coding.

We provided some methodological rigor through the structured observation approach. We also measured certain behavioral effects that occurred because of the researcher's presence. At the conclusion of the observation period both the manager and secretary were asked to complete a short questionnaire which ascertained how "typical" the manager's activities were during the study period. They generally reported that the days the managers observed were indeed typical. The only consistent difference reported was that managers went on slightly fewer tours and tended to spend somewhat less time in informal social encounters.

As noted previously, we compared the verb/noun categories assigned by the two raters for the managers they observed. These were generally similar, providing evidence for the consistency of the overall ratings.

Nevertheless, this type of study is, almost by definition, non-rigorous. It provides us with a rather fuzzy, big picture of the information systems manager's job. It says nothing about what separates a good manager from a bad one, or an effective organizational structure from an ineffective one. These are issues which future research needs to address.

Conclusion

In the introduction we saw the information systems manager's job evolve from a fairly low level, relatively unimportant service function to an important instrument of organizational change and profit making. Through this observational study of six current heads of the information systems function we gain some new understanding of this complex job as it exists today.

Today's information systems manager is clearly more of a manager in the classical sense than a technician. Interpersonal skills and the ability to motivate and guide subordinates are relied on heavily. The manager is surrounded by technical specialists who provide expertise as required. The manager is not preoccupied with the day-to-day operations of the data processing organization, but spends a great deal of time planning the overall strategy for the information systems function. A great deal of the manager's planning concerns human resources.

A very small portion of the information systems manager's contacts are with users at *any level*. There was some informal evidence that the managers' subordinates had responsibility for contact with operational users, particularly during development of new information systems. However, one can only conclude that the contact of information systems managers with functional management at their own level is noticeably absent. Such a conclusion is surprising in view of the plethora of literature advocating "top management involvement," on the user side, in development of new information systems.

Couger [6] found that information systems managers have low social needs; he hypothesized that this may interfere with communications. Our study simultaneously contradicts and supports Couger's findings. On the one hand, the managers in this study spent 79 percent of their time in verbal contacts, a number which is similar to Mintzberg's [13] findings for chief executive officers. Whether they enjoyed verbal contacts or not, there is no evidence that these information systems managers *avoided* verbal communications. On the other hand, their infrequent contact with users may in part be explained by Couger's findings. One may further speculate that they feel more comfortable "with their own kind," preferring to communicate with technical specialists and vendors. The data do not strongly support this conclusion, however; while it is true that the vast amount of the managers' contacts were with technical people, there is little evidence of "shop talk."

While this study provides some insights into the nature of the information systems manager's job, the conclusions that can be drawn are limited. There is no indication from this study of whether the managers were "effective" in their jobs. Readers, especially information systems managers, are encouraged to compare the activities reported here to their own "typical day" and to draw their own conclusions about their managerial role in today's organization.

Finally, our research suggests a variety of "problems" that future research efforts can constructively address. These include the following:

1. Distinguishing the characteristics of information systems managers that separate good and poor performance.
2. Developing organizational structures that will better integrate the roles of the information systems manager and the user managers served.
3. Considering the implications of minicomputer proliferation and developing strategies for effectively utilizing this powerful resource.
4. Developing strategies for dealing with the information systems budget during periods of economic decline or for shrinking industries.

5. Developing appropriate decision support systems and office automation systems to assist the manager of the information systems resource.

We see the information systems manager's role as primarily that of "manager." Good technical support from subordinates replaces much of the manager's need for "hands-on" technical skills. Despite the advocacy of "user involvement," however, much remains to be learned about the relationship between the information systems manager and user management.

Discussion Questions

1. Give some reasons for the high incidence of systems development failures and high turnover rate among MIS/DP managers in the early 1970s.
2. Describe the activities of MIS/DP managers as reported in this study. Do you find the results surprising?
3. What proportion of time do MIS/DP managers spend with personnel, and on personnel matters?
4. Given the importance of managerial activities as shown in this study, is a technical background unimportant? Explain.

References

[1] Anthony, R. N. *Planning and Control Systems: A Framework for Analysis*, Harvard University Press, Cambridge, Massachusetts, 1965.

[2] August, R. J. "DP Needs Managers, Not Technicians," *Infosystems*, Volume 23, Number 5, May 1976, pp. 55-56.

[3] Blee, M. "Where Do DP Managers Go From Here?," *Datasystems*, November 1974, pp. 10-13.

[4] Bouchard, T. J. "Field Research Methods: Interviewing, Questionnaires, Participant Observation, Systematic Observation, Unobtrusive Measures," in *Handbook of Industrial and Organizational Psychology*, Marvin D. Dunnette, ed., Rand McNally, Chicago, Illinois, 1976, pp. 363-413.

[5] Bristol, D. C. "The Applicability of Mintzberg's Managerial Role Theory to Describing Educational Administrator Behavior," unpublished doctoral dissertation, University of Massachusetts, Amherst, Massachusetts, 1979.

[6] Couger, J. D., Zawacki, R., and Oppermann, E. B. "Motivation Levels of MIS Managers Versus Those of Their Employees," *MIS Quarterly*, Volume 3, Number 3, September 1979, pp. 47-56.

[7] *Dun's Review*, "Getting Control of the System," Volume 110, Number 7, July 1977, pp. 68-81.

[8] Ferreira, J. and Collins J. F., Jr. "The Changing Role of the MIS Executive," *Datamation*, Volume 25, Number 13, November 25, 1979.

[9] Gilbert, J. C. "Can Today's MIS Manager Make the Transition?," *Datamation*, Volume 24, Number 3, March 1978, pp. 141-151.

[10] Halbrecht, H. (as told to Richard L. Nolan). "New Breed," Appendix to Nolan, R. L., "Business Needs a New Breed of EDP Manager," *Harvard Business Review*, Volume 54, Number 2, March-April 1976, pp. 123-133.

[11] Hallum, S., Scriven, D. D. "EDP Objectives and the Evaluation Process," *Data Management*, Volume 14, Number 5, May 1976, pp. 40-42, 50.

[12] McCall, M. W., Jr., Morrison, A. M., and Hannon, R. L. "Studies of Managerial Work: Results and Methods," Technical Report Number 9, Center for Creative Leadership, Greensboro, North Carolina, May 1978.

[13] Mintzberg, H. *The Nature of Managerial Work*, Harper Row, New York, New York, 1973.

[14] Murray, T. J. "The New Top Managers," *Dun's Review*, Volume 113, Number 6, June 1979, pp. 92-94.

[15] Nolan, R. L. "Plight of the EDP Manager," *Harvard Business Review*, Volume 51, Number 3, May-June 1973, pp. 143-152.

[16] Nolan, R. L. "Business Needs a New Breed of EDP Manager," *Harvard Business Review*, Volume 54, Number 2, March-April 1976, pp. 123-133.

[17] Rue, J. "Power Politics and DP," *Datamation*, Volume 22, Number 12, December 1976, pp. 51-52.

[18] Scott Morton, M. S. "Organizing the Information Function for Effectiveness as Well as Efficiency," Center for Information Systems Research, Report 17, MIT, Cambridge,

Massachusetts, 1975.
[19] Sommerfield, W. A. "DP Management Comes of Age," *Infosystems*, Volume 23, Number 6, June 1976, pp. 54-56.
[20] Stewart, R. "The Use of Diaries of Study Manager's Jobs," *The Journal of Management Studies*, No. 2, 1965, pp. 228-235.
[21] Taggart, W. M., Sibley, W. "A 'Balanced' Orientation for the Information Systems Manager," *MIS Quarterly*, Volume 3, Number 2, June 1979, pp. 21-23.
[22] Wetherbe, J. C., and Whitehead, C. J. "A Contingency View of Managing the Data Processing Organization," *MIS Quarterly*, Volume 1, Number 1, March 1977, pp. 19-25.

READING 42

Changing Role of the Corporate Information Systems Officer

article by
ROBERT I. BENJAMIN,
CHARLES DICKINSON, JR.,
and JOHN F. ROCKART

IS managers hardly need to be told that their world is changing. Change is everywhere—a harsher, more competitive business environment; rapidly evolving information technology; and increasingly knowledgeable, demanding, and diverse user constituencies. The problem for IS managers is not one of acknowledging change; it is one of adapting to it successfully. The purpose of this article is to report on a recent research effort that describes the adaptation made by corporate information officers (CIO's). The results of this research suggest that our sample of CIO's, working in very successful large corporations, are rapidly developing a new role for themselves—one that is radically different from the traditional role of the IS Manager.

Source: Reprinted by special permission of the *MIS Quarterly*, Volume 9, Number 3, September 1985, pp. 177-188.

In describing this new role of the CIO, we shall draw upon two types of material: first, a set of predictions about the new role itself, and second, findings from the CIO research.

Our research model was exploratory and designed to provide some validation for the conclusions reached in an earlier article by Rockart, Bullen and Ball [8]. Our sample was small but of very high quality. A questionnaire was sent to approximately 25 CIO's in a variety of large U.S. and Canadian corporations, of whom 20 (in a few instances their chief aides) responded. Because most of the CIO's have had a long term connection as sponsors of the Center for Information Systems Research (CISR) at the Sloan School, MIT, we were able to place high confidence in the care they took in responding to the survey. As a further step in eliminating ambiguities, the survey results were reviewed with most of the respondees at a CISR workshop in May of 1983.

The sample is clearly not a random one, and is not large enough for meaningful statistical analysis.

The sample is representative of a number of business sectors (Table 1A), however the results must be viewed in the light of two built-in biases. First, the respondents are from very large corporations with large IS budgets (Tables 1, B & C). Second, as CISR sponsors they have frequently been in contact with each other to discuss issues such as this one. From our many contacts outside of CISR we believe the respondee sample is reasonably representative of large corporations, and is at the leading edge in understanding the changing role of the corporate information officer.

Table 1 Basic Company Information

A. Industry

Category	Number	%
Manufacturing	9	45
Banking	3	15
Insurance	2	10
Petrochemical	2	10
Government	1	5
Other	3	15
Total	**20**	**100**

B. Revenues

Category	Number	%
More Than $5 Billion	10	50
$.5 to $5 Billion	9	45
N/A (Government)	1	5
Total	**20**	**100**

C. IS Budget

Category	Number	%
More Than $100 Million	12	60
$10-50 Million	6	30
$50-100 Million	2	10
Total	**20**	**100**

The Changing World of the CIO: Predictions

While CIO's have coped, some more successfully than others, with the changes in their world during the last several years, researchers and consultants have attempted to understand and describe these changes. Some strong perspectives have emerged on the direction that leading-edge organizations have been taking. It is useful, therefore, to summarize the traditional view of IS as a backdrop to our research findings.

Traditional View of IS Role

In 1974, Davis [1] described the IS organization as consisting of an executive with three responsibilities; analysis, programming, and operations. In 1981, Gruber and Synott [4] describe an organization with four responsibilities; data processing, telecommunications, methods, and systems development. Both of these traditional views of the IS organizational are functional in perspective, the latter one merely adding the telecommunications function.

In 1982, Nolan [5] identified a number of critical IS issues based on interviews with senior managers; balancing the supply and demand for computing resources as well as rationalizing the managing of IS as a profit center, measurement of effectiveness, centralization, planning and control, project selection, leadership, and (in terms of future opportunities) forecasting and administrative costs. As in most writing to this point, the issues highlighted were almost all aimed at improving the delivery of current large data center-based paperwork processing services.

Current Perspectives

Nolan [6], has suggested that IS is currently in a period of "technological discontinuity" as it makes the transition from a traditional DP technology (characterized by mainframe computers and common software under the control of a centralized data processing organization) to a user-dominated technology. Just as the traditional DP technology has its own learning curve (which provided the basis for Nolan's original description of the stages of DP growth [7]), so does the new, user-dominated technology. The complexity of the current IS environment is caused by the discontinuity and change associated with the transition from one learning curve to another.

Nolan, and others who have participated in his research, identify several implications for IS management:

- The computer infrastructures of organizations are shifting dramatically to the new user-dominated technologies.
- Senior management is looking to corporate IS for leadership in making the transition across technologies.
- Companies are being forced to shift from narrow DP planning to enterprise-wide computer architecture planning.

As Nolan points out, a major issue for companies as they pass through this "window" of technological discontinuity is one of leadership—effective management of the transition from traditional technology to the user-driven technologies.

Benjamin [1] draws upon Nolan's framework, but is more specific about the types of changes or discontinuities that IS is experiencing as it moves from one technology to the other. He describes five trends:

- There is a powerful movement in the direction of greater distribution and complexity of processing environments in all major organizations today. This trend is increasing with the introduction of newer, lower cost, more powerful technologies.
- Unprecedented user demand for IS resources has been generated by the explosive growth in workstations, software packages, and easy-to-use languages. This demand is now driving IS resource management.
- New ways of developing systems, where the user can develop and operate many applications independently, are radically changing the power balance between the IS department and the user organizations.
- In contrast to the communications task of the 70's (the connection of workstations to specific applications on mainframes), the communications task of the 80's is much more complex. It consists of interconnecting a range of applications to a single workstation, interconnecting the heirarchy of processing environments, and making databases accessible wherever needed in the organization.
- In the long run, of most fundamental significance is the realization that IS has become a factor in business strategy. Today's information technologies, coupled with advances in data communications, have made information systems a weapon to be considered in the fight for competitive advantage. Accordingly, IS management must develop an outward business-strategy perspective, in addition to its traditional operational focus.

Rockart, Bullen, and Ball [8] emphasize this evolving staff orientation for IS management—in particular for the CIO. Drawing upon the combined thinking of a group of successful CIO's and established researchers in the field, they theorized about the evolving CIO role. (It should be noted that of the 18 respondents in their panel only four were respondents in the survey reported here.)

This new role, as Rockart, *et al.* envision it, contains a new set of requisite managerial attributes for the individual CIO. More specifically, they make three "predictions" regarding this emerging role:

1. **Decentralization of line responsibilities to divisions and departments**—The new management environment will make it impossible for the CIO to maintain direct line management control over computer-based technology throughout the company. Accordingly, "line management of local hardware and much of the software development will be thrust into divisions and departments" [8, p. 14].

Nonetheless, the CIO will necessarily retain direct, line responsibility for several critical areas associated with the information infrastructure of the firm. These areas will include the communications network, corporate data management, common software development (including a changing array of start-up projects), and the corporate computing facility.

2. **Staff orientation**—The new emphasis on

staff-oriented responsibilities will result in the need for organizations to have a focal point for planning and facilitating the organization's move into the information era (or, in Nolan's terminology, into the advanced stages of user-dominated technologies).

The CIO will increasingly focus on strategies and planning. He/she will be oriented towards facilitating, guiding, and promoting change—but will not control it. Techniques utilized by the CIO to guide, facilitate, and promote will include; communication and education processes, standards (e.g., for data, communication, privacy and security), and other indirect controls (e.g., steering committees, policies, and guidelines, and individual persuasion). Rather than being the "owner" of a centralized IS technology, the CIO will become the "gate-keeper" and "integrator" of an increasingly diverse spectrum of technological resources which will be decentralized throughout the firm.

3. Corporate responsibility for information resource policy and strategy—Increasingly, the CIO will be a member of the top management team. He/she will have broad responsibility for developing policies and strategies for the information resources of the firm, just as the CFO (chief financial officer) has similar responsibility for the financial resources of the firm.

This clearly suggests that the CIO will not simply be the custodian of the data. Rather, he or she will be the corporate officer who truly understands the interconnection of the information flow to the business. The CIO will have "the responsibility of assuring that new opportunities presented by the technology are seized and that capital expenditures for information resources are ranked according to business needs" [8, p. 5].

If these predictions are true, Rockart, *et al.*, suggest that the emerging role for the CIO will require a set of managerial skills and attributes which, though, *useful* to the IS executive in the past, will become absolutely *critical* in the future. It will not be enough that the CIO have a considerable understanding of the technology. In addition, the CIO must be a general-business oriented manager with considerable political, organizational, and communication skills.

Research on the CIO Role

Research Model

The CIO model developed by Rockart, Bullen and Ball, was developed to identify a range of issues associated with the transitional management of the IS function in the 1980's. In particular, the predictions about the emerging CIO role and the associated managerial attributes for this role were intended to assist practicing CIO's in adapting successfully to a radically changed environment.

Although these predictions may be helpful, their practical value is limited until tested and validated by the actual experiences of successful CIO's in a variety of corporate environments. Our research on the emerging role of the CIO was thus undertaken to determine whether these predictions are, in fact, borne out by the actual experiences of successful CIO's in large corporate environments.

Research Findings

Our research was undertaken to test the three predictions of Rockart, *et al.*, to determine whether or not they are validated by the day to day experiences of practicing, successful CIO's. Accordingly, we will discuss the findings of this research in the context of each prediction.

Decentralization of Line Responsibility

1. Distribution of Line Activities to Subsidiary IS Units and User Management—Results from the CIO questionnaires indicate that a decentralization of line activities is taking place. CIO's were asked to indicate the location of responsibility (corporate IS, subsidiary IS groups, or user management) for an extensive list of staff and line activities. These were grouped into four general IS management functions (planning, managing, internal services, and user services).

Table 2A shows those activities where the CIO's were at least 60% agreed on whether they were centralized or distributed. The data shows clearly that major elements of line responsibility (development and operation of application systems, and line management of hardware and software) have been distributed to subsidiary IS groups and user management. It is generally agreed by the CIO's that subsidiary IS units are responsible for the operation of mainframe and minicomputer hardware, selection, and maintenance of applications software, and implementation of the system life cycle, as well as implementation of end user support. In addition, they are seen as having the responsibility for such line planning functions as budgeting (multi-year and annual) and architecture design for applications.

In spite of this significant pattern of decentralization, some key line activities are not distributed to subsidiary IS units and user management. Most of these activities are associated with developing and maintaining the information utilities that constitute the IS infrastructure for the firm. In addition, they identified line tasks in support of the corporate staff such as executive support systems.

There were a number of activities that the data did not identify clearly as corporate or distributed (Table 2B). These activities are generally associated with new evolving technologies (telecommunications, personal computers and office systems) and activities where the transistion to decentralized operations is still evolving (e.g., applications planning).

The distribution of responsibilities is a general trend that has focused on movement between corporate and distributed IS. Some movement of responsibilities is taking place between subsidiary IS and user management as well. This is shown in Table 2C as activities that at least 30% of the CIO's perceived user management to be responsible for. They emphasize a heavy user management role in applications, office and personal computers, and external databases and timesharing.

2. IS Budget—CIO's were asked to indicate the percentage of the entire IS budget that is under their direct control, both at present and estimated for three years in the future. In addition, they were asked to indicate the percentage of their budget which is dedicated to service utilities such as data centers, corporate applications, systems programming, and voice or data telecommunications. The premise in asking for this budget information was that the size of budget, and the trend over the next three years, would corroborate or weaken the CIO's own stated perceptions of their line/staff relationships. The results of these budget-related questions are shown in Table 3.

The data suggests that corporate IS is playing a less dominant role than it has in the past in terms of overall expenditures, and that this trend will continue in the future. The average corporate-controlled IS budget in the 20 firms is only 48% of the entire IS expenditures in the firm. Additionally, in the next three years it is expected to drop to 44%. Even today corporate IS does not control the majority of IS expenditures for the firm. These figures are consistent with the specific line/staff trends discussed previously.

Increasing Staff Orientation. In order to test the prediction of increased staff orientation, CIO's were asked to describe their *most critical* responsibilities. An average of three responsibilities was provided by each CIO. In addition, they were asked to indicate how they felt these responsibilities would be different three years from now. Our concern in both of these questions was to determine whether these critical responsibilities were primarily staff- or line-oriented.

The CIO responses, summarized in Table 4, clearly indicate that staff responsibilities are predominant in both instances. Of the 62 responses for current critical responsibilities, 40 (or 66%) fall into categories that are staff-oriented; only 21 (or 34%) can be classified as line responsibilities. Furthermore, to the extent that the CIO's anticipated change in the next three years most CIO's responded in a manner that was even more heavily weighted in favor of staff-oriented categories (13 of 15 responses). For a more detailed description of the responses see Benjamin [2].

The current line responsibilities cited by the CIO's may be organized into three categories. The first, creating and maintaining information utilities, reflects the residual line activities that were identified earlier. Responsibilities cited by CIO's included managing the corporate-wide computing center, world-wide networks and data, and the like. The other two categories of line responsibility are associated with the direct provision of information

Table 2A Distribution of IS Activities Centralized vs. Distributed Greater Than 60% Consensus by CIO's

Activity	Corporate IS	Distributed IS
Planning the IS Function		
• IS Strategic Planning	72	
• IS Multi-year Budgets or Project Plans		67
• IS Annual Budgets or Project Plans		67
• Technology Scanning/Anticipation	87	
• Architecture Planning Applications		73
• Application Portfolio		
a. Plan		88
b. Prioritize		89
Managing the IS Function		
• Mainframes/Mini		
a. Approval	61	
b. Standards	83	
c. Operations		72
• Personal Computers		
a. Selection		67
b. Operations		88
• Telecommunications/Voice		
a. Approval	68	
b. Standards	61	
• Telecommunications/Data		
a. Approval	88	
b. Standards	83	
Managing the IS Function		
• Office Systems Operations		88
• Systems Life Cycle		
a. Standards	61	
b. Implementation		79
• Applications Software		
a. Selection		72
b. Approval		61
c. Standards		69
• National/Multinational Vendor Contracts	76	
• Security/Privacy Standards	70	
IS Internal Services		
• Consulting Services/Technical Expertise	71	
• Information Exchange	88	
IS User Services		
• IS Education		
a. Senior management	66	
b. Line users	61	
• End User Support		62
• Executive Support	72	
• External Databases		88
• Timesharing		
a. Internal	63	
b. External		82

Table 2B Centralized vs. Distributed Activities Without 60% Consensus by CIO's

Architecture Planning

Hardware
Database

Mainframe/Minis

Selection

Personal Systems

Approval
Standards

Telecommunications/Voice

Selection
Operations

Telecommunications/Data

Selection
Operations

Office Systems

Selection
Approval
Standards

Application Software

Standards

IS Internal Services

Personnel Management
Education Training of IS

IS User Services

Office Systems
Implementation of Common Systems

Table 2C User Management Responsibilities Greater Than 30% Perception by CIO's

Application Portfolio	
Plan	33%
Prioritize	78%
Personal Computers	
Selection	50%
Approval	34%
Operations	84%
Telecommunications/Voice	
Operation	33%
Office Systems	
Selection	36%
Operations	76%
Applications Software	
Approval	33%
External Databases	53%
External Time Sharing	64%

Table 3 IS Budget Distribution

Budget Responsibility	Current Budget	Budget in 3 Years
Corporate IS		
Service Utilities	28%	26%
Other Corporate	20%	18%
Other IS Functions	52%	56%

services, either at the corporate level (e.g., operation of corporate systems, providing end user computing environment for corporate) or for the organization as a whole (e.g., develop and maintain administrative systems on a worldwide basis, total responsibility for data processing operations and systems development).

Within the current staff activities, planning responsibilities are particularly prominent. Over 40% of the staff-oriented responsibilities are associated with technology planning (e.g., information architecture, evaluating new technology) or IS strategic planning, (e.g., linking to the strategic plan of the corporation, providing support for corporate goals). Although the preponderance of responses in the strategic planning category reflect an emphasis on supporting business strategy, only two responses emphasized a responsibility to influence the strategy of the firm (e.g., influence product strategy, increase use of

Table 4 Critical Line and Staff Responsibilities of CIO's: Current and Future

Current Line Responsibilities	Current Frequency	Change
1. Create/Maintain Information Utilities	7	+2
2. IS Services, Organization-Wide	6	—
3. IS Services, Corporate	8	—
Total, Current Responsibilities	21 (34%)	
Total, Future Change (Projected)		23 (30%)
Current Staff Responsibilities		
1. Technology Planning	6	+1
2. IS Strategic Planning	12	+3
3. Literacy/Education on Information Technology	6	—
4. Human Resource Management	3	—
5. Consultation/Support	7	+9
6. Standards/Control	6	—
Total, Current Responsibilities	40 (66%)	
Total, Future Change (Projected)		53 (70%)

computer as tool to increase productivity/profitability of the corporation). This was inconsistent with the response of the CIO's to their selected key initiatives (discussed later) where influencing corporate strategy was one of their three highest ranking initiatives.

In addition to the planning responsibilities, CIO responses also emphasized such traditional staff functions as consultation and support (e.g. providing consulting to CEO, establishing end user computing, advising on effective utilization of computer and telecommunications technologies). These comprise over a third of the staff-oriented responsibilities identified by the CIO's. In addition, the CIO's felt that the category of consultation and support was going to be significantly more important in the future.

The remaining critical responsibilities identified by the CIO's fall into the staff-oriented categories of human resource management (e.g., attract, retain, and develop talent, develop competent people for key jobs in affiliates) and literacy or education on IS technology (e.g., see to it that the company is trained in computer technology, educate key executives on possibilities). The human resource category of responsibilities represents a rather traditional staff function. However, the responsibilities associated with fostering a growing literacy and understanding of IS technology represents an emerging need to understand and communicate the rapidly changing potential of information systems.

The CIO's view of critical responsibilities three years from now is little changed from today with some additional emphasis on consulting and planning activities. The staff-oriented picture of the CIO's role that is developed out of the list of critical responsibilities is consistent with the data that describes the distribution of corporate IS activities to subsidiary IS and user management. Inspection of Table 2 shows that the residual activities left under Corporate line up well with the staff activities described above.

What emerges from this aggregated listing of critical responsibilities, both at present and as anticipated for the future, is a rather sharply defined picture of the CIO as a high-level manager who is primarily concerned with issues of long-range planning, consultation, and support to a broad set of constituencies throughout the organization.

Corporate Responsibility for Information Resource Policy and Strategy

1. Reporting Relationships—In order to gauge CIO standing in the corporate hierarchy, CIO's were asked to indicate their reporting relationship to other top managers, particularly the CEO. The results of this question are summarized in Table 5, and compared to a 1968 survey reported by Davis [3, pp. 374-375]. The table summarizes the response to both surveys in terms of absolute numbers of respondents and percentage of respondents, indicating the number of levels a CIO is removed from the CEO, and where the CIO reports; finance or another key function.

These results suggest two significant findings. First, the CIO is becoming an integral part of the top management team. Sixteen of the 20 CIO's surveyed are positioned within two levels of the CEO—and four of them report directly to the CEO. This finding indicates that although only 4 of 20 CIO's reports to the CEO, the chief manager of the IS function is no longer buried mid-range on the organizational chart.

Second, the CIO reporting relationship is outside the traditional reporting pattern for IS executives—that of finance. Sixteen of twenty of the CIO's report to an area other than finance (e.g., operations, engineering, chief of staff). These organizational reporting paths are very consistent with the culture of the organization. To cite one illustration, the CIO of a major chemical corporation with a strong research and engineering tradition reports to the senior vice president of research and engineering.

2. Importance of Selected IS Initiatives—CIO's were asked to rate the importance of selected IS initiatives (specific areas requiring concentrated attention) on a scale of 1 (little importance to me as CIO) to 5 (critical to my success as CIO), both now and 3 years in the future. The mean ratings for each of these initiatives and the standard deviation is shown in Figure 1.

Table 5 Reporting Relationship of CIO

Levels from CEO	Reporting to Finance		Reporting to Other		Total	
	1983	1968	1983	1968	1983	1968
1.	n/a	n/a	4/20%	12/12%	4/20%	12/12%
2.	4/20%	19/20%	8/40%	12/12%	12/60%	31/32%
3.	0	36/37%	4/20%	18/19%	4/20%	54/56%
Total	**4/20%**	**55/57%**	**16/80%**	**42/43%**	**20/100%**	**97/100%**

The three initiatives rated most important by the CIO's were end user services, telecommunications, and corporate strategy. CIO's have some confusion about the importance of end user services in the short term (note the large standard deviation), but little uncertainty about its importance in the long term. CIO's also place considerable importance on initiatives in the areas of office systems and personal computers, which are special forms of end user services.

Eleven out of the 20 companies surveyed are in industries where CAD/CAM is significant

Figure 1 Importance Ratings for Major IS Initiatives Current and In 3 Years

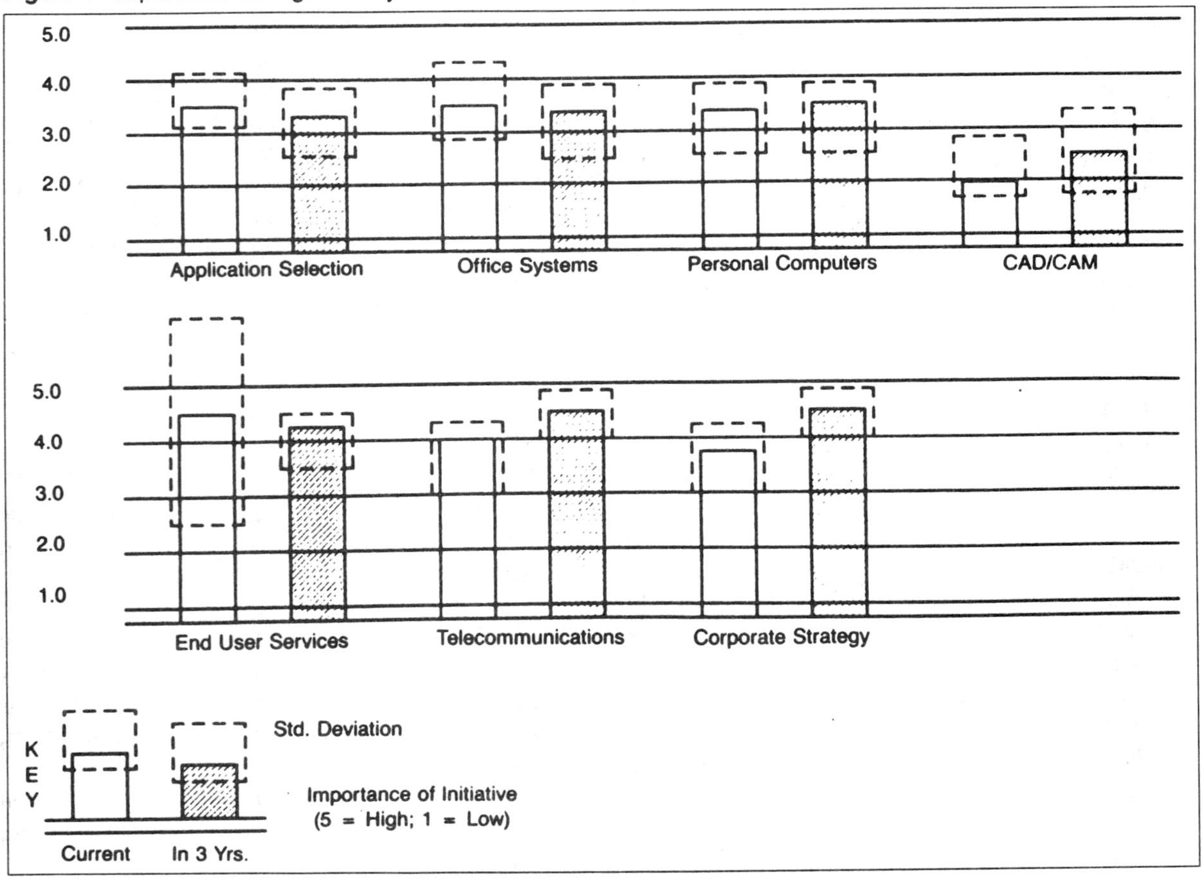

(manufacturing and petrochemicals); they give it considerable importance as an initiative.

Directional change in initiatives is consistent with the predictions in the first section of this article. Application selection will be of lower concern as the CIO distributes responsibility, and telecommunications and corporate strategy will be of increasing concern as the CIO moves into a staff role. It is interesting to note that the three year view of end user services, telecommunications, and corporate strategy initiatives have little dispersion, indicating that the CIO's have a consistent sense of where they are heading.

Conclusions and Future Research

This research survey, conducted with 20 CIO's from major companies, gives strong evidence that a changing role for the chief information officer is winning acceptance. This confirms the predictions made by Rockart, Bullen and Ball, and the more general predictions of Nolan and Benjamin. Of most importance to the IS executive and to senior management is that the pace of this change is faster than was anticipated. It was predicted to be transitional through the end of the decade but, in fact, describes reality for many leading companies today. Specifically:

• The distribution of corporate IS activities to subsidiary IS and user management is proceeding rapidly. Our research demonstrates this from both a budgetary and from a functional point of view. CIO's are concentrating their line activities where interconnection is required—corporate-wide applications, corporate data networks, and the like.
• The CIO, as evidenced by the responses received, accomplishes primary goals through staff activities.
• The CIO's are proactive executives who, in general, report to the CEO or one level below, and are aligned through their reporting relationships to the strategic and operational elements of the business. Their strongest personal initiatives are in areas of strategic importance; end user computing, telecommunications, and strategic planning (linking IS to the business, and gaining competitive advantage through use of information technology).

As with all research, the examination of the data and conclusions raises a number of interesting research questions.

• To what extent is the pattern of distribution of the IS function related to the size of the companies (which were very large in this sample), to the type of industry, and to organizational cultures?
• To what extent will the distribution of responsibility from subordinate IS to user management follow the pattern of distribution of responsibility from corporate to subordinate IS?

One final comment in concluding this report. The trends in leadership (large, sophisticated organizations) appear strong, and IS organizations that do not take them into account may encounter significant difficulty in coping with the transitional changes of the '80's.

Discussion Questions

1. Contrast the traditional perspective of the IS role with current perspectives.
2. How are the line management responsibilities of a CIO predicted to change in the new management environment?
3. How is the role of "gate-keeper" different from the role of owner of the technology?
4. Does a CIO have a central role in developing and planning corporate strategy? What does your answer imply for the organizational location of the CIO?

References

[1] Benjamin R. I. "Managing Through a Decade of Discontinuity," *Information Systems News*, August 22, 1983, p. 20.

[2] Benjamin R., Dickinson C., and Rockart J. *Changing Role of the Corporate Information Systems Officer*, Working Paper #113, Center for Information Systems Research, Massachusetts Institute of Technology, Cambridge, Massachusetts, March 1984, appendix 1.

[3] Davis G. B. *Management Information Systems*, McGraw-Hill, New York, New York, 1974, p. 374.

[4] Gruber W. H. and Synnott W. R. *Information Resource Management*, John Wiley & Sons, New York, New York, 1981, p. 183.
[5] Nolan R. L. *Managing the Data Resource Function*, (2nd Ed.), West Publishing Company, St. Paul, Minnesota, 1982, pp. 346-360.
[6] Nolan R. L. *Managing the Advanced Stages: Key Research Issue*, to be published as part of 75th Anniversary Colloquium papers; Harvard Business School, Cambridge, Massachusetts, July 1983.
[7] Nolan R. L., and Gibson C. F. "Managing The Four Stages of EDP Growth," *Harvard Business Review*, January-February, 1974.
[8] Rockart J. F., Bullen C. V., and Ball L. "Future Role of the Information Systems Executive," *MIS Quarterly*, Volume 6, Special Issue, December 1982, pp. 1-14.

SECTION FOURTEEN

Behavioral Issues

READING 43

Changing Systems and Behavior

article by
EDGAR G. WILLIAMS

Creating and innovating, the handmaidens of change and progress, do not always contribute to stable modifications of existing systems or to the smooth introduction of newly designed ones.

The early stages of implementation often prove difficult, appear to be less economical in the short run, and on the surface, less effective. How often have you heard the comment, "Why don't they leave well enough alone?" Chances are good that we have all heard that statement at one time or another, and chances are equally as good that the person saying it has found a new system or a new method less to his liking than a previous one. It may well be that the new system is a bit more difficult; it may well be that all of the "bugs" have not been anticipated or obviated—thus causing it to be more cumbersome and requiring closer attention. Either of these results will make it appear to the individuals involved that the change is a step backward rather than forward.

On the other hand, the new system or modification may be properly planned and designed, yet great difficulties may be experienced in getting it installed and operating smoothly because of the people involved. The real cause for the problem may be an individual who views the new system as a threat to his personal security; it may not match his skills as well as that which it replaced; or he may even have some emotional hang-up in that the degree of participation that he enjoyed in creating, planning, or implementing the new system may be viewed by him as being totally inadequate.

Two types of problems are commonly associated with the introduction of a new management system or the modification of an existing one: those that relate to the system itself and have to do with its nature and design, and those that have to do with people who either are, or think they are, going to be affected by the innovations and changes inherent in

Source: Business Horizons, August 1969, pp. 53-60.

making the newly designed system work. The purpose of this article is to discuss some of the ways and means by which "people problems" may be avoided.

As a creator of change, the manager must undestand that planned change, orderly change, is his immediate goal. There are four general reasons for designing orderly change:

1. To improve the means for satisfying somebody's economic wants
2. To increase profitability
3. To promote human work for human beings
4. To contribute to individual satisfaction and social well-being.

What is change in this sense? Simply put, change is a modification of existing relationships; it is an alteration of the status quo. The most difficult relationships to adjust or accommodate to, when one views change in this respect, are organizational or behavioral in nature.

If we are going to manage for change successfully, the values that result must contribute directly to the ultimate objectives of the business firm. Technological and/or managerial innovations make change essential. It is essential to competitive well-being and growth. Planned growth usually has a direct relationship to profitability. Profitability, in turn, has much to do with the personal satisfactions that individuals and groups get out of their interactions and individual contributions of energy and ideas. These satisfactions are the means toward social improvement, which, whether one likes it or not, is one of the most compelling long-run reasons for the introduction of change into a business environment.

Important Variables in Change

Change involves a number of variables. The most common types of change have to do with machinery and equipment, methods and procedures, work standards, personnel and organizational adjustments, interrelationships with those who hold authority and power, responsibility and status, and changes in objectives (in direction, plans, and policies). The systems manager may be involved with one, or even all, of these at one time or another. To be a real change agent, he must be able to influence others in a positive fashion. This skill is tested as he anticipates and designs ways and means of overcoming what in many cases is a natural reluctance or resistance to anticipated change.

Not all change is resisted by all people. Some welcome change. It provides them with hope for adjustment in existing work situations; alterations in relationships that exist among their associates; and opportunities to become more successful in line with their personal aspirations.

Resistance to Change

Probably there are more people who resist change for one reason or another than there are who accept it when first it is introduced. Resistance tends to focus on human relationships rather than on the structural and procedural changes in the systems themselves or the accompanying changes outside the systems. People resist change because it upsets their established patterns of behavior. They often see it as a threat to their security.

Economic Reasons

Some resistance is based on economic fear—the fear of becoming temporarily displaced or unemployed. Individuals may see a reduction in their work hours, which they relate to reduction in income; they relate this, in turn, to an attack on their economic security. They may look upon the new system as a work accelerator of some kind which speeds up the normal leisurely pace which they have been enjoying and puts them, as they would say, on a treadmill. They may come to the conclusion that the new system will not improve their material well-being in any way, and they say, "Well, why should I go along with it? It doesn't mean anything to me." *There may be some truth to that, too.*

Economic reasons for resisting change cannot be separated completely from the more personal reasons. Barriers to change, from the viewpoint of an individual, are perceptual, emotional, or cultural in nature. Perceptual barriers have to do with the mental limitations of the individual and his ability to visualize what the proposed changes may mean to him; he may be unable to visualize the total picture and never really understand how he fits into it.

Emotional Barriers

Emotional barriers include fears and biases. If people do not understand new equipment and new methods and have heard from others how they have worked, or not worked, apprehensiveness may develop. It is normal also to bring prejudices that have built up during one's lifetime to the job as a result of personal experience and exposure to others. Moreover, he may perceive the change as one involving greater effort or a higher degree of difficulty—thus adding to his resistance.

Cultural Barriers

Cultural barriers are the limitations and hang-ups that individuals have as a product of their culture. It is often unhandy, but we must learn to accept people in the same sense that we accept the system. We have to accept the whole man; we cannot employ part of him. We cannot hire a portion of a man to work for us during the day any more than we can take a portion of a system and equate it to a total system. Therefore, when we pay a man's salary we are buying not only his work effort but his fears, biases, and social inhibitions as well. Ways must be found to make the system work with and for him.

Perceptual Barriers

Individuals resent implied criticism. When somebody comes in and says, "Look, we're going to change the way this is being done; we're going to go to a different type of machine; we're going to alter the procedures or we're going to change the policies," there is the possibility that the individual will feel that the new development implies personal criticism. Therefore, the reasons for the change must be carefully explained in advance, in order that he will have a chance to think about it and to ask questions.

The individual may also fear that the need for either mental or physical skills involved in the job will be diminished by the substitution of systems and hardware. It may be, too, that an individual will resist because he anticipates greater monotony and boredom after the systems analyst has completed his task. Sometimes this is true. Yet, sometimes, we can go in the other direction and enlarge the dimensions of the job and make it more meaningful and satisfying.

The individual may not be happy about the time and effort that will be required of him to refrain or to relearn. An excellent example of this situation exists now in colleges and universities—particularly in business schools. We have brought in, over a period of time, a large number of mathematicians and behavioral scientists. We have introduced their disciplines and related information into all of our courses, and now suddenly we have a group of top professors who, if they are not obsolete, run a tremendous risk of becoming obsolete unless they are willing to relearn and to be "retooled" in the behavioral sciences and in mathematical analysis. According to a colleague, many of us are engaged in a footrace between obsolescence and early retirement, and the only way that we are going to win that race is to change our attitudes toward relearning.

Probably the greatest single personal barrier is that individuals do not undestand or refuse to accept the reasons for the change or the need for it. Unfortunately, it is not always easy to equate the reasons and the needs and to communicate them in meaningful and compelling language.

The Social System

Several social reasons support resistance in the development or modification of management systems. New social relationships will develop on the job as well as off the job, because existent relationships cannot very well be shut off in most communities when work ends at night. Individuals do not want present social relationships altered. They may resent what seems to them to be undue outside influence on their little informal organizational groups. They may feel that there is nothing to be gained as individuals by cooperating, or it may be that they resist because others are resisting (a form of "me-tooism").

Overcoming Resistance

Usually, when initiating a new system, some resistance to change can be anticipated. The planner can overcome this condition to the extent that he can minimize disrupting well-established interpersonal relationships by bringing people together with common or similar frames of reference well before the new system is introduced. He can alleviate resistance to the extent that he presents himself to the people who are going to be affected as an assistant in helping to overcome some of the problems that they perceive in meeting their objectives and to the extent that he minimizes threats and assists in calming anxiety.

It is normal for an individual to be concerned when there is a change in the offing; but it is not normal for that individual to let anxiety keep on developing to the point it serves as real fear. There is a difference between the two conditions: fear is introduced from an element that is external to an individual. He becomes afraid of something outside himself. Anxiety grows from within—a sort of self-induced dread. Those of us interested in the development of new systems and their proper implementation can anticipate the fear. We can also anticipate the development of some anxiety and we must do whatever we can to aid the individual in controlling his own dread of what is liable to happen to him under the new set-up.

In general, we can overcome resistance to the extent that we can generate feelings of personal acceptance in the people who are going to be involved and to the extent that we use appropriate timing and strategies in planning and implementing the changes.

Influencing Behavior

Let us examine the problem of influencing behavior, the real problem when systems men ask individuals to change their behavior. When we introduce a new system or modify the present one, we are asking people to do two things: unlearn the old and accept and learn the new. Too often we forget and do not give enough attention to the first requirement. We are quite willing to ask them to accept and learn the new, but fail to spend enough time trying to get them to unlearn the old. This problem is highlighted by the "persistency of set." Having learned to do something one way often makes it difficult to learn the new method, approach or technique. This "set" or behavior pattern persists and complicates new learning.

Factors in Learning

New learning is based on a number of factors. One must first get the individual's attention, and the individual must have the desire to learn. Learning cues, which automatically trigger certain responses in people, are another factor. If we are going to change a system, we are going to have people learning something new; this means that we have to change the cues as well, because people tend to do what they have done before. As a change agent, the systems man must find out what it is that triggers desired behavior. He should try to anticipate the responses he would like to have, then work backward and figure out what will cue that response. Then he must ascertain what is going to appeal to the specific individual in terms of personally satisfying values. Somehow, wants and needs must be related to the rewards that are available. Individual expectations can be matched with available opportunities and the system can be fully implemented.

To help individuals change their behavior patterns, the reasons for the proposed change must be made clear to them; the new behavior must appear necessary and real incentives must be provided. This does not necessarily mean financial incentives; it may be that nonfinancial incentives will prove most valuable. If we are going to get people to accept a new order of things, we must remember to remove the rewards for their old behavior patterns. If we continue to reward people for doing what they have in the past, they will continue to behave that way. We must remove the old rewards at the same time that we are trying to induce changes in behavior. To stimulate individuals to change their behavior adequate time and improved methods for retraining must be allowed plus adequate time to make the transition from the old to the new.

Finally, the systems manager must demonstrate sympathetic understanding of the problem that the individual is experiencing or likely to experience as a result of the change. He can't just say, "Oh, hell, Joe, that's no problem," or "That's your problem, you worry about it." If he wants to get his new system introduced smoothly, he had better offer a certain amount of sympathetic understanding to the individuals involved.

The Role of the Group

Groups in themselves are often effective change agents. When a group and its various subgroups have harmonious relationships and well-understood objectives and goals, the group itself may become the prime mover in getting a change effected. When a shared feeling for the need for change has been generated from within the group, the group itself will often cause the change to be implemented and implemented smoothly. This should provide a tip-off to the systems man who is picking an appropriate timing strategy. Whether he chooses a cautious action strategy, a mass offensive strategy or some other form of strategy, he may be able to utilize what some people have called the "boring from within" concept—plant the idea and get strength from inside the group, and then have the group ask for the change. Impetus for change that comes from within the group itself is probably the strongest and most effective way of producing it.

Recent research shows that when a decision involves some risk to all members of a group, the group as a whole is more willing to venture into a change than is the individual leader of that group. The leader's sense of responsibility seems to make him cautious, and the group itself proves more ready to take the risk. There must be a lesson here, too, for those of us who are planning the introduction of a new way of doing things that is likely to affect a sizable group of people. The reluctance to assume risks represents one of the major obstacles that we must contend with in dealing with individual managers.

In planning for change we should make clear the need for the change and try to provide a climate in which others feel free to identify with such needs. Relevant group participation in clarifying and expanding the concept of these various needs must be encouraged. We are obligated to state the objectives to be achieved in clear, concise, and, if possible, quantitative terms. We must establish broad guidelines for achieving the objectives, guidelines in terms of administrative policies that can be communicated and procedures that can be readily understood.

A word of caution seems advisable at this point. It is possible to overplan for change. We can plan to the point where no room is left for the exercise of any intelligent initiative on the part of those who are going to have to work with the change and make it operate. Therefore, in planning we will do well to determine the actions that are necessary—who-when-where—and then leave how to last and as much as possible to those persons directly concerned with implementation and operation.

Rewards or benefits to individuals and to the group must be carefully communicated. To materialzie these benefits or rewards, the opportunities that are inherent in the change must be related to the expectations of the people involved. In order to match expectations and opportunities, the systems manager may have to go all the way back to a consideration of the basic human wants and needs of individuals and give consideration to the different kinds of growth with which he is to deal.

People can make any change work if they want it to work. The key to successful, orderly, planned change lies in the systems manager's understanding of human behavior—individually or collectively.

Discussion Questions

1. Must organizations respond in an orderly way only to changes planned from within? What steps can be taken to ensure an orderly response to unanticipated changes arising from external causes?
2. Compare this author's views on motivating employees to accept change with those expressed by Bookep and other authors in previous articles. Do the reasons for resisting change tend to be rational or emotional? Can such resistance be overcome by explaining to people the reasons for the change?
3. How can the dynamics of group behavior be used to appropriately deal with the problems of change in an organization? What difficulties

might systems people encounter if they adopt this kind of strategy?

READING 44

The Implementation Process: A Change Approach

article by
ROBERT W. ZMUD and JAMES F. COX

Introduction

The major objective in implementing an MIS is to realize the intended benefits of the MIS. The difficulty associated with achieving this aim tends to be directly related to MIS complexity, which is comprised of technical and organizational aspects. Technical considerations involve issues such as the processing environment, data structures, integration with other computer-based systems, inquiry languages, security considerations, *etc.* Generally, the larger the MIS and the more system interfaces required, the greater the technical complexity. Organizational issues refer to the dependence of the organization upon the MIS, integration with other organizational systems, impact upon the duties and responsibilities of organizational members, impact upon socio-political structures, *etc.* Generally, as responsibilities rather than procedures are affected by the MIS, and the higher up the organizational hierarchy the individuals are that are directly affected by the MIS, the greater the organizational complexity.

MIS implementation is commonly viewed as involving a series of related activities. Each activity, usually referred to as an implementation stage, involves quite different tasks; specific techniques have evolved for accomplishing these tasks. In this article these stages are defined as: initiation, strategic design, technical design, development, conversion, and evaluation. *Initiation* includes project definition and justification. *Strategic design* refers to establishing the scope and requirements of a project, *i.e.*, design attributes visible to the users. *Technical design* involves translating the strategic design into hardware, software, and process specifications, *i.e.*, design attributes not visible to the users. *Development*

Source: Reprinted by special permission of the *MIS Quarterly*, Volume 3, Number 2, June 1979, pp. 35-43.

concerns the acquisition of hardware, the acquisition and construction of software, and the testing of both hardware and software. *Conversion* relates to the insertion of the new information system into the organization. Finally, *evaluation* assesses the effectiveness and efficiency of the MIS.

The techniques that have been developed for accomplishing implementation activities are predominantly concerned with facilitating the technical difficulties that arise. Practical experience and research both indicate, however, that the more serious obstacles to implementation success lie outside the technical boundary [1, 5, 7, 11, 13, 15, 23, 24, 29]. When the source of MIS complexity lies not with technical issues but with organizational issues, the *process* of implementation, *i.e.*, the roles adopted by participants and the interactions among participants, becomes a greater concern than the particular techniques employed during implementation.

This article proposes explicit specifications of process requirements believed necessary when organizational complexity becomes a major concern when implementing an MIS. The intent in presenting these specifications is to provide a synthesis of the more recent literature regarding MIS implementation and to suggest fertile areas for research. As the majority of the references are normative or anecdotal in nature, a strong need does exist to develop a better understanding of the roles required of organizational members and the relationships to be developed among organizational members in order to achieve MIS success.

Implementation As A Change Process

Organizational Change

Several authors conclude that introducing a computer-based information system into an organization results in profound changes to the social as well as technical fabric of the organization [3, 4, 13, 17, 18, 32]. One view, in fact, holds that it is the *intention* of many MIS projects to change the role behaviors of organizational members [16, 22]. In support of this belief, Edstrom [12] has found a high congruence between perceived MIS success and the amount of organizational change.

Implementation Protocols

Boland [3] has identified two extreme implementation protocols. One protocol, termed the *traditional approach*, identifies the systems analyst as the major force in implementation. Directing each of the implementation stages, the systems analyst engages in learning, analysis, and synthesis activities while the intended user of the MIS is only passively involved through responding to specific inquiries by the systems analyst. Evidence is available, although limited, which indicates this approach is commonly observed in practice [4]. The second protocol, termed the *change approach*, emphasizes the joining together of the systems analyst and the user as a problem solving team to discover an appropriate solution through mutual teaching and criticism.

Another way of differentiating the two protocols is with regard to the stress placed on each implementation stage. The traditional approach emphasizes the technical design and development. The change approach shows a greater concern for the beginning and ending stages, *i.e.*, initiation, strategic design, conversion, and evaluation.

Both approaches, and numerous other alternatives, are viable implementation procedures. While the choice depends to some extent on the technical and interpersonal skills of the individuals involved, the main criterion is the character of the MIS being implemented [3, 17, 22]. An information system that (1) automates a well-defined procedure, (2) is independent of other organizational systems, and (3) results in little organizational change, is appropriate for the traditional approach; implementation would probably be more efficient, since fewer individuals would be involved, and as effective as any other, since the systems analyst would be best suited to handle any technical difficulties that arise. The change process is the preferred method when the (1) organizational activity involved is ill-defined, (2) the MIS must interface with other organizational systems, and most importantly, (3) substantial organizational change is expected; the issues of central importance are interpersonal, political, sociological, and psychological in scope. The effectiveness of adopting such a perspective was empirically demonstrated by Boland [3]. With the maturing nature of the MIS function in organizations, an increasing proportion of implementation efforts can be described by this latter set of characteristics.

A Change Approach to Implementation

Clearly, where substantial organizational change is intended, implementing an MIS without the support of organizational members will not be successful: desired behaviors will not be adopted and the effort may, in fact, prove counter-productive [9, 32]. Personnel tend to accept such change only if they perceive their superiors to be supportive of the change, understand what is about to happen, and themselves contribute to what will transpire [6]. Additionally, the systems analyst cannot truly assume responsibility for another person's behavior. Responsibility for internalizing required behavior patterns, therefore, must lie with the MIS user and not with the systems analyst [4].

The change approach to MIS implementation strives to create an environment in which change will be accepted through the active involvement of affected organizational members, an intensive education program, and, most importantly, the assigning of project responsibility to the MIS user. Additionally, a sense of mutual trust and commitment must develop between participants so that a free exchange of beliefs and opinions is possible. If such an "openness" does not evolve, the capability of participants to identify and resolve critical implementation problems will be severely limited.

Involvement

While the organizational members involved in specific MIS implementations varies considerably, the following participant classifications have been observed: top management, functional management, operating management, operating personnel, systems analyst, and systems personnel. *Top management* refers to those persons with authority over all organizational members and resources involved in an implementation effort. *Functional management* has direct authority over the area within which the MIS is being introduced. *Operating management* and *operating personnel* refer to those users whose organizational roles will be directly associated with the MIS once it becomes operational. The *systems analyst* is the technical specialist most intimately associated with the implementation effort. *Systems personnel* include all other systems analysts and programmers involved in the implementation effort. The normative nature of these participant classifications and their role specifications, with a subsequent need for research studies to examine their validity, must be emphasized.

While the active involvement of all participants is necessary, the level of involvement varies as a function of both participant class and implementation stage. Four levels of involvement are suggested: consultation, influence, commitment, and responsibility. *Consultation* involves participants responding to questions and offering advice in those areas in which they are expert. *Influence* finds participants able to exercise choice among design alternatives. *Commitment* finds participants accepting an MIS as requiring their attention as an organizational obligation. Finally, *responsibility* refers to a participant accepting the *success* of the MIS or a certain implementation stage as a primary organizational obligation. Involvement prescriptions for implementation participants are outlined in Table 1.

While these role specifications indicate various levels of involvement, the main intent is to specify with whom implementation accountability lies. Responsibilities can be assigned for the entire project, for each implementation stage, and for tasks within a stage. A single individual, however, should be accountable for the entire project; and a single individual should be accountable for each of the implementation stages.

While top management is ultimately responsible for organizational activity, their direct role in implementation is to develop a sense of commitment within implementation participants. This is accomplished by exhibiting an appreciation for the project and establishing an environment that encourages involvement by and interaction among participants [14].

The functional manager is accountable for organization resources consumed during and after implementation and will directly realize the benefits derived from the MIS. This manager should bear responsibility for the overall implementation effort.

Table 1 Role* Prescriptions for Implementation Participants

Implementation Stage	Top Management	Functional Manager	Operating Managers	Operating Personnel	Systems Analyst	Systems Personnel
Entire Project	CM	R	CM	I	CM	CM
Initiation	I	R	I	CN	I	CN
Strategic Design	I	R	CM	I	CM	CN
Technical Design		I	I	CN	R	CM
Development		I	I	CN	R	CM
Conversion	CN	R	CM	I	CM	I
Evaluation	I	R	CM	CN	CN	CN

* The symbols in the body of the table are interpreted as follows: R—responsibility; CM—commitment; I—influence; and CN—consulting. A blank cell indicates the participant would typically not participate in that activity.

The functional manager's direction of the initiation, strategic design, conversion, and evaluation stages, in particular, is crucial because these activities link organizational activities and resources to a project.

Since the eventual success of an MIS ultimately derives from the behaviors of operating managers and operating personnel, these individuals must be committed to the implementation effort. The activities most dependent upon the contributions of these individuals are those associated with strategic design and conversion. Consequently, operating managers should be responsible for these implementation activities where their organizational responsibilities are affected and operating personnel must be allowed influence where the MIS affects their organizational duties.

The role played by the systems analyst is perhaps the most difficult. The systems analyst not only bears responsibility for the technical tasks, *i.e.*, technical design and development, but must also serve as a catalyst for the involvement of the other participants. Thus, interpersonal skills and an understanding of the functional area involved become as important as technical competence, and the sytems analyst must remain committed to the implementation effort *through* the successful introduction of the MIS into the organization.

The contributions of other systems personnnel primarily involve specific tasks during technical design and development. In addition, these individuals may take part in conversion when their particular skills are required.

Roles similar to those described above are imposed upon participants initially; however, there is some desirability in keeping the prescriptions flexible enough so that task boundaries are based upon individual competencies and accepted through mutual consensus [26]. The danger exists, of course, that too much flexibility could result in political forces, which are inevitable in organizational life, circumventing what might otherwise be more effective arrangements of responsibilities.

Education

In order for participants to be able or willing to contribute to an implementation effort, they must understand *why* the MIS is being introduced and *how* the project will affect them during and after implementation. Without such knowledge, ignorance and uncertainty will lead to resistance to involvement and eventual disassociation from the MIS [11]. Additionally, participants often require exposure to specific knowledge or techniques in order to perform their assigned tasks.

Training programs must consequently be organized to fulfill these educational requirements. Some programs will be of a general nature and not related to particular implementation efforts. Examples include sessions to (1) introduce computer and information systems concepts, (2) present an organizational overview that enables individuals to appreciate how their department and other departments interact and contribute toward organizational goals, and (3) aid organizational members in developing interpersonal skills.

An even greater need exists, however, to provide training sessions specifically directed toward each MIS project. At least six areas of concern can be identified: (1) an overview of the MIS; (2) the functional area in which the MIS is being introduced; (3) technical EDP training to introduce techniques; (4) project management concepts; (5) the impact of the MIS upon individual users; and (6) conversion procedures. A suggested plan associating *minimum* training requirements with participants for particular implementation stages is presented in Table 2. A blank cell in this table does not indicate that further training is inappropriate, but that prior education and experience along with the information gained from informal interactions with other participants generally proves sufficient. The normative nature of these prescriptions again needs to be emphasized.

Top management needs to be presented with an overview of the proposed MIS to enable its proper evaluation regarding the MIS "master plan." This orientation insures that correct decisions are made in setting policies and directives regarding the allocation of resources among alternative projects. Additionally, top management must be appraised of conversion procedures in order that any concurrent evaluations of organizational subunits are considered in the conversion effort.

Prior to the implementation effort, the functional manager should develop a basic understanding of technical issues relevant to the MIS under consideration. This should primarily involve hardware and software considerations needed in evaluating design alternatives, but should also cover implementation problems that have been observed in the past or are anticipated with particular design features. Additionally, as it is likely the functional manager may have not experienced project

Table 2 Educational* Requirements for Implementation Participants

Prior To:	Top Management	Functional Manager	Operating Managers	Operating Personnel	Systems Analyst	Systems Personnel
Initiation	O					
Strategic Design		T, M	O, T, M	O	F, T	O, F
Technical Design			P	P	T, M	T
Development					T	T
Conversion	C		C	C		
Evaluation						

* The symbols in the body of the table are interpreted as follows: O—overview of information system; F—exposure to functional area; T—technical (EDP) training; M—project management; P—personal relationship with information systems; C—conversion plan and conversion impact.

responsibilities in the past, training in project management concepts and methods may need to be provided.

In order for operating managers to contribute to the design effort, they need to acquire a thorough understanding of the scope and objectives of the MIS, to be exposed to certain technical and project management considerations needed to complete their project assignments, and to understand the impact the MIS will have on them and their subordinates upon its introduction. The operating managers must also become acquainted with alternative means of conversion so that they can participate in planning and implementing the conversion effort.

Operating personnel require training sessions that provide an overview of the MIS as well as specific instruction pertaining to each individual's personal relationship with the MIS. If both topics are not covered, operating personnel may not fully understand why change is occurring and may fail to contribute their unqiue insights to the design effort. These individuals must also be informed of their roles in the conversion effort as well as what to expect during conversion.

The most crucial training to be provided the systems analyst is the development of a familiarity with the functional area in which the MIS is being introduced. If such an understanding is not achieved, the systems analyst's capability to work with the operating managers in arriving at an effective design and to aid all participants in accomplishing their tasks will be severely hampered. Also, the systems analyst may need exposure to unfamiliar technical and project management issues that are expected to be utilized in the implementation effort.

Other systems personnel need to be exposed to an overview of both the MIS and the functional area in order that they understand how their implementation tasks relate to the entire project and to the organization. Without such training, user requirements and design specifications may not be fully understood.

The educational processes desired in a change approach to implementation go beyond the training programs described above. The aim of such formal education is to provide a common ground by which participants will be able to learn from one another through open exchange of suggestions, inquiries, and criticisms. Many valuable design and conversion insights arise only after participants get beneath the surface relationships among an information system and the organizational activities being served. If such a synergistic exchange of knowledge and experience does not occur, it is unlikely the full benefits of the MIS will be realized.

Structural Considerations

The organizational structures normally utilized to facilitate MIS implementation are those associated with project management [8]: interdisciplinary and interorganizational teams drawn together temporarily for specific tasks. Historically, a systems analyst is designated as project manager while the functional managers plays a supportive role by releasing subordinates to the project manager.

The role prescriptions presented earlier, however, demand a different structural arrangement. The functional manager becomes the project manager while the systems analyst, in addition to providing technical expertise, serves as the expediter of the implementation effort by coordinating participant activities.

Exactly what forms of structural arrangements are best suited for these prescriptions and the impact of these arrangements on the job behaviors of participants are unknown. Research investigating these topics, in particular, is advocated.

Case Histories of Applying The Change Approach to MIS Implementation

Many manufacturing organizations have implemented computer-based material requirements planning (MRP) systems that facilitate the planning and control of manufacturing activities [27]. MRP implementations, however, have not all been successful [12, 19, 22]; and at least one source suggests that the proportion of fully implemented MRP systems is low [31].

Both practitioners and consultants indicate that organizational, and not technical, difficulties, are to blame for most MRP failures [19, 20, 25, 28, 30, 31]. It is virtually impossible to implement an

MRP system without altering the organization: the manufacturing environment is affected as informal systems are formalized and as semi-independent functions are integrated; job descriptions are newly created, drastically revised; or totally eliminated; power and authority relationships are changed; performance becomes more visible; *etc.* What often follows are misconceptions, misusage, and mismanagement of the MRP system. Success in such situations is unlikely as MRP systems must be used well if they are to be effective [27].

Existing evidence indicates that those organizations acknowledged to have experienced the greatest success in implementing MRP advocate implementation philosophies similar in part to those expressed earlier in this article. Bevis, for example, describes the implementation effort at the Tennant Company as being directed by a committee composed of a corporate officer, two systems analysts, and representatives from production control, purchasing, finance, customer service, market research, and engineering [2]. Furthermore, users, not systems personnel, were assigned responsibility for both implementation and operation, and over 100 employees completed an audio-visual training program.

Two additional examples are provided by Hall and Vollman [19]. In one organization, the vice president of manufacturing directed the company's implementation effort, a top management steering committee provided overall direction, and key users were freed from operational responsibilities to participate full time in the implementation effort. In the second organization, the project teams who designed and installed the MRP system were largely composed of middle managers who understood the product line and procedures.

A final example is that of Ingersoll-Rand [10]. The project team in this case was led by two key managers, the plant controller and the manager of manufacturing engineering, who were freed from their normal duties; overall direction was provided by a steering committee consisting of divisional management representatives. Also, an intensive counseling and education program involving outside consultants, audio-visual individual training, classroom instruction, and hands-on training was established by the Corporate Systems and Data Processing Group.

Summary

The implementation of many MIS's radically alters the duties and responsibilities of organizational members. The resulting impact affects both formal and informal relationships among personnel as well as their particular relationships with and attitudes toward the organization. In such instances, implementation becomes a difficult, frustrating, and often unsuccessful exercise. This article discussed an approach to MIS implementation the authors believe necessary in situations where a substantial amount of organizational change is expected. The change approach to MIS implementation focuses upon the *process* of implementation, *i.e.*, the responsibilities and activities of and the interactions among participants. Key considerations include the necessity of (1) the user assuming overall responsibility for implementation, (2) the active involvement of all affected organizational members, (3) a thorough and continuing education program, and (4) establishing mutual trust among participants so that a free exchange of ideas is possible.

Finally, it is important to reiterate that there is no "best" way to implement an information system. When substantial organizational change is expected, a process similar to that described in this article is advocated. With projects involving little, if any, organizational change, more traditional processes which emphasize technical concerns and the assignment of project responsibility to the systems analyst will be adequate.

Discussion Questions

1. What is the meaning of "implementation" in the context of this article? How is this meaning different from other uses of the term in MIS literature?
2. Why might organizational development theories be applicable to the implementation of information systems?
3. Describe the role of users (operating personnel) in implementation. In which stages is user involvement at its highest?
4. Contrast the educational requirements of functional and operational managers in implementation. Why are they different?

References

[1] Alter, S. L. "How Effective Managers Use Information Systems," *Harvard Business Review*, Volume 54, November 6, November-December 1976, pp. 97-104.

[2] Bevis, G. E. "A Management Viewpoint of the Implementation of a MRP System," *Journal of Production and Inventory Management*, Volume 17, Number 1, March 1976, pp. 105-116.

[3] Boland, R. J., Jr. "The Process and the Product of System Design," *Management Science*, Volume 24, Number 9, May 1978, pp. 887-898.

[4] Bostrom, R. P. and Heinen, J. S. "MIS Problems and Failures: A Socio-Technical Perspective; Part I: The Causes," *MIS Quarterly*, Volume 1, Number 3, September 1977, pp. 17-32.

[5] Carter, D. M., Gibson, H. L. and Rademacher, R. A. *A Study of Critical Factors in Management Information Systems for U.S. Air Force*, Colorado State University, Fort Collins, Colorado, 1975.

[6] Caruth, D. L. "Basic Psychology for a Systems Change," *Journal of Systems Management*, Volume 25, Number 2, February 1974, pp. 10-13.

[7] Churchman, C. W. and Schainblatt, A. H. "The Researcher and the Managers: A Dialectic of Implementation," *Management Science*, Volume 11, Number 4, February 1965, pp. B619-B87.

[8] Cleland, D. I. and King, W. R., *System Analysis and Project Management*, McGraw-Hill, New York, 1975.

[9] Coleman, M. L. "System Modification in an Operational Environment," in *Proceedings IFIP-INFOPOL-76*, J. Madey (ed.), Elsevier North-Holland, New York, 1977, pp. 33-338.

[10] Davis, E. W. "Ingersoll-Rand Company: MRP Implementation at the Mocksville Plant," in *Case Studies in Material Requirements Planning*, American Production and Inventory Control Society, Washington, D.C., 1978.

[11] Dickson, G. W. and Powers, R. F. "MIS Project Management: Myths, Opinions and Reality," *California Management Review*, Volume 15, Number 3, Spring 1973, pp. 147-156.

[12] Donovan, R. M. and King, S. "Are You Ready for MRP?" *Management Review*, Volume 66, Number 10, October 1977, pp. 46-50.

[13] Edstrom, A. "User Influence and the Success of MIS Projects: A Contingency Approach," *Human Relations*, Volume 30, Number 7, July 1977, pp. 589-607.

[14] Ein-Dor, P. and Segev, E. "Information-System Responsibility," *MSU Business Topics*, Volume 25, Number 4, Autumn 1977, pp. 33-40.

[15] Garrity, J. T. "Top Management and Computer Profits," *Harvard Business Review*, Volume 41, Number 4, July-August 1963, pp. 6-8ff.

[16] Ginzberg, M. J. "Redesign of Managerial Tasks: A Requisite for Successful Decision Support Systems," *MIS Quarterly*, Volume 2, Number 1, March 1978, pp. 39-52.

[17] Ginzberg, J. J. "Steps Towards More Effective Implementation of MS and MIS," *Interfaces*, Volume 8, Number 3, May 1978, pp. 57-63.

[18] Hedberg, B. "Computer Systems to Support Industrial Democracy," in *Human Choice and Computers*, E. Mumford and H. Sackman (eds.) American Elsevier, New York, 1975.

[19] Hall, R. W. and Vollman, T. E. "Planning Your Material Requirements," *Harvard Business Review*, Volume 56, Number 5, September-October 1978, pp. 105-112.

[20] Johnson, M. L. "Paring the Myth from MRP," *Industry Weekly*, April 3, 1978, pp. 77-80.

[21] Keegan, D. P. "Some Second Reflections on MRP," *Price Waterhouse and Co. Review*, Volume 23, Number 3, Fall 1977, pp. 32-43.

[22] Keen, P. G. W. and Scott Morton, M. S. *Decision Support Systems: An Organizational Perspective*, Addison-Wesley, Reading, Massachusetts, 1978.

[23] Lucas, H. C., Jr. *The Implementation of Computer-Based Models*, National Association of Accountants, New York, 1976.

[24] Manley, J. H. "Implementation Attitudes: A Model and a Measurement Methodology," in *Implementing Operations Research/Management Science*, R. L. Schultz and D. P. Slevin (eds.), American Elsevier, New York, 1975.

[25] Maranka, P. "Your New Materials Management System—Let's Get the System User and the Computer Together," *Journal of Production and Inventory Management*, Volume 13, Number 2, June 1972, pp. 5-18.

[26] Mumford, E. and Pettigrew, A. *Implementing*

Strategic Decisions, Langman, London, 1975.
[27] Orlicky, J. A. *Material Requirements Planning*, McGraw-Hill, New York, 1975.
[28] Plossl, G. W. "The Best Investment—Control, Not Machinery," *Journal of Production and Inventory Management*, Volume 18, Number 2, June 1977, pp. 1-7.
[29] Schultz, R. L. and Slevin, D. P. "Implementation and Organizational Validity: An Empirical Investigation," in *Implementing Operations Research/Management Science*, R. L. Schultz and D. P. Slevin (eds.), American Elsevier, New York, New York, 1975.
[30] Wacker, J. and Hills, F. S. "The Key to Success or Failure of MRP: Overcoming Human Resistance," *Journal of Production and Inventory Management*, Volume 18, Number 4, December 1977, pp. 7-16.
[31] Wight, O. W. *Production and Inventory Management in the Computer Age*, Cahners, Boston, 1974.
[32] Vertinsky, I., Barth, R. T. and Mitchell, V. F. "A Study of OR/MS Implementation as a Social Change Policy," in *Implementing Operations Research/Management Science*, R. L. Schultz and D. P. Slevin (eds.), American Elsevier, New York, New York, 1975.

READING 45

A Behavioral Analysis for Planning MIS Implementation

article by
MARY LIPPITT NICHOLS

Introduction

Managing toward successful implementation of a new system requires understanding the effects of the new system on its potential adopters. In order to understand the effects, the change agent, who may be the MIS practitioner, must be able to obtain data which describes the current situation *through the eyes of the potential adopter*, so that changes adopters would feel as a result of a new system can be identified, and the consequences of the changes on the liklihood of a successful implementation can be assessed. This article describes in considerable detail an interview based approach to obtaining this useful descriptive data from potential adopters.

Source: Reprinted by special permission of the *MIS Quarterly*, Volume 5, Number 1, March 1981, pp. 57-65.

The approach described here is consistent with socio-technical theory, which holds that the organization's operating system is an emergent blend of its technical and social systems [24, 25], and is a direct descendent of basic research in the behavioral sciences on communication networks and group structures.

The approach is disarmingly simple. There are three data components—all gathered through interviews with potential adopters. The components are 1) the specific task activities each potential adopter performs, 2) the interactions they have with others as they carry out these activities, and 3) their feelings about these task activities and interactions which define their "role." Since the label "user" is somewhat presumptuous when our concern is implementation, the clumsier, but more appropriate, phrase "potential adopter" will be used.

The article first outlines existing implementation research, then describes the three data components, provides guidelines on the interview process through which the information is gathered, describes how the data can be used, and concludes with a short case study of a system implementation in which the approach was used.

Implementation Research

Some of the earliest implementation research investigated the relationships between cognitive style and personality characteristics of adopters and nonadopters [5, 6, 7, 10]. Another stream of behavioral research looks at the contextual factors surrounding system implementation, and attempts to identify the critical factors associated with successful implementation. In a review of fourteen factor studies up to 1975, Ginzberg noted that 140 factors were reported, but 73% of those factors did not appear in more than one study [8], so it is difficult to see that we are "accumulating knowledge" in the theory builder's sense.

The problem common to both the psychological and factor streams is that statistically significant relationships between variables reported in a study can be expected to hold across a large sample chosen at random from a population. Unfortunately, that is not the situation implementers face. To them, every situation is unique, and their career and the organization's effectiveness do not progress on a statistically significant number of MIS successes over a large sample of trials. For both, each implementation should be a success.

Keen [11] describes another source of knowledge about implementation as "conventional wisdom" gleaned from case studies of unsuccessful implementations. But as Keen [12] and Ginzberg [8] note, these negative models of single implementations can lead to ambiguous conclusions, evidenced by the differences between Ackoff [1] and Argyris [2, 3]. From such case studies, Ackoff concludes that successful implementation requires adequate power in the change agent, while Argyris concludes that the change agent should rely less on power and more on interaction with the potential adopter.

Another relevant stream of research addresses the role of the change agent. The dominant framework is the Lewin [14] and Schein [22] three stage process of change, in which behavior is unfrozen, moved, and refrozen. This framework was extended by Kolb and Frohman [13], who identify seven stages to the consultant's change process, consisting of "scouting, entry, diagnosis, planning, action, evaluation, and termination." These frameworks are conceptually appealing, but both provide only generalized guidance to a change agent who is responsible for implementing an MIS, but is not an organizational development specialist.

There has been relatively little research which focuses on the effects of implementation. Effects on the decision itself, and variables surrounding it, such as the amount of information requested, have been studied, along with some effects on the organizational context. The primary variable in the latter category has been effects of system implementation on the distribution of power among units [9, 18, 19, 20].

Behavioral Data for Implementation

Each of the research streams described above addresses legitimate variables which deserve attention as researchers and practitioners seek the keys to successful implementation. However, this article assumes that the basic variables which describe the effects of a system are those which measure the changes in potential adopters' task activities, and their interactions with other people in carrying out those activities. The approach used for obtaining this data assumes that the best source of information on activities, interactions, and feelings about them is the person experiencing them.

The theoretical basis for the approach is found in communication network experiments initiated by Bavelas [4] and Shaw [23], and later extended by Mackenzie [16, 17] and others. As a result of these experiments we have learned that when people are presented with a task, they respond by performing certain task activities and forming communication structures for getting the work done efficiently and in a *need-satisfying* manner. Using this as a conceptual lens, we can look upon an organization as consisting of a large set of dynamic structures, where structures are patterns of interaction. Different structures for different sets of tasks can be seen, and these structures can be seen to change as the tasks change slightly, as individuals' preferences, based on needs, are altered, and/or as the demands of the situation change [16, 17]. These structures are very flexible, yet they can be stable as long as they remain need-satisfying to participants. Applications of these ideas in the field of organizational design have been made by Lippitt and Mackenzie [15]. A new MIS affects these most basic patterns of task activities and interactions. To assess the potential effects of a new MIS, the person(s) charged with implementation responsibility needs three pieces of information:

1. the specific task activities the potential adopters actually perform,
2. the interactions/communications the potential adopters engage in, in performing those activities, and
3. how the potential adopters feel about each of the activities and interactions.

The specific task activities of potential adopters comprise the first component and may be numerous. It is data reflecting the detailed task activities through which responsibilities are met, not data about general responsibilities, which are relevant to implementation success. General responsibilities may not change with the introduction of a new system, but specific task activities will surely change.

The second component of the database, consisting of potential adopters' interactions with others in carrying out their task activities, is a critical element because the interactions facilitate both work and social needs. Implementation of a system may directly affect these communication structures by changing the work flow so that people who formerly had to interact no longer need to do so. The change agent should bear in mind that these structures may serve indirect functions.

In the case study a manager was encountered who must physically inspect the raw material inventory regularly. He gets to know the warehouse workers as he does his visual inspection. Through his visits to the warehouse he established good relationships with the workers, gained their confidence and support, which paid off when he was in a bind, learned of problems before they would normally surface, got some much needed exercise, greeted friends whom he enjoyed, and got a welcome break from the sterility of the administrative offices. A new system which would eliminate this useful and satisfying routine would thus produce several undesirable changes from his point of view. This is important data for a change agent to have as implementation of changes is planned. The data is directly related to potential adopters' perceptions of what makes them effective in their current positions, and what brings them satisfaction in it.

Having gathered detailed data on the activities potential adopters perform and who they interact with, the third relevant piece of information is how potential adopters feel about each of those activities and interactions. These feelings are simply classified as "like, dislike, or indifferent." Some changes will be perceived as positive, such as when tedious undesirable activities are eliminated from someone's role as a result of a new MIS. However, some changes are perceived as negative, such as the change which removed the manager's need to walk to the warehouse regularly. The strength of the analysis rests in the ability to look at the changes through potential adopters' eyes. Although an activity might have appeared to be merely a tedious one to the designer or a change agent, potential adopters might have some reason to feel it confers status among their peers, gains their boss's appreciation, or is intrinsically rewarding. The reason potential adopters report that it is a well-liked part of their role is not important—the fact is they like it, and it might be changed. The key to obtaining the data for this type of analysis rests in the effectiveness of the interview.

The Interview

Interviews should be conducted with the personnel who are targeted to use the MIS, and who will be affected by its implementation. The interviews should be conducted by someone who is perceived as neutral. Selecting an interviewer who will be perceived as neutral may not be an easy task, depending upon the degree of knowledge the potential adopters have about a proposed system and their attitudes toward it. In cases of little information or favorable attitudes, a member of the design group, or an outside staff member, might be perceived as acceptably neutral. Neither person should be seen as having a prior stake in the design of the system. On the other hand, where attitudes are already resistant, an outside consultant or even an interviewer selected by the potential adopters, would be a more appropriate choice. In any case, the interviews must be held privately. There are four key phases in the interview process:

1. preparation,
2. entry,
3. conducting the interview, and
4. closing.

Preparation

To prepare for the interview, the key organizational task and decision processes which will be affected by the MIS should be identified. The change agent may find it helpful to flow chart these processes. A major benefit of thinking in terms of "processes" is that it frees the analyst from thinking of the organizational "hierarchically" and of individuals' work as being within their domain of "authority" or "responsibility." These concepts never bear a perfect relationship to how work actually gets done, and can be misleading to the analyst. The processes, on the other hand, are much more transparent. They allow the analyst to see *who* is involved, either directly or indirectly, in the processes to be affected by the MIS, and therefore aid in identifying the appropriate personnel to interview. The processes also cause the analyst to think in terms of what specific task activities and interactions might be involved in achieving each milestone in the process. Then in the interview the analyst can ask the potential adopters what they do *vis-a-vis* a particular milestone.

Another critical aspect of the preparation phase of the interview is for the interviewer to adopt the appropriate attitude toward the task. The key to establishing an effective relationship is to come to the interviewees needing to learn from them. The relationship and information will be easily distorted if the interviewees perceive that the interviewer is there to sell them on the system, or wants to hear something which agrees with the interviewer's feelings about the system, or is going through the process and is not really interested in the information the interviewees possess.

Entry

The most successful entry to the interview is to simply state that, "I am trying to be of help in the implementation/design of the XYZ system. In order to be of help I need your help in understanding what you do. Could you just take me through a day and tell me in as much detail as you can what you do?"

People typically are pleased to have someone inquire and find it easy to talk at considerable length about what they do, provided the interviewer does not suffer the disabilities discussed above in association with the interviewer's attitude. The lower in organizations that this author has interviewed, the more anxious people are to talk about the many activities they see themselves performing.

Conducting the Interview

The interviewer's objective in this phase of the process is to get the potential adopter to identify all of the task activities performed, and the interactions associated with performing these activities. The interviewer can rely on the task and decision processes identified in the preparation phase to prompt the potential adopters to look at all aspects of their individual roles. The interviewer may need to remind the potential adopters of the interviewer's interest in learning of *specific* activities from them rather than merely broad responsibility areas. In gathering information on interactions the interviewer must be alert to opportunities to probe for the existence of important informal structures, as in the case of the manager performing raw material inventory inspections who engaged in many productive and satisfying interactions in the process of inspections.

The focus throughout this phase of the interview must be on *objective* information—*i.e.*, "what do you do" and "who do you talk with or work with?" If the interviewer probes for feelings or rumors, or in any other way departs from questions which can be answered objectively, the interview gets sidetracked and the interviewee may begin to doubt the motives of the interviewer and become guarded.

Closing

Following the collection of objective data, the final phase of the interview seeks data on potential adopter's feelings about the activities they perform and the interactions in which they participate. Many of these feelings will have been expressed voluntarily during the course of the interview. At the close of the interview, it is effective to signal that the interview is about over by ceasing notetaking, sitting back and making the following kind of statement: "We all have things about our jobs that we like and dislike. Of the activities you have told me about, and the communications you maintain, which do you like and which do you dislike?" Apparently this signal allows the potential adopters to feel they are going to get the last word, so not only does the interviewer get candid responses, but often the potential adopters lean forward and give the interviewer information about potential problems they see. Sometimes the problem is with their boss, or higher management, or sometimes they convey rumors they have heard which will have a bearing on implementation. In the case study, several operations-level people who were interviewed warned that supervision in the warehouse was sloppy, but that this author would not likely hear that from the warehouse people. They were concerned that this was the "weak link" in making the system successful.

Use of Data

The three pieces of data obtained in the interview can be useful at several stages of the MIS development cycle. As part of the *feasibility study* for a new system, this data could help management determine the need for and willingness to accept a new system. A forecast of serious implementation problems might, in some cases, have persuaded managements to scrap systems that created serious problems and were eventually abandoned or unused anyway.

In the initial *design phase*, the designers anticipate and hopefully avoid implementation problems that arise because the system does not serve its users' task needs and because it does not meet their personal needs.

The data is also useful *after the system is designed*, but prior to its implementation. At this stage potential adoption problems can be identified and some can be avoided in the way user procedures are developed. Where that is not possible, dissatisfaction with prospective changes in activities and interactions can be handled head-on by working with an individual to overcome any dissatisfaction or by enhancing the user's role in some other way. It may also be the case that the activity changes to be produced will not fit properly with the current mode of organizing, or the system of controls and rewards. A clear example of this lack of fit will emerge in the case to be described.

If the new system is already designed, the basic analysis performed on the data is to compare, on an individual-by-individual basis, the prospective user's reported activities and interactions before the system implementation, with the activities and interactions anticipated by the designers after implementation, assuming it is adopted by the prospective user. These role changes are then assessed against the potential adopter's stated preferences for activities and interactions, and the analyst must make a judgment about whether and how the system can be adjusted to the prospective adopter's needs, how the organizational context can be adjusted to accommodate the needs, or how the prospective adopter can be brought to adopt the system.

A Case Study Using the Behavioral Analysis

A Product Tracking System (PTS) had been under development by the corporate systems design group of a large multi-plant manufacturer for two years when the author became involved in the project. The author's role was to interview potential adopters of the PTS in order to anticipate areas of resistance to the changes and to recommend steps management could take to achieve a more successful implementation. The purpose of the system is to provide the ability to accurately track the product as it comes off the production line or is received as a finished product from another plant, through warehousing and shipping, and then to provide the ability for recall in the event of such a need after shipping. The information on the system serves as input to operations planners, who use it to plan production schedules, order raw materials, and schedule shipments; by accountants who use it to maintain inventory control; and by warehouse dispatchers, supervisors, and fork lift drivers who use it for warehousing operations. The system was being designed and introduced into a single plant as a prototype for use in other plants.

It could, perhaps, go without saying that the first step in the implementation study was to seek the support of the plant manager. This was readily accomplished. Flow charts of the task and decision processes were developed and used to identify the people who would be significantly affected by the PTS. They included six operations planners, three accountants, the warehouse dispatcher and five warehouse floor supervisors, two warehouse clerks, and two data input operators in accounting. A total of nineteen people were interviewed. While forklift drivers in the warehouse were to be affected by the system because they would get their dispatching orders from a terminal screen rather than a dispatcher, it was infeasible to interview them due to potential union complications.

Each interview proceeded in the manner described earlier. The interview focused first, and foremost, on specific, objective reporting of activities and interactions, without seeking for feelings until the objective data was available so the objective and subjective data could be specifically related.

It is not the intent of this article to claim that the approach outlined here is better than some other unspecified approach. It has been my experience, however, that it is *effective* in producing useful data and that it is *efficient*. The case study of the PTS reported in the following paragraphs involved one and one-half days of interviewing, with no prior contact with any plant personnel. The interviews provided a very rich picture of what people experienced in their jobs, what motivated them, and what management practices existed. This picture was then translated into a set of recommendations for managing the implementation process, and these too are described.

Operations Planners

Interviews with the operations planners followed an interesting pattern. At the outset they described activities which their manager could have related to the MIS team, or which could easily have been inferred from the job descriptions, namely, that they manually updated production and inventory reports, and then used these reports to prepare production schedules, raw material orders, and to schedule shipments of finished products. However, when asked how much time this consumed, they reported that it required an average of three hours daily, and then they perked up and reported that most of the rest of their time is devoted to solving problems and dealing with "emergencies," such as raw materials that have not arrived on schedule or orders that cannot be filled with the existing inventory. Solving these problems required that they be on the phone talking with various people throughout the day, and they also interacted with each other a good deal in order to juggle orders and schedules.

Even before reaching the last portion of the interview in which they were asked which of the activities and interactions were desirable or undesirable, the answers were obvious. They reported that the elimination of manual updating of reports was desirable and would make their jobs much easier, but they all reported that they found their jobs very challenging, and that the problem solving, which was termed by PTS designers as "fire-fighting" was very rewarding. Comments from the planners included "I like being able to respond to people, to make decisions, and I enjoy the personal telephone contact," and "I like the problem solving, the variability, and decisions in my work." Several reported that they like the personal contacts required by their jobs, and their problem solving required interaction personally and over the telephone with each other, warehouse people, production people, other plants, salesmen, and others. They were the hub of activities in the plant and derived a good deal of status from that.

The intent of the PTS was to eliminate the need for the time consuming updating of reports and to significantly eliminate the amount of emergency work they do. System designers intended that ultimately the operations planners' job would be planning oriented rather than reactive. Clearly, the PTS would change the "character" of the work they experience. Since much of it involved communication with others, it should be remembered that the work life of whomever was previously on the other end of the communication would change after implementation as well. In this case it was not worth investigating, but in some cases it might be more critical.

Warehouse

It became apparent that the warehouse was the key to the success of this system. The warehouse dispatcher received production and shipping reports from operations planners, and then issued orders to forklift drivers, telling them the bay rows in which finished products were to be stored and the bay rows from which goods were to be retrieved in order to be shipped. The new PTS would generate loading and storing orders automatically and the dispatcher would become a supervisor.

The forklift supervisors were not influenced directly by the PTS, but the operators whom they supervised were directly affected. However, since the operators could not be interviewed, for reasons involving the plant's labor relations, the supervisors were interviewed to learn what the operators do, and to learn what motivates their behavior. What was learned from the supervisors was very interesting. In addition to recounting what operators do, they reported that an estimated 25% of the lift drivers do not store and retrieve pallets from the rows they were assigned by the dispatcher. It appeared that there were no incentives for drivers to be accurate in the storage and retrieval of a product. Indeed, the incentives worked the other way. By picking from "convenient" rather than assigned rows, and otherwise, "cutting corners," drivers were able to finish a load and break for a cigarette. Furthermore, this warehouse had been touted within the company for its high productivity. The accuracy and thoroughness required by the new system would, at least in the short run, tend to be perceived as lowering their speed and productivity.

The activities of the supervisors themselves were straightforward supervisory activities, described by one as the "good cop role." They interacted with all of the drivers and all of the supervisors, which is not surprising because they are not responsible for supervising a particular crew, but instead for roaming the floor and checking loading docks.

Administration

The accountants reported that they did a great deal of handposting and verifying of reports, which they did not like. The PTS would require significantly less of this, and free them to do more work on trouble-shooting projects than they can do now. They reported that they liked the problem solving work in the projects they did have time to tackle, and were optimistic about being able to do more of it when the new system was operating. There appeared to be no changes in the work of Administration personnel that would hamper successful implementation.

Recommendations

The data obtained in the interviews provided a clear picture of how potential adopters saw their jobs; how they had adapted them to the plants' management practices, such as the incentive for the warehouse personnel to emphasize speed; what communication structures supported their work; and how their jobs and communications fit their own personal need structures, *e.g.*, operations planners like fire-fighting. Against this backdrop, the effects of the new PTS were assessed, and recommendations were developed regarding what management should do to attain both adoption and continued effective use of the PTS. The following are the key recommendations which were made.

The most threatening problem area was the lift drivers in the warehouse. If they were not conscientious in following loading and storing orders generated by the PTS, and if they did not take time to report adjustments due to damage, *etc.*, the information in the system would be inaccurate and its value as a planning and accounting tool completely undermined. The two key recommendations involved 1) creating incentives in the warehouse compatible with the *accuracy* needs of the new PTS, and 2) developing accountability for accuracy. A specific recommendation made to management was to place accountability for accuracy on the supervisors by dividing the drivers into teams and assigning them to a supervisor, who then plays the role of team leader rather than warehouse policeman. Being accountable for their teams, supervisors would then have incentives to build norms that support the accuracy objectives, to build *esprit de corps* in teams, and to spend more time assuring the accuracy of the orders going into the cars and trucks. In addition, the basis of recognition for the warehouse must shift, at least temporarily, away from productivity to success in making the PTS work. Repeatedly it can be seen that when quantity is rewarded, there is a tendency to drive out quality and accuracy. Certainly this was the state of affairs in the plant, so the entrenched reward system worked at cross purposes to successful implementation.

With respect to operations planners, it appeared that their motivation and commitment to their work would probably assure their adoption of the PTS. However, the recommendation to management was that they be alert to opportunities to provide future sources of challenge and responsibility to operations planners to substitute for the current challenges that the PTS will eliminate.

Summary

The data, data gathering procedures, and guidelines for using it, are not offered as a sure-fire solution to implementation problems for the practitioner. It may be most appropriate to view the approach as a means to act upon all of the good and sensible things which socio-technical theorists and behavioral scientists have been saying we should be concerned about, and that MIS practitioners are coming to accept and want to act upon. The approach is offered as a step toward the goal of successful implementation when it is used relatively skillfully. Indeed, one of its advantages is that it is specific and straightforward, and can be used "relatively skillfully" by organizationally sensitive, if even untrained, change agents.

The interview procedure is the central feature of the approach which opens it to practitioners/change agents who need not be organization development specialists. The interview, if conducted as described, appears to be successful for several reasons:

1. The questions about activities and interactions which serve as the heart of the interview are objective and non-threatening.
2. Potential adopters find the questions easy to respond to.
3. The questions give potential adopters an opportunity to convey to an apparently interested person the rich detail of how they work and how much they do.
4. These objective questions contribute to a climate of trust, in which candid and reliable expressions of what satisfies them in their work are more likely to come.
5. The approach helps convey the attitude that the interviewer needs to learn from the potential adopter, and is interested in basic and important things.

What the approach does then is place in the hands of the practitioner/change agent a rich source of insight into the *effects* of a new system on the working lives people would experience if the system were adopted by them. This insight can then help the analyst anticipate, avoid, or smooth potential adoption problems.

Besides the valuable uses for data on activities and interactions at several stages of the MIS development cycle, the process of gathering the data itself is beneficial. Behavioral scientists learned long ago in the famous Hawthorne studies that the mere expression of interest and concern by a researcher/change agent has a positive influence on behavior and attitudes [21]. Thus, it was not surprising to find in the field study that potential adopters responded very favorably to the interview itself; the management reported later that it had received supportive feedback from employees. The exact effect would be difficult to measure, but research has repeatedly shown it to be positive.

Discussion Questions

1. How does a behavioral analysis contribute to success in MIS implementation?
2. Describe the process of conducting a behavioral analysis. What are the objectives and who are the participants?
3. Under what circumstances should the change agent be internal? external?
4. What does this approach suggest regarding the educational and skill requirements of systems developers?

References

[1] Ackoff, R. L. "Unsuccessful Case Studies and Why," *Operations Research*, Volume 8, Number 4, March/April 1960, pp. 259-263.

[2] Argyris, C. "Resistance to Rational Management Systems," *Innovation*, Number 10, November 1970, pp. 28-34.

[3] Argyris, C. "Management Information Systems: The Challenge to Rationality and Emotionality," *Management Science*, Volume 17, Number 6, February 1971, pp. B275-292.

[4] Bavelas, A. "Communication Patterns in Task-Oriented Groups," *Journal of the Acoustical Society of America*, Volume 22, Number 6, November 1950, pp. 725-730.

[5] Churchman, C. W. and Schainblatt, A. H. "The Researcher and the Manager: A Dialectic of Implementation," *Management Science*, Volume 11, Number 4, February 1965, pp. B69-87.

[6] Dickson, G. and Wynne B. "Managers and Managing Machine Information Systems," Management Information Systems Research Center Working Paper Series, WP-72-04, University of Minnesota, Minneapolis, Minnesota, March, 1973.

[7] Doktor, R. H. and Hamilton, W. F. "Cognitive Style and the Acceptance of Management Science Recommendations," *Management Science*, Volume 19, Number 8, April 1973, pp. 884-894.

[8] Ginzberg, M. J. "A Process Approach to Management Science Implementation," Ph.D. Dissertation, Sloan School of Management, MIT, Boston, Massachusetts, 1975.

[9] Hedberg, B., Edstrom, A., Muller, W., and Wilpert, B. "The Impact of Computer Technology on Organizational Power Structures," in E. Grochla and N. Szyperski, eds., *Information Systems and Organization Structure*, Walter de Gruyter, New York, New York, 1975.

[10] Huysmans, J. H. "The Effectiveness of the Cognitive Style Constraint in Implementing Operations Research Proposals," *Management Science*, Volume 17, Number 1, September 1970, pp. 92-104.

[11] Keen, P. G. W. "Implementation Research in MIS and OR/MS: Description Versus Prescription," Stanford Business School Research Paper No. 390, Stanford, California, 1977.

[12] Keen, P. G. W. and Scott Morton, M. S. *Decision Support Systems, An Organizational Perspective*, Addison-Wesley, Reading, Massachusetts, 1978.

[13] Kolb, D. A. and Frohman, A. L. "An Organization Development Approach to Consulting," *Sloan Management Review*, Volume 12, Number 1, Fall 1970, pp. 51-65.

[14] Lewin, K. "Group Decision and Social Change," in T. M. Newcomb and E. L. Hartley, eds., *Readings in Social Psychology*, New York, New York, Henry Holt & Co., 1947, pp. 330-344.

[15] Lippitt, M. E. and Mackenzie, K. D. "Authority-Task Problems," *Administrative Science Quarterly*, Volume 21, Number 4, December 1976, pp. 643-660.

[16] Mackenzie, K. D. *A Theory of Group Structures, Volume I: Basic Theory*, Gordon and Breach, New York, New York, 1976a.

[17] Mackenzie, K. D. *A Theory of Group Structures, Volume II: Empirical Tests*, Gordon and Breach, New York, New York, 1976b.

[18] Mumford, E. and Pettigrew, A. *Implementing Strategic Decisions*, Longman, New York, New York, 1975.

[19] Pettigrew, A. M. "Information Control as a Power Resource," *Sociology*, Volume 6, Number 2, May 1972, pp. 187-204.

[20] Pettigrew, A. M. *The Politics of Organizational Decision Making*, Tavistock Publications, London, England, 1973.

[21] Roethlisberger, F. J. and Dickson, W. *Management and The Worker*, Harvard University Press, Cambridge, Massachusetts, 1939.

[22] Schein, E. H. "Management Development as a Process of Influence," *Industrial Management Review*, Volume 2, Number 2, Spring 1961, pp. 59-77.

[23] Shaw, M. E. "Communication Networks," in Leonard Berkowitz, ed., *Advances in Experimental Social Psychology*, Volume 1, Academic Press, New York, New York, 1964, pp. 111-147.

[24] Trist, E. L. and Bamforth, K. W. "Some Social and Psychological Consequences of the Long Wall Method of Coal-getting," *Human Relations*, Volume 4, Number 1, February 1951, pp. 1-38.

[25] Trist, E. L. "On Socio-Technical Systems," in Warren G. Bennis, Kenneth D. Benne, and Robert Chin (eds.), *The Planning of Change*, Holt,

Rinehart and Winston, Inc., New York, New York, 1969, pp. 269-282.

UNIT FIVE

MIS and Society

The implications of management information systems are not limited to individual business firms. Serious concerns are beginning to be voiced about the growing influence of information technology on society as a whole. This issue is addressed in Unit Five.

Section Fifteen (Social Issues) covers the effects of MIS on society, and the problems that occur in the confrontation between information technology and the rights and prerogatives of individuals. These legal and ethical implications will be an area of growing attention and concern in the years to come.

SECTION FIFTEEN

Social Issues

READING 46

Four Ethical Issues of the Information Age*

article by
RICHARD O. MASON

Today in western societies more people are employed collecting, handling and distributing information than in any other occupation. Millions of computers inhabit the earth and many millions of miles of optical fiber, wire, and air waves link people, their computers and the vast array of information-handling devices together. Our society is truly an information society, our time an information age. The question before us now is whether the kind of society being created is the one we want. It is a question that should especially concern those of us in the MIS community for we are in the forefront of creating this new society.

There are many unique challenges we face in this age of information. They stem from the nature of information itself. Information is the means through which the mind expands and increases its capacity to achieve its goals, often as the result of an input from another mind. Thus, information forms the intellectual capital from which human beings craft their lives and secure dignity.

However, the building of intellectual capital is vulnerable in many ways. For example, people's intellectual capital is imparied whenever they lose their personal information without being compensated for it, when they are precluded access to information which is of value to them, when they have revealed information they hold intimate, or when they find out that the information upon which their living depends is in error. The social contract among people in the information age must deal with these threats to human dignity. The ethical issues involved are many and varied; however, it is helpful to focus on just four. These may be summarized by means of an acronym—**PAPA.**

Source: Reprinted by special permission of the *MIS Quarterly* , Volume 10, Number 1, January 1986, pp. 486-498.

Privacy: What information about one's self or one's associations must a person reveal to others, under what conditions, and with what safeguards? What things can people keep to themselves and not be forced to reveal to others?

Accuracy: Who is responsible for the authenticity, fidelity, and accuracy of information? Similarly, who is to be held accountable for errors in information and how is the injured party to be made whole?

Property: Who owns information? What are the just and fair prices for its exchange? Who owns the channels, especially the airways, through which information is transmitted? How should access to this scarce resource be allocated?

Accessibility: What information does a person or organization have a right or a privilege to obtain, under what conditions, and with what safeguards?

Privacy

What information should one be required to divulge about one's self to others? Under what conditions? What information should one be able to keep strictly to one's self? These are among the questions that a concern for privacy raises. Today more than ever cautious citizens must be asking these questions.

Two forces threaten our privacy. One is the growth of information technology, with its enhanced capacity for surveillance, communication, computation, storage, and retrieval. A second, and more insidious threat, is the increased value of information in decision making. Information is increasingly valuable to policy makers; they covet it even if acquiring it invades another's privacy.

A case in point is the situation that occurred a few years ago in Florida. The Florida Legislature believed that the state's building codes might be too stringent and that, as a result, the taxpayers were burdened by paying for buildings which were underutilized. Several studies were commissioned. In one study at the Tallahassee Community College, monitors were stationed at least one day a week in every bathroom.

Every 15 seconds, the monitor observed the usage of the toilets, mirrors, sinks, and other facilities and recorded them on a form. This data was subsequently entered into a database for further analyses. Of course the students, faculty, and staff complained bitterly, feeling that this was an invasion of their privacy and a violation of their rights. State officials responded, however, that the study would provide valuable information for policy making. In effect the state argued that the value of the information to the administrators was greater than any possible indignities suffered by the students and others. Soon the ACLU joined the fray. At their insistence the study was stopped, but only after the state got the information it wanted.

Most invasions of privacy are not this dramatic or this visible. Rather, they creep up on us slowly as, for example, when a group of diverse files relating to a person and his or her activities are integrated into a single large database. Collections of information reveal intimate details about a person and can thereby deprive the person of the opportunity to form certain professional and personal relationships. This is the ultimate cost of an invasion of privacy. So why do we integrate databases in the first place? It is because the bringing together of disparate data makes the development of new informational relationships possible. These new relationships may be formed, however, without the affected parties' permission. You or I may have contributed information about ourselves freely to each of the separate databases but that by itself does not amount to giving consent to someone to merge the data, especially if that merger might reveal something else about us.

Consider the study that was circulating during the early 1970s. It's probably been embellished in the retellings, but it goes something like this. It seems that a couple of programmers at the city of Chicago's computer center began matching tape files from many of the city's different data-processing applications on name and I.D. They discovered, for example, that several highly paid city employers had unpaid parking fines. Bolstered by this revelation, they pressed on. Soon they uncovered the names of several employees who were still listed on the register but who had not paid a variety of fees, a few of whom appeared in the files of the alcoholic and drug abuse program. When this finding was leaked to the public, the city employees, of course, were furious. They demanded to know who had authorized the investigation. The answer was that no one knew. Later, city officials established rules for the computer center to prevent this form of invasion of privacy from happening again. In light of recent proposals to develop a central federal databank consisting of files from most U.S. government agencies, this story takes on new meaning. It shows what can happen when a group of eager computer operators or unscrupulous administrators start playing around with data.

The threat to privacy here is one that many of us don't fully appreciate. I call it the threat of exposure by *minute description*. It stems from the collection of attributes about ourselves and use of the logical connector "and." For example, I may authorize one institution to collect information "A" about me, and another institution to collect information "B" about me; but I might not want anyone to possess "A and B" about me at the same time. When "C" is added to the list of conjunctions, the possessor of the new information will know even more about me. And then "D" is added and so forth. Each additional weaving together of my attributes reveals more and more about me. In the process, the fabric that is created poses a threat to my privacy.

The threads which emanate from this foreboding fabric usually converge in personnel files and in dossiers, as Aleksandr Solzhenitsyn describes in *The Cancer Ward*:

> Every person fills out quite a few forms in his life, and each form contains an uncounted number of questions. The answer of just one person to one question in one form is already a thread linking that person forever with the local center of the dossier department. Each person thus radiates hundreds of such threads, which all together, run into the millions. If these threads were visible, the heavens would be webbed with them, and if they had substance and resilience, the buses, streetcars, and the people themselves would no longer be able to move. . . . They are neither visible, but material, but they were constantly felt by man. . . .
> Constant awareness of these invisible threads naturally bred respect for the people in charge of that most intricate dossier department. It bolstered their authority. [1, p. 221].

The threads leading to Americans are many. The United States Congress' Privacy Protection Commission, chaired by David F. Linowes, estimated that there are over 8,000 different record systems in the files of the federal government that contain individually identifiable data on citizens. Each citizen, on average, has 17 files in federal agencies and administrations. Using these files, for example, Social Security data has been matched with Selective Service data to reveal draft resisters. IRS data has been matched with other administrative records to tease out possible tax evaders. Federal employment records have been matched with delinquent student loan records to identify some 46,860 federal and military employees and retirees whose paychecks might be garnisheed. In Massachusetts welfare officials sent tapes bearing welfare recipients' Social Security numbers to some 117 banks to find out whether the recipients had bank accounts in excess of the allowable amount. During the first pass some 1,600 potential violaters were discovered.

Computer matching and the integration of data files into a central databank have enormous ethical implications. On the one hand, the new information can be used to uncover criminals and to identify service requirements for the needy. On the other hand, it provides powerful political knowledge for those few who have access to it and control over it. It is ripe for privacy invasion and other abuses. For this reason many politicians have spoken out against centralized governmental databanks. As early as 1966 Representative Frank Horton of New York described the threat as follows:

> The argument is made that a central databank would use only the type of information that now exists, and since no new principle is involved, existing types of safeguards will be adequate. This is fallacious. Good computermen know that one of the most practical of our present safeguards of privacy is the fragmented nature of present information. It is scattered in little bits and pieces across the geography and years of our life. Retrieval is impractical and often impossible. A central databank removes completely this safeguard. I have every confidence that ways will be found for all of us to benefit from the great advances of the computermen, but those benefits must never be purchased at the price of our freedom to live as individuals with private lives. [2, p. 6].

There is another threat inherent in merging data

files. Some of the data may be in error. More than 60,000 state and local agencies, for example, provide information to the National Crime Information Center, and it is accessed by law officers nearly 400,000 times a day. Yet studies show that over 4 percent of the stolen vehicle entries, 6 percent of the warrant entries, and perhaps as much as one half of the local law enforcement criminal history records are in error. At risk is the safety of the law enforcement officers who access it, the effectiveness of the police in controlling crime, and the freedom of the citizens whose names appear in the files. This leads to a concern for accuracy.

Accuracy

Misinformation has a way of fouling up people's lives, especially when the party with the inaccurate information has an advantage in power and authority. Consider the plight of one Louis Marches. Marches, an immigrant, was a hardworking man who, with his wife, Eileen, finally saved enough money to purchase a home in Los Angeles during the 1950s. They took out a long-term loan from Crocker National Bank. Every month Louis Marches would walk to his neighborhood bank, loan coupon book in hand, to make his payment of $195.53. He always checked with care to insure that the teller had stamped "paid" in his book on the proper line just opposite the month for which the payment was due. And he continued to do this long after the bank had converted to its automated loan processing system.

One September a few years ago Marches was notified by the bank that he had failed to make his current house payment. Marches grabbed his coupon book, marched to the bank, and in broken English that showed traces of his old country heritage, tried to explain to the teller that this dunning notice was wrong. He had made his payment he claimed. The stamp on his coupon book proved that he had paid. The teller punched Marches' loan number on the keyboard and reviewed the resulting screen. Unfortunately she couldn't confirm Marches' claim, nor subsequently could the head teller, nor the branch manager. When faced with a computer generated screen that clearly showed that his account was delinquent, this hierarchy of bankers simply ignored the entries recorded in his coupon book and also his attendant raving. Confused, Marches left the bank in disgust.

In October, however, Marches dutifully went to the bank to make his next payment. He was told that he could not make his October payment because he was one month in arrears. He again showed the teller his stamped coupon book. She refused to accept it, and he stormed out of the bank. In November he returned on schedule as he had done for over 20 years and tried to make his payment again, only to be told that he was now two months in arrears. And so it went until inevitably the bank foreclosed. Eileen learned of the foreclosure from an overzealous bank debt collector while she was in bed recovering from a heart attack. She collapsed upon hearing the news and suffered a near fatal stroke which paralzyed her right side. Sometime during this melee Marches, who until this time had done his own legal work, was introduced to an attorney who agreed to defend him. They sued the bank. Ultimately, after months of anguish, the Marches received a settlement for $268,000. All that the bank officials who testified could say was, "Computers make mistakes. Banks make mistakes, too."

A special burden is placed on the accuracy of information when people rely on it for matters of life and death, as we increasingly do. This came to light in a recent $3.2 million lawsuit charging the National Weather Service for failing to predict accurately a storm that raged on the southeast slope of Georges Bank in 1980. As Peter Brown steered his ship—the Sea Fever—from Hyannis Harbor toward his lobster traps near Nova Scotia, he monitored weather conditions using a long-range, single sideband radio capable of receiving weather forecasts at least 100 miles out to sea. The forecasts assured him that his destination area near Georges Bank, although it might get showers, was safe from the hurricane-like storm that the weather bureau had predicted would go far to the east of his course. So he kept to his course. Soon, however, his ship was engulfed in howling winds of 80 knots and waves cresting at 60 feet. In the turbulence Gary Brown, a crew member, was washed overboard.

The source of the fatal error was failure of a large scale information system which collects data from high-atmosphere balloons, satellites, ships, and a series of buoys. These data are then transmitted to a National Oceanographic and Atmospheric Administration computer which analyzes them and produces forecasts. The forecasts, in turn, are broadcast widely.

The forecast Peter Brown relied on when he decided to proceed into the North Atlantic was in error because just one buoy—station 44003 Georges Bank—was out of service. As a result, the wind speed and direction data it normally provided were lost to the computer model. This caused the forecasted trajectory of the storm to be canted by several miles, deceiving skipper Peter Brown and consequently sending Gary Brown to his death.

Among the questions this raises for us in the information age are these: "How many Louis Marcheses and Gray Browns are there out there?" "How many are we creating everyday?" The Marches received a large financial settlement; but can they ever be repaid for the irreparable harm done to them and to their dignity? Honour Brown, Gary's widow, received a judgment in her case; but has she been repaid for the loss of Gary? The point is this: We run the risk of creating Gary Browns and Louis Marcheses every time we design information systems and place information in databases which might be used to make decisions. So it is our responsibility to be vigilant in the pursuit of accuracy in information. Today we are producing so much information about so many people and their activities that our exposure to problems of inaccuracy is enormous. And this growth in information also raises another issue: Who owns it?

Property

One of the most complex issues we face as a society is the question of intellectual property rights. There are substantial economic and ethical concerns surrounding these rights—concerns revolving around the special attributes of information itself and the means by which it is transmitted. Any individual item of information can be extremely costly to produce in the first instance. Yet, once it is produced, that information has the illusive quality of being easy to reproduce and to share with others. Moreover, this replication can take place without destroying the original. This makes information hard to safeguard since, unlike tangible property, it becomes communicable and hard to keep it to one's self. It is even difficult to secure appropriate reimbursements when somebody else uses your information.

We currently have several imperfect institutions that try to protect intellectual property rights. Copyrights, patents, encryption, oaths of confidentiality, and such old fashioned values as trustworthiness and loyalty are the most commonly used protectors of our intellectual property. Problem issues, however, still abound in this area. Let us focus on just one aspect: artificial intelligence and its expanding subfield, expert systems.

To fully appreciate our moral plight regarding expert systems it is necessary to run back the clock a bit, about 200 years, to the beginnings of another society: the steam energy—industrial society. From this vantage point we may anticipate some of the problems of the information society.

As the industrial age unfolded in England and Western Europe a significant change took place in the relationship between people and their work. The steam engine replaced manpower by reducing the level of personal physical energy required to do a job. The factory system, as Adam Smith described in his essay on the pin factory, effectively replaced the laborer's contribution of his energy and of his skills. This was done by means of new machines and new organizational forms. The process was carried even further in the French community of Lyon. There, Joseph Marie Jacquard created a weaving loom in which a system of rectangular, punched holes captured the weaver's skill for directing the loom's mechanical fingers and for controlling the warp and weft of the threads. These Jacquard looms created a new kind of capital which was produced by disembodying energy and skill from the craftsmen and then reembodying it into the machines. In effect, an exchange of property took place. Weaving skills were transferred from the craftsman to the owner of the machines. With this technological innovation, Lyon eventually regained its position as one of the leading silk producers in the world. The weavers themselves, however, suffered unemployment and degradation because their craft was no longer economically viable. A weaver's value as a person and a craftsman was taken away by the new machines.

There is undoubtedly a harbinger of things to come in these 18th-century events. As they unfolded, civilization witnessed one of the greatest outpourings of moral philosophy it has ever seen: Adam Smith's *Theory of Moral Sentiments* and his *Wealth of Nations*, the American Revolution and its classic documents on liberty and freedom, the French Revolution and its concern for fraternity and equality, John Stuart Mill and Jeremy Bentham and their ethical call for the greatest good for the greatest number, and Immanuel Kant and his categorical imperative which leads to an ethical utopia called the "kingdom of ends." All of this ethical initiative took place within the historically short span of time of about 50 years. Common to these ideas was a spirit which sought a new meaning in human life and which demanded that a just allocation be made of social resources.

Today that moral spirit may be welling up within us again. Only this time it has a different provocator. Nowhere is the potential threat to human dignity so severe as it is in the age of information technology, especially in the field of artificial intelligence. Practitioners of artificial intelligence proceed by extracting knowledge from experts, workers, and the knowledgeable, and then implanting it into computer software where it becomes capital in the economic sense. This process of "disemminding" knowledge from an individual, and subsequently "emminding" it into machines transfers control of the property to those who own the hardware and software. Is this exchange of property warranted? Consider some of the most successful commercial artificial intelligence systems of the day. Who owns, for example, the chemical knowledge contained in DYNDREL, the medical knowledge contained in MYCIN, or the geological knowledge contained in PROSPECTOR. How is the contributor of his knowledge to be compensated? These are among the issues we must resolve as more intelligent information systems are created.

Concern over intellectual property rights relates to the content of information. There are some equally pressing property rights issues surrounding the conduits through which information passes. Bandwidth, the measure of capacity to carry information, is a scarce and ultimately fixed commodity. It is a "commons." A commons is like an empty vessel into which drops of water can be placed freely and easily until it fills and overflows. Then its capacity is gone. As a resource it is finite.

In an age in which people benefit by the communication of information, there is a tendency for us to treat bandwidth and transmission capacity as a commons in the same way as did the herdsmen in Garrett Hardin's poignant essay, "The Tragedy of the Commons," (subtitled: "The population problem has no technical solution; it requires a fundamental extension in morality"). Each herdsman received direct benefits from adding an animal to a pasture shared in common. As long as there was plenty of grazing capacity the losses due to the animal's consumption were spread among them and felt only indirectly and proportionally much less. So each herdsman was motivated to increase his flock. In the end, however, the commons was destroyed and everybody lost.

Today our airways are becoming clogged with a plethora of data, voice, video, and message transmission. Organizations and individuals are expanding their use of communications because it is profitable for them to do so. But if the social checks on the expanded use of bandwidth are inadequate, and a certain degree of temperance isn't followed, we may find that jamming and noise will destroy the flow of clear information through the air. How will the limited resource of bandwidth be allocated? Who will have access? This leads us to the fourth issue.

Access

Our main avenue to information is through literacy. Literacy, since about 1500 A.D. when the Syrians first conceived of a consonant alphabet, has been a requirement for full participation in the fabric of society. Each innovation in information handling, from the invention of paper to the modern computer, has placed new demands on achieving literacy. In an information society a citizen must possess at least three things to be literate:

One must have the intellectual skills to deal with

information. These are skills such as reading, writing, reasoning, and calculating. This is a task for education.

One must have access to the information technologies which store, convey, and process information. This includes libraries, radios, televisions, telephones, and increasingly personal computers or terminals linked via networks to mainframes. This is a problem in social economics.

Finally, one must have access to the information itself. This requirement returns to the issue of property and is also a problem in social economics.

These requirements for literacy are a function of both the knowledge level and the economic level of the individual. Unfortunately, for many people in the world today both of these levels are currently deteriorating.

There are powerful factors working both for and against contemporary literacy in our organizations and in our society. For example, the cost of computation, as measured in, say dollars per MIPS (millions of instructions per second), has gone done exponentially since the introduction of computers. This trend has made technology more accessible and economically attainable to more people. However, corporations and other public and private organizations have benefited the most from these economies. As a result, cost economies in computation are primarily available to middle and upper income people. At the same time computer usage flourishes among some, we are creating a large group of information-poor people who have no direct access to the more efficient computational technology and who have little training in its use.

Reflect for a moment on the social effects of electronically stored databases. Prior to their invention, vast quantities of data about publications, news events, economic and social statistics, and scientific findings have been available in printed, microfilm, or microfiche form at a relatively low cost. For most of us access to this data had been substantially free. We merely went to our public or school library. The library, in turn, paid a few hundred dollars for the service and made it available to whomever asked for it. Today, however, much of this information is being converted to computerized databases and the cost to access these databases can run in the thousands of dollars.

Frequently, access to databases is gained only by means of acquiring a terminal or personal computer. For example, if you want access to the *New York Times Index* through the Mead Corporation service you must first have access to a terminal and communication line and then pay additional hookup and access fees in order to obtain the data. This means that the people who wish to use this service possess several things. First, they know that the database exists and how to use it. Second, they have acquired the requisite technology to access it. And third, they are able to pay the fees for the data. Thus the educational and economic ante is really quite high for playing the modern information game. Many people cannot or choose not to pay it and hence are excluded from participating fully in our society. In effect, they become information "drop outs" and in the long run will become the source of many social problems.

PAPA

Privacy, accuracy, property, and accessibility—these are the four major issues of information ethics for the information age. Max Plank's 1900 conception that energy was released in small discrete packets called "quanta" not only gave rise to atomic theory but also permitted the development of information technology as well. Semiconductors, transistors, integrated circuits, photoelectric cells, vacuum tubes, and ferrite cores are among the technological yield of this scientific theory. In a curious way quantum theory underlies the four issues as well. Plank's theory, and all that followed it, have led us to a point where the stakes surrounding society's policy agenda are incredibly high. At stake with the use of nuclear energy is the very survival of mankind itself. If we are unwise we will either blow ourselves up or contaminate our world forever with nuclear waste. At stake with the increased use of information technology is the quality of our lives should we, or our children, survive. If we are unwise, many people will suffer information bankruptcy or desolation.

Our moral imperative is clear. We must insure that information technology, and the information it handles, are used to enhance the dignity of mankind.

To achieve these goals we must formulate a new social contract, one that insures everyone the right to fulfill his or her own human potential.

In the new social contract, information systems should not unduly invade a person's privacy to avoid the indignities that the students in Tallahassee suffered.

Information systems must be accurate to avoid the indignities the Marcheses and the Browns suffered.

Information systems should protect the viability of the fixed-conduit resource through which it is transmitted to avoid noise and jamming pollution and the indignities of "The Tragedy of the Commons."

Information systems should protect the sanctity of intellectual property to avoid the indignities of unwitting "disemmindment" of knowledge from individuals.

And information systems should be accessible to avoid the indignities of information illiteracy and deprivation.

This is a tall order; but it is one that we in the MIS community should address. We must assume some responsibility for the social contract that emerges from the systems that we design and implement. In summary, we must insure that the flow of those little packets of energy and information called quanta that Max Plank bequeathed to use some 85 years ago are used to create the kind of world in which we wish to live.

Discussion Questions

1. Why is privacy an increasingly important issue?
2. Why is accuracy sometimes a life-and-death issue?
3. Why are property rights an issue?
4. Why is access an important social issue?

References

1. Solzhenitsyn, Aleksandr I. *The Cancer Ward.* New York: Dial Press, 1968.

2. U.S. House of Representatives. *The Computer and Invasion of Privacy.* Washington, D.C.: U.S. Government Printing Office, 1966.